W9-CZI-850

Situating Semantics

Essays on the Philosophy of John Perry

Situating Semantics
Essays on the Philosophy of John Perry

edited by Michael O'Rourke and Corey Washington

A Bradford Book
The MIT Press
Cambridge, Massachusetts
London, England

MIT Press books may be purchased at special quantity discounts for business or sales promotional use. For information, please e-mail special_sales@mitpress.mit.edu or write to Special Sales Department, The MIT Press, 55 Hayward Street, Cambridge, MA 02142.

This book was set in Stone Serif and Stone Sans on 3B2 by Asco Typesetters, Hong Kong, and was printed and bound in the United States of America.

Library of Congress Cataloging-in-Publication Data

Situating semantics : essays on the philosophy of John Perry / edited by Michael O'Rourke and Corey Washington.
    p. cm.
"A Bradford book."
Includes bibliographical references and index.
ISBN 978-0-262-15118-4 (hardcover : alk. paper) — ISBN 978-0-262-65111-0 (pbk. : alk. paper)
1. Perry, John, 1943–. I. O'Rourke, Michael, 1963–. II. Washington, Corey.

B945.P454S58   2007
191—dc22   2006033526

10 9 8 7 6 5 4 3 2 1

Contents

Acknowledgments

We would like to thank all of our colleagues who have contributed to this volume and have stuck with the project through the five years it has taken to bring it to fruition. We are extremely grateful to our editor at the MIT Press, Tom Stone, who has seen this project through from its earliest moments. We are also very appreciative of the initiative of Eros Corazza, a contributor, who first proposed a volume of this type on John's work nearly ten years ago.

We think we speak for all of the contributors in saying that, most of all, we would like to thank John Perry, not just for his contributions to this volume but, more importantly, for his nearly four decades of influential and engaging contributions to philosophy. Whether we have agreed with him or not, we have all benefited enormously from his intelligence and insight. John is also one of the few people in any academic field who is both enormously respected for his intellectual contributions and just as highly appreciated for his warmth and personality. Over the years, we have learned from nearly everything he has written and laughed uproariously at his wonderful jokes.

1 Situating Semantics: An Overview of the Philosophy of John Perry

Michael O'Rourke and Corey Washington

Perry: A System Builder Step by Step

Contemporary analytic philosophers are not known as system builders. For the most part they have focused on particular problems in specific subdisciplines—for example, the role of emotions in virtue ethics, opaque contexts in modal logic, bivalence in the philosophy of quantum mechanics—and published their results in relatively short journal articles, making little effort at larger syntheses. Some take this approach because they see it as more scientific; others because they believe synoptic synthesis is impractical or even unachievable. Their practice stands in marked contrast with analytic philosophy in the modern period and contemporary philosophy in other traditions. Writers in the former category—such as Leibniz, Locke, Spinoza, Hume, and Kant—and in the latter—such as Husserl, Heidegger, and Derrida—have developed expansive views that explain human nature, language, our place in the world, and sometimes the world itself. These projects were sweeping in scope and comprehensive in aim, presenting entire worldviews.

Recent decades have seen a few analytic philosophers merge the two approaches by developing systems piecemeal. W. V. O. Quine, Donald Davidson, David Lewis, and Hilary Putnam are representative of this current. These writers have focused on narrow topics across a range of subjects, finding solutions that fit together like a mosaic into a broader and more systematic picture. We believe that John Perry's work falls within this new tradition. For nearly four decades, Perry has worked on a range of topics in metaphysics, epistemology, and the philosophies of language, mind, and action. He has approached all his subjects from a point of view that is squarely analytic, concentrating on explaining specific phenomena by using common sense concepts and the apparatus of modern logic. The product of these efforts is a systematic account of human nature that respects our basic intuitions about the world while doing justice to the complex demands of human experience.

A few bottom lines underwrite all of Perry's work. He maintains that an account of human nature must be both naturalistic and centered on the self. In his hands, this account is rooted in a sophisticated, information-based semantic theory that reveals many so-called philosophical problems to be the products of overly simple or incorrect theories of meaning. The outlook defined by these assumptions appears in his earliest writings and remains a factor throughout his work. In this introduction, we present a comprehensive overview of Perry's philosophical system, representing it as a theory of the self. After describing his idea of the self, we present the detailed theory in three stages, focusing in turn on content, action, and persons. With the theory in place, we proceed to demonstrate how his ideas about content can be used to fend off challenges involving consciousness and self-knowledge. We close by noting which aspects of Perry's system are addressed by the various contributions to this volume.

Perry's Self

John Perry sets out in his work to "explain human thought and action, including language, memory, and intention."[1] This theory—the "human-theory"—is the inheritance of each of us who master language and wield concepts of self, action, and attitudes, and Perry seeks to articulate and develop it into a form that establishes its coherence with physicalism. Perry's version of the human theory sees the human agent as a being in time, understood both synchronically and diachronically. Synchronically, it models the agent as a physical input/output system that converts perceptual inputs into practical outputs via the intercession of folk psychological states (e.g., beliefs, desires, and intentions). Diachronically, it models the agent as something that retains its identity across time. Thus, the notions of *self*, *identity*, and *time* play central roles in the theory.[2] Since his work on the human theory frames his contributions to metaphysics, epistemology, and the philosophies of language and mind, we can introduce his results and the explanatory system he develops with an integrated description of the self.

Perry's account of the self is grounded in two fundamental assumptions. First, there is physicalism, the view that all entities and events are fundamentally physical. Embracing physicalism about the self means accepting that, whatever appearances there may be to the contrary, thoughts like perceptions and beliefs must at the very least supervene on physical states. Perry commits to physicalism as his philosophical starting point, calling himself an "antecedent physicalist." As such, he will remain so committed unless he sees some "clear reason" to give it up.[3] Second, Perry assumes the prima facie legitimacy of common sense; indeed, he develops a version of common sense about the self, according to which the self is a physical system endowed with cognitive skills and capacities, made out in folk psychological terms, that support and integrate perception, action, and communication. Let us call this view of the self "physicalist common sense," or PCS.

In Perry's version of PCS, humans think about, talk about, and act in the world as conscious organisms that retain their identity over time. A person's thoughts include perceptual states, which we share with many other types of organisms, and higher level states like beliefs and desires that may set us apart. These thoughts cause, and are caused by, events in the world. Among their effects are actions, including linguistic utterances, that convey informational content from person to person. These particular effects are expressions of the person and mesh with the thoughts that cause them in interesting ways. Further, these persons remain identical over time in a way that is keyed to memory. Perry's account of personal identity is sympathetic to considerations Locke and Shoemaker raise in favor of the central role of memory in our concept of a person; it emphasizes, however, that memory itself is a causal notion; so, whatever we can do with the concept of personal identity in speculation and imagination, in reality it is rooted in the ongoing history of a complex organism.[4]

Persons, then, are persisting physical systems that perceive, think, and act—that is, they are complex input/output systems that interact causally with the world. We acquire information content (IC) through perception and language, storing this content as beliefs and later use these beliefs to advance our goals and satisfy our desires. A distinctive feature of Perry's view, exemplified here, is the importance of classification. He sees our ability to classify phenomena as one of the most basic features of human beings. Consider that perception and action are essentially classificatory in nature. We distinguish what we perceive into necessary/unnecessary, friend/foe, pleasant/unpleasant, and so forth, and our actions are likewise dependent on our ability to discriminate and categorize what is success conducing from what is not. Understood as discrimination and categorization, classification can be understood as a practice we engage in to order our experience—this is how we "keep things straight."

Our ability to carry out these classifications depends on contentful states, that is, states that carry information about the world and, directly or indirectly, control action. For Perry, these states can be understood as operating at three different levels. At the first level, we have perceptions and other states whose neural foundations are genetically hardwired or otherwise developmentally determined. These states drive activity without the intercession of conscious, language-like thought.[5] When we operate at this level, we are within the causal flow, with perceptions flowing in and behaviors flowing out, unmediated by explicit consideration of beliefs or desires. To the extent that our behavior at this level is successful, it is because we are attuned to our environ-ment; that is, our contentful states and the relations between them accurately reflect particular features of and regularities in the environment, respectively. Human agents operate on the first tier, but most living things operate *only* on this tier.

The second tier is occupied by those first-tier systems that can classify their own states and experiences by using propositions and concepts. These systems have access to beliefs and language-type, detachable representations that can be used to keep track of events past, present, and future. Representations of this sort make planning, reason-ing, and memory possible. Human beings, perhaps along with certain other complex organisms,[6] generally operate as second-tier systems. The third tier is attained by those second-tier systems that are interested in the self, for example, folk theorists, philoso-phers, and psychologists. At this level, we seek to classify processes and states of the mind. Here we not only use propositions and concepts to classify things by their con-tent, but also reflect on these practices, make them explicit, and extend them with a view to identifying nomological patterns. This is the level at which Perry works as he develops his views and designs a theory that is meant to explain the operation of human agents on all three tiers.[7]

Consider an example. Imagine that Josh is walking along an empty sidewalk, think-ing about soccer. After a few blocks, he turns into a busy marketplace, the sidewalk giv-ing way to a concourse filled with people. Head down, he moves through the crowd. As he goes, he automatically keeps track of the people near him. He modifies his trajectory and his movements to avoid the trajectories and movements of the people in his path, and he does so without consciously thinking about it. Throughout this complicated negotiation, he has continued to obsess about soccer. After a few minutes of this, he hears his name called out. Looking up, he scans the crowd before his eyes fix on a friendly face illuminated by a smile. He now believes that his friend Mary is in the market with him, and he raises his hand and says, "Hello, Mary!" This simple example illustrates the first two tiers described above: (a) our ability to classify without con-scious thought, a first-tier ability, and (b) our ability to classify using occurrent beliefs and consciousness, a second-tier ability.

Perry thinks this development of PCS is sensible but acknowledges that it faces a range of problems. For example, any physicalist account of the self must address con-sciousness and free will, both of which seem intractable unless one's physicalism is loosened in some way. Second, the prospect that we remain the same self across time does not sit well with the physical changes marking the growth and maturation of an individual. There are also knotty epistemological concerns such as subjectivity, point of view, and self-knowledge, each of which seems more congenial to dualism than physicalism. Problems like these have driven philosophers away from views like PCS and toward dualism, nominalism, or eliminativism in metaphysics and subjectivism, relativism, or skepticism in epistemology.

Perry resists the temptation to give up on PCS. He allows that the problems it faces are real but works hard to keep his solutions consistent with common sense while acknowledging that certain necessary refinements take the account beyond the naive folk picture. He locates this complexity, by and large, in his semantics, arguing that we can see the philosophical concerns that trouble PCS as creatures of language that can be handled with suitably sophisticated semantic analyses. We are sophisticated beings in a complex world, and our theory must be subtle enough to model this, but we can introduce the subtlety into the model without having to complicate the world beyond recognition.

The "Human Theory"

Much of Perry's most prominent work over the past three decades has concerned the philosophy of language and mind, but in the background of all this has been his interest in the nature of the self and its place in the world. As we noted above, he has been out to produce a "human-theory," that is, a systematic account of what we are as rational, cognitive agents and how we function in a dynamic world. His work on this theory is closely related to his semantic concerns, which generally relate to cognition and communication, two characteristically human activities. Humans are the proper object of a "human-theory," but what does Perry take humans to be?

In Perry 2002, he supplies an answer to this question, proposing the following as a "philosophical hypothesis":

(i) human beings are naturally occurring information-content harnessing devices; (ii) our system of using propositional attitude reports as explanations of actions (including internal acts such as theoretical or practical inferences) is a system of dual-purpose indirect classification, which involves attunement to the way humans work as information-content harnessing devices; and (iii) our concept of persons and personal identity reflects this attunement.[8]

In what follows, we will use this hypothesis to frame our description of Perry's self. We will emphasize the idea that humans are naturally occurring, IC-harnessing devices that can be attuned to their surroundings, wielding a dual-purpose indirect classification system in the interest of goal-directed activity, explanation, and understanding. In short, human persons are semantic beings capable of action. His theory of the self is a physicalist one. Within it, however, he is committed to accommodating our commonsense intuitions about consciousness, identity, and freedom, among other things, as we will see later. In this section, we elaborate Perry's hypothesis, focusing on three salient dimensions: (a) the theory of content that explains what it is we harness, (b) the theory of action that connects our semantic abilities with our practical abilities, and (c) the theory of persons that unifies the elements into a full account of the self.

Theory of Content

Entrance into the theory of content is typically by way of metaphysics (e.g., what meaning and reference are, etc.) or epistemology (e.g., how we know what a sentence or utterance means, etc.). For Perry, the way in is through metaphysics. As he sees it, the world is chock-full of meaning, understood as informational content. "Reality consists of situations," he tells us, and it is his understanding of situations that underpins his understanding of content. We begin this part with a description of situation theory and then follow that with Perry's account of information and IC. We close by considering his substantial contributions to semantic theory, detailing the role played by IC.

Situation theory   The theory with which Perry's name may be most closely associated is probably situation semantics, a framework for explaining phenomena related to meaning that he developed with Jon Barwise in the late 1970s and early 1980s. The reigning paradigms for the semantic values of sentences at the time were truth-values as extensions and, for philosophers who followed developments in possible worlds semantics, functions from possible worlds to truth-values as their meanings or intensions. Other fact-based accounts were available, but they were widely regarded as having been discredited by "the slingshot," an argument deployed by Church, Quine, Davidson, and others that contends that, on plausible assumptions, facts collapse into truth-values and so cannot be tenably taken as the *extension* of truth values. Barwise and Perry called this small argument "the slingshot," in honor of Davidson's use of it to slay a giant, namely, Reichenbach fact-oriented semantics. On the issue in question, however, Barwise and Perry sympathized with Reichenbach rather than Davidson. On many other issues, they were influenced by Davidson, including his emphasis on truth-conditions as a central part of semantics and his advocacy of what Barwise and Perry called, after a remark of Davidson's critical of Fregean approaches, "semantic innocence."[9]

The central element of this account is the idea that sentences designate types of situations. There was no single problem that the introduction of situations was designed to solve; rather, Barwise and Perry saw a semantics based on situations as providing a framework within which certain conceptual problems could be given the right kind of solutions. It was the desire to supply perception and belief semantics with an innocent account that forced the introduction of situations (Barwise and Perry 1980). The "innocence" in question is what Davidson calls "our pre-Fregean semantic innocence,"[10] the idea that a word makes the same contribution to the content of a sentence or utterance, regardless of where in the sentence it occurs. Though Frege and others had solutions to these conceptual problems, Barwise and Perry viewed the solutions as fundamentally misguided because they were not innocent.

To illustrate the difference consider the following pair of sentences:

(1a)   Sally believes Scott wrote *Waverly*.

(1b)   Sally believes the man who wrote twenty-nine *Waverly* novels wrote *Waverly*.

Sentence (1b) might be true, while (1a) is false. This is puzzling on the assumption that the referent of an expression aids in determining the truth value of the enclosing sentence, given the fact that Scott is the man who wrote twenty-nine *Waverly* novels. Frege's well-known and very noninnocent solution is that embedded expressions do not have their usual referents but refer instead to what is normally their sense. In contrast, Barwise and Perry account for the difference by holding that the embedded sentences stand for different situations types. The property of being a man is, for example, a constituent of the situation designated by the embedded sentence in (1b), but not (1a). The basic reason for preferring an account like Barwise and Perry's over Frege's is a reason for thinking that semantic innocence holds, namely, that words mean something different in embedded contexts just seems implausible, to them as to Davidson.

With the development of situation semantics, semantic innocence became a fundamental tenet of Perry's philosophy of language. Situations have met a rather different fate. They have persisted as part of his metaphysics but, for a variety of reasons, have ceased to be the designate of utterances, their role taken up by various types of propositions. Metaphysically, "real" situations remain the basic components of reality for Perry. As the world divided into facts for early Wittgenstein, it divides into situations for Perry. What many think of as the basic metaphysical building blocks of the world—namely, individuals, properties, and relations—are "uniformities" or "invariants" across situations in this worldview. States of affairs are possibilities, conceived within a family of such uniformities; that is, they are possibilities for the properties and relations recognized therein to hold of the individuals recognized therein. A situation, a chunk of reality, *supports* a state of affairs. For example, the state of affairs in Perry's yard on 15 May 1980, supports the state of affairs ⟨Running, Mollie, 1 = yes⟩, making the latter factual. Situations can be typed by the kinds of states of affairs they support.

In addition, one type of situation can *involve* another; that is, if there is a situation of the involving type, there is a situation of the involved type. Such involvements are called "constraints."[11] Constraints are "systematic relations" that hold between situations; more specifically, they are contingently existing, law-like relations that hold between specific types of situations.[12] They come in various types: necessary/logical; nomic/physical (e.g., natural laws); or conventional. These relations are a central part of Perry's metaphysics and epistemology. First, reality consists of situations knitted together by constraints—they are the relations that bind individuals, properties, and relations into the complex, overlapping patterns that constitute the world as we know it. Second, our knowledge of this world is grounded in our appreciation for the ways in which situations are so related. Indeed, as we shall see, attunement to these relations enables us to extract meaning from the facts we encounter in the world.

Information and information content Perry's situation-based, physicalist metaphysics is the foundation for his semantic theory. The meanings of our detachable representations—that is, our thoughts and words—are grounded in a naturalistic meaning that is fundamentally relational and implicative, where this is rooted in the involvement of situations. By moving in this direction, he rejects the idea of an internal, psychological theory of meaning and opts instead for an external theory of meaning that focuses on the "described world."[13] Meaning is all around us, underwritten by the existence of physical, logical, and conventional relations among situations. We get to meanings from situations with the help of *information*, where information is understood as what must be the case for the information carrier to have occurred as it did, given the way the world works. Though information first appears in "Frege on Demonstratives" in the form of singular contents of utterances, it remains mostly a crude metaphor until *Situation and attitudes*. The transforming event was the publication of Dretske's (1981) *Knowledge and the Flow of Information*, which had a strong influence on Perry's later writings. His use of information is in part a reaction to strengths and weaknesses in Dretske's account.

As Dretske defines information, an event e of type E carries the information *that p* if events of the type occur *only if* events of type F occur and an event of type F makes p true.[14] So defined, information has two distinctive features: it is indeterminate and it is infallible (i.e., it cannot be false). Both of these features distinguish information from meaning and, in particular, the semantic content of linguistic items and mental states. First, if an event carries the information *that p*, it also carries an indefinite number other pieces of information that are logically implied by p. In contrast, the fact that p logically implies q does not mean that a belief *that p* is also a belief *that q*. Second, to say that semantic content can be false is to say that a bearer can have the content that p even if p is not the case. Falsehood is antithetical to the very concept of information, for, if something isn't true, it isn't information. These pose important challenges for Perry, who wishes to construct an information-based account of semantic content.

Perry takes information to be carried by physical aspects of the world.[15] Information is carried by facts or, more specifically, by situations that "carry information by virtue of making certain states of affairs factual."[16] The information carried by facts consists in the conditions that must have been realized by actual situations, given the way that situations are related to one another in the world, that is, given the constraints that bind situations to one another. This presupposes a largely stable set of constraints, each of which is regular and systematic as we have seen. The stability of this set of constraints ensures that one situation can dependably indicate how things stand with another. This situation-based account of information enables Perry to meet the first challenge posed above. An event can carry the information *that p* without carrying all logical consequences of p. As we have seen, information is always relative to constraints, and a constraint linking situations of type A to situations of type B does not link A-type situations to situations whose obtaining is logically implied by B-type situations. For example, a constraint linking being alive and breathing does not link events of being alive to situations involving mathematical propositions even if these situations are logically implied by the situation of something breathing. So, if the obtaining of a situation carries the information *that p* relative to constraint C, it does not carry all information that is logically implied by p, thereby meeting the first challenge.

Information is a significant step in the semantic direction for Perry, but it is only a step. We can read information off of facts in the world, and thereby learn things about the way the world works. But as the second challenge indicates, information is true *essentially*—if it isn't true, it can't be information. Because information must be true, "X carries the information that P" implies P; however, this is not the case with the meanings of our thoughts and words. To say of an utterance U of sentence S that it means P is not to imply P. Thus, the "carrying information" relation cannot be used to model the relevant "meaning" relation. Perry aims to model meaning insofar as we traffic in it, and an essentially truthful medium won't fit the bill. Our thoughts and our words can be true or false, and so semantics must meet the second challenge by doing justice to this bivalence. Thus, he needs something that (a) tracks the regularities in our experience and (b) can be false, because we often get things wrong. To do this job, Perry introduces IC, which he uses to classify representations that can get the world wrong.[17] This move is necessary to ensure that the concept of information used as the basis of Perry's semantics has the intensional profile required by the second challenge. By introducing IC, Perry is able to capture the failure of the inference from means *P* to *P* while remaining committed to an external, information-based, semantic approach.

Following Perry, we turn to the standard issue home mousetrap for an example of IC, set in the context of action. Ideally, a constraint links the property of the cheese-carrying tray being depressed to the state of a mouse being on the trap. Given this constraint, the occurrence of this state of the tray carries the information that there is a mouse on the trap. When the state obtains in ideal circumstances and the trap snaps back, the necessary conditions in the environment obtain and the action is successful. But the connection between states of devices and organisms, on the one hand, and the external environment is obviously not infallible. The constraints that are operative in the real world are partial, not exceptionless, correlations. The tray may get depressed even if there is no mouse present, and so this state can be false, unlike carriers of information. The problem arises even more radically for the beliefs and other "executable" and "detachable" representations in complex, natural organisms—that is, representations that structure and shape our behavior underneath the level of consciousness and those that we can detach from the causal commerce of behavior and consider reflectively. In these organisms, success in the paradigm case depends on desires and beliefs, which provide longer-term representations of more stable regions of the environment, in addition to perceptions and tendencies to act. If our actions succeed in satisfying our desires, it is generally because our beliefs are correct. Beliefs, however, can be at least as unreliable as perceptions. We can represent the world as being *thus and so* when it is not, which is to say that we can *mis*represent the world. The states of the mouse trap and the complex agent do indicate how things stand in the world, relative to constraints, but because of their fallibility, they cannot be said to carry information. Rather, they carry representational content that Perry calls IC.

Perry develops this notion of IC, distinguishing between reflexive and incremental IC. Reflexive IC is relative to constraints, and incremental IC to both constraints and specific circumstances. To take an example from Israel and Perry 1991, given the principles of how they are formed, X rays carry a variety of different types of information. Consider an X ray of a dog with a broken leg. The X ray contains the *reflexive* IC that the dog *it* was taken of has a broken leg, relative to constraints based on how X rays work and animal anatomy. This is reflexive IC, since the content carried by the X ray is explicitly relative to itself. It contains the *incremental* IC that Mollie has a broken leg relative to all of that plus the circumstance that the X ray is *of* Mollie. We get to incremental IC by *loading* items from the context into the appropriate positions in the reflexive content—for example, Mollie into the position in the reflexive content occupied by "the dog it was taken of."[18]

So developed, IC is crucial to an adequate understanding of our classificatory behavior. As we noted, Perry believes we are "naturally occurring IC harnessing devices," and it is via our classificatory behavior that we harness IC. We naturally classify objects and events that we encounter, and our classificatory behavior is generally systematic and rational, keyed to the attributes of what we are classifying. We can classify these objects and events *directly*, in terms of their attributes, or *indirectly*, in terms of the information they carry about the attributes of *other* objects and events. Indirect classification is essentially connected to meaning: the information an object O carries about some other object or event is a semantic property, a type of meaning that can be attributed to O.[19] As before, when we move from idealized situations to the actual messy world, the flawless constraints that underlie information must be replaced by the partial correlations that actually obtain and that support IC. In developing his theory of IC in Perry 2001b, he focuses on situations involving utterances that can be indirectly classified in different ways, depending on how one perceives them in relationship to the surrounding world. Alternative classifications yield alternative ICs.

Semantic content   To this point, we have seen that Perry takes us to use information and IC to classify situations indirectly in terms of what they tell us about other situations. As noted above, IC is the more relevant for Perry's purposes, as it allows him to characterize mind and language. Recall that, when we classify, we attend to certain attributes of the situation classified. When we classify indirectly, we attend to those attributes that indicate how things stand with a systematically related situation, where this relation is cashed out in terms of constraints. Indirect classification is the foundation of Perry's semantic story, and here we lay that out in more detail. We begin by surveying the semantic problems Perry has addressed during the past thirty years, concentrating on the development of his view. We then detail the mature view, presented most explicitly in Perry 2001b.

The problems   Perry's knack for finding problems is on display in his early work in the philosophy of language, which focuses on demonstrative and indexical phenomena. In Perry 1977, he argues that statements containing indexicals and demonstratives, like those in (2), cause serious problems for Frege's semantic theory, based as it is on time-, self-, and location-independent senses and thoughts.

(2a)   I am David Hume.

(2b) This is Edinburgh.

(2c) It is now 1775.

The problem in a nutshell is that Frege requires indexicals to function as *complete* senses in the sentences in which they occur. Because complete senses determine references for Frege, the senses of the sentences in (2) must change with utterance context, since their truth-values change with the context. It is implausible to suppose that the sense of any of the words in (2a), for example, change with context because what speakers know when they understand these expressions does not change. According to Frege, the sense of 'I' should complete the incomplete sense of 'am David Hume' (ignoring tense), but its features make it ill-suited to serve in this role. The upshot is that, *pace* Frege, indexicals must not have complete senses.

Perry addresses similar themes in Perry 1979 in the context of the then current concepts of *de re* and *de dicto* belief, the problem of quantifying in, and the "new theory of reference." He maintains that action explanation poses problems for the standard analysis of beliefs as relations between individuals and context independent propositions:[20] we cannot account for why people act the way they do if we accept this picture of the attitudes. In order for a belief to lead to an action, the believer-actor must be related to the content of the belief in a context-dependent way one might express by using the word 'I'. For example, believing that *Hume is thirsty* (i.e., standing in relation to this proposition) cannot in and of itself lead Hume to ask for a glass of water and then proceed to drink it. He will only take these steps if he believes that *he* is Hume and so, from his perspective, that "I am thirsty." However, what distinguishes the last belief from the first is not the proposition believed but how it is believed. It must be believed in a way that only Hume can believe it—something that the conventional picture cannot capture. To resolve this problem, Perry proposes that beliefs, like utterances, have multiple contents and that some of these contents are essentially indexical and self-locating, in that they specify where one is, who one is, or when it is in a way that that connects the believer viewed subjectively to individuals, time and places viewed objectively. In this early work, Perry argues that we need a level of meaning for utterances and thoughts patterned after Kaplan's concept of character, which different thoughts and utterances, with different contents and truth-values, can have in common. As he describes in "Situating Semantics: A Response," in this volume, this view evolved into the reflexive-referential theory.

The important concept of unarticulated constituents emerges in Perry 1986. Having realized that explanations of our actions and many of our statements require self-reflexive contents, Perry notices that many of our statements lack explicit components that function reflexively, picking out features of the statements. Consider his principal examples, weather and time reports. He argues that proper treatment of these requires one to incorporate the location where the report is made into the semantic content. This is so even though the reports themselves contain no elements that refer to these locations. The same is true of *thoughts* about time or weather. Thoughts on these topics may be about the location where they occur even though they lack an element that picks out these locations. Perry describes these unrepresented components of contents as "unarticulated constituents" and argues that they are pervasive features of language. Unarticulated constituents go on to become basic building blocks of Perry's account of how humans use language and perform actions.

In Perry's early work in the philosophy of language, the picture is that utterances and thoughts have two fundamental semantic properties: their meanings or roles, corresponding more or less to Kaplan's level of character, and their contents, the proposition a believer believes or a speaker expresses. For reasons Perry explains in his "Response," this evolved into the reflexive-referential theory, in which the meaning gives rise to multiple contents in a systematic way, each content capturing what the world must be like for the thought or utterance to be true. The most basic contents are conditions on the thought or utterances themselves, and so are "reflexive"; at the other end of the spectrum, we have the conditions put on the subject matter of the thoughts or utterances, taking all of the facts that determine reference as given. Evolution toward this view began with his response to Wettstein's criticisms of Perry 1986. In "On Sense and Reference," Frege observed that true identities like (3a) might be informative, whereas those like (3b) almost never are:

(3a)   Tully is Cicero.

(3b)   Tully is Tully.

How this is possible was a puzzle for Frege under the assumption that the semantic values of the names are objects, since, granting this view, the claims made by (3a) and (3b) would appear to be the same. The puzzle, which seems to have been solved by Frege's distinction between sense and reference, was reopened by Ruth Marcus, Keith Donnellan, Saul Kripke, David Kaplan, Howard Wettstein, and other direct reference theorists who argued that the contribution of names to propositions expressed by utterances are individuals rather than senses or properties.

Perry describes utterances like (3a) and (3b) as differing in *cognitive significance*. A necessary condition for two utterances to differ in cognitive significance is that a rational speaker can take distinct attitudes toward them. He argues that one can explain the fact that a person may learn something from (3a) but not (3b) by focusing on what he has come to call the "reflexive truth conditions" of the utterances. Reflexive truth conditions are what one grasps about an utterance purely in virtue of knowing certain facts about its structure and meaning. They are what one can grasp without knowing the context in which the utterance was produced, not knowing some or all of the connections that determine the reference of the names, and perhaps not even knowing the meanings of some of the expressions. Knowing only that 'Tully' and 'Cicero' are names, utterances of (3a) and (3b) have the truth conditions in (3a′) and (3b′), respectively:

(3a′)   The referent of this utterance of 'Tully' is the same as the referent of this utterance of 'Cicero'.

(3b′)   The referent of this utterance of 'Tully' is the same as the referent of this utterance of 'Tully'.

Perry also came to recognize that he needed to postulate more structure in the mind to adequately deal with semantic and doxastic phenomena, especially the concepts of saying and believing the same thing (Perry 1980). In the earliest work, beliefs were simply classified by the sentence "accepted," that is, the sentence that the believer would use to express the belief. The first postulated structure was a mental *file* that is associated with repeated references to what the believer takes to be the same object. A mental file is a cognitive structure whose function is to unite information on a common topic. Because the names 'Tully' and 'Cicero' may head different files, containing different information, accepting (3a) may lead to the merging of distinct files and a reorganization of the audience's mental life with dramatic results. Such a rearrangement may occur with (3b), only if the two tokens of 'Tully' head different files, a far less likely occurrence. Perry contrasts the truth conditions of an utterance with the proposition it expresses, with the latter capturing something of the intuitive notion of *what is said* and which will involve individuals under theories of direct reference. Unlike the truth conditions, the proposition expressed will be the same for (3a) and (3b), if both are true.

   A number of the foregoing ideas are applied to puzzles of belief in Crimmins and Perry 1989. In the years since *Situations and Attitudes* was published, the aforementioned assumption of semantic innocence gained a foothold in the philosophical community. Somewhat earlier, direct reference—the idea that names, pronouns, and demonstratives contribute individuals to claims made—also became popular. The problem Crimmins and Perry take on here is one generated by the joint assumption of semantic innocence and direct reference. These appear to conflict with the fact that one can change the truth-value of a belief report by substituting coreferential expressions into the embedded clause:

(4a) Miles Hendon believed that Edward Tudor was of royal blood.

(4b) Miles Hendon believed that *he* was of royal blood (pointing to Edward Tudor).

(4c) Edward Tudor was of royal blood.

(4d) He was of royal blood (pointing to Edward Tudor).

If these contexts are innocent, then 'he' and 'Edward Tudor' make the same contribution to the content of utterances of (4a) and (4b) that they make to utterances of (4c) and (4d). According to the theory of direct reference, this contribution is just the individual Edward Tudor. If this is so, however, then (4a) and (4b) should always have the same truth value, since the sentences are identical in all respects except that (4b) contains 'he', where (4a) has 'Edward Tudor', and, under these assumptions, these expressions are semantically equivalent in the sense that they make the same contribution to the proposition expressed by the reports. This consequence runs up against the fact that (4a) can be true while (4b) is false.

Crimmins and Perry reconcile innocence and direct reference with facts about substitutivity by complicating the semantics. They begin with the assumption that beliefs are concrete mental particulars whose parts include *notions*, roughly the mental equivalents of singular terms that stand for the topics of beliefs (e.g., Edward Tudor), and *ideas*, which are essentially mental predicates that stand for what is attributed to the topic (e.g., being of royal blood). Though the embedded clauses in (2a) and (2b) express the same proposition when taken alone, reports containing them do not. The content of the former report contains an 'Edward Tudor' notion, whereas the content of the latter is a demonstrative notion, corresponding to however Miles is thinking of the person indicated at the moment. Crimmins and Perry argue that the notions and ideas that make up a belief described in a report are unarticulated constituents of the proposition expressed by the report. Hence, the reports make different claims. The authors account for the truth of the first claim and the falsehood of the second by assuming that Miles has two mental files for Edward Tudor that Miles does not realize are of the same individual. If one file contains what he believes about Edward Tudor, when thought of under that name and as the successor to the crown, (2a) will be true. If the second file contains what Miles believes about him, taken as the poorly dressed boy in front of him, (2b) will be false. This solves the problem.

The account For Perry, semantic contents are ICs, and these are propositional tools used to get at patterns and regularities in nature, functioning as classificatory media. Given this, there is no reason to think that we should find only one IC associated with each situation we classify. In fact, given the density of relationships in which real situations stand, it is to be expected that there will be multiple ways to classify a given situation in terms of what it indicates about other situations and, so, multiple ICs associated with it. As noted above, this is in fact Perry's view, and it has a significant influence on the shape of his reflexive-referential semantic theory, which applies to both linguistic and cognitive representations. In Perry 2001b, he examines situations involving utterances of sentences. These utterances can be indirectly classified in multiple ways, with alternative classifications yielding alternative ICs; each IC is properly understood to be a semantically evaluable content of the utterance because each purports to carry representational information about situations related to the utterance. Following Austin, Strawson, and Grice, Perry takes success and not truth to be the principal semantic standard for evaluating utterances. Thus, each of these ICs is a success condition on the utterance, that is, each indicates what must be the case for the utterance to have occurred, given the way the world works.[21]

This flies in the face of traditional semantic accounts of utterances, according to which they have a single, truth-evaluable semantic content and then possibly additional pragmatic contents. Success, though, includes truth, especially when one focuses, as Perry (2001b) does, on simple, indicative statements.[22] With these, the speaker will have wanted in most cases to express a truth, among other things. Thus, Perry is able to take success conditions for utterances of indicative sentences to include *truth* conditions. These ICs serve as conditions satisfaction of which ensures the truth of the utterance, given how the linguistically relevant parts of the world work. The speaker may wish to do more with the utterance than express a truth, though, and this would be reflected in success conditions that are more traditionally pragmatic in character.

In Perry 2001a, we are given a systematic means of identifying these ICs, namely, the "Content Analyzer."[23] This is a schematic formula that can be used to pick out truth and other success conditions associated with success-evaluable representations. The formula is:

(CA)   Given *such and such*, Φ is $\langle$true$\rangle$ iff *so and so*.

Filling this out, Perry notes that "Φ is any truth-evaluable representation, *such and such* are facts about the representation, and *so and so* is the content assigned to Φ, given those facts. So and so is what *else*, in addition to such and such, has to be the case for Φ to be true."[24] While Perry casts this in terms of truth conditions, it can generate success conditions as well. The *such and such* deliver background conditions that constrain how the world is supposed to work by making explicit the aspects of the world that are relevant to our determination of why the linguistic or cognitive representation was tokened. As you vary the *such and such*, you will get different truth conditions on the right-hand side of the formula. There appears to be no predetermined limit on how one might vary these conditions, which implies that there is no predetermined limit on the number of ICs associated with a given representation. These contents reveal different ways in which the representation is systematically related to other situations, and the density of relations in the world could generate an unlimited number of contents. However, the contents identified by Perry reflect his own interests and purposes, which are more limited.[25]

An example will help us get at the types of contents that receive the most attention in Perry's work. As noted above, this account applies to linguistic and cognitive representations, but we focus on the former for the purposes of this example. Consider the following sentence S, "You are listening to me," uttered by someone within earshot of you as you walk down the hall. Call this utterance "$U(S)$." Using CA, we can identify the following ICs associated with $U(S)$:

1. Given that S is interpreted relative to English syntax (and not some strange code), $U(S)$ is true iff the referent of 'you' in $U(S)$ is listening to the referent of 'me' in $U(S)$.

2. Given that S is in English and 'you', 'are listening', and 'me' are interpreted conventionally, $U(S)$ is true iff the addressee of $U(S)$ has the property of listening to the speaker of $U(S)$.

3. Given that the speaker is Jack and the addressee is Jill, $U(S)$ is true iff Jill is listening to Jack.

4. Given that Belief(P) and Desire(Q) caused the production of $U(S)$, $U(S)$ is true iff the person addressed by the believer of P and the desirer of Q is listening to the selfsame believer and desirer.

5. Given that Jack wants Jill to acknowledge Jack's awareness, $U(S)$ is successful iff Jill comes to believe that Jack believes Jill is listening to him.

Contents (1) and (2) are *reflexive*, since the conditions specified on the right side of the iff make mention of the utterance itself. Contents of this sort structure the production and interpretation of utterances, as they express those semantic aspects of sentences uttered that must be respected if we are to use them properly. These are the aspects we know how to exploit in producing successful utterances. These contents can also be where interpretation stops, in the case where we lack information about the intended referent of 'you', for instance.[26] Contents (3), (4), and (5) are *incremental*, in that they do not make mention of the utterance; they are obtained from reflexive contents by *loading* them with items drawn from the context of utterance. Content (3) is *referential*, because it is loaded with the referents of the referring terms 'you' and 'me' in

S. Content (4) is *architectural*, which is to say that it concerns "part of the same device, as opposed to something that is outside the device."[27] A representation has this content by virtue of its relation to other elements in the system that gives rise to it, and, in the case of an utterance, this includes the representational states of the speaker that are causally responsible for its production. Finally, content (5) is *pragmatic*. This content specifies a success condition that is not a truth condition, as its satisfaction is not necessary for the truth of $U(S)$.[28] This reveals that the informational structure of situations is rich and multifaceted, supporting indirect classification of many types and for many different purposes. The classifications vary in terms of their distance from the event itself—they can be quite reflexive or more incremental.[29]

Perry's reflexive-referential theory is a theory of the ICs of representational states and events, such as beliefs and utterances. Take an utterance like $U(S)$ above. The sentence type *S* is associated with a *meaning*, or a function from context to content, where the *content* is a success condition.[30] Among the ICs associated with the utterance will be (a) truth-evaluable contents that correspond to the different ways in which its truth orients us to the world, relative to various constraints and (b) success-evaluable contents that correspond to the different ways in which its success as a speech act orients us to the world, relative to various constraints. The *total content* is the total impact this utterance has on the systems of which it is a part, measured as a complex aggregate of the various ICs that are associated with it.[31]

We can close this section by characterizing what in general the final deliverable of a semantic theory should be, following a suggestion made in Perry 2002.[32] A semantic theory will specify the meanings of representations, where these can be states or events. One way to model this specification is in terms of functions that deliver ICs as their values. Focusing on events, take a representation event *e* of type *E*. (The same could be done for states, *mutatis mutandis*.) For this, there will be functions of the form

$$Y_E^x(a, t, F, e) = P.$$

Y assigns *P* to *e*, an event token produced by *a* at *t* in context *F*. The superscript *x* indicates what aspect of *e* the function *Y* concerns, where this corresponds to the *such and such* mentioned above in connection with the CA. In other words, *x* is a classification parameter that varies with the constraints relative to which we are evaluating the IC of *e*. (Presumably, the context variable *F* will vary with *x* as well.) For example, if we are interested in all informationally relevant constraints, *P* would be a proposition delivering the total content of *e*. For Perry, then, a semantic theory would fully specify these *Y* functions.[33] As *e* will have constituent structure, the theory must model regularities associated with the structural elements across $e_i \in E$. Each such element will have an associated meaning and a contextually determinable range of contributions to associated ICs. The theory must provide systematic rules on constituent contribution that constrain these Y functions, ensuring that the propositional values are structured accordingly.[34] Each significant representation e will be associated with a range of ICs, and a semantic theory's job will be to determine this associated range by implying specified Y functions as theorems from axioms about the relevant constituent elements of e. Perry's work in semantics to date can be seen as a systematic attempt to develop a theory that does just this.

Theory of Action

Let's revisit Perry's philosophical hypothesis, focusing for now on the first two conditions. The first condition characterizes human beings as IC harnessing devices, which implies that we can capture IC and put it to use. The second focuses on a particular practice of human beings—namely, the practice of using beliefs and desires to explain action—but in doing so it calls attention to three important facts about the self: (a) it engages in action, including explanation using detachable, language-like representations; (b) the actions it engages in are meaningful, given that they can be indirectly classified for the purposes of explanation and understanding; and (c) we are attuned to these facts, which is to say that we *know how* we work as agents. On this view, we are input/output systems that take in IC via perception, using it to guide action via both executable representations that underwrite our know-how, marking us as first-tier systems, and detachable representations that figure into our propositional attitudes and mark us as second-tier systems. In this section, we focus our attention on the second condition and, in particular, the role of action in relation to IC. We begin by attending to the cognitive background of action (i.e., how IC is harnessed and put to use) before turning to a particularly important problem for a PCS account of action: the meshing problem.

Action and its cognitive background   We are systems that *act*, where this is more than merely behaving. As a fan of folk psychology, Perry is committed to the idea that actions stand in complex relationships with cognitive representations, including beliefs, desires, and intentions. A robust account of action will depend, then, on an adequate account of these relationships, and that requires spending more time with the cognitive representations that figure into our IC transactions as well as the epistemic states they support. We create, store, process, and apply representations. Perry understands representations to be causally efficacious states of the system, and he believes they play the roles they do in our cognitive economy *because* of their representational content. Thus, we are intentional systems, that is, systems that employ representations because of what they are *about*. Further, since we can misrepresent the world, we are also intensional systems, in that we employ ICs some of which are false. Finally, as we indicated previously in this section, the representations we employ come in different forms: (a) representations with executable contents to which we are attuned but that we cannot detach from the physical states that have them; (b) representations with perceptual content of the kind associated with Humean perceptual impressions; and (c) representations with detachable, language-like contents, such as beliefs and desires. Type (a) is grounded in genetics or custom, and together with (b) mark us as tier-one systems.

These representations underwrite our epistemic capacities. We can be said to know about ourselves and our world precisely because we can make use of representations. But they support knowledge in different ways. Types (a) and (b) underwrite procedural knowledge, or *know-how*. Perry takes know-how to be knowledge of "facts about 'way-of' relations," that is, knowledge of how you bring about X by way of Y.[35] This knowledge does not consist in possession of a formula, or in explicitly represented (or even representable) knowledge, but rather in *attunement* to methods of bringing about results. If S brings X about by way of Y—for example, brings a swish about by way of a shot or a 300-yard drive about by way of a swing—then we can think of S as participating in a system that comprises those individuals, properties, and relations necessary for the bringing about of X by way of Y. Attunement to methods of bringing about Y requires that we "track" the relevant information carried by the states of this system. For example, to know how to settle a soccer ball with your right foot requires that you take information in via perception and then allow that information to guide how you position your right leg and your foot while receiving the ball; this typically happens very quickly and need not require any explicit, conscious representation. That is, one need not be able to say what it was that one just did to know how to do it. Here we are part of a system that involves us and a speeding soccer ball, and we are attuned to a method that concerns states of this system, namely, the method of bringing about a settled soccer ball by way of the right foot. As Perry puts it, "my being attuned to the system is a bit like my becoming part of the system."[36] As such, causation flows through us, guided by our perceptual impressions and executable representations, both of which are keyed to constraints operative on the system and are sensitive to changes in states of the system.

Type (c) representations figure into our propositional knowledge, or *know-that*. This type of knowledge marks second tier systems, as described in section II. These represen-

Table 1.1
Perry's classification of the states of an IC harnessing device.

	Thoughts	Actions
Causation	Representational States	Executions
Informational Content	Propositional Contents	Accomplishments

tations are epitomized by beliefs, understood to be cognitive states that can be indirectly classified by propositions structured in terms of ideas and notions (i.e., ideas of individuals). These exist to retain information and facilitate cognition and action. They can be linked to incoming information or to each other, or they can stand alone and be unlinked. If two beliefs are linked—say, by virtue of containing the same notion and so by being about the same individual—they form a *file*, which is a distributed collection of information that purports to be about the same object. We typically take IC in via perception, detach it from the perceptual experience and store it in a file, making it available for later use when we re-encounter and recognize the denotation of the belief. This is what Perry refers to as the "Detach and Recognize Information Game."[37] Perhaps the most important notion we have is the notion we have of ourselves, that is, our *self-notion*. As we will see below, this notion functions as a kind of roundhouse for the distribution of IC from perception through action.

The representations we employ and the knowledge that depends on them are crucial to our operation as IC harnessing devices. It is by virtue of these representations that we are able to take IC in via perception, manipulate it via thought, and channel it out via action in ways that are guided explicitly by our propositional knowledge and implicitly by our procedural knowledge. As IC harnessing devices that operate in the world, Perry argues that we can be classified in two ways, namely, informationally and causally. This is true for all stages of the IC harnessing process (i.e., for our thoughts as well as for our actions). Table 1.1 summarizes Perry's classifications.

Viewed causally a thought is a *representational state* with local physical properties. Seen from the point of view of a content-based explanation, what is relevant is the thought's *propositional content*. The causal aspect of an action is the physical movement, what Perry calls an *execution*. Executions of movements help us *accomplish* things; seen from this perspective, actions are designated *accomplishments* and are often characterized in terms of their content, for example, picking up the glass. Accomplishments are typically understood relative to the IC of the agent's intentions, which represent an agent's goals. Intentions are a type of thought and so have a causal and informational aspect. As representational states, they cause executions, and as propositional contents, they locate those movements in the context of a larger plan, thereby revealing what the executions mean for that agent, that is, what goals they accomplish for her.[38]

The meshing problem   By calling us "IC harnessing devices," Perry announces that the informational aspects of our thoughts and actions are relevant to our operation. That is, IC is causally relevant for him—he is no epiphenomenalist about the informational aspect of human agents. As Perry sees it, we function as we do because the two aspects of our thoughts and actions *mesh*. Our representational states structure our cognition and behavior in ways that are attuned to regularities and success conditions. Thus, cognition and action play out causally in ways that are 'sensitive' to content, according to Perry, and this is what constitutes meshing. As it turns out, though, meshing is more easily described than defended. A cogent defense requires an adequate response to the *meshing problem*, first posed in Fodor 1980. As Fodor states it, the puzzle concerns the viability of explanations of actions in terms of transparent contents. For example, we can explain why Perry reaches out, picks up the cup in front of him, and brings it to his lips for a drink by attributing to him mental states with transparent contents: he acted as he did because he believed of the cup, *c*, *that it was filled with water* and he desired *to drink water* and that these lead him to form the volition to pick up *c*. These contents involve relations between mental states and entities external to Perry. What makes this type of explanation puzzling is that the ability of mental states to cause actions rests on their local physical properties (their 'formal characteristics', in Fodor's terms) and not their relations to entities outside of the agent's body. The connection to *c* plays is irrelevant to the capacity for Perry's belief to cause his action. So, if explanations like this capture important generalizations, it can only be because these external contents are so aligned with their formal characteristics that they can act as surrogates for them, that is, mesh with them. How they can be counted on to do this is the meshing problem.

   To see why the meshing problem is a problem, it is useful to note what might happen if formal properties and external relations came apart. If this occurred, sensible combinations of mental states might cause inappropriate actions (e.g., states with the contents described above could cause Perry to scratch his head) or strange combinations of states cause appropriate actions (e.g., the belief that the earth is flat and the desire to watch television cause Perry to reach out and take a drink). An adequate solution must show how a state comes to have a particular external content just when it has the formal properties enabling it to cause actions that can be rationally explained using those external contents.

Fodor's solution to the problem sees the formal properties of a mental state as a common source of for both its causal properties and its content, thus tying the force behind causal explanations of action to contents used to rationalize those actions and accounting for their alignment. Israel and Perry agree that explanation by means of external contents is possible, "The belief and the desire make sense of the action. The action will promote the satisfaction of the desire if the belief is true."[39] But they think Fodor's solution will not work. They note that not only are transparent contents external, they are circumstantial—that is, determined by context—as Putnam's "twin" examples and many of Perry's writings hammer home. This leads to an even more radical version of the problem:

How can causal and content properties of tokens mesh, if the content properties of a token depend on both its form and on such particular external circumstances, while causal properties depend on form alone? If contents are sensitive to external circumstances, and so classify persons who are internally similar as different, and those who are internally different as similar, how can content-based principles of rationality mesh with causal laws?[40]

Since external contents are a function of formal properties and external circumstances and causal properties a function of only formal properties, formal properties alone cannot explain how causal properties and external contents yield parallel explanations of actions.

A solution to the meshing problem must show how the causal properties and transparent contents of mental states are linked so that the causal properties will result in an action when and only when the transparent contents explain that action. Perry's solution to the problem, developed first in collaboration with David Israel, proceeds in two stages. First, it captures the fact that the causal power of mental states reside in their local physical/formal properties by formulating a generalization in terms of the reflexive truth conditions of mental states, linking these states with the actions they cause. As with utterances, the reflexive truth conditions of mental states are explicitly tied to the structure of the state and so can reflect the local causal properties that account for actions in the most fundamental way. Second, applying the idea of multiple contents detailed above, it provides a systematic link between reflexive truth conditions and incremental truth conditions that ensures the viability of explanations by means of the latter whenever explanations by means of the former are viable. This solution takes incremental contents to be natural elaborations of reflexive contents that capture the local physical properties of mental states. Reflexive ICs lead to more and more

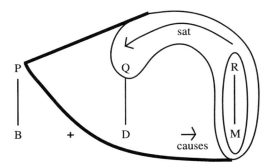

Figure 1.1
A representation of the way in which content and causation mesh in the context of intentional action.

incremental ICs when external objects replace descriptive contents that pick the objects out, that is, as more and more facts about the connections between the believer's ideas and the external world are loaded.

This is not to say that the IC is causally efficacious in its own right (it isn't); rather, what is required is that the causal powers of the representational states be determined by the IC they carry. This determination has a causal feel to it but can be distinguished from the efficient, push/pull causation that is the focus of causal talk in this domain. Dretske's (1988) distinction between *triggering* and *structuring* causation can help us here. Representational states that participate in causal exchanges, producing effects, are *triggering* causes, but their roles in these exchanges are structured by the IC they carry; that is, the exchanges in which they participate and how they participate in them are shaped by their informational profile.[41] Thus, IC functions as a type of *structuring* cause, determining the triggering causal powers of the states that carry it. It is for this reason that we can explain our actions as we do—we treat actions as signals in a system that is architecturally rigged to transfer IC from perceptions and internal states to actions aimed at satisfying the goals of the system.

By way of summary, we can turn to Perry 2002, where we find a detailed discussion of what he calls the "Meshing Principle."[42] For our purposes, we can examine Perry's formulation of the principle by inspecting figure 1.1. The belief state B and desire state D cause a movement M (bottom row). Because reflexive truth conditions capture the causal properties of states, the link between the reflexive truth conditions of B and D, on the one hand, and the reflexive description of M as an execution describe this causal connection. At the same time, the belief and desire have incremental contents P and Q, respectively, and the movement can be characterized in terms of the results it produces, R (top row). Given that content and causation mesh, when B and D cause M, B will have a content that ties M to a result the achievement of which will satisfy the content of D. That is, the agent will believe that by executing movement M, one will accomplish R and thereby satisfy the desire D as specified by Q. The content of B ties M to R and R to Q, which is the content of D, and so D motivates the agent to execute M in a way that is guided by B. Thus, causal connectedness suffices for content connectedness, and the result is a coherent IC harnessing system that meshes causation and content.

Theory of Persons

As we learned from Locke, a philosophical theory of persons must provide an analysis relating the concept 'person' to the concept 'human being'. Perry accepts this challenge, and in fact complicates it by suggesting that 'the self' need not be another way of getting at the concept 'person'. A person, for Perry, is "a physical system with the unity physical systems can possess, not a unity based on some other inner agent and perceiver or mysterious principle."[43] And whereas 'self' can be used as "a prefix for names of activities and attitudes," establishing a difference between the concepts 'self' and 'person', Perry opts for the "straightforward" view that the self just is the person.[44] As a physicalist, it is not open to Perry to identify the person/self with some "mysterious principle" that is essentially unrelated to the human being. Human beings are "live human bodies," but as we have seen, much of Perry's work has been devoted to developing an account of these in all their complexity. In particular, his PCS version of folk psychology, the "human-theory," is anchored in the view of human beings as IC harnessing devices who are attuned to themselves as such and who have self-concepts that reflect this attunement. The theory that emerges from his work, then, is that the person/self just is the human being in the typical case—although they are not conceptually identical, they coincide in normal experience. Further, this person/self/human being must be understood as a complicated, physical system that traffics in IC, harnessing it for cognition and action, a fact that accounts for the explanatory relevance of propositional attitudes.

So understood, a person's actions are structured by the IC of cognitive states and are performed in the service of system goals. We can now say a bit more about how the physical nature of the system helps to structure these actions. Our pursuit of our goals in the world is structured fundamentally by what Perry calls *epistemic/pragmatic* (E/P) *relations*, which are subjective relations that support "subject dependent ways of knowing" and "subject dependent ways of acting."[45] For example, the relation *in front of me* is an E/P relation. (Other examples include *now*, *here*, *on my skin*, etc.) There are certain ways of knowing about things in front of oneself to which one is attuned—for example, square your head so that you are looking forward and open your eyes, reach forward and feel with your hands, or turn your head to one side and cup your hand to your ear. There are also certain ways of acting on something in front of oneself to which one is attuned. For example, if one wants to give a plate to someone who is standing in front of oneself, one reaches forward with plate in hand, presenting it to the intended recipient. In general, where R is an E/P relation, it will support "normally R-informative ways of perceiving/knowing" as well as R-effecting ways of acting. Perry argues that the R-informative ways of knowing and the R-effecting ways of acting are architecturally connected to a type of buffer that serves as a roundhouse for information that is obtained in R-informative ways and so becomes potentially R-effecting, and this buffer becomes a standing idea, or notion, of the individual that happens to be occupying that subject-relative place at any given time. Returning to our example, one perceives the thing in front of oneself and acts on it in a way that is guided by an idea of that thing as *the thing in front of me*, making this the *in front of me* notion. One may also know about it under some other guise, but knowing about it in this way is what accounts for how the perceptual information taken in structures the actions one performs on the individual in that place.

E/P relations are a reflection of two things: (a) we are subjects that perceive and act, and (b) we are systems that have a physical architecture. Given (b), we should expect (a) to be dependent on that architecture. For Perry, this dependence is cashed out in terms of E/P relations—this is his way of developing an embodied theory of cognition and action, akin in interesting respects to that of Merleau-Ponty.[46] E/P relations underwrite architecturally rigged IC channels involving input and output functions. These channels convey IC in ways that do not require conscious recognition of the sort typically associated with detachable representations. As such, we modify our behavior in R-effecting ways based on the R-informative IC we have taken in, and all of this is often done under the level of conscious radar. Thus, it is clear that our attunement to ourselves and our environment depends on these relations, as does our know-how.

For our purposes, perhaps the most important example of an E/P relation is *identity*, with its associated R-notion, the self-notion. What we get with *identity* is a type of R-relation that figures prominently into cognition and action in a special way. We don't need an objective self-notion for many types of actions—the information flows in at the subjective level, from normally self-informative ways of perceiving to normally self-effecting ways of acting without involving detachable representations. This is guaranteed architecturally by the physical nature of the type of system we are, reflecting the fact that we are "points of origin" on the world and can channel IC from that point of view without having to render it objectively. Our understanding of what it is to be a person, both at a time and across time, is rooted in our self-notion. The detached concept we have of persons arises in the first instance out of our own attached, subjective experience and, so, is a reflection of our self-notion. In Perry's view, our concept of the person will be accurate to the extent that it reflects our own attunement to how our self channels IC from world to action.

One important aspect of our concept 'person' that grows out of our own subjective experience is the relation of different stages of the same person, that is, the relation of *personal* identity. Identity as an E/P relation is a short-term, subjective instance of this more general relation. Identity in our own case is grounded in the structured flow of IC from perception through action, a temporally extended event that is experienced subjectively as involving the self-same person. Although these events are often brief, they can be longer in duration—our understanding of our own persistence over time is dependent on our continuous and unified experience of IC-mediated interactions with our environment. The same is true of selves experienced objectively—we understand how humans act and react based on our belief that they remain unified across changes in circumstance. We know that putting a piece of cake in front a hungry dessert fan will typically result in the disappearance of the cake and that tossing a ball at a boy with a glove will typically result in catching behavior. Whether subjective or objective, though, these events are understood as involving different stages of the same human. Indeed, our working knowledge of how humans work—our "human-theory"—comprises hedged regularities such as these involving different human stages that are "H-related," that is, different stages of the same human.

But *why* are different stages of humans so related? What explains this relationship? For Perry, the answer to this question involves another relation, the "P-relation," that is, "the relation which explains (or, if known, would explain) the approximate validity of the principles about humans that we subscribe to."[47] This is his analysis of "the unity relation for persons, that relation which obtains between two stages if and only if there is a person of which both are stages" or, in other words, his analysis of the relation of personal identity. Perry takes the P-relation to be a causal one, involving the familiar causal pathways of memory and anticipation. This fact illuminates the importance of bodily identity, since it typically underwrites causal connectedness, conditions our intuitions about personal identity, and indeed, structures our commonsense understanding of what it is to be a person. To be sure, bodily identity is neither conceptually necessary nor sufficient for personal identity—the often creative literature on personal identity has made a strong case for this—but in most cases with which we are familiar, bodies and person stick together. In those thought experiments where they come apart, our concept of person can be challenged, leaving us with little that we can confidently say. As the P-relation resides in the explanans, though, we associate our concept of person with it in these challenging circumstances—like a good theoretical tool, it gives us guidance in the difficult circumstances while doing justice to common sense.

Common sense dictates that we take human beings to be perceiving, thinking, acting subjects who have a perspective on the world they occupy. We are reasonable beings with minds that move us intelligently through the world. We are both effects and causes, responding to our environments in ways conducive to our own survival and, in the best cases, our own pleasure. Perry accepts this characterization and models us with it in mind.[48] But, whereas Hume and the moderns took Aristotle's "rational animal" characterization as the starting point for their theories of human nature, Perry is better described as taking humans to be a complex type of "semantic animal." Granted, Perry believes that any organism that is responsive to its environment—quite probably any living organism—is a semantic being, in that its responses must reflect at least a hardwired sensitivity to the informational/causal character of the world. We are the same, in that we are also tier-one systems with hardwired responses to aspects of our environments, including those that are reflected in the E/P relations that account for our subjective perspective on the world; however, we are so much more than this. As tier-two and -three systems, we can also traffic in IC detached from the causal influences of the present moment and stored for later manipulation and use. We are IC-harnessing devices that are attuned to this fact, and so, when we traffic in meaning, we can know that we are doing it and thereby display a greater degree of flexibility and control—that is, *intelligence*—over ourselves and our environment. IC also accounts for the fact that we are goal driven, as it is our ability to take the IC we've stored, manipulate it, and generate representations of how we would like things to be that motivates us to act as we do. In sum, then, we are the reasonable, goal-driven creatures we are because we are able to harness IC and employ it in complex ways.

Problems for the Self

Perry treats problems faced by PCS in various places—consciousness in Perry 2001a, free will in Perry 2004, subjectivity and self-knowledge in Perry 2002. In this section, we focus on the details of two of these, namely, consciousness and self-knowledge.

In Perry 2002, we are told that the "straightforward view... that the self is just the person and that a person is a physical system... has been challenged on (at least) two fronts."[49] On one front, we find consciousness, and, on the other, self-knowledge. The problem posed by consciousness is that purely physical accounts seem ill equipped to explain the existence of qualia, those aspects of experience that are responsible for "what it is like to be" a conscious agent.[50] Dualists argue that this appearance of inadequacy is real and, as a result, physicalism must not be the whole story—there must be something nonphysical about human beings as well. Perry disagrees, making his case at length in Perry 2001a against three attacks on physicalism: the Zombie Argument (Chalmers 1996), the Knowledge Argument (Jackson 1986), and the Modal Argument (Kripke 1980).

We focus especially on his response to the Knowledge Argument, which follows the scientist Mary from her black and white room out into the world of color. Jackson uses this to argue that a physicalist account cannot tell us all there is to know about conscious experience. By hypothesis, Mary learns all there is to know about the physical character of color and color perception while in the black and white room, but she still seems to learn something new when presented with red for the first time; arguably, a new fact about the world, what it is like to see red. If this is so, there must be nonphysical facts. Perry feels the intuitive tug of this argument but denies that it is sufficient to upset his antecedent commitment to physicalism. His approach is to acknowledge that Mary learns something new while denying that she learns a new fact. If she knew all there was to know about color and color perception before seeing red, then, Perry contends, she knew what it was like to have a red visual experience, that is, she knew (a): "Q_R is what it is like to see red," where 'Q_R' is a context independent way of referring to a particular mental state. When she sees red for the first time, she learns something that can be expressed as (b): "This$_i$ is what it is like to see red," where 'this$_i$' refers to the perceptual experience that Mary has upon seeing red, the same state designated by 'Q_R'.

Utterances of these two sentences by Mary express the same fact—that is, have the same incremental truth conditions—but Mary is now in a position to know of this fact in a different way. Further, this new way puts her in a position to make an inference to (c): "Q_R is this$_i$," which is to say that the red qualia that she knew about before, from her studies, is the very subjective character she is now experiencing. Once again, this has the same incremental truth condition as (a), so it does not deliver a new fact; however, it puts her in a position to recognize the red subjective character when she sees it again. It does this via Mary's newly acquired attunement to its *reflexive* content, namely, that (c) is true iff the subjective character one has when seeing red is the subjective character to which I (i.e., Mary) am attending when producing this utterance. Thus, upon seeing red, Mary acquires new "recognitional or identificational knowledge" of the color red that is not cashed out in terms of subject matter but in terms of reflexive content. There is no new fact, but there is new knowledge of the old fact, and so Perry can maintain his antecedent physicalism while doing justice to the intuitions behind Jackson's case.[51]

Self-knowledge is a different type of problem for PCS. Whereas consciousness threatens to force the antecedent physicalist to embrace something nonphysical, self-knowledge suggests that the physicalist account might not just be incomplete, but wrongheaded. If the self is just the person, and the person is just a physical being, then knowledge of the self should be the same kind as knowledge of any other physical being. Self-knowledge, however, appears to have a very different character. In particular, it is essentially indexical and immune to "certain sorts of misidentification," as Descartes underscored years ago. It also plays a unique cognitive role vis-à-vis the actions performed by the agent who has it. These features differentiate it from knowledge of other things by emphasizing its subjective character. While Rebecca and Natalie could have the same knowledge of a coffee cup, Rebecca could not have the same knowledge of Natalie that Natalie has of herself. The self would appear to be a very different type of thing than other things, by virtue of its essential subjectivity. Physicalism, which appears to make no allowance for this, is once again confronted with a problem, but this time it is more serious. If this charge is correct, then physicalism can make no headway toward a proper account of the self. Perry resists the critique, arguing that the physicalist can indeed account for self-knowledge without compromising any of its essential principles.

Once again, Perry's semantics leads the way to a solution. As we have seen, on Perry's view we traffic in IC, taking it in, processing it, and producing more of it as we act. We are IC-harnessing devices, but it is important to note, we are devices with a point of view. This is analyzed in terms of input/output channels underwritten by E/P relations and mediated by *R*-notions—these convey information from perception through action in ways that are mostly automatic and dependent on attunement. The E/P relation *Identity* and the self-notion emerge as most important for our purposes once again. E/P relations and their associated notions are a physicalist's way of building subjectivity into an objective model, and Perry argues that they account for the problematic aspects of self-knowledge. The essentially indexical character of self-knowledge is explained by Perry in terms of the mediation of the self-notion, which is what we refer to when we use the first person pronoun 'I'. The self-notion also ensures immunity to misidentification, given that this notion, while associated with the indexical 'I', can only serve as the repository for information about the agent himself. (This is reflected in the fact that when the agent uses 'I', he can only refer to himself.) Finally, the intermediary role of the self-notion, routing IC from self-informative perception through self-effecting action often without the intercession of conscious, detachable knowledge, qualifies it as occupying a "unique" practical role in the life of the agent. Thus, Perry's IC-based, semantic conception of human cognition shapes his response to this problem, a response that allows him to build subjectivity into his PCS account of the self.

Conclusion

"What I had in mind by 'the human-theory' is basically 'folk-psychology,'" Perry tells us, "the set of commonsense principles that we apply to explain and predict human behavior." This theory comprises a "body of commonsense concepts and principles" that, in his view, qualifies as "an amazing intellectual accomplishment,"[52] and he has worked to develop a physicalist account of this theory. In this chapter, we have argued that his physicalist account is rooted in his information-based account of meaning, that is, that Perry situates semantics at the very heart of the human theory. Semantics explains the information content of our attitudes and utterances, our goal-driven practical activity, and our explanatory and predictive successes. As we have seen, Perry takes humans to be IC harnessing devices, and it is IC—a semantic concept—that makes possible our complex experience. We perceive, think, and act, engaging with the causal/informational structure of the world as three-tier physical systems, the operation of which is guided by procedural and propositional knowledge. The result, then, is a systematic account of human nature, one that combines sophisticated metaphysical and epistemological work in the service of common sense.

The following thirteen chapters address aspects of Perry's philosophical system, followed by his replies. Part I concerns general, background themes that are of central importance to the project. In chapter 2, Robert Audi discusses a Humean, instrumentalist account of reasons, noting that this is related to Perry's work both in being Humean and in being a contribution to a general theory of the self akin to the one Perry advocates. Chapters 3 and 4 both address identity. Patricia Blanchette begins by evaluating the prospects for the commonsense view of identity that Perry favors in the context of mathematics. Genoveva Marti follows with a discussion of the semantic implications of the Law of Identity, which is central to much of the metaphysical and semantic work that Perry has done over the past three decades.

Martí's discussion serves to segue into Part II, which focuses on semantic themes from Perry's system. This section opens with a chapter on content from François Recanati, who defends the value of relativized propositions as a theoretical tool to be used in grappling with problems of indexicality. This chapter combines an interest in content with an interest in indexicals and, so, is similar to the chapter by Ludlow that follows it. In chapter 6, Peter Ludlow focuses his attention on temporal indexicals, arguing that Perry's theory cannot accommodate them and so fails to be general in scope. While sympathetic to the idea of multiple utterance contents, Ludlow advocates a Fregean, sense-based approach that, he argues, accommodates temporal indexicals. Chapter 7, by Cara Spencer, focuses primarily on indexicals. Spencer argues that there is no clear correlation between indexicals and the special kind of thought with which they are typically associated, implying that the Problem of the Essential Indexical is really not about indexicals at all. Chapters 8, 9, and 10 are primarily concerned with unarticulated constituents. In chapter 8, Herman Cappelen and Ernie Lepore argue that the "unarticulated constituent position" is inconsistent and that, *pace* Perry, the meaning of the articulated elements of the sentence determines truth conditions. In chapter 9, Taylor argues against the Crimmins/Perry approach to belief reports that depends on unarticulated constituents, urging him to return to "the wisdom of his earlier days." Chapter 10 finds Stephen Neale presenting a detailed and comprehensive examination of unarticulated constituents in the context of concerns about location and location-dependent language. This chapter includes critical discussions of Recanati, Stanley, and Taylor, all in defense of Perry's view. The final chapters of this section are more general in scope. Chapter 11, by Kent Bach, is a sustained critique of themes that emerge in Perry 2001b, the most complete and comprehensive statement of his semantic theory.

Part III contains three chapters that examine various aspects of the application of Perry's semantic theory to issues that arise in the philosophy of mind. The first of these, by Eros Corazza, defends a modified version of Perry's view that we can have thought without representation. The final two chapters concern the view of consciousness developed in Perry 2001a. In chapter 13, Brian Loar presents a congenial account that aims to further clarify qualia by saying just what phenomenal concepts are and how they figure into our thinking about qualia. In his contribution, an extended critical discussion of the Loar/Perry view, Michael McKinsey argues that physicalism is not up to the task of explaining qualia, when all is said and done.

Part IV consists of a detailed, thematic response from John Perry, along with a comprehensive bibliography of his publications.

Notes

1. Perry 2002, p. 67.

2. This approach resonates with the view of John Locke, an important influence on Perry, according to whom one must first locate the *principium Individuationis* for a type of thing before locating the conditions that secure the identity of that thing across time. See Locke 1975, Bk. II, ch. 17.

3. Perry 2001a, pp. 26–29.

4. See Locke 1975 and Shoemaker 1963.

5. A classic example of this type of automatic behavior is found in D. M. Armstrong's essay, "The Nature of Mind." See Armstrong 1997, p. 231.

6. Perry leaves it an open question whether having language-type representations of this sort requires having a language; if not, then that increases the number of second-tier occupants.

7. Cf. Dennett 1996, ch. 4, for a similar classification scheme.

8. Perry 2002, p. 185.

9. For an extended discussion of these issues see Barwise and Perry 1981 and Perry 1996. See also Neale 2002.

10. See Davidson 2001.

11. In addition to real situations, Barwise and Perry also recognize "abstract" situations in *Situations and Attitudes*. Unlike "real" situations, which are parts of aspects of reality, "abstract" situations are set-theoretical constructs out of uniformities across real situations (viz., objects, properties, locations, and truth-values). Abstract situations are used to classify real situations. Complicating matters, Barwise and Perry also introduced a subclass of abstract situations, called "actual" situations, to "model" real situations. So within the formal theory, it looks like situations are intrinsically composed of objects, properties, locations, and truth-values, rather than these being uniformities across situations. In later versions of the theory, all of this was abandoned, along with many other aspects of the formal theory. In later works that explicitly address situation theory, Perry follows Barwise's later work in taking situations to be primitive. He develops situation theory as a theory of the above mentioned "supports" relation between these primitive situations and states of affairs or "infons" (to be discussed below), roughly atomic propositions to the effect that a sequence of objects do or do not stand in a certain relation at a certain locations. See Israel and Perry 1990, 1991.

12. The notion first appears in Barwise and Perry 1983, pp. 97–99.

13. Ibid., p. 4.

14. The foundation of Dretske's theory of information *content* is Claude Shannon's (1948) theory of information *quantity*. Under Shannon's theory events in the world correlate with others to varying degrees and, as a result, carry differing amounts of information about them. The quantity of information that one event carries about another reflects the degree to which the former reduces uncertainty about the latter. An event carries n bits of information if it reduces the range of possibilities as to what is occurring with the second by a factor of 2^n. So, if there were initially four possibilities as to what was involved in the second event—for example, it could rain, sleet, hail or be clear in Palo Alto on Sunday, 22 August 2004—and new information showed that, in fact, the only possibilities are rain and sleet, the new information reduces the uncertainty by half (a factor of 2^1) and, therefore, carries 1 bit of information. If the new data show that rain is the only possibility, it reduces the uncertainty by a factor of $4 = 2^2$ and carries 2 bits of information.

See Shannon 1948. To go from information quantity to relatively specific information contents, one has to narrow the focus to event types that are perfectly correlated or, more likely, use perfect correlation as an idealization. Dretske 1981.

15. Perry 1990 and Israel and Perry 1990, 1991. Cf. Shannon 1948 and Dretske 1981.

16. Israel and Perry 1990, p. 18, note 2.

17. See Israel and Perry 1990, Israel and Perry 1991, and Perry 2002, ch. 9. It is instructive to compare the information/information content distinction to the distinction between "natural" and "non-natural" meaning in Grice 1957, as well as the knowledge/belief distinction from epistemology.

18. This is analogous to the fact linking an utterance of a time or weather report to a place that makes the place an *unarticulated constituent* of the content of the report. Relative to this circumstantial fact, Mollie is an unarticulated constituent of information carried by the content of the X ray—though the X ray is of her leg, no part of the X ray refers to her. For more about unarticulated constituents, see the discussion of semantic content, as well as the chapters by Cappelen and Lepore, Neale, and Taylor.

19. Indirect classification has an essential connection to meaning, but classification in general and meaning are closely related in the following way: without classification, we would not traffic in meaning, and without meaning, there would be no systematic classification. Whatever else we are, we are creatures who communicate, and whether you are on the sending end of a message or the receiving end, you engage in classification. Selecting the code and mode of a message requires that we classify our audience, the interpretation context, and our thoughts—failure on any of these fronts might result in miscommunication, or perhaps worse. On the flipside, classification is systematic when it proceeds in a regular and nomological fashion; when it involves events in the world, this typically requires that we respect the natural categories we find there. As we go, we build and maintain meaningful representations of the world we experience so as to control our interaction with it; after all, it is much easier to classify what we encounter efficiently and successfully when we have a key.

20. A word or two about the metaphysical status of propositions is warranted here. Perry employs concepts and propositions, among other technical devices, to classify representational states. These devices are abstract objects introduced to capture generalizations across states and events; for example, a proposition is an abstract object used "to classify states and events by the requirements their truth (or some other form of success) impose on the rest of the world" (Perry 2001b, pp. 20–21). As Perry understands these, they are not "denizens of a Platonic 'third realm,'" but are objects that derive their reality from their role in our classificatory practices. As such, they are akin to latitudes and longitudes, or weights and lengths. Thus, the technical tools of the analytic philosopher interested in meaning, viz., concepts, propositions, etc., are introduced into Perry's theory as artifacts of our classificatory practices.

21. For a critical discussion of this utterance-based approach to semantics, as well as Perry's somewhat cavalier attitude toward the semantics/pragmatics distinction, see Bach's chapter in this volume.

22. Perry 2001b, p. 2.

23. Perry 2001a, p. 125.

24. Ibid.

25. One area of investigation that calls for further attention is the range of associated contents. Is the world a Leibnizian place, with each utterance a monad reflecting the rest of the world? Or is it more limited? And, if it is more limited, is the range of associated contents for a given utterance systematically constrained in some way? If so, what content framework can be identified?

26. For critical discussion of the role played by reflexive contents in Perry's theory, see Ludlow's chapter in this volume. It should be said, though, that Ludlow is sympathetic to the idea of multiple utterance contents.

27. Perry 2002, p. 179.

28. When Perry introduces pragmatic and architectural content in Perry 2002, p. 179, he does so in a way that suggests they are incremental. However, given that each IC can itself be complex, there is reason to think that one will encounter ICs that are reflexive in one part and either pragmatic or architectural (or both) in another. This suggests that we should expect to find ICs that are heterogeneous, i.e., reflexive and either pragmatic or architectural. (One might say that they are "lumpy" in a sense that is a bit more generic than the one introduced on p. 29, Perry 2001b.)

29. Another important type of content not in evidence here is *network content*, which is associated primarily with utterances of sentences involving proper names. In Perry's view, names are associated with *notions*, or ideas of individuals. The properties we associate with the referent of a name are stored in conjunction with these notions in memory, as a cognitive file. If we have a name associated with a notion, we can share IC with others by using this name. The result is what Perry calls a "notion-network," or an intersubjective network of notions all anchoring IC about the referent of a particular name. (See Perry 2001b, chs. 7 and 8.) These networks support the community-wide use of a name, underwriting a kind of information economy involving the transfer of IC about the *origin* of the network, i.e., what is taken to be the referent of the name. (Perry's discussion of "information games" is relevant here—see note 37 below.) Notion-networks are complicated things in their own right. They are typically associated with a single name and its referent, which is the origin of information; however, they could be associated with a single name and several different sources of information, creating what Perry (2001b) calls a "mess" (136). *Network content* is reflexive IC associated with an utterance of a sentence containing a proper name (or pronoun—see Perry 2001b, pp. 150–152) into which facts about the network have been loaded. For instance, an utterance U_1 of the sentence S_1, 'Jacob Horn does not exist' would have the network IC "that *the network that supports the use of the name 'Jacob Horn' in* [U_1] *has no origin*" (Perry 2001b, p. 149).

30. See Perry 2001b, ch. 2.

31. For more on total content, see Perry 2002, p. 232.

32. See pp. 172–173. See also Perry 1986 and Israel, Perry, and Tutiya 1993.

33. This approach is similar to the one Davidson (1984) defends.

34. Typically, a constituent of *P* will be articulated, which is to say that there will be some constituent element of *e* that has the propositional constituent as its semantic value. As we have noted, however, Perry argues that there are *unarticulated* constituents.

35. Perry 2001a, p. 153.

36. Perry 2002, p. 183.

37. Perry 2001a, pp. 135–139. See also Perry 2001b, 143–146, and Perry 2002, 224–228, for more on this and other information games.

38. For the full account of this distinction insofar as it is applied to action, see Israel, Perry, and Tutiya 1993. See also Perry 2002, ch. 9.

39. Israel and Perry 1991, p. 307.

40. Ibid., p. 301.

41. Dretske 1988, pp. 42–44.

42. Perry 2002, pp. 171–174.

43. Ibid., p. 191.

44. Ibid., pp. 189–191.

45. Ibid., pp. 197–202.

46. See Merleau-Ponty 1962. This work also resonates with certain aspects of Heidegger 1996.

47. Ibid., p. 149.

48. See Perry 2002, pp. 186–188, for a related discussion of pleasure and original intentionality.

49. Ibid., p. 191.

50. The antiphysicalist literature pressing this point is old and vast. For two recent flash points, see Nagel 1974 and Chalmers 1996.

51. For similar approaches, see Nemirow 1989 and Lewis 1990.

52. Perry 2002, p. 167.

References

Armstrong, D. M. 1997. "The Nature of Mind." In P. A. Morton (ed.), *A Historical Introduction to the Philosophy of Mind*. Peterborough, Ontario: Broadview Press.

Barwise, J., and J. Perry. 1980. "The Situation Underground." In J. Barwise and I. Sag (eds.), *Stanford Working Papers in Semantics*, vol. 1. Stanford, Calif.: Stanford Cognitive Science Group.

Barwise, J., and J. Perry. 1983. *Situations and Attitudes*. Cambridge, Mass.: MIT Press.

Chalmers, D. 1996. *The Conscious Mind*. New York: Oxford University Press.

Crimmins, M., and J. Perry. 1989. "The Prince and the Phone Booth: Reporting Puzzling Beliefs." *Journal of Philosophy* 86: 685–711. Reprinted in Perry 1993.

Davidson, D. 1984. "Truth and Meaning." In his *Inquiries into Truth and Interpretation*. Oxford: Clarendon Press.

———. 2001. "On Saying That." In his *Inquiries into Truth and Interpretation*, 2nd ed. Oxford: Oxford University Press.

Dennett, D. 1996. *Kinds of Minds*. New York: Basic Books.

Dretske, F. 1981. *Knowledge and the Flow of Information*. Cambridge, Mass.: MIT Press.

———. 1988. *Explaining Behavior*. Cambridge, Mass.: MIT Press.

Fodor, J. 1980. "Methodological Solipsism Considered as a Research Strategy in Cognitive Psychology." *Behavioral and Brain Sciences* 3: 63–72.

Grice, P. 1957. "Meaning." *Philosophical Review* 66: 377–388.

Heidegger, M. 1996. *Being and Time*. Trans. J. Stambaugh. Albany: SUNY Press.

Israel, D., and John P. 1990. "What Is Information?" In P. Hanson (ed.), *Information, Language, and Cognition*. Vancouver: University of British Columbia Press.

———. 1991. "Information and Architecture." In J. Barwise, J. M. Gawron, G. Plotkin, and S. Tutiya (eds.), *Situation Theory and Its Applications*, vol. 2. Stanford, Calif.: CSLI Publications.

Israel, D., J. Perry, and S. Tutiya. 1993. "Executions, Motivations, and Accomplishments." *Philosophical Review* 102: 515–540.

Jackson, F. 1986. "What Mary Didn't Know." *Journal of Philosophy* 83: 291–295.

Kripke, S. 1980. *Naming and Necessity*. Cambridge, Mass.: Harvard University Press.

Lewis, D. 1990. "What Experience Teaches." In W. G. Lycan (ed.), *Mind and Cognition: A Reader*. Oxford: Blackwell.

Locke, J. 1975. *An Essay Concerning Human Understanding*, 4th ed. Oxford: Clarendon Press.

Merleau-Ponty, M. 1962. *Phenomenology of Perception*. Trans. C. Smith. New York: Humanities Press.

Nagel, T. 1974. "What Is It Like to Be a Bat?" *Philosophical Review* 83: 435–450.

Neale, S. 2002. *Facing Facts*. Oxford: Oxford University Press.

Nemirow, L. 1989. "Physicalism and the Cognitive Role of Acquaintance." In W. G. Lycan (ed.), *Mind and Cognition: A Reader*. Oxford: Blackwell.

Perry, J. 1977. "Frege on Demonstratives." *Philosophical Review* 86: 474–497. Reprinted in Perry 1993.

————. 1979. "The Problem of the Essential Indexical." *Noûs* 13: 3–21. Reprinted in Perry 1993.

————. 1980. "A Problem about Continued Belief." *Pacific Philosophical Quarterly* 61: 317–332. Reprinted in Perry 1993.

————. 1986. "Circumstantial Attitudes and Benevolent Cognition." In J. Butterfield (ed.), *Language, Mind, and Logic*. Cambridge: Cambridge University Press. Reprinted in Perry 1993.

————. 1990. "Individuals in Informational and Intentional Content." In E. Villanueva (ed.), *Information, Semantics, and Epistemology*. Cambridge: Blackwell. Reprinted in Perry 1993.

————. 1993. *The Problem of the Essential Indexical*. New York: Oxford University Press.

————. 1996. "Evading the Slingshot." In A. Clark, J. Ezquerro, and J. Larrazabal (eds.), *Philosophy and Cognitive Science: Categories, Consciousness, and Reasoning*. Dordrecht: Kluwer Academic.

————. 2001a. *Knowledge, Possibility, and Consciousness*. Cambridge, Mass.: MIT Press.

————. 2001b. *Reference and Reflexivity*. Stanford, Calif.: CSLI Publications.

————. 2002. *Identity, Personal Identity, and the Self*. Indianapolis: Hackett.

————. 2004. "Compatibilist Options." In J. Keim Campbell, M. O'Rourke, and D. Shier (eds.), *Freedom and Determinism: Topics in Contemporary Philosophy*, vol. 2. Cambridge, Mass.: MIT Press.

Shannon, C. 1948. "The Mathematical Theory of Communication." *Bell System Technical Journal* 27: 379–423 and 623–656.

Shoemaker, S. 1963. *Self-Knowledge and Self-Identity*. Ithaca, N.Y.: Cornell University Press.

Part I

2 Prospects for a Naturalization of Practical Reason: Instrumentalism and the Normative Authority of Desire

Robert Audi

Practical reason is, above all, our capacity for rational action. Theoretical reason is, above all, our capacity for knowledge and rational belief. The theory of practical reason attempts to provide an account of the basis of rational action and, more broadly, to clarify the connection between practical and theoretical reason. Insofar as the central concern of ethics is the nature, content, and authority of moral reasons for action, ethics may be viewed as a major branch of the theory of practical reason. Ethics will not be explicitly considered here, but what emerges concerning practical reason will have important implications for ethical theory.

It would be widely agreed that the notion of rational action is normative, but the consensus that this agreement reflects may go little beyond a point of classification. A major issue that continues to divide ethical theorists is whether the notion of rational action is *irreducibly* normative or, instead, equivalent to some non-normative concept, such as a complicated psychological one. If the latter is the case—if, for instance, rational action is explicable in terms of its causal relations to the agent's desires and beliefs—then on the face of it, the notion of rational action is *naturalizable*.[1]

This is an age of naturalization projects. To be sure, these projects are not new. Some would consider them at least as ancient as Aristotle. One might certainly take Hume as seeking to naturalize reason. It is well known that his empiricism in epistemology and semantics can be viewed as an attempt to place reason under the natural guidance of experience, and, particularly in semantics and philosophy of mind, John Perry has provided sophisticated accounts that fulfill at least the spirit of Hume's enterprise. But what account can Humeans give of *practical* reason? It is not clear that Hume countenanced *practical* reason at all, which may partly explain why at most a very small proportion the leading proponents of a broadly Humean approach in philosophy, including Perry, have not sought to naturalize practical reason along Humean lines. But Hume did attribute to theoretical reason an important practical role in guiding action: it serves as an instrument of "passion." Given this conception of its role in action, Hume is commonly seen as a founder of instrumentalism in the theory of practical reason.[2] Just what a Humean instrumentalism amounts to, however, needs more clarification than it has received.

I suggest that, whatever else underlies the vitality of Humean instrumentalism, one incentive, particularly in recent decades, is the hope of naturalizing the notion of a (normative) reason for action and, perhaps through this, the moral domain (if not moral concepts, then at least moral properties). I do not, however, present a specifically Humean instrumentalism nor consider moral concepts directly. Instead, I explore some versions of instrumentalism that are broadly Humean but are in any case among the most plausible contenders to represent instrumentalism as a contemporary naturalistic position in the theory of practical reason. I begin with some preliminary considerations about reasons and, in that light, formulate a plausible version of instrumentalism conceived as providing an account of basic reasons for action and, thereby, of rational action. I then pose some difficulties for the view. Given the magnitude of these difficulties, I sketch an alternative position. This is mainly for comparison and contrast; my space is too short for detailed development of an alternative. Finally, in the light of my overall exploration of practical reason, I make some concluding suggestions about the prospects for instrumentalism and about the associated attempt to naturalize practical reason. If the issues are seen as I propose, this will facilitate the application of major elements in Perry's philosophy to the task of a Humean naturalization of practical reason, and I will outline a direction that Perry or others following his lead might go in developing this position.

The Diversity of Reasons for Action

There are at least five main kinds of reason for action (and similar conceptual categories may be identified for belief, which is analogous to action this respect). First, there are *normative reasons*: reasons (in the sense of objective grounds) there *are* to do something, reasons for anyone, or at least anyone of a certain general description; there is, for instance, reason (for normal persons) to wear coats in a cold wind, to do errands for sick friends, and to make amends for wrongdoing. Second, there are *person-relative normative reasons*: these are reasons there are for a specific person, say, for *me*; there is a reason for me to do an errand, namely, that it will help my friend. These are normative reasons conceived in application to individual persons and particular situations. A third category is that of *possessed reasons*: reasons someone *has*, such as my reason to wear a coat, which I have in virtue of needing warmth. A possessed reason is subjective if grounded merely in what someone wants. Reasons that are so grounded are sometimes called *internal* to contrast them with normative reasons viewed as *independent* of what the agent wants and in that sense external and objective; but 'internal' can be misleading here because some possessed reasons are also normative and because normative reasons must be *capable* of being possessed by someone or other and hence of being in that sense internal.

These three cases call for brief comment before we consider the last two. I take the kinds of reasons in question to be, strictly speaking, abstract elements—in the case of contents of beliefs and other cognitive attitudes, propositions, and in the case of the contents of desires and of other conative attitudes, states of affairs. Such abstract elements are not likely candidates to be causal factors. Normative reasons are objective: when a normative reason is propositional, it is true; when it is not propositional, it in some way corresponds to a truth. For instance, suppose there is an objective reason for me to help a friend and that it is expressed, as it might be, infinitivally: to fulfill my promise. This reason corresponds to the truth that it is a promissory duty to relieve this suffering. (If doing this is not a duty or is in no way good, then there only appears to be an external, normative reason to do it, though I could still have a motivational reason for doing it and might act on it.) As to the third case, that of reasons one has, these are expressed by one's intentional states, such as desire, hope, and intention, and they are possessed in virtue of being the contents of the appropriate intentional states. These psychological states may or may not exercise causal power.

The fourth case we should consider for purposes of understanding practical reason is that of *explanatory reasons*: reasons *why* an action occurs, say, why one puts on a coat. These are typically also reasons one *has*; but something very different—say, certain brain manipulations—might explain why one does something, without constituting or providing a reason one has to do it. (Such manipulations might even do this via a wayward causal chain running through the agent's desires and beliefs.) Finally, the richest kind of reasons for action are *motivating reasons*: reasons *for which* we do something, such as take a cool swim.[3] These are not only reasons we have, but also reasons that actually motivate our doing something on the basis of them and thereby ground a motivational explanation of our doing it. They are explanatory, possessed, and commonly also normative.

From the point of view of the theory of practical reason, the main focus of analysis is normative reasons for action—*practical reasons*. Roughly, practical reasons are the kind that determines what we have (some) normative reason to do. Correspondingly, they determine what it is *rational* for us to do when, in virtue of one or more of them, we have *adequate* (normative) reason for an action, as where we have a practical reason to do something and no such reason not to. (The notion of its being *ir*rational *not* to do a particular thing yields a concept of what we might call a *compelling* reason, but we can leave this notion aside here.[4])

It is useful to speak of *reason states* in reference to desires (and other attitudes) that express the sorts of abstract elements that constitute reasons of the five kinds just described. Some such states yield no actions: we are not actually moved by every reason for action we have. Possessed reasons for action, however, whether normative or not, are internal to one's motivational system in a way that makes their producing action tendencies at least expectable.

It is often thought that desires can provide all five kinds of reason. But clearly some desires do not. Irrational desires, even if they can motivate, do not provide normative reasons. Virtually every theory of practical reason grants this at least for the case in which the agent can readily see that the desired object is impossible to realize—for instance, because it is internally inconsistent.[5] An irrational desire of this sort surely does not provide any kind of normative reason for action aimed at satisfying it. A normal desire, by contrast, for instance to read beautiful poetry, can provide a normative reason, at least *for* certain people. (It can also provide a subjective, explanatory, and motivating reason, but that point is not my concern here.[6])

Suppose, however, that we exclude irrational desires as providers of (normative) reasons for action. What range of other desires—those that, if not rational, are at least not irrational—can provide reasons for action? This question brings us to instrumentalism as a theory of practical reason.

Some Versions of Instrumentalism

For instrumentalism, as I understand it, all and only intrinsic desires, that is, desires for something for its own sake—or at least all and only *noninstrumental* desires—provide basic reasons for action (in both cases irrational desires are ruled out). An instrumental desire—say, to rent a car—*can* provide a nonbasic reason for action; but a reason for action is basic only if the desire expressing it is not instrumental, as this one normally would be: we normally want to rent cars only as a means to some further end. The central claim of instrumentalism, then, is roughly this: the function of practical reason is to serve intrinsic desires, and, accordingly, rational action is action that is optimally instrumental in doing this, that is, in serving intrinsic (hence noninstrumental) desire.

In Humean terms, practical reason does its job well when it is an efficient slave of passion. I have in mind not only Hume's famous claim that "Reason is, and ought only to be the slave of the passions," but also passages in which he makes it clear that 'passion' encompasses what he called the "calm passions," the kind such that "What we call strength of mind, implies the prevalence of the calm passions above the violent."[7]

There are many variants of instrumentalism; some are subjective, some objective. The simplest version is objective in the (limited) sense that it takes an action to be rational for an agent if and only if the action is *in fact* at least as good as any alternative in achieving satisfaction of the agent's intrinsic desires. There are various kinds of such optimal satisfaction of intrinsic desire. This may, for instance, be a matter of satisfying a single intrinsic desire that is stronger than any competing set of desires the agent has at the time, or of satisfying a *set* of intrinsic desires whose combined strength is greater than that of any set of such desires satisfiable by an alternative action open to the agent.[8]

It is more plausible, however, to conceive what is rational for us as relative to what we *believe* will optimize our intrinsic desire satisfaction. This version of instrumentalism, like its objective cousin just stated, is also naturalistic. It construes the rationality of an action as simply a kind of fit between the action-type in question and the agent's basic desires and instrumental beliefs. The position seems, however, both too permissive and excessively subjective. Suppose the beliefs in question are patently irrational and would be abandoned by the agent on a brief examination of their content. Here it is quite implausible to consider the action rational for the agent.

The implausibility of this highly subjectivist view is confirmed by its failure to satisfy two reasonable constraints on a theory of rational action. First, such a theory should account for the sense in which a full-bloodedly rational action is a candidate for *advisability*—or at least minimal *approvability*—and, especially, for the inadvisability of certain nonrational actions.[9] Second, it should enable us to explain why performing full-bloodedly rational actions counts toward—or at least never counts against—being a rational person. To illustrate, we would normally advise anyone we care deeply about not to perform an action we take to be irrational. We also tend to advise against actions where we consider the person's underlying belief(s) to be irrational (at least if, as is reasonable, we think this renders the action deficient in rationality).[10] Moreover, if we take anyone to act on an irrational instrumental belief, we consider this prima facie evidence of some deficiency in the person's rationality at the time (and the evidence seems, other things equal, to be stronger than that provided by simply *having* such an instrumental belief). Thus, the highly subjectivist notion of rational action just stated will not enable instrumentalism to meet the suggested constraints.

As it happens, there is no standard instrumentalist resolution of the problem of what constraints to impose on the crucial instrumental beliefs. A plausible tentative formulation might be this: for a qualifiedly subjective instrumentalism, an action is rational

for you if and only if, given what you *rationally* believe on the basis of your total relevant evidence, the action optimizes your intrinsic desire satisfaction. Alternatively, one
could speak here of what you *would* rationally believe on appropriately considering
that evidence.[11] If, as I suspect, such ideas must be restricted further by a plausible
instrumentalism (say, by requiring well-developed inferential skills as a condition
for some of the needed rational beliefs), that should in any case not affect what follows, since my main concern is to assess the basic instrumentalist idea that practical
reason is an instrument of desire. If that idea is unsound, the question of rules for
determining a good instrument—a producer of optimal action—is, though still important, secondary.

As against the simple objective formulation, the two just stated rely on the normative notion of rational belief. Instrumentalism so conceived can thus yield a fully naturalistic account of rational action only if the notion of rational belief admits of a
naturalistic analysis. Reliabilist theories of justification in epistemology are perhaps
the best candidates to fulfill that aim (assuming that success in naturalizing justification can be extended to rationality). I believe it is far from clear that they succeed; but
here it is sufficient simply to point out that, if I am right about the richness of the raw
materials instrumentalism requires to provide a plausible account of rational action,
then the project of instrumentalist naturalization of practical reason is not self-
contained: it requires supplementation by a major epistemological theory.[12]

There is a further problem confronting the project of an instrumentalist naturalization of practical reason. Suppose my supreme desire is to write beautiful poetry. Then
what constitutes a rational action for me is arguably not a "descriptive" matter, at least
of the kind plausibly considered naturalistic; 'beautiful' is normative in a way that
seems to defy such characterization. One Humean reply might be that what I really
want is to write poetry I will consider beautiful. But this move has at least two defects.
To write a poem that I will consider beautiful need not be what I want; and, insofar as I
am aware that thinking a thing beautiful does not imply that it is beautiful, this will
not be what I want. Nor need I, as a practically rational agent, accept a theory that commits me to this kind of psychologistic conception of the objects of normative desires,
such as a theory that says that to want an apparent intrinsic good is equivalent to
wanting something one will believe to have certain properties.[13]

There are passages in Hume that might encourage a reductive naturalist response
here. At the opening of part III of the *Treatise*, for instance, he says, "We come now to
explain the direct passions, or the impressions, which arise immediately from good or
evil, from pain or pleasure."[14] If (as one reading of this suggests) the very concepts of
good and evil are roughly equivalent to those of pain and pleasure, then regardless of

my *theory* of normative notions, the content of my normative desires could be naturalistically expressed (in the aesthetic case it would perhaps be in terms of the pleasure or pain of *disinterested* reading, viewing, or otherwise experiencing the object in question). Difficulties for such a reductive analysis are well known. I doubt that they can all be overcome, but I cannot pursue them here.[15]

Suppose it is granted that a reductive analysis of normative concepts cannot be achieved. As desirable as this might be for a kind of radical naturalization of practical reason, it is not needed for a modest naturalization project. Just as reductive materialists in the philosophy of mind may take mental properties, but not mental concepts, to be ultimately physical, naturalists about practical reason may take the property of rationality in action and related properties, but not the corresponding concepts, to be natural rather than irreducibly normative.[16] Arguably, then, cognitive and conative ("passional") properties might be natural, even if the corresponding concepts are not. More modestly still, the claim might be that if, without relying on your normative concepts or anyone else's, we can tell what you want and what you believe, we can thereby determine, in a naturalistic way, what is rational for you. What is crucial is that you act optimally in the service of your desires, not what they are or whether they have normative content.

The Permissiveness of Instrumentalism

Quite apart from whether the notion of rationality is naturalizable in any strong sense requiring a naturalistic reduction of concepts or even properties, then, instrumentalism can claim to provide a *criterion* of rational action. The plausibility of this claim tends to diminish, however, once we reflect on a striking implication that is often either unnoticed or underappreciated. Unless one has some undermining belief (or ground for some undermining belief) that makes an intrinsic desire irrational, the desire is a source of a reason for action to satisfy it *regardless* of its content; and for instrumentalism, reason, being instrumental, apparently cannot yield such undermining beliefs except in two ways: either by indicating the impossibility (or sufficient improbability) of realization of the desire or by indicating that its realization will (or may) prevent greater overall satisfaction of the agent's intrinsic desires.[17] Satisfying one intrinsic desire might, for example, prevent satisfying two others whose combined strength is greater. Neither of these defeaters of (at least some of) the reason-providing power of intrinsic desire concerns its content. If I have a strong enough intrinsic desire to waive my umbrella at an airplane, doing this may be rational even if it makes me miss my train. I may, after all, have only a weaker desire to get to the conference on time.

From this defeasibility of the reason-giving power of a desire, it does not follow that an undefeated desire is rational in any positive sense. Instrumentalism uses a kind of good-unless-proven-bad standard for desires: a noninstrumental desire can be irrational when theoretical reason indicates impossibility or inefficiency; otherwise it is rational. But noninstrumental desires are rational on this view only in the weak sense that they are not irrational. Their positive normative status consists solely in their power to render certain actions and certain other desires instrumentally rational. Moreover, for the most cautious instrumentalism, not only are objects of intrinsic desire not considered intrinsically good because so desired; they do not even define what is good *for* the subject (either in, e.g., the perspectival sense of constituting a good from the subject's point of view or in the doxastic sense of being good on the subject's beliefs). Of course, we can (intrinsically) desire something that is not instrumentally good for us *relative to* our overall desires, which it might fail to satisfy at all; and we can fail to want intrinsically something that is, as where we do not recognize it as an instance of something we do intrinsically desire. Nevertheless, the relativized notion of good operating here does no noninstrumental work.

Intrinsic goodness, then, has no standing in the theory; instrumental goodness is the only kind of goodness recognized. It is desire, not desirability, that grounds the rationality of action. In part, the point is that intrinsic desires *confer* rationality on actions and instrumental desires; they do not *transmit* it. They have none to transmit.

For many people, however, it is natural to think that if a desire of any kind provides one with a reason to act, then one believes—or at least has some reason to believe—that there is some positive characteristic of the desired object that one should (if rational and properly responding to one's available evidence) believe the object to have. This has been called a "desirability-characteristic."[18] Moreover, even apart from this fairly strong normative constraint, an intrinsic desire is plausibly thought to be a desire for its object *on account of* some such property or ascribed property; and its capacity to ground or even express a reason for action arguably depends on what sort of property this is.

One may be reminded here of the view that (at least in noninstrumental cases) we desire things only under the aspect of the good.[19] But suppose this is so. It does not imply that any desired object (or anything else) *is*, qua desired, good, or even that the *ground* of rational action is desire for something conceived as good. Certainly instrumentalism denies any such normative constraint on desires. It does not even require, as a condition for rational action, conceived as action serving intrinsic desire, that one believe one *has* the desire(s) or that one want the object in question *for* any particular property of it, much less that realizing the desire will be enjoyable or worth while in any other way.

Once this instrumentalist indifference to content is fully clear, we may quite reasonably ask whether just any intrinsic desire really does provide a reason, as opposed to a motive, for action, where (for our purposes here) a reason is roughly a consideration that counts to some degree toward the rationality of an action based on that reason. In pursuing this question, I want to begin by setting aside some false supports for instrumentalism. Doing this will both clarify the view and indicate where it most needs grounding.

First, I believe instrumentalism gains unwarranted plausibility from a fact about our natural constitution. Given some apparently deep elements of our psychology, we just do not commonly tend to want things, intrinsically, unless we either take them to have certain sorts of qualities or at least are drawn to them *for* certain qualities, and in either case these qualities tend to be very much the sorts in virtue of which—on objectivist theories incompatible with instrumentalism—it is rational to some degree to want to realize the objects of the desires in question. So far as pleasure and the avoidance of pain account for our intrinsic motivation, these points seem obvious; for we are naturally drawn to pleasure and averse to pain and both apparently provide noninstrumental reasons for action. As Hume noted, "when we have the prospect of pain or pleasure from any object, we feel a consequent emotion of aversion or propensity, and are carry'd to avoid or embrace what will give us this uneasiness or satisfaction...'Tis from the prospect of pain or pleasure that the aversion or propensity arises toward any object" (Hume 1888/1978, 414). Whether this is psychologically correct or not, there surely are noninstrumental normative reasons to realize pleasures and avoid pains. I am not endorsing hedonism, but hedonists are apparently right in this much: the fact that something is painful is a reason—even if not a conclusive reason—to avoid it, and the fact that something is pleasurable is a reason to pursue it.

Second, since the intrinsic desires of normal persons tend to be, in some pretheoretical sense, prima facie rational, it seems correspondingly plausible to say, of virtually any of their representative intrinsic desires, that these desires provide at least some reason to act. To see that they tend to be prima facie rational, consider how large a proportion of them correspond (as Hume saw) to *needs*, for instance needs for food, clothing, shelter, and for human relationships, where such needs are normatively conceived as constituting (normative) reasons for action. If the notion of need in question does not itself ground noninstrumental reasons, many needs *are* such that their nonfulfillment obviously produces pain, and their fulfillment obviously produces or tends to produce pleasure. We would again have a case in which instrumentalism may seem more plausible than it should because the category of actions it takes to be rational for normal agents is, extensionally, at least largely coincident with the category of actions that would be rational for them on the basis of very different normative criteria.

There may be a still deeper explanation of the plausibility of instrumentalism, one that has not to my knowledge been noted. Intrinsic desire seems to have a noncontingent (perhaps even a priori) connection with certain feelings. For instance, if we come to believe that we will not get something we intrinsically desire, we tend to feel disappointment.[20] If I intrinsically want to attend a play, I tend to feel disappointment on hearing that all the tickets are taken. Similarly, if, regarding something I intrinsically wanted, I suddenly realize I have missed a chance to get it, I tend to feel regret, which is a retrospective counterpart of prospective disappointment. Now, even if feelings of disappointment and regret are not *necessarily* unpleasant, clearly—and this is arguably a conceptual truth—there is prima facie practical reason to avoid disappointment and to avoid incurring regret. On the plausible assumption that rational agents in general believe that, if they do not get something they intrinsically want—at least if it is something they want on balance—they will tend to be disappointed, they thereby have some reason to act to get it. But here the *ground* of their reason is not the desire itself; it is the hedonic or other valuational consideration constituted by the prospect of disappointment or, in some cases, perhaps, of regret after the fact (I take such regret to be typically unpleasant). If instrumentalism gains plausibility from this point, it is trading in part on the merits of an incompatible theory, one for which the kind of experience an action will bring us is relevant to what reason there is for us to perform it.

It is also instructive to compare desire as instrumentalists conceive it with belief. The theoretical analogue of noninstrumental desire is noninferential belief. First, both are intentional and, in that sense, representational. Second, each is in a sense foundational: it is not based, through any practical or theoretical inferential link, on another element of its kind. Hence, third, each is, functionally speaking, a potential psychological and normative ground for another such element: another belief can be inferentially grounded in the belief, and another desire can be instrumentally grounded in the desire. Notice, however, that our actual noninferential beliefs are based mainly on sources that, unlike wishful thinking, apparently confer some degree of justification (I ignore skepticism here). By contrast, a belief's merely being noninferential surely does not confer any degree of rationality on it. Why should desire differ in this respect?

To be sure, a *merely* noninferential belief is analogous not to an intrinsic desire but to a merely noninstrumental one. The real theoretical analogue of an (occurrent) intrinsic desire is a belief of a proposition *on account of* something in the experiential context of the belief, something that characteristically gives it intuitive plausibility for the subject, as does a supporting sensory experience (or, in the a priori case, a sense of self-evident truth). I believe there is a printed surface before me not merely noninferentially, but because my visual field contains a series of typescript letters on a white surface. (This is not to deny that one can believe something on the basis of experiential qualities that do not lend it support, as one can desire something on the basis of qualities that one should not, by one's best lights, find attractive.)

To someone uncommitted to any theory of practical reason, it may seem that there is no harm in granting the instrumentalist the thesis that any intrinsic desire that is not objectionable on broadly logical grounds (say, by having a clearly impossible state of affairs as its object) has some degree of rationality or at least provides some reason to act in order to satisfy it. But, as will be apparent shortly, we are not bound to do so, either by the analogy between practical and theoretical reason or on any other count. We might, to be sure, grant such an intrinsic desire a tiebreaker role. This seems most plausible for cases where there are already equally good reasons for and against an action and a tie-breaking desire tips the balance one way or the other, perhaps saving us from the fate of Buridan's ass. Even here, however, once we distinguish the causative power to produce one option rather than another from the normative power to make one option *preferable*, we can see that the disappointment factor may be doing the normative work. The disappointment likely to be attendant on failing to satisfy one's stronger desire(s) is a bad thing.

Desire Satisfaction Viewed as a Ground of Rational Action

We can better appraise instrumentalism, and we can sharpen the contrast between it and more objective theories, if we carry the contrast between them further, in a direction that is largely unexplored. For instrumentalism, since the function of reason is to serve desire, reasons for action are grounded *only* in desire. This is not (as noted earlier) because the satisfaction of intrinsic desire is considered intrinsically *good*. For one thing, positing an intrinsic good is apparently incompatible with naturalism, at least if the existence of intrinsic goodness entails that there are irreducible value properties or that there is synthetic a priori knowledge of them (as Moore and Ross thought), or both. Second, even apart from that, anyone who countenances intrinsic goodness would be at best unlikely to be an instrumentalist. For quite apart from any actual desires, intrinsic goodness would surely provide reasons for action, such as preservation of the things that have it, *whether or not* these things are desired.[21]

To see that the existence of intrinsic goods would provide non-desire-based reasons, notice that it is at best scarcely coherent to acknowledge such goods and deny their reason-giving power. Imagine someone saying "I can see that your enjoying a quiet walk in the country is intrinsically good, but that is no reason to take one" or "Crossing the stream of hot lava would give you painful burns, which I grant are intrinsically bad, but what reason is that to avoid it?" An instrumentalist can try to accommodate these examples by positing an appropriate desire, but—even if it could be shown that there must be one in each case—that would not show that the *ground* of the reason is the desire, and normative objectivists would deny that it is. They might, to be sure, impose, in addition to external, objective grounds of reasons, "internal" criteria for reasons—for instance, that the agent be *capable* of believing that the wanted object has certain desirable qualities, or at least capable of wanting it—but these constraints are not substantive and would still leave this objectivist position far from instrumentalism.[22]

Instrumentalism in its pure form is at once very permissive about what sorts of objects intrinsic desires may have and very restrictive in its grounding of reasons: they stem exclusively from actual desires. On the second count in particular, it is more odd than is usually realized. It implies that if, for even a moment, we were bereft of desires, we would have no reasons for action. We would not even have a reason to step out of the way of an advancing lava flow, though we might know that we *would* want to avoid the burns it promises to cause.

It is common for philosophers in the instrumentalist tradition to deal with this permissibility problem by ascribing reason-giving power to *hypothetical* desires, such as those one would retain or acquire upon suitable reflection—for instance, reflection concerning one's actual options and the probabilities of realizing them, given one's abilities.[23] That such desires may provide reasons is a plausible claim; but ascribing this normative power to them must be seen as a major departure from the aseptic functionalism of pure instrumentalism. For the pure theory, the function of reason is to serve desire, not to serve hypothetical desires, or even those "durable" actual ones that would be retained upon such hypothetical conditions as reflection on their objects. Hypothetical desires, not being actual, are not even calm passions. And why should durable desires be privileged over passing ones that are far stronger?

To see a rationale for the functionalist notion that is central in instrumentalism, one might think of instrumentalism as based on the conception of foundational desires as something like agitations that naturally tend toward quiescence. The means of achieving quiescence that it calls for, the actions we naturally and—for instrumentalism—rationally tend to perform, may be of any specific kind. This will depend on the kind of agitation we experience and on what, in the situation of action, attracts our attention in the right way and generates suitable instrumental beliefs: as we are actually constituted, an appropriate action may warm shivering flesh, rest tired limbs, and allay acute anxiety. We bundle against the cold, sleep to rest the body, and talk with friends to relieve anxiety. One might posit an evolutionary explanation for such patterns; that would suit the naturalistic aim of much instrumentalist theorizing. If, on the other hand, the function of reason is not to serve the desires we actually have, and if in the end that function is construed hypothetically, so that some desires are suitable foundations of rational action and others are not, then we are owed an account of the added conditions that does not presuppose an independent standard of practical reason. What might that account be?

One good explanation of why certain hypothetical noninstrumental desires should have the normative power to confer rationality on action or would-be action is, in general terms, that realizing their objects is *valuable*, for instance, enjoyable, beautiful, intriguing, and so forth. It may be replied that a better explanation is that one naturally *tends* to want them—for instance, to want to enjoy exercise or to avoid burns—even at a time when one in fact has no such wants. But what if, owing to neural manipulation, one did not want, or even tend to want, to avoid burns? It could still be claimed that the *natural* thing is to have such desires and that the theory of practical reason applies only to beings that do. Suppose we allow this reply (though if pressed fully into service it leads in the direction of a noninstrumentalist, list theory of rationality). Imagine that at present I do want to avoid being burned but I have a stronger desire to be burned, although I *would* want even more not to be burned, once the lava reached me. It still seems that I have either no reason at all to let myself be burned or at least far better reason to avoid the lava than to wait for it. But, for instrumentalism, why should a mere tendency to want have any force in comparison with an actual want, even if the potential (nonexistent) want is stronger?[24]

If the instrumentalist grants that it should, one might suspect that a tacit attribution of value or disvalue is subliminally at work. After all, being burned is virtually universally taken to be a terrible thing. Even apart from this, it is commonly taken to be a bad thing—and a paradigm of imprudence—to do or permit something now, because of our present desires, when it will frustrate desires we will later have which are vastly stronger and, at least in that way, more important to us.[25] Neither notion of badness— neither the valuational nor the prudential notion—is derivable from pure instrumentalism. The first notion presupposes a value as a desire-independent ground of action (at least a ground independent of actual desire); the second apparently presupposes a desire-satisfaction criterion of value (roughly, of goodness and badness).

The second notion may seem to be a good resource for instrumentalists. The desire satisfaction view of goodness may indeed seem equivalent to instrumentalism, since it grounds the rationality of action in its relation to intrinsic desire. But (as suggested earlier) they are quite different positions: instrumentalism does not countenance intrinsic goodness at all,[26] for that would be something—here, desire-satisfaction—that, in some normative sense, we *ought* to want for its own sake.

It might seem trivially true that we do want desire-satisfaction, since it may seem self-evident that a desire is by its nature something we want to satisfy. But (leaving aside the regress problem generated by the view that desiring something entails having a desire to satisfy the desire for it) even if it is self-evident that when we want something, we want to bring it about, and even if this entails satisfying the desire, it does not follow that having a desire entails—much less *is*—desiring to satisfy the desire. A person can have a desire without even having the concept of desire; and some people, at least, might, upon considering either their desires in general or one in particular, not desire the relevant conative satisfaction.

Two Types of Motivating Ground

Intrinsic desire is commonly contrasted with instrumental desire, and the latter is often taken to exhaust the category of extrinsic (noninstrumental) desire. It does not. Intrinsic desire (the kind Hume had in mind in speaking of passions), is desire for something for its own sake, where this implies wanting it on account of something taken to be intrinsic to it, such as the refreshing qualities of water. But (as indicated earlier) a desire can be merely noninstrumental: neither intrinsic nor instrumental, as where a desire utterly isolated from one's interests is induced by posthypnotic suggestion and one has no idea why one has it.

If we keep in mind that there are two kinds of noninstrumental desire, we can see that at least for pure instrumentalism, it makes no difference whether a desire is intrinsic or merely *noninstrumental*. Suppose one forgets why one wanted something, such as to go to the garage, but still does this. The action is a response to the desire and may occur even when one has forgotten, but does not realize one has forgotten, why one is going there, yet also has no (intrinsic) desire to do it for its own sake. Since one has forgotten this, the action, although plainly in some way desire-based, is not a candidate to be rational as a means to any further end. Still, *that* one desires something other than as a means (noninstrumentally) is all that matters. Such a desire—call it a *residual desire*—can have a clearly attainable object, and it defines a goal for action as clearly as does an intrinsic desire. We can act to realize a residual or other merely noninstrumental desire, get what we want in so acting, and do so efficiently or inefficiently in the same sense that applies to instrumental action in general.

This apparent commitment of instrumentalism to the reason-giving power of merely noninstrumental desires is entirely consistent with the related *psychological* point that believing one does not know why one wants to go to the garage can *eliminate* the desire to, especially if one realizes that one originally wanted to do it only as a means. Normatively, the desire is, for instrumentalism, still not only not irrational but capable of providing a perfectly good reason for action, say to open the door.

A consequence of conceding reason-giving power to a merely noninstrumental desire is this. Even though this desire is not intrinsic and (typically) would be easily given up upon realizing that one has no idea why one has it, wanting to do something purely as a means to realizing such a desire would provide a reason for this action *derivatively* from the "grounding" of this instrumental desire in the noninstrumental desire to which it is subordinate.[27] *Is* there, however, any (normative) reason to perform the second action—say, to ask someone to move a car so that one can enter? Doing this might be reasonable on the basis of wanting to recall what one wanted, but *not* in order to fulfill the merely noninstrumental desire to enter.[28]

It might be replied that a merely noninstrumental desire is "alien," in the sense that one does not identify with it and is even in some way uncomfortable with it or has a second-order desire—or disposition to form a second-order desire—not to have it. But not all merely noninstrumental desires are like this. It feels natural to want to enter my garage, even when I cannot remember my original reason.

A deeper point is this: a pure instrumentalist is apparently unable to account for why a desire's feeling alien should matter in this way or why the desire's being unwanted or potentially unwanted by the agent should bear on its capacity to ground rational action. It is not as if the higher-order desires automatically had greater normative authority; they are, from the point of view of pure instrumentalism, simply further desires. The higher-order strategy also invites an apparently vicious regress (since the second-order desire could be similarly in need of grounding at the third order, and so forth). But the main point is that merely noninstrumental desires can guide action and cry out for satisfaction no less urgently than intrinsic ones.

The implied parity in normative power between intrinsic and merely noninstrumental desires leads to a further oddity of instrumentalism: I can have reason to enter the garage, since I want to, but be utterly unable to say on what account I want to. I may be able to explain the *genesis* of the want as undoubtedly due to, say, finding myself without some tool I needed. But at present the desire itself seems utterly ungrounded: it is neither instrumentally grounded nor based on an attraction to its object on account of any of its intrinsic features. Surely the rational thing is to regard it, not as providing a reason for the desired action, but, at best, as giving one a reason to find the reason one *had* for that action.

A possible response here is that the *belief* that one had a reason (or potentially has one now) may serve as one's reason to enter the garage. This at best applies to *rational* belief of the kind in question; a nonrational belief to this effect might motivate entering the garage, but a plausible instrumentalism will surely require a rational belief here. Even that, however, cannot be taken to entail any actual desire; it is thus not a basis for a purely instrumental reason. We cannot simply assume—and a Humean would not assume—that believing one has a reason must be accompanied by a desire to do what one believes one has reason to do. This might hold for a perfectly rational person, but—even apart from the case of very young children who can have reasons before they have the concept of a reason—ordinary rationality is compatible with a kind of weakness of will that allows such a disparity between belief that one has a reason to do something and desire to do it.[29]

It is also instructive to consider the belief analogue of a merely noninstrumental desire. Suppose I forget my premises for a thesis that, without them, does not seem plausible to me. Suppose further that I also have no sense of remembering it, so that the belief is not grounded in memory in the way some beliefs for which one has no other ground are. Quite reasonably, I am puzzled by my own belief. I may have faith that there *is* a justification for the belief (in the sense of a ground for its propositional object); but it is surely not justified now. It would seem, indeed, that one's having no idea why one believes something or what one wants something *for*, or wants to do a deed for, in general tends to be a defeater of the rationality of holding the belief or desire. In the kind of case imagined, where the belief is ungrounded and merely noninferential, it is surely incapable of providing a reason for believing something further, just as a merely noninstrumental desire to do something provides no reason for pursuing that action.[30] If instrumentalism cannot solve this *parity problem*—if it cannot properly motivate distinguishing mere noninstrumental desires from intrinsic ones in relation to providing reasons for action—it becomes still less plausible.

Instrumentalism and the Practical Authority of Theoretical Reason

Some of the points that have emerged so far indicate that, as Kant and others have seen, practical reason is not isolable from theoretical reason.[31] This is not surprising if one thinks of reasons for action as requiring that desire be guided by belief, which in turn can provide *adequate* guidance only if it meets certain standards appropriate to theoretical reason—say, being based on good evidence. But there is a further point. It concerns the capacity of theoretical reason to discern not just routes to what is desired—a role Hume himself attributed to reason—but what, in some apparently normative sense, is desirable.

Recall the case of a mere noninstrumental desire. In good part because the agent does not want the object *for* anything, it is counterintuitive to construe this ungrounded desire as providing a (normative) reason for action. There is nothing about the object that makes the agent see it as desirable or even inclines the agent in its direction. In that light, it seems reasonable to believe that the desire is not rational, that is, to hold this normative assessment of it from the point of view of theoretical reason.

We might put part of the point like this. Theoretical reason overlaps, or at least bears on, practical reason in providing certain standards for rational desire. Less metaphorically, the requirements for rational beliefs *about action*—the requirements for a sound theoretical perspective on practical matters—seem to demand that, for rational desire, there be a ground, at least in the minimal sense of something that indicates, if only from the agent's perspective, the desirability of the object. This is, however, by no means all theoretical reason demands. It also supplies (as already indicated) both negative and positive criteria *for* an appropriate ground. If, for instance, I believe that doing something will be intensely annoying, I thereby have a noninstrumental reason for wanting to avoid it.

Once more, we find a parallel between practical and theoretical reason. With belief as with desire, there is surely the same requirement that there be a ground for a normative reason; this is why merely noninferential beliefs have no power to provide reasons or confer rationality. There are surely also specific negative and positive criteria. If, for example, a belief contravenes sensory experience, as where my visual field contains nothing but white and black, yet I believe there is only blue before me, I have a reason in that very fact (a defeasible reason, to be sure) to give up the belief. And if a belief accords with my sensory experience, as where I have a visual experience of people in the room and believe that there are people in the room, I have a reason in that very fact to hold the belief.

How might we account for the normative practical authority of theoretical reason? Broadly speaking, we might say that in both the theoretical and the practical spheres there are features of experience that apparently play basic normative roles; and at least in the practical sphere they play that role in part *through* the agent's beliefs about such features (though the content of the beliefs need not be normative, e.g., involving goodness or value as such). This indispensable part that beliefs play in the realm of action implies that theoretical reason has a kind of authority over practical reason, a kind that instrumentalists from Hume onward have apparently been unable to account for.[32] As I have described the normative power of beliefs, it gives a special place to experience, and that supports a kind of *internalist* theory of normativity. Nevertheless, although experience is here understood internally, this role is independent of actual desire and is the same for us all. In that respect the theory I am developing is *objectivist*.

Hedonic Value and Intrinsic Desire

It may be thought that the suggested experientialist view of rational intrinsic desire, at least so far as it depends on a hedonistic understanding of value, may in the end be tarred with the same brush as instrumentalism. For it might seem that when we take seriously the phenomenology of pleasure and pain, there really is nothing distinctive about either of them, over and above the intrinsic qualities of the experiences yielding these responses. To enjoy a symphony, it may be held, is not to experience anything different from listening to it and simply wanting to continue listening to it for its own sake; hence, to take enjoyment as a source of the rationality of an intrinsic desire is in effect to grant reason-giving power to the having—or, anyway, the satisfying—of intrinsic desire.[33] If this is so, and if pain is similarly explicable in conative terms, such as aversion to the experience in question, then in a sense instrumentalism swallows up hedonism: it accounts for the appearance of intrinsic good and evil in terms of their necessary connection with desire as the real foundation of practical reason.

But should we accept the conative conception of pleasure—the view that to take pleasure in something is simply to have an intrinsic desire to continue it? Does the difference between enjoying a walk and simply taking one consist just in what one intrinsically wants regarding the walk? I think not. Surely I can enjoy it without wanting to continue it for its own sake. Two quite different kinds of example show this (both can be adapted to deal with a counterpart conative theory of pain, but in the interest of brevity I leave that aside).

One case occurs when I am *disposed* to want to continue listening but do not in fact want this (or its absence) because I have had no occasion to form such a want. I may *like* what I am doing, but if, for instance, no one asks me whether I want to continue, no such specific desire need form.[34] Liking is often prior to wanting, both normatively and psychologically. It need not be a consequence of desire satisfaction. Far from it: liking something is often both a cause and a ground of desire for it.

Second, at the *last* moment I enjoy listening, need I even be disposed to continue to want to listen? Surely not. I may know from experience how long I can enjoy it, and at the end of that time I may foresee the onset of satiety. Even apart from such self-knowledge, we can enjoy hearing (or singing) a song through the very last note but, at that point, be quite ready to go on to something else. Perhaps depression might also result in enjoyment's ceasing to yield a desire for continuation.

There are more positive reasons to reject the conative theory of pleasure. Is there not a certain enthusiastic feeling, or perhaps a sense of reward, that partly constitutes the kinds of enjoyments I have described, or at least a pervasive sense of absorption that goes with such things as enjoyment of listening to a symphony? Is it not because of this and similar feelings that one *does* want to continue? And when I am disappointed by, for instance, a walk and I do not enjoy it, is the problem just that it turned out that I did not want to continue it for its own sake? Is there not a difference in the experience itself and, often, a feeling of disappointment?

Admittedly, the enthusiasm, the spontaneously engaged focus, the sometimes zesty feeling that goes with enjoying, for instance, certain music, may be grounded in elements of the experience that can be nonhedonically characterized. My enjoyment in playing a sonata derives from hearing its characteristic sounds, from the feel of the keys under my fingers, from the sense of being part of the rhythmic movement, from awareness of the integration of melody and harmony. But these surely are phenomenally distinct pleasurable activities and sensations, and they need not depend on what one wants at the time. It may be that the tendency to want to continue enjoyable activities for their own sake is the only—or at any rate the most prominent—thing they have in common. But this point is explainable in terms of the tendency's being produced by the pleasure; it does not imply that any such desire is partly constitutive of pleasure.

We should also look at the conative theory of pleasure from the other direction: can one not want to continue something for its own sake without enjoying it? Consider a stimulating and informative, but also sobering, conversation with a lawyer informing one about a property transfer. Granting that one might not be able to want to continue it for its own sake if one were utterly suffering throughout, it still appears that pleasure (or pain avoidance) is not the only case in which one has such an intrinsic want to continue something that, at the time, one is not enjoying. Even without pleasure, there can be an appreciation of insight, a sense of intriguing discovery for oneself, a spontaneous feeling of worthwhile engagement in the process.

A different kind of consideration emerges from a hypothetical case. Perhaps through posthypnotic suggestion, but certainly if one's brain were suitably manipulated, one might be able to have an intrinsic desire to continue doing something even if one believed doing so would not be enjoyable or good in any way, but, for instance, one simply felt impelled to do the thing, as where a kind of idle curiosity motivates action. Thus, an intrinsic desire to continue something not only does not entail that one is

enjoying it; it does not even imply that one *attributes* to the experience anything pleasurable or good in any sense. Here an intrinsic desire to continue doing something *also*
fails to give one a reason for the action or activity in question. Indeed, a non-desire-
based consideration gives one a reason *against* it. The case runs counter to instrumentalism as well as to the conative theory of pleasure.

Desire, Belief, and Reasons for Action

Once again, it is illuminating to compare desire with belief. As different as they are,
their parallels are far-reaching. We have seen that the cognitive analogue of intrinsic
desire is not mere noninferential belief, but the normal kind of noninferential belief,
such as the kind grounded in perceptual experience. Consider my belief that there is a
printed surface before me. It is noninferentially grounded in my visual experience and
is a natural response to it, as least where I see such a surface and am seeking a typical
example of an experiential belief. On the same perceptual basis, I could have formed
the belief that there are more than twenty-two words on this page; but although I had
a disposition to form this belief upon considering whether there are, I did not form it
until the proposition occurred to me as I sought an example. Belief formation is (normally) a discriminative response to experience.[35] Our cognitive system is selective in
what it inclines us to attend to or otherwise "cognize," and we tend to form beliefs
mainly on matters relevant to what we are doing or are inclined to do. Perhaps for
both evolutionary and pragmatic reasons, we form only a small proportion of the
beliefs that we could justifiedly form given our experiences. Here nature is at once psychologically economical and normatively generous. It does not clutter our map of the
world with needless detail, but it gives us the wherewithal to draw indefinitely many
routes as our travels call for them.

I suggest that intrinsic desire is similar to experiential belief in this respect. What we
want for its own sake we want for certain of its qualities; we do not just want it on no
account at all, as in the case of the object of a merely noninstrumental desire. Mere desire, even if stronger than any competing motivation, should not put a destination on
our itinerary any more than mere belief should put a route on our map. Insofar as naturalism attends to what is natural in our psychology, these points are surely congenial
to it.

Much as a merely noninferential belief tends to be neither justified nor capable of
conferring justification on any belief grounded in it, a merely noninstrumental desire
will tend to be neither rational nor capable of conferring rationality on any desire or
action grounded on it. If such a desire is a response to experience at all, it is not dis-

criminative: whatever its history may be, the desire is not grounded in anticipation of pleasure, aversion to pain, engagement in conversation, aesthetic contemplation, or any other aspect of experience for which one might want the object in question.

These points about desire and experience suggest a partly metaphysical explanation of why mere desire does not provide normative reason for action. Desires are, broadly speaking, dispositional properties. It is not essential to having them that they be manifested in consciousness, though they tend to be.[36] Indeed, as dispositions, desires—by contrast with their manifestations in consciousness—are not part of our lives at all. This can be so even if their *objects* are realized (we need have no inkling of their realization). What is in this way not part of our lives does not *by itself* provide us with normative reasons for action. The most distinctive way desires (at least noninstrumental, and especially intrinsic, desires) come into our lives is through our having, under suitable conditions, consciousness of their objects and of aspects thereof that make the objects appealing or otherwise meaningful to us. When we are lonely, for instance, seeing a friend may activate our desire to converse, so that we feel an urge to do so. There is no reason why the mere consciousness of *having* a desire, as opposed to a consciousness of something desirable in its object, should give us a reason to act, any more than mere consciousness of having a belief, as opposed to a consciousness of its plausibility or of a ground for it, should give us a reason to believe the proposition that is its object.

With a merely noninstrumental desire, moreover, consciousness of its object reveals no property of it that indicates, even to the subject, anything desirable or attractive about it. Why put a destination on your itinerary if you have no notion of what to do there? The desire enters one's life through consciousness of the bare inclination it sustains, not through consciousness of anything that makes its object something one can view as an end. At the time, the desire is scarcely intelligible even to oneself.[37]

Pure instrumentalism, by contrast with the objectivist view I have outlined, has no adequate way to explain why a merely noninstrumental desire should not play the same role in conferring rationality as our intrinsic desires, which are (normally) discriminative responses to experience. Modified instrumentalist theories may reject this parity in normative power; but they then owe us an account of how, apart from assumptions that undermine instrumentalism entirely, one can deny such parity between intrinsic desires and merely noninstrumental ones.[38]

Conclusion

We have seen what are, at the very least, serious difficulties for instrumentalism in the theory of practical reason. I have argued, moreover, that even the initial plausibility of the theory may derive largely from the coincidence between, on the one hand, its own verdicts about reasons and rational action and, on the other hand, verdicts that are in fact explained by an incompatible, objectivist view.

Might a Humean—or at least Hume himself—modify Humean instrumentalism in a way that both makes it more plausible in itself and retains its naturalism? At one point he says, "Desire arises from good consider'd simply and aversion is deriv'd from evil," and in the same passage he speaks of "good and evil, or in other words, pain and pleasure."[39] Given his hedonistic theory of motivation (even apart from his apparent identification of the good with the pleasurable and the bad with the painful), it is open to Hume to give to the experience of pleasure and pain a role in relation to practical reason analogous to that of sensory experience in relation to theoretical reason. As the latter figures essentially in determining the very content of our thoughts (in ways Perry has explicated), the former might figure in determining the content of our desires and intentions directed toward the good (or at least toward what we conceive as good or desirable in some apparently normative way). This view would at least produce the basis of an account of practical reason that is extensionally plausible, for commonly hedonic experience *is* crucial both in producing our conception of the good and the bad and of motivating us. The approach would also preserve the instrumentalist idea that (practical) reason serves desire (including aversion as "negative" desire), though it would (hedonically) constrain the objects of desires that can ground rational action.

To work this approach out would require a semantics for evaluative terms and an account of deontic ones, such as 'obligation' and 'impermissibility', by appeal to the former. Here again we might look to Perry as offering a sophisticated Humean perspective.[40] Although Perry's naturalism in semantics and philosophy of mind do not commit him to a Humean view in the theory of practical reason or even to a naturalistic account of it, his work provides a possible avenue toward a Humean naturalism. I cannot try to map this path here but hope that its possible directions will be explored.

Suppose I am correct, however, in thinking that instrumentalism is mistaken, and suppose G. E. Moore was right to reject a naturalistic reduction of evaluative properties (above all, goodness). It does not immediately follow that practical reason cannot be naturalized, nor have I suggested that—in philosophical psychology—a moderate Humean theory of *motivation* cannot be sustained, one which says that desire as well as belief is essential in the explanation of every intentional action.[41] Humean instrumentalism may claim more: that practical reason has a naturalistic anchor, at least to the extent that, as even the arch nonnaturalist, Moore, granted, moral properties are consequential on (supervene, in one sense, on) natural ones and, in the order of psychological explanation as opposed to normative justification, the latter are basic. This anchoring, however, falls far short of a full naturalization, even of a modest kind.[42] Normative properties, even if they are anchored in the natural world, can still be very different from natural properties.[43]

If the functionalist route to full naturalization that instrumentalism provides is impassible, there is at least one other route—also found, if only by implication, in Hume's *Treatise*. I refer to noncognitivism. On this view, there are neither normative properties to be naturalized nor any normative propositions to possess truth value; rather, normative vocabulary is expressive, not "descriptive."[44] Insofar as noncognitivism is motivated by naturalistic aims, there is a certain irony here: the noncognitivist strategy of naturalization succeeds only at the cost of dramatically shrinking the prize. If everything real can be shown to be natural, that would appear to be only by subtracting value and normative reasons from the target domain: the entire realm of the normative—or, if epistemology can be "reductively" naturalized, at least of the practically normative—is transferred to the ontologically innocuous realm of expressive discourse.

I cannot even begin to assess noncognitivism here, but it should be clear that sustaining it has considerable theoretical costs even if there are no decisive objections.[45] Among these costs is denying truth value to statements that appear both to ascribe properties and figure in logical relations with propositions in a way that requires having truth value. Another is the burden of devising a semantics that adequately accounts for the meaning of normative sentences conceived noncognitively and a logic that intuitively accounts for their apparently standard inferential behavior. These tasks may be achievable, but I am not confident of that. If the project of naturalizing practical reason forces us either to complicate our semantics and our logic or to embrace instrumentalism, then surely we have additional good ground for regarding the kind of objectivist theory of normativity I have partially outlined as a more plausible candidate to yield a sound understanding of practical reason.

Acknowledgments

This paper was originally written for a conference on practical reason at the University of Munich. A later draft was delivered at the annual meeting of the Italian Society for Analytic Philosophy in 2000, and various versions were read at the following universities: Brown, Georgia State, Indiana, Missouri, Nebraska, Rome, St. Andrews, Saint Louis, and Washington. The present version reflects additions that bring out the connection of the paper to the work of John Perry, and it is dedicated to him, with appreciation for philosophical exchanges that go back many years. I am grateful to colleagues and students in these audiences for helpful reactions, and for a number of critical comments I thank Roger Crisp, Jamie Dreier, Brad Hooker, and Ernest Sosa.

Notes

1. The notion of naturalism is not altogether clear, but the use made of it in this paper is broad enough to avoid presuppositions that should not be made here. I have indicated various ways it may be construed in Audi 2000.

2. For accounts of Humean instrumentalism see ch. 3 of Audi 1989; Fumerton 1990, esp. chs. 4–6; and Cullity and Gaut 1997. For a broad characterization of instrumentalism and responses to it, see the introduction by Cullity and Gaut. The chapters by James Dreier, "Humean Doubts about the Practical Justification of Morality," and Peter Railton, "On the Hypothetical and Non-Hypothetical in Reasoning about Belief and Action," defend certain elements of instrumentalism, and Dreier's brings out the limitations of instrumentalism as a route to providing reasons to be moral (or alternatively, "justifying morality"). Cullity's "Practical Theory" critically examines Bernard Williams's well-known version tracing to his much-discussed "Internal and External Reasons," in Williams 1981; and Gaut's "The Structure of Practical Reason" assesses a Kantian constructivist response to instrumentalism (represented in the volume by Christine Korsgaard's paper), and sketches a broadly Aristotelian alternative to both.

3. These five kinds of reasons are introduced and discussed in my 1986 article, reprinted in 1993a and, in a different way, in Audi 2001a, esp. ch. 5, on which this chapter draws significantly. I might add that since motivating reasons as here described operate in producing or sustaining action, one might also call them *activating reasons*; and since subjective reasons may or may not activate behavior, but are the appropriate kind to motivate it, one could call them *motivational* as opposed to motiva*ting*. We could also distinguish a sixth variety: *inclining reasons*, those that produce a tendency to act, and are in that sense (causally) operative, but do not yield action itself. But for our purposes there is no need to complicate the terminology in the text.

4. What about the possibility of a reason so minor that, by itself, it cannot count toward the rationality of an action? I am inclined to think that if a candidate for such a minor reason deserves the name "reason," then there is a possible action minor enough in some circumstance to enable that reason to count toward its rationality. When browsing in a bookstore, the slightest curiosity about a book's cover can make it rational to take the book from the shelf.

5. I do not say that a desire whose object the person knows or believes to be impossible is irrational, because I think that, for an object we believe is impossible, we can have only a *wish* rather than a desire (apart from such lapses as temporary forgetting of the belief). We could consider *any* such conative attitude irrational, but I leave open that one might believe, for instance, one cannot square the circle and still rationally wish one could. In any case—and this is the main point here—such a wish would not render action to achieve its object rational.

6. Beliefs can also provide all five kinds of reason, either for further belief or for action, though they may do so for action only because of what one does or should want, where the 'should' is

that of rationality. To be sure, beliefs, by contrast with wants, are not quite as naturally described as reasons for action. I think this is because, apart from what one wants or should, in some presumably objective sense, want, there cannot be reasons for action. Even if, for example, a belief that listening to an aria will be enjoyable provides, by itself, a reason to listen to it, it also provides a reason to want to listen it, and it could not yield the former reason apart from producing the latter. By contrast, a belief can express a reason for a further belief quite apart from what one wants or even should want, or from any non-cognitive attitudes; and this evidential role of beliefs is usually taken to be their primary reason-giving function.

7. See Hume 1888/1978. The famous claim is on p. 415; the point about strength of mind on p. 418.

8. Two points of clarification will help. First, I assume for the sake of argument that we may speak of combined desire strengths at least in a way that enables us to make comparative determinations of strength. Second, my focus is the rationality of an action *for S*, not *S's acting rationally*; I take the latter to be more complex, requiring that the action be *based on* the reason(s) in virtue of which it is rational. Supporting argument on the latter point is given in my "Rationalization and Rationality," in Audi 1993b. Detailed explication of the instrumentalist notion of desire satisfaction, and indeed of rational action in general, is provided by Fumerton 1990, esp. ch. 4.

9. For a naturalistic defense of a neo-Humean position on practical reason that takes advisability into account, see Hubin 2001. He says, for example, that "there may be a fact of the matter about what action is rationally recommended for an agent.... On my view, it is the agent's values that play this role in determining what is rationally advisable for an agent. Other neo-Humeans focus on desires or preferences ... at bottom, there is a fact—a brute fact—about the agent's subjective, contingent, conative states ... the property of advisability just is the property of being properly related to these brute facts" (pp. 466–467). For a defense of instrumentalism that stresses the idea of what we intrinsically want as "dear to our heart," see Fehige 2001.

10. Only normally rather than always, because we might think that (e.g., by good luck) acting irrationally might bring splendid results.

11. Cf. Fumerton (1990): S has most reason to X provided "The collective weight of S's ends that might (relative to S's evidence) be satisfied (frustrated) by X, when the value of each end is adjusted for the probability (relative to S's evidence) of its occurring, is greater than the collective weight of ... any of the alternatives" (101), where "an end for S ... [is] something that S *wants or values for its own sake*" (94).

12. For a plausible attempt to present a detailed naturalistic epistemology see Goldman (1986). I have critically appraised the attempt to naturalize epistemology in Audi 1993b, esp. chs. 6, 10, and 12, and in Audi 2001b.

13. An important question that arises here is how, if at all, a self-concept must enter into the object of desire. I have discussed this in detail Audi 2001a, esp. ch. 4. Questions about how conceptions of the self enter into propositional attitudes are also treated in detail in the work of John Perry. For a short statement of his position on some of the central issues, see Perry 1990.

14. On p. 399. There are also hedonistic passages in Hume 1960. See, e.g., p. 134. He says, in part: "Ask a man *why he uses exercises*; he will answer because he desires to keep his health. If you then enquire *why he desires health*, he will readily reply *because sickness is painful*. If you push your enquiries further and desire a reason *why he hates pain*, it is impossible he can ever give any. *This is an ultimate end*, and is never referred to any other object . . . beyond this it is an absurdity to ask for a reason. It is impossible there can be a progress *in infinitum*; and that one thing can always be a reason why another is desired. Something must be desirable on its own account." This makes it sound as if pain provides a reason for action on its own account, even if we cannot help wanting to end it. Indeed, Hume even uses the notion of the *desirable* as if it did not derive from the *desired* in the way required by his instrumentalist theory.

15. Even if G. E. Moore and others are correct in rejecting naturalistic analyses of normative notions, a Humean can try to bypass the problem they pose for an instrumentalist naturalization of practical reason by arguing that the we can ascertain the natural base properties of, say, a beautiful poem and in that light argue that wanting to write a beautiful poem is "practically equivalent" to wanting to write poetry with the relevant properties. But is there a finite, definite list of these properties? And even if, to have the concept of beautiful poem, I must have a sense of relevant base properties—not all of them, presumably—I don't have to want to write it under that description. And suppose I want to write a kind of beautiful poem that surprises me. Am I not in effect supposing there might be base properties for beautiful poetry not now in my ken?

16. I have discussed the possibility of naturalizing moral properties, including those with apparently normative content, such as a belief that one ought (morally) to do something, in "Ethical Naturalism and the Explanatory Power of Moral Concepts," reprinted in my 1997. For related discussion of what naturalism requires in the case of mental and physical properties, see, e.g., Kim 1998 and Perry 2001.

17. Cf. Hume's claim that "'Tis only in two senses that any affection can be call'd unreasonable. First, When a passion . . . is founded on the supposition of objects, which really do not exist. Secondly, When in exerting any passion in action, we chuse means insufficient for the design'd end." See Hume 1888/1978, p. 416. In ch. 2 of Audi 1989, I have discussed and clarified Hume's position on rational action, which is subtler than this quotation suggests. It is noteworthy that (as one might expect from the hedonistic elements in his work) he seems to think there are some commonsense grounds for criticizing even logically unobjectionable beliefs that go against experience. He says, e.g., that "none but a fool or a madman would ever pretend to dispute the authority of experience or to reject that great guide of human life." See Hume 1977, p. 23. It appears that Hume has in mind *normative* authority here, and one might think he might say something similar about experience as a guide to logically and instrumentally unobjectionable intrinsic desires.

18. The term occurs in Anscombe 1957, but the idea is at least as old as Aquinas's (Aristotelian) view that we want things under the aspect of the good.

19. Thomas Aquinas comes to mind here. His overall view is ramified and complex, but it includes many far-reaching points in the vicinity of the view cited in the text—e.g., that "the object of the appetitive power is the appettible good, which varies in kind according to its various

relations to reason" (Aquinas 1981, Q. 60, art. 1, reply obj. 1); "nothing stands firm with regard to the practical reason, unless it is directed to the last end which is the common good" (Q. 90, art. 3, reply objection 3); and "*good* is the first thing that falls under the apprehension of the practical reason, which is directed toward action (since every agent acts for an end, which has the nature of good)" (Q. 94, art. 2.)

20. I argue for this in "The Concept of Wanting," in Audi 1993a.

21. I am here allowing that an intrinsic good might "provide" a reason without *constituting* one. Suppose, e.g., that we adopt T. M. Scanlon's "buck-passing" view of goodness and value (hence presumably of basic reasons for action as well), on which reasons are constituted by the specific things in virtue of which something is good—say, being enjoyable—not by its goodness as such. See Scanlon 1998, esp. pp. 95–100. We can still speak, however, of intrinsically good things as providing the reasons, though in *virtue* of their grounds. We could also distinguish between elements' directly and indirectly constituting reasons and between specific and general reasons. I might do a thing because (for the reason that) it is good even if I think it is good only *on account of* some particular property of it. Suppose, moreover, that I do it only because I believe you when you tell me it will be good. It would appear that even if, given an inquiry into the status or basis of my reason, I would pass the buck to you, my generic reason—to do something good—is where the buck stops for me. To be sure, it stops there *on* your authority; but that does not make my reason *doing what you suggest.*

22. Instrumentalists may argue that pain and pleasure *entail* positive and negative (aversive) desire, respectively, and hence must supply reasons for action. I think there is no such entailment (in part because pain and pleasure are prior to the conceptualization needed to have the relevant desires). In any case, the relevant desires by themselves need not confer reasons for action just *because* they are non-instrumental desires; the instrumentalist would still need an argument to show that it is not because of their content, e.g., being for something good, that they provide reasons. The next section bears directly on this issue.

23. Hume appears to do this, for reasons I have indicated in ch. 2 of Audi 1989. Certainly R. B. Brandt does it in Brandt 1979. Brandt's position constitutes a good foil for the neo-Humean one defended by Hubin 2001.

24. The problem can also be raised in relation to Buridan's ass: if I am caught between two obviously incompatible things that I want equally, say to escape the fire by land and to escape it by sea, and I have no third want providing a reason to break the tie, then I have no reason to break it; and unless nature comes to my aid by giving me, say, a desire to avoid the increasingly hot dilemma, I have no reason even to break the tie to save my life.

25. On this point Parfit 1984 is instructive. A more recent statement of his view is Parfit 1997.

26. Perhaps one should say that instrumentalism does not countenance intrinsic goodness *Hume's common sense to the contrary notwithstanding.* See some of my quotations from Hume in the text and, for a passage that treats pain as an intrinsic evil, note 14. No doubt there are other striking departures by instrumentalists from the theory as usually conceived, but current defenders are

more guarded. If instrumentalism did countenance intrinsic goodness, it would also fail as a naturalization project unless there are adequate naturalistic criteria for such goodness. One problem would be the normative content one mentioned in the text. But supposing this is soluble, the theory seems to me to lack plausibility in any case, for reasons of a kind indicated below in arguing for the failure of merely noninstrumental desires to provide (automatically) normative reasons for action.

27. The reason is, however, *entirely* derivative. Otherwise, even where one wants A purely as a means to B, one could be credited with two reasons to A—that one wants to A and that one wants to B—which could outweigh an intrinsic desire to C stronger than the desire to A. At that rate one could prefer swimming to boating, but, since the strength of one's desire for the latter, together with the strength of one's desire to rent a boat, as a means to it, could be greater than the strength of one's desire to swim, one could have better reason to go boating. And this could be so even if one has forgotten why one wanted to go boating (say, to meet a friend across the lake) and would hardly know what to do with the boat having rented it. Here conative agitation unsettles me after all, even though I do not know its cause or how to achieve quiescence.

28. If this case of a merely noninstrumental desire is one in which an object of desire is *not* desired under any aspect of goodness, the case also suggests why the view that, normally, what is intrinsically wanted is wanted under the aspect of goodness is plausible.

29. I have defended this kind of view of normative belief in relation to action in, e.g., "Weakness of Will and Rational Action," in Audi 1993a.

30. Granted there are cases in which we apparently know something from memory even when we have forgotten our grounds, but I believe that knowledge and justification are different in this respect, as I argue in Audi 1995. Thus, *even if* a memory belief meets the defeating condition described in the text, it may still constitute knowledge; but I take this to be compatible with failure to be rational or confer rationality on any belief based on it.

31. As Kant put it in one place, "we should be able to show at the same time [i.e., in a critique of practical reason] the unity of practical and theoretical reason in a common principle, since in the end there can be only one and the same reason, which must be differentiated solely in its application." See Kant 1948, sect. 391, p. 59.

32. I have argued for these points in some detail in, e.g., chs. 3 and 11 of Audi 1997.

33. The implicit view of pleasure I take from Brandt (1979), who may have been influenced by Mill's contention (which, as he may have realized, may not represent Mill's considered view) that "desiring a thing and finding it pleasant, aversion to it and thinking of it as painful...are two parts of the same phenomenon—in strictness of language, two different modes of naming the same psychological fact." See ch. 4 of Mill 1871/1998. I am not aware that the use I make here of Brandt's view of pleasure has been proposed by anyone else. For a good survey of views on the nature of pleasure see Alston 1967.

34. This point will not seem plausible if one does not distinguish dispositional propositional attitudes from dispositions to form them. For a theory of the difference and a case for positing fewer of the former and more of the latter, see Audi 1994.

35. I say "normally" because a belief can be induced by, say, brain manipulation. I should add that the relevant experience includes belief formation or contemplation of one's beliefs or their propositional objects: this can be crucial for inferential, as opposed to experiential, belief formation. The suggested discriminative-response theory of belief formation (which I merely sketch here) is introduced and defended in Audi 1994.

36. An "occurrent desire," then, is not a desire constituted by a set of conscious events; it is a desire manifesting itself in such a set of events.

37. To be sure, if I intrinsically want something I am surprised or ashamed to want, I might find the desire scarcely intelligible, but the case is very different. Here I do not fully understand myself because I *do* understand being attracted to the object; in the case of merely noninstrumental desire, I understand the desire only in a historical sense, but I very likely do understand myself—e.g., as forgetful.

38. For a discussion bearing on this problem (but not, I think, solving it), see Nozick 1993, esp. pp. 133–151. I should add that I have not meant to suggest that solving the parity problem would be *sufficient* to sustain a naturalistic instrumentalism. Suppose my doubts can be overcome and a naturalistic account of normative reasons for action is viable. Then the notion of a reason for action can be "factually" analyzed by appeal to, above all, desires and beliefs. But what would be the status of the analysis itself or of such higher-level propositions as that agents are rational in doing what optimally satisfies their noninstrumental desires? I do not think these could be empirical, and I doubt that they can be shown to be analytic. If they are synthetic a priori, then the instrumentalist naturalization of practical reason will be consistent with a metaphysical view that posits non-natural facts and with a rationalist epistemology. A recognition of this may be why some naturalists take the view that naturalism must go all the way down (as it may for a noncognitivist view of normativity). For a well-developed pragmatic naturalism with much attention to practical reason, see, e.g., Harman 1999, esp. the essays in part I.

39. Hume 1888/1978. Suppose Hume (as it seems here) *identifies* the properties of good and evil with those of pleasure and pain; if he does, we should take him at this point to be maintaining a reductive naturalism in the theory of value. Some may think this view is doomed from the start, but the criteria for property identity are neither fully developed nor uncontroversial so far as they are. In the mental-physical case, we find John Perry maintaining (regarding the knowledge argument purporting to show that "phenomenal" self-knowledge could not be of physical properties), "At the heart of each case is an informative identity either known or not known. It is natural to suppose that the key is the two different ways of thinking of the object, location, property, or state involved" (Perry 2001, 113). If predicates as different as the mental and physical ones in question can designate the same property, one might expect less difficulty in arguing that value properties like goodness and badness are natural ones.

40. See, e.g., Perry's "Individuals in Informational and Intentional Content," in Perry 1993. He notes at one point, "Hume recognizes, and emphasizes, that an individual may mentally conjoin types that are not constantly conjoined. To mentally conjoin T and T' is something like believing that T and T' are constantly conjoined. But it is more primitive than belief. It is not the result of a rational process" (286). A similar account can be given of how pleasure can be mentally conjoined

with something one has enjoyed, but not constantly (or pain with, e.g., a single hot stove one has touched). The process is not rational, but given the uncontroversial rationality of pursuing pleasure and avoiding pain, it can be seen as a way that nature puts practical reason under the guidance of the good and the bad—so far as these are identifiable with pleasure and pain—in something like the way theoretical reason is under the guidance of the true and the false.

41. Two qualifications belong here. First, even a Humean theory of motivation may allow that belief may not be required for every *basic* action, since at least some of these may be "automatic" in a way that frees them from the need to be guided by anything like an instrumental belief. Second, to require desire in the explanation of an intentional action is not to preclude the possibility that some desires are produced by belief. Even if Hume himself took "reason" to be inert, it would be quite un-Humean to place a priori restrictions on what can be caused by belief.

42. It is important to note that the failure of naturalization in the domain of practical reason would not entail its failure with respect to the mental, even in the strong sense in which that entails a strong version of physicalism about phenomenal properties. For instance, John Perry's "antecedent" physicalism might still be maintained. For a recent statement see his 2001, esp. ch. 8. Moreover, moral properties need not be naturalizable in order for *moral explanations* to be. For an account of how the latter is possible despite the apparent impossibility of the former, see my "Ethical Naturalism and the Explanatory Power of Moral Concepts," in Audi 1997.

43. I do not mean to suggest that it is easy to distinguish natural from non-natural properties, and this is a good place to add that, for Moore, the natural category was wider than it is in general currently taken to be, since it included all but value properties. Theological properties would thus be natural for Moore. And if, as it appears, there are normative theological properties, it is not clear how they may be plausibly held to be consequential on (non-Moorean) natural properties.

44. If one thinks that normative judgments characteristically motivate, that descriptive judgments cannot motivate, and that expressive judgments characteristically do so, one has additional reason—as Hume surely did—for noncognitivism. I leave this issue aside here, but have treated it in detail in ch. 10 of Audi 1997.

45. A widely discussed difficulty is the Frege-Geach problem, concerning the (apparently propositional) behavior of normative sentences in conditionals. For a sophisticated contemporary statement of noncognitivism see Gibbard 1990. For criticism of Gibbard's position, see Sinnott-Armstrong 1993; van Roojen 1996 (a critique of Simon Blackburn's noncognitivism more than of Gibbard's); and Dreier 1999.

References

Alston, W. 1967. "Pleasure." In P. Edwards (ed.), *The Encyclopedia of Philosophy*. New York: Macmillan.

Anscombe, G. E. M. 1957. *Intention*. Oxford: Blackwell.

Aquinas, T. 1981. *Summa Theologica*. Trans. Fathers of the English Dominican Province. Foster City, Calif.: Christian Classics.

Audi, R. 1986. "Acting for Reasons." *Philosophical Review* 95: 511–546.

———. 1989. *Practical Reasoning*. London: Routledge.

———. 1993a. *Action, Intention, and Reason*. Ithaca, N.Y.: Cornell University Press.

———. 1993b. *The Structure of Justification*. Cambridge: Cambridge University Press.

———. 1994. "Dispositional Beliefs and Dispositions to Believe." *Noûs* 28: 419–434.

———. 1995. "Memorial Justification." *Philosophical Topics* 23: 31–45.

———. 1997. *Moral Knowledge and Ethical Character*. Oxford: Oxford University Press.

———. 2000. "Philosophical Naturalism at the Turn of the Century." *Journal of Philosophical Research* 25: 27–45.

———. 2001a. *The Architecture of Reason*. Oxford: Oxford University Press.

———. 2001b. "An Internalist Theory of Normative Grounds." *Philosophical Topics* 29: 19–45.

Brandt, R. B. 1979. *A Theory of the Good and the Right*. Oxford: Oxford University Press.

Cullity, G., and B. Gaut, eds. 1997. *Ethics and Practical Reason*. Oxford: Oxford University Press.

Dreier, J. 1999. "Transforming Expressivism." *Noûs* 33: 558–572.

Fehige, C. 2001. "Instrumentalism." In E. Millgram (ed.), *Varieties of Practical Reasoning*. Cambridge, Mass.: MIT Press.

Fumerton, R. 1990. *Reason and Morality*. Ithaca, N.Y.: Cornell University Press.

Gibbard, A. 1990. *Wise Choices, Apt Feelings*. Cambridge, Mass.: Harvard University Press.

Goldman, A. 1986. *Epistemology and Cognition*. Cambridge, Mass.: Harvard University Press.

Harman, G. 1999. *Reasoning, Meaning, and Mind*. Oxford: Oxford University Press.

Hubin, D. C. 2001. "The Groundless Normativity of Instrumental Rationality." *Journal of Philosophy* 98: 445–468.

Hume, D. 1888/1978. *A Treatise of Human Nature*. Ed. L. A. Selby-Bigge. Oxford: Oxford University Press.

———. 1960. *An Enquiry Concerning the Principles of Morals*. LaSalle, Ill.: Open Court.

———. 1977. *An Enquiry Concerning Human Understanding*. Ed. Eric Steinberg. Indianapolis: Hackett.

Kant, I. 1948. *Groundwork of the Metaphysics of Morals*. Trans. H. J. Paton. London: Hutcheson.

Kim, J. 1998. *Mind in a Physical World*. Cambridge, Mass.: MIT Press.

Mill, J. S. 1871/1998. *Utilitarianism*. Ed. R. Crisp. Oxford: Oxford University Press.

Nozick, R. 1993. *The Nature of Rationality*. Princeton, N.J.: Princeton University Press.

Parfit, D. 1984. *Reasons and Persons*. Oxford: Oxford University Press.

————. 1997. "Reasons and Motivation." *Proceedings of the Aristotelian Society* (supplement) 71: 99–130.

Perry, J. 1990. "Self-Notions." *Logos* 11: 17–31.

————. 1993. *The Problem of the Essential Indexical*. Oxford: Oxford University Press.

————. 2001. *Knowledge, Possibility, and Consciousness*. Cambridge, Mass.: MIT Press.

Scanlon, T. 1998. *What We Owe to Each Other*. Cambridge, Mass.: Harvard University Press.

Sinnott-Armstrong, W. 1993. "Some Problems for Gibbard's Norm-Expressivism." *Philosophical Studies* 69: 297–313.

Van Roojen, M. 1996. "Expressivism and Irrationality." *Philosophical Review* 105: 311–333.

Williams, B. 1981. *Moral Luck*. Cambridge: Cambridge University Press.

3 Mathematical Objects and Identity

Patricia Blanchette

Introduction

In what might be called the "straightforward" view of identity and of objects, identity is *universal* in the following sense: If α is an object and β is an object, then either they are the same object, or they are not—that is, either $\alpha = \beta$ or $\alpha \neq \beta$. Hence if 'a' stands for an object and 'b' stands for an object, then either 'a = b' is true, or 'a = b' is false and similarly for all other object-designating terms. In brief, we have the following two principles:

Universality of Identity (UI): For any objects α and β, either $\alpha = \beta$ or $\alpha \neq \beta$.

Bivalence of Identity-Statements (BI): If two terms refer to objects, then the identity-statement linking those terms is either true or false.

Both of these principles are presupposed in much of our ordinary thinking and discourse about everyday objects. Difficulties arise with respect to vagueness and ambiguity, but these will arguably have more to do with our linguistic resources than with the objects themselves. The objects themselves, according to the straightforward view, are each identical with themselves and with no other thing, and as long as our terminology has been supplied with clear and precise reference, our identity-sentences similarly are precisely true or false, though of course we may not always know which.

In an important challenge to the straightforward view, Peter Geach has argued that there simply is no univocal identity-relation of the kind purportedly involved in UI and BI.[1] "It makes no sense," says Geach, "to judge whether x and y are 'the same' or whether x remains 'the same' unless we add or understand some general term—the same *F*."[2] As Geach sees it, x may be the same *lump of clay* as y without being the same *statue* as y, and, in general, x may be the same F as y while being a different G from y.

As John Perry has taught us, however, a clear-headed examination of the issues reveals that the kinds of puzzles Geach has in mind provide no reason to give up on the straightforward view.[3] Although our discourse does involve frequent and helpful use of phrases of the form "the same F," the role of the predicate F in such cases is that of helping individuate the objects concerned and not of introducing a relativized version of identity. To say that x is the same F as y is to say that x and y are both Fs, and that x is identical with y. The straightforward view has no difficulty, in the end, with statues and lumps of clay.

The purpose of this chapter is to examine a somewhat different challenge to the straightforward view, one that arguably arises with respect to mathematical objects. In particular, a certain view about the connection between mathematical objects and mathematical truth, a view shared by various accounts of the nature of those objects and of that truth, entails that there are mathematical objects α and β such that there is no fact of the matter whether α is identical with or distinct from β. The associated identity statements, those that on the view in question contain successfully referring singular terms and yet fail to have truth-values, come in a variety of kinds, of which a few examples are:

(i) $2 = \{\varnothing, \{\varnothing\}\}$;

(ii) $\langle \text{Smith}, \text{Jones} \rangle = \{\{\text{Smith}\}, \{\text{Smith}, \text{Jones}\}\}$;

(iii) $7_N = 7_Q$ (i.e., the natural number 7 = the rational number 7);

(iv) $\varnothing_Z = \varnothing_N$ (i.e., the empty set of ZF set theory = the empty set of NGB set theory);

and perhaps, but more questionably,

(v) $2 = $ my coffee cup.

The question to be addressed in what follows is whether the view in question is compelling, and hence whether we have good reason to take mathematical objects to provide counterexamples to UI. The question lurking in the background is whether there is in the end a tension between realism about mathematical (and other, associated abstract) objects and the straightforward view of identity.

Numbers and Structures

One of the peculiar features of mathematical discourse is that the precise nature of its objects taken in isolation is essentially irrelevant to its body of truths. What is important about the objects of mathematics, if there are such things, is that they are *ordered* in certain ways, that is, that they collectively form structures of certain kinds, or exhibit multiply instantiable patterns. What matters, to the truths of mathematics, about the natural number 2 is that it comes third in the natural-number sequence and that infinitely many things bear the ancestral of the successor relation to it; this, along with purely structural features of the successor relation, is enough to determine all of 2's mathematical properties. Similarly for at least a large part of the mathematical universe: its objects, once characterized in terms of their role in an overarching pattern (one that can be instantiated by any number of different structured collections of objects), are thereby characterized as fully as mathematics requires or allows.

The approach to mathematical ontology that takes this feature of mathematics most closely to heart is the approach called *structuralism*. Structuralism comes in a variety of stripes, some of which are consistent with the straightforward view of identity and some of which are not. The version of structuralism that is most clearly in tension with the straightforward view of identity is also perhaps the clearest example of the general view we need to investigate here, the view that takes mathematical objects to be, necessarily, counterexamples to UI. We begin, then, with a look at structuralism.

The central idea behind structuralism is that the concern of mathematics is abstract structure. For example, the concern of number theory is the structure or pattern instantiated by any ω-sequence; the concern of analysis is the elaboration of the properties had by any ordered collection that instantiates the abstract structure of the real line, and so on. One version of structuralism, and one that does not offer a conflict with UI, is what has come to be called *eliminative* structuralism, namely, the view that every mathematical statement is an implicitly universal generalization, one that makes a claim about every instance of a given pattern. '$3 = 2 + 1$,' in the context of number theory, will mean essentially, "For any collection Σ of objects and relation ρ on Σ, if Σ is an ω-sequence with respect to ρ, then Σ's fourth entity (with respect to the ρ ordering) is the result of applying the ρ-addition function to Σ's third and second elements (in, again, the ρ-ordering)." On this view, the mathematical singular terms do not pick out specific objects, but instead are used to talk about whichever objects play a certain role in each instance of the pattern. On this view, mathematics is not about specific objects like numbers. As Benacerraf puts it,

[N]umbers are not objects at all, because in giving the properties (that is, necessary and sufficient) of numbers you merely characterize an *abstract structure*—and the distinction lies in the fact that the 'elements' of the structure have no properties other than those relating them to other 'elements' of the same structure...To *be* the number 3 is no more and no less than to be preceded by 2, 1, and possibly 0, and to be followed by 4, 5, and so forth....*Any* object can *play the role of* 3; that is, any object can be the third element in some progression....

...Number theory is the elaboration of the properties of *all* structures of the order type of the numbers. The number words do not have single referents. (Benacerraf 1965, 291)

In brief, there are, on this view, no numbers. Statements like our (i)–(v) will count as meaningless, since they cannot be understood as generalizations about systems of a specific structural type. But, because their singular terms are taken not to refer, they are not counterexamples to BI and give us no reason to suppose that UI is false.[4]

Eliminative structuralism faces the well-known problem that if the patterns in question are not instantiated (if, for example, there aren't enough things in the world), then the universally quantified conditionals will all be vacuously satisfied, with the result that such sentences as '2 + 2 = 90' will end up true, and arithmetic will be inconsistent. The consistency of mathematical theories, on this straightforward structuralist account, ends up depending unhappily on the size and complexity of the universe. Solutions to this problem can be had either by adding a modal element to the analysis, in the way pursued by Hellman (so that mathematical claims are essentially about *possible* instances of patterns), or by assuming from the outset a rich collection of sets (or categories, etc.) to serve as instances of the patterns.[5] Both approaches face well-known difficulties, the first turning on the need for an explication of the introduced modality, and the second on the arguably self-defeating exemption of set-theoretic discourse from the structuralist analysis.

A different strain of structuralism provides reasons to reject both UI and BI. This approach, defended most clearly by Stewart Shapiro, will be of particular interest to us because it seeks to recognize the sense in which mathematical discourse is ''about structure'' without giving up on the idea that there are such mathematical objects as numbers, points, and so on.

For Shapiro, a structure is very like a traditional Platonic universal: it is instantiable (by systems of objects and relations) but exists independently of any particular instantiations. Consider the general structure, or pattern, shared by every ω-sequence. This pattern, in Shapiro's view, is the subject matter of number theory. The *places* in the pattern are the numbers. Thus '4 = 3 + 1' is not syntactically misleading; it expresses a genuine identity, namely, the identity between the fifth position in the natural-number pattern and the result of applying the addition function (a function definable in terms of the order relation on the pattern) to two others, specifically the fourth and second positions in that pattern.

Here is Shapiro's view of identity-sentences like '$2 = \{\emptyset, \{\emptyset\}\}$':

Again, a number is a place in the natural-number structure. The latter is the pattern common to all of the models of arithmetic, whether they be in the set-theoretic hierarchy or anywhere else. One can form coherent and determinate statements about the identity of two numbers: $1 = 1$ and $1 \neq 4$. And one can look into the identity between numbers denoted by different descriptions *in the language of arithmetic.* For example, 7 is the largest prime that is less than 10. . . . *But it makes no sense to pursue the identity between a place in the natural-number structure and some other object, expecting there to be a fact of the matter* [emphasis added]. Identity between natural numbers is determinate; identity between numbers and other sorts of objects is not, and neither is identity between numbers and the positions of other structures. (Shapiro 1997, 79)

A similar picture of mathematical objects is expressed by Michael Resnik, also a structuralist, whose view of these objects is summarized as follows:

The objects of mathematics, that is, the entities which our mathematical constants and quantifiers denote, are themselves atoms, structureless points, or positions in structures. And as such they have no identity or distinguishing features outside a structure. (Resnik 1997, 201)

So for Shapiro and Resnik, number-talk is not to be viewed as shorthand for something else; it really is talk about specific objects, each with its own distinguishing properties. (The natural number 2 is the third element in the natural-number progression; it's even; it's prime, and so on.) But there is something very "incomplete" or "partial" about them; their only properties are those that stem from their specific patterns. (One wants to say: " . . . from their *places* in those patterns," but of course they *are* the places; they do not *have* places.) And, most important for our purposes, as Shapiro and Resnik see it, the properties "being identical with α" and "being distinct from α," for α not a natural number, simply do not apply to natural numbers. Similarly for other mathematical objects.

Structuralism in general offers an extremely compelling account of mathematical discourse. Its primary virtues include the fact that it takes very seriously what is evident when doing any mathematical work, namely, that mathematics is concerned not with its objects taken in isolation, but with those objects insofar as they collectively exhibit various patterns. The noneliminative brand of structuralism favored by Shapiro and Resnik, further, has the virtue of taking mathematical discourse at face value, of rejecting the idea that we can only make sense of what the mathematician says by saying that she doesn't really mean what she seems to mean. Our question, in what follows, will be whether these compelling features of the account require us, if we are to take them to heart, to conceive of mathematical objects in a way that violates UI and BI.

Because the structuralist holds that part of what it is to *be* the natural number 2 is to be a place in the natural-number pattern, it seems that there is a straightforward way for the noneliminative structuralist to accept the meaningfulness of cross-structure identity statements and to say that they are all false. On this approach, our structuralist says that since an essential feature of an abstract position in a pattern is the pattern it's a position in, no positions in distinct patterns are identical. Because the natural number 2 is a position in the ω-sequence pattern, and the set $\{\emptyset, \{\emptyset\}\}$ is a position in a very different pattern, they are different objects, and our identity sentence (i) is perfectly meaningful and straightforwardly false. Similarly for (v): since my coffee cup is not a position in a pattern, 2 is not my coffee cup, and (v) is false. Call this position "robust structuralism."

It is difficult to tell from their texts exactly why Shapiro and Resnik favor their own structuralist position, one that conflicts with UI, to robust structuralism. But the following three considerations are closely connected with things they say, and each serves as a reason to be at least somewhat hesitant about robust structuralism.

First of all, it is a standard part of mathematical practice to take some mathematical objects (e.g., sets) as stand-ins for, or representatives of, others (e.g., numbers). In a context in which this is being done, for example in a reduction of arithmetic to set theory, the "standing-in-for" relation is treated as the identity-relation: one asserts, in the context of such a reduction, that $2 = \{\varnothing, \{\varnothing\}\}$. And although it is one thing to stand back and say that the identity here asserted is strictly speaking neither true nor false (though perhaps "true in the present context"), it is arguably quite another (and less palatable) to say that the identity is strictly speaking *false*, while treating it as true for present purposes. The point here is just that there is something jarring about the idea that all reductions assert straightforward falsehoods, rather than deciding, for contextually delimited purposes, the truth value of genuinely indeterminate identities. Hence, there is something uncomfortable about saying that these identities are all strictly speaking false. I don't think anyone would claim that this is a terribly strong reason in its own right. But it is interestingly connected to the third, more interesting reason, to which we'll get shortly.

The second reason is that if one takes the robust structuralist viewpoint, one has to say that identities like (iii) are all false. The natural number 2 is not identical with the integer 2; the empty set of a theory that includes the axiom of choice is distinct from the empty set of a theory that includes the negation of that axiom; and it will be impossible to make straightforward sense of such disputes as, for example, how "high" a given cardinal falls in the set-theoretic hierarchy, since any differences in the overall structure in which it resides will mean that it's a different cardinal under discussion. In short, there is a certain presumption in a good deal of mathematical discourse that cross-structural identity-claims are not all false. This presumption may well be easier to give up than is, for example, UI, so again perhaps we have reached a (vague) principle whose virtues need to be weighed against that of UI when assessing the reasonable commitments of a noneliminative structuralist. But there is more to be said before summing up the weights. (It's worth noting in passing that the considerations of this paragraph are arguably reasons to reject Shapiro's and Resnik's account of cross-structural identity-statements as meaningless; the presumption just noted is in fact not just that not all such identities are false, but further that some of them are true.)

The third reason to reject the idea that all identity sentences like (i)–(v) are false turns on the idea that perhaps motivates all of the serious resistance to UI in the mathematical context. This is the idea that the essential properties of mathematical objects are just those properties that mathematics reveals. Where mathematical investigation has no place, on this view, questions about its subject matter become meaningless. And mathematical investigation clearly has nothing to say about the kinds of cross-structural identities we've been discussing.

Essentially the same point can be made by appeal to the history of newly developed areas of mathematics. As Shapiro puts it:

Suppose that mathematicians develop a new field. Call its objects "hypernumbers." Analogues in (reconstructed) history are the study of negative, irrational, and complex numbers, and quaternions. It would surely be pompous of the philosopher to suggest that the field of hyperarithmetic is somehow illegitimate and is destined to remain so until we know how to individuate hypernumbers. The mathematicians do not have to tell us, once and for all, how to figure out whether, say, the additive identity of the hypernumbers is the same thing as the zero of arithmetic or the zero of analysis or the empty set. It is enough for them to differentiate hypernumbers from each other. (Shapiro 1997, 81)

Shapiro surely has a point, and I suspect that it is a central part of the motivation for taking mathematical objects to be "partial," both on Shapiro's part and more generally. Mathematics is silent about identities of the kind (i)–(v), and there is arguably something silly about the metaphysician asking questions about mathematical objects about which mathematics itself has nothing to say. The fundamental idea here is that since there's no mathematical fact of the matter, there's no fact of the matter.

It's worth noting that this consideration applies independently of structuralist concerns. Whether the structuralist approach to mathematics is the right one or not, still mathematics has nothing to say about the identity, for example, of the natural number 2 with any particular set or real number. So if we take it that mathematics is the source of all essential truth about mathematical objects, we must conclude that there is no truth here to be discovered and, hence, that, if there are mathematical objects, then UI is false.

It's time to take stock. As we've seen, structuralism's various subspecies bear different relations to the doctrines UI and BI. In brief:

• Eliminative structuralism: Compatible with UI/BI, essentially because it rejects the idea of mathematical objects altogether.

• Noneliminative structuralism:

• Shapiro's version: Incompatible with UI/BI, since it takes mathematical objects to have "only structural" properties.

• Robust structuralism: Compatible with UI/BI; rejects the idea that all of the essential properties of mathematical objects are those revealed by mathematics.

Because the point of this chapter is essentially to investigate whether realism about mathematical objects provides reason to reject UI, we will leave the eliminative version of structuralism aside in most of what follows. If the only reasonable account of mathematical discourse were an antirealist, eliminative one, then of course our question would be moot. But I take it that this is at least not obviously true and further that the (in)compatibility of a tenable realism with UI will be an important issue in assessing the coherence of the various realist positions.

Next, we turn to an apparently very different conception of mathematical objects, to see how a similar tension between UI and mathematical realism arguably arises in a very nonstructuralist context.

Frege's Mathematical Objects

Frege held that the numbers were objects. He also held that arithmetic is reducible to (something very like) naive set theory. Does this mean that Frege held each number to be a particular set-like entity, that is, a particular extension? At first glance, the answer might seem to be "yes." In the *Grundlagen*, Frege claims that each natural number is the extension of a particular second-level concept; for example, 0 is the extension of that second-level concept under which fall all those first-level concepts under which nothing falls; similarly for the other natural numbers. In addition, Frege prefaces his definitions of the numbers with a discussion that seems to show him holding essentially our UI. The relevant passages are worth looking at in a little detail.

The first relevant passage concerns a preliminary, and ultimately rejected, means of defining numbers. This preliminary method would not have defined each number independently, but would instead have defined the series of open sentences of the form 'the number ____ belongs to the concept....' Among the reasons Frege gives for rejecting this series of definitions is this:

we can never—to take a crude example—decide by means of our definitions whether any concept has the number Julius Caesar belonging to it, or whether that same familiar conqueror of Gaul is a number or is not....It is only an illusion that we have defined 0 and 1; in reality we have only fixed the sense of the phrases "the number 0 belongs to," "the number 1 belongs to;" but we have no authority to pick out the 0 and 1 here as self-subsistent objects that can be recognized as the same again. (Frege 1884, 68)

In short, a definition that fails to give truth conditions to statements of the form "$0 = X$," for arbitrary substitutions of X, is for that reason unacceptable as a definition of zero.

The second passage concerns a proposed, and ultimately rejected, means of defining *directions*. The preliminary proposal is to define directions by stipulating that 'the direction of $a =$ the direction of b' is to be synonymous with the statement 'a is parallel to b.' The definition is rejected because, says Frege,

> In the proposition "the direction of a is identical with the direction of b" the direction of a plays the part of an object, and our definition affords us a means of recognizing this object as the same again, in case it should crop up in some other guise, say as the direction of b. But this means does not provide for all cases. It will not, for instance, decide for us whether England is the same as the direction of the Earth's axis—if I may be forgiven an example which looks nonsensical. Naturally no one is going to confuse England with the direction of the Earth's axis; but that is no thanks to our definition of direction. That says nothing as to whether the proposition "the direction of a is identical with q" should be affirmed or denied, except for the one case where q is given in the form of "the direction of b." (Frege 1884, 78)

The problem, again, is that the proposed definition fails to give truth conditions to all of the identity sentences that can be formed using the newly defined terms. In demanding that an acceptable definition of numbers, or of directions, give sense to *all* identity statements involving the newly defined terms, even far-fetched ones of the kind Frege cites, Frege seems to have in mind the principle BI, motivated essentially by UI. A definition of a term t that fails to make sense of a statement of the form $\ulcorner t = t' \urcorner$, where t' is an unproblematically referring singular term, has failed to determine what object t stands for and is therefore unacceptable.

This account of Frege's understanding of reference and of identity is further confirmed by his views that identity is a univocal relation, that an open sentence of the form $\ulcorner \_\_\_\_ = t \urcorner$ refers to a first-level concept as long as t refers to an object, and that all first-level concepts are "total," which is to say that for each object o and each first-level concept C, either o falls under C or it does not. The combination of these views delivers an account of identity that implies both UI and BI. Hence we might reasonably expect Frege's view to be that his identity sentences of the form $\ulcorner n =$ the extension of $C \urcorner$, for n, a numeral, have a determinate truth value. The point of the Fregean reduction would presumably have been to figure out precisely which extensions the numbers were and to say so.

But, as has often been remarked, there are real difficulties with understanding Frege's project as that of uncovering and then recording particular number-extension identities.[6] Frege says in the *Grundlagen* that he could have carried out the project without appealing to extensions, a strange thing to say for someone engaged in the kind of simple "discovery" process just mentioned. Perhaps more significantly (particularly in light of his later repudiation of the claim that he could have done without extensions altogether), Frege's later formal version of the reductionist project, the 1893/1903 *Grundgesetze*, gives a rather different series of identity statements regarding the natural numbers. In the later work, the numbers are no longer the extensions of second-level concepts but are rather the extensions (value ranges) of first-level concepts and hence are presumably quite different objects.[7] Frege does not claim to have changed his mind about the identity of the numbers but simply remarks, as is certainly the case, that the new method is technically more streamlined.

Finally, Frege's discussion of the issues surrounding the appropriate means of defining, for example, the complex numbers reveals that as far as he is concerned, there is a good deal of leeway involved in the choice of particular objects to which one "reduces" the numbers in question.[8]

What, then, are we to make of the famous "Julius Caesar" issue in the *Grundlagen*, namely, the claim that a definition of a singular term t (in our case, a name of a direction or of a number) is unacceptable if it fails to determine t's reference in such a way that all the identity questions about that referent have determinate answers? This looks a good deal like a view that can only be motivated by UI. But the arbitrary nature of Frege's identification of extensions (value-ranges) as numbers makes it seem that, on his view, these kinds of "cross-category" identifications are not fixed, that is, that there is a certain indeterminacy about such identities as those between natural numbers and extensions. An even more pronounced indeterminacy arises in *Grundgesetze*, in which Frege's definitions of his singular terms suffice to determine truth conditions only for those very few identities expressible in the limited formal language; though the definitions of the numerals '0' and '1' suffice to give truth-conditions to the sentence '$0 = 1$,' they leave it entirely indeterminate whether, for example, 0 is Caesar. Either the definition has left the term '0' ambiguous, so that though every object is determinately identical with or distinct from Caesar (in accordance with UI), the definition does not pin down any particular object as the reference of '0,' or the definition assigns to '0' a particular object, but one that is neither identical with nor distinct from Caesar, in violation of UI. Neither of these options, to say the least, fits comfortably with Frege's overall views about identity and about reference.

There is a great deal more to be said about the correct interpretation of Frege; but this is not the place for detailed Frege scholarship. For our purposes, we can sum up the situation as follows: although Frege stands as one of the paradigmatic mathematical realists, and would appear in contexts other than those involving mathematical reduction to be a firm believer in UI, it is at least not obvious that we can understand his account of mathematical objects as itself being consistent with UI. And what *is* obvious is that his account of the numbers, which he takes to reveal their nature and not just their overall structure, does not depend on their being determinately identical with or distinct from all (other) objects. It is essential to his formal, proof-theoretic purposes that every sentence of his formal language have a truth-value; because this includes identity-sentences, this may explain the apparent UI flavor of the *Grundlagen* passages quoted above. But it is no part of his program to explain the numbers in such a way that they bear determinate identity-relations to objects not named in the formal language— which, in the case of *Grundgesetze*, includes just about every ordinary object. Despite the fact that Frege holds the straightforward view of identity in general, the striking point about his mathematical reduction is that its account of the numbers does not even give sense to, let alone determine the truth conditions of, the kinds of cross-type identity sentences we have been interested in here. Further, nothing about the mathematical success of that reduction requires that sense be made of such identities.

The essential thing to understand, in order to grasp numbers of a certain kind, says Frege, is the meaning of identity-sentences linking numbers *of that kind*. Frege's claim about cardinal numbers is as follows:

How, then, are numbers to be given to us, if we cannot have any ideas or intuitions of them? Since it is only in the context of a proposition that words have any meaning, our problem becomes this: To define the sense of a proposition in which a number word occurs.... If we are to use the symbol *a* to signify an object, we must have a criterion for deciding in all cases whether *b* is the same as *a*, even if it is not always in our power to apply this criterion. In our present case, we have to define the sense of the proposition "the number which belongs to the concept *F* is the same as that which belongs to the concept *G*." (Frege 1884, sect. 62)

It is interesting that Frege's reference to "all cases" above turns out to be "all cases in which the objects in question are both cardinal numbers." And regarding numbers of other kinds, similarly:

In the same way with the definitions of fractions, complex numbers and the rest, everything will in the end come down to the search for a judgement-content which can be transformed into an identity whose sides precisely are the new numbers. In other words, what we must do is fix the sense of a recognition-judgement for the case of those numbers. (Frege 1884, sect. 104)

And in the developed *Grundgesetze* analysis of arithmetic, as Richard Heck has shown in detail, the only essential feature of the cardinals that is appealed to is their identity conditions with one another: the (cardinal) number belonging to the concept F = the (cardinal) number belonging to the concept G iff there's a one–one function from F onto G.[9]

In short, Frege's concerns are the mathematician's concerns, and nothing in his analysis settles or presupposes "cross-category" identities of the kind we have been examining. Frege is concerned precisely with the questions Shapiro takes to be meaningful, namely, those of the identity of a mathematical object with another of the same kind. This should be no great surprise, in some sense, since Frege was a mathematician. But he was also a philosopher and claimed to be giving an account of the nature of the numbers and of arithmetical knowledge. It is for this reason significant that his account of the numbers is by no means supportive of the universality of identity as applied to those objects. The central point for our purposes is that Frege's reductive project does not presuppose the truth of UI and does not, it is important to note, entail that identity statements of the kind we have been looking at have truth values. This despite the fact that the singular terms in these statements unquestionably, from Frege's point of view, refer to objects. If one were to take it that something like a Fregean reductionist program could reveal all of the essential properties of numbers, one would have to conclude that UI is false.

Abstraction

A number of so-called abstract objects are understood, arguably, via a process of abstraction. The colors and other properties are things had in common by objects similar in a certain way; we understand *red*, perhaps, by "abstracting away from" differences among similarly colored objects and paying attention to what they have in common. Similarly, perhaps, for such things as sentences, words, beliefs, books, songs, and so forth: they are all understood via understanding a certain similarity relation between inscriptions, tokens, and so forth. And so, on some views, with numbers, sets, and mathematical objects generally: cardinal numbers are what equinumerous collections have in common; sets are what coextensive concepts have in common, and so on.

In each case, arguably, the terminology and the objects in question (if there are such objects) are introduced in terms of an equivalence relation that holds between other, already understood things. If this is an accurate account of any of the examples just cited or others like them, what we see is the introduction of a function f (color-of, number-of, word-tokened-by, etc.) that takes us from an object, property, and so forth to a "new" object, in a way that is explained in terms of an equivalence relation R (same-color-as, equinumerous-with, equiform-with, etc.): $f(a) = f(b)$ iff $R(a, b)$.

If in fact objects and their names can be successfully introduced in this way, then we have the beginning of an argument "from abstraction" against UI: If all there is to know about the objects $f(a)$ and $f(b)$ is that they are identical iff $R(a, b)$, then one can know all there is to know about those objects without knowing anything that confers truth conditions upon, or makes meaningful, statements about the identity of these objects with objects of other kinds. And, arguably, we do come to know about objects in this way: to know what colors are is to know under what conditions two things have the same color; to know what a word is is to know when two inscriptions are inscriptions of the same word; to know what a cardinal number is, perhaps, is to know when two properties share the same cardinal number. In none of these cases does the arguably comprehensive knowledge about the objects reached "via abstraction" include anything that gives sense to cross-category identity statements. So if anything like this process of abstraction is an accurate picture of our acquisition of knowledge about objects, it seems that the objects in question will provide ready counterexamples to UI. Indeed, there is a sense in which the kinds of arguments against UI coming out of Shapiro's and Frege's work are instances of this general argument that "abstracted" objects are counterexamples.

Again, we have at this point a conditional: *If* there are objects $f(a)$ and $f(b)$ all of whose essential properties follow from their satisfaction of the biconditional $f(a) = f(b)$ iff $R(a,b)$, then UI is false.

Contra

All of the serious reasons we have seen so far for giving up UI have a similar flavor. From a certain structuralist viewpoint we have the idea that since the only properties and relations participated in by numbers are those that are "purely structural" and that cross-category identities are not structural in the relevant sense, these identities neither determinately hold nor fail to hold. From a certain viewpoint motivated by the success conditions of a reduction like that given by Frege, we have the idea that all that is essential to numbers of a certain kind (rationals, reals, etc.) is given by the identity statements linking numbers of that kind, and hence that since no other identity statements are entailed by these, the "other" identity statements are indeterminate in truth-value, despite referring to determinate objects. And from a generally abstractionist viewpoint, we have the idea that entities of a certain kind are identical with or distinct from only entities of that kind, since only these states of affairs are settled by the abstraction principle for that kind. In each case, the idea is that for a collection C of entities, the statements that reveal all of the essential characteristics of members of C neither entail nor contradict identity statements linking members of C with (some) nonmembers, with the result that these identity statements, though they refer to determinate objects on each side, have no truth-value.

The first difficulty with this form of argument is most easily seen with respect to the general case of "abstracted" objects. The abstractionist case against UI relies on the assumption that the terms of the form $f(a)$ are in fact names of objects, that is, that the sentences of the form $f(a) = f(b)$ are really identity sentences and not mere shorthand for something else. But the assumption that terms of the form $f(a)$ are in fact understood entirely in terms of the equivalence between statements of the form $f(a) = f(b)$ and those of the form $R(a, b)$ is most plausible in cases in which these are the *only* contexts in which the operator f and its associated terms are meaningful. And it is in just these cases that it is most natural to understand the sentences $f(a) = f(b)$ as syntactically misleading ways of expressing $R(a, b)$, that is, ways that are not really about objects $f(a)$ and $f(b)$ at all. If it really were true that the only contexts in which color words occur meaningfully were (or were reducible to) those of the form 'the color of a = the color of b,' and that each of these sentences were evidently synonymous with the associated '$R(a, b)$,' our motivation for taking 'the color of a' to be a genuinely referring singular term would be fairly slight, and certainly overridable by any ensuing conflict with UI.

Actual cases of objects known by abstraction are not in fact quite as neat, typically, as the paradigm just discussed. Words are not known merely as what typographically similar inscriptions have in common: we refer to them also in contexts having to do with utterance, with belief, and so on. Similarly for colors and numbers: perhaps one can "reduce" all discourse involving numerical and color terminology to discourse having to do with equinumerosity and color similarity, but this certainly takes some argument—and the more successful the argument, the less obvious it is that we are talking about objects in the first place. In short, there is a tension in the abstractionist case between the view that color-talk, word-talk, and so forth is genuinely object-referring and the view that this kind of talk is really understood entirely in terms of associated equivalence relations. The argument against UI requires that a case be made for both views simultaneously, and it is at least not obvious that this can plausibly be done.

More serious difficulties follow from the purportedly "partial" nature of the objects in question. With respect to the mathematical realm, the case against UI requires that mathematical discourse be viewed as about genuine objects but objects about which nothing can be said truly or falsely aside from what is provable or disprovable mathematically. The first thing to note about this position is that it is maintained by nobody. It is generally agreed, for example, that mathematical objects (if they exist) are *abstract*, that they have no spatial location and bear no causal relations to anything. For Frege, it is important that the numbers are not ideas; for most of us it is obvious that they are not actual numeral inscriptions. None of these claims follows from nor conflicts with any truth of mathematics, and hence, if mathematics is to be the source of all truths about mathematical objects, none of the traditional claims just mentioned should be regarded as either true or false. Similarly for the generally abstractionist picture: If the only essential properties of $f(a)$ are those conferred by the criterion that $\forall x[f(a) = f(x)$ iff $R(a,x)]$, then—for the kinds of f, a, and R, we have been discussing—there can be no fact of the matter about whether $f(a)$ is abstract, about whether it has a size, and so on. In short, if the realist about the kinds of "partial" objects in question wants to take, for example, the body of mathematical truths, or the body of truths following from an abstraction principle, to be the source of all essential truths about these objects, then he must reject some of the standard characterizations of those objects, saying that there is no fact of the matter about many aspects of those objects.

One might balk at this point. Suppose we have defined 'concrete' in some relatively clear and comprehensive way, with the intention that every object either satisfies it or fails to do so, and have said that 'abstract' is just to mean "not concrete." It should, one might think, follow from this that every object is either concrete or abstract. Similarly, of course, for any other pair of predicates designed to cover between them all the objects there are. The fan of partial objects—that is, the one who rejects UI—must, if he is to argue along the lines given here, disagree. The mathematical objects must stand as a counterexample with respect to any such pair of predicates that's not defined in mathematical terms.

Perhaps most troubling, the mathematical opponent of UI must reject the *bivalence* of a large number of properties, that is, the idea that, given an object and a property, either the object has the property or it does not. This rejection of bivalence arises for three reasons:

(1) Because the mathematical case against UI turns on holding that the only essential properties of mathematical objects are those revealed by mathematics, the opponent of UI must hold that the nonmathematical (potentially essential) properties are neither had by nor lacked by any mathematical object. Because 2's being abstract is neither entailed by nor inconsistent with any truth of mathematics, it's not the case that 2 is abstract, and it is not the case that 2 is not abstract.

(2) For a large number of cases, the mathematical opponent of UI will hold that there are objects α, β, and γ such that: (i) β is neither identical with nor distinct from α, and is neither identical with nor distinct from γ, while (ii) there is some property P such that $P(\alpha)$ and not $P(\gamma)$. In such a case, the opponent of UI must hold that it is not the case that $P(\beta)$, and it is not the case that not $P(\beta)$. Because 2 is neither identical with nor distinct from my clearly nonabstract coffee cup, 2 cannot be abstract (else

it would clearly be distinct from the coffee cup); and since 2 is neither identical with nor distinct from some clearly-abstract object (choose one), similarly 2 cannot be nonabstract.

(3) For any pair $\langle \alpha, \beta \rangle$, forming a counterexample to UI, the property *being identical with* β is neither had nor lacked by α.

The question, now, is whether such a position is coherent.

It might seem that failures of bivalence are not unusual. The most familiar (apparent) cases of failures of bivalence concern arguably vague properties, ones whose boundaries are not sharply delimited, properties like *bald*, *tall*, and the like. Perhaps we should say of a person with a quite small number of hairs that he is neither bald nor nonbald. We needn't enter here into the question whether cases like this are in fact to be traced to actual property vagueness or merely to linguistic ambiguity; the essential point for us is that the mathematical cases in question are not of either kind. The properties mentioned in (1) and (2) above can be sharpened up to perfect precision, and still they will neither hold nor fail to hold, in the anti-UI view, of the mathematical objects.

Furthermore, vagueness is of no help in trying to make sense of the kind of failure of bivalence entailed by the failure of UI. Say that an object x is "in the penumbra of" P if x neither has nor lacks P due to P's vagueness. Suppose that α, β, and γ are as described in (2) (i) and (ii) above. The opponent of UI cannot maintain that β is in the penumbra of P, since α and γ are clearly not in that penumbra, and hence would, on this account, both be distinct from β.

A different intuition that might be thought to underwrite the coherence of failures of bivalence is the intuition that properties come with a "range of application" only within which things either have or lack those properties. For example, one might hold that numbers are just the "wrong kind of thing" to have or lack colors, that coffee cups are the "wrong kind of thing" to be prime or nonprime, and so on.

Despite the naturalness (to some) of this claim, particularly with respect to examples like those of number and color, there are serious difficulties with the general doctrine. First of all, the notion of *kind* that it depends on cannot be made out coherently without conflicting with the rejection of UI it was intended to underwrite. Recall that 2's being neither identical to nor distinct from my coffee cup entails that it is not the case that 2 is abstract, and 2's being neither identical to nor distinct from some clearly abstract object entails that it is not the case that 2 is not abstract. The explanation of this state of affairs is, again, supposed to be that the object in question (here, 2) is not a member of that kind to which abstractness and non-abstractness apply. But if this is right, then, since my coffee cup *is* clearly of that kind, it follows that 2 is not, after all, identical with my coffee cup. If it's indeterminate whether $2 = \{\{\varnothing\}\}$, and indeterminate whether $2 = \{\varnothing, \{\varnothing\}\}$, then *having two members* is a property that 2 neither has nor lacks. So, on the explanation just given, 2 is not the right kind of thing to either have or lack the property. But since both $\{\{\varnothing\}\}$ and $\{\varnothing, \{\varnothing\}\}$ are exactly the right kind of thing, again our counterexample to (UI) falls apart.

Neither a notion of vagueness nor the idea that properties come with a range of application can help to make sense of the kind of failure of bivalence entailed by the mathematical rejection of (UI). The question, now, is whether this failure of bivalence can be made sense of at all. And it is difficult to see how it can, in the end. That is, it is hard to see how it can make sense to say of an object that it neither has nor lacks a sharply delimited property. For to say of an object that it doesn't have a property is just to say that it lacks it. (Being the "wrong kind of thing" to have property P is just an emphatic way of lacking P.) To say of an object that it neither has nor lacks a sharply delimited property, then, is simply to contradict oneself.

If this is right—that is, that there is no sense to be made of the kind of failure of bivalence just discussed—then the mathematical argument against UI is a failure. Further, if it is true, as just argued, that each sharply delimited property is had by or lacked by each object, then it is a short step to affirming UI, for, if β is an object, then *being identical with* β is a sharp property, and hence is had or lacked by each object α.[10]

Mathematics and UI

Mathematics offers us a particularly interesting case of objects that appear to be only "partially determined," in the way relevant to counterexamples to UI. Because mathematical discourse can easily be seen as forming a clearly separable subset of the rest of our talk, and because it is easy to view the objects of mathematics as entirely revealed by the body of mathematical truths, it is tempting to conclude both that we can easily isolate the class of statements that exhaust the character of those objects, and that this character leaves open the truth values of statements like (i)–(v).

If the considerations of the preceding section are on the right track, though, this conclusion is misguided. Whether we take the character-revealing truths about mathematical objects to be those determined by structure or those that follow from the truth conditions for identity statements about numbers of a given type, or even to be the whole body of mathematical truth, the claim that they reveal all the truths about those mathematical objects is incoherent. Because it can never be true to say of an object that it neither has nor fails to have a given sharply delimited property, it can never be the case that all of an object's characteristics (or even all of its essential characteristics) are revealed by the kinds of collections of truths we have been discussing. And because the mathematical argument against UI supposes that the nature of mathematical objects is in just this way entirely revealed by such a limited collection of truths, that argument does not get off the ground.

This does not help very much in settling the right account of discourse apparently about mathematical and other abstract objects. But it helps a little. If structuralism is essentially on the right track, then either the eliminative version or something like the robust version is the way to go. That is, the structuralist options are either to deny the existence of mathematical objects, or to take it that whereas mathematics is essentially about structure, there is more to its objects than is given by the truths about its structures. That all mathematical truths are structural can no longer be taken as a reason to suppose that all truths about mathematical objects are structural. Independent of the issue of structuralism, the upshot for the mathematical realist is the same: the fact that the mathematical truths only partially determine the properties of mathematical objects means that one cannot simultaneously hold that mathematics is about peculiarly mathematical objects and that the nature of these objects is given entirely by pure mathematics.

Is there, then, a tension between UI and realism about mathematical objects? In general, the realist about mathematical objects must say that these objects, like objects generally, are entirely determinate with respect to all (sharply delimited) properties and hence that each is determinately identical with or distinct from each object, independent of type. Because this determinacy is not to be afforded by the limited domain of mathematical truth, the realist must hold either that much about mathematical objects is in principle unknowable (an unattractive option), or more simply that much of what is to be known about these objects is to be delivered by nonmathematical, presumably by philosophical, reflection. The kinds of considerations that have reasonably convinced us that 2 is not an idea, not an inscription, and not a coffee cup, will need to be brought to bear in order to shed light on the question of whether $2 = \{\varnothing, \{\varnothing\}\}$, and presumably to answer it in the negative. Unless there are difficulties of principle with this kind of extramathematical investigation—a question for a different occasion—there is no clear reason to take the truth of UI as a reason to be skeptical about the existence of mathematical objects.

Conclusion

The reasons considered here for taking mathematical objects to be "partially determined" are reasons for adopting a crucial part of Geach's position about identity within the context of mathematical discourse. They are reasons to say that, where F is a mathematical predicate like 'natural number', 'cardinal number', 'set', 'ordered pair', and so forth, the truth of sentences of the form 'x is the same F as y' is not attributable to the holding of the straightforward identity relation between the object(s) referred to by each singular term. The reasons are not Geach's own; unlike Geach's, the considerations raised here do not lend support to the view that there is no identity relation *simpliciter*. But in underwriting the rejection of the universality of that relation as characterized in UI, the reasons would stand with Geach's own considerations in support of the idea that when we say "a is the same F as c" and "b is the same G as d," we have not thereby engaged in discussion about any relation that determinately holds or fails to hold between a and b. For Geach, as for the proponent of the partial-mathematical-objects picture discussed here, determinate reference to object a and to object b does not entail the meaningfulness of the question of their identity. If the considerations raised here are telling, though, we learn about the proposed mathematical account just what John Perry has taught us about Geach's proposal: the considerations in its favor are far from compelling, and the revisionist account of identity it recommends is beset by serious difficulties.

Acknowledgments

A version of this chapter was read at the Metaphysical Mayhem conference in Syracuse, New York, August 2002. Many thanks to the audience for helpful comments, and particularly to Joseph Melia for detailed commentary and helpful discussion.

Notes

1. See Geach 1962 and 1967.

2. Geach 1962, 39.

3. See Perry 1970 and 1978.

4. This reaction to the identity-sentences is not the only one possible for someone with an eliminative structuralist position. As Charles Parsons sees it, these identities can in fact be made sense of, as long as the context of discussion provides a "background structure" sufficiently rich to make sense of both terms. In the context of a reduction of arithmetic to set theory, for example, one might have in mind a structure that interprets both '2' and '$\{\varnothing, \{\varnothing\}\}$', in which case the identity-sentence will not be meaningless. It will have a truth-value in the context of this particular discourse but, of course, will have a different one elsewhere. Common to both approaches, however, is the view that sentences like '$2 = \{\varnothing, \{\varnothing\}\}$' have no fixed truth-value and that this is due not to anything incompatible with UI or with BI, but rather to the fact that the terms flanking the identity sign have no (fixed) reference. See Parsons 1990.

5. For the former, see Hellman 1989. For a discussion of all of these issues, see Parsons 1990.

6. See, e.g., Parsons 1965 and Benacerraf 1981.

7. For further discussion of this point, see my 1994.

8. See, e.g., Frege 1884, sects. 100*ff.*

9. See Heck 1993.

10. It is worth noting that the vagueness of an object β (if such a notion makes sense), as perhaps exemplified, for example, by clouds and mountain ranges, does not imply that the property *identical with* β is nonsharp. Those objects identical with β are exactly those that share its (vague) boundaries. For discussion of this point, see Morreau 2002.

References

Benacerraf, P. 1965. "What Numbers Could Not Be." *Philosophical Review* 74: 47–73. Reprinted in P. Benacerraf and H. Putnam, eds. 1983. *Philosophy of Mathematics*, 2nd ed. Cambridge: Cambridge University Press. Page references are to this reprinting.

———. 1981. "Frege the Last Logicist." *Midwest Studies in Philosophy* 6: 17–36.

Blanchette, P. 1994. "Frege's Reduction." *History and Philosophy of Logic* 15: 85–103.

Frege, G. 1884. *Die Grundlagen der Arithmetik*. Breslau: W. Koebner. Translated as *The Foundations of Arithmetic*, ed. J. L. Austin. Evanston, Ill.: Northwestern University Press, 1978.

———. 1893/1903. *Grundgesetze der Arithmetik*, Band I/II. Jena: H. Pohle. Partially translated as *The Basic Laws of Arithmetic*, ed. M. Furth. Berkeley and Los Angeles: University of California Press, 1964.

Geach, P. 1962. *Reference and Generality*. Ithaca, N.Y.: Cornell University Press.

———. 1967. "Identity." *Review of Metaphysics* 21: 3–12.

Heck, R. 1993. "The Development of Arithmetic in Frege's *Grundgesetze der Arithmetik*." *Journal of Symbolic Logic* 58: 579–601.

Hellman, G. 1989. *Mathematics without Numbers*. Oxford: Oxford University Press.

Morreau, M. 2002. "What Vague Objects Are Like." *Journal of Philosophy* 99: 333–361.

Parsons, C. 1965. "Frege's Theory of Number." In M. Black (ed.), *Philosophy in America*. London: George Allen and Unwin.

———. 1990. "The Structuralist View of Mathematical Objects." *Synthese* 84: 303–346.

Perry, J. 1970. "The Same F." *Philosophical Review* 79: 181–200.

———. 1978. "Relative Identity and Relative Number." *Canadian Journal of Philosophy* 7: 1–14.

Resnik, M. 1997. *Mathematics as a Science of Patterns*. Oxford: Clarendon Press.

Shapiro, S. 1997. *Philosophy of Mathematics*. New York: Oxford University Press.

4 Substitution, Identity, and the Subject-Predicate Structure

Genoveva Martí

One of the many important tasks of semantics is to provide an account of the substitution patterns of a language—that is, to furnish an explanation of the conditions under which semantic values of complexes are preserved when components are replaced. The importance of this issue is plain: we only have to recall the debates regarding substitutivity between proponents of direct reference theories and advocates of some version of Fregeanism, as well as the disagreements among different proponents of direct reference theories as regards substitutivity in belief reports.[1]

This is why it is important to articulate an acceptable principle of substitution. A traditional statement of the principle of substitution holds that codesignative singular terms should be intersubtitutable *salva veritate*. In the past I have argued that such a principle is not connected properly to some pretheoretical data about the function of referring terms.[2] In this chapter I argue that such a principle does not gain support either from other, more fundamental, laws. I end by defending the adequacy of a different principle of substitution.

Some Background

Five pages into Frege's "On Sense and Reference" (1892/1960), he presents a problem to which he proceeds to offer an elegant solution. Sixty-one years later, Quine opens his 1953 work by addressing the same problem, to which, he argues, there is no solution. The problem that both philosophers address is the puzzle, or apparent puzzle, of failures of the principle of substitution. According to the principle of substitution (PS) codesignative terms should be intersubstitutable *salva veritate*, however the substitution of codesignative terms such as 'Hesperus' and 'Phosphorus' may fail to preserve the truth value of a sentence such as 'John believes that Hesperus is a star'. According to Frege, the failure is only apparent for the terms of the attempted substitution are not codesignative in the context in question. Were we to intersubstitute expressions with the same oblique designatum, truth value would certainly be preserved. Quine, on the other hand, regards the failure as real. Attempts to restore PS are in general futile, for failure of PS signals that the occurrences of expressions are not purely referential, that truth value depends on not just the entities designated, but also the expressions used to designate them. The 'believes that' context in the above sentence is thus opaque, and the substitution of a term for another inside it makes about as much sense as the attempted substitution of 'three times three' for 'nine' in 'canine'.[3]

In some ways, it might be more accurate to say that neither Frege nor Quine regard the failures of substitution as problematic. For Frege, because there really are no failures of substitution. For Quine, because they are just indicative of the fact that the terms of the attempted substitution do not really occur, qua significant terms, in the context in question, but the important point for my purposes is that, even though for different reasons, both Frege and Quine take PS to be a principle that one should expect to hold. Violations or apparent violations of that principle are taken to pose prima facie puzzles, and they require an explanation. This has continued to be—with slight variations, rare exceptions, and some discussions about which kinds of terms the principle is meant to apply to—a relatively standard position in the field.[4] And rightly so, one should think, for the principle of substitution has two major sources of support. And both sources are explicitly mentioned right at the beginning of Quine 1953. On the one hand, the principle is supported from above, so to speak, for it is supposed to be equivalent to, or to follow from, the undeniable Law of Identity (LI), or Principle of Indiscernibility of Identicals. Thus, in Quine's own words,

One of the fundamental principles governing identity is that of *substitutivity*—or, as it might well be called, that of *indiscernibility of identicals*. It provides that, *given a true statement of identity, one of its two terms may be substituted for the other in any true statement and the result will be true.* Quine (1953, 139; emphases original)

The second source of support comes from below, for the principle of substitution is supposedly firmly grounded on pretheoretical intuitions regarding the aboutness of language and the role of terms whose standard function is to designate:

the basis of the principle of substitutivity appears quite solid; whatever can be said about the person Cicero ... should be equally true when said about the person Tully ... this being the same person. Quine (1953, 139)

The idea conveyed in this passage is, I think, extremely powerful: we have designative, or singular, terms in language to talk about things. The use of a singular term enables a speaker to affirm or deny things about the entity designated by the term in question, and the truth or falsity of what is asserted should depend, one would presume, on whether the object designated is as it is claimed to be or stands in the relations it is claimed to stand; that is, truth or falsity should depend on the object, not on its name nor on how it is specified.

That, I believe, is a pretheoretical datum that anyone who thinks about reference and truth conditions can hardly deny.[5] A different question, of course, is whether the powerful intuition does provide any support to the principle of substitution, as Quine contends. In the past, I have argued that it does not, and thus I have argued against the lawlike status of the principle of substitution by severing it from its alleged intuitive basis.[6] Now I want to argue also that the principle is not supported from above, namely, that it is neither the same principle as, nor follows from, the law of identity. I am definitely not the first one to pursue this line of argument. In Cartwright 1971,[7] Richard Cartwright argues that counterinstances to the principle of substitution are not counterinstances to the law of identity, establishing thus that the former is neither equivalent to nor follows from the latter. My argument, however, differs from his, for I will concentrate on the alleged derivation of the principle of substitution from the law of identity and argue that something goes amiss in the intermediate steps.

In the next section, I focus on the principle of substitution, the law of identity, and their alleged connection. For ease of exposition, and as it is customary, I will discuss formal or symbolic counterparts of these two principles. I will then argue that what is a seemingly harmless and unproblematic derivation of the formal counterpart of substitution from the formal statement of the law of identity takes for granted certain assumptions about which features of sentences—and of the claims they express—are relevant or irrelevant in the process of derivation. Then, in the following section I explain why when it comes to natural language sentences those features are indeed relevant and why the fact that they are disregarded should make us conclude that the principle of substitution of codesignative terms does not follow from the law of identity.

Before I plunge into that discussion, though, I need to make an aside. There is a question regarding which terms the principle is supposed to apply to. According to Frege and Quine those include names, as well as definite descriptions, so among the terms that Quine uses to illustrate the discussion we find 'the number of planets', and in Frege's case, with characteristic precision, 'the planet which is accompanied by a moon whose diameter is greater than the fourth part of its own'.[8] Many of us would be disinclined to include definite descriptions, at least in their typical attributive uses, among the terms the principle of substitution is supposed to apply to. For instance, if one espouses Russell's or Carnap's analyses of sentences containing definite descriptions, one will not accept that questions about the intersubstitutivity of items of the form *the F* with other expressions even arise. Russell himself pointed out why in his solution to the first puzzle of "On Denoting." When we consider the complete analysis of a sentence containing a definite description, we do not find a unit corresponding to the description to substitute for. Definite descriptions are not singular terms; they are not terms at all.[9]

There are reasons not to include definite descriptions among the instances of terms covered by PS even if one is suspicious, as I am, of the Russellian contextual analysis. For one can hold the position that Russell's analysis is correct if understood as a statement of the truth conditions of a sentence of the form *the F is P*, and incorrect as an analysis of the sentence itself or of the claim it expresses. On such a view, definite descriptions constitute syntactic and semantic units that contribute to the content of sentences. Certainly, that contribution is not the object the description applies to, the denotation, but a complex of conditions and properties with the constitutive requirement of uniqueness. It is a proposition containing one of those complexes that is evaluated in actual and counterfactual circumstances, and the possibly different truth values of the proposition in those circumstances depend on whether the Russellian truth condition is satisfied, that is, on whether there is at least one object that satisfies *F*, no more than one such object, and it satisfies also *P*.[10]

So regarded, *the F* is indeed a syntactic and semantic unit, but even so there is, as I said, good reason not to include definite descriptions in the domain of application of PS. This is pointed out by Ruth Barcan Marcus when she argues that, independently of whether one analyzes descriptions away or not, definite descriptions should be excluded because of their "predicative role."[11] In the discussion that follows, I will simply put this issue aside and focus on proper names since undeniably PS applies to them, if it applies at all. I will eventually return to definite descriptions and to the reasons why what Marcus identifies as their essentially predicative nature matters in the discussion of PS.

The Two Principles and Their Alleged Connection

LI asserts that identicals are indiscernible. It is difficult to state the law in a way that does not make one say incoherent things, such as "if two things are identical," which is why it is useful to resort to a semiformal statement of the principle, using free variables, that is:

(1)   if x and y are the same thing, whatever is true of x is true of y.

Variables are not, properly speaking, terms in a language; they are placeholders, rather like holes in a sentence that need to be filled with objects, producing a partly objectual and partly linguistic entity, a valuated open formula. In Kaplan's words, open formulas "are incomplete, a way station on the road to sentences....There are two parallel ways of completing them: closure (the syntactic way) and valuation (the semantic way)."[12]

The presence of *x* and *y* above indicates that there are two different holes to fill, not two different designating terms. Of course, valuated open formulas are strange creatures: they are hybrids of words and things, but the advantage of using variables is that it is immediately apparent that the antecedent of (1) is true only when *x* and *y* are assigned one and the same object, and then it is obviously true that φ applies to it if and only if φ applies to it.

Open formulas such as *x is green* are often compared to sentences containing demonstratives, such as 'this is green', for they both show the same degree of incompleteness that Kaplan talks about: they fail to make any claim about the world until the demonstrative and the variable are made to take a value, until an object is demonstrated or assigned. The comparison with demonstratives is somewhat helpful; it suggests that an assignment of an object to a variable can be conceived as the result of a pointing. From this perspective, LI could also be stated as follows: if you point at the same thing twice, then anything true of the thing pointed at first, is also true of the thing pointed at second. Thus, the following open formula

(2) $x = y \rightarrow [\Phi(x) \equiv \Phi(y)]$

is satisfied by all assignments of individuals to the variables and consequently the formula's universal closure is true:

(3) $\forall x\, \forall y\, \{x = y \rightarrow [\Phi(x) \equiv \Phi(y)]\}$.

It is important to stress that LI, in all its guises, is a principle about things and the conditions of satisfaction of simple or complex predicates applied to them. It is not a principle about words and the conditions under which the semantic properties of the expressions those words occur in are, or should be, preserved.

Still, it may be argued that PS follows from LI, and this seems to be the case, for a simple application of Universal Instantiation (UI) to the latter formal statement of LI produces:

(4) $t = t' \rightarrow [\Phi(t) \equiv \Phi(t')]$.

Observe that if *t* and *t'* are any two codesignative terms the antecedent of (4) is true, and therefore, as the consequent states, their intersubstitution is truth preserving. If we step now from formal counterparts to natural language sentences, it seems that on the basis of (4) we may conclude, for any two terms *a* and *b* (for example, 'Cicero' and 'Tully'):

(5)   If *a* is *b* then ... *a* ... just in case ... *b* ...,

where the blanks around *a* and *b* stand for any context in which the terms occur; (4), it appears, is just a more formal looking counterpart of (5).

Since two terms *a* and *b* are codesignative just in case *a is b* is true, (5) is just a version of PS:

(PS)   If *a* and *b* are codesignative terms, *a* and *b* are intersubstitutable *salva veritate*.

As Quine predicted, we have derived PS from LI.

Different things can be said at this point. Some may observe that the antecedent of (4) contains a statement of identity, whereas many natural language sentences that conform to the antecedent of (5) are arguably not identity claims. So in fact (4), which is deemed acceptable and follows from LI, is not unambiguously captured by (5) and consequently it does not lead to PS. According to this line of argument, what we should actually accept instead is a principle that modifies or implements substantially the principle discussed by Quine. A principle of substitution supported by LI would assert that any two terms that generate a true claim of identity are intersubstitutable *salva veritate*. If sentences such as 'Cicero is Tully', do express an identity claim, then the terms in question should be interchangeable in every context. Observe that, from this point of view, if definite descriptions, as some philosophers have argued, are not the kinds of terms that one can use to express claims of identity, then they are excluded from the class of substitution instances of PS. This is one way of interpreting the line taken by Ruth Barcan Marcus in Marcus 1975, where one of the reasons she proposes to exclude definite descriptions is the fact that "the logical form of an identity sentence flanked by a description . . . is not given by '$x = y$'" (107).

I do not intend to address the discussion as to whether (5) and PS should or should not be endorsed on their own merits. The question here is whether they follow from LI. Moreover, my aim is not to argue about whether certain terms should be expected to be intersubstitutable *salva veritate* or whether the proponents of certain theories about the semantic role of terms such as names are committed to something like (5), at least for certain expressions. Rather, my aim is to discuss whether the expected intersubstitutivity constitutes a principle that derives its support from LI. I will argue that it does not. But I will not question the adequacy of (5) as a counterpart of (4), because it is my view that something rather important happens even before we get to (5), in the process of reasoning from (1) to (4).

Variables, Singular Terms, and Logical Subjects

To proceed, it will be helpful to focus on the relationship between an open formula, $\Phi(x)$, $\Phi(t)$, and some natural language counterpart of the latter, '. . . Cicero . . .'. There are some differences here that are easy to disregard. For instance, the following is, on the surface, correct: if Φ holds true of a certain individual i assigned to x, then $\Phi(t)$ should be true as long as t designates i. The argument seems impeccable: Φ—or being-a-Φ, or Φ-ness—applies to i and so it applies to the designatum of t. And, similarly, if 'Cicero' designates i we would expect '...Cicero...' to be true as long as the blanks are the natural language counterpart of Φ.

This is then taken as the springboard to argue that if t' and 'Tully' also designate i we would expect $\Phi(t')$ and '...Tully...' to be true, too. For the question here is only whether Φ-ness or its natural language counterpart applies to i.[13] If any alteration of truth value occurs, one can only conclude either that the contexts surrounding the terms are simply not sensitive just to designata—conclusion à la Quine—or that the terms involved, contrary to appearances, do not after all designate i—conclusion à la Frege. But rather than concentrating on the substitutivity issue, I would like to focus on the first part, the impeccable argument, for if we think of $\Phi(t)$ and '...Cicero...' as any sentence that results from filling a gap with a singular term, the argument, I contend, cannot be applied.

The valuated $\Phi(x)$, because it is a hybrid entity only partly linguistic, is interpreted as an attribution of a simple or complex predicate to an object. In the valuated $\Phi(x)$, Φ as a unit is attributed to a subject, the value of x. The valuated $\Phi(x)$ is truly subject-predicate no matter how complex Φ is, i is the subject, and Φ stands for what is attributed to that subject. My use of "subject-predicate" is Russellian in that what is relevant here is not the grammatical structure of the linguistic entity per se (obviously so, since the valuated formula is not a linguistic entity). This is a point about logical structure, or equivalently, a point about the structure of propositional content.[14]

$\Phi(x)$ under an assignment is subject-predicate because the value of x is the subject to which Φ or, to be precise, the interpretation/content of Φ, is attributed. The value of x is, in other words, the subject (the *logical* subject, we could say to emphasize the difference with the purely grammatical notion of subject) of the content of $\Phi(x)$ under the assignment in question.

Even if t happens to designate one of the objects that satisfy $\Phi(x)$, we do not have any guarantee that the content or logical structure of $\Phi(t)$ is subject-predicate; $\Phi(t)$ could be the sentence $Qa \,\&\, Pb$, a sentence whose structure, as its truth conditions reveal, is not naturally interpreted as subject-predicate, that is, as a claim in which a complex predicate is attributed to a logical subject designated by b.[15] The natural language counterpart of $\Phi(t)$ differs from the valuated open formula in the same way. Take as an example 'Mat is green and Pat is yellow'. What this sentence *says* is that something and something else is the case; what makes it true is the co-occurrence of two states of affairs. I take it that it is obvious that the sentence does not claim that the designatum of 'Pat' has the property-like entity expressed by 'Mat's-being-green-and-yellowness'.[16] The structure of the content expressed by 'Mat is green and Pat is yellow' is conjunctive; it is not the structure of a claim in which a complex property is attributed to a subject. Thus, the designatum of 'Pat' is not the logical subject of the claim expressed by 'Mat is green and Pat is yellow', and the impeccable argument from above, quite simply, does not apply to it.

I argue that when we move from Qa & Pb to the valuated open formula Qa & Px, things change again quite radically. What makes the latter true when a certain individual i is assigned to the free variable is i's satisfaction of a complex predicate, for Qa & Px is, in fact, a one-place predicate. No matter how complex an open formula is, satisfaction splits the universe into two disjoint sets of things: those who satisfy the open formula and those who do not, in a fashion similar to the way in which a property does (issues of vagueness aside). The valuated open formula *has* to be interpreted as attributing a property-like entity to the value of a free variable. In other words, Qa & Px has to be interpreted as λy (Qa & Py) x, which reveals its subject-predicate logical structure.[17] And, if there are natural language counterparts of valuated open formulas, the same goes for them.[18] In 'Mat is green and . . . is yellow', filling the gap with the designatum of 'Pat' results in an attribution of a complex predicate to that object. In other words, in the content of the valuated 'Mat is green and . . . is yellow' the designatum of 'Pat' is indeed the logical subject. It is obvious also that both in the formally stated open formula and in its natural language counterpart, how an individual is assigned to the variable, or the gap, is immaterial. The value is the same, whether the object assigned is called 'Hesperus' or 'Phosphorus', or even for that matter, 'the Morning Star'.[19]

Variables are often compared to directly referential terms. The basis of the comparison is the observation that when a variable is assigned a value what counts for evaluation and what counts for truth conditions is the value, neither any form of designation nor mode of presentation of it. Directly referential terms are similar to variables under an assignment, in that the object designated, and neither the designator nor any mode of presentation associated with the designator is what figures in the truth conditions.

But there is one aspect in which directly referential terms, or some directly referential terms at least, differ from variables. For what is distinctive of a variable under an assignment is that it makes its value into the logical subject to which the rest of the open formula is attributed, no matter how complex that is. This is not the way the way directly referential terms, in general, behave. For instance, proper names are the paradigm of directly referential term, but it is at the very least doubtful that the sentence

(6)   Historians believe that many Romans did not think that the speeches delivered
       by Cicero were interesting,

makes a subject-predicate claim in which Cicero is the logical subject to which being believed by historians to have delivered speeches not taken to be interesting by his fellow countrymen—or something equally convoluted—is ascribed.[20]

In emphasizing too much the similarities between directly referential terms and variables, we may end up confusing two very different claims. One thing is to argue that an expression is directly referential, that it contributes its referent and only its referent to the determination of the truth conditions, or to the content of a sentence. A different thing is to argue that an expression makes its referent the logical subject of the content of any sentence in which it occurs, that is, that any sentence in which, say, 'Cicero' occurs should be understood as expressing a content in which a property is ascribed to a subject, the referent of 'Cicero'. That a term is directly referential does not entail that the presence of the term in a sentence automatically makes the content of the sentence subject-predicate.[21]

To sum up, the difference between the valuated $\Phi(x)$ and $\Phi(t)$—or natural language counterparts of those—is that the pure structure subject-predicate that makes an object the logical subject of the former may not recur in the latter. This gets lost in the reasoning from (1) to (4) above and it gets lost in the inference from LI to PS. To be more specific, the application of UI to the universal closure of

(2) $x = y \rightarrow (\Phi(x) \equiv \Phi(y))$

to obtain

(4) $t = t' \rightarrow (\Phi(t) \equiv \Phi(t'))$

may annul the subject-predicate structure of the valuated $\Phi(x)$ and $\Phi(y)$, as long as $\Phi(\ )$ is understood as usual, that is, as any context whatsoever in which a singular term may be placed. So, what gets lost in the inference from (1) to (4), to put it simply, is the connection to LI, a principle about things and their possession of properties, a principle appropriately expressed in purely subject-predicate terms, whose undeniable legitimacy is intimately connected with deeply rooted commonsense assumptions about property instantiation and property attributions.

But, how can be blame UI if, after all, UI is a logical law? Well, let us recall that UI is also the law that leads from the necessary $\forall x \exists y \, x = y$ to the contingent $\exists y \, George = y$. In this case, we realize that there is a presumption behind the application of UI; when that presumption, which is not a logical law and it is not the expression of a necessity, is brought to the surface as a condition for the application of UI, then we get the law of instantiation characteristic of free logic, a law that allows us to derive the necessary, albeit trivial $\exists y \, George = y \rightarrow \exists y \, George = y$. What I wish to highlight with this illustration is that often what seems to be a process of impeccable reasoning takes for granted assumptions that do not have the generality of logical laws. In the case that concerns us here, that is, the reasoning from LI, another assumption of the application of UI surfaces: the supposition that structure is irrelevant.

That supposition underlies also the application of Existential Generalization (EG). EG is the mirror image of UI, and its effects on structure are also the mirror image of UI's effects. To illustrate this, consider the sentence

(7)   John believes that Cicero was an orator.

Some philosophers contend that proponents of theories of direct reference that regard belief reports as expressions of a relation between an agent and a singular proposition are committed to the inference from (7) to a sentence of the form:

(8) $\exists x$ (John believes that x was an orator)

and consequently, to the intersubstitutivity of names in belief reports.[22] But the matter is, on my view, more complex: UI is suspect because its application erases the subject-predicate structure present in the valuated $\varphi(x)$. EG has the opposite effect: it forces a subject-predicate structure where it is not naturally present. The natural de dicto reading of (7) is not subject-predicate, but the application of EG produces a sentence that states that there is an object of which the complex predicate 'believed by John to be an orator' is true.

Losing the subject-predicate structure of the valuated $\varphi(x)$ severs the connection of our reasoning about substitution with LI. The application of EG does the inverse: it imposes conclusions about substitutivity that are supported by LI by altering the structure of the sentences under discussion and of the claims they express.

Logical Subjects, Aboutness, and Substitution

But why should it matter? Why should it make any difference to substitution whether or not we lose somehow the subject-predicate structure? After all, in the first-order language that we have been using here to represent LI and PS it does not make any difference whether Φ is an atomic predicate or a complex one. If t and t' designate the same object, and that is the object assigned to x, $\Phi(x)$ so valuated, $\Phi(t)$ and $\Phi(t')$ will all have the same truth value, alleged differences in structure notwithstanding. And even in natural language, it does not matter whether we are considering a sentence such as 'Mat is green and Pat is yellow' or just 'Pat is yellow'. If 'Pat' and 'Nat' designate the same drawing on a piece of paper, their intersubstitution in these two sentences preserves truth value. So, it may be argued, it is really only when we get verbs of propositional attitude or other intensionality creating operators that we may start getting things wrong. It is, as Quine contends, the context of occurrence that causes unexpected behavior in terms.

Now, this is a good point to remind ourselves of the focus of the discussion here. I am not denying that the substitution of 'Nat' for 'Pat' in 'Mat is green and Pat is yellow' results in a sentence with the same truth value. I am not discussing whether we should or should not expect 'Pat' and 'Nat' to be intersubstitutable. The question here is: Should the alleged intersubstitutivity be expected on the basis of a principle derived from LI?

More specifically, after we have seen how we progress from the statement of LI to the statement of PS, we can ask the more precise question: should the potential difference in structure between the valuated formulas that constitute instances of LI and the sentences that constitute instances of PS affect our expectations as regards the intersubstitutivity *salva veritate* of codesignative terms? The answers to these two questions are, respectively, no and yes.

The reason takes us back to the intuitive basis of support for PS that Quine puts forward, the remarks on aboutness that open Quine 1953: "whatever can be said about the person Cicero...should be equally true of the person Tully..., this being the same person." This is undeniable. If I say something about Cicero, I am saying the same thing about Tully, and the truth of what I say about him should depend on him and on what is said about him, period. Now, the idea of *saying something about Cicero* immediately conjures up simple sentences such as 'Cicero was an orator' or 'Cicero was Roman'. Undeniably, for that kind of sentences Cicero is the subject, the logical subject, of the content, and it makes all the sense in the world to say that the sentences *say something about Cicero*.

But the intuitive remark loses completely its intuitive bite if we start applying it to any sentence whatsoever that contains the word 'Cicero', such as (6). To say that sentences like (6) say something about Cicero is tantamount to the assumption that, as long as the word occurs in it, the sentence makes a subject-predicate claim, that it ascribes a property to Cicero. In the case of (6), specifically, that it says *of* Cicero that he has the property of being believed by historians to have delivered speeches not taken to be interesting by his fellow countrymen. It is easy to see that the extremely plausible support that makes the intersubstitutivity of 'Cicero' and 'Tully' appear so natural in simple sentences, sentences that express subject-predicate contents, does not support the same intersubstitution in complex sentences like (6). This is why the change of structure does matter in natural language: because the support for intersubstitution *salva veritate* that derives from LI and is encapsulated in Quine's intuitive remarks applies only if the content expressed by a sentence has the structure subject-predicate.

If Cicero is the logical subject of '...Cicero...', the substitution of 'Tully' for 'Cicero' will preserve truth value.[23] But in such a case the structure of the claim is the structure of the valuated $\Phi(x)$. If $\Phi(x)$ is true when Cicero is assigned to x, it surely is true too when Tully is assigned to x. The difference between the variable and the name is that the variable can, and always does, make its value a logical subject, whereas the name can, but not always does, make its referent a logical subject. That a term can contribute its referent as logical subject does not entail that it does contribute the logical subject of a content no matter where the term appears in the structure of the sentence.

Now, it goes without saying that there may be other reasons why one may wish to argue that terms that can contribute logical subjects, such as 'Cicero' and 'Tully', should be interchangeable *salva veritate* in any sentence whatsoever. Thus, some proponents of direct reference theories argue that proper names contribute their referents and only their referents to the truth conditions or the contents of sentences in which they occur, and that intersubstitution of coreferential proper names should preserve truth value on the basis of identity of the proposition expressed. Other semanticists defend different versions of so-called hybrid theories that acknowledge and explain the failure of substitution of coreferential directly referential terms in certain contexts.[24] My contention is that, whatever the reasons are to accept or reject the across the board intersubstitutivity *salva veritate* of terms such as 'Cicero' and 'Tully', they do not follow from the fact that, in general, $\Phi(x) \equiv \Phi(y)$ is true if the variables are assigned the same object, whatever the means of assignment. In other words, the reasons are not connected to LI or to a principle of substitution based on it.

Singular Terms and Logical Subjects

Are there in natural language expressions that force the structure subject-predicate no matter where in a sentence they appear? The question is important, for if there are such expressions their codesignativeness should guarantee their intersubstitutivity, according to the argument put forward here. The kinds of expressions forcing such a structure are valuated free variables, and there are no variables in natural language. Variables are devices of an artificial language. Although their behavior can be usefully compared to the behavior of some natural language terms, no expression in natural language behaves exactly like a free variable, that is, a variable expecting, so to speak, to be valuated.[25] Directly referential devices are a bit like free variables, but as I have argued above, proper names, directly referential devices *par excellence*, differ from valuated free variables in that names do not force the structure of a content to become subject-predicate.

Demonstratives, in particular, have often been likened to free variables, so maybe demonstratives are the kind of expressions we are looking for. There are nevertheless important differences: demonstratives are expressions in a language governed by semantic rules; the reference of a demonstrative in a particular occasion of use is systematically determined according to the relevant rule. On the other hand, assignments of individuals to variables, the way in which something like a referent is determined for a variable, are just functions. There is nothing rule-like in an assignment function and it is quite a stretch to compare assignments to the character rules that govern the use of demonstratives (even if Kaplan, as was customary in the intensional semantics tradition that he championed, represents characters as functions).

Still, Russell himself recognized the special status of 'this' and 'that'. Undoubtedly, Russell's reasons to treat 'this' and 'that' in any way special had to do a lot with his epistemology, but I do think that some of his reasons are purely semantic, and they have to do exclusively with what he perceived as the raw capacity of those expressions to contribute the subject of discourse. For it could be argued that no matter where 'this' or 'that' appear in a sentence they unavoidably make the referent the subject of discourse, the logical subject of which the rest of the sentence is predicated. Consider a sentence such as 'Many people think that this is one of the greatest books ever written', pointing to Yourcenar's *Mémoires d'Hadrien*. The book has become here the logical subject; the book is that about which we are talking and that to which something is being attributed. Thus, recapitulating Russell, but changing what is a potentially misleading terminology, we could say that 'this' and 'that' are the only *logically proper subject terms* in that they are the only terms that always contribute logical subjects.

Nice at this would be, I am afraid it is not the right conclusion. As Perry's work on demonstratives shows, things are considerably more complex.[26] Among other things, two consecutive pointings at the *Enterprise* may make true utterances of 'Mary believes that this is the *Enterprise*' and 'Mary does not believe that this is the *Enterprise*', which strongly suggests that, at least on some readings of the sentences involved, the *Enterprise* is not, after all, the logical subject of the claims in question. For if the claims were about the *Enterprise*, if they attributed a complex property to that ship, we should then ask the questions that Cartwright (1971) keeps asking: which is the property P possessed by this ship that this ship lacks? What is supposed to be true of this ship that is not true of this ship?[27]

As close as 'this' and 'that' may come to being logically proper subject terms, the fact is that in natural language there simply does not seem to be anything that behaves exactly like a free variable, something whose function is to impose the structure subject-predicate when that structure is not naturally present.[28] In some ways, that is as we should expect. For what makes it possible for free variables to function in that way is the fact that, technically speaking, they are not expressions in the language; they are just gaps waiting to be filled.

Definite Descriptions

It should be clear now also why definite descriptions, at least in their standard attributive uses, never make their denotation the logical subject. Definite descriptions are, using Marcus's words, essentially predicative, and so they characterize individuals by their properties. Their function is not to provide a subject to which things can be truly or falsely attributed. They are attributive in and of themselves, and they differ from names in that names "have a logically irreducible use. They permit us to entertain a separation in language of the object under discussion from its properties."[29] With Russell, we can say that sentences of the form *the F is P* are not logically subject-predicate, but only grammatically so. This does not have to mean that definite descriptions should be analyzed away; it does not have to mean that descriptions fail to be syntactic and semantic units, or that they are pseudo-terms. But it does mean that the object selected by the definite description is not the logical subject of the claim expressed by *the F is P*, for *the F* does not contribute its denotatum to the logical form, the content, or the assertion expressed.[30] By the same intuitive remarks on the aboutness of discourse that fuel Quine's high regard for the principle of substitution, two sentences such as *the F is P* and *the G is P* are not about the same things: they do not have the same subject (as long as F and G are not synonymous), even if the individual that happens to satisfy uniquely F and G is one and the same. For each of the definite descriptions contributes a different complex of attributes, and thus a different subject matter, to truth conditions and content. Therefore, there is no reason to expect *the F* and *the G* to be intersubstitutable *salva veritate* in any context. And, of course, if names do contribute their referents as logical subjects, then there is also a difference in aboutness between *the F is P* and *Cicero is P* even if Cicero satisfies F uniquely—and even if Cicero uniquely satisfies F as a matter of necessity.

   As an aside: in spite of all this, we have to note, as Russell does, that when the description takes primary scope, when sentences such as 'John believes that the president of the housing committee is a spy', are interpreted *de re* as synonymous with 'the president of the house committee is such that John believes that he is a spy', what Russell calls "the verbal substitution" of descriptions preserves truth value. Typically the explanation of these cases stresses that the definite description in the *de re* reading is not under the scope of the propositional attitude verb. Firmly convinced as we are that failures of PS are caused by the presence of operators that create so-called *intensional* contexts and that PS would not fail if it weren't for the presence of such operators, we accept this explanation without question.[31] A different explanation is that even though, for the reasons mentioned by Marcus, the content of the *de re* 'the president of the house committee is such that John believes that he is a spy' does not have the denotation of the definite description as its subject, the grammar of the sentence mimics the structure of a subject-predicate content, and we speakers use it assigning to it a similar semantic behavior. For, from an intuitive point of view, we use terms primarily to talk about objects so that we can predicate things of them. This is why the subject-predicate structure is privileged and why, on the basis of the law of identity, we think that predicating the same of one and the same object cannot lead us from truth to falsehood. The powerful intuition stays with us, even when the terms we are using are inadequate to guarantee that an object is the subject matter independently of any mode of specification.[32]

A Principle of Substitution

Is there any principle of substitution that in some way follows from or is connected to the law of identity? I think that there is, but it does not look at all like the traditional PS. The argument put forward here suggests that the following is a candidate to replace PS:

(PS*)   If the referent of t is the logical subject of '$...t...$' and t' is the kind of term that can contribute a logical subject to truth conditions and content, then the substitution of t' for t in '$...t...$' should preserve truth value, if t and t' are co-referential.

As a principle of substitutivity, this is considerably more modest and guarded than PS. It may be, however, not modest and guarded enough to be correct, as a new look at the Giorgione/Barbarelli cases shows.

It would be difficult to argue that in the sentence

(9)   Giorgione was so called because of his size.

Giorgione, or Barbarelli for that matter, is not the subject of the attribution, the logical subject in short. Now, we have been working here on the assumption that proper names are terms that can contribute logical subjects, and it would be not very promising to deny that 'Giorgione' and 'Barbarelli' are names. But Quine is right: the substitution of 'Barbarelli' for 'Giorgione' in the sentence in question alters its truth-value. This is a counterexample to PS*, so it would seem that, even when we try to formulate a principle of substitution sensitive to the content and significance of the law of identity, we still get a principle with counterexamples. Of course, it becomes more and more tempting to follow Quine's line and blame the context.

Actually, the explanation of the Giorgione cases was already suggested by Cartwright (1971),[33] and his account gives us the key reason why PS* as it stands is insufficient. There isn't such a thing as the property of being so called because of one's size, Cartwright argues. (9) and

(10)   Barbarelli was so called because of his size

attribute different properties to the same subject. The substitution of 'Barbarelli' for 'Giorgione' in this case does not alter the logical subject, but it does alter what is attributed to it. There is more than one way to account for that change in the predicate. A standard explanation postulates that (9) is actually shorthand for

(9′)   Giorgione was called 'Giorgione' because of his size

and substitution of the two names in (9′) preserves truth value just as one would expect. A less traditional and, to my mind, better explanation is the one that, if I read him correctly, Cartwright suggests. (9) and (10) are quite fine as they stand and there is no need to suppose that they disguise sentences like (9′). But we need to acknowledge that the substitution of expressions in a sentence may alter the semantic values and the semantic contributions of *other* expressions in the sentence. As it so happens, 'is so called because of his size' is a predicate sensitive to the word in the grammatical subject position. Which property is attributed by that predicate to the subject depends on which word is used to designate the subject. There is traditionally some resistance to accept explanations of this type, which has to do, I think, with misconceptions about compositionality. It is taken for granted that the substitution of expressions cannot alter the semantic contribution of other expressions at the same level of composition, that is, that if $A\wedge B$ is a compound and C has the same semantic value as A, the substitution of C for A cannot alter the semantic value of B. The assumption is that the composition of semantic value works in plateaus that jointly determine only the semantic value of the next level up. The semantic value of the compound $A\wedge B$ may be altered by the substitution of C for A, but such substitution in no way can modify the semantic contribution of B. That can only be modified by a replacement of B itself, or by a replacement of one of the components of B, if B is a complex expression. In other words, there is no horizontal alteration of semantic value. This presumption automatically disallows horizontal accounts like the one suggested by Cartwright, but the presumption is not forced upon us by the acceptance of a principle of composition, a principle that holds that the semantic value of a complex depends on the semantic values of its components and the way in which they are structured.[34]

It is interesting to note that Cartwright's horizontal account of Giorgione cases goes hand in hand with the Crimmins-Perry account of substitutivity in belief reports. The substitution of 'Tully' for 'Cicero' in 'John believes that Cicero was an orator' does not alter the content of the subordinated clause: the two proper names make the same contribution to that content. That very substitution, however, may alter other ingredients relevant in the interpretation of the report.[35]

A horizontal account, I suggest, may help explain the puzzles brought to attention by Saul (1997). Compare 'John went into the booth' and 'John came out (of the booth)' with Saul's 'Clark Kent went into the booth' and 'Superman came out (of the booth)'. The first two sentences make simple subject-predicate claims: they attribute, respectively, the properties of walking into (out of) a place to a given individual. Truth and falsehood depend here on whether that individual performs the actions of entering and exiting a phone booth. It could be argued that Saul's sentences should not be described as making the same kinds of simple subject-predicate claims, claims in which those properties are attributed to some individual, let's call him Rudy. For instance, the property attributed to Rudy by the second sentence, one could argue, is the considerably more complex property of walking-out-as-super-hero-world-savior. An explanation along these lines would account for the allegedly different behavior of 'Clark Kent went into the booth' and 'Superman came out of the booth' in terms of the alteration of the attribute expressed by the predicate, a change due to the different associations of the terms 'Clark Kent' and 'Superman', in a way similar to the way in which 'Giorgione' and 'Barbarelli' alter the predicate attributed in (9) and (10).[36]

In any case, one general lesson is manifest: any phenomenon for which a horizontal explanation is adequate provides counterinstances to PS*, so it is easy to see that PS* cannot be the final word about substitutivity, and we need a more refined principle:

(PS**)   If the referent of t is the logical subject of '...t...', t' is the kind of term that can contribute a logical subject to truth conditions and content, t and t' are co-referential and the substitution of t' for t does not alter what is attributed to the designatum of t by the context surrounding t, then the substitution of t' for t in '...t...' should preserve truth value.

I think that this is the principle of substitution that comes closer to being the linguistic counterpart of the law of identity. For it captures, by appeal to terms and predicates, what the law of identity captures about objects and properties: that if we attribute a property to an individual and again we attribute the same property to the same individual, the two attributions are bound to be equally true or equally false. It is a very modest principle. We are not likely to get a lot of semantic mileage out of it. But I think this what we should expect from a principle that follows from the very obvious and uncontroversial law of identity.

Acknowledgments

In 1986 I started writing a dissertation on intensional semantics under the direction of John Etchemendy. It was John Perry, though, who upon reading a footnote of the proposed introduction commented that my remarks on substitution, aboutness, and identity were a bit cryptic and perhaps should be expanded. After more than a hundred pages of expansion Etchemendy decided the footnote had better be the whole dissertation. Since then, the discussion of these questions has infused my work. I am grateful to the editors of this volume for giving me the opportunity to thank John Perry for, among many other things, planting the seeds of this topic in my mind.

The writing of this essay has been partly supported by grant BFF2002-02846 from the Spanish MCYT and by the European Science Foundation EUROCORES program "The Origin of Man, Language and Languages." I am grateful to members of the research group LOGOS for discussions. Besides the people already mentioned in the text, I thank Graeme Forbes for helpful comments on a distant ancestor of this essay. Versions of this essay were given at the 2002 meeting of the European Society for Philosophy and Psychology in Lyon, the 2003 meeting of the Society for Exact Philosophy in Vancouver, and the 2003 Summer School on Analytic Philosophy in Florence. I am grateful to the audiences for helpful discussions. I am especially grateful to Professor Ruth Barcan Marcus for her comments and criticisms.

Notes

1. See Salmon 1986, Soames 1987, and Crimmins and Perry 1989.

2. See Martí 1989.

3. Frege's presentation of the apparent problem and its solution is summarized in the first paragraph of 1960 (67). Quine's argument extends throughout "Reference and Modality," although his conclusions are presented in the first section of the paper.

4. For instance, Anthony Appiah (1987) exemplifies the standard position when he reviews traditional examples of failures of substitution and concludes: "I rehearse this familiar story because it seems to me that the fact that this is a problem, that there is something here to explain, gets lost from time to time in recent semantic theorizing." The point is that whether one thinks that the

failures are real or apparent, whether one thinks the issue is tractable or intractable, the traditional examples of apparent failures of substitution are instances of a semantic phenomenon that requires explanation.

5. It is important to stress that, in the end, the intuitive datum is not part of Quine's *official* theory—Quine does not have nor want a *theory of reference*, in the way in which Frege or Russell do. But he nevertheless relies on that datum to establish a point about the naturalness of the principle of substitution on his way to argue that contexts in which the principle fails, such as modal contexts, are deviant. In Martí 1997, I discuss the fundamental role of the principle of substitution and its sources of support in Quine's argument against the coherence and significance of modal discourse.

6. See Martí 1989.

7. This essay is reprinted in Cartwright 1987. References are to the original edition.

8. Frege 1960 (67–68).

9. It is indeed surprising that Quine includes descriptions in his examples of failures of PS, given that he accepts the Russellian analysis. In fact, it is even more surprising that Quine discusses PS and its failures at all, for on Quine's view all singular terms, including proper names, are analyzed away contextually. So, technically, the Principle of Substitution of codesignative singular terms has virtually no instances. Now, once singular terms have been analyzed we are left with general terms, and there may be other principles regarding intersubstitution of coextensional terms. But surely such principles of extensionality are not PS and they definitely do not seem to gather any support from LI or from the pretheoretical considerations on aboutness that Quine appeals to in "Reference and Modality." And Quine himself recognizes it: in Quine 1964 he points out that certain constructions (the so-called *opaque* contexts) do not allow the substitution *salva veritate* of singular terms with the same designatum, they do not allow the intersubstitution *salva veritate* of sentences with the same truth-value, and they do not allow either the intersubstitution *salva veritate* of general terms with the same extension; and then he goes on to say: "all three failures are called failures of *extensionality*. A reason for stressing the first is that *one rightly expects substitutivity of identity in discourse about the identical object*, whereas no such presumption is evident for full extensionality" (151, emphasis added).

10. This is Kaplan's position as regards the content of *the F is P*. For instance, in Kaplan 1989 (494), he claims that the constituent of a proposition corresponding to a definite description is "some sort of complex, constructed from various attributes by logical composition." The view is already proposed in Kaplan 1972, where the modified Frege-Strawson and the modified Frege-Carnap analyses treat descriptions as terms and assign Russellian truth conditions to the sentences containing them, preserving the equivalence between *the F is P* and its Russellian counterpart.

11. See Marcus 1975. Reprinted in Marcus 1993.

12. Kaplan 1986. The discussion of the role of variables and valuation here and later in this section is based on by Kaplan's remarks in that work. See especially section ix.

13. This is, roughly, Quine's aboutness argument from "Reference and Modality" (1953, 139): whatever can be said about Cicero should be equally true when said about Tully, this being the same person.

14. Two points: (1) The claim that a sentence expresses a subject-predicate proposition does not per se entail that the proposition it expresses has objectual components. Independent of whether propositional constituents are objectual or fully conceptual, it should be possible to distinguish a subject-predicate assertion from, say, a conjunctive one. However, if propositional content is conceived as essentially conceptual, it is not clear how to highlight what is special about the content of a valuated open formula, which is why here I have taken a Russellian conception of content. (2) In any case, nothing too substantial should be read into my use of the notion of content. As I see it, the appeal to content and its objectual constituents is no more than a convenient metaphor. To paraphrase Wettstein's remarks on the issue: to say that an object is what figures in the content expressed by a sentence may come to no more than saying that a predicate is directly applied to an object (see Wettstein 2004, 10). In fact, it is this fundamental idea of applying a predicate directly to an object without the mediation of other attributes that I intend to stress here.

15. There is another sentence $\lambda x (Qa \& Px)b$, with a different logical structure that in an extensional language will be equivalent to our original $Qa \& Pb$. This other sentence does express the attribution of a complex property to the designatum of b. The point here is that the logical form of the two sentences is different. Why the differences matter will be discussed later on.

16. The violence to language is premeditated. Also, the qualification "property-like entity" is here to stress that not all expressions that qualify syntactically as predicates can be coherently interpreted as expressing properties. Observe, again, that there is an interpretation of 'Mat is green and Pat is yellow', in which the complex predicate is attributed to the designatum of 'Pat', an interpretation to which the impeccable argument does apply. On that interpretation the sentence has the logical form $\lambda x (Qa \& Qx)b$, a subject-predicate logical structure.

17. I thank Paolo Casalegno for discussions about this point.

18. Whether there are really any natural language counterparts to open formulas will be discussed below.

19. What is said here about the subject-predicate logical structure appears to apply in general, mutatis mutandis, to relations and their terms. Arguably, 'John loves Mary' expresses a relational content, with 'John' and 'Mary' contributing the terms of the relation, whereas 'John is singing and Mary is reading' does not express a relation between John and Mary (even if some formal representation of it can be made to do so). For our purposes here, i.e., the discussion of the inference from LI to PS, only the structure subject-predicate is relevant, since LI is a principle about things and attributions stated in purely subject-predicate terms. In any case, there are reasons to be cautious in extending the reasoning to relations, but the discussion of this issue would take us far from the topic of this essay.

20. That reading is possible, and it is also possible to make a claim in which the complex predicate is attributed to Cicero. And if the complex predicate is attributed to Cicero, then the in-

tuitive argument connected to LI does apply: whatever is true of Cicero should be equally true of Tully. But the latter, although possible, is neither the only reading of (6) nor its most natural interpretation.

21. But the claims tend to be conflated, often by proponents of theories of direct reference. For instance, Soames (2002) endorses the view, attributed to Donnellan, that proper names are exportable from propositional attitude contexts. So, a sentence such as 'John believes Cicero was an orator' entails 'Cicero is such that John believes that he is an orator', a *de re* reading that expresses a subject-predicate proposition.

22. Those who question the claim of intersubstitutivity must then furnish arguments to block the substitution. More on this in the last section.

23. This rests on two assumptions: (1) that 'Tully' is also an expression that can make its referent a logical subject and (2) that the substitution of 'Tully' for 'Cicero' does not alter the attribute ascribed. The latter is a reasonable assumption, although, below, I will raise some doubts about it. For the moment, we can carry on with the oversimplification.

24. Nathan Salmon and Scott Soames are representatives of the former position. Mark Crimmins and John Perry present a version of the latter.

25. Anaphoric pronouns do come to mind, but they act like bound, not valuated free variables.

26. See Perry 1977 and 1980.

27. Perhaps I should remind the reader here that my aim is not to explain why substitutivity fails, if it does, but just to note that if the claim expressed were truly and simply subject-predicate, the substitution would go through. We could ask Cartwright's question and answer "nothing."

28. Although arguably we do perform speech acts that can be captured adequately only with something very much like a valuated open formula, like, for instance, when observing my guest's reaction to the big tiger in the room, I look at it and say what could be put as '___ stuffed' (thanks for the example and the observation to Barry C. Smith). As Strawson (1971) puts it: "There is...the method of uttering a single word or attributive phrase in the conspicuous presence of the object referred to; or that analogous method exemplified by...the painting of the words 'unsafe for lorries' on a bridge."

29. Marcus 1975 (107).

30. I am focusing on standard, attributive, uses of definite descriptions, and putting aside any discussion regarding whether descriptions can be used as purely referential devices (and whether what is said here about names applies to them as well).

31. I have argued against the assumption that failures of PS are due to intensionality creating operators governing that-clauses in Martí 1993.

32. The intuitive importance of separating in language the subject from its properties (to put it in Marcus's terms) explains also why the hard core Fregean position that denies any structure to

assertions is a historically fascinating, but deeply unsatisfactory view as a conception of how natural language functions.

33. See Cartwright 1971 (123–124).

34. The assumption comes rather from a way of cashing out compositionality in terms of recursive semantic rules, an assumption that is not clearly motivated, unless one counts as a motivation the fact that our life as semanticists would be much simpler if it held.

35. Those who question the claim of intersubstitutivity in sentences such as 'Cicero is believed by John to be an orator' may appeal to a horizontal account and argue that the substitution of 'Tully' for 'Cicero' alters the properties attributed to the subject. (This is not a move that I endorse, as I do not think that the substitution is questionable in such cases.) This is one of the substitution-blocking strategies mentioned in note 22. I am grateful to Crispin Wright for suggesting that kind of strategy (even though I don't endorse it) and to Stephen Schiffer for discussion of this issue at the 2003 Summer School in Florence.

36. I do not endorse this approach either as, on my view, the phenomenon is not semantic. But it seems to me that some explanations of the supposed difference in truth value rely on this strategy. This kind of approach is what, on my view, inspires Graeme Forbes' responses to Saul's cases in terms of attires, appearances or ways of self-presentation (Forbes 1997, 1999). Forbes characterizes his treatment as Fregean but I think it is not Fregean at all: the appeal to appearances does not alter the reference of 'Clark Kent' and 'Superman': one and the same individual crosses the threshold of the phone booth on each occasion. If appearances play a semantic role at all, they do not change the subject of the claim, they qualify it, in the way an attribute does. They belong to the predicate part of the claim. I am grateful to Julian Dodd and the audience at the Centre for Philosophy in Manchester for comments that led me to consider the Saul cases.

References

Appiah, A. 1987. "Why Componentiality Fails: A Case Study." *Philosophical Topics* 15: 23–45.

Cartwright, R. 1971. "Identity and Substitutivity." In M. K. Munitz (ed.), *Identity and Individuation.* New York: New York University Press.

———. 1987. *Philosophical Essays*. Cambridge, Mass.: MIT Press.

Crimmins, M., and J. Perry. 1989. "The Prince and the Phone Booth: Reporting Puzzling Beliefs." *Journal of Philosophy* 86: 685–711.

Forbes, G. 1997. "How Much Substitutivity?" *Analysis* 57: 109–113.

———. 1999. "Enlightened Semantics for Simple Sentences." *Analysis* 59: 86–91.

Frege, G. 1892/1960. "Über Sinn und Bedeutung." *Zeitschrift für Philosophie und Philosophische Kritik*. NF 100: 25–50. Translated as "On Sense and Reference." In P. Geach and M. Black (eds.), *Translations of the Philosophical Writings of Gottlob Frege*. Oxford: Blackwell.

Kaplan, D. 1972. "What Is Russell's Theory of Descriptions?" In D. F. Pears (ed.), *Bertrand Russell*. Garden City, N.Y.: Anchor Books.

———. 1986. "Opacity." In L. E. Hahn and P. Schilpp (eds.), *The Philosophy of W. V. O. Quine*. Chicago: Open Court.

———. 1989. "Demonstratives." In J. Almog, J. Perry, and H. Wettstein (eds.), *Themes from Kaplan*. New York: Oxford University Press.

Marcus, R. B. 1975. "Does the Principle of Substitutivity Rest on a Mistake?" In A. Anderson, F. Fitch, R. Marcus, and R. Martin (eds.), *The Logical Enterprise*. New Haven, Conn.: Yale University Press.

———. 1993. *Modalities*. Oxford: Oxford University Press.

Martí, G. 1989. "Aboutness and Substitutivity." *Midwest Studies in Philosophy* 14: 127–139.

———. 1993. "The Source of Intensionality." *Philosophical Perspectives* 7: 197–206.

———. 1997. "Rethinking Quine's Argument on the Collapse of Modal Distinctions." *Notre Dame Journal of Formal Logic* 38: 276–294.

Perry. J. 1977. "Frege on Demonstratives." *Philosophical Review* 86: 474–497.

———. 1980. "A Problem About Continued Belief." *Pacific Philosophical Quarterly* 61: 317–332.

Quine, W. V. O. 1953. "Reference and Modality." In his *From a Logical Point of View*. Cambridge, Mass.: Harvard University Press.

———. 1964. *Word and Object*. Cambridge, Mass.: MIT Press.

Russell, B. 1956. "On Denoting." In his *Logic and Knowledge*. London: George Allen and Unwin.

Salmon, N. 1986. *Frege's Puzzle*. Cambridge, Mass.: MIT Press.

Saul, J. 1997. "Substitution and Simple Sentences." *Analysis* 57: 102–108.

Soames, S. 1987. "Direct Reference, Propositional Attitudes, and Semantic Content." *Philosophical Topics* 15: 47–88.

———. 2002. *Beyond Rigidity*. Oxford: Oxford University Press.

Strawson, P. F. 1971. "On Referring." In his *Logico-Linguistic Papers*. London: Methuen.

Wettstein, H. 2004. *The Magic Prism*. Oxford: Oxford University Press.

Part II

5 Relativized Propositions

François Recanati

Introduction

The Essential Indexical

In *The Logical Syntax of Language*, Carnap said he was dealing "only with languages which contain no expressions dependent upon extra-linguistic factors" (Carnap 1937, 168). Carnap's disciple Bar-Hillel lamented that this "restricts highly the immediate applicability" of Carnap's views to natural languages since "the overwhelming majority of the sentences in these languages are indexical, i.e. dependent upon extra-linguistic factors" (Bar-Hillel 1963, 123). Bar-Hillel ventured the hypothesis that "more than 90 per cent of the declarative sentence-tokens we produce during our life-time are indexical sentences and not statements" (Bar-Hillel 1954, 76; a "statement," in his terminology, is a sentence that expresses the same proposition whichever context it occurs in).

Despite his emphasis on the pervasiveness of indexicality, Bar-Hillel accepted that "a judgment [i.e., an ordered pair consisting of a sentence and a context] with an indexical sentence as first component can always, without loss of information, be transformed into a judgment with a statement as a first component, keeping the second component intact" (Bar-Hillel 1954, 76). Thus if, in context c, John says "I am hungry" and thereby expresses the proposition that John is hungry at t (the time of c), he can express the same proposition in the same context by uttering "John is hungry at t." Bar-Hillel follows Carnap here:

The logical character of [nonindexical sentences] is . . . invariant in relation to spatio-temporal displacements; two sentences of the same wording will have the same character independently of where, when, and by whom they are spoken. In the case of [indexical sentences], this invariance can be attained by means of the addition of person-, place-, and time-designations. (Carnap 1937, 168)

The thesis that indexical sentences can always be rephrased into a context-invariant form without loss of information deserves a name. Let us call it the *transformability thesis*. It used to be very commonly accepted until fairly recently. In the late sixties, a general principle—the principle of "Expressibility" (Searle) or "Effability" (Katz)—that entails the transformability thesis as a special case was put forward. According to that general principle, *whatever may be conveyed by uttering a sentence S in a context c can also be literally expressed, in a context-independent manner, by means of a fully explicit sentence S'*. One consequence of the principle is that "cases where the speaker does not say exactly what he means—the principal kinds of cases of which are non-literalness, vagueness, ambiguity, and incompleteness—are not theoretically essential to linguistic communication" (Searle 1969, 20). Indexicality also counts as theoretically dispensable.[1] In principle, we can always replace an indexical expression by a nonindexical one. Instead of saying, "Thank God, he's gone," I can say, "The man who just asked the stupid question about the relation betwen the mental and the physical has, thank God, left the room" (Katz 1977, 20); and instead of saying, "That man is a foreigner," I can say, "There is one and only one man on the speaker's left by the window in the field of vision of the speaker and the hearer, and he is a foreigner" (Searle 1969, 92). To be sure, that way of speaking would not be very convenient in practice. As Katz puts it, indexicality "allows speakers to make use of contextual features to speak far more concisely than otherwise" (Katz 1977, 19).

But the problems raised by the transformation of indexical sentences into a context-invariant form are not as light as the Katz quotation suggests. The transformation "poses formidable problems," Bar-Hillel said (Bar-Hillel 1963, 123)—it's not just a matter of inconvenience or verbosity. The transformability thesis says that, for any sentence S, context c, and proposition p that S expresses in c, there is a sentence S' such that in every context (including c) S' will express that same proposition p. In other words, c and p remaining constant, it is always possible to replace S by a nonindexical sentence S': that is the gist of the transformability thesis. Still, Bar-Hillel pointed out, there is a sense in which S *cannot* be replaced by S'. Consider a very simple example: the replacement of 'I am hungry' (S) by 'John is hungry at t' (S'). S and S' express the same proposition (that John is hungry at t) in every context in which John is the speaker and t is the time of utterance; but that does not mean that S and S' can be freely interchanged in all such contexts. If the users do not *know* that John is the speaker and t the time of utterance, the sentences S and S' will not be taken to express the same proposition and, hence, they will not be intersubstitutable *in the communicative situation*. S will be actually replaceable by S' only in a small subset of the above set of contexts—namely, the contexts in which (1) John is the speaker and t the time of utterance and (2) the language users are aware of that fact. In general there is a pragmatic constraint on the transformation from indexical to nonindexical: the language users must know the relevant facts in virtue of which S and S' express the same proposition. But it is far from obvious that this constraint *can* be satisfied if the transformation from indexical to nonindexical is to be complete. In the examples I gave above ('The man who just asked the stupid question about the relation betwen the mental and the physical has, thank God, left the room' and 'There is one and only one man on the speaker's left by the window in the field of vision of the speaker and the hearer, and he is a foreigner') the transformation was clearly not complete: there remained various sources of indexicality in the replacing sentences. Arguably, if we try to get rid of *all* indexicals, we will be in a position to do so only by invoking facts that are *not* known to the language users, that is, by violating the pragmatic constraint.

That difficulty, and the pragmatic constraint on which it is based, can be dismissed as irrelevant. Thus Goodman writes:

Against such translations, it is sometimes urged that they do not really convey the content of the originals. A spoken 'Randy is running now' tells us that the action takes place at the very moment of speaking, while a 'Randy runs [tenseless] on October 17, 1948, at 10 P.M., E.S.T.' does not tell us that the action takes place simultaneously with either utterance unless we know in addition that the time of the utterance is October 17, 1948 at 10 P.M. E.S.T. Since—the argument runs—we recognize the tenseless sentence as a translation of the tensed one only in the light of outside knowledge, we have here no genuine translation at all. But this seems to me no more cogent than would be the parallel argument that 'L'Angleterre' is not a genuine translation of 'England' because we recognize it as a translation only if we know that l'Angleterre is England. (Goodman 1951, 268–269)

Goodman's quotation makes clear what is at issue: there are aspects of the intuitive "content" of the original that are left aside in the nonindexical translation, and at the same time "outside knowledge"—that is, information that is not part of that intuitive "content"—is exploited in producing the nonindexical translation. How is that intuitive notion of the "content" of the original utterance, what it "tells us," related to that of the "proposition" that it expresses and that the nonindexical translation is taken also to express? Can we discard the intuitive difference in content between the original and its nonindexical translation, as Goodman suggests, on the grounds that they express the same proposition, much as 'l'Angleterre' and 'England' denote the same country?

When we say that 'I am hungry' and 'John is hungry at t' "express the same proposition" with respect to a context c in which John is the speaker and t the time of utterance, we mean that they *have the same truth-conditions*. Both are true iff John is hungry at t. This is captured by saying that they express the same "singular proposition," consisting of John, the time t, and the two-place relation of being hungry at a time. But if we have in mind more fine-grained propositions of the sort Frege was concerned with (what he called "thoughts"), then it is unlikely that those utterances express the same proposition, even if they have the same truth-conditions. As far as Fregean thoughts are concerned, considerations of 'cognitive significance' play a crucial role alongside truth-conditional considerations.

Let us assume that John is rational. At *t* he may well assent to 'I am hungry' while, at the same time, dissenting from 'John is hungry at *t*'. (That is possible if, lacking the relevant outside knowledge, he does not know who he is, or what time it is. For example, he may mistakenly believe that he is Peter, and that the current time is *t'*.) By Fregean standards, the fact that that is possible shows that the two sentences do not express the same "thought", even with respect to a context in which John is the speaker and *t* the time of utterance. Following this line of argument, it can be shown that *no transformation from indexical to nonindexical is possible without affecting the cognitive significance of the utterance and therefore changing the thought it expresses.* One of the first philosophers to have made this point was Arthur Prior, who used an example very similar to Katz's "thank God" example, in support of the opposite conclusion:

One says, e.g. "Thank goodness that's over," and not only is this, when said, quite clear without any date appended, but *it says something which it is impossible that any use of a tenseless copula with a date should convey.* (Prior 1959, 84; emphasis mine)

The same point was to be made forcefully by Castañeda some years later, and, following Castañeda, by Perry in a sequence of insightful and influential papers.[2] As a result of their work, the transformability thesis is as commonly rejected nowadays as it was accepted in the first half of the twentieth century. The irreducibility and indispensability of indexicals is widely acknowledged.

Relativized Propositions

"The essential indexical," Perry says in his well-known essay by the same name, "is a problem for the view that belief is a relation between subjects and propositions conceived as bearers of truth and falsity" (Perry 1979, 34). If we individuate propositions in truth-conditional terms (in such a way that two utterances express the same proposition iff they are true in the same circumstances), then, indeed, the essential indexical poses a problem for the view that belief is a relation to propositions. How can it be that a rational subject believes P while disbelieving Q if P and Q, having the same truth conditions, are said to be the same proposition?

To solve that problem there are a number of options available. First, we can make the belief relation triadic: we can say that propositions are believed under "guises" or "modes of presentation." Replacement of an indexical by a nonindexical expression in the asserted sentence affects the guise, even if the proposition expressed is the same. The problem is solved because a rational subject may both believe and disbelieve the same proposition, provided he believes it under one guise (*P*) and disbelieves it under another guise (*Q*). This is the solution advocated by Perry himself, and by most philosophers in the so-called Russellian camp. Alternatively, we can keep the belief relation dyadic, but, departing from Russellianism and the "coarse-grained" individuation of propositions in terms of objects and properties, follow Frege in building propositions ("thoughts") out of "senses" or modes of presentation, thus making them directly answerable to cognitive considerations. For that solution to work, special, nondescriptive senses of the sort invoked by the "neo-Fregeans" must be associated with indexical expressions.[3] A middle course is also available (Recanati 1993, 1995). We can keep the belief relation dyadic by incorporating the modes of presentation into the singular proposition, alongside the objects and properties of which they are modes of presentation. The resulting "quasi-singular proposition" will be truth-conditionally equivalent to, but cognitively distinct from, the original singular proposition.

There is yet another option, which I want to discuss in this chapter. We can shift to *relativized propositions*, as Prior suggested in his treatment of tensed sentences. According to Prior, tensed sentences express propositions that are true or false only relative to a time. Such propositions are incomplete, by Fregean standards: they are best thought of as propositional functions (taking times as arguments) or as predicates (of times). Incomplete though they are, we can maintain that *they are* the contents of tensed sentences. The relevant time, without which no truth-value can be determined, is arguably not a part of the content of the sentence, but an aspect of the *circumstance* in which the content is evaluated. We can treat indexical sentences in the same way, by holding that they express relativized propositions: propositions true at some indices but not at others. Thus if John is hungry at t_1, 'I am hungry' is true at $\langle$John, $t_1 \rangle$. The proposition expressed by that sentence is a relativized proposition, that is, a function from indices to truth-values. Such a proposition is very different from the unrelativized proposition that John is hungry at t_1; hence it is no mystery that one can believe the relativized proposition expressed by 'I am hungry' while disbelieving the unrelativized proposition expressed by 'John is hungry at t_1'.

The relativized-proposition view bears family resemblances to the classic analysis of indexical sentences due to Montague and Scott (Montague 1968; Scott 1970). Montague and Scott take the content of an indexical sentence to be not a proposition in the standard sense (a function from possible worlds to truth-values), but a function from *points of reference* to truth-values, where a point of reference consists of several coordinates besides a possible world: a time, a place, a speaker, and so forth. The relativized proposition approach is also closely related to the Loar-Lewis theory of *de se* beliefs as self-ascriptions of properties (Loar 1976; Lewis 1979). In his original sketch of the theory, Loar says that *de se* belief is a relation to propositional functions, rather than to complete propositions. Lewis generalizes this point and argues that the object of the attitudes are not (classical) propositions, but properties.

Relativized propositions show up twice in Perry's writings. In Perry 1979 he says that

the problem [i.e., the problem which the essential indexical raises for the view that belief is a relation to propositions individuated in truth-conditional terms] is not solved . . . by moving to a notion of proposition that, rather than true or false absolutely is only true or false at an index or in a context (at a time, for a speaker, say). (Perry 1979, 34)

We shall consider Perry's argument to that effect in some detail in the section "Relativized Propositions and *De Se* Belief." The second appearance of relativized propositions in Perry's work is in his paper "Thought without Representation" (1986b). In that paper, Perry himself appeals to relativized propositions, in order to deal with what he calls unarticulated constituents (or at least a subclass of them). According to Perry, if my four-year-old daughter says "it's five o'clock" (or believes it), the proposition she expresses or believes is relativized to a time zone, but the time zone is not an aspect of the content she expresses or believes. It is truth-conditionally relevant but is best construed as an aspect of the circumstance with respect to which what she says or believes is evaluated. Perry himself expresses that point by saying that her thought "concerns" a particular time zone but is not "about" it. This is exactly the sort of thing that Prior wanted to say about times.

Has Perry changed his mind about the usefulness of relativized propositions? Not necessarily. He carefully distinguishes between indexicality and unarticulated constituency as two different forms of context sensitivity, and it may be that relativized propositions can only be appealed to in dealing with the latter. This is one of the issues I will consider in "Relativized Propositions and *De Se* Belief," when I discuss Perry's attitude toward relativized propositions. First, however, I will sketch a framework in which relativized propositions play a central role ("Relativizing Contents"). The framework I will sketch builds upon ideas put forward by Perry himself in Perry 1986b.

Relativizing Contents

Possible Worlds

The notion of circumstance of evaluation is familiar from modal logic. In modal logic, propositions are evaluated relative to "possible worlds." The possible worlds are necessary to truth-evaluation, but they are not themselves represented in the propositions that we evaluate. Thus 'I am French' is true, with respect to a world w, iff I am French in w; but the sentence 'I am French' talks only about me and the property of being French. The world of evaluation is not a constituent of the content to be evaluated.

One can bring the world into the content by making the statement more complex. The complex sentence 'Possibly, I am French' tells us that *in some possible world* I am French. The modal statement I make by uttering that sentence is about possible worlds, not merely about me and the property of being French. In hybrid logic (a variety of modal logic), one can even make statements "referring" to specific possible worlds.[4] But the worlds that are thus introduced into the content of the complex statement (via modal operators such as "possibly") are used in evaluating the *simple* statement that is embedded within the modal statement. The modal statement itself is evaluated with respect to possible worlds, and it shares with the simple statement the property that *the worlds with respect to which it is evaluated are not themselves represented in the statement under evaluation*.

To appreciate the unarticulated character of the circumstance of evaluation in the modal framework, it is worth looking at what happens when we (standardly) translate a modal statement into first-order logic, by explicitly quantifying over possible worlds. Thus translated, 'Necessarily p' becomes '$\forall w\, p(w)$', 'Possibly p' becomes '$\exists w\, p(w)$', and so forth.[5] All complete sentences are transformed into predicates (of worlds). A simple categoric statement such as 'Rain is wet' will be represented as '$p(w)$', where 'p' is the proposition that rain is wet transformed into a predicate of worlds, and 'w' is a free variable to which the actual world is contextually assigned as default value.

The big difference between the modal statement and its standard extensional translation is that, in the extensional framework, the circumstance of evaluation (the world) becomes a constituent of content. The contrast between content and circumstance is lost. This is too bad, for that contrast makes a lot of sense. To evaluate a sentence, we determine whether the state of affairs it describes obtains in some "reality" that serves as circumstance of evaluation. But that reality—the actual world, say—is not itself, or at least doesn't have to be, among the constituents of the state of affairs in question, that is, among the entities that are talked about and articulated in the content of the proposition. The world comes into the picture for purposes of evaluation, but the thoughts that are evaluated need not be metaphysically elaborated thoughts *about* the world. Indeed the users of the language need not even have the ability to entertain such thoughts. Only the theorist needs to be able to talk about the world of evaluation, in her metalanguage. The thoughts that are evaluated "concern" the world, but they need not be "about" it in the sense in which they are about the entities they represent.

Let us consider a simple language without modal operators or other means of talking about worlds; let us go further and assume that the users of the language don't possess the reflective abilities necessary for thinking about modal issues. They entertain only nonmodal thoughts such as that expressed by 'Rain is wet'. The possible-worlds semanticist who studies their language will still need to think and talk about the possible worlds relative to which the sentences of the language are evaluated; but, contrary to what the standard extensional translation suggests, mention of the possible worlds in question will be confined to the theorist's metalanguage.

Now suppose the users of the object language become sophisticated and start thinking about metaphysical issues. Suppose they come to talk and think about what is *actually* the case as opposed to what *might be* the case. Such modal talk can be formally represented in two ways, as we have seen: by using sentence operators or by explicitly quantifying world variables in the object language. If we use the modal framework and introduce modal operators such as 'actually' or 'possibly', *nothing will be changed for the fragment of the language that does not involve those operators*. The sentence 'Rain is wet' will still be a simple, modally innocent sentence. The language will simply have been enriched by the introduction of new resources enabling us to construct more complex sentences. But if we use the standard extensional framework and represent modal sentences ('It might be that...', 'Actually...') by means of explicit quantification over possible worlds, as suggested above, then, unless special precaution is taken to avoid that consequence, *a change of language takes place*, not merely an enrichment. In the new language, *all* sentences (including simple sentences) now contain a hidden argument-place for a world. Modal innocence is lost.

I think this move is (almost) as damaging as the previous one—the ascription of thought and talk about possible worlds to modally innocent subjects. Even if the users of the language are sophisticated enough and can think about modal issues, it is misleading to suggest that they *always* think and talk about such issues even when they entertain simple thoughts or utter simple sentences such as 'Rain is wet'. By forcing us to construe, for example, the assertion that rain is wet as involving a covert argument-place, which the actual world fills, the extensional translation blurs the cognitively important distinction between the simple, modally innocent assertion 'Rain is wet' and the modal assertion 'Actually, rain is wet'. To maintain that distinction, we have to see modal sentences as *constructed from* simple sentences by the application of modal operators to them. In this way we can analyze the ability to use and understand modal sentences as resting on two distinct abilities: the ability to use and understand simple sentences and the ability to imagine other possible worlds and to contrast the actual world with them. The first ability is independent of the second: we can use and understand simple sentences (e.g., 'Rain is wet') even if we lack the ability to think thoughts about the actual world (in Perry's sense of 'about').[6]

Time and Tense

The difference we have found between two ways of representing modality can be found also between two ways of representing tense, one that preserves temporal innocence in simple sentences and one that does not.

In tense logic, tense is represented by means of sentence operators.[7] Alternatively, tenses can be represented by adding extra argument-places for times.[8] If we choose the latter course, it is no longer possible to consider adjectives such as 'warm' or 'yellow' as denoting properties; they have to be considered as denoting relations—relations between the objects that have the alleged properties and the times at which they have them. As Michael Dummett has pointed out, this relational approach significantly departs from our habitual way of thinking:

We think of adjectives such as 'warm', 'smooth', 'slender' and so on as denoting *properties*; properties that a thing may have at one time, and not at another, but nevertheless properties rather than relations between objects and times. And this goes with the way in which we come to understand such adjectives.... We do not begin by learning in what relation an object must stand to an arbitrary time for it to be warm or wet at that time, and then, having learned what time is referred to by the adverb 'now', derive from this a grasp of what it is for it to be warm now. Rather, we first learn what it is for something to be warm, wet, smooth or slender, that is to say, for the predicate 'is warm (wet, smooth, slender)' to be applicable to it, where the verb 'is' is in the true present tense. From this we advance to an understanding of what is meant by saying of an object that it was or will be warm, etc., at some other time. The advance is made by our acquiring a general grasp of the past and future tenses. That is to say, to understand 'was warm' or 'will be warm', we apply to our prior understanding of what is meant by saying that something is warm our general comprehension of what it is to speak of how things were or will be at another time. In so doing, we are in effect treating the tenses (and other indications of time) as operators applied to sentences in the present tense of which we have previously acquired an understanding, just as the tense-logical semantics treats them. We could not learn the language in any other way. (Dummett, forthcoming, 16–17)

Dummett's complaint about the relational treatment of tenses parallels my complaint about the extensional rendering of modal talk. The relational treatment threatens temporal innocence, just as overt quantification over possible worlds (without variadic functions) threatens modal innocence.

In the temporal case there is a possible objection, due to the fact that tense is (to put it crudely) obligatory in English—or nearly so. Since it is, one may argue that time shouldn't be treated like modality: there are simple, nonmodal sentences, whose characteristics must admittedly be preserved and captured, but there is no such thing as nontemporal talk and, hence, no such thing as temporal innocence.

From the tense-logical point of view, that objection is misguided. The present tense is not a tense like the past or the future. It is more primitive and, in a sense, temporally neutral. Someone can think "It is hot in here" even if she has no notion of time whatsoever, hence no mastery of the past and the future. If this is right, mastery of genuine temporal talk rests on two distinct abilities: the ability to use and understand simple sentences (i.e., sentences in the present) and the ability to think about times and to constrast the past and the future with the present. As in the case of modality, the first ability is independent from the second.

It is true that, when we say or think "It is hot in here," we talk (or think) about what is presently the case; we characterize the situation *at the time of utterance*. Yet this is not part of what the sentence itself expresses. The content of the sentence, from the tense-logical point of view, is a function from times to truth-values. When the sentence is uttered, the function is applied to the time of utterance. That is so *whether the sentence is in the present or any other tense*. Even if I say "It was hot" or "It will be hot," I characterize the time of utterance (and, in relation to it, some earlier or later time). The time of utterance, which the sentence is used to characterize, is the time with respect to which we *evaluate* the sentence. The best thing I can do here it to quote Prior:

> If tenses are formed by attaching prefixes like 'It has been the case that' to the present tense, or to a complex with a present tense "kernel," it is not always true to say that what is in the present tense is understood as a characterisation of the time of utterance; rather, it characterises whatever time we are taken to by the series of prefixes. The *presentness* of an event, we may say, is simply the *occurrence* of the event, and that is simply the event itself. But every complete tensed sentence characterises the time of utterance in some way or other, and other times only through their relation to that one. (Prior and Fine 1977, 30)

To sum up, the time of utterance is not represented, it does not feature in the content of tensed sentences; it only comes into the picture as the circumstance with respect to which the content of a tensed sentence is evaluated.

Fregean Qualms

Another possible objection, voiced by Evans, concerns the fact that a tensed sentence like 'It is hot', 'It has been hot', or 'It will be hot' is not evaluable as true or false, unless we are given a particular time. In the absence of a time specification, the sentence is only "true at" certain times and "false at" others. Such a sentence, therefore, is *semantically incomplete* by Frege's lights:

A thought is not true at one time and false at another, but it is either true or false, *tertium non datur*. The false appearance that a thought can be true at one time and false at another arises from an incomplete expression. A complete proposition or expression of a thought must also contain a time datum. (Quoted in Evans 1985, 350)

As Evans points out, the problem of semantic incompleteness does not arise in the modal case. Even if a thought is said to be "true at" one world and "false at" another, as in modal logic, this does not prevent it from being true (or false) *tout court*. It is true *tout court* iff it is true-at the actual world. But the "thought" that it is hot cannot be evaluated as true or false *tout court*. In the absence of a contextually supplied time it can *only* be ascribed relative, "truth-at" conditions. Only a particular, dated utterance of such a sentence can be endowed with genuine truth-conditions. What this shows is that the time of utterance is part of the (complete) content of the utterance;[9] hence it cannot be expelled out of the content and treated like the world of evaluation. So the objection goes.

According to Dummett, Evans's objection to Prior is based on a misunderstanding. Prior was concerned only with *sentence-types* and *their* contents. The content of a sentence-type is a function from times to truth-values. Hence a sentence-type has only relative truth conditions: it is true at some times and false at other times. To introduce a notion of absolute truth, one thing we can say (though not, according to Dummett, what Prior himself would say)[10] is that, when a sentence is uttered, the function that is its content is applied to some contextually provided time (typically, the time of utterance). The time in question serves as circumstance of evaluation for the utterance: the utterance is true *tout court* iff the sentence is "true-at" the contextually provided time. As Dummett points out, "The variable truth-value and the absolute truth-value attach to different things; it is the type sentence that is true at one time, false at another, but the utterance that is true or false simpliciter" (Dummett, forthcoming, 44).

Since there are two distinct levels, corresponding to the sentence-type and the utterance, there is no harm in taking the utterance to possess a "content" also (content$_u$), distinct from that of the sentence (content$_s$). For example, we can treat the utterance as expressing a structured proposition consisting of (1) the contextually provided time as subject and (2) the content of the sentence-type, predicated of that time. But, if we do so, we must acknowledge the unarticulated nature of the "subject" in the content$_u$ of tensed utterances. As Prior says, "tensed propositions are understood as directly or indirectly characterising the *un*mentioned time of utterance" (Prior and Fine 1977, 30).

Hence there is a trade-off: if we want to restrict ourselves to what is linguistically articulated, we must focus on the content$_s$, which is "semantically incomplete" by Frege's lights—it corresponds to the content of a predicate rather than to that of a complete sentence in a logically perfect language. If, following Frege, we want to focus on the complete content of the utterance, what makes it truth-evaluable in absolute terms, we must acknowledge the role played in that content (content$_u$) by unarticulated constituents corresponding to the circumstances in which the content$_s$ is evaluated.

Situations

Let us take stock. For purposes of semantic evaluation we need a circumstance as well as a content. Even Frege, who was unconcerned by modalities and thought of the actual world as the only world there is, was aware of that fact. He took fictional sentences to be unevaluable, for the following reason: since the author of a fictional statement does not attempt to characterize the actual world, we are given a content without any circumstance of evaluation for it. The obvious conclusion to draw from Frege's remarks on fiction is that, to get a truth-value, a content is not sufficient; we need to connect that content with the actual world, via the assertive force of the utterance, in virtue of which the content is presented as characterizing that world. Frege was aware not only that we need a circumstance in addition to a content, but also that the circumstance is not, and cannot be, an aspect of the content articulated in the sentence. If a sentence lacks the force of a serious assertion because the speaker does not attempt to characterize the actual world but is engaged in a different enterprise (e.g., poetry), making the content of the sentence more complex by means of operators such as 'it is true that' will not change the situation. Whether or not an utterance is serious and characterizes the actual world is a pragmatic matter—a matter of "force," not a matter of (narrow) content.

Once it is admitted that we need a circumstance over and above the content to be evaluated, we can part from Frege and, following Prior, tolerate contents that are not "semantically complete" in Frege's sense, that is, endowed with absolute truth conditions. We can, because the circumstance is there that enables the content to be suitably completed. Thus the content of tensed sentences is semantically incomplete, yet the circumstance (the time) relative to which such a sentence is evaluated is sufficient to complete it. It follows that we must distinguish two levels of content. The content we evaluate with respect to the circumstance is the content$_s$; it may, but need not be, semantically complete by Frege's lights. What is semantically complete in any case is the content$_u$. It consists of the content$_s$ *and* the circumstance with respect to which the content$_s$ is evaluated.

Situation theory, as I understand it,[11] follows those ideas to their consequences. It generalizes and systematizes them, in two main directions:

(1) There is no reason why only times and worlds should be accepted as features of the circumstance of evaluation. Why not also, for example, *locations*? If I say, "It's raining," the location is unarticulated, but it is relevant qua feature of the circumstance of evaluation: what I say (or think) is true iff it is raining *at the contextually provided location*. Why not also consider the *agent* of the speech act (the speaker) or of the thought act (the thinker) as (part of) the circumstance of evaluation, to handle the cases in which the content to be evaluated is a property of agents that the speaker or thinker self-attributes? Why not extend the notion also to ordinary objects? If, talking about my car, the mechanics tells me, "The carburetor is in good condition but there is a problem with the front wheels," my car is a crucial feature of the circumstance of evaluation. It is true (or false) *of my car* that the carburetor is in good condition, and so forth. The same thing could have been said of another car, but as things turn out it is my car that figures in the content$_u$ of the mechanics's utterance.

Rather than list all the features that may figure in a circumstance of evaluation, let us follow Barwise, Perry, and others and use the word 'situation' to denote any entity or complex of entities that can play that role. Anything counts as a situation provided, for some sentence S, it makes sense to ask whether or not what S expresses is true *in it* (or "of it" or "at it" or "with respect to it"). Ordinary situations—restricted portions of the actual world—are, of course, the paradigmatic case of a situation in this generalized sense.

(2) When the content of the sentence is semantically incomplete, it is the utterance that is the proper bearer of (absolute) truth-value. Thus, tensed sentences only have relative truth-values, they express relativized propositions, and we need to shift to utterances to get absolute truth-values and absolute propositions. One might think that, *with sentences that are not relevantly context-sensitive and whose content is not semantically incomplete*, there is no need to invoke a double layer of content. The content of the sentence, insofar as it has an absolute truth-value, is the only thing we need. Situation theory, however, rejects that viewpoint. In situation theory, the content of a sentence (whatever the sentence) is a function from situations to truth-values. Hence the relativity of truth, construed as a property of sentences: the same sentence may be true relative to a situation and false relative to another one. That is so *even if the sentence itself is not relevantly context-sensitive or semantically incomplete*. Even when the sentence is truth-evaluable in the absolute sense—when it is "semantically complete" by Frege's lights—situation theory says there is a principled distinction between the content$_s$ of

the sentence and the content$_u$ of the utterance. In such a case, the content$_s$ will be a "classical" proposition (a function from possible worlds to truth-values), and the content$_u$ will contain a situation in addition to that proposition. What the utterance "says" is that *the situation in question supports the proposition in question.* It follows that two distinct evaluations are possible, in such cases. We can evaluate the sentence itself (i.e., evaluate the proposition with respect to the actual world), or we can evaluate the utterance, that is, evaluate the proposition *with respect to the situation figuring in the content$_u$.*

I cannot refrain from quoting my favorite example here (from Barwise and Etchemendy 1987). Commenting upon a poker game I am watching, I say: "Claire has a good hand." What I say is true iff Claire has a good hand in the poker game I am watching (at the time of utterance). But suppose I made a mistake and Claire is not among the players in that game. Suppose further that, by coincidence, she happens to be playing poker in some other part of town and has a good hand there. Still, my utterance is not intuitively true, because the situation it concerns (the poker game I am watching) is not one in which Claire has a good hand. But we can say that the *sentence* is true, or at least true at the time of utterance: for it says that Claire has a good hand, and Claire *has* a good hand (somewhere). The unarticulated constituent that distinguishes the content$_u$ from the content$_s$ makes all the difference here, and it accounts for our intuitive classification of the utterance as nontrue.

This sort of approach can easily be extended to deal with standard problems such as that of quantifier domain restriction. It is natural to hold that 'all *F*s are *G*' expresses a proposition that is true (in a world, at a time) iff all the *F*s are *G* (in that world, at that time). Thus 'All students are French' expresses the proposition that all students are French. Many theorists feel compelled to give up this natural view and claim that the sentence is semantically incomplete or covertly indexical, so that it expresses no proposition (independent of context).[12] They say so because they are impressed by the fact that the truth-conditions of an utterance of that sentence typically involve a contextually restricted domain of quantification. In the situation-theoretic framework, however, we can stick to the simple and straightforward view regarding the proposition expressed by 'All the *F*s are *G*' while fully acknowledging contextual domain restriction. The two layers of content enable to do just that. The sentence is said to express a proposition that is evaluable with respect to an arbitrary world-time pair—the proposition that all students are French—but that proposition can also be evaluated with respect to the specific situation that features in the content$_u$. That is what happens when we evaluate an utterance of this sentence, instead of evaluating the sentence itself.[13]

Unarticulated Constituents of What?

Barwise versus Perry

The framework I have sketched owes much to Perry's pioneering paper "Thought without Representation," where he introduces the notion of an unarticulated constituent and the distinction between *concerning* and *being about*. That distinction comes out most clearly in the case of the Z-landers, a small group of people who "do not travel to, or communicate with residents of, other places" (Perry 1986b, 212) and have no name for Z-land, the place where they live. As Perry points out, Z-land is an unarticulated constituent of the content expressed by the Z-lander's utterance "It's raining." The utterance is true iff it is raining in Z-land. But the Z-landers do not have a concept or idea of Z-land as opposed to other places. Their weather thoughts "concern" Z-land, not by virtue of containing a representation of Z-land (in which case they would be "about" Z-land), but by virtue of their *being in* Z-land. The unarticulated constituent is unarticulated not only linguistically but also mentally: it is a constituent of content directly provided by the environment.

In such cases the mental representation, considered in abstraction from the environment that it concerns, expresses less than a complete proposition. The Z-landers think "It is raining": the content thus articulated is not fully prepositional—it is a propositional function, which is truth-evaluable only with respect to a particular place (determined by the environment). Now, as Perry pleasantly says, "there is a little of the Z-lander in the most well-traveled of us" (Perry 1986b, 216). The difference between the Z-landers and us is that we do have a notion of the place where we live, as opposed to other places; so we are capable of entertaining a thought *about* the place where we are, such as 'It's raining in Paris, but not in Saint Tropez'. Perry's point, however, is that when we are in Paris (or Palo Alto) and we say or think "It's raining," we need not think *reflectively* about the place we're in. We can think "It's raining" and *let the place we are in complete the content of our thought*.

The framework I have sketched owes much also to Barwise's paper "Situations, Facts, and True Propositions" (1989), in which the two layers of content I have mentioned (content$_s$ and content$_u$) are systematically told apart. What I call the "content$_u$," Barwise, in that paper, dubs the "Austinian proposition." (That terminology was already used in Barwise and Etchemendy 1987.) The structure of the Austinian proposition is

$$s \models p,$$

where 's' is the situation that the utterance concerns, 'p' is the (typically relativized) fact that the utterance presents as obtaining in that situation, and '$\models$' is the support relation, that is, the relation that holds between a situation and a fact whenever the fact obtains in the situation.[14] This is very much in the spirit of Perry (1986b), yet in his paper Barwise says that Perry and he disagree. Before proceeding, I will attempt to locate the points of disagreement and to clarify my position regarding them.

Barwise gives the following example to illustrate his disagreement with Perry. Suppose Holmes and Watson face each other. In between stand the salt and the pepper. Holmes says, "The salt is left of the pepper," because the salt is left of the pepper from Holmes's perspective. From Watson's perspective, the pepper is left of the salt; however, Watson is mistaken as to which shaker is which, and he wrongly says, "The salt is left of the pepper." Holmes and Watson apparently "say the same thing," but Holmes is right and Watson wrong. Some unarticulated constituent must be involved, which accounts for the difference in truth-value. This unarticulated constituent is the perspective: the salt is on the left from Holmes's perspective, but it is not on the left from Watson's perspective. (That is why Holmes is right and Watson wrong.) Thus far Barwise and Perry agree, but now a decision has to be made: the unarticulated constituent may be fed into the content to be evaluated (the right-hand side in the Austinian proposition), or into the situation that the content concerns.

On the first option, both Watson and Holmes are talking about the same "objective" situation (the situation they share), but they state different facts about that situation. The facts they state are, respectively:

Holmes: Left-of (salt, pepper, perspective H)

Watson: Left-of (salt, pepper, perspective W)

Watson's and Holmes's perspectives turn out to be (unarticulated) constituents of the facts they state. According to Barwise, that is the view Perry favors.

On the second option, taken by Barwise, Holmes and Watson assert the same (relativized) fact:

Left of (salt, pepper)

However, Holmes and Watson talk about *different situations*. The situations are individuated in terms of Holmes's and Watson's subjective perspectives on them. The Austinian propositions expressed by Watson's and Holmes's respective utterances are:

Holmes: Holmes's perspective $\models$ 《Left of (salt, pepper)》

Watson: Watson's perspective $\models$ 《Left of (salt, pepper)》

According to Barwise, the superiority of the second option comes from the fact that, if we take the first one, "we have nothing in the theory that classifies the similarity in attitudes of Holmes and Watson in cases like these. And it is this similarity that leads them to make the same bodily movements, reaching in the same direction, though toward different objects, when they want the salt" (Barwise 1989, 240).

Whatever we think of "perspectival situations" and the specific problems they raise,[15] there is a more fundamental issue at stake. According to Barwise, Perry *generally* treats "unarticulated constituents" as constituents of the content to be evaluated rather than as aspects of the situation with respect to which the content is evaluated. Unarticulated constituents, for him, are things the statement or belief is "about" rather than things the statement or belief "concerns." If this is right, then Perry must have changed his mind since Perry 1986b, for that paper's main point was that more cases of unarticulatedness can be handled in terms of the "concerning" relation than one might as first suppose. Not only can the case of the Z-landers, or the case of children saying or thinking "It's five o'clock" even though they have never heard of time zones, be so handled. The same thing holds for the case of *anyone* saying or thinking "It's raining" and grabbing his or her umbrella, or of *anyone* saying or thinking "It's five o'clock" and deciding to have tea. In all such cases, Perry held that we can appeal to relativized propositions and the concerning relation. In his paper, however, Barwise suggests that Perry has changed his mind, and he ascribes to him a position in sharp conflict to that put forward in Perry 1986b regarding examples such as 'It is raining' or 'It's five o'clock':

My four year old daughter Claire knows what it means to be 7 AM, since that is when she is allowed to wake us up. And she can believe that it is 7 AM. Now the point is that she has no idea about time zones. But to account for the truth of her belief, we somehow have to build in the dependence of the proposition on time zones. It can either be an aspect of her situation, or the fact she states and believes. If [following Perry] we take the unarticulated constituent route, we end up saying that the fact she notes when she notes that it is 7 AM has something like Pacific Daylight Time as a constituent. This seems to me quite contrary to the situated perspective on inquiry, which would see it as an aspect of the situation she is in. (Barwise 1989, 241)

Was Barwise right to ascribe to Perry a view so clearly at variance with that put forward in Perry 1986b? The fact that Perry has stopped using the notion of "concerning" in subsequent papers lends some support to the claim that he has changed his mind on those issues (though he never said so explicitly); however, Barwise certainly goes too far when he suggests that Perry would put the time zone on the content side rather than the situation side. I think Perry's new frame of mind is better captured by saying that he would rather not use the Austinian framework (with its two sides) at all. Be that as it may, it is important to realize that, even in Perry 1986b, he remained very cautious and resisted the sort of generalization that characterizes Barwise's approach and mine. Not all instances of unarticulatedness, he then suggested, can be handled in terms of the concerning relation. In the next section, I will present what I take to have been Perry's criterion, at the time of Perry 1986b, for picking out the cases that can be so handled.

Perry's Criterion: The NCC

Though he did not discuss the issue explicitly, the following passage seems to me representative of Perry's view regarding the cases which can and those which cannot be handled by appealing to relativized propositions and the concerning relation:

> In cases in which the same unrepresented parameter is relevant to a whole mode of thinking or discourse, we should classify each specific belief or utterance with a propositional function. The truth-value would be that of the proposition obtained by applying the function to the value of the parameter fixed by facts about the whole system. (Perry 1993, 221)

This actually covers two sorts of case. There are, on the one hand, the cases in which the subject has no representation whatsoever of the relevant parameter, which only the theorist can articulate. That is the "Z-lander" sort of case. There are also the cases in which the subject herself can articulate the relevant parameter, but need not do so because the value of the parameter is fixed by the environment or the architecture of the system in a uniform manner, that is, without any need for the subject herself to *cognitively discriminate* the situation of concern from other possible situations. That is what happens in the mode of thinking or discourse that specifically concerns local weather:

> In those parts of our life where there is an external guarantee that the weather information we receive and our actions will concern our own locale, there is no reason for our beliefs to play the internal coordinating role they need to at other times. When I look outside and see rain and grab an umbrella or go back to bed, a relatively true belief, concerning my present surroundings, will do as well as a more articulated one, about my present surrounding. (Perry 1986b, 216)

> Those belief states that directly control behavior for local weather merely *concern* local weather, rather than being about it. All believers who had just seen rain and were about to open their umbrellas [should] be reckoned as believing the same propositional function, but the truth conditions of their beliefs...differ with their location. (Perry 1986b, 217)

So 'It's raining' expresses a propositional function when it is uttered in talking about local weather. Even though 'It's raining', in such circumstances, turns out to have the same truth-conditions as 'It's raining here', they are not synonymous: 'It's raining' expresses a place-relative propositional function, while 'It's raining here' articulates the place that therefore goes into the evaluated content instead of being simply part of the circumstance of evaluation.

The cases that presumably cannot be handled in this way, according to Perry, are the cases in which it is incumbent upon the subject to discriminate what his thought or statement is tacitly about, because there are several possible options and no external fact to pick out one. That is what happens in the mode of thinking or discourse about nonlocal weather.

Suppose, for example, that my son has just talked to my older son in Murdock on the telephone, and is responding to my question, "How are things there?" Then his remark ["It is raining"] would not be about Palo Alto [the place where he is], but about Murdock.... My son's belief [is] about Murdock, and his intention [is] to induce a belief in me that [is] about Murdock by saying something about Murdock. Here it is natural to think that we are explaining which unarticulated constituent a statement is about, in terms of something like the *articulated* constituents of the beliefs and intentions it expresses. (Perry 1986b, 211)

Perry's position may be reconstructed and tentatively justified as follows. In this sort of case it is not the location of the speaker, but his intentions and beliefs, that determine the place on which the truth-value of the statement depends. Since that is the case, the place in question must be mentally represented, hence it is an articulated constituent of the content of the belief the utterance expresses. Assuming that the content of the utterance is the same as that of the belief it expresses, it follows that the place is a constituent of the content of the utterance even if it is not articulated in the utterance itself (but only in the belief that the utterance expresses).

I do not accept this piece of reasoning, and I reject its conclusion: I think Murdock is the place the mentioned utterance *concerns* rather than a constituent of its content (narrowly speaking). I have no quarrel with the assumption that the content of an utterance is the same as that of the belief it expresses nor with the premise that Murdock must be mentally represented if the speaker is to be credited with the appropriate communicative intentions. Still, there is a premise in the above reasoning that I find unpalatable. The fact that something is mentally represented, hence articulated in *some* mental representation, does not entail that it is represented or articulated *in the mental representation whose truth-value depends upon that thing*. It may be articulated in some *other* mental representation. Thus, the fact that Perry's son must think of Murdock and intend to say something about Murdock when he utters "It is raining" possibly entails that Murdock is articulated in some mental representation of his, but it does *not* entail that the belief he expresses by his utterance "It is raining" is the locus of that articulation.

In general, the contextual facts that fix the value of the situational parameter for a given mental representation may well be cognitive factors involving other mental representations. To take an example I have used many times, suppose I say, "Berkeley is a nice place. There are bookstores and coffee shops at every corner." This is a two-sentence discourse. Berkeley is an articulated constituent of the first statement and an unarticulated constituent of the second statement. Nothing prevents us from saying that the second statement *concerns* the place the first sentence explicitly mentions. The fact that that place is cognitively discriminated via the mental representation corresponding to the *first* sentence does not entail that it is articulated also in the mental representation corresponding to the *second* sentence. On the contrary, the fact that the subject has just entertained a representation explicitly about Berkeley contributes to explaining why the second representation concerns that city. Likewise, I think it is the mental representation corresponding to Perry's question 'How are things there?' not that corresponding to his son's answer 'It is raining' that articulates Murdock. The place thus articulated in the question can serve as the situation that the answer concerns.

Given all this, my policy is to (try to) handle *all* cases of unarticulatedness, or as many as possible, by feeding the unarticulated constituents into the situation of concern. In many cases, the situation that an utterance or thought concerns will be determined not by external facts like the location of the speaker, but by cognitive factors such as the topic of the conversation or what the thinker is mentally focussing on. In such cases, admittedly, the situation s that the representation R concerns will itself have to be somehow represented or articulated—it will have to be cognitively discriminated—but that would raise a problem only if that entailed that s is articulated *in R*. As we have just seen, that consequence does not follow. I therefore reject the principle which Perry seems to accept in his discussion of unarticulated constituents and the concerning relation:

No Cognitive Concerning (NCC): For an unarticulated constituent to go into the situation of concern, it must be contributed by the environment rather than cognitively discriminated.

Relativized Propositions and *De Se* Belief

Perry's Argument
Can we use the relativized-propositions framework to deal with the essential indexical? Can we say that an utterance such as "I am hungry" expresses an Austinian proposition, the right-hand-side of which is occupied by a relativized proposition, true only at a time and an agent? According to Perry, if we say so, that will not help us solve the problem of the essential indexical. We cannot, in this way, properly capture the *de se* belief that is expressed by saying "I am hungry."

Perry's argument proceeds in two steps. First, Perry attempts to establish that the subject does not merely believe the relativized proposition. The belief could not be evaluated as true or false if its content was exhausted by that proposition. For the belief to be evaluable, we need a situation of concern over and above the relativized proposition. In particular, we need a time and an agent, such that the relativized proposition is *believed to be true with respect to that time and to that agent.* Second step: Perry shows that, as soon as we bring the agent into the picture, the problem of the essential indexical reappears: "Once we have adopted these new-fangled propositions, which are only true at times for persons, we have to admit also that we believe them as true for persons at times, and not absolutely. And then our problem returns" (Perry 1979, 44). The problem returns because there are different ways of thinking of the person relative to which the relativized proposition is believed to be true. When Perry thinks, "I am making a mess" at time t_1, he believes the relativized proposition "x is making a mess at t" to be true for himself at that time. But all the shoppers who watch him make a mess also believe that relativized proposition to be true for Perry at t_1. Both Perry and the shoppers believe, at t_1, the Austinian proposition

$$\langle \text{Perry}, t_1 \rangle \models \langle\!\langle x \text{ is making a mess at } t \rangle\!\rangle$$

Appealing to Austinian propositions consisting of a situation and a relativized proposition does not therefore solve the problem. Whether we use classical propositions or Austinian propositions, it seems that we need guises over and above the usual propositional constituents to distinguish Perry's first-person belief from the other shoppers' third-person beliefs.

Evidently, one should block the argument at step 1 and maintain that the content of the belief is the relativized proposition. Only in that way can we hope to solve the problem of the essential indexical, for the very reason that Perry gives at step 2. The position I take is therefore the same as that defended a long time ago by Richard Feldman in his reply to Perry:

Perry takes the doctrine of indexed propositions to entail that we do not simply believe such propositions, but rather believe that they are true at some index. However, we need not understand the doctrine in that way. Contrary to what Perry says, we ordinarily do not believe that indexed propositions are true at some index. We simply believe them. In Perry's example, when I realized what was happening I first came to believe the proposition *that I am making a mess.* Of course, I was then believing it a certain place and time and in a certain possible world. And it was true for me in that world at that place and time. Prior to my realization, I did not believe this proposition at all, although I may have believed some other proposition about this proposition. That is, I may have believed the meta-proposition that the proposition *that I am making a mess* is true at some index, namely, one containing the guilty shopper and that time. Similarly, the shopper watching me does not believe the proposition *that I am making a mess*, but he may believe some proposition about this proposition. For example, he may believe that it is true at an index containing me and then. So, on this view, the proposition *that I am making a mess* is one that I came to believe at the appropriate time and my coming to believe it can help to explain why I straightened my sack. (Feldman 1980, 82)

Indeed, in the situation-theoretic framework, the cognitive content of the belief (that which accounts for the subject's behavior) is captured by the right-hand side in the Austinian proposition—that is, by the relativized proposition. The situation is needed only to account for the belief's truth-conditions. So what the guilty shopper believes, on the situation-theoretic account, is the relativized proposition true at an agent x and a time t iff x is making a mess at t.

To be sure, that proposition is not semantically complete: it can be truth-evaluated only with respect to an agent and a time. In his reply, Feldman says that the agent and the time are, simply, the agent and time of the context. The agent is the person who believes the relativized proposition, and the time is the time at which the agent believes it. Now Perry had anticipated such a position, and he responded to it in advance: "All believing is done by persons at times, or so we may suppose. But the time of belief and the person doing the believing cannot be generally identified with the person and time relative to which the proposition believed is held true" (Perry 1979, 44).

This is the critical issue indeed. According to Feldman, an agent-relative proposition can only be evaluated with respect to the agent in the context of belief (i.e., with respect to the believer himself). So the agent does not have to be represented in order to play its role in fixing the belief's truth-conditions: It is provided by the environment. This is also the position defended by Loar (and by Lewis). According to Loar, there is a primitive relation, the "self-ascriptive belief relation," between believers and propositional functions (Loar 1976, 358). Whenever a person stands in that relation to a propositional function, she entertains a *de se* belief, true iff the propositional function is true of *that person*. Here again, we find that *the index with respect to which the relativized proposition is evaluated is bound to be the "index of the context"* (to use the terminology from Lewis 1980). Only if we accept this constraint, which I call the reflexive constraint, can we hope to solve the problem of the essential indexical by appealing to relativized propositions.

According to Perry, there is no reason to accept the reflexive constraint, for we can hold relativized propositions true with respect to noncontextual indices. That is what he thinks happens in the supermarket example: the guilty shopper takes the relativized proposition 'x is making a mess' to be true with respect to himself, but the other shoppers who watch him also take the relativized proposition to be true with respect to him. The difference—or, more cautiously, one difference—between the guilty shopper who holds a first-person belief and the other shoppers who hold a third-person belief is that, for him but not for them, the context of evaluation and the context of belief coincide. Now the simple fact that they need not coincide shows that the problem of the essential indexical (i.e., the problem of characterizing the first-person perspective) cannot be solved simply by appealing to relativized propositions. So the argument goes. As Perry puts it,

The time of belief and the person doing the believing cannot be generally identified with the person and time relative to which the proposition believed is held true. You now believe that *that I am making a mess* was true for me, then, but you certainly do not believe it is true for you now, unless you are reading this in a supermarket. Let us call *you* and *now* the context of belief, and *me* and *then* the context of evaluation. The context of belief may be the same as the context of evaluation, but need not be. (Perry 1979, 44)

The issue, however, is very far from settled. We cannot consider Perry to have demonstrated the possibility of a divergence between the circumstance of evaluation and the context of belief, by actually providing a couple of examples; for the examples he provides are controversial (to say the least). As we have seen, Feldman *denies* that the other shoppers are belief-related to the relativized proposition "*x* is making a mess at *t*": they are, at best, related to a meta-proposition about it. Loar and Lewis would make the same denial. So the question we must ask is: Are there good theoretical reasons for accepting, or for rejecting, the reflexive constraint?

The Reflexive Constraint

If the situation a representation concerns was always fixed by environmental facts like the time of thinking/speaking or the location or identity of the thinker/speaker, that would be sufficient to justify the reflexive constraint. There would be no divergence between the context of belief and the situation of evaluation; the index with respect to which a representation is evaluated would always be the index of the context. But I argued that the situation of concern may be fixed by cognitive factors. One may entertain the place-relative representation 'It is raining' in the course of thinking about a place distinct from the place where one is. In such a case the index relative to which the representation 'It is raining' is evaluated is not the index of the context, because the "place" coordinate of the index has been shifted to the place currently under focus.

Here we spot an inconsistency in Perry's position (as I have reconstructed it). On the one hand, he holds that some unarticulated constituents do not belong to the situation of concern because they are not fixed by environmental factors but by cognitive factors. He therefore accepts the principle I called NCC. On the other hand, when he insists that the problem of the essential indexical cannot be solved by appealing to relativized propositions, he argues that the reflexive constraint must be rejected. This is inconsistent because the NCC and the reflexive constraint are two sides of the same coin. The NCC tells us that the situation of concern is fixed by environmental facts, not cognitive factors. The reflexive constraint tells us that we are not free to choose the situation of concern, which is determined by environmental facts and cannot be shifted. Were the NCC correct, as Perry (1986b) suggests, it would follow that the reflexive constraint holds and that the sort of divergence between the context of evaluation and the context of belief that Perry (1979) invokes cannot arise. His argument against relativized propositions would collapse.

Be that as it may, I reject the NCC: the utterance/thought "It is raining" *may* concern all sorts of place, whether or not the speaker/thinker happens to be in that place; hence there may well be a divergence between the context of belief and the situation of evaluation, as Perry claims. That is the view Prior held with respect to times. A time-relative proposition of the sort expressed by tensed sentences need not be evaluated with respect to the time of utterance. If we prefix the sentence with a temporal operator, the relativized proposition will be evaluated with respect to the time we are taken to by the operator, which shifts the time coordinate of the index. Even if we consider only sentences uttered in isolation, we can easily transport ourselves in imagination to a time distinct from the time of utterance, and evaluate the time-relative proposition with respect to the time thus imagined.

Since I reject the NCC, and the reflexive constraint that goes with it, it seems that I should accept Perry's conclusion: that the problem of the essential indexical cannot be solved by appealing to relativized propositions. Those, like Loar and Lewis, who believe that the problem can be solved in this way take the reflexive constraint for granted: what determines the individual with respect to which the self-ascribed propositional function (or property) is evaluated is an environmental fact: the individual in question is bound to be the person who does the self-ascribing (the agent in the context of belief). There is no way in which one can, as it were, vary the person of evaluation by applying the propositional function to someone else. Thus the type of case imagined by Perry—the other shopper's applying the propositional function 'x is making a mess' to Perry—cannot arise. But for me, given the framework I adopt, such a situation ought to be possible.

Remember what I said in "Relativizing Contents." 'The carburetor is in good condition' may well express an object-relative propositional function, true of a certain car. The car here is the situation that the relativized proposition concerns. Similarly, I may comment on someone's appearance and say: "Very handsome!" Here, arguably, I express a person-relative proposition (a property), true of persons at times, and I apply it to a certain individual whom my utterance concerns. Whether or not such a view is sustainable, it is clearly in the spirit of what I said in that section. Now if we accept that there are such person-relative propositions, which can be evaluated with respect to whichever persons they happen to concern, it is clear that the problem of the essential indexical cannot be solved merely by appealing to such propositions. For the person whose appearance I comment upon when I say (or think) "Very handsome!" may happen to be myself, seen in a mirror and mistaken for someone else. In such a situation, arguably, I believe the propositional function 'x is very handsome' of myself, yet I do not believe the sort of thing that I could express by saying "I am very handsome." I entertain a *de re* belief about myself, not a *de se* belief. I conclude that, without something like the reflexive constraint to anchor the situation of concern to the context, the problem of the essential indexical cannot be solved by appealing to relativized propositions (unsupplemented by guises or something of that sort).

A last move is available to the propositional relativist, however. One may grant that the reflexive constraint does not hold in general, while maintaining that it holds in a specific domain: the indexical domain. One of the differences between 'It is raining' and 'It is raining here' is that, whereas the first sentence can be evaluated with respect to a place different from the place of the context, the second sentence cannot: the indexical 'here' rigidly anchors the situation of evaluation to the context.[16] As far as indexicals are concerned, the reflexive constraint holds: the coordinates of the evaluation index that correspond to indexicals cannot be shifted but are set, once for all, by the context. It is interesting to note that Feldman, who maintains the reflexive constraint against Perry, models index-relative propositions by indexical sentences. To believe a relativized proposition, for him, is to accept an indexical sentence such as 'I am making a mess':

The idea [of believing a relativized proposition] may be clarified if we drop talk of propositions altogether and simply talk of sentences. What I came to believe was the sentence 'I am making a mess'. I did not believe it before. I came to believe it at the same time I became prepared to say it. Note that I need not have become prepared to say-it-at-an-index or say that it is true at an index. I may have no thoughts about indices at all. I just became prepared to say this sentence. Of course, there was a time, place, etc., at which this happened. Similarly, I did not come to believe that the sentence is true at an index. I simply came to believe it. This coming to believe may have occurred at some index, but the index is not in any sense a part of the content of my belief. (Feldman 1980, 82–83)

Since he equates relativized propositions with indexical sentences, it is understandable that Feldman sticks to the reflexive constraint, for it is a property of indexical sentences that the relevant coordinates of the index are anchored to the context and cannot shift.

At this point someone like Feldman, who thinks the problem of the essential indexical can be solved by appealing to relativized propositions, may argue as follows. It is true that the unarticulated constituents which go into the evaluation index are shiftable; hence if we think of *de se* belief on the model of 'It is raining' the problem of the essential indexical will not be solved, because the reflexive constraint will not hold. But we need not think of *de se* belief on the model of 'It is raining'. We may think of it on the model of 'It is raining here'. This is an indexical sentence, and that guarantees that the reflexive constraint holds. Why not, then, say that there are two sorts of relativized propositions? Sentences like 'It is raining' express one sort of relativized propositions—the sort that does not conform to the reflexive constraint. Admittedly, *de se* belief cannot be accounted for by appealing to such propositions, but there is another sort of relativized propositions: those corresponding to indexical sentences like 'It is raining here'. The difference between them and the first sort of relativized propositions is that they satisfy the reflexive constraint. Hence, *de se* belief can be construed as involving such propositions.

This intriguing move raises an obvious objection (though not an insuperable one, as we shall see in the next section). In what sense does 'It's raining here' express a place-relative proposition? Insofar as the place is articulated (by the indexical 'here') is it not a constituent of the content articulated by the sentence? This suggests that we really have two different phenomena at issue. First, there is indexicality, in both language and thought. The reflexive constraint belongs there, as does the phenomenon of *de se* belief. Second, there is unarticulated constituency and relativized propositions (again, in both language and thought). This is a different phenomenon altogether.

The position I have just stated is plausible, and it is a charitable reconstruction of Perry's view. On Perry's view, there is no hope of solving the problem of *de se* belief by appealing to relativized propositions, even though relativized propositions can be appealed to for dealing with 'It is raining' and similar cases. It makes sense to posit relativized propositions only if the constituent the proposition is relative to is not articulated in the (linguistic or mental) representation expressing the proposition; for if it is articulated, indexically or otherwise, then there is no reason to expel it out of the proposition and make it part of the situation of concern.

Having made as strong a case as I could for Perry's view, I will now attempt to show that we can, after all, account for *de se* belief by appealing to relativized propositions. We can, because the obvious objection I have just raised to what I called "the last move of the propositional relativist" can be met. We can maintain that there is a class of relativized propositions for which the reflexive constraint holds. The only thing we have to do to meet the objection is to clearly distinguish the propositions in this class from the propositions expressed by indexical sentences: we have to ensure that the relevant situational constituent (that to which the proposition is said to be relative) is not articulated, indexically or otherwise, in the sentence or mental representation to which we assign the relativized proposition as content. Still, what characterizes the new class of relativized propositions is the unshiftability of the situational constituent: that distinguishes them from the relativized propositions expressed by sentences such as 'It is raining', which are relative to a *shiftable* situational component.

Context-relative Propositions

Let us assume that the problem can be solved, that is, let us assume that *there are* relativized propositions which can be used to model *de se* belief. Such propositions must have two main properties:

1. Qua *relativized* propositions, they must not contain the thinker/speaker as a constituent. So the proposition expressed by an indexical sentence such as 'I am making a mess' is ruled out because the first-person pronoun articulates the self. In the relevant relativized proposition, the self must be unarticulated—just as the place is unarticulated in 'It is raining'. It must be found only on the situational side.

2. The evaluation index (or the relevant coordinate of the index) must be anchored to the context so as to be unshiftable. In other words, the reflexive constraint must hold. Only if that is the case will the Perry counterexamples (involving a divergence between the context of belief and the situation of evaluation) be avoided.

The two requirements seem to conflict. For we have seen that the property of unshiftability characterizes indexicals as opposed to unarticulated constituents. It seems that the second requirement demands that indexicals be used to anchor the index to the context, while the first requirement (unarticulatedness) prevents indexicals from being used.

The conflict is merely apparent, however; there is a way of anchoring the index to the context without using explicit indexicals and thereby articulating the relevant constituent. The trick consists in sorting relativized propositions according to the type of situation of evaluation they need.

Tensed sentences express time-relative propositions. Sentences like 'It is raining' express place-relative (or time-and-place-relative) propositions. I claimed that still other sentences express object-relative propositions. The last type I mentioned is that of person-relative propositions. When I mentioned it, I said that appealing to such propositions does not account for *de se* belief, because the person with respect to which such a proposition is evaluated can be thought of in many different ways or under many different guises. In particular, she can be thought of in a first-person way or in a third-person way. So what is distinctive of *de se* belief is not captured merely by appealing to person-relative propositions.

This difficulty can be met, by introducing a new sort of situation for propositions to be relative to. Just as we distinguished persons from (other) objects, we can distinguish subjects, or "first" persons, from other persons. This is not an ontological move. I am not suggesting that we appeal to Cartesian egos in order to account for *de se* belief in the relativized-propositions framework. A subject is an ordinary person. What distinguishes him or her from other persons is only the contingent role he or she plays with respect to a tokening of the relevant relativized proposition.

Whenever a proposition is tokened, that is, grasped through an occurrent representation expressing that proposition, the person doing the grasping fills the subject or first-person role with respect to that tokening. There are other roles associated with the tokening: there is not only the person who grasps, but also the place, time, and so forth at which the event takes place. This corresponds to the standard notion of context. My suggestion is that we make room for a new type of relativized propositions, namely *context-relative propositions*, which can be evaluated only with respect to entities bearing the relevant contextual relations to the token under which the proposition is grasped.

The place-relative proposition expressed by 'It is raining' is not context-relative because the location with respect to which it is evaluated is not constrained to be the place of the context; it may be any place currently under focus. But there is no reason why there could not be a special sort of place-relative proposition, exhibiting the property of context-relativity. Instead of being evaluable with respect to any place, such a proposition would be evaluable only with respect to the place of the context. Similarly, a time-relative proposition that is also context-relative could be evaluated only with respect to the time of the context. For context-relative propositions, the reflexive constraint holds: the index of evaluation is anchored to the context. Yet the feature of context with respect to which the proposition is bound to be evaluated remains unarticulated: it is not a constituent of the proposition, contrary to what happens when an indexical sentence is used.

Since a context-relative proposition can be evaluated only with respect to entities bearing the relevant contextual relations to the token under which the proposition is grasped, such a proposition cannot be directly evaluated; it can be evaluated only if tokened, because a proper evaluation index can be assigned to the proposition only relative to a tokening of that proposition. There is, as it were, a double relativization here. Not only is the proposition evaluated relative to some index, but the index itself can be assigned only relative to a tokening of the proposition.

So far we have made room for a new class of propositions (context-relative propositions). Only if there are linguistic or mental representations expressing them will the notion of a context-relative proposition be useful in theorizing about language and thought. Such representations, if they exist, are *intermediate* between indexical representations and situation-relative representations such as 'It is raining' (which can be evaluated with respect to any place and time). Like indexical sentences, their truth-value depends upon a feature of the context—for example, the time or the place of the tokening. Whether we evaluate the indexical sentence 'It is raining here and now', or the context-relative sentence ^{c}It is raining^c,[17] in both cases we must look at the place and time of the context to check whether or not the sentence is true. But the relevant feature of context is explicitly represented in the indexical case, whereas it remains unarticulated in the context-relative case, just as the situation of concern remains unarticulated in situation-relative sentences. Context-relative representations exhibit both unshiftability (a property they share with indexical sentences) and unarticulatedness (a property they share with situation-relative sentences).

Do such representations exist? As far as natural language is concerned, that is far from obvious. It may be that, in natural language, we find only indexical sentences ('it's raining here and now') and situation-relative sentences ('it's raining'), but no context-relative sentences.[18] Be that as it may, there is no reason why there shouldn't be context-relative representations in thought. Quite the contrary: There is every reason to believe that *there are* context-relative representations in thought. The most basic kind of representation with which a perceiving-and-acting organism must be credited presumably belongs to that category.

An organism that (like most animals) does not have the reflective capacity to think of itself as a person among other persons yet perceives and acts should be credited with a primitive form of egocentric thinking. That is one of Perry's major insights, in Perry 1986b and elsewhere. In Perry 1986a, he writes:

The information that we get at a certain spot in the world is information about objects in the neighborhood of that spot in a form suitable for the person in that spot. As long as this is the only source of information we have about ourselves, we need no way of designating ourselves, indexical or insensitive. Our entire perceptual and doxastic structure provides us with a way of believing about ourselves, without any expression for ourselves. (Perry 1986a, 148–149)

Though relative to the subject, perceptual representations are not just person-relative representations, for they are not applicable to persons other than the subject of the context (the first person). They can *only* be evaluated with respect to the context in which they are entertained—the perceiving subject and the time and place of the perception. In other words, they are context-relative representations, satisfying the reflexive constraint.

Shall we say that only organisms devoid of an explicit representation of themselves entertain such context-relative representations, while we entertain more sophisticated, indexical representations containing the word 'I' or a mental analogue? Perry gave us a reason not to make that move. Just as "there is a little of the Z-lander in the most well traveled of us," there is a little of the simple perceiving-and-acting organism in the most reflectively self-conscious of us. What Perry says about our thoughts concerning the local weather easily generalizes to perception-based thought, whether it is about the weather or anything else:

> What each of us gets from perception may be regarded as information concerning ourselves, to explain connections between perception and action. There is no need for a self-referring component of our belief, no need for an idea or representation of ourselves. When a ball comes at me, I duck; when a milk shake is put in front of me, I advance. The eyes that see and the torso or legs that move are parts of the same more or less integrated body. And this fact, external to the belief, supplies the needed coordination. The belief need only have the burden of registering differences in my environment, and not the burden of identifying the person about whose relation to the environment perception gives information with the person whose action it guides. (Perry 1986b, 219)

Again, perceptual representations are context-relative. They satisfy the reflexive constraint, but they do so in virtue of brute architectural facts, not through the use of explicit indexicals.

If we, sophisticated organisms endowed with language, want to verbally express a context-relative thought, and there are no context-relative sentences, what can we do? We have to use either a situation-relative sentence or an indexical sentence. If a situation-relative sentence is available that is the most appropriate tool. The difference between a situation-relative sentence and a context-relative sentence is very small when the situation of evaluation happens to be the situation of utterance. It is a purely counterfactual difference: the situation-relative sentence *could* be used to characterize another situation than the situation of utterance, while a context-relative sentence could not. The difference between a context-relative sentence and an indexical sentence is more substantial, since the indexical sentence articulates the relevant contextual feature and makes it part of the content. That is why one would not express the context-relative thought ᶜIt is rainingᶜ, prompted by the perception of rain, by saying "It is raining here and now." We would naturally say, "It is raining" (unless there is a good reason to explicitly represent the place of the context). But there are context-relative thoughts for which no situation-relative sentence is available. Self-relative thoughts are a case in point. If I want to express a self-relative thought, to the effect that I am hungry (or cold, or what have you), I can hardly say "Hungry!" or "Cold!", for that is not proper English. I have to use an indexical sentence and say: "I am cold", or "I am hungry." In contrast to 'it's raining here', which makes sense only if there is a good reason to explicitly represent the place of the context (typically because of an intended contrast between that place and some other place), I can use an indexical sentence such as 'I am hungry' to express a context-relative thought because, given the lack of an appropriate situation-relative sentence, there is no clear alternative. In this way, we can perhaps explain why Wittgenstein and some of his followers have insisted that there are two uses of 'I': a subjective use whereby an indexical sentence 'I am F' expresses a self-relative propositional function, and a more objective use whereby it expresses a proposition with the subject as a constituent. The word 'I', they say, is a genuine referring expression only in the second type of case.

This leads us back to the problem of the essential indexical. I have shown that, by appealing to context-relative propositions, we can account for *de se* belief. But the problem of the essential indexical is not thereby solved in its full generality, for it arises also with respect to the "objective" use of indexical sentences. If I entertain an indexical (rather than context-relative) thought and express it by uttering the sentence '*I* was born in Paris (in contrast to you, who were born in Chicago)', my utterance expresses a proposition with me as constituent. Yet the indexical is no less essential in that sentence than in any other: if we replace it by a nonindexical expression, we affect the cognitive significance of the utterance. As Perry might say, "our problem returns." What this shows, presumably, is that we need modes of presentation anyway. To the extent I am concerned, that is fine. My aim, in this chapter, was not to cast doubt on the usefulness of modes of presentation as a theoretical tool; it was merely to advertise, and start exploring the potential of, *another* theoretical tool, the usefulness of which has not been sufficiently appreciated.

Acknowledgments

I am grateful to the participants in the Indexicality seminar in Paris (especially Stéphane Chauvier, Jérôme Dokic, Paul Egré, and Isidora Stojanovic) for their comments on earlier versions of this paper, and to the European Science Foundation EURO-CORES programme "The Origin of Man, Language and Languages" for supporting this research.

Notes

1. At least this follows from the principle of effability as formulated by Katz. Searle's formulations are not as clear-cut. On the relations between the two principles, see Recanati 2003.

2. See Castañeda's and Perry's collections of papers, Castañeda 1999 and Perry 1993.

3. Such senses are of "limited accessibility," since they "can only be expressed in special circumstances" (Perry 1979, 45).

4. On hybrid logic, see Blackburn et al. 2001, ch. 7.

5. To keep things simple I skip accessibility relations (or rather, I leave them implicit).

6. The important thing, I said, is to see modal sentences as constructed from simple sentences by means of operators. Now this is something we can do *even if we want to represent modal talk extensionally*. The apparatus of variadic functions presented in Recanati 2002 enables us to do that. In that paper, I analyzed 'Everywhere I go it rains' as resulting from the application of a locative variadic operator to the sentence 'It rains'. That operator does two things. First, it modifies the adicity of the predicate in the sentence it applies to: it adds an extra argument-place for a location, which can be represented by a free variable. Second, it introduces a restricted quantifier that binds that variable. The operator can be paraphrased as 'for every location l such that I go to l, in l it is the case that'. 'Necessarily it rains' can be represented in the same hybrid way, by applying to the sentence 'It rains', a sentence operator that can be rendered as: 'for every world w, in w it is the case that'. Since the variable 'w' is introduced by the variadic operator, we don't have to treat the emergence of modalities as a radical change in the language, but simply as an enrichment of it; an enrichment which does not affect the simple (nonmodal) sentences, hence preserves modal Innocence.

7. Barbara Partee (1973) says that examples like "I did not turn off the stove" (in which reference is made to a specific time) speak against a treatment in terms of operators, because modal operators cannot capture the referential nature of (some uses of) tenses. But the referential/quantificational issue is orthogonal to the question, whether or not we should use operators. Even if standard modal operators are quantificational rather than referential, nothing prevents the introduction of 'referential' operators in the modal framework. See Prior 1967, 1968 and Blackburn 1994.

8. There is a third option: tenses can be represented as temporal predicates of events. If we like Davidson's analysis of adverbial modification, that is a natural move to make.

9. Or, in a Fregean framework, part of the expression of such a content.

10. "The simplest way to introduce a notion of absolute truth is to follow the analogy with possible words semantics and stipulate a type sentence to be true simpliciter just in case it is true-now. Tense-logic, in the hands of its inventor, could be regarded, without violation of its principles, as a semantics exclusively of statements uttered at one particular time" (Dummett, forthcoming, 19).

11. By "situation theory" here, I do not mean the official doctrine expounded in Barwise and Perry's 1983, but a body of ideas developed a few years later and centered around the notion of 'Austinian proposition' (Barwise and Etchemendy 1987; Barwise 1989; Recanati 1997, 1999, 2000; Dokic, forthcoming; see also Perry 1986b, where some of these ideas originate).

12. See e.g. Stanley and Szabo 2000.

13. A well-known difficulty for the situation-theoretic approach to contextual domain restriction comes from the fact that distinct quantifiers in a single sentence may involve distinct restrictions. The answer to that difficulty consists in associating sub-sentential expressions with (local) circumstances of evaluation. See, e.g., Recanati 1996.

14. I use 'fact' and 'proposition' interchangeably. A fact, for me, is the content of a statement (the "fact stated").

15. The main problem perspectival situations raise is that they are not "objective" enough to play the role of situation; or so it may be thought. That difficulty can (perhaps) be overcome by viewing perspectival situations as "reflexive situations" that include a viewer with a perspective *on* the situation. Be that as it may, I am not specifically concerned with perspectival situations in this chapter. I use them only for illustrative purposes.

16. There are apparent exceptions to that principle (e.g., shifted indexicals in free indirect speech), but I will not deal with them here.

17. The "context-quotes" I am using here make a situation-relative sentence context-relative by anchoring the unarticulated constituents of the evaluation index to the context.

18. There is no certainty here. Maybe some expressions (e.g., the verb 'to come' or expressions like 'in two days') can be treated as contributing to the expression of a context-relative proposition.

References

Bar-Hillel, Y. 1954. "Indexical Expressions." Reprinted in Bar-Hillel 1970.

———. 1963. "Remarks on Carnap's Logical Syntax of Language." Reprinted in Bar-Hillel 1970.

———. 1970. *Aspects of Language.* Jerusalem: Magnes Press.

Barwise, J. 1989. "Situations, Facts, and True Propositions." In his *The Situation in Logic.* Stanford, Calif.: CSLI Publications.

Barwise, J., and J. Etchemendy. 1987. *The Liar: An Essay on Truth and Circularity.* New York: Oxford University Press.

Barwise, J., and J. Perry. 1983. *Situations and Attitudes.* Cambridge, Mass.: MIT Press.

Blackburn, P. 1994. "Tense, Temporal Reference and Tense Logic." *Journal of Semantics* 11: 83–101.

Blackburn, P., M. de Rijke, and Y. Venema. 2001. *Modal Logic.* Cambridge: Cambridge University Press.

Carnap, R. 1937. *The Logical Syntax of Language.* London: Routledge and Kegan Paul.

Castañeda, H.-N. 1999. *The Phenomeno-Logic of the I: Essays on Self-Consciousness.* Ed. J. Hart and T. Kapitan. Bloomington: Indiana University Press.

Dokic, J. Forthcoming. *Steps Toward a Theory of Situated Representations*. Typescript, Paris.

Dummett, M. Forthcoming. *Existence, Possibility and Time*. Typescript, Oxford.

Evans, G. 1985. "Does Tense Logic Rest on a Mistake?" In his *Collected Papers*. Oxford: Clarendon Press.

Feldman, R. 1980. "Saying Different Things." *Philosophical Studies* 38: 79–84.

Goodman, N. 1977. *The Structure of Appearance*, 3rd ed. Dordrecht: Reidel.

Katz, J. 1977. *Propositional Structure and Illocutionary Force*. New York: Crowell.

Lewis, D. 1979. "Attitudes *De Dicto* and *De Se*." Reprinted (with a postscript) in Lewis 1983.

———. 1980. "Index, Context, and Content." In S. Kanger and S. Öhman (eds.), *Philosophy and Grammar*. Dordrecht: Reidel.

———. 1983. *Philosophical Papers*. Vol. 1. New York: Oxford University Press.

Loar, B. 1976. "The Semantics of Singular Terms." *Philosophical Studies* 30: 353–377.

Montague, R. 1968. "Pragmatics." In R. Klibansky (ed.), *La Philosophie Contemporaine, 1: Logique et Fondements des Mathématiques*. Florence: La Nuova Italia.

Partee, B. 1973. "Some Structural Analogies Between Tenses and Pronouns in English." *Journal of Philosophy* 70: 602–603.

Perry, J. 1979. "The Problem of the Essential Indexical." Reprinted in Perry 1993.

———. 1986a. "Perception, Action, and the Structure of Believing." Reprinted in Perry 1993.

———. 1986b. "Thought without Representation." Reprinted in Perry 1993.

———. 1993. *The Problem of the Essential Indexical and Other Essays*. New York: Oxford University Press.

Prior, A. 1959. "Thanks Goodness That's Over." Reprinted in Prior 1976.

———. 1967. *Past, Present, and Future*. Oxford: Clarendon Press.

———. 1968. "Now." *Noûs* 1: 101–119.

———. 1976. *Papers in Logic and Ethics*. London: Duckworth.

Prior, A., and K. Fine. 1977. *Worlds, Times and Selves*. London: Duckworth.

Recanati, F. 1993. *Direct Reference: From Language to Thought*. Oxford: Blackwell.

———. 1995. "Quasi-Singular Propositions: The Semantics of Belief Reports." *Proceedings of the Aristotelian Society*. Supplement 69: 175–194.

———. 1996. "Domains of Discourse." *Linguistics and Philosophy* 19: 445–475.

———. 1997. "The Dynamics of Situations." *European Review of Philosophy* 2: 41–75.

————. 1999. "Situations and the Structure of Content." In K. Murasugi and R. Stainton (eds.), *Philosophy and Linguistics*. Boulder, Colo.: Westview.

————. 2000. *Oratio Obliqua, Oratio Recta. An Essay on Metarepresentation*. Cambridge, Mass.: MIT Press.

————. 2002. "Unarticulated Constituents." *Linguistics and Philosophy* 25: 299–345.

————. 2003. "The Limits of Expressibility." In B. Smith (ed.), *John Searle*. Cambridge: Cambridge University Press.

Scott, D. 1970. "Advice on Modal Logic." In K. Lambert (ed.), *Philosophical Problems in Logic*. Dordrecht: Reidel.

Searle, J. 1969. *Speech Acts*. Cambridge: Cambridge University Press.

Stanley, J., and Z. Szabo 2000. "On Quantifier Domain Restriction." *Mind and Language* 15: 219–261.

6 Understanding Temporal Indexicals

Peter Ludlow

In Ludlow 1999 (ch. 3) I offered a treatment of temporal indexicals that was in the spirit of work by Gareth Evans (1981, 1982). In arguing for the position, I held that accounts which failed to incorporate *indexical content* (in the sense of Perry 2001) were inadequate and that token-reflexive accounts of content would not work as theories of indexical content. I held that the only way out was to develop a theory that incorporated Fregean senses, and I offered that Perry's famous (1977) considerations against employing Fregean senses in accounts of indexicals like 'today' and 'tomorrow' were not decisive after all.

Over the past decade, however, Perry has developed a theory of indexicals that weds a traditional "direct reference" story with a token-reflexive (or more accurately, a variation on that theme with the simpler label "reflexive") account of indexical content. This hybrid theory, which Perry calls "reflexive-referential," promises to at once avoid the weaknesses of stand-alone token-reflexive theories of indexical content and at the same time avoid the weaknesses of direct reference accounts of temporal indexicals (in particular, their failure to provide an account of cognitive significance). If Perry's new theory works, we can have our cake and eat it, too. That is, if it works.

In this chapter, I will argue that Perry's theory, though ingenious, will not work for temporal indexicals. (I will not directly consider other kinds of indexicals here.) I will argue that although the *reflexive contents* offered by Perry are certainly more robust than plain *referential contents*, it is arguable that they are not, for all that, robust enough to handle temporal indexicals.

I also develop a worry that I raised (1999) for trying to further augment reflexive theories of content like Perry's. The basic idea is that the reflexive content cannot be bolstered without exploiting more basic notion of indexical *senses*. In effect, bolstering reflexive theories requires smuggling in a notion of indexical sense.

Next, I return to the issue of whether Fregean senses are really all that problematic in giving accounts of indexical content. I will argue that, at the end of the day, the basic

Fregean story about indexicals—one which employs a notion of indexical sense—doesn't look so bad after all and indeed (taking a leaf from Perry) can be wedded to a theory of referential content yielding what we might call a *sense-referential* theory of indexicals. I will concede, however, that following considerations in Perry 1977 and Heck 2002 the Fregean picture cannot stand in its entirety—parts of it shall have to be given up.

Finally, I will take up the question of whether ecumenical theories like Perry's and the one I propose here can really have their cake and eat it, too. I will argue that the move of ignoring or discarding indexical contents and relying solely on referential contents in certain counterfactual situations is too simple and that developing a theory that employs modal discards is more subtle than it appears at first glance. For example, I will show that there are cases where we crucially cannot discard indexical contents in other possible worlds, and hence the modal profile of temporal indexicals is not a simple matter of discarding the reflexive contents.

That sounds like a lot of ground to cover. Maybe it is. In any case I will proceed as follows. In the next section, I will briefly review Perry's reflexive-referential theory of indexicals. Then, I will raise the worry that reflexive-referential content is too thin to work in a theory of temporal indexicals. In the section that next follows, I will argue that if we augment Perry's theory of reflexive content to fold in more of the indexical content, we may well be introducing senses through the back door; such augmentation may have to appeal to a more basic notion of indexical sense. Then, I will develop the sense-referential theory of indexical content. Finally, I will consider whether either theory (sense-referential or reflexive-referential) can really have its cake and eat it too.

Perry's Reflexive-Referential Account of Indexical Content

Suppose that I am sitting in my office one day, painfully aware that I have an important meeting with the president of the university at 3:00 PM. I might even utter (1) under my breath as I shuffle papers and take care of academic administrative minutia.

(1)   I have a meeting with the president at 3:00 PM.

As I dither about in my office, I realize that the clock on my wall hasn't moved off of 2:30 in a while. Puzzled I check the clock on my computer. It says that it is 3:00. I double-check the time online. I conclude that it is in fact 3:00 PM and I utter (2).

(2)   Oh no, I have a meeting with the president now!

I immediately get up and race to the president's office.

Arguably, my utterance of (2) reflects a piece of knowledge that my utterance of (1) does not and this additional piece of knowledge played a role in my actions. The thought that I expressed by my utterance of (1) was not enough to get me up out of my chair. It was only by coming to have the thought that I express by my utterance of (2) that I formed the intention to immediately run over to the president's office.

Obviously there is something more to my utterance of (2) than there is to my utterance of (1) but the big question is whether this "something more" is something *semantic*. *Fregeans* think that it is. That is, the semantics must reflect the difference in cognitive significance between my utterance of (1) and my utterance of (2). Accordingly, or so says the Fregean, the semantics must give different truth conditions to my utterances of (1) and (2), perhaps (to a first approximation) along the following lines.

(1-F1)   An utterance u, at 3:00 PM of 'I have a meeting with the president at 3:00 PM' is true iff (the individual picked out by the sense of 'I' in u) has a meeting at 3:00 PM.

(2-F1)   An utterance u, at 3:00 PM of 'I have a meeting with the president *now*' is true iff (the individual picked out by the sense of 'I' in u) has a meeting at (the time picked out by the sense of 'now' in u).

I say that these are Fregean glosses only to a *first* approximation (that is also what (1) in the 'F1' stands for), because I have used descriptions like 'the time picked out by the sense of u' to express the senses of the indexicals and these glosses are surely inadequate; eventually I'll need a better way of expressing or displaying the sense. For now, let's just assume that there will be something more illuminating than what is offered by these descriptions.

For *referentialists* like Kaplan (1979, 1989, 1990), Soames (1987, 2002), and (in an earlier incarnation) Perry (1979), the problem with (1-F1) and (2-F1) are not that they load too little information into the semantics, but rather that they load *too much* into the semantics. Referentialists think that this extra bit of indexical content does not make it into the truth conditions. On their view, the truth conditions for (1) and (2) would fundamentally look the same:

(1-R)   An utterance u, by s, at t, where $t = 3:00$ PM of 'I have a meeting with the president at 3:00 PM' is true iff s has a meeting with the president at t.

(2-R)   An utterance u, by s, at t, where $t = 3:00$ PM of 'I have a meeting with the president *now*' is true iff s has a meeting with the president at t.[1]

What about the difference in cognitive significance between (1) and (2)? Perhaps, as Wettstein (1986) has argued, it is a mistake to think that the something extra is semantical. On such a view there is semantics and there is psychology, and it is just "sloppy thinking" (Kaplan 1990) to mix the two.

But what is the harm of mixing them? Plenty, according to the referentialists, and the central problem has to do with the modal profile of these utterances. As Kaplan (1979) stressed, if the indexical content of a demonstrative (or indexical) makes it into the truth conditions, then what are we to say about examples like the following?

(3)   You are the person I'm addressing with this utterance

We surely don't want (3) to have an analysis like (4), because (4) appears to be a necessary truth while (3) does not.

(4)   The person I'm addressing with this utterance is the person I'm addressing with this utterance.

Clearly there are counterfactual environments where someone else might have been standing before me when I make my utterance, so (3) is only contingently true. But (4) does not appear to allow this possibility; it appears to be a necessary truth.

Thus our dilemma. If we include the extra bit in our semantics—if we make it part of the truth conditions—we mess up the modal profile of the sentence. If we leave out the extra bit, we don't seem to have a way of accounting for cognitive significance. Now, of course, referentialists will say that this is not a problem because the issue of cognitive significance can be dealt with in other ways, and the Fregean will say that this is not a problem because there are fancier stories to tell about the modal profile of utterances containing indexicals. Perry, however, suggests a third route. Maybe both sides are right—or, rather, partly right and partly wrong.

Why suppose that utterances have only a single content? They might have many. In fact, Perry suggests that utterances have at least three kinds of content:

The *indexical content* (sometime he calls this *content-M*) of an utterance corresponds to the truth-conditions of the utterance given the facts that fix the language of the utterance, the words involved, their syntax and their *meaning*.

The *referential content* (sometimes he calls this *content-C* and sometimes the *official content*) of an utterance corresponds to the truth-conditions given all of these factors, plus the facts about the *context* of the utterance that are needed to fix the designation of indexicals.

The *designational content* (sometimes he calls this *content-D*) of an utterance corresponds to the truth-conditions given all of these factors, plus the additional facts that are needed to fix the *designation* of the terms that remain (definite descriptions in particular, but also possessives, etc.).

Before I get to Perry's punch line, let me say a little bit more about the natures of indexical content and referential content (designational content will not concern us here). Referential content (or "official content") consists in the content that referentialists find kosher. So, for example, the official content of (2) is as given in (2-R). Indexical content is *not* what I have given in (2-F1). Perry enlists a modified version of Reichenbach's token-reflexive theory of content where the indexical content of (2) would be something akin to (2-X).

(2-X)   This utterance *u*, at 3:00 PM of 'I have a meeting with the president *now*' is true iff the utterer of *u* has a meeting with the president at the time *u* is uttered.

Perry's theory departs from Reichenbach in that it is not the utterance *tokens* that are constituents of the descriptions in (2-X), but rather the utterances themselves—that is, the acts of uttering (actually Reichenbach equivocates on this point). Perry could have called his theory "utterance-reflexive" or more generally "act-reflexive," but I will follow his usage and simply call it *reflexive*. Finally, Perry generalizes the theory to non-indexicals like names (2001, chs. 5–7), however names do not concern us here, so I will set them aside.

Of course, the Kaplanesque worries about the modal profile of (2-F1) carry over mutatis mutandis to (2-X), and we did not even need Kaplan to tell us this; the point was made (pre-Kaplan) by Casteñada 1967 (87):

Reichenbach, for instance, claims that the word "I" means the same as "the person who utters this token." This claim is, however, false. A statement formulated through a normal use of the sentence "I am uttering nothing" is contingent: if a person utters this sentence he falsifies the corresponding statement, but surely the statement might, even in such a case, have been true. On the other hand, the statements formulated by "The person uttering this token is uttering nothing" are self-contradictory: even if no one asserts them, they simply cannot be true.

So (2-X) apparently can't be the content of (2) either.

Now to Perry's punch line. Since we have (at least) two kinds of contents, we can rely upon the reflexive content to give us an account of the cognitive significance of the utterance, but we don't need to keep the reflexive content around all the time. In fact, when we want to consider the modal profile of a sentence (i.e., when we want to evaluate it in a counterfactual situation) we can simply discard (ignore) the reflexive content and rely on the referential content. This is the sense in which Perry thinks we can have our cake and eat it, too. We can account for both the cognitive significance and the modal profile of an utterance if we simply get clear that these involve different contents of the same utterance!

That is the theory in a nutshell. Now I want to consider whether it really works.

Is Reflexive Content Too Thin?

Perry's theory may do just fine for certain kinds of indexicals, and maybe even for names, but temporal indexicals (including tenses themselves) are another matter. First, a point about basic tenses like past and future. Prima facie it may not be so obvious that tenses have indexical content, but this is a point that was noticed by Smart (1966, 133–134), and he proposed an extension of Reichenbach's (1947) theory of token-reflexives to account for tenses:

> Let us replace the words "is past" by the words "*is* earlier than this utterance." (Note the transition to the tenseless "is.") Similarly, let us replace "is present" and "now" by "*is* simultaneous with this utterance," and "is future" by "*is* later than this utterance."...Notice that I am here talking of self-referential *utterances*, not self-referential *sentences*. (The same sentence can be uttered on many occasions.) We can, following Reichenbach, call the utterance itself a "token," and this sort of reflexivity "token-reflexivity." Tenses can also be eliminated, since such a sentence as "he will run" can be replaced by "he *runs* at some future time (with tenseless "runs") and hence by "he *runs* later than this utterance." Similarly, "he runs" means "he *runs* (tenseless) simultaneous with this utterance." and "he ran" means "he *runs* (tenseless) earlier than this utterance." All the jobs which can be done by tenses can be done by means of the tenseless way of talking and the self-referential utterance "this utterance."

Could we execute the same strategy using Perry's notion of reflexive content? Here's the worry: consider the old chestnut from Prior 1959—'Thank goodness that's over'— said after a visit to the dentist or after sitting through a particularly dreadful meeting with the university president. To keep things as uncomplicated as possible, we can consider an indicative version of this:

(5)   I am thankful that my root canal is over with.

According to Perry's theory, for an utterance u, of (5), at time t, by Ludlow, we have a reflexive content akin to the following,

(5-X)   The utterer of u is thankful that the event of his root canal is earlier than the time of u.

And a referential content as in (5-R).

(5-R)   Ludlow is glad that the event of his root canal is earlier than u (at time t).

The first thought is, well, are (5-X) and (5-R) really something to be glad about? That is, why should I care about the relative ordering of my utterance and my root canal? One might respond that this objection has no force, because at a minimum my utterance of (5), by having (or being associated with) the reflexive content in (5-X), temporally situates me with the time of that very utterance and therefore places me well after the root canal.

But, of course, it can and has been argued that the contents expressed by (5-R) and (5-X) do no such thing, either individually or in concert. Famously, Prior, in his "thank goodness" paper concluded (p. 17) with the claim that token-reflexive theories do not capture what I express with my utterance of (5). The question is, why did Prior consider reflexive content (or at least Reichenbach's token-reflexive content) to be inadequate?

For a B-theorist or four-dimensionalist,[2] my location just is my space-time worm, and, although that includes my utterance of (5) as a temporal segment, there are still big chunks of my space-time worm that are eternally situated earlier than that root canal. The only thing that an utterance actually claims to be safely situated later than the root canal is the utterance itself (utterance *event*, for Perry) and the part of my space-time worm that overlaps with the utterance. The problem is that we still want to know why *that* utterance and the corresponding part of my space-time worm are supposed to be special and why I should be glad about the fact that *that* utterance and worm segment are a safe temporal distance from the unpleasant event.

It is perfectly well open to Perry to argue that explaining why I am glad is not really part of the goal here. Many facts could explain my being thankful; perhaps I am delighted that I now possess free samples of mint-flavored floss, or perhaps I enjoy having fresh memories of the smell of dental gauze. Perry presumably will say that all this is very fine but that the reflexive content of my utterance is what makes my utterance of 'I'm thankful that's over' true. It doesn't do more than that and it isn't supposed to do more than that. The reflexive content certainly is not supposed to *explain* why I am relieved.

We can refine Prior's objection, however, by introducing explanatory talk directly into the crucial utterance, as in (5′).

(5′)   I am thankful *because* my root canal is over with now

Someone who utters (5′) clearly is not talking about mint-flavored floss or the smell of dental gauze, but they do seem to be offering an account of the reason for their thankfulness, and that appears to be that they are thankful *because* the root canal *is past*, quite independently of whatever other reasons they may have for being thankful. More to the point, isn't (5′) basically what I am saying when I utter (5)? So isn't the explanatory part of (5) somehow crucial to a proper analysis of it?

Is it plausible to say that this is illusory and what makes (5) and (5′) true is that the state of affairs described by the *reflexive* content of 'my root canal is over with now' is what causes me to be thankful? Well, presumably that is an option for Perry, but now one has to worry about the stability of Perry's project; precisely what amount of explanatory role is semantic content supposed to play? For Kaplan, Wettstein, and other direct reference theorists, the answer is simple: none. But for Perry, accounting for cognitive significance is a very important part of semantics. Thus he writes:

I cannot accept that a semantic theory can be correct that does not provide us with an appropriate interface between what sentences mean, and how we use them to communicate beliefs in order to motivate and explain action. A theory of linguistic meaning should provide us with an understanding of the properties sentences have that lead us to produce them under different circumstances, and react as we do to their utterance by others. (2001, 8)

Perry then offers the following "cognitive constraint on semantics":

If there is some aspect of meaning, by which an utterance u of S and an utterance u' of S' differ, so that a rational person who understood both S and S' might accept u but not u', then a fully adequate semantics should say what it is. (2001, 9)

It is clearly open to Perry to relax his cognitive constraint, but then the question arises as to how much of a role cognitive significance is supposed to play. The answer would have to be "some—not too much of a role, but just the right amount"—where the "right amount" is being determined by either Perry's theory or his intuitions, or both. But wouldn't the consistent strategy be to try and augment the theory with additional content so as to account for Prior's "thank goodness" case? Here is a possible amendment: just add a new kind of content to the mix.

The *sense content* (we can call this the *content-S*) of an utterance corresponds to the mode of presentation or sense displayed by truth-conditions of the utterance.

This results in a very ecumenical theory. We would now have the "official" referential content, the reflexive content, and Fregean sense content among others. Of course, I owe an account of how sense content is supposed to be handled in a semantic theory, and I will get to that in "Fregean Senses Reconsidered." First however, I want to argue against a possible repair job for the reflexive-referential theory. In the next section I will try to show that it would be a mistake to think one can augment the theory of reflexive content without sliding into a sense content position.

Why More Robust Reflexive Content Presupposes Sense Content

One might think that Perry's reflexive content is more austere than it needs to be—indeed, more austere than past token-reflexive accounts have been. Would the situation be better if we jazzed up the reflexive content of (5) in the following way?

(5-XX)   The utterer of this utterance u is thankful that the event of his root canal is earlier than the time of u—*this very utterance!*

That is, maybe it would help if we added some reflexivity in the way that we describe u. Perry avoids this strategy, and I think it is easy to understand why. The problem comes in with the way we go about identifying (reflexively) an utterance. In (5-XX), for example, we used the phrase 'this very utterance'. Question: just how innocent is that indexical 'this'?

Arguably, the answer to the question is that the appearance of the indexical in the metalanguage is not innocent at all, for it amounts to smuggling in a closet disquotational treatment of indexicals. For Evans (1981), Rumfitt (1993), Ludlow (1999), and Heck (2002), deploying indexicals in the metalanguage is precisely how one would want to proceed, but for reflexive content advocates like Perry, as well as for direct reference theorists, that is basically giving away the store.

We might ask whether we are really giving away the store just because we are deploying 'this' in the metalanguage. It is true enough that the kinds of indexicals being deployed in the metalanguage (e.g., 'this') may be different than those found in the utterance of the object language sentence (we have, in the case of (5-XX), traded in a 'now' for a 'this'), but this isn't much of a victory. Furthermore, on closer scrutiny even this small victory may be illusory, since the 'this' being deployed in the metalanguage doesn't look much like the indexical we use when pointing to nearby objects; we aren't pointing at anything, there is no act of indicating, and we don't appear to have any relevant referential intention.

What is going on when we use 'this' in (5-XX)? As I suggested in Ludlow 1999, it seems as though in cases like (5-XX), when one says 'this very utterance' one is really saying 'the utterance happening now' or, more accurately, 'the utterance I am producing now'. If that isn't how the utterance is identified, then how?

One might think that the referent of 'this very utterance' in (5-XX) might be given by the reflexive content of 'this very utterance'—perhaps along the lines of 'the utterance being produced by the speaker of u at the time u is produced'. But this won't work, for now the reflexivity is lost again—the whole reason for pursuing this strategy was to get at the indexical content in a richer way, and this spell-out adds nothing to that end.

As I stated earlier, it is understandable that Perry avoids this gambit, leading as it does to what looks like sense content in sheep's clothing. But, whereas this outcome may be undesirable to Perry, is there any reason why *we* should reject it? In other words, why shouldn't we simply shed the sheep's clothing and become full-on content-S advocates?

Fregean Senses Reconsidered

At the end of "Is Reflexive Content Too Thin?" I argued that Perry's theory might be augmented with the addition of sense content, but how is such content to be introduced into a semantic theory? In this section I want to sketch a possible way of displaying sense content within a semantic theory.

Before sketching the proposal, I will review some familiar arguments from Perry 1977, and, following discussion in Heck 2002, I will concede that certain aspects of the Fregean project will have to be given up (in particular the identification of a meaningful utterance with a single sense or thought), but I will hold that the resulting picture is no worse off for that. That is to say, we can reject certain of Frege's doctrines and still retain a useful notion of sense content.

I will then argue that a theory incorporating *both* referential content and sense content can give us what Perry was looking for. In effect, Perry was right to advocate being ecumenical, he just happened to advocate the wrong kind of ecumenicalism (or perhaps he wasn't ecumenical enough!).

To set up the discussion properly, I want to begin with an outline of the Fregean project as laid out in Heck 2002. According to Heck, Frege was committed to the following doctrines.

(1a)   There can be different Thoughts that "concern the same object" and ascribe the same property to it. For example, the Thought that Superman flies and the Thought that Clark Kent flies are different, even though Superman is Clark Kent.

(2a)   Sentences of the form 'N believes that a is F' and 'N believes that b is F' can have different truth-values, even if 'a' and 'b' refer to the same object.

(3)   Sense determines reference.[3]

(4)   The sense of a sentence is what one grasps in understanding it.

(5)   The sense of a sentence is a Thought.

In Heck's view not all of these doctrines can be maintained. In particular, we shall have to abandon the idea, implicit in doctrine (4) that there is a single thought associated with the understanding of a sentential utterance. To see why, we might begin with the considerations raised in Perry 1977. The point of departure for Perry's discussion is the following passage from Frege 1956.

If someone wants to say the same today as he expressed yesterday using the word 'today', he must replace this word by 'yesterday'. Although the thought is the same, the verbal expression must be different so that the sense, which would otherwise be affected by the differing times of utterance, is readjusted. The case is the same with words like 'here' and 'there'. In all such cases the mere wording, as it is given in writing, is not the complete expression of the thought, but the knowledge of certain accompanying conditions of utterance, which are used as means of expressing the thought, are needed for its correct apprehension. The pointing of fingers, hand movements, glances may belong here too. The same utterance containing the word 'I' will express different thoughts in the mouths of different men, of which some may be true, others false.

Perry argued that Frege gets into trouble by trying to identify the sense of a sentence (utterance) with a thought. Why? Well, because 'yesterday' and 'today' presumably have different senses, and it therefore follows that 'Today is a fine day' and 'Yesterday is a fine day' must have different senses—since they are *composed* of different senses. But if I can express the same thought today with an utterance of 'yesterday is a fine day' that I expressed yesterday with an utterance of 'today is a fine day', then thoughts cannot be associated with senses. This is clear. Different senses are deployed in expressing the same thought so thoughts are not in a one-to-one correspondence with the senses of sentences.

It seems that Frege has to give something up. He can either give up the one-to-one identification of senses with thoughts, or he can give up the idea that the two utterances can express the same thought. Of course, Evans (1981) argued that there is no dilemma for the Fregean here:

there is no headlong collision between Frege's suggestion that grasping the same thought on different days may require different things of us, and the fundamental criterion of difference of thoughts which rests upon the principle that it is not possible coherently to take different attitudes towards the same thought. For that principle, properly stated, precludes the possibility of coherently taking different attitudes towards the same thought *at the same time.*

Evans appeared to be saying that thoughts are to be identified with senses—but with different senses at different times. This strategy loosens the link between senses and thoughts by identifying thoughts with different senses at different times (and more generally in different contexts).

An alternative strategy that I suggested in Ludlow 1999 (and mistakenly attributed to Evans) would be to hold that indexical expressions like 'today' can be used to express or display senses, but they do not express the same sense on each occasion of use. This second strategy holds the sense associated with a thought constant, but allows that different indexical expressions can display the same sense—albeit on different occasions of use. Both strategies appear to ameliorate the worry articulated by Perry. Or do they?

As we will see, neither of these strategies is capable of salvaging the Fregean project in its entirety. To see why, however, we need to begin introducing the details of these proposals. Although I am parting company with Evans on a couple of key points, I am following his lead in thinking of senses as being displayed by the theorems of a Tarskian or Davidsonian T-theory. I don't think it is accurate to say that Evans' deployment of such theories is accidental, and in fact I know of no semantic theory that is actually capable of characterizing the kinds of senses required.

Here is the idea: given a T-theory for a language *L*, we want to be careful to distinguish (a) what the truth conditions literally state, (b) the way in which the truth conditions are represented, and, finally, (c) the sense displayed by the truth conditions so represented.

To see how this works, consider the following example, pertaining to names, discussed by McDowell (1980) and Lepore and Loewer (1987). The idea is that whereas theorems (7) and (8) in some sense state the same truth conditions, they do so in different ways, so that they "display" different senses.

(7)   'Cicero is bald' is true iff Cicero is bald.

(8)   'Cicero is bald' is true iff Tully is bald.

What one wants from an adequate T-theory is that it gives the truth conditions in such a way that the senses of the object language sentences are correctly displayed in the metalanguage.

Matters are a little more involved when we move to the introduction of indexicals in the metalanguage. Following Rumfitt (1993) and Ludlow (1999), I would propose that we can simply disquotationally enter the indexical expression into the right-hand side of a biconditional. So, for example, we might have axioms and theorems like the following.

(9)   Val(x, '*I*') iff $x = I$

(10)   Val(T, 'I walk') iff I walk

Of course this *appears* hopelessly naive. If we deployed such an axiom, wouldn't we get absurd results when interpreting the utterances of others? For example, if someone says 'I walk', it is no good for me to have a T-theory that interprets that utterance as saying that *I* walk. But that appears to be what a theorem like (10) delivers.

Likewise, if someone leaves me a voice mail on Monday saying 'Little Rupert went to the dentist today', if I only retrieve the voice mail today (several days later) it is no good for me to interpret this as saying that Little Rupert went to the dentist *today*. So presumably axioms like the following for temporal indexicals are also problematic.

(11)   Val(x, 'today') iff x is true today.

Or so goes the objection. However, I do not think this objection has much bite. In the first place, if we are talking about language (I-language) in the sense of Chomsky 1986, and if, as I suggested in Ludlow 1999, the primary use of I-language is not communication but thought, then axioms like the above are entirely appropriate for I-language tokenings. Such axioms are also entirely suitable for the interpretation of any speech that we *produce* or intend to produce. The only drawback for such axioms appears to be in the interpretation of the utterances of others.

In Ludlow 1999, I argued that even if we are concerned with interpretation of other individuals, it is far from clear that these kinds of axioms are inadequate. For example, it is a plausible position to maintain that when we interpret the remarks of another, we amend the axioms of our T-theory to account for the position of the speaker. Accordingly, we might have conditionalized axioms like the following, where S is a sentential clause modified by the adverb 'today'.

(12)   If yesterday s left a message m, having the form 'S is true today', then in m 'S is true today' is true iff S was true yesterday.

This sort of paraphrase might allow us to track the indexical utterances of others from different spatial and temporal vantage points.

In Ludlow 1999, I thought that this would be enough to salvage the identification of a sense with a thought. The idea was that a single thought having a single sense would have to be represented in different ways from different spatiotemporal perspectives. Applying this idea to T-theorems, the idea was that the way the theorem is represented helps determine what sense is displayed but that the particular representation cannot be identified with the sense, for that sense must be displayed in different ways at different times.

The problem for this proposal (which I should have anticipated) comes in when something happens that causes us to "lose track" of how a particular sense should be displayed. In the above case we were able to keep track of the sense of (12) because we knew that the message was left yesterday, but we are not always in a position to know when the message was left and may be mistaken about when it was left. This brings us to cases like Rip van Winkle, postcards, answering machine messages and the like. As Kaplan (1979) noted, these cases present serious difficulties for stand-alone sense based accounts of indexicals.[4] Consider first the case of Rip van Winkle, who goes to sleep one day saying to himself 'today was a fine day'. When he awakes twenty years later, he may want to express what he expressed by the utterance that he made before he fell asleep. He may try to do this by saying 'yesterday was a nice day', but in doing so Rip fails to express what he did with his original utterance because he has lost track of the relative temporal position of his original utterance.

For Evans (speaking of beliefs rather than utterances here) this was a bullet that we should bite:

I see no more strangeness in the idea that a man who loses track of time cannot retain beliefs than in the idea that a man who loses track of an object cannot retain the beliefs about it with which he began. (1981, 87n–88n)

I don't see this as a reasonable move. Unless we assume some technical notion of recollection, Rip certainly does recall his earlier belief (and what he expressed) in some interesting sense.

We needn't bite this bullet, however, if we follow Heck's lead and reject the idea that there is a something like "the [unique] Thought" that is expressed by an utterance. Perhaps a more plausible picture emerges if we suppose that "a given utterance can differ in cognitive value for two speakers without their being unable to communicate successfully." There may be limits to the variation that successful communication can tolerate: "speakers cannot associate with an utterance just any Thought that determines the right singular proposition... and still understand it." If we want to hang on to plank (4) of the Fregean project, then speakers will have to deploy demonstrative thoughts (senses) to understand the utterance[5]; however, "no *one* of the different Thoughts different speakers might permissibly associate with an utterance is plausibly taken to be its meaning: none of them is privileged over the others."

Notice that having a demonstrative thought is still crucial for understanding the utterance. So for example, while Rip may not be able to express what he expressed with his original utterance via the sense he deployed predormatively, he may well express its content (or one of its contents) by deploying another sense. When he wakes up, he might express it by uttering the words 'that was a fine day', thereby deploying a new demonstrative sense.

Heck's point is that it is a mistake to suppose that there is a single thing that one must thereby grasp or that constitutes the one thought expressed by an utterance. These thoughts must, of course, be related in some interesting way, but we should resist the pull to say that there must therefore be The Meaning of the utterance.

But why do we want to find something to call the meaning? What we (relatively) uncontroversially have are speakers who associate Thoughts with utterances and restrictions upon how the different Thoughts they associate with a given utterance must be related if they are to communicate successfully: to put it differently, we have the fact that utterances have cognitive value for speakers, and we have communicative norms determining how the cognitive values a given utterance has for different speakers must be related if we are to understand them. (Heck 2002, p. 31)

This is a programmatic suggestion, and one might rightly ask how Heck intends to flesh out the details here. Just how are these various Thoughts supposed to be related?

A plausible answer to this challenge can be borrowed from a discussion of propositional attitudes that was offered in Larson and Ludlow 1993. On the Larson and Ludlow proposal, the referent of a that-clause was an interpreted logical form (ILF)—a linguistic structure corresponding to the syntactic form of the utterance, but interpreted, so that semantic values are assigned to the syntactic components of the structure. In the case of ILF theories, the puzzle was to show how two completely different ILFs (for example, one with English words and one with Italian words) could count as having correctly characterized the attitude of an agent or an utterance by that agent. The answer in Larson and Ludlow 1993 was a theory that took account of the hearer's interests, the speaker's goals, shared knowledge about the structure of the agent's beliefs, and so forth.

The application of this idea here would be motivated by the following rationale: just as one can *correctly* describe a single belief or utterance in a number of different ways (i.e., via a number of different that-clauses), so too one can understand an utterance in many different ways. There is no single correct content by which to characterize an utterance, and so too there is no single correct way via which one can grasp or understand an utterance.

Here is how the Larson and Ludlow proposal worked for the contents of beliefs (that-clauses of belief reports). The basic idea was that belief reports are not intended to identify some object in the agent's head or even any object at all that is to count as the object of the agent's belief. Rather, the idea is that a belief report is true (a content is correctly attributed to an agent) just in case that content serves the interests of the person who receives the belief report. Accordingly, the correct way of expressing a belief will depend not just on the agent A, but upon the interests of the hearer H as determined by the speaker S.

Larson and Ludlow identified several rules of thumb in characterizing which component of an ILF will be relevant in a given attitude report. For example, if H is interested in information that A has about the world (for example the distance to the Venus), then H will be indifferent to the choice of 'the Morning Star' versus 'the Evening Star' in an attitude ascription concerning Venus. By contrast, if H is interested in explaining or predicting A's behavior, for example, whether A will assent to an utterance of 'The Morning Star is the Evening Star', or whether A will act in a way compatible with the knowledge that the Morning Star is the Evening Star, then H may well be interested in the syntactic expressions that S uses to characterize A's belief.

In cases like this, where prediction or explanation of behavior is the goal, Larson and Ludlow envisioned the speaker's choice of syntactic constituents in an ILF to involve a two-stage process vis-à-vis the hearer H. First S determines the way in which H models

A's belief structure. Then *S* "negotiates" with *H* the expressions to be used in speaking of the components of that model. Both steps involve complex subprocesses. For example, in inferring *H*'s model of *A*'s belief structure, *S* would appear to draw at least on all of the following:

1. *S*'s knowledge of *H*'s interests;

2. general principles of common sense psychology that *S* supposes that *H* believes;

3. knowledge that *S* knows *H* to have about *A*.

Suppose *S* knows *H* to be interested in the behavior of *A*—for example, in whether *A* will train her telescope on a particular region of the dawn sky. Then, by general principles of commonsense psychology, which *S* supposes *H* to share, *S* may infer that *H* will deploy a fine-grained model of *A*'s psychology—one that distinguishes Morning Star beliefs from Evening Star beliefs. *S* may also rely upon information supplied directly by *H* or some other source. For example, *S* may learn that *H* knows that *A* is unaware that the Morning Star is the Evening Star.

In the second stage of selecting an ILF, *S* and *H* must agree on expressions used to speak of the components of *H*'s model of *A*'s belief structure. Expressions used in attitude ascriptions will be tacitly "negotiated" by participants in the discourse, following quite general principles holding of discourses of all kinds.

In Ludlow 1999, I argued that this strategy could be extended in a natural way to attitude and discourse reports incorporating indexical expressions. The key addition was a theory of the hearer's spatiotemporal perspective. When reporting what the agent said or thought, one needs to know where the hearer is relative to the agent one is reporting on. If on Wednesday the agent says 'It is fine today', then when we give reports to a hearer on Thursday we shall want to report the same statement, but relative to the hearer's temporal position. Thus we get '*A* said that it was a fine day yesterday'. Roughly, then, we will want the theory to keep track of the following:

1. *S*'s knowledge of *H*'s spatiotemporal position;

2. *S*'s knowledge of *H* and *A*'s relative positions;

3. *H*'s knowledge that *S* knows *A*'s spatiotemporal position (with standard assumptions about common knowledge).

All of this remains programmatic, of course. My goals here remain similar to Heck's—to show how one might approach attitude reports and discourse reports as having multiple contents rather than a single content.[6]

As noted in this section (and as Heck has highlighted), if a Fregean believes that an utterance has only a single content (thought), then this picture is certainly not canonically Fregean. On the other hand, it seems to me that we retain an important part of the program (and certainly the part that is crucial for handling "thank goodness" cases), as long as we still have a workable notion of sense content.

Can We Really Have Our Cake and Eat It Too?

As noted in "Perry's Reflexive-Referential Account of Indexical Content," a key advantage of Perry's proposal is that by having two kinds of content, we can use one sort of content for the modal profile of the utterance and the other kind of content to get the cognitive significance right. To illustrate, consider an utterance u of a sentence like (3) ('You are the addressee of this utterance'). Suppose, for example, that u is an utterance of (3), by me, addressing John Perry; in that case, we would have the following two contents (again ignoring designational content):

(3-R) Perry is the addressee of u.

(3-X) The addressee of this utterance u is the addressee of this utterance u.

Now, it is clearly metaphysically possible that Perry not have been in front of me when I spoke, or even in the neighborhood. This is fine, because (3-X) plays no role in the modal profile of my utterance. Good thing, too, because (3-X) is true in every possible world. We're safe, because what we evaluate in other possible worlds is (3-R), and of course there are worlds where Perry is not my addressee.[7]

It is clear that the sense-referential proposal that I have advocated here should have the same advantages. We can rely on the referential content of an utterance (and discard its sense content) when we are interested in the modal profile of the utterance. The question is whether this have-your-cake-and-eat-it strategy really works, either for the reflexive-referential theorist or the sense-referential theorist. Here matters are subtle.

The chief worry has to do with cases where we need the reflexive or sense content in another possible world. (In "Is Reflexive Content Too Thin?" I argued that reflexive content is not enough to give the cognitive content of temporal indexicals, but for now, let's set aside that objection and, in our current spirit of ecumenicalism, suppose that both theories give us all we'll ever need to account for the cognitive significance of temporal indexicals. In fact, from here on out, I will simply use the phrase "reflexive/ sense content" to highlight that we are both in the same boat here.) Now, what are we to do with an utterance of (13), said after I learned I didn't need a root canal after all, and the time of the initially scheduled root canal had past:

(13) By now I would have been relieved that it was over.

We want to evaluate the nonmodal portion of this in another possible world (that is, we want to evaluate 'I'm relieved that's over' in a possible world in which I had a root canal), but we can't exactly discard the reflexive/sense content when we do so, because we need it in that world of evaluation—obviously so, if we want to explain why I'm relieved in that counterfactual situation.

There is a kind of "hacky" response that is possible here. One can say we don't always discard the reflexive content; we only do so under certain circumstances—like when the reflexive/sense content messes up the modal profile of the utterance. But this won't work, since it is possible to find examples where we need to keep some reflexive content *and* discard some reflexive/sense content, lest the modal profile goes haywire. This requires some stage setting, but bear with me.

Imagine that we are entertaining a possible state of affairs in which you have an evil doppelgänger. In this possible state of affairs, if I unknowingly address the doppelganger today I shall be subjected to a root canal operation on the following day. Suppose you ask me what, under such circumstances, my reaction would be on the day after tomorrow, having entirely avoided the root canal. I respond by uttering (14).

(14)   By then I would been relieved that you had been the addressee of this
          utterance.

Clearly, there would have been no relief in the fact that the addressee of the utterance had been the addressee of the utterance. One needs go with the reflexive/sense content for the tense, but the referential content is what is crucial for the evaluation of the indexical 'you'.

Well, it might be objected that reflexive/sense content need not be discarded across the board, and in fact may be deployed for some indexicals, yet discarded for other indexicals—all within the same utterance. This solution strikes me as even "hackier" than what we have been considering up to now, but here again we can find counterexamples to the proposal.

To set this one up I need to introduce a stock objection to token reflexive theories, show how Perry's theory could handle that objection, and then go on to consider some more complex cases where I think the theory founders. The stock objection (discussed in Castañeda 1967, Smith 1993, and Craig 1996) revolves around the possibility of utterances of (15).

(15)   There are no utterances now.

Pretty clearly, reflexive content all by itself is not going to fare well in an analysis of (15).

(15-X)   There are no utterances at the time of this utterance.

Whatever we might want to say about (15) it is clearly not necessarily false, so (15-X) cannot be what we carry to other possible worlds for evaluation. So far this is not a problem for Perry, since he can simply employ his referential content:

(15-R)   There are no utterances at *t*.

The problem comes in when we consider more complex cases that combine the "no utterance" argument with the "thank goodness" argument.

Imagine the following case. You ask me to consider a counterfactual situation in which utterances are excruciatingly painful to me. Not just my utterances. Not just your utterances. Anybody's utterances. If someone is talking somewhere on planet Earth I am in pain, and the pain is worse than getting a root canal. You then ask me to consider the possibility that at some time everyone in that world goes mute. There are no more utterances and I am no longer in pain. You ask me what I would think then. I respond by uttering (16).

(16)   I would be relieved that there were no longer any utterances.

Now we are in a real jam. We need to keep the reflexive content to deal with the "thank God that's over problem," but we need to discard it because of the "no utterance" problem.

But Perry (personal correspondence) offers a way out. We needn't suppose that my relief be earlier than the time of the utterance. It might be enough to say that it is earlier than the time of the corresponding thought token so that the theory is not really utterance-reflexive (as I suggested above), but rather thought-reflexive. This in effect takes a leaf from a proposal due to Higginbotham, with his introduction of tensed thoughts:

If e is the event of my affirming to myself with a sense of relief, "My root canal is over" (or: "over now"), then the thought that I think is indicated in [(A)].

[(A)] (s) s is the situation of my root canal's being over & the time of s includes (the time of) e

The thought that I have when I affirm with a sense of relief that my root canal is over is a thought whose very existence depends upon the existence of a certain episode in my mental life: it contains that episode as a constituent, and could not exist without it. (Higginbotham 1995, 228–229)

The problem for Perry is that we have now stepped away from an utterance-reflexive analysis, and are now adopting what is in effect a *thought*-reflexive analysis for what was an utterance in the actual world. For a sense-reflexive analysis there is a similar worry: why are we now talking about the senses of thoughts rather than the senses displayed by utterances?

I don't mean to say that these kinds of worries can't be ameliorated—obviously, I hope that they can. My only point here is that the worries are underwritten by some very subtle and complex issues about the modal profile of these utterances and that it will require some care to sort them out (whether one is advocating a reflexive-referential theory like Perry is or a sense-referential theory like I am).

Conclusion

Perry's strategy of endowing a semantic theory with both reflexive and referential (and other) contents may not succeed in the specific form he advocates, but it suggests a more general strategy of hybrid theories of content—like the sense-referential theory that I advocated above. Naturally, this requires avoiding standard objections to senses and perhaps also allow that a single utterance can be accurately associated with multiple senses (Thoughts). Following considerations I raise in the previous section, I think this can be done—at least in principle.

Although there are technical worries about handling certain complex cases involving modal discards, these are difficulties that are shared by all ecumenical approaches. It is difficult to draw strong conclusions at this stage, but I would offer that sense-based accounts of temporal indexicals remain promising on a number of counts and are very much worth investigating further.

Acknowledgments

I am indebted to John Perry, Nathan Oaklander, Stacie Friend, Thomas Hofweber, Jessica Wilson, Jason Stanley, and the students in my winter 2003 graduate seminar in the philosophy of language at the University of Michigan for lots of criticism, some of which I even grasped and incorporated.

Notes

1. Here I am assuming that variables do not display sense content. If Heck (2002) is right this assumption may not be so innocent.

2. A canonical example would be Mellor 1981.

3. Heck (2002, p. 3) allows that this may be understood in a weak way: "On the weakest interpretation of (3), it speaks of 'determination' only in a mathematical sense: it claims only that senses are related many-one to references."

4. See also Perry 1997, for discussion of these cases.

5. Another possibility would be to give up the idea that it is via the sense of a sentence alone that one grasps the meaning of a sentence, or more accurately, that it is the sense that one grasps in understanding the sentence. It is arguable that it is not part of the doctrine of identifying thoughts with senses that recalling a thought or even expressing what you once thought requires that you continue to have access to the sense content. Surely recollection of thoughts, like recollection of everything else, might be partial. Likewise expressing a kind of type identity between thoughts (like expressing type identity between everything else) must be a context-sensitive enterprise in which sense content may or may not figure. The point of the sense-referential theory would be that there are some contexts (not all contexts) in which access to a thought must be mediated by sense content. So sense content is necessary to the identity of a thought, although not always necessary to understanding that thought. To illustrate, on this proposal Rip could express what he did with his original utterance without benefit of sense content. He could do so by expressing the referential content only of that original utterance (crucially referential content that is determined by the sense which he no longer has access too). Likewise, if we receive an undated postcard or an answering machine message from a friend saying "I wish you where here now," it is entirely reasonable to suppose that we have access to some aspects of the content of the writing if not the sense content. Even if one supposes that we have lost the referential content in these cases, there is still Perry's designational content to be recovered, so there is always some sense in which we can say we know what our friend was saying. In this respect, the path shown by Perry is navigated as handily by the sense-referential theory as by the reflexive-referential theory. Of course, not all Fregeans will be happy giving up the idea that senses are always necessary for understanding an utterance, and for current purposes I'll take the more "Frege-friendly" path of giving up the idea that there is a single sense or thought associated with an utterance.

6. In Ludlow 1999, I mistakenly thought that what these abilities allowed us to do was to keep track of a *single* thought or sense in many formal guises. For example I thought that ILFs with different structures could be used to characterize "the same" belief or attitude, as for example, when I hear A and B utter sentences of different structure, and I say that A said what B said. I thought that this robust theory of our use of 'believes' underwrote our ability to keep track of a single belief under the guise of different that-clauses. As noted above, considerations in Heck 2002 have convinced me that the talk of a "single belief" here is not much more than unmotivated reification. The obvious move here is abandon the idea of a single content, and endorse the idea of multiple contents. Of course this is a general idea that has been endorsed by a number of writers recently, albeit in different contexts. See for example Neale 1999.

7. Here I am assuming that utterances are not individuated widely, so that the addressee is not an essential component of an utterance. This assumption is, of course, open to challenge.

References

Castañeda, H.-N. 1967. "Indicators and Quasi-Indicators." *American Philosophical Quarterly* 4: 85–100.

Chomsky, N. 1986. *Knowledge of Language*. New York: Praeger.

Craig, W. L. 1996. "Tense and the New B-Theory of Language." *Philosophy* 71: 5–26.

Evans, G. 1981. "Understanding Demonstratives." In H. Parret and J. Bouveresse (eds.), *Meaning and Understanding*. Berlin: W. de Gruyter. Reprinted in *Collected Papers*. Oxford: Oxford University Press.

———. 1982. *The Varieties of Reference*. Oxford: Oxford University Press.

Frege, G. 1956. "The Thought." Trans. A. M. and M. Quinton. *Mind* 65: 289–311.

Heck, R. 2002. "Do Demonstratives Have Senses?" *Philosophers' Imprint* 2. Http://www.philosophersimprint.org/002002/.

Higginbotham, J. 1995. "Tensed Thoughts." *Mind and Language* 10: 226–249.

Kaplan, D. 1979. "On the Logic of Demonstratives." *Journal of Philosophical Logic* 8: 81–98.

———. 1989. "Demonstratives." In J. Almog, J. Perry, and H. Wettstein (eds.), *Themes from Kaplan*. Oxford: Oxford University Press.

———. 1990. "Thoughts on Demonstratives." In P. Yourgrau (ed.), *Demonstratives*. Oxford: Oxford University Press.

Larson, R., and P. Ludlow. 1993. "Interpreted Logical Forms." *Synthese* 95: 305–356.

Lepore, E., and B. Loewer. 1987. "Dual Aspect Semantics." In E. Lepore (ed.), *New Directions in Semantics*. London: Academic Press.

Ludlow, P. 1999. *Semantics, Tense, and Time: An Essay in the Metaphysics of Natural Language*. Cambridge, Mass.: MIT Press.

McDowell, J. 1980. "On the Sense and Reference of a Proper Name." In M. Platts (ed.), *Truth, Reality, and Reference*. London: Routledge and Kegan Paul.

Mellor, D. H. 1981. *Real Time*. Cambridge, Mass.: MIT Press.

Neale, S. 1999. "Coloring and Composition." In K. Murasagi and R. Stainton (eds.), *Philosophy and Linguistics*. Boulder, Colo.: Westview.

Perry, J. 1977. "Frege on Demonstratives." *Philosophical Review* 86: 474–497. Reprinted in Perry 2000.

———. 1979. "The Problem of the Essential Indexical." *Noûs* 13: 3–21. Reprinted in Perry 2000.

———. 1997. "Rip van Winkle and Other Characters." *European Review of Philosophy* 2: 13–40. Reprinted in Perry 2000.

———. 2000. *The Problem of the Essential Indexical*. Stanford, Calif.: CSLI Publications.

———. 2001. *Reference and Reflexivity*. Stanford, Calif.: CSLI Publications.

Prior, A. N. 1959. "Thank Goodness That's Over." *Philosophy* 34: 12–17.

———. 1967. *Past, Present, and Future*. Oxford: Oxford University Press.

Reichenbach, H. 1947. *Elements of Symbolic Logic*. New York: Macmillan.

Rumfitt, I. 1993. "Content and Context: The Paratactic Theory Revisited and Revised." *Mind* 102: 429–453.

Smart, J. J. C. 1966. "The River of Time." In A. Flew (ed.), *Essays in Conceptual Analysis*. London: Routledge and Kegan Paul.

Smith, Q. 1993. *Language and Time*. Oxford: Oxford University Press.

Soames, S. 1987. "Direct Reference, Propositional Attitudes, and Semantic Content." *Philosophical Topics* 15: 47–87.

———. 2002. *Beyond Rigidity: The Unfinished Semantic Agenda of Naming and Necessity*. Oxford: Oxford University Press.

Wettstein, H. 1986. "Has Semantics Rested on a Mistake?" *Journal of Philosophy* 83: 185–209.

7 Is There a Problem of the Essential Indexical?

Cara Spencer

Some time ago, John Perry raised a problem for the traditional picture of belief, according to which having a belief is just standing in a certain relation, the belief relation, to a proposition. Perry's problem concerns indexical belief, that is, belief expressible with a sentence containing an indexical pronoun such as 'I', 'here', or 'now', or a demonstrative pronoun such as 'this' or 'that'.

The received view is that indexical belief presents a *special* problem for the traditional picture of belief, and Perry's arguments show us what this problem is. What is surprising about the received view is that it conflicts with what most philosophers are inclined to say about other putative cases of natural language indexicality, of which there are many. For instance, Mark Richard identifies propositional attitude verbs as indexicals (1990, 107); Tyler Burge offers us an indexical theory of proper names (1973), as well as an indexical theory for the word 'true' (1979a); Scott Soames argues that vague predicates are indexicals (1999, 2002); and Hilary Putnam asserts that his theory of natural kind terms "can be summarized as saying that words like 'water' have an unnoticed indexical component" (1975b, 234). Yet, these philosophers have tended not to conclude that beliefs expressible with these "indexicals" present any special problem for the traditional picture.[1] At most, these putative cases of indexicality are thought to require a distinction between narrow content, determined by the internal state of the thinker, and wide content, determined by the thinker's internal state and relevant facts about the context. The received view thus stands in a prima facie tension with a familiar stance toward indexicality more broadly construed.

Two responses to the tension are available. One might say that even though a variety of natural language expressions are in some sense indexicals, indexical belief narrowly construed is nevertheless uniquely problematic for the traditional picture. Or one might deny that indexical belief has any special status and claim, instead, that Perry's arguments merely use the paradigm example of indexical belief to illustrate that the pervasive indexical element in thought eludes the traditional picture. Here, I split the difference. I largely accept Perry's arguments that indexical belief presents a problem for the traditional picture, but I deny that the problem has anything special to do with indexical belief narrowly construed. Perry's problem arises quite generally for what is commonly called singular belief.[2] In support of this claim, I consider Perry's two central arguments against the traditional picture, which I call the Explaining Behavior Argument and the Belief State Argument. I show that both arguments are extensible to belief expressible with natural kind terms and proper names, which, along with indexical belief, are the paradigm cases of singular thought. Although Perry's arguments do not isolate any *unique* problem for the traditional picture, they nonetheless provide some reason for thinking that indexical belief, narrowly construed, has a special status. Its special status does not derive from its content, but rather from its special role in the explanation of action. That questions about belief content have been a locus of concern about indexical belief has obscured this point, which has nothing specifically do to with its content.

The Explaining Behavior Argument

We can briefly state the central claims of the traditional picture of belief in (1)–(3).

(1)   *A*'s having the belief that *s* is *A*'s standing in the belief relation to the proposition that *s*.

(2)   Propositions have truth conditions.

(3)   If someone can take different cognitive attitudes toward the proposition that *s* and the proposition that *s**, then the proposition that *s* and the proposition that *s** are distinct.

As characterized here, the traditional picture is a simplified version of Frege's account, in that it includes in (2) the view that propositions are bearers of truth value and in (3) an epistemic criterion of difference for propositions similar to Frege's own proposal. On the Fregean view, a proposition is composed of the senses of the words in a sentence that expresses the proposition. It is commonly supposed that Frege held that names and indexicals have descriptive senses, by which he is supposed to have meant that thinkers think of the bearer of the name or the referent of the indexical as the satisfier of some definite description. Because indexicals shift reference with context, and sense determines reference on the Fregean view, the sense of an indexical must also shift with context. Perry (1979, 38) claims that the traditional picture can capture this in (4):

(4) All singular terms have descriptive senses, where an utterance of a singular term *a* in a context *c* has a descriptive sense if and only if there is a nonindexical definite description whose constant sense is that expressed by *a* in *c*.

Descriptive Sense follows from (4), and it is the direct target of Perry's argument.

Descriptive Sense For any natural language sentence '*a* is *F*,' where *a* is a singular term, and any context of utterance *c*,[3] there is a nonindexical definite description 'The *G*' such that 'The *G* is *F*' expresses the same proposition as '*a* is *F*' does when uttered in *c*.

There are several good reasons to reject *Descriptive Sense*, only some of which specifically have to do with indexicals. Most importantly, definite descriptions are not referring terms.[4] This alone ensures that definite descriptions and singular terms will not make the same semantic contributions to propositions expressed by sentences containing them. Then there are Kripke's (1980) well-known arguments against descriptivism about proper names, which, if sound, show that *Descriptive Sense* is false.

Perry offers a different sort of reason for rejecting *Descriptive Sense*. His central argument is what I call the Explaining Behavior Argument, which appeals to the following psychological criterion of difference for propositions *PCD*:

PCD The propositions that *s* and that *s** are distinct if and only if attributing the belief that *s* to someone would explain behavior that attributing the belief that *s** would not explain.[5]

Perry invites us to consider the now-familiar case of the messy shopper, whose torn sack of sugar is leaving a trail on the supermarket floor. He follows the sugar trail around the store, hoping to find the messy shopper and tell him what a mess he is making. After following the trail of sugar up and down the supermarket aisles, the shopper soon realizes that *he* is the messy shopper he is trying to catch. Only then does he reach into his cart to adjust his sugar sack. All along, he believed that the person with the torn sugar sack was making a mess, but he then came to believe something different, something he would express by saying "I am making a mess." These must be different beliefs, because the second, unlike the first, explains why he reached into the cart to adjust the sugar sack. The first only explains this action on the assumption that he has another belief he would express by saying "I am the shopper with the torn sack."

The argument appears to run as follows:

(P1) We can explain the shopper's action (in context *c*) of reaching into his cart to adjust the sugar sack by attributing to him the belief he would express by saying "I am making a mess" in context *c*.

(P2)   There is no description 'the F' that applies to the shopper such that we can
       explain the shopper's action of reaching into his cart to adjust the sugar sack
       by attributing to him the belief that the F is making a mess.

(C)   By *PCD*, The proposition the shopper would express in context c by saying "I am
       making a mess" is distinct from any proposition expressed by 'The F is making a
       mess' for any description 'the F' that applies to the shopper.

(C) directly conflicts with *Descriptive Sense*, and thus with the traditional picture
of belief, which is understood to include *Descriptive Sense*. It follows that indexical belief is a counterexample to this picture.

To evaluate this argument, we need to consider what Perry has in mind in saying
that we can explain an action by ascribing an indexical belief to the agent, but not
by ascribing a descriptive belief to the agent. Perry is clearly not saying anything
about the pragmatics of action explanation. An action that cites only a descriptive
belief can be useful and informative to an audience. Nor is he saying that agency
requires the agent to have just one belief, which happens to be indexical. An explanation may only *cite* one belief, but it presupposes that the agent has many other
relevant beliefs and desires, some of which may be indexical and others of which may
not be.

Perry could have two different claims in mind. He could be saying that indexical
belief (and presumably desire as well), plays some special, privileged, or basic role in
intentional agency, in that explanations that cite descriptive beliefs depend on the
agent's having certain indexical beliefs, but not vice versa. Cheryl Chen has recently
suggested that we interpret Perry as defending this claim.[6] So we might read Perry to
endorse something like the following *Action Explanation Dependence Claim*:

Action Explanation Dependence Claim: An explanation of an action X that ascribes to its
agent the belief that the F should do X assumes that the agent has a belief he or she
could express by saying "I am the F," but one that ascribes the latter belief does not
assume that the agent has any descriptive beliefs about him- or herself.

If *Action Explanation Dependence Claim* is true, indexical beliefs play one role in the explanation of action, and descriptive beliefs play a different role. Hence, indexical beliefs
cannot be a species of descriptive belief.

But Perry is usually taken to mean something different, that *PCD* is essentially equivalent to the Fregean individuation principle in (3), both of which individuate belief
contents by the psychological roles of beliefs that have those contents.[7] On this reading, *PCD* and (3) distinguish the proposition the messy shopper expresses in saying
"I am making a mess" from the proposition that the F is making a mess in just the

same way they distinguish the proposition that Hesperus is in the east from the proposition that Phosphorus is in the east. They are different because someone can believe one without believing the other, or, equivalently on this view, because we can explain behavior by ascribing a belief in one but not by ascribing a belief in the other.

If this is right, then perhaps we can render Perry's argument this way:

(P1*) For any candidate description 'the G' that applies to an individual A, it is possible for A to believe the proposition she would express by uttering "I am F" in context c without believing that the G is F.

(P2*) By (3), the proposition A would express by uttering "I am F" in c is distinct from any proposition expressible by 'The G is F' for any description 'the G' that applies to A.

(P3*) 'I' is a singular term, so by *Descriptive Sense*, any proposition expressible in any context by 'I am F' is identical to some proposition expressible by 'the G is F.'

Since we have arrived here at a contradiction, we infer that the traditional picture in (1)–(4) is false, and specifically that *Descriptive Sense* is false.[8]

On this interpretation, it is easy to see how Perry's argument is extensible to other kinds of belief. Since proper names are singular terms of natural language, *Descriptive Sense* requires that for any proper name there is some nonindexical definite description that provides its sense, and, as Kripke has famously argued, there need not be any such description. For any description—say, 'the sixteenth president of the United States,' which applies to Abraham Lincoln—we can imagine believing that Abraham Lincoln gave an address at Gettysburg without believing that the sixteenth U.S. president did so. The same could be said for any uniquely identifying description of Lincoln we might consider.[9] Descriptive names like Gareth Evans's 'Julius' aside (1979), competent users of proper names need not possess any uniquely identifying descriptions of their bearers.

The Explaining Behavior Argument explicitly concerns only singular terms, but it also undermines descriptivism about natural kind terms. Anyone competent with the term 'water' knows it to be a clear, odorless liquid found in lakes, streams, and reservoirs. This description, however, does not uniquely identify water, since it applies equally to XYZ. Competent speakers need not know any other descriptions that uniquely identify water, they can have beliefs about water, which they can express with that very term. Although the Explaining Behavior Argument does show that the traditional picture of belief, understood as the conjunction of (1)–(3) and *Descriptive Sense*, cannot accommodate indexical belief, it equally well shows that it cannot accommodate beliefs expressible with proper names and natural kind terms. Thus, it captures no distinctive problem about indexical belief.

The Belief State Argument

In a footnote added to "The Problem of the Essential Indexical" in 1993, Perry says that his original focus on descriptive senses may have been misleading. "The significant point," he says, "is not that the demonstrative could not be regarded as an abbreviation for a description. It is rather that the sense of a demonstrative cannot be one that determines its reference independently of context. It does not matter whether these senses are identified by definite descriptions, or expressions of some other type, or cannot be identified linguistically at all" (1993, 15 n. 4). Perry offers a different argument for this view. Since it moves from considerations about belief states, I call it the Belief State Argument.[10] Where the Explaining Behavior Argument targets the conjunction of (1)–(3) and *Descriptive Sense*, the Belief State Argument targets (1)–(3) and a principle about the relation between belief content and psychological explanation, which I call *Propositions and Belief States*.

The guiding idea of the Belief State Argument is that the traditional picture requires the propositional content of a belief to do double duty. It characterizes the thinker's psychological state and provides the truth conditions of the belief. Perry's point is that the content of indexical belief cannot play both of these roles, no matter what we take the content to be. The problem is not so much with any particular account of the proposition as it is with the dual role of belief content, which makes conflicting demands on the content of indexical belief.

As I have suggested, it is natural to suppose that if the contents of beliefs are individuated as (3) requires, then we will be able to explain someone's behavior by citing his or her beliefs (and other propositional attitudes). If it is impossible to take different cognitive attitudes toward what s expresses and what s^* expresses, there could not be, for any agent, any internally discriminable difference between believing what s expresses and believing what s^* expresses. But the only differences in belief that make a difference to behavior are differences the agent can discriminate. This is why (3) and *PCD* are often taken to be equivalent.

As it turns out, however, (3) does not make the right kinds of distinctions between beliefs to yield important generalizations about their psychological roles. Perry (1980) suggests that internal belief states, which in his view determine psychological roles, can be classified with reference to the sentences that typically would be used to express them.

When we believe, we do so by being in belief states. These states have typical effects, which we use to classify them. In particular, we classify them by the sentences a competent speaker of the language in question would be apt to think of or utter in certain circumstances when in that state. To accept a sentence S is to be in a belief state that would distinguish speakers who would think and utter S from those who would not. (1980, 53–54)

If two believers are internally similar in the right way, with respect to the right class of behavioral and cognitive dispositions, then Perry says that they are in the same belief state. Saying which class of behavioral and cognitive dispositions is the right class is not easy, but the rough idea is that these classes correspond to sentences accepted rather than propositions believed. Speakers who have a belief they would express by uttering *s*, that is, who accept *s*, are in the belief state associated with *s*. These speakers all have some set of behavioral and cognitive dispositions in common, which according to Perry is in principle identifiable without reference to the disposition to utter *s*.

With the notion of a belief state in hand, we can see why (3) does not characterize them. Grant that everyone who has a belief he or she could express by uttering "I'm in Paris" is in the same belief state. If two of them, Alfred and Bert, expressed this belief, then clearly someone could take different cognitive attitudes toward what Alfred's utterance expresses and what Bert's utterance expresses. Perhaps she thinks that although Bert knows where he is, Alfred is confused; he's really in London. So (3) would classify these as different propositions (as (2) would at any rate require), even though Alfred and Bert are in the same belief state.

Why should it be a problem that belief states do not always correlate with propositions believed? The conceit of the traditional picture is that two beliefs have the same psychological role if and only if they have the same propositional content. So if belief states determine psychological role, they must also determine propositional content. Thus it would be impossible for two thinkers to be in the same belief state and thereby have beliefs that differ in propositional content. But this is precisely what happens with indexical belief.

Which commitments of the traditional picture give rise to the problem? In addition to (1)–(3), it is the view that belief states determine the propositional content of the belief. I state this as *Propositions and Belief States*.

Propositions and Belief States If *A* and *B* are in the same belief state, then *A* and *B* thereby have beliefs with the same propositional content.

An additional principle, *Sentences and Belief States*, individuates belief states along the lines suggested by Perry's sentential classification scheme. This thesis is not intended as a part of the traditional picture; rather, it is supposed to be an independently plausible principle that causes trouble for the traditional picture.

Sentences and Belief States Fix a language *L*; if two speakers of *L*, *A* and *B*, accept the same sentence of *L*, then *A* and *B* are both in the belief state that this sentence classifies.

The sentences of *L* to which *Sentences and Belief States* applies must be free of obvious kinds of ambiguities and context-dependence that undermine its intuitive force. If *A* and *B* both utter "I'll meet you by the bank," and *A* means to refer to a place that charges high fees, and *B* means to refer to the edge of a river, then clearly *A* and *B* are not in the same belief state with respect to this sentence. Other kinds of context-dependence also present a difficulty for *Sentences and Belief States*, so they too are excluded from its purview. For instance, suppose *A* and *B* accept the sentence 'John ought to have been here by now'. *A* might mean that he expects John to be here by now, and *B* might mean something quite different, that John is under some moral obligation to be here by now. In this case, it would be unnatural to say that *A* and *B* are in the same belief state. It is important to note that the context-sensitivity of indexicals is *not* supposed to threaten their univocality in the way that these context-dependencies do. A person who uses an indexical to express a belief is supposed to be thinking of the referent of that indexical in a certain way, and this way of thinking of the referent associated with an indexical is supposed to be constant throughout its uses, even though the object so thought of differs from use to use.

Perry suggests that if we accept *Sentences and Belief States*, then we should also say that indexical belief is a counterexample to the traditional picture of belief. He invites us to consider the case of Hume and the delusional Heimson, who thinks he is Hume.

Let us imagine David Hume, alone in his study, on a particular afternoon in 1775, thinking to himself, "I wrote the *Treatise*." Can anyone *else* apprehend the thought he apprehended by thinking this? First note that what he thinks is true. So no one could apprehend the same thought, unless they apprehended a true thought. Now suppose Heimson is a bit crazy, and thinks himself to be David Hume. Alone in his study, he says to himself, "I wrote the *Treatise*." However much his inner life may, at that moment, resemble Hume's on that afternoon in 1775, the fact remains: Hume was right, Heimson is wrong. Heimson cannot think the very thought that Hume thought to himself, by using the very same sentence. (1977, 16–17)

Perry uses this example to state what I call the Belief State Argument. Consider the following pair of propositions:

p = the proposition Hume asserts in uttering "I wrote the *Treatise*."

q = the proposition Heimson asserts in uttering "I wrote the *Treatise*."

Suppose that Hume believes *p* and Heimson believes *q*. According to *Sentences and Belief States*, Hume and Heimson are thereby in the same belief state, as clearly Hume and Heimson are both speakers of English, and they utter the same sentence, which is free of any obvious ambiguities that undermine the intuitive force of *Sentences and Belief States*. But the traditional picture, understood as including *Propositions and Belief States*, says that Hume and Heimson must thereby have beliefs with the same propositional content. Evidently this is not the case, as p and q differ in truth value, so (2) requires that p and q are distinct.

Does the Belief State Argument identify any special problem about indexical belief? To identify the problem, we should first consider why, and for which kinds of sentences, *Sentences and Belief States* is plausible.

Even for some indexical sentences, there is no interesting sense of 'same belief state' in which everyone who assertively utters the same indexical sentence is in the same belief state. The various individuals who assert, "he is my mail carrier" (or who would be disposed to assert it under certain conditions) might think of the various referents of 'he' in similar ways, but they need not. One might see his mail carrier down the street while he thinks or expresses this thought. For him the sense of 'he' is something akin to that of a perceptual demonstrative.[11] Another might have a more complex representation of her mail carrier, since she also recognizes him in his after-work gig as the regular pianist at her local bar. Perhaps she says, "he is my mail carrier" during a conversation about his piano playing. Since the man they are talking about is nowhere in sight, the sense of 'he' is not akin to that of a perceptual demonstrative. Speakers can identify someone in a variety of ways—either demonstratively, descriptively, or perhaps based on a recognitional ability—while using 'he' or 'she' to refer to that person. If belief states determine ways of thinking of the objects the belief is about, it would also be unnatural to say that all those who accept the sentence 'he is my mail carrier' are in the same belief state.

Perceptual demonstrative uses of 'this' and 'that' illustrate another problem for *Sentences and Belief States*. Much as there is a characteristic way of thinking of oneself associated with 'I' and a characteristic way of thinking of a location associated with 'here', there is a characteristic way of thinking of objects identified by demonstration. These beliefs are paradigmatically expressed with sentences containing 'this' or 'that'. We can make demonstrative reference to an object anywhere in our immediate environment, regardless of its position in egocentric space. Nonetheless, its position in egocentric space will affect some of our behavioral dispositions toward it. Consider an example: Lisa and Judy are near a precariously balanced vase. Both think, "that is about to fall over." Are they in the same belief state? If Lisa and Judy want to stop the vase from falling, they would both reach for it to move it somewhere else. Suppose that Lisa is standing with the vase in front of her and slightly to her right, and Judy is standing almost directly opposite her, also facing the vase, but with the vase just perceptibly further to her right. The vase occupies similar, but not identical, positions in their egocentric spaces. When they reach for the vase, they move in slightly different directions. This is a difference in what they do, an intentional difference, and, as such, there should be a belief-desire explanation for it. On Perry's view, belief states rather than propositions believed do the work of psychological explanation. So the intentional difference between Lisa and Judy should be a difference in their belief states (or desire states), rather than the contents of their beliefs or desires. The most attractive explanation is that Lisa and Judy are in different belief states about the location of the vase in relation to them, but there is no reason to think that they would have to accept different sentences about the vase's location in egocentric space. The difference between the vase's location in Lisa's and Judy's egocentric spaces may be large enough to affect their intentional actions with respect to it but small enough to allow that Lisa and Judy accept all of the same sentences about its location in egocentric space. This natural explanation directly conflicts with *Sentences and Belief States*.[12]

The indexicals 'here' and 'now' present different problems for *Sentences and Belief States*, because of their nonindexical context-sensitivity. These terms refer to the place or time of the utterance, but the boundaries of the place or time vary in different contexts. My hemisphere, my city, and my office chair can all be the referent of 'here'. This means that sentences containing 'here' do not classify belief states in the straightforward way *Sentences and Belief States* claims. As I noted, *Sentences and Belief States* does not apply to sentences containing nonindexical context-sensitivity. Because indexicals like 'here' and 'now' themselves are context-sensitive in nonindexical ways, *Sentences and Belief States* does not classify believers in the same belief states in virtue of the 'here' and 'now' sentences they accept. At least, it does not classify them as it currently stands.

My concern about the Belief State Argument is that it underspecifies the problem about indexical belief. As Perry says, indexical belief presents special difficulties for the traditional picture of belief because thinkers of indexical thoughts need not be able to identify the objects these thoughts are about in any context-independent way. A thought can be indexical in this sense even though there is no sentence that precisely captures the context-dependent way in which the thinker identifies the objects her thought is about. We saw this with thoughts expressible with 'he', 'she', and the demonstratives 'this' and 'that'. With 'here' and 'now', which are context-sensitive in several ways, it is simply difficult to determine whether sentences correspond to belief states in the way Perry suggests. Perhaps at a certain level of abstraction, and when certain nonindexical information has been "filled in" from the context, the words 'here' and 'now' specify ways of thinking of locations or times. But it is not clear that this is the level of abstraction that would help to explain behavior as psychological roles should.

While I think these examples show *Sentences and Belief States* to be limited in scope, I do not think they undermine its use in the Belief State Argument. At least with respect to beliefs about oneself, beliefs expressible with 'I', I think the generalization holds. Is this anything unique about indexical belief? Only if indexicals are the only sorts of natural language expressions that work like 'I', in that they present a contextually determined referent in a uniform way, and a way that slots into psychological explanations.

But for familiar reasons, this appears not to be the case, because sentences containing natural kind terms plausibly classify belief states in the same way. Putnam (1975b, 234) and Burge (1979b) have shown that natural kind terms have what Putnam has called an "indexical component," in that the references of uses of such terms are partially determined by context. Suppose Hume is again in his study. In a prescient burst of scientific genius, he declares, "water is H_2O." On Twin-Earth, Twin-Hume makes the same declaration, only what he says is false, because the watery presenting substance on Twin-Earth is XYZ rather than H_2O. Hume and Twin-Hume assert different propositions, but it seems clear that Hume thinks of H_2O in just the same way Twin-Hume thinks of XYZ.

Two features of indexical thought drive the Belief State Argument. First, indexicals are associated with context-sensitive modes of presentation. These are modes of presentation of particular objects, but which object they present on any particular occasion is not determined by the mode of presentation alone, because they stand in need of some sort of contextual supplement.[13] Second, an indexical is also supposed to present its various contextually determined referents in the same context-sensitive manner.

I have argued that some indexicals don't have the second feature, because they present their various referents in different ways in different contexts. That's why different people can accept the same indexical sentence—for instance, one containing 'he' or 'she' or the demonstratives 'this' and 'that', even though they thereby have beliefs that differ in their psychological roles. So the Belief State Argument is too narrow to raise a special problem about indexical belief per se. It is also too broad, because it applies to belief expressible with natural kind terms just as it does to some indexical belief. Thus the argument does not raise a special problem about indexical belief.

Still, we might ask why the second feature should be of any concern. The traditional picture is an account of attitude content. The contents of attitudes are expressed with sentences, but apart from this the traditional picture is not particularly concerned with sentences.[14] Perry claims that although sentences offer a useful means for classifying belief states, these states are in principle identifiable without reference to sentences. So if we want to characterize the content of a thought, why should an association between a mode of presentation and a word make any difference? Wouldn't it be the special features of the mode of presentation itself that are relevant, and not its association with linguistic entities that are not part of the content of thought? If indexical belief presents a special problem for the traditional picture of belief, then the problem must have to do with the kind of content an indexical belief has, rather than with the association between its content and words used to express it.

Suppose we accept that the second feature is irrelevant to any special problem that indexical belief might present for the traditional picture. This leaves us with the first special feature of indexical thought, that it involves thinking about an object in a context-sensitive way. If any other expressions have this feature, this will further undermine the claim that indexical belief presents a unique problem for the traditional picture. We have already seen that belief expressible with natural kind terms has this first feature. And it seems clear that proper names, in at least some of their uses, have this first feature as well. When someone has a belief about an individual that could be expressed using a proper name, the thinker is presented with that individual in some way or other, even if this way is irrelevant to the semantics for proper names. The thinker might think of the bearer of the name as the satisfier of some uniquely identifying condition. The thinker might also represent the bearer of a name as some individual who bears that name and stands in a certain relation to him or her, perhaps as someone he or she met sometime in the past, or someone a friend has often talked about. In both of these cases, the way the thinker thinks of the bearer of the name varies with context, even though the name has the same bearer throughout its uses.[15]

Some would object that the Belief State Argument cannot be extended to these two cases because indexicals are individuated differently from proper names and natural kind terms. When different people use 'I' they are all using the same word, but when Oscar and Twin-Oscar use 'water' they are not. Oscar's use of 'water' might sound like Twin-Oscar's use of it, but this is merely coincidental, like one use of 'bank' might sound like another, even though they are uses of different words. If Oscar and Twin-Oscar use different words when uttering 'water' then clearly they do not accept the same sentences expressible with these different words, so the Belief State Argument simply does not apply in the way I have suggested.

I agree with the objector that we shouldn't say that Oscar and Twin Oscar use the same word because they spell or pronounce certain word tokens in the same way.

What matters are the semantic and syntactic properties of the words they use. Does Oscar's use of 'water' have the same semantic and syntactic properties as Twin-Oscar's? Clearly the syntactic properties are the same in virtue of the design of the thought experiment. Are the semantic properties the same? If the semantic value of an occurrence of a word is its referent (if it is the sort of word to have one), then they differ in semantic value. But clearly this is not the conception of semantic value that makes sense of the original claim that different uses of 'I' are uses of the same word, because these uses also differ in referent. Instead, we might say that semantics treats indexicals and natural kind terms differently because competent speakers know that 'I' refers to the speaker, but they do not know that 'water' refers to the watery substance around here, or the substance that plays the water role around here. They just know that 'water' refers to water. Thus our semantics should assign a rule to the indexical 'I': $\mathrm{Val(I)}_c = \mathrm{speaker}_c$. But the semantics for English assigns a context-insensitive value to 'water', and the semantics for Twin-English assigns a different context-insensitive value to the orthographically identical expression (but distinct word) 'water'.

On this view, facts about a thinker's internal state do not determine which natural kind terms he or she is using. This severs the connection between psychological states and sentences accepted, which drives Perry's Belief State Argument. For Perry, the internal state is essentially independent of the sentence that classifies it. By hypothesis, the Twin-Earth scenario is already one in which the two thinkers are in the same internal states. The problem for the traditional picture is that belief states do not determine the propositional content of the belief, that is, that *Propositions and Belief States* is false. Indexical belief and belief expressible with natural kind terms and proper names all provide counterexamples to this view.

A Special Status for Indexical Belief?

I have argued that Perry has not provided any argument in support of the received view that indexical belief presents a special problem for the traditional picture of belief. This is not to say that Perry's arguments are flawed in some way. Rather, my view is that they do not show what they are commonly taken to show. They do point to problems for the traditional picture, but the problems are not about indexical belief per se. The problems are about singular thought in general, which includes indexical belief as well as belief expressible with proper names and natural kind terms. The traditional picture cannot accommodate these thoughts because we invoke thought content to explain behavior, but the psychological role of singular thought cannot be specified independently of the thinker's causal or spatiotemporal relation to the objects (or kinds) the thought is about.

Is there any reason to think indexical belief has a special status among the singular beliefs? Some of Perry's discussion of the special role of indexical belief in explaining behavior may point us in the right direction. In discussing the messy shopper, Perry claims that we cannot explain why he reaches into his cart to adjust his sugar sack by ascribing to him the belief that John Perry is making a mess. Why? Because this explanation only works on the assumption that he also believes what he would express by saying, "I am John Perry."

I suggested two ways of interpreting this observation: Perry could mean that indexicals and definite descriptions just have different senses, so naturally beliefs expressible with indexicals and beliefs expressible with definite descriptions slot into psychological explanations in different ways. On this construal, Perry's argument is similar to the familiar argument due to Frege, that the belief that Hesperus = Hesperus is not the same as the belief that Hesperus = Phosphorus, because someone can have the former without having the latter.

Another interpretation of Perry's observation points toward a special status for indexical thought. Some of Perry's remarks lend support to what I called the *Action Explanation Dependence Claim*, which I restate here.

Action Explanation Dependence Claim: An explanation of an action X that ascribes to its agent the belief that the F should do X assumes that the agent has a belief he or she could express by saying "I am the F," but one that ascribes the latter belief does not assume that the agent has any descriptive beliefs about him- or herself.

The guiding idea is that indexical belief plays a basic role in the explanation of action. All of the descriptive beliefs in the world won't guide an agent in selecting an action unless she also has some suitably related beliefs she recognizes to be about herself and her immediate environment, that is, unless she also has some indexical belief. *Action Explanation Dependence Claim* just makes this point more precise.

As I suggested above, there is a straightforward argument from *Action Explanation Dependence Claim* to Perry's conclusion that indexicals do not have descriptive senses, even though it is not the argument usually attributed to Perry. And similar arguments are plausibly available for some, but perhaps not all, types of indexical belief. It is plausible, for instance, that an ascription of a belief that A should do X at t only explains A's doing X if A also believes that it is now t. To explain why Professor X arrived at the department office at noon, we might say that Professor X believes that the meeting starts at noon. As above, this success of this explanation depends on Professor X

having another belief, one he would express by saying "it is now noon" at the time of action. The same could be said for beliefs expressible with 'here'.[16]

Merely adopting *Action Explanation Dependence Claim* in the service of antidescriptivism about indexicals ignores its full relevance to the issue. If it is true, at least some indexical beliefs have a special status that distinguishes them from beliefs expressible with proper names or natural kind terms. The analogue of *Action Explanation Dependence Claim* for these cases is not at all plausible. For instance, we can say that John went to the museum because he believed that the woman he met on the subway would be there. John need not also believe that the woman he met on the subway is, say, Mary, for this explanation to succeed. Similarly, we can say that John poured a bottle of water onto his plants because he believed that the liquid in the bottle he bought at the grocery store is good for plants. He need not be able to identify that liquid as water for this explanation to succeed.

Perry repeatedly calls our attention to the special status of indexical beliefs in action explanation, frequently insisting that other action explanations ultimately require grounding in an indexical belief that connects the terms in the other explanation to something the agent can identify indexically. He correctly insists that its special role in action explanations gives indexical belief a special status. But this observation is unrelated to Perry's arguments that the content of an indexical belief cannot be a proposition. A conflation the observation with these arguments, and an insistence that the problem about indexical belief is a problem about content, can hinder appreciation of this point.

Acknowledgments

This paper started as a dissertation chapter, and I am grateful to the members of my dissertation committee, Robert Stalnaker, Judith Thomson, and Alex Byrne, for very helpful discussion and comments. I am also grateful to Michael Glanzberg, Kirk Ludwig, and Michael O'Rourke for very illuminating conversations and helpful written comments about issues discussed here.

Notes

1. Lewis (1979) is one exception to this trend in calling attention to the parallels between Putnam's arguments and his own. More recently, Chalmers (1996) has suggested that the indexicality of natural kind terms is importantly similar to that of indexicals narrowly construed. As to whether attitude verbs, vague predicates, proper names or natural kind terms *really are* indexicals, I think there is no saying. The category of indexical expressions is typically demarcated by example.

'I', 'now', 'here', 'this', and 'today', among others, are offered as paradigm cases. The list is usually accompanied by the suggestion that it is not exhaustive, but those looking for instructions about how to complete the list are invariably left unsatisfied. Either it is supposed to be obvious what the list does and does not include, or it isn't supposed to matter much. Either way, unless we are told what makes indexicals categorically different from nonindexical expressions, it is unclear what it means to say that natural kind terms or proper names or other expressions are indexicals.

2. A *singular* belief about an object *o* is a belief that comes to be about the object *o* because the thinker stands in the right kind of causal or spatiotemporal relation to *o*. The right kinds of relations are various, and they include causal relations like perceiving *o* or remembering perceiving *o*, or, in the case of singular thoughts about natural kinds, perceiving samples of the same kind as what the thought is about. The right kind of relation may also be strictly spatiotemporal, as it is when a thinker has a thought about where he is. To determine which object or kind a singular belief is about, we need information about the context, specifically, information about which objects or kinds the thinker stands in the right relations *to*.

3. I understand a context to include a specification of the speaker.

4. The traditional Russellian account of definite descriptions treats them as quantifiers, but Fara (2001) has recently shown that this account is mistaken and that descriptions are predicates. Whether we treat definite descriptions as quantifiers or predicates, the point remains that they are not singular terms.

5. *PCD* is often assumed to be equivalent to (3). I consider this assumption in the next section.

6. See Chen 2002, for extensive discussion of this and the closely related claim that action is impossible without indexical belief. I am grateful to Cheryl Chen for drawing my attention to this interpretation of Perry.

7. See Evans 1981 and Tiffany 2000 for this interpretation of Perry.

8. This argument contains a merely technical problem as it stands. Perry grants that the sense of an indexical may shift with context, that is, that any two utterances of the same indexical, even in very similar contexts, could have different senses. This vastly limits the kind of counterfactual reasoning we can use to establish that an indexical sentence *s* uttered in a context *c* does not express the same proposition as nonindexical sentence *s'*. In particular, we cannot establish that these propositions (what *s* expresses in *c* and what *s'* expresses) are distinct by showing that there is some context *c'* in which *s* and *s'* express different propositions. For this inference is only valid if the indexical sentence *s* expresses the same proposition in *c* and *c'*, and Perry has granted to the description theorist that this may not be the case. Defending the argument as it stands involves distinguishing between reasoning counterfactually about a context of utterance and reasoning about a different context of utterance. The distinction will be difficult to draw if contexts of utterance include features of the speaker's mental states, and particularly if externalist scruples are taken seriously. The problem can be addressed in various ways, perhaps by showing how a context of utterance can be reidentified in another possible world, or by rejecting the claim that the sense of an indexical can shift with context and claiming instead that it shifts only with *relevant* shifts in the context, so that, for instance, the sense of 'I' in *c* differs from its sense in *c'* only when

the speaker of c is not the same as the speaker of c'. Perry might also say that it is possible that a thinker believes what he would express by saying "I am G" without correctly believing himself to satisfy any definite description. This would show that 'I' does not have a descriptive sense in that context, but it is not clear why it would follow that 'I' does not have a descriptive sense in *any* context.

9. Kripke's arguments that proper names and natural kind terms do not have descriptive senses are widely accepted, though recently some philosophers have challenged Kripke on this point. See Dummett 1989 and 1981, and Sosa 2001 for the view that proper names can be construed as descriptions that always take wide scope and Stanley 1997 for sympathetic discussion of view that they are rigidified descriptions. See also Soames 2002 for criticism of these approaches. The point I make here has also been explicitly raised by Tiffany 2000.

10. Lewis (1979) also offers a version of this argument but without the focus on sentences and their role in classifying belief states that is operative for Perry.

11. By "perceptual demonstrative," I mean an apparently directly referential use of a demonstrative to refer to an object that the speaker currently perceives. There is no linguistic indicator that a particular use of a demonstrative is a perceptual use, which suggests that for demonstratives, words are not always associated with particular ways of thinking of their referents.

12. A defender of *Sentences and Belief States* might observe that even though Lisa and Judy are the same with respect to their dispositions to utter various sentences about the location of the vase, the fact that they differ in their behavioral dispositions with respect to the vase is enough to show that they accept different sentences. As Perry has explained, someone can be in a belief state associated with a sentence without having the disposition to utter the sentence. This move threatens to turn Perry's substantive generalization in *Sentences and Belief States* into the truism that if two people share a certain (but unspecified) class of behavioral and cognitive dispositions, then they are in the same belief state. If agents need not stand in any particular cognitive relation to a sentence to count as *accepting* that sentence, then it is unclear what work sentences are doing in a principle like *Sentences and Belief States*.

13. When I say that indexicals are associated with modes of presentation, I simply mean that when a person expresses a belief with a sentence containing an indexical, the person also represents the referent of that indexical in some way or other. This mode of presentation need not be semantically relevant.

14. This is clearly the case if contents are taken to be unstructured entities like sets of possible worlds, but it also holds on a structured content view. On the latter view, contents are structured to mirror the structure of sentences that express them, but they are not themselves sentences.

15. An extension of the Belief State Argument to proper names would require a pair of thinkers A and B such that both A and B accept the same sentence containing a proper name and both represent the bearer of the name in the same way, yet the proper names in the sentences have different bearers. One might think that proper names are individuated so as to make such a case impossible. I consider this response in the text.

16. It is less plausible, however, that descriptions of an individual or object can never be substituted for indexicals like 'she', 'he', or 'that'. For instance, we might explain why *A* walked up to the bar by noting that she wanted to talk to *him*, or that she wanted to talk to the man in the gray T-shirt. It is not clear that the latter explanation is successful only if *A* has the further belief she would express by saying "He is the man in the gray T-shirt." In saying this, I am not saying that this occurrence of 'he' has the same sense as 'the man in the gray T-shirt'. The point is simply that we can explain why *A* walked up to the bar by ascribing the descriptive belief to her, and this explanation does not seem to require that she have a further indexical belief about the man in the gray T-shirt.

References

Burge, T. 1973. "Reference and Proper Names." *Journal of Philosophy* 70: 425–439.

———. 1979a. "Semantical Paradox." *Journal of Philosophy* 76: 169–198.

———. 1979b. "Individualism and the Mental." In P. French, T. Uehling, Jr., and H. Wettstein (eds.), *Midwest Studies in Philosophy 4: Studies in Metaphysics*. Minneapolis: University of Minnesota Press.

Chalmers, D. 1996. *The Conscious Mind*. New York: Oxford University Press.

Chen, C. 2002. "Why Perception Matters: The Case of the Global Clairvoyant." Unpublished manuscript.

Dummett, M. 1981. *The Interpretation of Frege's Philosophy*. Cambridge, Mass.: Harvard University Press.

———. 1989. *Frege: Philosophy of Language*. 2nd ed. Cambridge, Mass.: Harvard University Press.

Evans, G. 1979. "Reference and Contingency." *Monist* 62: 161–189.

———. 1981. "Understanding Demonstratives." In H. Parret and J. Bouveresse, (eds.), *Meaning and Understanding*. Berlin: Walter de Gruyter.

Fara, D. 2001. "Descriptions as Predicates." *Philosophical Studies* 102: 1–42. Originally published under the name "Delia Graff."

Kripke, S. 1980. *Naming and Necessity*. Cambridge, Mass.: Harvard University Press.

Lewis, D. 1979. "Attitudes *De Dicto* and *De Se*." *Philosophical Review* 88: 513–543.

Perry, J. 1977. "Frege on Demonstratives." *Philosophical Review* 8: 474–497. Reprinted in Perry 1993. Page references cited from this reprint.

———. 1979. "The Problem of the Essential Indexical." *Noûs* 13: 3–21. Reprinted in Perry 1993. Page references cited from this reprint.

———. 1980. "Belief and Acceptance." In P. French, T. Uehling, Jr., and H. Wettstein (eds.), *Midwest Studies in Philosophy 5: Studies in Epistemology*. Minneapolis: University of Minnesota Press. Reprinted in Perry 1993. Page references cited from this reprint.

———. 1993. *The Problem of the Essential Indexical and Other Essays*. New York: Oxford University Press.

Putnam, H. 1975a. "The Meaning of 'Meaning'." In K. Gunderson (ed.), *Minnesota Studies in the Philosophy of Science 8: Language, Mind and Knowledge*. Minneapolis: University of Minnesota Press. Reprinted in Putnam 1975b. Page reference from this reprint.

———. 1975b. *Mind, Language, and Reality: Philosophical Papers*. Vol. 2. New York: Cambridge University Press.

Richard, M. 1990. *Propositional Attitudes*. Cambridge: Cambridge University Press.

Soames, S. 1999. *Understanding Truth*. New York: Oxford University Press.

———. 2002. *Beyond Rigidity*. New York: Oxford University Press.

Sosa, D. 2001. "Rigidity in the Scope of Russell's Theory." *Noûs* 53: 1–38.

Stanley, J. 1997. "Names and Rigid Designation." In B. Hale and C. Wright, (eds.), *A Companion to the Philosophy of Language*. Oxford: Blackwell.

Tiffany, E. 2000. "What's So Essential about Indexicals?" *Philosophical Studies* 100: 35–50.

8 The Myth of Unarticulated Constituents

Herman Cappelen and Ernie Lepore

This chapter evaluates arguments presented by John Perry (and Ken Taylor) in favor of the presence of an unarticulated constituent in the proposition expressed by an utterance of, for example, (1):[1]

(1) It's raining (at t).

We contend that these arguments are, at best, inconclusive. That is the critical part of this essay. On the positive side, we argue that (1) has as its semantic content the proposition *that it is raining (at t)* and that this is a *location-neutral* proposition. According to the view we propose, an audience typically looks for a location when they hear utterances of (1) because their interests in rain are *location-focused*: it is the location of rain that determines whether we get wet, carrots grow, and roads become slippery. These are, however, contingent facts about rain, wetness, people, carrots, and roads—they are not built into the semantics for the verb 'rain'.

We're interested the semantics and pragmatics of (1) not because of an interest in weather reports in general or rain reports in particular. We find Perry's examples and discussion of them important as case studies in the relationship between three central components of all communicative interactions:

- The meanings of words (e.g., 'rain') and sentences they occur in (e.g., (1)).
- Facts about the subject matter of our sentences not "encoded" in the meanings of our words (in this case, facts about rain and our interest in the location of rain).
- Our intuitions about what is asserted, claimed, and said by utterances of sentences.

We will argue that (1) provides a particularly clear illustration of how nonsemantic (and more generally, nonlinguistic) facts about the subject matter of our sentences determine communicated content. It is difficult, in such cases, to distinguish those components of communicated content determined by the meanings of words used and those not so determined. The various devices we use to tease them apart in this case provide a model for how it can be done in other cases.

The chapter is structured as follows: We present a brief overview of Perry's (and other's) view of unarticulated constituents. We present one central argument for the thesis. We rebut that argument. We consider and rebut a second argument in favor of unarticulated constituents. We conclude with some general methodological remarks.

Unarticulated Constituents in Perry, Crimmins, Bach, and Austin

About (1) Perry famously says:

In order to assign a truth-value to my son's statement [of (1)] . . . I needed a place. But no component of his statement stood for a place . . . Palo Alto is a constituent of the content of my son's remark, which no component of his statement designated; it is an unarticulated constituent. (Perry 1986, p. 206)

[the location] is a constituent, *because, since rain occurs at a time in a place, there is no truth-evaluable proposition unless a place is supplied. It is unarticulated, because there is no morpheme that designates that place.* (Perry 1998, p. 9, emphasis added; cf. also Perry 2001, p. 45)

the task of identifying the unarticulated constituents of the proposition expressed by an utterance remains after all of the relevant semantic rules have been understood and applied. (Perry 1998, p. 10)

According to these passages, if we fail to add a location to what's expressed by an utterance of (1) we lack something truth evaluable, that is, we don't have a proposition. In what follows, one of our central concerns is with *the justification* for this claim. Perry provides a justification in these passages: his reason for opining that no proposition gets expressed without an added location is *that rain occurs at a time in a place.*

What exactly does he mean?

Here's our interpretation: it's a necessary truth about rain that it happens in a place at a time. Such necessary truths must, in some way, be encoded in the propositions expressed by utterances of (1). We call this *Perry's Argument for Nonexist*, and it will be further discussed below.

This isn't the only significant feature of this famous passage. Another important claim is that no expression in (1) refers to a location. This part of the claim is emphasized by Crimmins:

[where] an unarticulated constituent of the content of a statement is an item that is used by the semantics as a building block of the statement's content but is such that there is no (overt) expression in the sentence that supplies the object as its content. In a semantics that takes propositions to be structures containing objects and properties an unarticulated constituent is simply a propositional constituent that is not explicitly mentioned—it is not the content of any expression in the sentence. (Crimmins 1992, p. 16)

Crimmins's parenthetical remark, "(overt)," introduces a hedge where there is none in Perry. It seems to open the possibility that "hidden" in the logical/syntactic form of (1) there is an expression that refers to a location. This is not Perry's position. He says:

there is no basic problem with a statement being about unarticulated constituents. In particular, we do not need to first find an expression, hidden in the "deep structure" or somewhere else and then do the semantics of the statement augmented by the hidden expression. Things are intelligible just as they appear on the surface, and the explanation we might ordinarily give in nonphilosophical moments, that we simply understand what the statement is about, is essentially correct. (Perry 1986, p. 211)

We interpret him to mean that there is no lexical element that takes locations as its semantic value, not just no "overt" lexical element. We should emphasize that even though our arguments below are directed against Perry's view so interpreted, it works just as effectively against the view that there is a "hidden" variable in logical form. (We in particular have in mind the view suggested by Stanley [2000].)

Before evaluating this view, we want to mention how it can be generalized beyond weather reports. Perry and Crimmins mention a number of such examples, including but not limited to

It's 2 PM.

She's moving.

The central examples in Bach 1994 makes essentially the same point as Perry's but applied to a different set of examples. Bach says:

For example, sentences [2] and [3],

[2]   Steel isn't strong enough.
[3]   Willie almost robbed a bank.

though syntactically well-formed, are semantically or conceptually incomplete, in the sense that something must be added for the sentence to express a complete and determinate proposition (something capable of being true or false). . . . In these cases the conventional meaning of the sentence determines not a full proposition but merely a propositional radical; a complete proposition would be expressed, a truth condition determined, only if the sentence were elaborated somehow.

Perry, Crimmins, and Bach each appeals to some rather restricted subset of sentences to make their points. Various neo-Wittgensteineans, ordinary language philosophers, and other radical contextualists claim that *all* sentences suffer from the sort of incompleteness that Perry attributes to (1) and that Bach attributes to (2) and (3). This passage from Austin is representative (for more quotes along these lines see Cappelen and Lepore 2005, ch. 2):

> If you just take a bunch of sentences...impeccably formulated in some language or other, there can be no question of sorting them out into those that are true and those that are false; for...the question of truth and falsehood does not turn only on what a sentence *is*, nor yet on what it *means*, but on, speaking very broadly, the circumstances in which it is uttered. Sentences are not *as such* either true or false. (Austin 1962, pp. 110–111)

Our focus here will be on Perry's famous example (1). It is not entirely clear that our diagnosis of his example generalizes in any obvious way to these other cases. It might be that the specific diagnosis will vary from case to case—we won't take a stand on that issue here. We do, however, hold that the general strategies that can be used with respect to (1) can be, at least, useful heuristics in a wider range of cases. We return to the question of how to draw general lessons from this particular case at the very end of the paper.

Two Central Claims: Nonexpress and Nonexist

Perry is committed to something like Nonexpress:

Nonexpress: Let u be an utterance of (1) in context C. The semantic values of the lexical components of u (in C) and their compositional structure do not suffice to express a proposition.

Nonexpress is closely related to Nonexist. To articulate Nonexist, we'll use the following convention: Let an italicized that-clause denote *whatever* you get by *not* including the alleged unarticulated constituents—so *that it's raining (at t)* denotes whatever you get without adding the location:

Nonexist: There is no proposition for *that it's raining (at t)* to denote.

Another way to put Nonexist is as the claim that there's no location-neutral proposition of the form *that it's raining (at t)*. This is a claim about which propositions *exist* rather than about which proposition is or is not *expressed* by a certain English sentence. The two claims are intimately connected, as we've seen, since the argument for Nonexpress is based on Nonexist. We turn now to an evaluation of that argument.

Evaluation of Perry's Argument for Nonexist

If Nonexist is true, then Nonexpress seems immensely plausible. If there's nothing propositional expressed by (1) before a location is added, then, if a proposition is expressed, that proposition must contain something like an unarticulated constituent, if we assume, as Perry does, that there's no hidden lexical item in its syntactic/logical form. Assuming utterances of (1) do express propositions, we have what appears to be a good argument for unarticulated constituents.

For this argument to work, we need an argument for Nonexist (one that doesn't rely on Nonexpress). Absent such an argument, the central argument for Nonexpress is without a foundation. We have already encountered an argument for Nonexist in the quotes where Perry introduces the notion of an unarticulated constituent. He repeats this argument in several presentations. Above we called it Perry's Argument, and it's very simple: rain happens in a location, and so nothing propositional, no complete proposition, can be expressed by (1) unless a location is added.

We do not think this a strong argument. Our objection to it is not original. We take it from Taylor (2001). Taylor does not present it as an objection to Perry, but in fact it is. He points out something exceedingly obvious once you think about it—namely, that almost any kind of activity as a matter of necessity occurs in a location. This is true about, for example, boxing, kissing, spinning, breaking, and dancing. Taylor focuses on the latter example and notes that it is impossible for (4) to be true unless Nina danced *somewhere* last night.

(4)   Nina danced last night.

But it would be crazy to infer, on that basis alone, that the location of dancing is an unarticulated constituent of the proposition expressed by an utterance of (4). Or consider (5):

(5)   John drove to Cleveland last night.

The driving must have happened at a certain speed, but Perry would not, and should not, conclude from this that the speed is a component of the proposition expressed by (5).

The general point should be obvious: just because a certain kind of activity necessarily happens in a location (or at a velocity), it doesn't follow that that location (or velocity) is part of the propositions expressed by utterances of (4) and (5). More generally, there are plenty of facts that might be metaphysically required for a certain sentence to be true, but we don't want to build unarticulated constituents corresponding to all of these facts into the proposition we express by uttering such sentences. This would, potentially, create an indefinite number of unarticulated constituents in all the propositions we express with our utterances. So, what we have called Perry's Argument for the location being an unarticulated constituent of (1) fails.

Of course, you might think you don't need a real argument for Nonexist; you might think it's just *obvious* that (1) doesn't express a proposition. We don't share that sense of obviousness. It seems to us to be the result of limited imagination or theoretical prejudice—and in the next three sections we try to convince you of this by "softening" your philosophical imagination through thinking about 'rain' when it occurs as a mass term and in theoretical interpretations of questions such as 'Why does it rain?'

Two Exercises

Remember, all we are trying to achieve now is to show that the nonlocalized proposition exists. How does one go about showing that a proposition exists? We're not sure we have a complete and general answer to this question (does anyone?), but the following seems to *suffice*: If you (or anyone) can think that *p*, then *p* exists (and is a proposition). So, if we can get you to think the location-neutral proposition, then we have established that it exists.

At this point we are not trying to show that (1) expresses the location-neutral proposition. All we're trying to show is that there is such a proposition. We're doing this because the central argument for Nonexpress is based on Nonexist.

In what follows we'll try to get you to think *that it rains* by thinking about other occurrences of 'rain' where the location-neutral interpretation seems obvious. There are two exercises.

First Exercise: 'Rain' in Subject Position
First, consider 'rain' in subject position, as in (6)–(9):

(6)   Rain is Nina's favorite weather condition.
(7)   Rain is the topic of our next book.
(8)   Nina dreamed about rain yesterday.
(9)   I've missed rain since moving to Arizona.

We are not going to present a semantics for 'rain' in (6)–(9); all we want to do is point out that the most natural reading of 'rain' in these four sentences is *location-neutral*.

The natural reading of (6) is *not* one according to which Nina's favorite weather condition is rain *in l*. Nor is it a location general reading according to which her favorite weather condition is rain *in some location*. The same applies to (7)–(9). Try for yourself.

Can we say something more specific about that location-neutral interpretation of 'rain'? Again, we're not going to (because we don't need to) present a fully developed semantic proposal here; what we will do is give an intuitive characterization. We can, as a first stab, take 'rain' to refer to *a certain kind of activity* (and we'll remain neutral about what sort of things *kinds of activities* are). It is an activity that always takes place in a location—just as, for example, dance is an activity that always takes place in a location. But that fact isn't reflected in our interpretation of (6)–(9). It is, rather, a fact we know about that *kind of activity*. Let's call this kind of activity *R*.

How does this help us get clearer on the location-neutral proposition *that it's raining (at t)*? In the obvious way: on the present proposal, *that it's raining (at t)* is the proposition *that R is going on at t, that it Rs at t*, that is, *that it rains at t*. This is the *location-neutral proposition*.[2]

Remember, all we are trying to achieve at this point is get you to notice that it is possible to think the location-neutral thought. We're doing that to refute Nonexist (and we want to refute Nonexist to undermine one of the main arguments for Nonexpress). We're suggesting that going from *R* to *that R is going on at t* will help you grasp the location-neutral rain proposition.

Second Exercise: Read Theoretical Literature about Rain

To learn about how to think the location-neutral proposition, it also helps to read some theoretical literature about rain. This is where the continuity between uses of 'rain' as an abstract noun and as a verb becomes most salient. Here's a sample from a web page that tries to explain what rain is:

> For most areas of the world, rain is so common that few people stop to think about it. *Why does it rain?* Does all rainfall have the same causes? For those of us living in England, rain is a common subject of discussion and debate. (Http://www.krysstal.com/rain.html)

Focus on the question (10), as it occurs in the above passage:

(10)   Why does it rain?

The following seems obvious: The natural interpretation of question (10), at least in the context of the internet discussion about rain, is not location-*specific*, that is, it is not "Why does it rain *in location l*?" It also is not the location-*general* "Why does it rain *in some location*?" The natural interpretation of (10) is *location-neutral*. We're suggesting using that interpretation of 'rain' to get at the location-neutral reading of *that it's raining (at t)*.

Question (10) is not the sole example of an English sentence where the verb 'rain' takes a location-neutral interpretation. Below we argue that there, in the right settings, are utterances of, for example, (11) that require the same interpretation:

(11)   I don't care *where* it rains; I only care *whether* it rains.

That example is best presented with stage setting (and we provide that below), but even out of context, one can get the location-neutral reading of 'rain' in (11).

Taylor's analogy with 'dance' might help to clarify the point of focusing on examples like (10) and (11). Someone with a more theoretical interest in dance might ask question (12):

(12)   What is it to dance?

Since all dancing, as a matter of necessity, takes place in a location, any explanation of what it is to dance will be an explanation of what it is to dance *in some location or other*. But it does not follow from this metaphysical/physical fact that (12) has a location as an unarticulated constituent. That is to say, it is not the question, "What is to dance *in l (or in some location)*?" The natural interpretation of (12) is location-*neutral*. This, as Taylor points out, generalizes to occurrences of 'dance' in sentences like (4).

(4)   Nina danced last night.

We are suggesting that you try to make the same extension from (10) to (13):

(13)   It rained last night.

Let's take stock: We have no way to ensure that going through these two exercises will help you fix on the location-neutral proposition *that it's raining (at t)*. If it doesn't, we don't really have much more to say—there's a kind of standoff here. We claim to be able to think it; you claim not to be able to do so. We don't know how to make progress if that's the case. We are, however, quite confident that *we* are able to think the location-neutral thought, and that's enough for us. So, from now on we assume its existence.

Refuting Nonexist helps refute Nonexpress because most arguments for Nonexpress rely on Nonexist. There is, however, one influential argument for Nonexpress that does not obviously rely on Nonexist. This is an argument from Taylor 2001 that we call "the argument from feelings of incompleteness." We next turn to a presentation and evaluation of Taylor's argument.

Taylor's Argument from Feelings of Incompleteness

Taylor says:

The view which I favor supposes that the verb 'to rain' has a lexically specified argument place which is θ-marked THEME and that this argument place takes places as values. This is a way of saying that the subatomic structure of the verb 'to rain' explicitly marks rainings as a kind of change that places undergo. . . . Thus though:

[1]   It is raining.

is missing no syntactically mandatory sentential constituent, nonetheless, it is semantically incomplete. The semantic incompleteness is manifest to us as *a felt inability* to evaluate the truth value of an utterance of [1] in the absence of a contextually provided location (or range of locations). This *felt need* for a contextually provided location has its source, I claim, in our tacit cognition of the syntactically unexpressed argument place of the verb 'to rain'. (Taylor 2001, emphasis added)

We take the structure of Taylor's argument to be this: He starts with data that need explanation. The data are as follows: when we encounter utterances of (1), we feel unable to evaluate that utterance as true or false unless we are provided with a location for the rain. In what follows, we call this "the feeling of incompleteness." Taylor proposes the following explanation of the data: What he calls the "subatomic structure" of the verb 'rain' contains an argument place for a location. This argument is not articulated in the logical form of (1) (there's no expression corresponding to it), but without being provided with a location we're left with something incomplete and that incomplete object causes feelings of incompleteness.

We suspect that when the argument gets spelled in this way, it'll seem a little fishy to some readers. After all, what do we philosophers really know about what causes feelings of incompleteness? Or, come to think of it, does anyone have an idea of what the "subatomic structure" of a verb is? Taylor says very little about this notion, which is surprising, given how much work he thinks it does for him. We could rest our objections to Taylor's argument on the speculative nature of the alleged causal mechanism behind our feelings of incompleteness and his failure to provide any sort of an account of what the "subatomic structure" of a verb is, much less an account of how it can provoke feelings of incompleteness. But our objections are more generous in this sense: We'll grant Taylor that he might, at some point in the future, be able to specify what the "subatomic structure" of a verb is and that he'll be able to say something about the kind of causal mechanism through which it might elicit feelings of incompleteness in us. But even granting Taylor all of this, there are, we think, conclusive arguments for holding that Taylor has the wrong story about what, *as a matter of fact*, causes feelings of incompleteness when confronted by utterances of (1).

Our objection to him has two components: we first point out that the location-neutral readings of 'rain', as presented in (10) and (11), above are incompatible with Taylor's view. Second, we provide an alternative explanation for the feeling of incompleteness, one that makes Taylor's appeal to the subatomic structure of 'rain' otiose.

Part 1 of Objection

The first objection has, in effect, already been anticipated by us earlier: if in *some* sentences the only acceptable interpretation of 'rain' is a location-neutral interpretation, then the "subatomic structure" of 'rain' cannot require a location. If it did, it would do so in all its occurrences. We have already seen examples where it does not, the most obvious one being the occurrence of 'rain' in (11) and in (12) (see discussion below). This occurrence of 'rain' cannot be interpreted in a location specific way, that is, cannot be interpreted as 'rain [at l]'. Nor can it be interpreted in a location-general manner, that is, as 'rain [somewhere]'. This provides strong evidence against Taylor's view.

Part 2 of Objection

Of course, we don't disagree with Perry (and Taylor) about the empirical fact that speakers typically look for a location when they hear utterances of (1). Who could deny that! Nor do we disagree that when speakers hear such utterances, they feel a kind of "incompleteness" prior to a location being provided. Nor do we disagree with them that in some sense the metaphor of the utterance "demanding" a location is a good one. What we do disagree about, however, is the explanation of this feeling—its cause.

According to Taylor's interpretation (or elaboration) of Perry's view, this feeling of incompleteness is caused in us by the fact that the subatomic structure of 'rain' contains an argument place for a location. We have an alternative explanation: our interest in rain is *location focused* and, as a result, our interpretation of rain-talk is typically (but not invariably) *location focused*. Our interests are location focused in this sense: the location of rain is essential to our interest in it. It is only *at* the location of the rain that we get wet, that food grows or rots, that cars slide, and so forth. In almost all the different ways in which rain affects human life, its location is essential. These facts, and not the subatomic structure of the verb 'rain,' explain why we typically (but not always) focus on location.

Some evidence that an explanation along these lines is reasonable can be gathered from trying to imagine scenarios in which our interests in rain are *not* location focused. This is difficult to do, but here is a modest attempt:

The Rain-Ache Universe: This universe differs from ours in four respects:

a. Rain is never noticed by humans as wetness—as soon as rain touches any object it evaporates immediately—so there is no need for umbrellas or any other rain-protection instruments.

b. Food is not grown, so there is no need for rainfall for that purpose.

c. Whenever it rains, however, no matter where it rains, through some poorly under-stood causal mechanism, it causes headaches in humans. And humans don't need to be in the vicinity of rain to get a headache.

d. These headaches can be avoided by wearing yellow hats.

In the rain-ache universe, parents are prone to tell their kids things like: "If it rains, you have to wear a yellow hat." To avoid these epidemic headaches, humans place rain detectors around the entire globe[3] and put out daily warnings that say things like (14):

(14)   It will rain at 2 PM, so make sure to bring your yellow hats.

Sometimes when the rain detectors fail to pick up rain and a distinctive headache occurs, people say things like:

(15)   Oh, it's really raining today.
(16)   Ugh, it's raining; those rain detectors never work.

It might be difficult for us to get our minds around such a world, but it seems plausible to assume that those who speak about rain in this universe will do so without any in-terest whatsoever in the location of rain. The location will never be salient. The only thing they'll care about is not where it rains but whether it rains (Note to reader: think about how you interpreted the sentence before this parenthesis). They'll express that by uttering sentences like (11):

(11)   I don't care *where* it rains; I only care *whether* it rains.

They care about whether it rains because that causes headaches and, when it does, they have to wear yellow hats. Utterances of, for example, (14) will feel complete, even though no location is salient.

   If you share our intuition about this example, it shows two important things:

1. It provides evidence in favor of an alternative explanation of the feeling of incom-pleteness: we have that feeling because of contingent features of our way of life and the role of rain in it, and not because of any feature of the verb 'rain'.

2. When inhabitants of this world interpret utterances by inhabitants of the Rain-Ache universe, they interpret them as expressing location-neutral propositions. We take (11) to be a particularly clear instance—it is almost impossible not to read (11) in

a location-neutral way. This is further evidence (of the kind encountered with [10]) that the "subatomic structure" of the verb 'rain' lacks an argument place for location.

Summary

We have presented arguments against both Perry's and Taylor's arguments for Non-express. Along the way, we established the existence of a location-neutral proposition and established that some utterances of sentences containing 'rain' must have location-neutral readings. One conclusion we can draw from all of this—and one we do draw—is that the location-neutral proposition is the *semantic* content of (1) and that the verb 'rain' has a location-neutral semantic value (there is nothing in its sub-atomic structure that requires a location). If some occurrences of 'rain' are location-neutral and 'rain' is not ambiguous, then we should expect it to have a location-neural semantic value also when it occurs in 'It's raining'. Remember, Perry's only objection to this is Nonexist, that is, that there is no such thing as the location-neutral proposition. As soon as that view is off the table, it is hard to see how (1) could fail to express the location-neutral proposition, prior to the addition of a contextually salient location. Combine this with an alternative explanation of the feeling of incompleteness (as we provided above), and it's hard to see what objections there could be to treating the location-neutral proposition as the semantic value.

We should point out right away that it is possible that *our* disagreement with Perry is less serious than it might at first seem. There are two points over which we disagree:

• We disagree about the existence of a certain proposition, Perry doesn't think that the location-neutral proposition *that it's raining (at t)* exists; we do.

• As a result, we disagree about the explanation of our search of a location when we hear utterances of (1): Perry says: "[the location] is a constituent, because, since rain occurs at a time in a place, there is no truth-evaluable proposition unless a place is supplied." We provided an alternative explanation.

It is perfectly possible that our alternative explanation is acceptable to Perry. We suspect that the argument we focused on (the argument from Nonexist to Nonexpress) might be just a kind of throw away by Perry—something he'd give up easily when confronted by our objections. In which case, there's little substantive disagreement between us here. What we do *not* disagree with Perry about is that when normal speakers utter (1) the proposition they saliently assert is one that contains a component that does not correspond to any lexical component of the sentence. So, we concur with Perry that "Palo Alto is a constituent of the content of my son's remark, which no component of his statement designated," at least if 'remark' is interpreted to mean "what was saliently asserted by the utterance." We also agree that, so understood, "it [i.e., the location] is an unarticulated constituent."

Our disagreement with Taylor, however, is more fundamental: Taylor's argument from the Feeling of Incompleteness and his theory about the "subatomic structure" of verbs such as 'rain' must, if we are right, be abandoned. This is clearly not a throw away point for Taylor—it is, in effect, at the very center of his interpretation of Perry's theory of unarticulated constituents. As we see things, Perry is better off ignoring Taylor's proposed underpinning of unarticulated constituents. Instead, he should embrace the idea that a minimal, location-neutral proposition is expressed and combine that idea with an alternative, interest-focused, explanation for why the proposition that gets saliently asserted with an utterance of (1) has a location in it.

General Lessons

If our diagnosis of weather reports is correct, it has important corollaries. Below, we present these as rather grand and general claims. Of course, all we have shown is that these hold in one particular case. It goes beyond the scope of the present paper to establish them in the general form presented below—for further justification, see Cappelen and Lepore 2005:

• The example discussed in this chapter illustrates a general phenomenon: the proposition semantically expressed by an utterance of S can be very different from the proposition *saliently asserted* by that utterance. For most utterances of (1), the purpose of the utterance is not to assert or convey the semantic content. What is saliently asserted is a proposition of the form *that it's raining in l*. We suspect this phenomenon is ubiquitous in linguistic communication.

• Grice (1989) introduced a "quasi-technical" notion of "what was said" by the utterance of a sentence. He tied this notion closely to the meaning of the words in the sentence and their compositional structure—it is close to what we in this chapter (and in Cappelen and Lepore 2005) have called "the semantic content" (though nothing depends on that choice of terminology). The remaining components of the totality of the communicated content Grice explained by an appeal to conversational or conventional implicatures. In the case of (1), we have seen that "what was said" in Grice's technical sense can be very different from what intuitively is said (or asserted or claimed). For that reason, we think Grice's choice of terminology was extremely unfortunate. More often than not, what is intuitively *said* or *asserted* by an utterance is not

Grice would classify as "what was said." This, we suspect, has been the source of a great deal of confusion in the literature since Grice. We elaborate on that point in chapter 4 of Cappelen and Lepore 2005.

• Our diagnosis of Perry's example also provides an illustration of how speakers can, on a regular basis, sincerely utter a sentence that semantically expresses a proposition they do not believe. They utter it to communicate a proposition they do believe. Take the negation of the location-neutral proposition, that is, *that it's not raining*. It will (almost) always be false. Nonetheless, if we are right, every utterance of 'It's not raining' expresses that proposition. When speakers utter, "It's not raining," they use a sentence, the semantic content of which they do not believe, to assert a proposition that they do believe (e.g., *that it's not raining in l*). We believe this is a situation that does not occur only in connection with (1), but is ubiquitous in language (see Cappelen and Lepore 2005). This should come as no surprise; although our communicative goals are context-dependent in the extreme, the meanings of our words are stable. So we use stable meaning (i.e., semantic content) to perform speech acts, for example, make assertions, the content of which is shaped by the peculiarities of the particular contexts we find ourselves in.

• A further corollary, one that should be obvious by now, is that our intuitions about what speaker's saliently assert and our feelings about which propositions are expressed are extremely poor guides to semantic content. As we have seen, they are even worse guides to what propositions exist.

How do we study semantic content if it isn't salient to us? If our intuitions about what speakers say and assert are poor guides to the semantic content of sentences, what tools do we who study language have for finding semantic content? In reply we should first point out that this is a tricky question for *anyone* to answer, and it is, if anything, made *easier* by giving up the demand that a semantic theory capture or explain our intuitions about what speakers saliently say and assert in uttering sentences (for the difficulties raised by this demand, see Cappelen and Lepore 1997; 2005, ch. 4). Our strategy in this chapter has been to look for uses that are minimal in this sense: if some feature F seems to be part of what is said by most utterances of an expression e, but you can find contexts in which F isn't included in what is asserted by sentences containing e, then you know that F is not a stable part of the meaning of e. This is in effect a version of what Grice (1989, p. 44) called Contextual Cancelability—in this case used as a device for separating semantic content from other parts of communicated content. There are other strategies, some of which we outline in Cappelen and Lepore 2005; what they all have in common is an attempt to abstract away from the peculiarities of particular contexts of utterance and find contents that are common between them. We doubt, however, that there will a single, universal procedures that for each sentence, S, will provide a simple and informative account of S' semantic content. We can always express and grasp semantic contents disquotationally. Those who feel the need for more informative presentations of this content might have to work it out on a case-by-case basis, much as we just did for (1).

Notes

1. The 'at t' reflects the tense of the (1). We are simply making it explicit, say, in logical form.

2. In conversations with students (and even some colleagues) we often encounter the misunderstanding that the location-neutral proposition really is a *location-general* proposition—that is, that proposition *that it's raining somewhere*. This, it should be obvious, is *not* our view.

3. An example involving rain detectors (but no headaches) is in Recanati 2002. He uses his example for partly the same purposes as our Pain-Ache example, but Recanati is not defending the view we propose here. He says, for example, "Hearing it [i.e., the rain alarm], the weatherman on duty in the adjacent room shouts: 'It's raining!' *His utterance is true, iff it is raining (at the time of utterance) in some place or other*" (Recanati 2002; emphasis added). In other words, Recanati is arguing that the location-*general* proposition, not the location-*neutral* proposition, gets expressed. For reasons pointed out above, these propositions are importantly different. It is hard to see whether this proposal is even incompatible with Perry's view, given that Perry accepts that there is a proposition expressed by 'It's raining somewhere'; Perry can't think that proposition doesn't exist. That Recanati's only means to rule out the need for a *particular* location is also clear from this passage: "The fact that one can imagine an utterance of 'It's raining' that is true iff it is raining (at the time of utterance) in some place or other arguably establishes the pragmatic nature of the felt necessity *to single out a particular place*, in the contexts in which such a necessity is indeed felt" (Recanati 2002; emphasis added). There are a number of other fundamental points at which we disagree with Recanati's position and presentation of the issues in that paper, but this is not the place to go through them all in detail. For a discussion of the "big-picture" differences between the kind of view we defend and the kind of view Recanati defends, see our exchange in *Mind and Language* (Recanati 2006; Cappelen and Lepore 2006). Put simply: We see this as a partial defense of the kind of Semantic Minimalism we defend in Cappelen and Lepore 2005. For Recanati, it is an attempt to defend his brand of Radical Contextualism (Recanati 2004).

References

Austin, J. L. L. 1962. *How to Do Things with Words*. Ed. J. O. Urmson. Oxford: Clarendon Press.

Bach, K. 1994. "Conversational Implicature." *Mind and Language* 9: 124–162.

Cappelen, H., and E. Lepore. 1997. "On an Alleged Connection between Indirect Quotation and Semantic Theory." *Mind and Language* 12: 278–296.

———. 2002. "Indexicality, Binding, Anaphora, and *A Priori* Truth." *Analysis* 10: 271–281.

———. 2005. *Insensitive Semantics*. Oxford: Basil Blackwell.

———. 2006. "Reply to Critics." *Mind and Language* 21: 50–73.

Crimmins, M. 1992. *Talk about Belief*. Cambridge, Mass.: MIT Press.

Grice, P. 1989. *Studies in the Way of Words*. Cambridge, Mass.: Harvard University Press.

Perry, J. 1986. "Thought without Representation." *Proceedings of the Aristotelian Society* Supplement 60: 263–283. Reprinted in Perry 1993.

———. 1993. *Problem of the Essential Indexical and Other Essays*. Oxford: Oxford University Press.

———. 1998. "Indexicals, Contexts and Unarticulated Constituents." *Proceedings of the 1995 CSLI-Amsterdam Logic, Language and Computation Conference*. Stanford, Calif.: CSLI Publications.

———. 2001. *Reference and Reflexivity*. Stanford, Calif.: CSLI Publications.

Recanati, F. 2002. "Unarticulated Constituents." *Linguistics and Philosophy* 25: 299–345.

———. 2004. *Literal Meaning*. Cambridge: Cambridge University Press.

———. 2006. "Crazy Minimalism." *Mind and Language* 21: 21–30.

Stanley, J. 2000. "Context and Logical Form." *Linguistics and Philosophy* 23: 391–434.

Taylor, K. 2001. "Sex, Breakfast, and Descriptus Interruptus." *Synthese* 128: 45–61.

9 Misplaced Modification and the Illusion of Opacity

Kenneth A. Taylor

Preliminaries

In a number of groundbreaking publications, John Perry has stressed the importance of avoiding a class of fallacies that he and Barwise (1983) formerly called fallacies of misplaced information and that Perry (2001) now prefers to call subject matter fallacies. One commits a subject matter fallacy when one supposes that

the content of a statement or belief is wholly constituted by the conditions its truth puts on the subject matter of the statement or belief; that is, the conditions it puts on the objects the words designate or the ideas are of. (Perry 2001, 50)

Avoiding the bewitching influence of subject matter fallacies, Perry has argued, is one key to seeing that two alleged failures of referentialism—namely, its apparent inability to solve both what Perry calls the coreference problem and what he calls the no-reference problem—are really only apparent. The coreference problem is the problem of explaining how possibly, consistent with referentialism, coreferring expressions may differ in cognitive significance. The no-reference problem is the problem of explaining how possibly, consistent with referentialism, names entirely lacking a referent may be cognitively significant at all.

Naive forms of referentialism maintain that all there is to the meaning, semantic content, or cognitive significance of a name is its property of standing for a certain object. Referentialism of this sort has a prima facie problem on each of these fronts. The naive referentialist would seem to be committed to saying that sentences differing only by coreferring names must have the same cognitive significance and that sentence containing names with no reference must be entirely devoid of cognitive significance. By distinguishing what he calls *referential content* from what he calls *reflexive content*, Perry insists that the referentialist can offer satisfying solutions to both the coreference and no-reference problems. The reflexive content of an utterance is, roughly, a proposition about that very utterance and the conditions under which it is true. The referential content of an utterance, on the other hand, is typically a proposition about some *object*—the object that is the *subject matter* of the relevant utterance. Armed with this distinction, the referentialist can claim that even if there is no difference in referential or subject matter content between two sentences that differ only by the presence of coreferring names, there can still be differences in the reflexive contents of such utterances. And the crucial further claim is that, although *what is said* by an utterance is a matter of the referential or subject matter content of the utterance, the *cognitive significance* of an utterance is a matter of its reflexive content.

Perry makes a compelling enough case for the claim that the cognitive significance of an utterance should be explained by appeal to its reflexive content rather than by appeal to referential or subject matter content.[1] In fact, the case he makes is so compelling that one might have expected him to say something similar about apparent failures of substitutivity within propositional attitude contexts. After all, once one conjoins the thesis of referentialism with the notion of a subject matter fallacy, the pieces for such an approach would seem to be in place already. So, for example, one might begin by conceding that an utterance of

(1)   Jones believes that Hesperus rises in the evening

does not convey the same information, at least not in toto, as an utterance of

(2)   Jones believes that Phosphorus rises in the evening.

However, it is open to the referentialist to maintain that the difference in conveyed information has nothing to do with any difference in subject matter or referential content between the two reports. Instead, the referentialist can say that (1) and (2) attribute to Jones exactly the same relation to exactly the same singular proposition. Consequently, (1) and (2), as uttered at a given moment, should either both be true or both be false. To be sure, denying that (1) and (2) may differ in truth-value involves a bit of bullet biting. But the strategy Perry applies to the coreference problem in general is available here as well. He need only insist that despite their shared referential content, (1) and (2) need not convey the same information in toto. Some of the information conveyed by an utterance of (1) as opposed to (2) might be thought to be a matter of the *reflexive* content of (1) as opposed to (2). And because of the potential differences in reflexive contents of (1) and (2), there can be conversational contexts in which it is appropriate to utter (1) but inappropriate to utter (2), even though (1) is true when and only when (2) is true. The take-home message of such an approach would be to deny that our evident reluctance to utter reports like (1) and (2) interchangeably has anything to do with Fregean reference shifts,

Quinean opacity, or any other such subject-matter-level semantic peculiarities of embedded clauses. Indeed, one might have expected Perry to say that the mistake of many previously extant approaches to attitude statements is to assume that embedding somehow effects, for good or for ill, the subject matter of the relevant sentence. And one might have expected an avowed referentialist, like Perry, to deny this assumption. To think otherwise, one might have expected Perry to say, is to commit a subject matter fallacy.

In point of fact, Perry once did endorse such views. For example, in Barwise and Perry 1983, we find the following:

> But, a Lockean or Fregean might ask, "Does an innocent theory have any right to even *notice* what name is used in an attitude report? It is not the name but the individual referred to which gets into the interpretation of the report, so how can the name be in *any* way relevant, even to the *appropriateness* of the report?" [emphasis added]
>
> This objection contains an instance of *the fallacy of misplaced information* [emphasis added]. The change from TULLY to CICERO makes an enormous difference to the information made available by the report, and an innocent theory need not overlook this if it is combined with a relation theory of meaning. Part of the information you can get is the information that someone is called 'Cicero', and of course you do not get this information if 'Tully' is used instead. This is so even though the interpretation of the report stays the same. (Barwise and Perry 1983, 264)

For reasons he has never spelled out in complete detail, however, Perry rather quickly abandoned this approach to attitude statements and became convinced that reports like (1) and (2) can and do differ not just in total information conveyed, but also in subject matter.

Even in the face of Perry's altered convictions about what attitude reports state, he remained steadfast in both his commitment to referentialism and his commitment to Davidsonian semantic innocence. In collaboration with Mark Crimmins, Perry sought to reconcile the combination of innocence and referentialism with the essentially Fregean intuition about the attitude statements that he had earlier eschewed—namely, that propositional attitude statements that differ only by coreferring proper names may, nonetheless, differ in truth-value. The key to such a reconciliation is the supposed insight that there is more to an attitude statement than meets either the eye or the ear. The propositions expressed by an attitude report typically contains one or more unarticulated constituents, as Perry calls them, where a constituent of a proposition is unarticulated if it does not correspond to any constituent of the sentence (or utterance thereof) that expresses that proposition. The central thought is that, although a device of "direct reference" may retain, when embedded, the semantic role of standing for an object—thus preserving innocence—the embedding of such an expression somehow triggers the introduction into the expressed proposition of an unarticulated constituent. Moreover, at least in some contexts, distinct, but coreferring names may trigger the introduction of distinct unarticulated constituents. That is why, despite referentialism and semantic innocence, substitution of coreferring names is not guaranteed to preserve truth-value.

In this essay, I take issue with the Perry-Crimmins approach to propositional attitude reports and urge upon Perry a return to the wisdom of his earlier days.[2] In particular, I shall argue that the proposition strictly, literally expressed by a propositional attitude statement contains no unarticulated constituents. I doubt, in fact, that *any* proposition literally expressed by *any* sentence or utterance contains unarticulated constituents. However, although I will dwell at some length on some reasons to be skeptical about unarticulated constituents in the general case, my main aim is to show that even the most intuitively compelling motivations for positing unarticulated constituents in the general case have no force when it comes to propositional attitude statements. Propositional attitude statements simply lack the sort of felt semantic incompleteness to which Perry generally appeals in attempting to motivate the positing of unarticulated constituents. Although I reject the mechanism of unarticulated constituents, I shall argue that there is still a way to put notions and ideas at semantic issue in an attitude report. Moreover, just as Perry desires, that way of doing so is consistent with the conjunction of referentialism and semantic innocence. One merely has to deploy what I have elsewhere called a fulsomely *de re* ascription (Taylor 2002, 2003). And I will show that the device of fulsomely *de re* ascriptions actually provides a less problematic way to capture many of the quite correct insights about beliefs and their ascriptions that lie at the core of Perry's approach. In the end, then, my arguments may constitute less of a refutation of Perry's views than a friendly, if rather far-reaching, amendment to those views.

What Is an Unarticulated Constituent?

A constituent of a *proposition* is unarticulated when it is not the semantic value of any *syntactic* constituent of the *sentence* or *utterance* that expresses the relevant proposition. It is important to distinguish Perry's claim from the claim that unarticulated constituents are semantic values of "hidden" or "suppressed" constituents of some sort or other. On such approaches, although some propositional constituents would not be associated with any constituent at the level of surface syntax, they would be associated with syntactic constituents that show up in logical form or in what I have elsewhere called the subsyntactic basement of the lexicon (Taylor 2003). Such approaches amount to the view that there really are no unarticulated constituents, that a principle of full articulation holds at some level or other. Perry quite explicitly rejects any such view. As he puts it:

we do not need to first find an expression, hidden in the "deep structure" or somewhere else and then do the semantics of the statement augmented by the hidden expressions. Things are intelligible just as they appear on the surface, and the explanation we might ordinarily give in non-philosophical moments, that we simply understand what the statement is about, is essentially correct. (Perry 1986, 176)

It is clear what unarticulated constituents are *not*, on Perry's view. It is a little less clear exactly what they are and why he supposes that there are any of them. On this score, it may help to compare and contrast Perry's views with other views in the neighborhood. On the one hand, there is impliciture approach defended by Kent Bach (1994, 2001a, 2001b). Bach endorses what he has called the Syntactic Correlation Constraint on what is said by (an utterance of) a sentence. According to that constraint, what is strictly, literally said (by an utterance) must correspond to "the elements of [the sentence] their order, and their syntactic character." At first glance, that constraint may seem quite alien to the spirit of Perry's approach, since Bach's constraint fairly directly entails that there can be no unarticulated constituents in what is strictly literally expressed by (the utterance of) a sentence. However, the disagreement between Bach and Perry may not be as deep as it first appears. Bach's approach allows that certain sorts of "enriched" propositions—that is, propositions containing constituents not correlated with any either explicit or suppressed syntactic constituent of the relevant sentence—may be "pragmatically imparted," but not strictly expressed by (the uttering of) a sentence. Such propositions are one sort of "impliciture," as Bach calls them. Moreover, since Bach allows that a syntactically complete sentence may, nonetheless, be semantically incomplete, the "first" or even only fully truth-evaluable thing pragmatically imparted by an utterance of such a sentence may be an impliciture. To be sure, Bach insists that an utterance of a syntactically complete, but semantically incomplete sentence will not strictly literally express the relevant impliciture. Implicitures, he maintains, are extrasemantic pragmatic conveyances that go beyond what is strictly literally said in the uttering of a sentence.

The common ground between Bach and Perry is substantial. Both agree, for example, that a syntactically complete sentence, even one with no hidden or suppressed constituents, may be semantically incomplete in the sense that no complete proposition is determined merely by the interaction of its meaning, syntax, and the contextual provision of values for its explicit indexicals and the like. Moreover, both agree that a speaker, in uttering a semantically incomplete sentence, may nonetheless pragmatically impart a complete proposition. The one issue over which Bach and Perry appear to part company concerns what counts as what is strictly literally said by an utterance of a sentence. On Bach's view, the pragmatically imparted implicitures generated by utterances of semantically incomplete sentences are "extrasemantic" and, as such, form no part of what is strictly literally *said* by a speaker in making the relevant utterance. Perry, on the other hand, holds that the proposition pragmatically imparted by the utterance of a syntactically complete, but semantically incomplete sentence may, nonetheless, be what the speaker strictly literally says in making the relevant utterance. On Perry's view, but not on Bach's, pragmatics can play a role in constituting what is strictly literally said by an utterance, even when the relevant sentence is indexical-free. Bach, on the other hand, seems to want to deny any such role to context and pragmatics in constituting what is said by a speaker in uttering such a sentence.

Because Bach and Perry both agree that it will often be the case that nothing propositionally complete is yielded by the interactions of syntax, lexical meaning, semantic composition rules, and the contextual provision of values for explicit indexicals and demonstratives, it is not unreasonable to think that the real dispute between them, to the extent that there is one, boils down to what may amount to a merely verbal dispute over the proper ownership of the phrase 'what is said'. In particular, the question arises whether what is said by an utterance has, in all cases, to be something fully propositional. Bach evidently thinks that what is said need not be fully propositional, whereas Perry seems to think that what is said must always be something propositional. Because Bach allows that what is said by an utterance may fall short of a proposition, he has no particular motive to identify the "first" fully propositional content generated in a certain communicative circumstance with what is strictly literally said by the speaker in making the relevant utterance. By contrast, Perry seems at least tacitly to hold that a speaker hasn't yet said anything fully determinate until a determinate propositional content has been generated. Moreover, he seems willing to count whatever goes into generating an, as it were, "initial" proposition a determinant of what is said.

Now I doubt that there is a single intuitive notion of "what is said" against which to measure competing claims of this sort.[3] In particular, any merely intuitive notion of what is said is likely to be tied up with notions of samesaying and with the direct and indirect ascriptions of content to utterances in delicate ways difficult to untangle. For example, in some contexts, relative to certain communicative purposes, speakers would seem to count as saying the same thing again just in case their utterances express the same proposition. In other contexts, and relative to other communicative purposes, speakers would seem to count as samesayers just in case what one says about object *a* the other says about object *b*. So, for example, if I say of myself that I am hungry and you say of yourself that you are hungry, there would seem to be a sense in which we say the same thing and a sense in which we say different things. This suggests that on one way of assessing "what is said" by a speaker in making an utterance, it may be only complete propositions that count—just as Perry apparently believes—while on other ways of assessing what is said something less than a complete proposition may do—just as Bach apparently believes. But if that is right, then there may be no settling the apparent dispute between Perry and Bach, once and for all, independently of particular discourse contexts. Indeed, it would not be surprising if a fuller, more systematic exploration of the various ways in which we determine either what counts as what is said by a speaker or when two speakers count as having said the same thing again revealed that our practices fail to add up to anything fully precise and determinate. There may, in fact, be no isolable thing in our ascriptive practices against which we can directly test competing claims of the sort defended by Bach and Perry. Choosing between them may be a matter of who has the best, most comprehensive, most explanatory overall theory of meaning and communication. On that score, the jury is still out.[4]

Still, such disagreements as there are between Bach and Perry over what goes into what is said suggests that it may be more natural to assimilate Perry's views to those of radical contextualists like Recanati (2001, 2003b), Sperber and Wilson (1995), Carston (2002), and others. Radical contextualists tend to hold that the gap between semantically incomplete sentence meaning and pragmatically determined utterance content is bridged not by the provision of contextually determined values of either explicit or hidden parameters, but by so-called primary pragmatic processes such as free enrichment. Primary pragmatic processes are supposed to play a role in the very constitution of "what is said." Such processes are supposed to operate antecedently to the determination of a complete propositional content. As such, they are supposed to stand in sharp contrast with so-called secondary pragmatic processes. Secondary pragmatic processes are supposed to operate on an already constituted propositional content to yield something further—a conversational implicature, an indirect speech act—as output. One's first thought may be that primary pragmatic processes function mainly to assign contextually determined values for relatively tractable elements of a sentence such as tense, aspect, indexicals, demonstratives, and quantifiers in some relatively systematic and semantically constrained fashion. But the radical contextualist holds that there are primary pragmatic processes that enrich contents to include propositional constituents not tethered to any particular syntactic constituent of the relevant sentence.

The free enrichment of the radical contextualists bears a striking affinity to what Perry 2001 calls "content-supplemental" uses of context. We use context in a content-supplemental way, according to Perry, when context provides propositional constituents "after we have all the words and their meanings identified" (Perry 2001, 45). That is, context is used in a content-supplemental way when word meaning, sentence meaning and the contextually determined values of explicit indexicals and demonstratives still do not determine a "complete" content, that is, a content for which the question of truth and falsity meaningfully arises. Consider, for example, the supposed unarticulated location constituent introduced in context by one who utters:

(3)   It is raining.

Perry says that:

There is a debate about whether in such cases the 'logical form' of a sentence [like (3)] contains an argument place for the place, or does not. Francois Recanati and Jason Stanley have commandeered the term 'unarticulated constituent' for the purposes of this debate (Stanley 2000). Stanley claims that there is such an argument place in logical form, hence that the constituent is articulated; Recanati claims that there is no such place, hence it is not. I think it is a bad idea to use the term 'unarticulated constituent' for two different questions, and of course I like my use of it better.

On the issue in question, I am inclined to side with Recanati, I think. I conceive of things in the following way. Relations are ways of classifying variations and unknowns across phenomena, against a background of factors that are taken as unchanging or otherwise given. The words for relations will be lexicalized in a way that reflects what is taken as varying and unknown, at least in a typical case, or was at the time the words acquired their grammatical properties. So 'be simultaneous' has two argument places for events, and none for inertial frames. 'Rain' has tense, but no argument place for places. 'Be successful' has tense and an argument place for succeeder, but none for standards of success. We use adverbial and prepositional phrases of various sorts to get at additional relevant factors when we need to. In cases where this happens a lot, it will be easy. There are lots of ways to say where it is raining. In cases in which scientific or philosophical discoveries or insights lead to appreciation of unlexicalized factors, we appeal to phrases like 'relative to'. So events are simultaneous *relative to* inertial frames; the 49ers were unsuccessful last year *relative to* the common standards of success for athletic teams. (Perry 2001, 48)

This passage makes it pretty clear that Perry doesn't endorse anything like what I earlier called a principle of full articulation. But it also raises, I think, at least as many questions as it answers. To consider just one example, notice that Perry seems to grant that we can often, perhaps always, add explicit, syntactically optional modifiers or adjuncts to "complete" what would otherwise be incomplete. This means that *if* the speaker wants to explicitly *say* where it's raining, she can do so in a quite straightforward way. She simply adjoins to the verb a modifier that denotes a place. Given that a speaker may optionally adjoin a modifier and thereby explicitly specify where it is raining, it may seem fair to wonder whether it might not be the case that *whenever* a speaker utters (3) in some context *C without* adding an explicit place modifier, she conversationally implicates, by the very failure to add a modifier where one is called for, some proposition to the effect that it is raining at *m*, where *m* is a place denoted by some conversationally relevant modifier or other. The worry is that if we've already got the mechanism of conversational implicature available to explain how someone who utters (3) without a place modifier can, nonetheless, communicate a proposition to the effect that it is raining at a particular place and time, then its not immediately obvious what talk of unarticulated constituents is supposed to add to this essentially Gricean story.

At times, Perry seems to have in mind a view like Recanati's. Recanati holds that conversational implicatures are generated by so-called secondary, rather than by primary, pragmatic processes. Clear evidence that Perry has something like this distinction in mind can be found in his rejection of Nathan Salmon's view that apparent failures of substitutivity in propositional attitude contexts are pragmatically generated illusions. By contrast, Crimmins and Perry (1989) claim to assign to pragmatics what they call "a more honorable role." Pragmatic features do not, they claim, "create an illusion, but help to identify the reality the report is about." And they go on to suggest that there are at least two different jobs that the pragmatic factors can perform: the job of determining the truth conditional content of an utterance of a semantically incomplete sentence and the job of generating a conversational implicature.[5] As they put it:

Last, the move to unarticulated constituents emphasizes the importance of pragmatic facts about language to the study of what seem like purely semantic issues. In order to express claims, we exploit the tremendous variety of facts, conventions, and circumstances, of which the meanings and referents of our terms form just a part. So it is a mistake to relegate pragmatics to matters of felicity and implicature. In the case of belief reports, it is central to the understanding of truth and content. (Crimmins and Perry 1989, 232)

But it is fair to wonder whether Perry has some principled basis for deciding just when pragmatics is performing one rather than the other of these two distinct jobs. About all that Perry ever says by way of defending the view that unarticulated constituents are not pragmatic externalities, as I call them, but ingredients of literal truth-conditional content is that, absent those very ingredients, the relevant utterance would not say anything strictly truth-evaluable at all. In the case of (3), for example, Perry typically says things like the following:

In this case, I say that the place is an *unarticulated constituent* of the proposition expressed by the utterance. It is a constituent *because, since rain occurs at a time in place, there is no truth evaluable proposition unless a place is supplied* [emphases added]. It is unarticulated, because there is no morpheme that designates that place. (Perry 2001, 45)

But Perry's reasoning here is not altogether compelling. From the fact that rain occurs at a time in a place, it simply doesn't follow that there is no truth-evaluable proposition expressed by an utterance of 'it is raining' unless a place is supplied. To see why, consider other indispensable properties of rainings. Whenever it rains, it rains a certain amount and for a certain duration. But we can express a fully determinate proposition by an utterance of 'it rained' without having to specify how much rain fell or over what span of time the rain fell. It is unclear what explanation there is supposed to be, on Perry's view, of the fact that we must specify *where* it is raining in the case of the present tense 'it is raining' if we are to express a complete proposition, but we need not specify how much it rained or for how long it rained in the case of the past tense 'rained' in order to express a complete proposition.

One might be tempted to appeal here to Perry's distinction between argument *roles* of relations and argument *places* of predicates. He puts the distinction this way:

On the way I like to look at things, relations have *argument roles* or parameters. These are to be distinguished from the *argument places* or *variables* that predicates that express the relations may have. My picture of unarticulated constituents is that there are argument roles that are not represented by explicit argument places. We fill the *argument role* which is filled from context. (Perry 2001, 47)

But our current worry is that not every argument role demands contextual filling in, on pain of incompleteness. Perry might—but this is really just a guess—try to make something like the adjunct/argument distinction, not at the level of predicates but at the level of relations themselves. Armed with that distinction, he could perhaps argue that it's the arguments, and not the mere adjuncts of a relation, that must be supplied if the relation is to obtain at all.

This move seems unpromising. For any relation in *n* arguments with a claim to be the unmodified raining relation, there will be other relations in *m* arguments, for *m* distinct from *n*, that appear to have no lesser claim to being the or at least a raining relation. Consider the following two examples. There is a relation that holds between a place, a time, and a velocity just in case it is raining at the time, at that place, with that velocity. There is another, less "articulated" relation that holds between a time and a place just in case it is raining at that time at that place. Does one or the other of these relations have more of a claim to being *the* raining relation? Is the former relation merely a modification of the latter? If these questions are supposed to be purely metaphysical questions about relations rather than semantic questions about the lexical meaning of verbs, then I confess to not having the foggiest clue how to answer them. I suspect that Perry may not either. The problem is that if Perry is to explain, merely on the basis of the distinction between the argument roles of relations and the argument places of predicates, why this rather than that aspect of a raining requires contextual filling in on pain of semantic incompleteness of an utterance, he owes us answers to such questions.

Perry gets himself tied up in knots, I think, just because he denies that it's a fact about the verb 'to rain' that it demands contextual provision of a place, but not contextual provision of an intensity, amount or duration. That denial is, I think, motivated in part by a mistaken conception of where in syntax the argument places of a predicate may sit. He seems to suppose that where there is no sentence level syntactic constituent and no morpheme, there can be no argument place for a predicate. But there are, I think, reasons to believe that not every to-be-contextually-evaluated argument place is explicitly expressed in the syntax of the sentence. Sometimes, I claim, a to-be contextually evaluated argument place hides in what I call the subsyntactic basement of suppressed verbal argument structure (Taylor 2003). Take Perry's favorite verb as an example. On the view that I favor, the verb 'to rain' has a lexically specified argument place that is theta-marked THEME that takes places as values. My claim is that, in the lexicon, rainings are explicitly marked as a kind of change that places undergo. But from the point of view of sentence-level syntax, such lexically specified parameters are what I call subconstituents rather than constituents. No constituent of the sentence (3) need serve as an argument place for the verb 'rain'. Yet, despite the fact that this lexically specified argument place need not be expressed as a sentence-level constituent, it makes its presence felt by "demanding," on pain of semantic incompleteness, to be assigned a contextually supplied value. Thus, although Perry is right to say that (3) is missing no syntactically mandatory sentential constituent, it is, nonetheless, semantically incomplete. The semantic incompleteness is manifest to us as a felt inability to evaluate the truth-value of an utterance of (3) in the absence of a contextually provided location (or range of locations). This felt need for a contextually provided location has its source in our tacit cognition of the syntactically unexpressed argument place of the verb 'to rain'.

To be sure, there are many changes that places plausibly undergo that are *not* explicitly marked as such in the subsyntactic basement of the lexicon. Consider 'dancing'. It is certainly true that there can't be a dancing that doesn't happen somewhere or other. So one might plausibly conclude that a place undergoes a dancing when a dancer dances in that place. But suppose that, without saying where Laura danced, a speaker utters,

(4)   Laura danced the tango until she could dance no more.

Has the speaker left something out, something required for the semantic completeness of her utterance? The answer seems clearly to be no. One can say something fully determinate, something fully truth evaluable, by uttering (4) even if context provides no place as the place where the dancing took place. Why does (4) differ from (3) in this regard?

The answer, I suggest, depends not on language independent facts about *relations* but on language dependent facts about *verbs*. 'To dance' and 'to rain' relate differently to the places where rainings and dancings happen. Unlike 'to rain', 'to dance' does not stake out any proprietary claim on the place where a dance happens as the theme or undergoer of the dance. The theme or undergoer of a dancing is the dancer herself. The place where a dancing "takes place" is, from the lexical perspective, derivatively and indirectly associated with the dancing as the place where the *dancer* dances. When Laura is dancing in a place, the place does not undergo the dancing; only Laura does. Of course, she undergoes the dancing *in* a place, but that does not make that very place to be the theme of the dancing. Again, I take this to be a fact about the verb 'to dance', not a fact about the dancing as such. It is this fact about the verb, I submit, that explains why, despite the fact that one cannot dance without dancing somewhere or other, a sentence containing 'to dance' can be semantically complete, even if the place where dancing happens is not contextually provided. That a dancing must take place somewhere or other is a (mutually known) metaphysical fact about the universe—a fact that supervenes on the nature of dancing and the structure of space-time. But that metaphysical fact is not explicitly and directly reflected in the lexically specified thematic structure of the verb. To say this is, of course, not to say that the place where a dancer dances is never of conversational relevance to us. It is merely to say that such conversational relevance as the location of a dancing enjoys is not a direct consequence of lexically generated requirements on thematic/semantic completeness. That is why we use *optional adjuncts* rather than fill a *mandatory argument place* to specify where a dancing takes place.

Things are otherwise with the verb 'to rain'. The verb itself—in particular, its lexically specified thematic structure—is the source of the felt need for the contextual provision of a place or range of places where a raining happens. Facts about the lexically specified thematic structure of the verb directly entail that nothing fully propositionally determinate has been expressed by an utterance of a sentence like (3), unless a place is contextually provided. Notice, however, that although 'to rain' does demand, as a consequence of its lexically specified thematic structure, that a place be provided, it permits silence about the duration, intensity, or amount of the relevant raining.

If my hypothesis is correct, it will be an especially interesting and pressing matter to determine just why 'to rain' allows its mandatory theme to go unexpressed by any sentential constituent, even though the verb itself demands the contextual specification of a theme. For many, many verbs their lexically specified argument structured is realized by a suitable array of sentence level constituents. This must surely be the unmarked case. Why should some verbs, like 'to rain,' behave any differently? I admit that a fuller defense of my current hypothesis requires a principled answer to this question or a principled way of separating out the marked cases from the unmarked cases. Indeed, it may be thought that the very fact that we can say things like "it rained in Seattle" but not things like "Seattle rained" shows that the place where it rains is not, after all, lexically marked as the theme of the raining. But this argument turns on a suppressed principle, namely, Thematicity Requires Constituency (TRC). TRC is at least tendentious. I cannot, however, stop to argue it here. I will only say that TRC begs the question against the very possibility of lexically specified but syntactically suppressed thematic structure. To accept the existence of lexically specified but syntactically suppressed thematic structure is to allow that the lexicon may directly prohibit the possibility of "bare rainings." It does so by directly specifying both that a raining can't happen without happening somewhere and, more particularly, by specifying that the place where the raining happens *undergoes* the raining. Moreover, the lexicon may make such direct thematic specifications *without* thereby requiring that the relevant place be the value of an overt and syntactically explicit argument place. Indeed, I suspect, but again will not argue here, that something stronger is true. Not only does 'to rain' not *require* its theme to be expressed as the value of an explicit *argument*. It doesn't even *permit* its theme to be expressed by an explicit argument. It does, however, permit a place to be originally expressed by *an optional adjunct*. I suspect that the prohibition together with the permission explains why 'it is raining *in Seattle*' is okay, but 'Seattle rains' is not okay. It is as if the theme is "locked" in subsyntactic basement and can't be "raised" to the level of a surface theme-argument. Nonetheless, adjuncts can always be freely added. In particular, we can adjoin a phrase that specifies a place. The crucial further open question for this hypothesis is whether the allowable adjunct can be used to encode as such the thematic information that when it rains in a place the place undergoes the relevant raining.[6] I suspect that the answer is no but admit that much further argument is needed to establish the point.

Although I admit that to not having a knock-down argument in favor of the series of hypotheses just outlined, I think they are, nonetheless, plausible enough to suggest that Perry is probably half-right and half-wrong about the relationship between the argument roles of relations and the argument places of predicates. He is certainly correct to highlight the fact that a predicate may represent a more or less fulsome lexicalization of a relation. Likewise, he is certainly correct to highlight the fact that the indefinite modifiability of predicates via adjuncts gives us one way to accommodate the mismatch between the adicity of a relation and the adicity of the lexicalization of that relation. Perry's mistake, I think, is to suppose that the bare mismatch between predicate and relation itself somehow explains why some argument roles *must* be contextually supplied, on pain of semantic incompleteness, while others need not be. My alternative hypothesis is that it is typically the lexical structure of the verb itself, and not language independent facts about the relation or even facts about the mismatch between predicate and relation, that determine what must be supplied and what need not be supplied by context. The verb itself directs its own semantic completion by, as it were, demanding that occupants of certain argument roles, but not others, be supplied in context, sometimes, perhaps, as the value of sentence-level constituents, but not always. Indeed, in the kind of cases that motivate Perry's introduction of unarticulated constituents, we have lexically generated demands on thematic completeness not tied to explicit sentence-level constituents.[7]

Just why a given relation should be lexicalized via a predicate with certain argument places rather than others, whether they are expressed as sentential constituents or locked in the subsyntactic basement, will often be shrouded in the prehistory of our ancient conceptions of the way things are. As Perry himself points out, before the advent of relativity theory, our linguistic progenitors took simultaneity to be absolute rather than relative to an inertial frame. The discovery that our prior lexicalization of a given relation is insufficiently fulsome may sometimes lead to a more fulsome relexicalization of the given relation, but such discoveries need not lead to such relexicalization. The indefinite modifiability of predicts via adjuncts provides us the wherewithal to compensate for the underlexicalization of a given predicate in a highly flexible way that need not require more fulsome lexicalization of argument roles.

One final class of cases bears mentioning before we turn to propositional attitude statements. Sometimes a relation or property so rich in known complexity may be lexicalized by a predicate so thin in thematic structure that sentences containing that predicate may seem to us to express nothing determinate enough to count as complete proposition. Consider, for example, the predicate 'is red'. It would seem to be one thing for a table to be red, another thing for dirt to be red, still another thing for a book to be red. Red dirt is dirt that is *through and through* red. On the other hand, the redness of a table would seem to depend on the redness of its upward facing surface and not to depend at all on whether its legs are red or its downward-facing surface is red. Indeed, even if the downward-facing surface were entirely red that would not, on its own, suffice for the redness of a table. By contrast, the outside surfaces of the two covers of a book have an equal say in determining when a book is red. Neither the inside surfaces of the covers nor the pages themselves have any say in determining the color of the book. A book is a red book just in case *both* covers of the book are sufficiently red. If just one cover of the book is red, then it is a book with one red cover and one nonred cover, but it is not, it would seem, a red book. Moreover, just *how* red the relevant surface or surfaces must be in order that the object itself counts as red is a contextually variable matter. I am currently looking at a box of Sun-Maid raisins. No more than half of the total outer surface of the box is red. A large chunk of the outer surface consists of yellow, white and black lettering announcing the product itself and a picture of the sun maid, in all her rural glory, in front of a bright yellow sun, carrying a basket of green grapes. Although she wears a red bonnet, she is dressed mostly in white. The multicolored surface contains nearly as much red as nonred on it, maybe even slightly more nonred than red. Nonetheless, there are clearly contexts in which it would be true to say that the box is red. For example, suppose there were another box of raisins that was purple where the Sun-Maid box is red. It would surely be correct to call the Sun-Maid box the red box (of the two) and the other box the purple box (of the two). But there are also contexts in which the multicolored Sun-Maid box would be insufficiently red to count as a red box. Imagine, for example, an art project, the first step of which involves painting a box red. It seems pretty intuitively clear that if you painted the box to match the distribution of colors on a Sun-Maid box, you would have failed to follow the instruction given.

The foregoing considerations will suggest to the various advocates of unarticulated constituents, free-enrichment, implicitures and the like that a statement of the form

(5)   *x* is red

is semantically incomplete and must somehow be completed in context. But I want to suggest that instances of (5) aren't so much semantically incomplete but rather what I'll call modificationally neutral. An utterance of (5) makes the weakest possible positive statement about the redness of *x*. It is not, for that reason alone, semantically incomplete, however. It just that there is no modifier *m'ly* such that an utterance of (an instance of scheme) (5) will be strictly literally equivalent to an utterance of an instance of scheme (6):

(6)   *x* is *m'ly* red.

Strictly, when a speaker asserts merely that *x* is red, she has asserted neither that *x* is wholly red nor that *x* is partly red nor that *x* is just a little bit red nor that *x* is mostly red. In fact, she has asserted no modification of redness of *x* at all. She has simply asserted that *x* is red. However, because a modificationally neutral assertion of redness is the weakest possible assertion of redness possible, such an assertion would, in typical conversational contexts, be insufficiently informative. The mutual recognition by speaker and hearer of the uninformativeness of the speaker's modificationally neutral assertion, however, may well generate, by roughly Gricean means of a familiar sort, some more informative, because less modificationally neutral, pragmatic conveyances of one sort or another.

The fact that modificationally neutral assertions are minimally informative, together with the fact that speakers who make such assertions typically convey something more informative and less modificationally neutral, has, I believe, led many to see semantic incompleteness where there is only modificational neutrality. But the inference from neutrality to incompleteness is fallacious. Indeed, in the spirit of Perry himself, it is worth giving a name to the relevant fallacy. I will say that one commits a fallacy of misplaced modification when one infers from the modificational neutrality of a sentence to the semantic incompleteness of that sentence. One who commits a fallacy of misplaced modification is liable to believe that sentences with a perfectly determinate, though modificationally neutral semantic contents stand in need of contextual supplementation, even when there are no explicit or suppressed argument places for context to fix a value for. I suspect that all forms of so-called radical contextualism are founded on fallacies of misplaced modification.

On the other hand, some might claim that apparent semantic incompleteness is *always* really just unappreciated modificational neutrality.[8] The main benefit of this approach is that it enables one to explain contextual variability in what is communicated by utterances of a given sentence, while eschewing not only unarticulated constituents, but also any suppressed parameters of the sort I posit for verbs like 'rain'. If this were right, then one could almost certainly defend an old-fashioned Gricean way of marking the semantics/pragmatics divide, on the grounds of elegance and parsimony. Although I have great affinity both for clean and parsimonious theories and for a roughly Gricean approach to the pragmatics/semantics divide, I suspect that things are much messier than paleo-Griceans envision. Many putatively incomplete sentences are, in fact, not incomplete, but are complete and modificationally neutral. Failure to appreciate that fact can indeed lead one to posit both unarticulated constituents and hidden parameters where there are only Gricean implicatures or the like. But I do not think that all instances of apparent incompleteness can be handled in this way. Indeed the pure neutrality approach, as we might call it, faces pretty much the same obstacle, in the end, that bedevils Perry's unarticulated constituents. It cannot explain why *some* "extra" ingredients seem all but mandatory, whereas others, though they "enrich" the communicated contents remain *optional*. If all is implicature, why *must* information about place be contextually available before an utterance of (3) is conversationally acceptable, while information about duration or intensity need not be? I do not think the pure neutrality approach has much of a chance of answering such questions. But since I am not prepared to argue on this front at length in the current essay, I will for the nonce concede that deciding who has the better of this issue is a delicate matter, requiring detailed, construction-by-construction investigation of the marking of thematic roles.

Unarticulated Constituents and Belief Reports

Like many others, Crimmins and Perry maintain that at least some attitude ascriptions are what we might call notionally sensitive. In particular, they share the widely endorsed intuition that at least some belief ascriptions somehow put at semantic issue via the mechanism of embedding, the notions, conceptions, ideas, or modes of presentation via which the ascribee putatively cognizes the objects and properties her beliefs are of or about. Strikingly, however, Perry and Crimmins swim against a major current in much earlier thinking about belief reports by maintaining that nothing in either the logical syntax of the sentences with which we typically make belief ascriptions nor in the lexical semantics of the verb 'believes' serves to explain why notions and their ilk should be at semantic issue in any belief reports at all. In particular, they posit no Quinean lexical ambiguity for 'believes,' no Russellian scope ambiguity, no Fregean reference shifts. In fact, they take pains to state that although a *speaker* typically refers to a notion in making a belief ascription, the speaker's *words* typically do not refer to any notion.

  The thought, of course, is that the notions referred to by the speaker are unarticulated constituents of the proposition the speaker expresses in uttering the relevant sentence. As Crimmins and Perry put it:

in belief reports an *n*-ary relation is reported with an *n*-minus-one place predicate. On our account, the complex relation invoked in belief reports is a four-place relation: an agent believes a proposition at a time relative to a sequence of notions. But there is no argument place in the 'believes' predicate for the sequence of notions. The notions are unarticulated constituents of the content of that report. (Crimmins and Perry 1989, 220)

But certain urgent questions go entirely unasked by Crimmins and Perry. Just why should the utterance of a belief report invoke an unarticulated constituent at all? What is the utterance of a verb with three argument places *doing* expressing a relation in four argument roles? And just why does *that particular* additional argument role get

introduced into the content of the relevant assertion? It is hard to know how Crimmins and Perry would answer these questions.

It will help to contrast belief reports with Perry's favored examples of unarticulated constituents. In the standard case, the context must provide a value for an unlexicalized argument role, supposedly, because even after the values of the explicitly lexicalized argument roles are supplied, we still do not have anything semantically complete
enough to express a determinate proposition. That is, Perry maintains that, except that
a value for the absent argument role is added to the content of an utterance of the relevant sentence, the utterance would not yet express anything for which the question
of truth or falsity can even arise. The unlexicalized argument role must be filled if the
speaker is to say anything truth evaluable at all. So, for example, if a speaker were simply to utter 'it is raining' without either referring to a particular location or quantifying
over some range of locations, she would not yet have said anything that could be
evaluated for its truth or falsity. (And recall, this is not supposed to be a language dependent fact about *verbs* but a language independent fact about relations.)

But the same story does not explain why an unarticulated constituent is demanded
in the case of a belief report. Filling what Crimmins and Perry grant are the explicit
argument places of the verb 'believes' with a determinate time, agent and proposition
already yields, by their own admission, a fully determinate and truth evaluable
content—namely, the proposition to the effect that the agent believes the relevant
proposition at the relevant time. This content can be evaluated as either true or false,
period, without the need to provide some additional argument role for propositional
attitude statements, since, apparently, the *articulated* constituents relate a believer, a
time, and a proposition. The problem, on Perry and Crimmins view, is not that filling
in values for all the explicit argument places still leaves us with no complete content.
The problem from their perspective is that we don't yet have the *right* content. But
there is simply no obvious reason why, given that some such fully truth-evaluable content is already directly expressed once a time, agent, and proposition are specified,
there should be any remaining demand for the provision of an additional, unarticulated constituent. It is especially puzzling why such an additional constituent would
make its way into *what is strictly literally said* by the speaker in making the relevant
utterance rather than counting as some *extrasemantic pragmatic externality* of that
utterance.

I do not mean to deny that, on an occasion, an ascriber may mean to communicate
more by the utterance of an attitude report than the proposition that the ascribee
believes a certain proposition at a certain time. She may intend, for example, to convey
something about the evidence on the basis of which the ascribee holds the relevant be-

lief. She may intend to communicate something about the degree of conviction with which the ascribee holds the belief. She may even intend to communicate something about the notions or representations via which the ascribee holds the relevant beliefs. It is, of course, perfectly possible for the ascriber to state such further modifications of the ascribed belief by deploying explicit modifiers. We may say, for example, she believes such and such a proposition at such and such a time *with such and such degree of conviction* or *on the basis of such and such evidence*. Nor is it hard to imagine conversational contexts in which an ascriber merely implicates, in a roughly Gricean way, perhaps, without directly stating, that some such modification of the relevant belief attains. One can even imagine, as Perry and Barwise evidently did at one time, that the mere choice of words used in ascribing the relevant belief itself generates, in certain conversational settings, "external" implications to the effect that a certain modification of the ascribed belief obtains. But none of these possibilities supports the idea that unarticulated constituents are, as it were, agglomerated onto an already complete propositional content.

To be sure, it is open to Crimmins and Perry to argue that the notions via which an agent believes a given proposition at a given time are not merely so many modifications of an ascribed belief among others. Notions, they might say, are intrinsically privileged in such a way that absent either reference to particular notions or the provision of some constraint on notions, nothing truth evaluable is expressed via the utterance of a propositional attitude sentence. Because Crimmins and Perry think that beliefs are literally built out of notions and ideas, motivations for some such privileging of notions may not be all that far to seek within their framework. The real problem, however, for any such attempt to motivate the indispensability of notions to what is said by a belief ascription is that it puts the metaphysical cart before the semantic horse. It may well be true that beliefs are literally built out of notions and ideas, but it simply doesn't follow from that fact alone that a speaker hasn't yet said anything truth evaluable by an utterance of a belief ascription unless she refers to or 'constrains' the notions that figure as constituents of the ascribed belief. It may also be true, for example, that to have a(n) (explicit) belief is to token a Fodorian sentence in mentalese, but it certainly wouldn't follow from that fact about the nature of beliefs that we haven't said anything truth evaluable in making a belief ascription if we haven't yet specified what sentence or type of sentence the ascribee putatively tokens in a particular episode of believing.

Once again, there seems to be no grounds for the claim that belief report sentences are semantically incomplete and in need of contextual supplementation. We appear to be left with the claim that absent contextual supplementation, such sentences will not express the right sort of intuitively felt semantic content. Now, the foregoing considerations are not yet meant to show that belief reports do not invoke unarticulated constituents. They are meant to suggest that Crimmins and Perry have given no reason why utterance of a sentence whose main verb has three argument places should have, as part of its strict literal content, a relation in four argument roles. In place of a tractable explanatory mechanism, we are left with a sort of pragmatic alchemy whose workings are, I submit, quite mysterious.

Although they never take the question up in a direct and systematic way, Crimmins and Perry are not entirely unaware of the need for some explanation of just why and how unarticulated constituents are "called for" by some sentences and not others. Nevertheless, what they have to say in this regard is insufficient to draw any principled distinction between the garden variety pragmatic externalities of an utterance, externalities that are not part of the strict literal content of the utterance, from the so-called unarticulated constituents of the relevant utterance. We find such comments as the following, for example:

> Unarticulated constituency is one example of the incrementality of language. In the circumstances of an utterance, there always is a great deal of common knowledge and mutual explanation that can and must be exploited if communication is to take place. It is the function of the expression uttered to provide just that last bit of information needed by the hearer to ascertain the intended claim, exploiting this rich background. What is obvious in context we do not belabor in syntax—we do not elaborate it.
>
> This is by no means to transgress the intuition of the systematicity of language, which is commonly reflected in principles of compositionality. Since we finite creatures are able to make and understand a potential infinity of claims, there must be systematic features of our statements that explain our infinite abilities in something like a combinatorial fashion—in terms or our more finite abilities to understand the contributions of specific features of statements toward the claims made. But there is no reason to assume that these features of statements must all involve syntactic expressions. It is just as systematic for a form of speech, like a belief report or a report of rain, to *call for* a propositional constituent that meets, say, certain conditions of relevance and salience, as it is for a form of speech to have a syntactic expression *stand for* a propositional constituent. (Crimmins and Perry 1989, 221)

It is no doubt true that *communication* presupposes that a shared background of "common knowledge and mutual expectation" is in place. Indeed, I can think of no theorist who would deny this claim. But that universally acknowledged fact does not entail that belief report sentences "call for" the introduction of unarticulated constituents. *All* pragmatically generated content, of any sort whatsoever, presupposes such a background. Although knowing how to fruitfully exploit that background is at the very foundation of all communicative competence, granting that much takes us not one step further toward a justification for the appeal to the quite specific pragmatically generated content that Perry countenances under the rubric of unarticulated constituents.

It may be that Perry originally had in mind more modest explanatory goals than the ones to which I have been holding him here. The goal may have been to explain neither *how* unarticulated constituents get introduced into a content nor how to explain what about attitude sentences and their constituents *calls for* the contextual provision of occupiers of additional argument roles. Rather, the aim may have been simply to show that the contents of belief reports do contain such constituents—however they are introduced and for whatever reason they are demanded. Indeed, what one in fact finds when one looks for explicit arguments on behalf of unarticulated constituents in Crimmins and Perry (1989) are not so much direct arguments for the semantic incompleteness of belief report sentences, but more indirect arguments based on the widely shared intuition that belief ascriptions that differ only by coreferring names may, nonetheless, differ in truth-value. The central claim is that the mechanism of unarticulated constituents enables us to preserve this intuition by explaining how possibly the failure of substitutivity can be reconciled with both direct reference and semantic innocence. We are *never* offered an explanation of just what about a belief sentence either permits or demands the addition to the content of an utterance of that sentence an argument role attached to none of its constituents. And it may just be that the reader was supposed to be content with the thought that explanatory utility of the very idea of an unarticulated constituent is adequately demonstrated by cases of another kind.

On the Modificational Neutrality of Belief Reports

I have nothing principled to say against arguments designed to show how possibly certain apparently conflicting antecedent intuitions can be reconciled. I'm prepared to admit that *if* there were such things as unarticulated constituents in the contents of belief reports that might indeed enable us to reconcile certain apparently competing intuitions, just as Crimmins and Perry allege. But I shall spend the remainder of this section arguing that the standard puzzle cases about belief have been widely misdiagnosed. Almost all currently extant approaches to attitude statements, Crimmins and Perry's included, take the standard puzzle cases to show that in making a belief ascription an ascriber undertakes a commitment to specify the contents of the ascribee's head in what might be called a notionally sensitive, ascribee-centered way. The ascriber is supposed to undertake a commitment to specify the modes of presentation, concepts or notions under which the ascribee cognizes the objects (and properties) that her beliefs are about. Such an ascription will be true, the widely shared intuition goes, just in case the ascriber specifies either directly or indirectly both *what* the ascribee believes and *how* she believes it. This widely shared supposition has been the basis of a furious search for the mechanism, whatever it is, that explains just *how* an ascriber accomplishes the feat of putting the ascribee's notions at semantic issue in a belief ascription. I shall argue, however, that the search is misguided from the start. Belief ascriptions typically specify the ascribee's predicative commitments, as I call them, and nothing more. In ascribing a belief to another we specify what object or domain of objects the relevant belief is about and what properties the believer takes the relevant objects to have. We typically do not—at least not by the mere mechanism of embedding—either semantically specify or pragmatically implicate the modes of presentations, notions, or conceptions via which the ascribee cognizes the objects and properties relative to which she undertakes the ascribed predicative commitments.

My claim is not that it is impossible to put the ascribee's notions and ideas at semantic issue in a belief report. It is simply that embedding clauses do not do that sort of work. The way to put notions and ideas at semantic issue is via what I have elsewhere called a fulsomely *de re* ascription (Taylor 2002). In fulsomely *de re* ascriptions, the ascriber specifies what objects the ascribee putatively thinks about, what properties and relations the ascribee putatively takes those objects to have, and, at least indirectly, something about the notions or modes of presentation via which those objects are putatively thought about. Such ascriptions characterize the "how" of a belief, not via an embedded clause, but via unembedded modifying clauses. Fulsomely *de re* ascriptions take many forms. The following is one such form:

(7)   *a* believes of $n_1 \ldots n_n$, of which/whom he thinks ϕ_1'ly $\ldots \phi_n$'ly that $\psi(x_1 \ldots x_n)$.

where each n_j is a name and each ϕ_j (partially) characterizes, either directly or indirectly, some conception or notion of an object, and each x_j is anaphorically linked to n_j. Standard issue *de re* ascriptions of the sort more widely studied by philosophers are what I call truncated *de re* ascriptions. We get fulsomely de ascriptions from truncated *de re* ascriptions by adding certain modifying clauses. These modifying clauses, however, are adjuncts rather than arguments. So the claim is not that the sentences with which we make garden variety truncated *de re* ascriptions are in any way syntactically or semantically incomplete or that such sentences are in some way syntactically or semantically ambiguous. Such sentences are merely modificationally neutral in the sense outlined earlier on.[9]

My argument begins with an intuition pump of sorts. Consider Smith, a virulent racist, who refers in his thought and talk to people of African descent via a certain infamous derogatory term that begins with the letter *n*. I do not share Smith's derogatory attitudes. I assiduously avoid using the relevant term in my own thought and talk. Still, I may have occasion to ascribe to Smith an attitude of derogation toward people of African descent. I want, however, to do so without myself either derogating or endorsing Smith's derogation of people of African descent. If embedding did function to put the notions and conceptions of the ascribee at semantic issue, then it should be possible, it would seem, merely by embedding the offending phrase to say something about Smith's attitude toward people of African descent. And it should be possible to do so without my thereby representing myself as endorsing or adopting the ascribed attitude. It is, after all, the ascribee's notions, and not the ascriber's, that are supposed to be put at semantic issue via embedding.

This prediction, however, is not borne out by the facts. Even an embedded use of the "n-word," as in (8) below, would express only the ascriber's own derogation and does nothing to represent the ascribee as holding a derogatory attitude toward people of African descent:

(8)   Smith believes that niggers are such and such.

Notice that a standard (truncated) *de re* ascription like (9) below correctly reports certain aspects of Smith's belief—his predicative commitments—and that it does so without implying any derogation on the ascriber's part. That is, (9) correctly specifies both the objects Smith's belief is about and the properties Smith believes those objects to have:

(9)   Smith believes of people of African descent that they are such and such.

But (9) no more represents Smith as derogating people of African descent than (8) does. Sentence (9) is, in fact, explicitly silent on the character of Smith's notions of black people. In fact, (8) and (9) would appear to represent *Smith's* attitude toward people of African descent in pretty much the same way. What (8) does do that (9) does not is to express certain evaluative commitments on the ascriber's part. But I shall not argue that point at present. It is enough for our current purposes to note that the availability of (9) suggests the hypothesis that, in general, an ascriber can avoid taking on certain evaluative commitments expressed by the ascribee in her use of a derogatory or other expressive-evaluative term by going *de re* and thereby going silent on the character of the ascribee's notions. Correlatively, an ascriber can make it explicit that an evaluative commitment is her own by simultaneously going silent on the ascribee's notions, while using an expressive-evaluative to express her own evaluative attitudes. Imagine that Smith, the racist, wants to express his astonishment that Jones does not believe that black people, toward whom Smith but not Jones holds derogatory and racist attitudes, do not deserve to be rounded up and imprisoned. He might do so via a suitably stressed utterance of the following:

(10)   Jones does not believe that niggers deserve to be rounded up and imprisoned.

If Smith wants to be fastidiously explicit about which evaluations are whose, he might utter the following instead:

(11)   Jones does not believe of niggers that they deserve to be rounded up and
       imprisoned.

Sentence (11) makes it quite explicit that it is Smith, and not Jones, whose notion of black people includes negative and racist evaluations; (11) is, in fact, silent on the character of Jones's notion of black people.

It turns out that there is, after all, a way for an ascriber to have her cake and eat it too, by simultaneously representing the derogatory character of Smith's attitude and inoculating herself from expressing any such attitude. She merely needs to deploy a fulsomely *de re* ascription in the manner of (12) or (13):

(12)   Smith believes of people of African descent, to whom he refers via the infamous
       n-word, that they are such and such.

(13)   Smith believes of people of African descent, of whom he thinks under the title
       'nigger', that they are such and such.

The additional modifying clauses here indirectly characterize Smith's way of thinking about people of African descent. The offending word itself is not used, though it may be either described or mentioned. In so describing Smith's mode of derogation, as we might call it, the ascriber thus does not deploy the offending mode in either her own talk or her own thought about people of African descent.

It might be thought that too much is made here of the peculiar behavior of derogatory terms and other expressive-evaluatives. We already know that there are certain very special expressions—indexicals and demonstratives being the paradigm case—that resist embedding. And it may be tempting to think that derogatory and other evaluative expressions are just a different sort of special case and that nothing of general significance for embedding can be gleaned from such examples. I have argued against this view in detail elsewhere (Taylor 2002, 2003). I have argued that, even in the general case, embedding an expression (in subject place) does not free one from expressing various sorts of commitments that one otherwise would express using the same expression in unembedded contexts.[10] For example, even the existential commitments that one would normally express by the use of a definite description typically cannot be escaped merely through the mechanism of embedding.

Although I lack the space to elaborate and defend this last claim in detail, a brief discussion should suffice to convey a rough sense of my arguments. Suppose that Smith,
Jones, and Black are working a party as bartenders. They are instructed not to serve
anyone who has had too much to drink. There is a man in the corner, drinking martinis, who has clearly had a great deal to drink. Jones, however, takes the man to be a
woman and she takes him to be drinking gimlets rather than martinis. With evident
intent of alerting Smith to the man's state, Jones utters,

(14)   The woman in the corner drinking gimlets has had too much to drink.

Smith recognizes whom Jones has in mind, but she does not realize that Jones has
made a mistake until she is about to report Jones's belief to Black. Because Jones thinks
of the man in the corner drinking martinis under the description 'the woman in the
corner drinking gimlets', this description may be reasonably thought to partially characterize Jones's notions of the person in the corner. If embedding functioned to put
the ascribee's notions at semantic issue, that would seem to suggest that Smith should
be able to put Jones's notions of the man in the corner at semantic issue by embedding
the description 'the woman in the corner drinking gimlets'. But it is easy to see that
this prediction is not borne out by the facts.

Suppose that it is common ground between Smith and Black that there is no woman
in the corner drinking gimlets. Now consider

(15)   Jones believes that the woman in the corner drinking gimlets has had too much
       to drink.

as potentially uttered by Smith to Black. Smith would naturally be taken not merely to
ascribe to Jones a commitment to the existence of a gimlet-drinking woman in the
corner but also thereby to impute that she herself accepts or endorses the ascribed
commitment. Because the existential commitment that she would thereby impute to
herself conflicts with what is already common ground between Smith and Black, uttering (15) is a conversationally inappropriate way for Smith to report Jones's belief to
Black.

It would be wrong to conclude that by uttering (15) in the setting just imagined,
Smith imputes to Jones a commitment to the existence of a gimlet-drinking woman.
Varying the case ever so slightly shows decisively that Smith has imputed no such
commitment to Jones at all. Imagine a scenario in which the person Jones has in
mind and to whom she intends to refer via the description 'the woman in the corner
drinking gimlets' is, in fact, a woman drinking gimlets. Now suppose that although it is
mutually manifest to Smith and Black who Jones has in mind, they, nonetheless, mistakenly take Jones to be mistaken. Though Smith and Black mutually recognize that

Jones takes the person in the corner to be a gimlet-drinking woman, they take that person to be a martini-drinking man. Jones is right; they are wrong; but they are unaware of these facts. Now suppose that Jones utters (14), intending to alert Smith to the drunken reveler. From our better-informed perspective, it seems evident that Smith would speak truly if she were to report Jones's belief to Black via an utterance of (15). That, in fact, is just how *we*, who are in the know, would report Jones's belief. Sentence (15) is, however, unavailable to Smith as way of reporting Jones's belief. An utterance of (15) by Smith would quite clearly impute to *Smith* an existential commitment that she manifestly does not have. The preferred way for Smith to report to Black what Jones believes in the imagined setting is the false (16) rather than the true (15):

(16)   Jones believes that the man in the corner drinking martinis has had too much to drink.

By Smith's use of the description 'the man in the corner drinking martinis' in the utterance of (16), she commits herself to the existence of a martini-drinking man. She does not thereby ascribe such a commitment to Jones. Indeed, it is common ground between Smith and Black in the imagined setting that Jones mistakenly takes the relevant person not to be a martini-drinking man but a gimlet-drinking woman. We can even stipulate that it is part of the common ground that Jones takes there to be no martini-drinking man in the room at all. Now Smith does, to be sure, ascribe to Jones a predicative commitment to the effect that a certain person—the person whom Smith and Black take to be a martini-drinking man—has had too much to drink. But in so ascribing, Smith appears neither to refer to nor to specify nor to describe Jones's notions of the relevant person.

By parity of reasoning, it follows that even where there is doxastic agreement between ascriber and ascribee, the ascribee's notions of those objects are often simply not at semantic issue and cannot be put at semantic issue merely by the mechanism of embedding. When Smith utters (15) as a way of reporting Jones's belief to Black in a context in which Smith, Black, and Jones one and all take the martini-drinking man to be a gimlet-drinking woman, Smith expresses her own commitment to the existence of a gimlet-drinking woman, but she does not thereby succeed in ascribing such a commitment to Jones by that utterance. If the proposition that Jones is committed to the existence of a gimlet-drinking woman were not already part of the common ground in the imagined context of doxastic agreement, the mere utterance of (15) by Smith would not increment the common ground to include such a proposition. What Smith ascribes *to Jones* by an utterance of (15) is a predicative commitment to the effect that a certain person has had too much to drink. She does not thereby purport to specify how Jones thinks of the relevant person. By using the embedded description, Smith presents only *herself* to Black as cognizing the relevant object under the description 'the woman in the corner drinking gimlets.' In addition, she offers up that description to Black as a vehicle for Black and Smith to achieve mutual recognition of the object that Jones's belief is about. But she does not thereby use the embedded description either to represent, indirectly specify, or refer to Jones's notion of the relevant person. It is not Jones's notions that are at semantic issue in Smith's ascription but only Jones's predicative commitments.

Notice, however, that the machinery of fulsomely *de re* ascriptions enables us to ascribe existential commitments across such divides. Suppose, as above, that Smith intends to report Jones's belief about the martini-drinking man in the corner to Black. Suppose that Smith intends via her report to, as it were, arm Black for interaction with Jones by making it explicit just how Jones thinks of the martini-drinking man. It is, of course, commonly thought that it is via so-called *de dicto* ascriptions that we arm one another for interaction with the ascribee. But recall that Jones mistakenly takes the martini-drinking man to be a gimlet-drinking woman. Smith is aware that Jones is confused, but Black is not aware of Jones's confusion. If Smith were to report Jones belief by an utterance of (16), she would correctly and successfully ascribe to Jones a commitment to the effect that a certain person has had too much to drink, but her utterance would convey no information about Jones's confused notions of the relevant person. She would not thereby arm Black for interacting with Jones. Smith needs a way both to ascribe the commitment just mentioned and to convey information about Jones's confused notions, without thereby committing herself to Jones's confusions. She can do no better, I suggest, than to go fulsomely *de re*. She might, for example, utter something like the following:

(17)   Jones believes of the martini-drinking man in the corner, whom she mistakes for a gimlet-drinking woman, that he has had too much to drink.

In uttering (17), Smith undertakes, and manifestly so, a commitment of her own to the existence of a martini-drinking man; she ascribes to Jones a commitment to the existence of a gimlet-drinking woman, without herself thereby undertaking any such commitment; and she ascribes to Jones, also without herself undertaking, a predicative commitment to the effect that a certain person has had too much to drink. In so doing, Smith not only informs Black of Jones's doxastic commitments, but she does so in a manner that arms Black for interaction with Jones by explicitly conveying information about Jones's notions of doxastically relevant objects.

Now consider some belief reports involving embedded names. Suppose that Jones is an inept astronomer who proudly fancies herself the first to realize that Mars and

Venus are one and the same planet. Imagine that before her spurious "discovery" Jones is as linguistically competent as the rest of us. Like the rest of us, she uses 'Venus' to refer to Venus and 'Mars' to refer to Mars. Although her spurious discovery no doubt rationally commits her to some serious reconfiguration of her notions of Mars and Venus, it is not obvious that such reconfigurations would ipso facto cause her no longer to be numbered among the linguistically competent. Indeed, linguistically and cognitively speaking, Jones would appear to be no worse off than someone who believes that Hesperus is distinct from Phosphorous. If she is not, then when she makes such bizarre postdiscovery statements as

(18)   Mars is, after all, just Venus again

she is certainly speaking falsely, but she is still speaking, and presumably intends to be speaking, English.

Now suppose that Brown recognizes the nature of Jones's confusion and wants to inform Black of something about Jones's beliefs in a situation in which it is common ground between Black and Brown that Mars and Venus are distinct. For example, imagine that Jones has uttered the following:

(19)   I see that Venus is visible tonight

with evident intent of referring to the currently visible Venus rather than to the not yet visible Mars. It seems intuitively right to say that Jones has expressed a belief to the effect that Venus is currently visible. After all, she sees Venus in the evening sky and correctly uses the name 'Venus' to refer to the very object that she sees. At the same time, since Jones takes that very object to be Mars, it also seems right to say that Jones believes that Mars is visible in the evening sky. After all, Jones would accept both the sentence 'Venus is visible tonight' and the sentence 'Mars is visible tonight'. One's first thought might be to represent what Jones believes by (20):

(20)   Jones believes that Venus is visible and that Mars is visible.

But (20) is entirely silent about the character of Jones's confused notions of Mars and Venus. It does not depict, for example, the fact that by Jones's notional lights Mars and Venus are one and the same planet. To see this, just imagine that Brown does, but Black does not know that Jones takes Mars to be identical to Venus. An utterance of (20) would put Black in no position to infer that Jones takes Mars and Venus to be identical.

Once again, the fulsomely *de re* provides a way of depicting the character of Jones's confused notions of Mars and Venus, and a way of doing so without Brown having to own the relevant confusion as her own, as in:

(21)   Jones believes of Venus, which she takes to be identical with Mars, that it is visible tonight.

(22)   Jones believes of Mars, which she takes to be identical with Venus, that it is visible tonight.

One can easily imagine discourse situations in which one might prefer one of (21) or (22) over the other, with the choice being driven largely by pragmatic considerations relating to what is foreground or background in the relevant discourse situation.

Consider briefly a slightly different scenario. Suppose that Jones is even more clueless about the planets—Mars in particular. Sometimes when she sees it, she takes it to be Venus. Other times, she takes it to be Jupiter. Now suppose that on appropriate occasions she utters (23) and then (24), each with the evident intent of referring to Mars:

(23)   My how lovely Venus looks this evening.

(24)   My how lovely Jupiter looks this evening.

How should we report the belief expressed by Jones? Our procedures so far may suggest (25) and (26) below:

(25)   Jones believes of Mars, which she takes to be Venus, that it looks lovely this evening.

(26)   Jones believes of Mars, which she takes to be Jupiter, that it looks lovely this evening.

And these do get at something about the truth about Jones's state of mind. But because Jones sometimes takes Mars to be Venus and sometimes takes it to be Jupiter, one may want to know more. One may want to know whether, as it were, in this very episode of believing, Jones is taking Mars to be Venus or taking it to be Jupiter. This we can capture by expanding our ascriptions as follows:

(27)   Jones believes of Mars, which, in this very episode of believing, she takes to be Venus, that it looks lovely this evening.

(28)   Jones believes of Mars, which in this very episode of believing, she takes to be Jupiter, that it looks lovely this evening.

The Illusion of Opacity

I want to close this essay by suggesting that it is an illusion, brought on by a failure to perceive their modificational neutrality, that belief contexts block the free substitution of coreferring singular terms. I have argued at length for this sort of conclusion elsewhere—though without explicit appeal to the notion of modificational neutrality (Taylor 2002, 2003). I will not rehearse those arguments here, except to note that whether coreferring names are intersubstitutable in a given discourse contexts depends entirely on what dialectical constraints are operative between the discourse participants in the relevant contexts. In particular, I have argued elsewhere that there is a default, but overrideable coreference constraint on propositional attitude ascriptions. The default coreference constraint is the following:

Default Coreference Constraint

If a sentence of the form:

A believes that ... *n* ...

is dialectically permissible for a player *p* in a dialectical setting *D* at *t* and it is common ground between *p* and her interlocutors that *m* is in the coreference set of *n* for *A* at *t*, then a sentence of the form

A believes that ... *m* ...

is dialectically permissible for *p* in *D* at *t*,

where *m* is in the coreference set of *n* for *A* at *t* just in case *A* accepts the identity sentence *m* = *n* at *t* and acceptance is a certain belief-like attitude held toward *sentences* rather than toward propositions. The default coreference constraint says that belief ascriptions are defeasibly dialectically sensitive to facts about *ascribee* coreference sets, rather than to facts about either ascriber coreference sets or to facts about real world coreference. When attitude ascriptions are sensitive to facts about ascribee coreference sets, such ascriptions exhibit many of the hallmarks commonly associated with so-called *de dicto* ascriptions. But two points bear brief emphasis. First, being dialectically sensitive to facts about ascribee coreference sets is not the same as putting notions, ideas, or conceptions at semantic issue. Even when we try to make our ascriptions sensitive to facts about ascribee coreference sets, we still need not refer, specify, or quantify over the notions or ideas via which the ascribee cognizes the objects that are implicated in her beliefs. Second, there are many dialectical settings in which the default sensitivity of ascriptions to facts about ascribee coreference sets is overridden in favor of sensitivity to facts about the coreference sets that are elements of the common ground between speaker and hearer. In such dialectical settings, attitude ascriptions will exhibit many of the hallmarks of what are commonly called *de re* ascriptions. In particular, names that are known or believed by speaker and hearer to corefer will be freely interchangeable even if there are not known or believed to be coreferring by the ascribee. But the deeper point is that the substitutivity or lack thereof of coreferring names in attitude contexts really does nothing to show that names have any kind of different or additional semantic function within the context of belief ascriptions. Whether names are intersubstitutable in a given discourse contexts depends entirely on the dialectical standards operative in that particular context, or so I have argued at length elsewhere (Taylor 2002).

Finally, I will point out that the device of fulsomely *de re* ascriptions, together with the notion of modificational neutrality, provide a satisfying explanation of the case of Miles Hendon. Recall that Perry and Crimmins want to say that, although (29) below is false, (30) below is true, even though one and the same boy is referred to by 'he' and 'Edward Tudor'.

(29)   Miles Hendon believed that he was of royal blood.

(30)   Miles Hendon believed that Edward Tudor was of royal blood.

According to my own analysis, (29) and (30) have the same modificationally neutral content. Consequently, they are either both true or both false. Of course, whether (29) and (30) are interchangeable in a given discourse context depends on what coreference set is governing in the relevant context. In discourse contexts in which facts about ascribee coreference sets govern dialectical permissibility, they need not be interchangeable. In contexts in which facts about common ground coreference sets govern, they may be.

But we need not stop with the modificationally neutral characterizations offered of Miles's beliefs expressed by (29) and (30). Rather, (31) and (32) below capture further facts about Miles's beliefs, facts that differentiate between two different sorts of episodes of believing the singular proposition that Edward Tudor was of royal blood:

(31)   Miles Hendron believed of Edward Tudor, who, in this very episode of believing (demonstrating the belief he has when Edward is present and dressed as a pauper) he took to be a pauper, that he was of royal blood.

(32)   Miles Hendron believed of Edward Tudor, who, in this very episode of believing (demonstrating an episode of believing involving the deployment of 'Edward Tudor' in a thought or talk episode) he took to be the Prince of Wales, that he was of royal blood.

Clearly an utterance of (31) and an utterance of (32) can differ in truth-value, even though they may predicate belief in one and the same singular proposition. It may be, for example, that no episode of believing in which Miles takes Edward to be a pauper is also an episode of believing in which she takes Edward to be of royal blood—in which case (31) is false. Nonetheless but some or every episode of believing in which he deploys the name 'Edward Tudor' to refer to Edward is an episode in which he takes Edward to be the Prince of Wales—in which case (32) is true.

Now consider the claim expressed by

(33)   Miles Hendron did not believe that he was of royal blood

where (33) is said with reference to an episode of believing in which Miles takes Edward to be a pauper distinct from Edward. Perry and Crimmins seem to think that in such a scenario (33) expresses something unambiguously true. But this, I think, is a mistake. Miles has two Edward-related episodes of believing. In one such episode, he believes that he (Edward) is of royal blood. In the other, he believes that he (Edward) is not of royal blood. These two belief episodes are jointly metaphysically incoherent since they cannot be made jointly true in any metaphysically possible world. There is, however, an unambiguous truth about Miles's belief. And it is the sort of truth that Perry and Crimmins wrongly suppose that (33) unambiguously expresses. To state that truth explicitly, we need to resort to explicit quantification over belief episodes as in:

(34)   For no belief episode in which Miles takes Edward to be a pauper does Miles
        also predicate being of royal blood of Edward.

There may indeed be contexts in which a speaker who utters (33) is really trying to convey what is strictly, literally and unambiguously expressed by (34). Speakers often convey, and intend to convey, something nonliteral by literally stating something else. That, I suggest, is more likely to be what is happening in the case imagined by Perry and Crimmins. If so, there is no basis for concluding that an utterance of (33) in the relevant context strictly literally expresses, via the pragmatic alchemy of unarticulated constituents, what (34) expresses in a more fully articulated way.

To be sure, it follows on my account that strictly speaking (33) says something quite strong (and potentially informative). It denies that even the weakest, most modificationally neutral possible belief report about Edward and his bloodline is true of Hendon. Speakers will seldom be in possession of evidence to support any claim so strong. Indeed, one could possess evidence to that effect only if one were in a position to know that there is *no* notion of Edward deployed in *any* episode of believing by Hendon such that in that very episode of believing Hendon predicates being of royal blood of Edward. We are seldom in a position to know such things about even our own belief episodes—let alone the belief episodes of another. We are typically presented with *particular* episodes of believing, with a given content, without knowing how things are by the ascribee's other episodes of believing that involve the affirmation or denial of that very same content. Consequently, one who utters the strong (33) would typically be taken to be, and would typically be, engaging in a kind of overstatement. Because of the mutual obviousness of the overstatement, an utterance of (33) might indeed pragmatically convey something more like the weaker, more modificationally limited (34). But this possibility provides no basis for supposing that the content of an utterance of the non-quantificational (33) is an unarticulated version of the articulated content of the quantificational (34).

Conclusion

I have objected to a fair number of Perry's views here. Nonetheless, there are certain deep agreements between us. Like Perry, I believe that beliefs are mental particulars, built out of recurring constituents. Moreover, like Perry, I believe that our belief ascriptions must sometimes make reference to, quantify over, and partially characterize particular belief episodes and the structure of notion-like elements deployed in those episodes. Because belief episodes with the same propositional contents may differ radically in the recurring constituents therein deployed, belief reports must sometimes do more than specify the propositional contents of belief. About this, Perry is also correct. What I have been objecting to strenuously here, however, are mainly Perry's views about the *way* the language of belief reports works to achieve these effects. Simple, unmodified belief sentences have no hidden or explicit argument place where a "notional specifier" might go. And contrary to the view defended by Crimmins and Perry, there is no pragmatic mechanism that can magically render the ascribee's notions directly semantically relevant to the literal truth-value of any such sentence. Indeed, the real, but underappreciated, lesson of Kripke's justly famous puzzle about belief, I claim, is that embedding does nothing at all to effect the semantic functioning of singular terms. It does not shift their referents; it does not render them nonreferential; and it does not cause them to induce unarticulated constituents. Consequently, if we want to explain apparent failures of substitutivity and the like, we had better look elsewhere. Or so I have been arguing.

Notes

1. I do not mean by this remark to fully endorse Perry's argument. For my own approach to the coreference and no-reference problems see Taylor 2003, especially essays I, II, IV, and VI.

2. Indeed, the Barwise-Perry approach seems to me to fit more comfortably than the Crimmins-Perry approach with the more general theoretical framework outlined in Perry's recent work.

3. Bach's own notion of "what is said" is self-consciously pretty far removed from day-to-day communication. His is a highly theoretical notion quite distant from our intuitions about

what is communicated or even our intuitions about direct and indirect ascriptions of content. Consequently, he is unlikely to be moved by complaints of the sort issued here. But then it is fair to wonder just what is supposed to entitle him to his notion of what is said in the first place.

4. For an excellent discussion of a variety of issues connected to the notion of what is said, especially the interest-relative and context sensitive nature of direct and indirect characterizations of what is said, see Stojanivic 2003.

5. Although Perry's approach to unarticulated constituents has a certain affinity to Recanati's approach, Perry has not to my knowledge endorsed what I regard as the most questionable aspect of Recanati's view. Recanati argues that primary pragmatic processes differ in fundamental psychological character from secondary pragmatic processes. Secondary pragmatic processes, he takes to be conscious and inferential. Primary pragmatic processes, he takes to be subdoxastic and non-inferential. To my knowledge, Perry has nowhere appealed to anything like this sort of processing distinction. In addition, in some explicit remarks about how unarticulated constituents get conveyed to a hearer by a speaker, he seems to suggest that reasoning of the very same sort is involved both in the understanding of conversational implicatures and in the grasping of unarticulated constituents. See, for example, the discussion in Perry 2001, especially pp. 49–50.

6. This hypothesis has implications for the so-called binding argument in favor of suppressed constituents. It suggests, in particular, that there is no reason to expect that subsyntactic argument places will be "bindable" by sentence-level quantifiers. If such arguments are restricted to what I am calling the subsyntactic basement they are, in the sense, "beneath" the reach of quantificational constituents.

7. Perry sometimes writes things that suggest some agreement with the approach outlined here. For example, he notices that although the metaphysics of the winning relation requires both a victor and a vanquished, the grammar of 'won' does not require we identify the vanquished. By contrast the grammar of 'beat' does require that the vanquished be specified. The difference between 'beat' and 'win' on this score is due not to differences in the metaphysics of the beat relation as compared with the winning relation, but to differences in the fulsomeness of the lexicalization of the relevant relation by the relevant verb. Perry's point may be that, if an argument role of a relation is lexicalized as an argument place of a predicate, it will show up as an explicit sentence-level constituent. I see no reason to believe that this is so. At any rate, it begs the question against the very possibility of what we might call "subsyntactic lexicalization."

8. Cappelen and Lepore (2005) come pretty close to endorsing such a view.

9. To be sure, there are those who will claim that the distinction between fulsomely *de re* and truncated *de re* ascriptions cannot be exhaustive, since it leaves out so-called *de dicto* ascriptions. Although there may indeed be something to the *de re/de dicto* distinction, I have argued at length elsewhere that the fulsomely *de re* actually does much of the communicative work that philosophers have wrongly assigned to *de dicto* reports. Indeed, I have shown that even in conversational contexts in which a *de dicto* ascription is permissible, it typically merely partially characterizes a

reality that can be more fully and informatively characterized by a fulsomely *de re* ascription. I lack the space to repeat those arguments here, however.

10. I add the parenthetical phrase "in subject position" because I have recently come to realize that things work differently for ascribed predications, even predications involving derogatory predicates. If Smith says,

Jones believes *that bitch Sally* is about to get tenure,

Smith has himself derogated Sally, but he has not ascribed any derogatory attitude toward Sally to Jones. On the other hand, if Smith says,

Jones believes that Sally *is a bitch*,

Smith has not derogated Sally himself but he has ascribed a derogatory belief about Sally to Jones. This apparent asymmetry between predicates and terms has, I think, to do entirely with the fact that the predicative commitments specified in a belief ascription do purport to attach *entirely to the ascribee*. This is entirely in keeping with my view that belief ascriptions specify nothing but the predicative doxastic commitments putatively undertaken by the ascribee. Just as the commitments normally involved in the use of the expression in subject position can't be detached from the ascriber, so the commitments normally involved in the use of the expression in predicate position can't be detached from the ascribee. But I lack the space to argue this point in detail here.

References

Bach, K. 1994. "Conversational Impliciture." *Mind and Language* 9: 124–162.

———. 2001a. "Speaking Loosely: Sentence Nonliterality." In P. French and H. Wettstein (eds.), *Midwest Studies in Philosophy*. Vol. 25: *Figurative Language*. Oxford: Blackwell.

———. 2001b. "You Don't Say." *Synthese* 128: 15–44.

Barwise, J., and J. Perry. 1983. *Situations and Attitudes*. Cambridge Mass.: MIT Press.

Cappelen, H., and E. Lepore. 2005. *Insensitive Semantics*. Oxford: Blackwell.

Carston, R. 2002. *Thoughts and Utterances: The Pragmatics of Explicit Communication*. London: Blackwell.

Crimmins, M., and J. Perry. 1989. "The Prince and the Phone Booth: Reporting Puzzling Beliefs." *Journal of Philosophy* 56: 685–711. Reprinted in Perry 2000. Page numbers are to reprinted edition.

Perry, J. 1986. "Thought without Representation." *Proceedings of the Aristotelian Society* (Supplement) 60: 263–283. Reprinted in Perry 2000. Page numbers refer to reprinted version.

———. 2000. *The Problem of the Essential Indexical and Other Essays*, expanded ed. Stanford, Calif.: CSLI Publications.

———. 2001. *Reference and Reflexivity*. Stanford, Calif.: CSLI Publications.

Recanati, F. 2001. "What Is Said." *Synthese* 128: 75–91.

————. 2003a. *Literal Meaning: The Very Idea*. Cambridge: Cambridge University Press.

————. 2003b. "What Is Said and the Pragmatics/Semantics Distinction." In C. Bianchi and C. Penco (eds.), *The Semantics/Pragmatics Distinction*. Stanford, Calif.: CSLI Publications.

Sperber, D., and D. Wilson. 1995. *Relevance: Communication and Cognition*. London: Blackwell.

Stanley, J. 2000. "Context and Logical Form." *Linguistics and Philosophy* 23: 391–434.

Stojanivic, I. 2003. "What to Say on What Is Said." In P. Blackburn, C. Ghidini, and R. Turner (eds.), *Modeling and Using Context*. Berlin: Springer-Verlag.

Taylor, K. 2002. "*De Re* and *De Dicto*: Against the Conventional Wisdom." *Philosophical Perspectives: Language and Mind* 16: 225–265.

————. 2003. *Reference and the Rational Mind*. Stanford, Calif.: CSLI Publications.

10 On Location

Stephen Neale

Underarticulation

In *Smith v. United States* (1993), the United States Supreme Court handed down a decision that resolved a conflict among the circuit courts over the interpretation of the common word 'use' as it occurs in the phrase 'use a firearm'. This was for purposes of the provisions of a statute setting penalties for offenses where a defendant "during and in relation to" any crime of violence or drug trafficking "uses or carries a firearm."[1] The statute, 18 U.S.C. section 924(c)(1), mandates a five-year consecutive sentence, increased to thirty years if the weapon is "equipped with a firearm silencer or firearm muffler."

Petitioner John Angus Smith had attempted to trade an unloaded automatic weapon, a MAC-10, together with a silencer, for two ounces of cocaine and had been found guilty of drug trafficking. At no time did Smith brandish the weapon or threaten with it. The Supreme Court ruled that the exchange or barter of a gun for illegal drugs constitutes "use" of a firearm, thus agreeing with the opinion of the Court of Appeals for the Eleventh Circuit that the plain language of the statute "imposes no requirement that the firearm be used as a weapon" and disagreeing with the Court of Appeals for the Ninth Circuit that trading a firearm for drugs could not itself constitute "use" of that firearm during and in relation to a crime.[2] According to the Supreme Court, *any* use of the weapon to facilitate in any way the commission of the offence was sufficient. In consequence, Smith had certainly "used" a firearm in a drug-trafficking crime by attempting to trade it, and it made no difference that he had not "used" it in the way firearms are intended or designed to be used.

Interestingly, given my concerns here, the Court noted that the phrase 'as a weapon' appeared nowhere in the statute and wrote in its opinion, "Had Congress intended the narrow construction petitioner urges, it could have so indicated. It did not, and we decline to introduce that additional requirement on our own." The Court continued,

It is one thing to say the ordinary meaning of 'using a firearm' *includes* using a firearm as a weapon, since it is the intended purpose of a firearm and the example of use that most immediately comes to mind. But it is quite another to conclude that, as a result, the phrase also *excludes* any other use. Certainly that conclusion does not follow from the phrase 'uses...a firearm' itself.... That one example of 'use' is the first to come to mind when the phrase 'uses...a firearm' is uttered does not preclude us from recognizing that there are other uses that qualify as well. In this case, it is both reasonable and normal to say that petitioner "used" his MAC-10 in his drug trafficking offense by trading it for cocaine...the only question in this case is whether the phrase 'uses...a firearm' in § 924(c)(1) is most reasonably read as *excluding* the use of a firearm in a gun-for-drugs trade. The fact that the phrase clearly includes using a firearm to shoot someone, as the dissent contends, does not answer it.... We are not persuaded that our construction of the phrase 'uses...a firearm' will produce anomalous applications...§ 924(c)(1) requires not only that the defendant "use" the firearm but also that he use it "during and in relation to" the drug trafficking crime. As result, the defendant who "uses" a firearm to scratch his head...or for some other innocuous purpose, would avoid punishment for that offense altogether: Although scratching one's head with a gun might constitute "use," that action cannot support punishment under § 924(c)(1) unless it facilitates or furthers the crime; that the firearm served to relieve an itch is not enough.... Under the dissent's approach,...even the criminal who pistol-whips his victim has not used a firearm within the meaning of § 924(c)(1), for firearms are intended to be fired or brandished, not used as bludgeons.

The central issue here is one that falls squarely within the purview of the philosophy of language. It concerns whether the expression 'uses a firearm' is to be understood, in the context of this particular statute (and presumably elsewhere) as if it were tantamount to 'uses a firearm as a weapon'. The Court ruled that it should not. The issue may be set out in at least three ways: (i) In terms of what many philosophers discussing attributive uses of incomplete definite descriptions ('the murderer', 'the mayor', and so on) have called *ellipsis* (not to be confused with a *syntactic* notion in generative grammar often called 'ellipsis', 'deletion' or 'elision').[3] (ii) In terms of what Dan Sperber and Deirdre Wilson have called the *underdetermination* of propositions by the meanings of the linguistic forms we use to express them (even relative to assignments of referents to singular terms and the specification of any anaphoric links).[4] Or (iii) in terms of what John Perry has called *unarticulated constituents* of the propositions we express using sentences of natural language.[5] We are in the same territory with the concepts mentioned in (i)–(iii), although (a) Perry's conception of unarticulated constituents appears to involve subtleties relevant to the study of thought that elude simple talk of ellipsis and underdetermination, (b) talk of underdetermination appears to involve subtleties and allow for interpretive possibilities not obviously captured by talk of ellipsis and unarticulated constituents. I do not, however, want to get too embroiled in these matters here. If we want a label that is neutral, we could do worse than talk about *underarticulation*, but we shall have to be careful at times:

The Underarticulation Thesis (UT): What a speaker says (the proposition he expresses) by uttering an unambiguous, declarative sentence φ on given occasion is underarticulated by φ's syntax, the meanings of the morphemes in φ, the prosodic features of φ, the references to any referring expressions in φ (including those of an indexical nature), and the specifications of all anaphoric links.

Several things about this general characterization should be mentioned. (1) I assume here and throughout the standard view that propositions are true or false without relativization to times (or anything else).[6] And, in order to engage with Perry and other authors, I shall assume that propositions have objects, properties, and complexes built out of such things as constituents. Thus, the proposition that Scalia judges has Scalia himself and the property of judging as constituents. (2) I talk of "the proposition *a speaker* expresses." This is because I follow Austin, Grice, and Strawson in construing meaning, saying, asking, implying, referring, predicating, asserting, making statements, and expressing propositions as things *people* do on given occasions (usually *with* words), as intentional actions they perform.[7] (3) For simplicity, I shall start out using 'indexical' in its broad sense above to include any expression that may be used to refer to different things on different occasions of utterance, for example the words 'I', 'you', he', 'this', 'that', 'here', 'there', 'now', and 'then'.[8] (4) By 'anaphoric links', I mean (roughly) interpretive dependencies holding between expressions, including those that involve the binding of one expression (often a pronoun) by another.[9] (5) The word 'declarative' appears in this formulation for expository convenience only: I want to focus on *saying* (rather than *asking*, for example), on *statements* made (rather than *questions* asked) and on *propositions* expressed (rather than *issues* queried).[10] (6) Why "unambiguous"? Among the things a hearer or reader needs to do in order to identify what *S* is saying on a given occasion, is identify which *words S* is using. 'Bank' is the superficial form of either a single, ambiguous word of English or else two distinct unambiguous words, and I do not want one's position on this matter to impinge upon UT.[11]

The sort of thoroughly intentional, speaker-based usage of 'say', 'express', 'refer' and so on that I advocate is to be distinguished from (typically less intentional) talk of, for example, *sentences* expressing propositions relative to "contexts" and of *words* (or *phrases*) referring relative to these same entities, talk I find problematic because of the way it leads people to treat the wrong notions as basic within a theory of interpretation.[12] Perry talks of *uses*—particular dated uses or tokenings—of sentences expressing propositions (and of *uses* of words referring). I must admit, I don't care for this way of talking any more than I care for talk of sentences relative to contexts expressing propositions or talk of utterances of sentences doing so (or talk of words relative to contexts referring or talk of utterances of words doing so). However, because there is always understood to be a *user* in one of Perry's particular dated uses of a word or sentence, later I shall take the liberty of construing his talk of a particular use of a sentence X expressing the proposition that p (or saying that p) as replaceable by my talk of the user (e.g., the speaker) expressing the proposition that p (or saying that p) by using (e.g., uttering) X on a given occasion.

Similarly, I shall take Perry's talk of a particular use of a word (or phrase) X referring to someone or something as replaceable by my talk of the user (e.g., the speaker) referring to someone or something with X on that occasion of use.[13] I maintain that referring is an intentional act, something *speakers* do, that talk of an *expression* itself referring, and even talk of an expression referring relative to an utterance, a speech act, a "context," or a "tokening," is, at best, derivative. So when I use the word 'refer', I intend its subject to be an expression we use to refer to a speaker.

With Perry, I wish to allow for the (actualized) possibility of a user referring to some object without using any particular word or phrase to refer it. Perry's best known example involves an unarticulated *location*. Consider an utterance made by me right now of the following sentence:

(1)   It's raining

I could be expressing the proposition that it's raining in Reykjavík. Yet there is no part of sentence (1) that I would be using to refer to Reykjavík. Nonetheless, raining, as Perry stresses, is a binary relation between a time and a place. (Similarly, being a citizen, foreigner, resident, local, native, national, or patriot is a binary relation between a person and a place.) It doesn't just rain. (One cannot just be a citizen.) It rains at a time, in a place. (One is a citizen of a place.) This is why I can use (1) right now to express a true proposition about Reykjavík, or a false one about Paris; or use it tomorrow to express a false one about Reykjavík, or a true one about Paris.

Now suppose I had used (2) or (3) instead of (1):

(2)   It's raining in Reykjavík.

(3)   It's raining here.

It is natural to say that I would be using 'in Reykjavík' (or at least the 'Reykjavík' part) to refer to Reykjavík by uttering (2), and that I would be using the word 'here' to do so by uttering (3). But neither 'here' nor 'in Reykjavík' occurs in (1). Now I want to say, with Perry, that I referred to Reykjavík when I uttered (1). But what was I using to refer to Reykjavík?

Ordinary language suggests it would be quite correct to say I would be referring to Reykjavík. If we had a crossed telephone line and a third party said in response to my utterance of (1), "No it didn't, I was here in London all day; there was no rain," I suppose I might reply by saying, "I was referring to Reykjavík, not London." We need a distinction here between referring to *X with* an expression (typically a singular term) and merely referring to *X in uttering* an expression (typically a sentence). I referred to Reykjavík *in uttering* (1), but there is no constituent of (1) *with which* I would have referred to Reykjavík.[14] Or so I maintain.

Suppose I utter (4):

(4) It's raining here in Reykjavík.

Would I be referring to Reykjavík *twice*, once with 'here' and once again with 'in Reykjavík', and perhaps even a third time with the compound (if such it is) 'here in Reykjavík'? First impressions suggest I would be saying only *one* thing about Reykjavík, that it's raining here. But if I am really *referring* to it twice *with words* shouldn't we say that I referred to it twice *in* uttering (4) or at least explore the idea that I am *predicating* two things of it in uttering (4), (i) that it's raining here, and (ii) that I am there (i.e., here). If I were in *Genoa* today when I uttered (4), wouldn't I be saying something true (that it's raining in Reykjavík) and also something false (that I am in Reykjavík)?[15] Compare an utterance of (5):

(5) It's raining in Reykjavík today; it often rains here.

Surely I refer to Reykjavík twice when I utter (5), once with 'Reykjavík' and once again with 'here'. And in this case it would be perverse to deny that I am saying two distinct things about Reykjavík (that it's raining there [i.e., here] and that it often rains there [i.e., here]). We should have no qualms, then, about saying that I referred to Reykjavík twice *in* uttering (5). But if that is right, what precisely are the qualms about saying I referred to it twice *in* uttering (4)?

Similarly, I can use (2) now to express a true proposition about me and Great Britain, or a false one about me and Iceland, and in principle I could use it at some point in the future to express a true proposition about me and Iceland, or about me and the United States:

(6) I am a citizen.

To say that one cannot be a citizen without being a citizen of some particular place is *not* to say that we cannot express propositions involving this binary relation without having *particular* places in mind. We certainly can, because we can make *general* statements using quantifiers. Consider (7):

(7) Smith is a citizen of somewhere or other: he has a passport.

This fact will be important later.

Before getting to the details of Perry's discussion of (1) and the responses it has elicited, I want to touch on a more general issue in an informal way. Consider particular dated utterances of the parts of (8)–(10) below that are not in acute angled brackets:

(8)   The mayor ⟨of Reykjavík⟩ is underpaid.

(9)   Most people ⟨in Reykjavík⟩ think the mayor ⟨of Reykjavík⟩ is underpaid.

(10)   John is ready ⟨to leave ⟨Reykjavík⟩⟩.

The fuller expressions could easily be used to make more *explicit* the proposition a speaker wishes to express (which is not to say the speaker would always be doing a better job). Examples involving things other than locations are not hard to find:

(11)   I haven't drunk any wine ⟨tonight⟩.

(12)   The Russian ⟨judge⟩ voted for the Russian ⟨skater⟩.

(13)   ⟨In Egil's Saga⟩ Thorolfur is killed in England.

(14)   The ⟨former⟩ hostages were greeted at the White House.

(15)   ⟨The woman on⟩ table six wants her steak rare.

(16)   Every man who owns sheep vaccinates the sheep ⟨he owns⟩ every year.

To many who accept UT, much contemporary work in the philosophy of language seems to be in a grip of a gray and cramped picture of so-called compositional semantics, a picture too beholden to the study of formal languages and not sufficiently sensitive to certain facts about the use of natural language and our ordinary talk about what we are saying and what we are referring to (perhaps only implicitly) on given occasions. Problems discussed under the rubric of compositional semantics—construed as the study of the composition of the *propositional content* of a sentence (relative to a context) from the contents of its parts (relative to that context) and their syntactic arrangement—are products of specious questions in the philosophy of language, questions that have genuine and important counterparts in the philosophy of *mind*, mostly about inference and the way we identify the thoughts people attempt to express using sentences of natural language.[16] Our interpretive abilities are *so good* that we can reasonably expect our addressees (and often those who overhear) to identify the thoughts we seek to express, even when the linguistic meanings of the expressions we use fall short of delivering the precise concepts involved in the thought. Often a speaker will use a simple predicate, even if a richer one might be used, one that could, in principle, leave the hearer with less inferential work to do. (The use of the richer predicate is not guaranteed to speed up communication—it could slow it down).

A general theory of interpretation must answer the following question: how is it that we manage to identify the proposition a speaker seeks to express—let alone the ones he seeks merely to imply—by uttering a sentence X on a given occasion, given the precious little information we obtain by virtue of our knowledge of the meanings of the words in X and our knowledge of X's syntactic structure?[17]

Most of the people I know who publicly accept UT—*linguistic pragmatists*, to give them a name—do not do so *gleefully*. They did not wake up one Monday morning and decide it would be fun to abandon traditional compositional semantics, to claim that the propositions we express by uttering sentences are underdetermined by the meanings of unambiguous linguistic forms we use, even relative to "reference assignments" and "anaphoric assignments." It would be more accurate to say they threw in the towel. They are, for the most part, people who have great respect for syntactic theory—many of them have come from linguistics, after all—and for the idea that syntactic facts go well beyond what is revealed by superficial parsing. Many of them have done a good deal of traditional compositional semantics and tried to explain all manner of "contextual effects" the good old-fashioned ways, by judicious appeals to indexicality and hidden syntax or by bringing down the Gricean guillotine. Moreover, they have worried themselves sick about the relation between thought and language. In the face of what seemed like an invincible alliance of empirical and conceptual pressures, reluctantly, and with a distinct lack of glee, they concluded that something had to give. With the best will in the world toward syntactic theory, often embracing a distinction between a sentence's superficial form and its underlying form (and, with that, often enough the idea of aphonic items in syntax), they have seen no reasonable alternative to surrendering to UT. Content compositionality has ceded to mere content *systematicity*, and the relation between natural language sentences and sentences of Mentalese or the language of thought (for those who are happy with the idea of such a system of mental representation) now looks quite different, only the latter being truly compositional and rich enough to have truth-evaluable content;[18] various old puzzles about conjunctions, conditionals, descriptions, variable-binding, and deletion look less threatening; the possibility of explaining indexicality in terms of *perspective* has returned as unfettered appeals to indexicals and hidden syntax have faded. It is only at *this point* that excitement begins. It is doubly a mistake to identify it with the excitement of just tearing down an old order or advancing controversial theses. First, it is excitement at the prospect of *progress* of a sort, or the prospect of escaping from some narrow tunnel. Second, UT itself smacks of an old order, an order that winds through

Wittgenstein, Moore, Austin, Strawson, Grice, and Searle, in taking the use of language, and the way *speakers* say things and refer to things as the primary object of investigation.

Many people who are involved in the project of constructing semantic theories reject UT out of hand, but not, I think, for particularly good empirical reasons. Several related factors appear to be implicated in this, and I want to say something about two of them, interconnected holdovers from generative semantics: free-wheeling appeals to hidden syntax and to indexicality.

It is all too easy to claim that some seemingly troublesome expression is "indexical" (in a broad sense) and, unfortunately, appeals to "indexicality" have become semantic panaceas in various branches of philosophy. There are those in epistemology, for instance, who claim the verb 'know' is indexical, the strength of the justification required for felicitous usage altering with context.[19] And there are those in the philosophy of language, for instance, who claim there are unheard indexical expressions in the syntax of all sorts of natural language sentences, expressions that can refer to more or less anything the theorist chooses, without being in the least bit perspectival or descriptive.[20] Perspective has traditionally been a distinguishing feature of indexical (deictic, egocentric) expressions, and for good reason: indexicality needs to be *explained*.[21] As Perry 1986 points out, a nonindexical expression is one whose meaning specifies a contribution to propositional content that is constant across different uses; an indexical is one whose meaning specifies only *a relation to the user* that is constant across different uses, different entities capable of serving as the specified relatum and hence as contributions to propositional content, on different occasions of use. The indexicality of an expression is thus *explained* in terms of a perspective it signals. (The perspective may be higher order.) Much contemporary discussion of indexical expressions, by contrast, appears oblivious to this, being utterly unconstrained and grounded in nothing whatsoever, except the desire to obliterate some problem or paradox of interpretation.[22] The result, as we shall see, is interpretive vacuity and syntactic dogma, neither of which has much empirical value.

I mentioned a Gricean guillotine just above, and I had in mind, of course, the reduction or relegation of parts of what a speaker means on a given occasion to things he or she *implied* rather than said, the phenomena in question best explained in terms of Grice's (1961, 1989) maneuvers in connection with uses of, for example, 'and', 'or', 'the', 'seem' and 'try'. I find it very odd that some linguists and philosophers claim Grice actually *rejects* UT, that it conflicts with what he says about his pet notion of *what is said*. Certainly Grice did not see underarticulation as a phenomenon as broad as Perry, Searle, Sperber and Wilson, Carston, Récanati, or I see it, but it does not follow that he *rejected* the thesis. It would be an error to claim he is rejecting it in the following oft-quoted passage, which concerns a single example:

In the sense in which I am using the word *say*, I intend what someone has said to be closely related to the conventional meaning of the words (the sentence) he has uttered. Suppose someone to have uttered the sentence *He is in the grip of a vice*. Given a knowledge of the English language, but no knowledge of the circumstances of the utterance, one would know something about what the speaker had said, on the assumption that he was speaking standard English, and speaking literally. . . . But for a full identification of what the speaker had said, one would need to know (a) the identity of [the person] *x* [the speaker is referring to with 'he'], (b) the time of utterance, and (c) the meaning, on the particular occasion of utterance, of the phrase *in the grip of a voice*. (Grice 1989, 25)

As a matter of historical fact, (a) Grice saw UT as a necessary component of any viable response to Strawson's (1950) Argument from Incompleteness against Russell's Theory of Descriptions, just as Sellars (1954) did;[23] (b) he never intended to be seen as denying UT and was confident nothing in his "paltry corpus" conflicted with it; and (c) he thought the work of Austin, Searle, and Sperber and Wilson showed just how pervasive underarticulation was, even if he did think *some* data were better explained in terms of implicature. Of course, Sperber and Wilson (and those they have influenced) go much further than Grice, making it clear (i) that many cherished "relegations to conversational implicature" inspired by Grice—indeed some of Grice's own—had to be radically rethought and reclassified as parts of what is said and (ii) that the underdeterminaton of what is said by linguistic meaning and reference assignment is a wholesale and pervasive feature of the use of natural language.

Although underarticulation is an old idea, as far as I can ascertain, in more technical work in the philosophy of language it was not discussed in earnest until after the quest had begun to produce semantic theories capable of complementing the syntactic theories produced by Chomskyan linguists. It may well have been Sperber and Wilson who first stated the thesis outright and in terms relevant to the contemporary study of the semantics of natural language and the study of what is now often called Gricean pragmatics. What is interesting and novel about UT in the hands of people like Grice, Perry, Récanati, and Sperber and Wilson is the belief that holding it does not require throwing out the baby with the bathwater as Austin, Strawson, and Sellars did. The novelty lies in the realization that there is no inconsistency in combining UT with the thesis that the syntax and semantics of natural language can be tackled by drawing upon many of the great technical insights in linguistics and the philosophy of language made by Chomsky, Davidson, Evans, Harman, Lewis, Kamp, Kaplan, Kripke, Montague, Partee, Perry, Stalnaker, and others in the 1960s and 1970s. The general idea of providing syntactic and semantic *theories* is not itself under attack. As Crimmins and Perry (1989) so rightly stress, one can give up compositionality without giving up *systematicity*.

The justices on the U.S. Supreme Court might profit from a good dose of pragmatist philosophy of language and reflection on UT, and Perry might be the perfect person to get them started. Once he has explained to the Court what the issues boil down to for uses of (1)–(12), he could get them started on the unarticulated constituent Justice O'Connor tries to trample to death in the proposition expressed in stating § 924(c)(1), already clear from reflection on utterances of (13):

(17)   Smith used a gun.

It can't just rain, Perry might say; raining has to take place *somewhere, somewhen*. Similarly, you can't just *use* something, and you can't just use that something to do *something*, or just use it as *something*. You have to use it to do *something in particular*, or use as it as *something in particular*. The proposition we express by stating a regulation governing the use of firearms contains an unarticulated constituent just as much as the proposition expressed by an utterance of

(18)   Through the inspired use of his new nine iron, Moravcsik triumphed over
       Hampshire on the eighteenth.

It makes all the difference, Perry might say, whether Moravcsik holed out with an extraordinary nine-iron shot, smashed his nine-iron shot straight into Hampshire, or whacked Hampshire on the shin with the aforementioned implement during a heated debate in the heavy rough, forcing Hampshire to retire and concede the match. Some particular use, or particular range of uses, is understood when the verb 'use' or the noun 'use' or the adjective 'useful' is *used* (even in utterances of 'this has many uses' or 'you can use this to do all sorts of things'). That, I imagine, is how Perry might be inclined to reason, and I for one would be inclined to go along with him, for reasons I shall spell out.

Perry

Perry was a constant source of inspiration to me at Stanford, not only as a brilliant philosopher but also as a model dissertation director who somehow knew when to be hands-on and when to be hands-off—infallibly gauging my mood or commitment to any particular thesis—a phenomenally creative teacher and witty interlocutor from whom I have never stopped learning. I first met Perry in January 1984, in Jon Barwise's office. (I had left the Ph.D. program in linguistics at MIT in mid-year to go to Stanford because of all the excitement surrounding the recently founded Center for the Study of Language Information.) We chatted about Barwise and Perry's book *Situations and Attitudes*, which had just appeared, about context and implicature, and about the semantics-pragmatics distinction. One reason I felt at home so quickly was that Stanford seemed to be awash in sympathy for UT, which had been tenderly drummed into me by Deirdre Wilson when I was an undergraduate. Barwise and Perry appeared to be convinced there was no hope of constructing a viable theory of interpretation without taking into account entities not served up directly by individual words or phrases (although there were heated debates at the time about when such entities were constituents of the proposition expressed, or situation described, and when they merely placed constraints on those propositions). Some of the Stanford linguists seemed to feel the same way, particularly Geoffrey Nunberg and Stanley Peters. Discussions with Paul Grice in Berkeley revealed that he was resigned to UT, the case having been made convincingly, he thought, by the perfectly felicitous use of incomplete descriptions that he had discussed in a 1970 manuscript called "Lectures on Logic and Reality."[24] All right-thinking people, it seemed to me in 1984, probably accepted the thesis, although many may not have articulated it to themselves clearly. (How wrong I was!)

The more I talked to Perry and Barwise, to Grice, and to Christopher Peacocke (a fellow that year at the Center for Advanced Studies in the Behavioral Sciences) the more I got drawn into philosophy, and the more my enrollment in Stanford's doctoral program in linguistics looked like a flag of convenience. It was Peacocke who suggested I move over to philosophy full time and write a dissertation with Perry. There was a problem: although I'd attended a few philosophy lectures as an undergraduate, I'd never actually taken a philosophy course, written a philosophy paper, or taken any sort of philosophy examination. To my surprise, Perry and Barwise didn't seem to mind: they encouraged me to attend few seminars and see how things worked out. John Dupré, John Etchemendy, Dagfinn Føllesdal, and Pat Suppes all drew me further into philosophy over the next year; so did my golfing partners, Julius Moravcsik and Stuart Hampshire; and so did a remarkable new intake of philosophy graduate students, including Mark Crimmins, David Magnus, and Leora Weitzman. They absorbed me as one of their own, and in September 1985 I became a backdated member of their class, a beneficiary of Stanford's creative approach to problem-solving.

Once I had completed the coursework for the Ph.D. in philosophy, I began to work closely with Perry on my dissertation, which metamorphosed from something on situations and events, to something on event descriptions, and in turn to something on descriptions themselves. We met as regularly as possible on Friday afternoons in Perry's office in the Quad, where conversation took place in ordinary English and, often enough, in a cloud of pipe smoke, a sanctuary from the rigors of CSLI, where ZF, AFA, GPSG, HPSG, LF, LFG, DRS, DRT, and the like were taking their toll on my adviser. In the peace of the quad, we argued about sentences and utterances, facts and situations, indexicals and demonstratives, acquaintance and description, and, if Perry had not overdosed on CSLI that week, an occasional quantifier or donkey pronoun. I think the topic we found most vexing was incomplete descriptions. Barwise and Perry (1983) had pretty much sided with Kaplan (1978) and Wettstein (1981) in holding that Donnellan's (1966) distinction between attributive and referential uses of descriptions reflected a distinction between the expression of a general proposition and the expression of a singular proposition and was therefore of semantic significance and not "merely" of relevance to a theory of speaker's meaning. But I was siding with Grice (1969), Kripke (1977), and Davies (1981) in holding that the phenomena usually taken to demonstrate the alleged semantic significance of the distinction could be explained at least as well by invoking Grice's distinction between what a speaker *says* and what he *means*.[25] This made for fabulously productive arguments about partiality, persistence, quantifier domains, ellipsis, resource situations, multiple propositions, and so on, and Perry ended up supervising a dissertation, one of whose principal theses he rejected, or at least still questioned.

What Perry had to say about (1),

(1)   It's raining

sounded incontrovertible at the time and seemingly in harmony with what some philosophers had said about incomplete descriptions. Among the examples I discussed in my dissertation was one due to Evans (1982):

(2)   They ought to impeach the mayor.

Suppose Perry is driving through a city he has never driven through before, Reykjavík for example, and is horrified at the condition of the roads. He might utter (2) to express the proposition that the mayor *of Reykjavík* (or of *this city*) ought to be impeached. On my account, Reykjavík itself is an unarticulated constituent of the proposition Perry expressed, but the name "Reykjavík" is not a component of the sentence he uttered.[26] Another convincing example, it would seem, of the failure of isomorphism of form and content, a breakdown of the one-to-one mapping between the meaningful constituents of a sentence and the constituents of the proposition it is used to express on a particular occasion.

Perry's Unarticulated Locations

The basic idea behind talk of unarticulated constituents is easy to grasp *if* one can put down any syntactic or semantic axe one has to grind and restrict attention to the relation between the words we utter and the constituents of the propositions we express in so doing. Some of Perry's discussions, however, concern thought as much as language, and this means certain interpretive complexities arise. I want to start by summarizing what I take to be Perry's basic points about unarticulated constituents in words that are as neutral as possible on matters of syntax and thought. I shall then turn to Perry's own words and finally to the way of talking I myself favor.

Consider the following sentences:

It's raining / it's snowing / it's hailing.

It's foggy / it's cloudy / it's windy.

It's hot / it's humid / it's dull / it's overcast.

It's dark already / it's an hour before sunset.

It's 52 degrees / it's 6 Beaufort.

It's even windier than yesterday.

It's unusually warm for April / April has been unusually warm.

If I use any of these sentences right now to say something true or false, I make an "implicit" or "tacit" reference to a place or location (not necessarily my current location—we might be talking about somewhere else). It cannot just be raining: raining is a binary relation between a place and a time: it rains *somewhere* and *somewhen*. (Which is not to say it could not be raining everywhere on Earth at the same time. Perhaps there are *physical* reasons why this could not happen, but this is no part of the meaning of the verb 'rain'.) Similarly, it cannot just be cloudy, overcast, an hour before sunset, or 6 Beaufort: these are all binary relations between time and places.

The binary nature of the relations expressed by utterances of sentences such as those above would appear to have important consequences for a theory of interpretation. Suppose I use (1) to say something about the current weather here in Reykjavík:

(1)   It's raining.

In classical parlance, I say (or state) that it is raining *in Reykjavík*, I express the proposition (or make the statement) that it is raining *in Reykjavík*. The proposition that it's raining in Reykjavík is a proposition that *involves* Reykjavík, a *Reykjavík-involving* or *Reykjavík-dependent* proposition, despite the fact that there is no particular word or phrase in (1) that I am using to refer to (talk about) Reykjavík. Of course I could have used (2) instead to express the same proposition:

(2)   It's raining here.

Then I would have been using the indexical 'here' to refer to Reykjavík, so the story goes, but there was nothing wrong with my use of (1) to say that it's raining in Reykjavík.

Why insist that the proposition I expressed by uttering (1) is Reykjavík-involving? Because the truth or falsity of my remark—that is, the truth or falsity of the proposition I express on this particular occasion, depends upon whether or not it is raining *in Reykjavík* (and not, for example, on whether or not it is raining *in Genoa* or raining *somewhere or other on Earth*). Of course, I could use (1) to express the proposition that it is raining in Genoa. In certain contrived circumstances, *perhaps* I could use it to express the proposition that it is raining somewhere on Earth; certainly I could also use any of the following to do that:

(2′)   It's raining somewhere.

(2″)   It's raining somewhere or other.

(2‴)   It's raining somewhere or other on Earth.[27]

So where do *unarticulated constituents* come into the picture, and what are they? Mark Crimmins answers these questions about as concisely as they can be answered:

In a semantics that takes propositions to be structures containing objects and properties, an un-articulated constituent is simply a propositional constituent that is not explicitly mentioned—it is not the content of any expression in the sentence. (1992, 16)

And assuming such a "semantics," Reykjavík, the place I made "implicit" or "tacit" reference to by uttering (1), is an unarticulated constituent of the proposition I expressed.[28]

(i) Perry's label is excellent. To anyone exposed to some phonetics, the verb 'articulate' and its progeny will immediately conjure up thoughts about the mouth, the alveolar ridge, liquids, and vowel quadrilaterals, and spark memories of the threefold division in phonetics between the acoustic, the auditory, and the *articulatory*, the subject matter of articulatory phonetics being *the ways in which meaningful sounds are produced by the speech organs*.[29] Among the various uses of 'articulated', good dictionaries specify two that are interestingly related through the concept of something like *segmentation* or *distinctness*: (1) "attached by a joint; connected by joints; having segments united by joints," and (2) "uttered as articulate sound, distinctly spoken" (*Oxford English Dictionary* [*OED*]). This is perhaps clearer with the adjective 'articulate': (1)

"Jointed; united by a joint; composed by sections...distinctly jointed; having the parts distinctly recognizable" and (2) "Of sound: with clearly distinguishable parts, each having meaning. Of speech, expression, etc.: fluent and clear. Of a person: able to express himself or herself fluently and clearly" (*OED*).[30] Although I have not consulted him on this matter, I suspect Perry chose 'unarticulated' to connote the idea of a constituent of a proposition corresponding to nothing that was *articulated* in the sense of 'spoken' or 'pronounced'. Of course, this connotation does not mean he cannot employ the underlying idea (whatever that may be) *more widely*—for example in the realm of *thought*—for labels are just labels, and connotations are just connotations. There is always a risk in introducing a label for something, especially when one is in the early stages of describing a phenomenon or fleshing out an idea, but connotative labels are often helpful in those early stages, despite the damage they may do later, and we owe it to ourselves as interpreters of philosophical prose to exercise charity when we witness the genesis of philosophical ideas or labels, to put ourselves in the position of the creator, who is trying to get across (or just formulate to his own satisfaction) ideas that may be more general than those that finally emerge from the long labors of armies of critics descending upon the terrain.

(ii) *Being an unarticulated constituent of a proposition p* is an intrinsically binary relation, rather like being a foreigner. α cannot just be a foreigner: α is a foreigner *relative to a place*. Similarly, α cannot just be an unarticulated constituent of a proposition ⟨...α...⟩: α is an unarticulated constituent of ⟨...α...⟩ *relative to some representational entity X* (e.g., a sentence), more accurately, relative to some particular *tokening* or *instance X"* of *X* (e.g., a use, utterance, occasioning or what-have-you of a sentence). Take the proposition that it's raining in Reykjavík (now). Is Reykjavík an unarticulated constituent of that proposition or not? Wrong question. Relative to a use by me (now) of (1), by which I express the proposition that it is raining in Reykjavík, it *is*:

(1)   It's raining.

But relative to a use by me (now) of (2) or (3) by which I expresses the same proposition it is *not*:

(2)   It's raining here.

(3)   It's raining in Reykjavík.

Nor is Reykjavík an unarticulated constituent of the proposition expressed relative to my use (now) of (4) to express the proposition that it's raining in Akureyri:

(4)   It's raining there.

But perhaps it *is* relative to my use of (5) to say that Akureyri gets less rain that Reykjavík,

(5)   Akureyri gets less rain.[31]

Then again, it is *not* relative to my use of (5) to express the proposition that Akureyri gets less rain than London, or relative to my use of (6) to say that $3^2 + 4^2 = 5^2$:

(6) $3^2 + 4^2 = 5^2$.

We have in play three entities that can be construed as having *parts*, so let us forestall confusion by adopting certain conventions. Let us use 'portion' for a part of *a tokening* of a representation (e.g., a part of a particular dated use of the sentence (3) such as the subtokenings of 'Reykjavík' and 'in Reykjavík'). Let us use 'component' for a part of *the thing tokened* (e.g., a part of (3) such as 'Reykjavík' and 'in Reykjavík'). And let us use 'constituent' for a part of the thing expressed by the tokening (e.g., a part of the proposition expressed by a tokening of (3) such as Reykjavík itself).

The general concept of an unarticulated constituent makes sense only when we have *two* distinct entities that are meant to be standing in an asymmetric representational relation to one another, a *representing* entity X and a (partially) *represented* entity $\langle \ldots \rangle$, which X is taken to (partially) represent. We might now say the following on Perry's behalf:

A particular constituent a of a proposition $\langle \ldots a \ldots \rangle$ is unarticulated relative to a tokening X^u of X if, and only if,

(a) X^u represents (e.g., expresses, stands for, designates) $\langle \ldots a \ldots \rangle$; and

(b)   among the portions of X^u that correspond to (and represent) the constituents of $\langle \ldots a \ldots \rangle$, there is no portion that corresponds to a.[32]

(iii) According to the very general picture of language that Perry (1986, 207–208) assumes: (1) a use of a sentence stands for (or expresses) a proposition; (2) the meaning of a sentence X is systematically related to the meanings of X's components and their mode of composition; (3) the meanings of the components of X can be explained in terms of the relations between uses of these components and the things those uses stand for; so (4) the meaning of X is systematically related to the relations between uses of its components and the things those uses stand for; (5) the thing that a particular use C^u of a component C of X stands for is a constituent of the proposition expressed by the particular use X^u of X, of which C^u is a portion; (6) the meaning of X can be explained in terms of a relation between uses of X and propositions expressed by these uses. So where does talk of an unarticulated constituent a of the proposition $\langle \ldots a \ldots \rangle$ expressed by a use X^u come from in this picture if the use of no portion of X^u

stands for α? Answer: from X^u *as a whole*. X^u is *about* α (and any articulated constituents of $\langle\ldots\alpha\ldots\rangle$ that portions of X^u stand for) even though no portion of X^u stands for α. Thus, a particular use of (1) can be as much *about* Reykjavík as a particular use of (3).

(iv) There are just *two* ways in which an *articulated* constituent may get into the proposition expressed by an utterance of some sentence *X*. It is given either *directly* or *relationally* by the meaning of some component of *X*. More specifically, the meaning of a component of *X* is either of such a nature that it supplies the same *propositional constituent* on any occasion of use, or else of such a nature that it identifies the same *relation to the speaker* on any occasion of use, a relation that permits different propositional constituents bearing the relation in question to the speaker on different occasions of use. An expression that contributes in this relational manner is an *indexical*.

(v) As far as the propositions expressed by utterances of sentences are concerned, unarticulated constituents seem straightforward: a tokening X^u of *X* is just a particular dated *use* of *X*, in Perry's sense. When it comes to *thoughts*, matters are somewhat trickier. Suppose, as Jerry Fodor and others have maintained, there is a *language of thought*, a modality-neutral system of mental representation. In principle, if X^u is a token representation of this internal language (*Mentalese*, as it is often called), and $\langle\ldots\rangle$ is its propositional content, then it would seem that $\langle\ldots\rangle$ may contain what we might call an *unprojected* constituent α, a constituent that is not projected from any particular portion of X^u.[33]

(vi) No interesting thesis about *the syntax of natural language* is implied by the mere postulation of unarticulated constituents. (And no interesting thesis about the syntax of Mentalese is implied by the postulation of unprojected constituents.) But some philosophers are predisposed to see syntactic theses in the most unlikely places, so let me say a few words about this matter. For many linguists and philosophers of language, a particular theoretical stance on syntactic structure and on the identity conditions for sentences, dominates investigations of language and mind. I confess to being one of these people myself: I take the Chomskyan line that a sentence is best construed as a pair $\langle\pi,\lambda\rangle$ of representations, where π is a PF (or "Phonetic Form") to be read by the sound system, and λ an LF (or "Logical Form") to be read by the intentional system, where λ incorporates "whatever features of sentence structure (1) enter into the semantic interpretation of sentences and (2) are strictly determined by properties of sentence grammar" (Chomsky 1976, 305).

On this approach, the LF of an English sentence is not just some semiformal, semi-English representation of "semantic structure" or "truth-conditional content." It is meant to be the actual syntactic structure of the sentence, generated by a syntax for the language, a structure that it is the task of empirical linguistics to reveal. Although many linguists and philosophers of language take more or less this line, many others do *not*, having more conservative views on just how removed representations of syntactic structure can be from the "ordinary" representations of speech we find in our traditional orthography.[34] Now one thing is quite certain: *Perry was not assuming any particular syntactic theory when he first talked about unarticulated constituents.* He was trying to present in as straightforward a manner as possible, facts about what people are saying when they use simple weather sentences such as the one we "ordinarily" represent as (1), which we "ordinarily" say contains three words, 'it', 'is', and 'raining'. Of course, there is already a modicum of theory in our "ordinary" orthographic segmentation and classification of parts of speech. But we have to start *somewhere*; and Perry takes it for granted that the philosophers he is addressing—his original paper on this topic was for the Aristotelian Society—will assume the same starting point and be thinking about the issues without having any particular syntactic axe to grind. In short: talk of unarticulated constituents is not supposed to be beholden to any particular theory of what a sentence is: it concerns the relation between the propositions we express by using what are pretheoretically taken to be sentences of English. And so it involves no commitment to the view (or to the denial of the view) that in "underlying" or "deep" or "logical" syntax, sentence (1) contains an expression used to refer to a location, an expression that is "aphonic," "phonetically null," "phonologically empty," "silent," "implicit," "tacit," "covert," "hidden," or "buried," as far as surface syntax is concerned.

(vii) No interesting thesis in *psycholinguistics* about the process of interpretation is implied by the postulation of unarticulated constituents. In particular, it involves no commitment to the view (or to the denial of the view) that understanding a particular utterance of (1) involves mentally constructing or reconstructing a longer sentence such as 'it's raining here' or 'it's raining in Reykjavík'. It is an empirical question whether something like that does or does not take place, and no amount of a priori speculation is going to illuminate the matter.

(viii) Since it is possible to use sentence (1) here in Reykjavík to talk about the weather in Genoa or London, it cannot be the *extensional* fact of the speaker's location that determines the unarticulated constituent of the proposition the speaker expresses, but the speaker's *intentions* in uttering (1). A philosopher who espouses the language of thought hypothesis may well illuminate the unarticulated constituent of the proposition I express by uttering (1) by matching it with a component of the Mentalese representation constituting the thought to which I am giving expression. The proposition I express by uttering (1) contains an unarticulated location by virtue of the location's *irreducible role* in that thought.

The above characterization of Perry's proposal was all very compressed, of course, and my own Gricean bias crept in because I often talked about a *speaker* (rather than his words or his use of some expression, or his utterance of some expression) referring, saying, and expressing propositions. This will be important later. Perry, as I said, talks about *uses of expressions* designating objects, expressing propositions and so on (1986, 207–208).

Perry's Own Words

Let us turn now to Perry's own words, which appear to have been taken in different ways by different people.[35] In his earliest remarks on this topic, Perry begins by saying that he is going to study "the possibility of talking about something without designating it" (1986, 206). Only someone with the peculiar combination of grammatical and Gricean grievances I have about philosophers' uses of the verbs 'refer', 'denote', 'designate', 'predicate', 'say', 'imply', and 'mean' is likely to worry about this remark, and in any event it is just a rough pointer and should not be subjected to the sort of remorseless scrutiny to which philosophers are constitutionally prone to subject one another's remarks. So let me just say that I prefer to invoke a distinction between referring to X *in doing something* (e.g., in uttering "it's raining") and referring to X *with something* (e.g., with 'Reykjavík' or with 'here').[36] The latter is meant to be equivalent to using something (e.g., 'Reykjavík' or 'here') to refer to X, where the understood subject of 'refer' points to the agent rather than the tool.[37] So, I have two simple transpositions of Perry's remark: I am interested in "the possibility of referring to something without using a word to refer to it," alternatively "the possibility of referring to X without referring to X with a word." That is the way I shall talk later, and I hazard there is nothing here to alarm Perry.[38]

Back to Perry's own words. Concerning an utterance of (1) made by his younger son after looking out of the window one morning, Perry says,

What my son said was true, because it was raining in Palo Alto. . . . In order to assign a truth-value to my son's statement, as I just did, I needed a place. But no component of his statement stood for a place. . . . Palo Alto is a constituent of the content of my son's remark, which no component of his statement designated; it is an unarticulated constituent. (Perry 1986, 206)

This oft-quoted passage occurs *before* Perry introduces propositions as entities containing objects and properties, and before he talks about propositions expressed, and any perplexity one feels in reading it is probably due to these facts. We must be careful, however, with 'what my son said', 'statement' and 'remark'. The words 'statement' and 'remark' have an all too convenient act-object (perhaps process-product) ambiguity also found with 'use', 'utterance', 'assertion', and so on.[39] The word 'statement' is used in a head-spinning array of ways in philosophy, linguistics, and law. Sometimes occurrences can be replaced by 'sentence', and sometimes by 'use of a sentence' or by 'utterance of a sentence' (both of which also have the act-object ambiguity). And when it occurs in the contexts of certain verbs the situation worsens. Sometimes 'the statement made' (by a person? by a sentence? by a use of a sentence? by an utterance?) can be replaced by 'the proposition expressed', 'what is said', or 'what is stated'. All of this can make it exceedingly difficult to establish what a writer means when talking about the truth or falsity of a statement or about the components of statements, especially when debates about the bearers of truth and falsity are lurking in the shadows.

In the passage just quoted, Perry begins by talking of "what my son said" and "my son's statement" being true. If one is staunchly of the persuasion that propositions are the principal bearers of truth or falsity, this might well suggest that replacing 'what my son said' and 'my son's statement' by 'the proposition my son expressed' will preserve Perry's meaning. And although this might seem to sit well with his use of 'a statement made by the use of a sentence' (1986, 208), it would not sit well with his use of 'the propositional content of the statement made' and 'the propositions expressed by statements' (1986, 207) or with his use of 'the proposition the statement expresses' (1986, 208). And it would not square with the claim in the passage we are examining that "no component of [my son's] statement stood for a place," unless this occurrence of '[my son's] statement' were replaceable by something quite different from 'the proposition my son expressed', perhaps 'the sentence my son used' or 'the utterance my son produced'. Perry's use of 'component' rather than 'constituent' is surely pointed: propositions have *constituents*, sentences, or utterances thereof, have *components*.[40] At least that is the way I read him here and on page 207.[41]

Now what of the remark that "Palo Alto is a constituent of the content of my son's remark"? Easy: 'the content of my son's remark' is replaceable by 'the proposition my son expressed' (that is, Perry's 'my son's remark' in the original could itself be replaced by 'my son's utterance of the sentence 'it's raining''). And the final occurrence of 'of his statement' can be replaced by 'of the sentence he used, or of the utterance he produced'. The net result, on my reconstruction:

The proposition my son expressed was true, because it was raining in Palo Alto.... In order to identify the proposition my son expressed and evaluate it for truth or falsity, as I just did, I needed a place. But no component of the sentence he used stood for a place.... Palo Alto is a constituent of the proposition my son expressed, which no component of the sentence he used, or of the utterance he produced, was used to refer to; it is an unarticulated constituent.

This is how I have always understood Perry, at any rate.[42]

As far as Perry is concerned, the postulation of unarticulated constituents itself involves no commitment to the existence of (or to the denial of the existence of) "covert" expressions in syntactic structure, no commitment to a distinction (or to the denial of a distinction) between a sentence's superficial form (in contemporary jargon, its PF) and its underlying form (its LF):

there is no basic problem with a statement being about unarticulated constituents. In particular, we do not need to first find an expression, hidden in the "deep structure" or somewhere else and then do the semantics of the statement augmented by the hidden expression. Things are intelligible just as they appear on the surface, and the explanation we might ordinarily give in nonphilosophical moments, that we simply understand what the statement is about, is essentially correct. (1986, 211)

Notice that Perry does not say there is no hidden expression in sentence (1), only that on his proposal "we do not *need* [emphasis added] to first find" such an expression. Perhaps we will find good syntactic evidence for a hidden locative expression in the sentence, but Perry is simply skirting that issue here. If syntacticians come back to him with evidence, of course he will listen, but it would have to be *syntactic* evidence not just facts about how uses of (1) are *interpreted*. That much we know already, for it was precisely those facts that Perry pointed out to us in the first place.

There is one final feature of Perry's (1986) discussion we need to look at. Perry recognizes that the unarticulated constituent of the proposition a speaker expresses by uttering (1) need not be the *speaker's* location. So if this extensional fact does not determine the constituent, what does? I have already offered my own Gricean gloss on this: the speaker's communicative intentions. That Perry is attracted to the Gricean line seems evident enough:

It is simply facts about the speaker's intentions that, perhaps limited by what the speaker can expect the audience to figure out, that determines which place is being talked about. (1998, 9)

The intentions and beliefs of the speaker are clearly key factors. . . . it is natural to think that we are explaining which unarticulated constituent a statement is about, in terms of something like the *articulated* constituents of the beliefs and intentions it expresses. (1986, 210–211)

The second passage has given me a headache for many years, and I am not sure I have a better grasp of it today than I did in the mid-1980s. On a quick skim, the point seems perfectly clear and Gricean: speakers' intentions and beliefs determine unarticulated constituents. But the more one looks at the passage, the more one feels there is a lot more going on, elusive stuff. The final phrase is an awkward one to interpret as the pronoun 'it' appears to be anaphoric upon the indefinite description 'a statement' and in this context the pronoun is naturally read as if it were equivalent to an occurrence of the definite description 'the statement in question'. So, the final phrase contains a device that is meant to be read as if it contained the dreaded word 'statement'. We have talked of statements, construed as uses of sentences, as expressing *propositions*. Now we have to get our minds around the idea of statements expressing *beliefs* and *intentions*. We need to bear in mind a distinction Crimmins and Perry (1989) emphasize in their work on attitudes and attitude ascriptions between a belief itself (a concrete particular) and the *content* of that belief (an abstract object), the *object* of that belief, the *thing believed*. Concrete beliefs are cognitive structures, causally efficacious in our mental life. Belief contents are things we use to *classify* concrete beliefs. Since we have been talking about statements expressing *propositions*, talk of statements expressing *beliefs* and *intentions* might suggest that here Perry is talking about belief *contents*. But that does not seem to square with the idea of explaining "which unarticulated constituent[s] a statement is about" in terms of "the *articulated* constituents of the beliefs and intentions it expresses." I am a little worried about sticking my neck out here, and I am perfectly willing to be corrected, but my best guess as to what Perry means is this:

The intentions and beliefs of the speaker are clearly key factors. . . . it is natural to think that if a proposition $\langle \ldots \alpha \ldots \rangle$ expressed by a use of a declarative sentence X by a speaker S contains an unarticulated constituent α, we can specify α by reference to something like a constituent of a belief S with content $\langle \ldots \alpha \ldots \rangle$, whose content S intended to be expressing by his use of X.

Quite a mouthful, but I think it is not unreasonable to suppose that Perry had something like this in mind.

In more recent work, Perry has elaborated on his 1986 discussion. Sometimes when we are interpreting,

We lack the materials we need for [identifying] the proposition expressed by a statement, even though we have identified the words and their meanings, and consulted the contextual factors to which the indexical meanings direct us. Some of the constituents of the proposition expressed are *unarticulated*, and we consult the context to figure out what they are. (1998, 6)

A location is an unarticulated constituent of the proposition expressed by an utterance of (1):

It is a constituent, because, since rain occurs at a time in a place, there is no truth-evaluable proposition unless a place is supplied. It is unarticulated, because there is no morpheme that designates that place. (1998, 9; 2001, 45)

In such a case,

the task of identifying the unarticulated constituents of the proposition expressed by an utterance remains after all of the relevant semantic rules have been understood and applied. (1998, 10)

That is, there is a "postsemantic" (1998, 10) or "content-supplemental" (2001, 45) use of context in the utterance interpretation process. (The later label is meant to replace the earlier one.)

It is clear from these later remarks that Perry's position is in harmony with those of Sperber and Wilson (1986), Carston (1988), Récanati (1989, 1993, 2001), and Neale (1990) on one important point: the proposition expressed on a given occasion may be underarticulated by the meaning of the sentence uttered and the assignment of referents to all names, indexicals, and so on, and the fixing of anaphoric connections. We are as one on the general matter of linguistic underarticulation. And as far as the relation between sentence (1) and the proposition it is used to express on a given occasion is concerned, Perry's thesis that the proposition may well contain an unarticulated constituent seems to me correct.

Alternative Words

Transposed into the way of talking I favor, Perry's point about utterances of (1) is this: If I utter (1) (right now) to talk about the weather in Reykjavík (right now), to express the proposition (right now) that it is raining in Reykjavík (right now), then Reykjavík itself is a constituent of the proposition I express—on one common conception of propositions, at any rate—but the name 'Reykjavík' is not a component of the sentence I utter.[43] A pretty convincing example, it would seem, of the failure of *isomorphism of form and content*, a breakdown of the one-to-one mapping between the meaningful components of a *sentence* and the constituents of the *proposition* it is used to express on a particular occasion. In the direction we have been considering, a breakdown amounts to the postulation of an unarticulated constituent. In the opposite direction, a breakdown amounts to the postulation of a *nonprojecting articulant*. On direct reference accounts of demonstrative descriptions ('this barn', 'that tall, anemic man') and referential uses of definite descriptions ('the murderer', 'the man drinking champagne'), the nominals would be nonprojecting articulants.[44]

I am concerned mainly with unarticulated constituents here, although the postulation of nonprojecting articulants does raise all sorts of interesting questions, as we shall see. (Does Reykjavík occur twice in the proposition I express by uttering "it's raining here in Reykjavík"?) Unarticulated constituents have come under fire of late, and one of my goals here is to show that most of the criticism is misguided, that it fails to take into account many things that Perry and other underarticulation theorists have taken into account, sometimes only implicitly, but often explicitly. At the same time, I want to explain why I think there is an awful lot of syntactic, semantic, pragmatic, and (most important) conceptual work to do here if we are to provide an adequate theory of underarticulation.

Unarticulated Constituents and the Interpretation of Noun Phrases

Perhaps rashly, I just assumed the truth of UT in *Descriptions* without much comment, mentioning the fact in a few notes and elaborating by way of particular examples rather than by discussion of the underlying concepts.[45] The idea of an isomorphism of form and content in the use of natural language seemed to me, as I think it did to my teachers, either a useful methodological ploy, if used cautiously, or else a poisonous hangover from the age of formal language philosophy, out of place in a realistic examination of the use of natural language. At the time I was writing *Descriptions*, I toyed with the idea of seeing uses of (1) and (2):

(1)   It's raining.

(2)   They ought to impeach the mayor.

as involving the same general phenomenon, and numerous drafts of chapter 3 contained attempts to spell this out. Finally (and fortunately), I held off because I was nervous there might be something *syntactic* going on in (2) that was not going on in (1). Today, I'm inclined to think I made the right decision for the wrong reason. To place any weight on the similarity between (1) and (2) is to make certain *semantic* mistakes. (I am less sure now that it involves a syntactic mistake.) Important differences between uses of (1) and (2) will occupy me a good deal here. For the moment, however, I want to dwell on the superficial similarities.

    First, in both of the scenarios just described, the unarticulated constituent appears to be a *place*, Reykjavík. (A significant difference: with respect to my use of (1): Reykjavík is construed as a *geographical location*, whereas with respect to my use of (2) it is construed as a *geopolitical entity*.) Second, in the scenarios discussed, the unarticulated constituent was the place of utterance, but this is not something dictated by the meanings of the sentences themselves. I may utter (1) here in Reykjavík to express the proposition that it's raining *in Palo Alto*. Suppose Perry is here giving a lecture and is concerned about the weather back home because he has recently replanted his garden. It so happens that I am speaking on the telephone to Ken Taylor, who is in Palo Alto, and Taylor is lamenting the rain that has not let up for three days. I tell Perry I'm talking to

Taylor and inform him about the weather in Palo Alto by uttering (1). In *Descriptions*, I noted the parallel fact in connection with utterances of sentences such as (2). In the midst of a conversation we are having in Reykjavík about the quality of the roads in *Palo Alto*, Perry could use (2) to express the proposition that the mayor *of Palo Alto* ought to be impeached.[46]

The noun 'mayor' is just one among many that are frequently used in such a way that implicit reference to a place or a location is part and parcel of the speech act. No doubt all sorts of useful classifications can be made here, but for present purposes it will suffice to have a representative list of what I shall call *implicit geopols*: 'mayor', 'king', 'prime minister', 'president', 'senator', 'ambassador', 'citizen', 'resident', 'inhabitant', 'native', 'national', 'local', 'foreigner', 'alien', 'exile', 'refugee', 'guest', 'visitor', 'inmate'. The principle used in drawing up this list is roughly this: α cannot be an N without being an N relative to something β or some pair of things $\langle \beta, \gamma \rangle$. α cannot be a mayor without there being some place β that α is mayor *of*. α cannot be an ambassador without there being a place β that α is ambassador *from* and a place γ that α is an ambassador *to*. Some geopols have straightforward adjectival siblings ('foreigner'–'foreign', 'local'–'local'), others do not ('king'). Some have straightforward verbal siblings ('president'–'preside', 'resident'–'reside', 'visitor'–'visit'), others do not ('foreigner'). Sometimes meaning shifts occur between the noun and sibling ('presidential' does not mean 'is a president', for example). Some geopols admit of both informal and legal uses that could clash ('resident'). Some of them are, relative to somewhere or other it turns out, applicable to everyone ('foreign'), whereas others are not ('mayor'). I shall not try to impose any order here. (My private attempts have been unimpressive, to say the least.) Rather, I want to touch on some rather general issues about the syntax, semantics, and interpretation of geopols with a view to exposing certain things that will be useful when we return to weather verbs.

Consider a binary relation M that holds of a pair $\langle \alpha, \beta \rangle$ of objects iff α is a mayor of β.[47] M is related in *some* way to the meaning of the English noun 'mayor'—didn't I just use 'mayor' in the biconditional! Three possibilities come straight to mind. (i) The noun 'mayor' has as its meaning the *binary* relation M. (ii) It has as its meaning the *unary* relation $\lambda x \exists y M x y$. (iii) Some occurrences of 'mayor' have as their meaning M, other occurrences have as their meaning $\lambda x \exists y M x y$. On option (iii), there would be a similarity with the way the verb 'eat' is sometimes analyzed. Transitive occurrences have as their meaning a binary relation E that holds of a pair $\langle \alpha, \beta \rangle$ of objects iff α eats β. Intransitive occurrences have as their meaning the unary relation $\lambda x \exists y E x y$. Borrowing this terminology, let us say that the noun 'mayor' appears to have both transitive and intransitive uses.[48]

These options involve no intrinsic commitment to any interesting *syntactic* thesis about 'mayor'. For example, there is no commitment to treating all or some occurrences of 'the mayor', 'every mayor', and so on as containing an aphonic, indexical argument that speakers use to refer to different things on different occasions. That *might* be a syntactic position we find we want to accept for various *syntactic* reasons; but nothing in the *semantic* proposals themselves involves such a commitment. As Perry (1986, 1998, 2001) stresses, there is nothing *incoherent* in the idea of an expression having as its meaning an n-place relation while having m argument positions in syntax, where $m \neq n$. And on his view, this may explain the presence of certain unarticulated constituents. It is an *empirical* question whether natural languages actually contain expressions for which $m \neq n$, and we can have no time for a priori claims that they cannot.

The mere fact that (i)–(iii) come to mind so readily may suggest that geopols differ in some common and interesting way from 'table' and 'tree'. It is hard to imagine getting to the point of needing to choose among competing accounts of the relation between the meaning of the word 'tree' and a unary relation (property) T that holds of α iff α is a tree. Certainly nothing is a mayor or a tree unless it is *at* a location (geographically speaking), but nothing is a mayor unless it is *at* a location and also mayor *of* a location (geopolitically speaking). (For a caveat, see below.) And surely this is why we are tempted to start talking about a binary relation in connection with the meaning of 'mayor' but not in connection with the meaning of 'tree'.

So what are the right accounts of the syntax and semantics of 'mayor'? The issues here are complex. As far as grammar is concerned, it is clear that no mandatory overt argument is required: 'the mayor' is just as well formed as 'the mayor of Reykjavík'. Nonetheless, we cannot immediately discount the possibility that syntacticians will find evidence that the noun 'mayor' always co-occurs with an *aphonic locative* of some sort. On such an account, (2) might have the syntactic form we can sketch as (3), where e is the aphonic, the position it occupies in (3) being occupied by 'of Reykjavík' in (4):

(3)   They ought to impeach [$_{DP}$ the [$_{NP}$ mayor e]].

(4)   They ought to impeach [$_{DP}$ the [$_{NP}$ mayor [of Reykjavík]]].

And it might seem very natural to ally such a syntactic hypothesis with semantic hypothesis (i), the thesis that 'mayor' expresses the binary relation M. The idea would be that e is an aphonic indexical that might be used to refer to Reykjavík on one occasion, to London on another, and so on. Thus, (3) and (4) might be used on one occasion to express the location-involving proposition whose truth conditions are given helpfully by (5):

(5) [*the x*: M(*x*, *Reykjavík*)] *they ought to impeach x.*

But this will not do. There are several mistakes we must be careful not to make here. The first is that a felicitous (i.e., nonincomplete) use of a definite description based on a geopol always involves a *particular* unarticulated place. That this is incorrect is clear from the fact that the following *quantified* sentences might be used to express perfectly determinate propositions in response to questions about a particular man:

(6) Smith is the mayor of somewhere or other.

(7) Smith is the ambassador to some place or other from somewhere or other.

Notice that 'somewhere or other' takes large scope on the most natural readings of these sentences and that it is quantifying into the descriptions that secures uniqueness:

(6′) [*somewhere y*] [*the x*: *x mayor of y*] Smith = *x*.

(7′) [*somewhere y*] [*somewhere z*] [*the x*: *x ambassador of y to z*] Smith = *x*.[49]

The basic point here is that *the property of being a place* rather than a *particular place* is a component of the propositions expressed. This is a trivial consequence of the distinction between singular and quantified sentences. The contrast between 'Smith is the mayor of Reykjavík' and 'Smith is the mayor of somewhere or other' involves nothing that is not already involved in the contrast between 'Smith left his keys in Reykjavík' and 'Smith left his keys somewhere or other'.

It will hardly have gone unnoticed that there are much simpler sentences containing indefinite descriptions that would do as well as (6) and (7) in most communicative settings:

(6″) Smith is a mayor.

(7″) Smith is an ambassador.

And here it is clear that no *particular* locations would be involved.[50] (Notice that (6″) and (7″) are not *equivalent* to (6) and (7): unlike (6), (6″) is compatible with the existence of two mayors of the place Smith is a mayor of.)

The second mistake we must guard against here is thinking that that felicitous uses of incomplete definite descriptions based on implicit geopols will always involve unarticulated places (or other constituents that involve the concept of *place*).[51] Whatever property it is that correctly characterizes the entities that mayors or kings are mayors or kings *of*—places, communities, or whatever—a felicitous (i.e., nonincomplete) use of a definite description based on 'mayor' or 'king' need not involve the expression of a proposition containing either a *thing* with that property or *that property* itself as an unarticulated constituent. Suppose it is known to us that only one mayor has ever broken the bank at Monte Carlo. Surely I can make a felicitous, indeed true, assertion using (8):

(8)   the identity of the mayor who broke the bank at Monte Carlo is no longer known.

A more interesting example. Suppose I am to dine tonight with Ragga, who has quirky ideas about dinner parties. She tells me early this morning that there will be, exactly one mayor, one king, one ambassador, one sheriff, and so on for dinner, the identities of none of whom are known to her or to me in advance, because each is to be chosen by Ragga's well-connected sister later in the day. Ragga decides to arrange a seating plan in advance, even though she does not know who is coming. She says to me,

(9)   I want you to sit opposite the mayor, and between the king and the ambassador.

The proposition Ragga expresses is not the place-involving proposition that she wants me to sit opposite, say, the mayor of Reykjavík, and between the king of Norway and the British ambassador to Iceland. Nor is it the monstrous *property-of*-place-involving proposition whose truth conditions we might capture as follows:

(10)   [*somewhere t*] [*somewhere u*] [*somewhere v*] [*somewhere w*]
       [*the x: x mayor of t*] [*the y: y king of u*]
       [*the z: z ambassador of v to w*] *Ragga wants Stephen to sit opposite x and between y and z.*

The proposition Ragga expresses is something like the proposition that she wants me to sit opposite the mayor dining here tonight and between the king dining here tonight and the ambassador dining here tonight.

The use of geopol nouns with determiners other than 'the' or with no (phonic) determiner at all reinforces the point. When the official photographs are being taken at the opening of a meeting of heads of state, the following announcement might be made in connection with the general photograph:

(11)   All presidents and prime ministers in the middle, please, ambassadors to the left, private secretaries and local dignitaries to the right.

What these examples seem to demonstrate is that 'mayor' is not quite as different from 'table' as we might have thought initially. True, one cannot be a mayor without being the mayor *of* some place or community. But quite what follows about the syntax and semantics of 'mayor' is not yet clear. What we appear to have established so far is only that it is pretty pointless pursing the following combination: the meaning of 'mayor' is the binary relation M, and 'the mayor' has a syntactic structure [$_{DP}$ the [$_{NP}$ mayor e]] in which e is an aphonic, indexical, locative. Perhaps the *structure* is right, but e is not required to be a locative, its presence dictated not by the meaning of 'mayor' but by a quite *general* fact: *every* nominal co-occurs with an aphonic argument.[52] This is certainly an idea that needs exploring, but the fact that we have been led to it suggests the question of how we interpret utterances of 'the mayor' is not itself a question about unarticulated places or communities at all, even if, as seems correct, the meaning of 'mayor' crucially involves the property of place or community.

We have been led astray, I think, in our quest to understand the syntax and semantics of nouns like 'mayor', 'father', and 'murderer' by the general problem of quantifier incompleteness, of which the case of incomplete descriptions is an instance. And this is not surprising: the problem of incomplete descriptions has been treated by many people as if it were properly soluble only by saturating preexisting arguments, or at least filling pre-existing argument positions. For certain nouns, the argument position is intuitive, revealed by meaning ('mayor', 'father', and 'murderer'). For others it is not ('tree', 'table', 'cloud'), suggesting we dig deeper until we find it. I think this is mistake. We should be pursuing option (ii): the noun 'mayor' has as its meaning the unary relation $\lambda x \exists y M x y$. The difference between 'tree' and 'mayor' is not that the latter stands for a binary relation; the difference, rather, is that whereas 'tree' stands for a noncomposite unary relation, 'mayor' stands for a composite unary relation built around a noncomposite binary relation. This leaves us with the task of explaining the possibility of expressing the proposition that the mayor of Reykjavík will sit here by uttering (12) or (13):

(12)   [$_{DP}$ the [$_{NP}$ mayor]] will sit here.

(13)   [$_{DP}$ the [$_{NP}$ mayor [of Reykjavík]]] will sit here.

Let us take (13) first. The idea would be that 'of Reykjavík' is an *argument-affecting adjunct*. The noun 'mayor' is used to express the unary relation $\lambda x \exists y M x y$ and the expression 'of Reykjavík' is used to refer to Reykjavík; and so (in a way that needs to be elaborated) the whole NP 'mayor of Reykjavík' is used to express the unary relation $\lambda x M(x, Reykjavík)$; and so the sentence as a whole is used to express the proposition whose truth conditions are given helpfully by (13′), which can be simplified as the still more helpful (13″):

(13′)   [*the z*: $\lambda x M(x, Reykjavík)z$] *z will sit here.*

(13″)   [*the z*: $M(z, Reykjavík)$] *z will sit here.*

Now what of the NP 'mayor' in (12)? Here it would seem that a little more work is required. All we get from syntax and semantics is a proposition whose truth conditions are given by (14'), hence (14''):

(12') [*the z*: $\lambda x \exists y M(x, y)z$] *z will sit here.*

(12'') [*the z*: $\exists y M(z, y)$] *z will sit here.*

The problem is that (12'') is true only if there is exactly one mayor. *Now* we face the problem of incomplete descriptions. And *now* we can see where unarticulated constituents come into the picture. Consider two distinct utterances of (12). The first is made in a context in which someone is telling me where the mayor *of Reykjavík* is to sit. The second is made by Ragga in connection with her dinner party: she is telling me where the mayor who comes to diner tonight will sit. The structure of the unary relation expressed by 'mayor' means one very natural way of providing a complete interpretation of utterances of 'the mayor' is always lurking in the shadows. Interpretation does not *have* to take advantage of this, but in principle it can. And it is this that distinguishes, on the one hand, 'mayor', 'king', 'president', 'father', and 'murderer', from, on the other, 'tree', 'table', and 'cloud'.

In the light of our understanding of 'mayor', we should revisit and query the idea that the verb 'rain' is intrinsically and richly locative. I do not mean this in the uninteresting sense that we can sometimes express a proposition about no *particular* location using a sentence that contains the verb 'rain'. For that is easy enough, and we have a sentence tailor-made for such use: 'it's raining somewhere'. This fact is not interestingly different from the fact that we can sometimes express propositions about no particular *person* using sentences that contains verbs such as 'kill' and 'die'. We have sentences tailor-made for such use: 'the flood killed someone', 'someone died'.

Unarticulated Constituents and the Interpretation of Verb Phrases

How tight, then, is the connection between the interpretation of weather statements like (1) and (2) and the interpretation of quantified statements like (3) and (4)?

(1)   It's raining.

(2)   It's windy.

(3)   The mayor ought to be impeached.

(4)   Foreigners need a visa.

The following points seem clear enough: (i) In both types of cases, we are inclined to say that typically the proposition expressed contains a location as a constituent. (ii) In neither type of case are we tempted to say we are dealing with syntactic elision of the sort we find in, say, 'Perry is at Stanford and Crimmins is too'. (iii) In neither case are we tempted to say we are dealing with less than a complete, well-formed sentence (as we might be tempted to say when confronted with anacoluthon, for example, 'the mayor of... look there he is!'). Of course, we cannot afford to overlook the possibility that the purported failure of isomorphism between the meaningful constituents of (1)–(4) and the components of the propositions we express on particular occasions by uttering them is only *apparent*. It is no news that many generative linguists have argued for a distinction between the phonic and aphonic elements of a sentence, a distinction that makes perfectly good sense if a sentence is analyzed in the manner suggested by Chomsky, as a pair comprising a PF and an LF, the former relevant to sound, the latter to meaning.[53] It is at least arguable (a) that the sentence whose PF we represent in traditional orthography as (1) contains an indexical, locative aphonic in its LF, and (b) that when I used (1) to express the proposition that it was raining in Reykjavík I was using this aphonic to refer to Reykjavík, in much the same way as I could have used the phonic 'here'.[54] There is much to say about the aphonic indexical proposal, but there is much else of a syntactic, semantic, and pragmatic nature to say about weather statements first.

There are some obvious differences between the weather statements (1) and (2). In (1), we find a form of the verb 'rain'; in (2) we find the adjective 'windy'. To add intensity to (1) we can modify the verb with an adjective like 'hard'; to add intensity to (2) we can modify the adjective with 'very'. For the moment, I want to put aside adjectival weather statements and consider only verbal weather statements like (1). And I want to focus for a moment not on the unarticulated locations of propositions expressed by uses of verbal weather statements but on whether there might not be *additional* unarticulated constituents of these propositions. For the sake of argument, let us just assume, without prejudice, that raining is a relation that has at least two relata, places and times, and look at whether there might be a *third* relatum. Consider the following:

(5) It's raining cats and dogs.

(6) It's raining a very fine rain.

(7) It rains nitric acid on some planets.

(8) It's raining blood/frogs/pebbles.

(9) It's raining men (Hallelujah!) / money.

Statement (5) is an idiom, 'cats and dogs' understood as something like 'very hard'. But 'cats and dogs' is a DP nonetheless, just like 'a hard rain', 'nitric acid', 'blood', and so forth. Do we say that 'rain' optionally takes a DP complement? Or do we say it always does so and that such a complement is implicit in (1), that when I use that sentence to say that it's raining in Reykjavík, I am using 'rain' in some sort of default way to express the idea of raining the stuff it usually rains, namely, water?

The issues here seem similar to those involving 'eat' and 'mayor' discussed earlier. Consider a ternary relation R' that holds of a triple $\langle \alpha, \beta, \gamma \rangle$ of objects if, and only if, at time α, in place β, substance γ is being rained. R is related in *some* way to the meaning of the English verb 'rain'—didn't I just use 'rained' in the biconditional! Three possibilities. (i) The verb 'rain' has as its meaning the *ternary* relation R'. (ii) It has as its meaning the *binary* relation $\lambda y \lambda x \exists z R' xyz$. (iii) Some occurrences of 'rain' have as their meaning R', other occurrences have as their meaning $\lambda y \lambda x \exists z R' xyz$. Adapting earlier terminology, on this option the verb 'rain' appears to have both transitive and intransitive uses. None of these options seems particularly attractive, but somehow we need to explain the uses of (5)–(9).

Are we dealing with a single verb 'spit' in the following?

(10)   It's spitting.

(11)   Bill is spitting.

(12)   Bill is spitting blood.

Utterances of (10), where 'spit' is used as a weather verb (in British English, at least), seem no different from utterances of (1) in relevant respects: the proposition I express by uttering (10) might be the proposition that it is spitting *in Reykjavík*, a proposition that contains Reykjavík as an unarticulated constituent. But what about utterances of (11) and (12), which appear to contain the same verb? I have not checked, but I imagine the use of 'spit' as a weather verb evolved from its uses in sentences of the forms of (11) and (12), where there is no issue of an unarticulated constituent (except a potentially unarticulated spittle, of course).

That considerable work is going to be involved teasing apart syntactic, semantic, and pragmatic considerations involving the uses of verbs of interest here is reinforced by reflections on utterances of (13)–(15):

(13)   It's pouring today.

(14)   You're pouring today; I poured yesterday.

(15)   You're pouring the tea; I poured (it) yesterday.

Suppose Ósk and I take turns pouring afternoon tea, wherever we happen to be, and that we take afternoon tea just once each day. I may utter (14) or (15) to tell her that it is her turn today and to state my justification. But *the location* of my tea pouring yesterday does *not* seem to be an unarticulated constituent of the proposition I express: it does not seem relevant to the identity of the proposition I expressed *where* I poured our tea yesterday—which is not to say Ósk will not try to recall where we were yesterday afternoon at around 4:00 PM in order to see whether the proposition I am expressing is true. Under what conditions is it true? It is true if we were in our favorite café when I poured our tea, and equally if we were at Sindri's house, or at the side of the road on the way to Gullfoss. In this respect, utterances of (14) and (15) appear to be unlike utterances of (13).

Or are they? A modification of our example might suggest matters are more complicated than they first seem. Suppose Ósk and I take tea *twice* everyday, once at a friend's house outside Reykjavík and once in Reykjavík at our favorite café. And suppose that it is only when we take our tea in the café in Reykjavík that we ritually alternate the pouring. Could I utter (14) or (15) in such a scenario to express the proposition that today it is Ósk's turn to pour the tea *in Reykjavík*? (Or, perhaps, her turn to pour it *in our favorite café in Reykjavík*?) If so, then Reykjavík *would* appear to be an unarticulated constituent of the proposition I express. So perhaps it is a "pragmatic" or "context-sensitive" matter whether the proposition someone expresses by uttering (14) or (15) contains a location as an unarticulated constituent. Whether this is so is something we shall need to investigate, along with any repercussions our answer may have for utterances of (1)–(9).

One thing is certain: we are not going to get to the heart of the *interpretive* matter by simply embellishing the syntactic structures of English sentences with purportedly indexical aphonics. Perhaps there are good syntactic reasons for thinking that some of (1)–(9) *do* contain such devices and that when we utter such sentences we use these aphonics to refer to places, but a general theory of the commonsense nature of utterance interpretation still has to provide an account of *how* such devices are understood on occasions in which (1)–(9) are produced, just as such a theory has to explain how *phonic* indexicals like 'he', 'she', 'it', 'this', 'that', 'here', and 'there' are understood.

We are left with some pressing questions. First, is Perry right about the propositions we express when uttering sentence (1) containing unarticulated constituents? Second, how much uniformity is there in the way locations "get into" the propositions we express by uttering sentences (1)–(9). Third, how are we to reconcile the seemingly "pragmatic" absence or presence of an unarticulated location in the propositions I express using (14) or (15) in the different scenarios involving Ósk and the tea pouring. Fourth, are there consequences of this unarticulated constituent business for the theory of *reference*? Did I *refer* to Reykjavík when I uttered (1)–(9) even though I did not use any expression to refer to Reykjavík? Did I *refer* to it when I uttered (14) in the second tea-pouring scenario? Fifth, what are the consequences of all of this for the theory of syntax? There would appear to be three broad options for any particular linguistic construction, the *subsyntactic* option, the *syntactic* option, and the *parasyntactic* option. I shall suggest that the first of these, proposed by Taylor 2001 is the most attractive.

Locations

With the name 'Reykjavík', we may refer to a geographical location, to a geopolitical entity, or perhaps to a still more complex entity altogether. We can certainly talk non-redundantly about Reykjavík's location, and talk sensibly, in certain contexts, about digging up Reykjavík and relocating it in southeastern Iceland.[55] The idea that there is a single entity that we always refer to when we use this name is surely incorrect.[56]

When we talk about the weather, we tend to be more interested in locations themselves, and these will be my principal concern here. But we need to take into account a few facts about reference to geopolitical entities if we are not to slip. Consider (1):

(1)   Reykjavík has more than 100,000 inhabitants.

Suppose I use this to express a proposition about a geopolitical entity. The proposition is *singular* and may be contrasted with the *general* propositions I express by uttering (2) or (3):

(2)   Every capital city has more than 100,000 inhabitants.

(3)   Many capital cities have more than 1,000,000 inhabitants.

The proposition I express by uttering (1) is *singular* (or *object-dependent*) in the following sense: there is a particular object x—namely, Reykjavík (the geopolitical entity)—such that if x did not exist the proposition in question would not exist. There is an object x—namely, Reykjavík, such that the truth-value of the proposition in actual and counterfactual situations depends upon how things are with x. Given the way the world is, the proposition is true. But there are possible states of the world in which Reykjavík (the geopolitical entity) has fewer that 100,000 inhabitants, and so possible states of the world in which that proposition is false (it is not a necessary truth that Reykjavík has more 100,000 inhabitants).[57] On the Russellian conception of propositions that Perry and many who have discussed his work find appealing, to say that this proposition is Reykjavík-dependent is to say that it contains Reykjavík as a constituent.

The propositions I express by uttering (2) and (3), by contrast, are *general* (or *object-independent*). To be sure, there have to be particular objects, cities, that have populations in excess of 100,000 for the propositions to be true. But that does not make the propositions singular in our sense. There is no object *x* upon whose existence the existence of the propositions depends. (The propositions do not contain any particular city as a constituent.) The truth-value of the proposition in a counterfactual situation might depend upon how things are with cities *distinct* from any actual capital city and might *not* depend on how things are with any actual capital city (suppose every country had a different capital)—if Akureyri were capital of Iceland, for example, then the truth or falsity of the proposition I express by uttering (2) would depend (in part) on how things are with Akureyri rather than Reykjavík.

I want now to discuss some very important points about the use of 'singular' (and, 'object-dependent') in philosophical exposition. These points are going to be central to much of what is to come, so I want to spell them out in a way that should preclude various common forms of misunderstanding. Typically, we use 'singular' with what I shall call a *linguistic wink*. Compare (4) and (5):

(4)   Reykjavík enchants many people.

(5)   Many people are enchanted by Reykjavík.

Strictly speaking, the propositions I express by uttering (4) and (5) are both *Reykjavík-dependent*. But, in point of fact, philosophers will often want to *contrast* (4) and (5), declaring the proposition I express by uttering the former to be singular (object-dependent) and the one I express by the latter to be general (object-independent). Why? Because 'singularity' ('object-dependence') is often used to classify a particular proposition bearing in mind the *grammatical subject* of some particular sentence used to express it. (The linguistic wink.) So, although the distinction between singular and general propositions is meant to be a *metaphysical* one, in point of fact it is often treated as if it corresponded to a *linguistic* distinction between sentences with referential subjects and those with quantificational subjects. In consequence, although the proposition I express right now by uttering (5) is, strictly speaking, Reykjavík-dependent, we often classify it as *general* because it is not what (5) and (4) have in common that interests us, but what (5) and (6) have in common:

(6)   Many people snore.

(In Perry's 2001 terminology, the general proposition I expresses by uttering [6] is "lumpy," as it contains an object as well as properties, but is not singular.) If there are philosophers who share our interests and maintain that I express the same proposition whether I utter (4) or (5), they will call it a singular proposition when winking at (4) and a general one when winking at (5).

Since quantified expressions may contain referential expressions as parts, we must take care when we consider utterances of a sentence like (7):

(7)   Many people who live in Reykjavík are enchanted by it.

Strictly speaking the proposition I express by uttering (7) is Reykjavík-dependent, but often we will not classify it as singular in our discussions because we are actually winking at the *entire* subject expression, which is quantificational, not at one of its parts, 'Reykjavík', which happens to be referential. That is, we are not interested in what (7) has common with (4), but in what it has in common with (6) and (5). (The proposition I express by uttering (7) is "lumpy".) Further caution must be exercised because of unarticulated constituents. Consider (8) and (9):

(8)   Many people who visit are enchanted by Reykjavík.

(9)   Many visitors are enchanted by Reykjavík.

I may use (8) or (9) to express the proposition that many people who visit *Reykjavík* are enchanted by Reykjavík, although in the right circumstances I might use it to express the proposition that many people who visit *Akureyri* are enchanted by Reykjavík. Either way, the propositions are city-dependent, although we will often want to classify them as general when winking at their entire subject expressions.

The linguistic wink route to classification seems useless when discussing the propositions we express by uttering (10)–(12) because the subject expression, in surface syntax at least, is pleonastic 'it', which appears to function as neither a referential nor a quantificational expression:

(10)   It's snowing in Reykjavík today.

(11)   It's snowing here today.

(12)   It's snowing today.

If I am using (10)–(12) to express the proposition that it is snowing *in Reykjavík* today, the proposition I express is surely Reykjavík-dependent. So let us simply stipulate that this proposition is singular, contrasting it with the general propositions I express by uttering (13) or (14):

(13)   It's snowing today in every capital city I visited last year.

(14)   It's snowing today in every city north of Reykjavík.

Of course, the proposition I express by uttering (14) is Reykjavík-dependent, but we are winking at 'every capital city except Reykjavík' (not at 'Reykjavík') when we say the proposition expressed by a use (14) is general.

We must take care in some cases to specify *which* location we have in mind upon whose existence a proposition depends. Suppose we are discussing (15):

(15)   A man from Copenhagen told me it's snowing.

It may be the *Reykjavík*-dependence of the proposition I express by uttering (15) that we are interested in, not the *Copenhagen*-dependence. As we shall see, when discussing locations we have to be careful in all sorts of ways.

The seemingly simple distinction between singular and general propositions is famously complicated by consideration of the propositions we express using sentences with definite descriptions as subjects. According to Russellians, the word 'the' is a quantificational device on a par with 'every' or 'no', so the proposition I express right now by uttering (16) is general:

(16)   The city which hosted the most famous chess match in history has over 100,000 inhabitants.

There is no object x upon whose existence it depends. There is no object x such that the truth-value of the proposition in actual and counterfactual situations depends upon how things are with x. Assuming, for the sake of argument, that the Fischer-Spassky match is the most famous chess match in history, the proposition is true, but it does not contain *Reykjavík* as a constituent. The proposition is Reykjavík-independent: in a counterfactual course of history in which the most famous chess match in history was played in Helsinki, the proposition would be true if Helsinki had a population that exceeded 100,000 in that world, and Reykjavík would not be relevant to this.[58]

When we talk about the weather we tend to be interested in geographical locations rather than geopolitical entities (although one can easily engineer cases for which matters are otherwise). So I want to start talking now about *location*-singular and *location*-general propositions. The problem with location-singularity is that it is unclear what is involved in using *existence* to characterize it. (Of course, it is not entirely clear what is involved in using existence to characterize *object*-singularity either, but the situation with locations seems to me if anything worse.) Nonetheless, we can, I think, get what we want from talk of the truth-values of propositions in actual and counterfactual situations. We can distinguish the location-singular proposition I express by uttering (17) from the location-general propositions I express by uttering (18) and (19):

(17)   It rained last week in Reykjavík.

(18)   It rained last week in every city I stayed in.

(19)   It rained last week in the city I was staying in.

The truth-value at an arbitrary possible state of the world of the proposition I express by uttering (17) depends upon how things are with Reykjavík at that world. Not so the propositions I express by uttering (18) and (19), even though the only city I stayed in last week was Reykjavík, and it rained there. At worlds in which I happened to be staying only in London last week, the proposition is true if it rained *in London* last week.[59]

With these preliminaries out of the way, we can now address concerns raised by those who maintain that the proposition I express by uttering (20) does not contain an unarticulated constituent:

(20)   It's raining.

Suppose I utter (20) in response to a question about the weather in Reykjavík, intending to communicate that it is raining here. The philosopher who denies that the proposition I expressed is location-singular (Reykjavík-dependent), who denies that it contains Reykjavík as an unarticulated constituent, has an immediate problem: he needs to tell us exactly what proposition I *did* express, but this is a task he has effectively blocked himself from executing. (a) He cannot say it is a location-singular proposition at all, for if it were, it would surely be the *Reykjavík*-dependent proposition that it is raining *in Reykjavík*, which contains Reykjavík. (It would be absurd to claim it was the proposition that it is raining in Iceland or in the Northern Hemisphere, for example.) (b) He cannot say it is the location-general proposition that it's raining *in the place Stephen Neale happens to be* because in many possible states of the world this proposition differs in truth-value from the proposition I expressed when I uttered (20). (There cannot be possible states of the world in which one and the same proposition has two different truth values.) Similarly, it cannot be the location-general proposition that it is raining *in the place the speaker happens to be.* (c) He cannot say it is the location-general proposition that it is raining *somewhere or other* (the proposition that $\exists x(x$ *is a location &* *it is raining in/at/on x*)) for then the proposition I expressed would be almost trivially true, which it is not. The only circumstances, on such a proposal, in which one could express a false proposition by uttering (20) would be when it's raining nowhere in the universe![60] (d) He cannot say it is the location-general proposition that it is raining *everywhere* (the proposition that $\forall x(x$ *is a location* $\supset$ *it is raining in/at/on x*), for then the proposition I expressed would be almost trivially false, which it is not.

If there is no location-singular proposition that I expressed and no location-general proposition that I expressed, then what proposition did I express, and what are the conditions of its truth, actually and counterfactually? (e) He cannot say it is the proposition that it is raining simpliciter, because *there is no such proposition*, propositions being the sorts of things that are evaluable for truth or falsity on any theory that is engaging the issues. *Without a location (or quantification over locations) no such evaluation is possible.* In summary, there appears no alternative to Perry's position that Reykjavík is an unarticulated constituent of the proposition I expressed. Until we get from the philosopher who rejects Perry's position a sensible answer to the question "what proposition did I express when I uttered (20), and what are the conditions of its truth, actually and counterfactually?," we are perfectly justified in ignoring him.

Lest there be any misunderstanding here, it should be pointed out that Perry's opponent cannot wriggle out here by arguing that the *location* of the rain I am talking about when I utter (20) is no more a constituent of the proposition expressed than its *intensity* or its *temperature.* Suppose of necessity it is true that rain always has an average temperature and an average intensity (gentle, hard, or whatever) and that the rain coming down in Reykjavík right now is 5° Celsius and hard (according to some specified measure). It would still be a mistake to claim that its intensity and temperature are on a *propositional par* with its location when it comes to the proposition I expressed by uttering (20). Whether it is raining hard in Reykjavík or raining gently in Reykjavík, the proposition that *it is raining in Reykjavík* is true. The actual intensity of *no current (falling) rain anywhere* is relevant to the truth or falsity of this proposition; and similarly the actual temperature of *no current (falling) rain anywhere* is relevant to the truth or falsity of this proposition. By stark contrast, the actual *location* of some current (falling) rain *is* relevant: some of it has to be *in Reykjavík.* This asymmetry is striking and reinforced from the other direction. Consider the proposition I express by uttering (21) now:

(21)   It's raining hard.

Here the actual intensity of some current rain *is* relevant to the truth or falsity of the proposition I expressed. *But so is the location.*

On a related note, Taylor (2001) points out that the relation a location bears to an utterance of (20) is quite different from the relation a location bears to an utterance of (22):

(22)   Laura danced the tango all night last night.

When dancing takes place it must be at a location, even if it is only on an aircraft speeding between Reykjavík and New York. Must the proposition expressed by someone who utters (22) contain an unarticulated constituent, a location without which it makes no sense to ask about truth and falsity? Taylor's response is a resounding "No":

One can say something fully determinate, something fully truth-evaluable by uttering [(22)] even if context provides no place as the place where the dancing took place. Why does [(22)] differ from [(20)] in this regard?

The answer, I think, has to do with how 'to dance' and 'to rain' relate to the places where rain-ings and dancings happen. 'To dance' does not mark the place where a dance happens as the undergoer of the dance. The theme or undergoer of a dancing is the dancer herself. The place where a dancing "takes place" is merely the place where the dancer dances. When Laura is danc-ing in a place, it is not the place that undergoes the dancing. . . . That a dancing must take place somewhere or other is a (mutually known) metaphysical fact about the universe—a fact that supervenes on the nature of dancing and the structure of space-time. But that metaphysical fact is not explicitly represented in the subsyntactic structure of the lexicon. This is not to say that the place where a dancer dances is never of conversational relevance to us. It is merely to say that such conversational relevance as the location of a dancing enjoys is not a direct consequence of lexically generated requirements on semantic completeness. (2001, 54)

I concur. It matters not a bit whether Mary danced the tango in a swanky club in Bue-nos Aires, in a dive in Reykjavík, at home in Palo Alto, on a glacier, or in Russian sub-marine cruising the depths of the Indian Ocean: if she danced the tango all night last night, she danced the tango all night last night. Taylor goes on:

Things are quite otherwise with the verb 'to rain'. I take the verb itself, and its subsyntactic lexical structure, to be the source of the felt need for the contextual provision of a place or range of places where a raining happens. Facts about the subsyntactic lexical structure of the verb directly entail that nothing fully propositionally determinate has been expressed by an utterance of a sentence like [(20)] unless a place is provided. It is, of course, an interesting and important question just why 'to rain' allows its theme to go syntactically unexpressed at the level of sentence-level syntax, despite the fact that the verb demands the contextual specification of that theme. But that is an interesting and difficult *linguistic* question, not an interesting and difficult *philosophical* one. (2001, 54)[61]

I shall say more about Taylor's discussion later. Right now I want only to stress my gen-eral agreement on the matter of the difference between the verbs 'dance' and 'rain': a use of the latter, and only the latter, demands a particular location (or quantification over locations) in order for a use of a sentence containing it to express a proposition.

There is another issue that needs to be taken up, however. For all that has been said so far, there may be some occasions on which the location of dancing *is* an unarticu-lated constituent of the proposition expressed by a use of a sentence containing the verb 'dance'. That could be the case when (23) is used, of course, but this is not what I have in mind:

(23)   It rained last night the whole time Laura was dancing the tango.

I might use (23) to express the location-independent proposition that it rained last night wherever it was that Laura danced the tango, the whole time Laura was dancing the tango. (This proposition is true if Laura traveled by fast boat from some point in the Atlantic due north to Reykjavík last night, dancing the tango the whole way, as long as it rained the whole way.) But I might use (23) to express the location-dependent proposition that it rained *in Reykjavík* last night the whole time Laura was dancing the tango, wherever Laura may have been dancing the tango last night Reykjavík time (i.e., GMT). (This proposition is true if Laura traveled by very fast boat last night [GMT] from anywhere on Earth to Reykjavík, dancing the tango the whole way, as long as it rained the whole time in Reykjavík.) Reykjavík is an unarticulated constituent of *that* proposition. And if Laura happened to be dancing the tango *in Reykjavík* all night last night, the location is still an unarticulated constituent of the proposition expressed. But this is an accident as far as 'dance' is concerned: it has nothing to do with the demands imposed by the meaning of 'dance' (or those imposed by the metaphysics of dancing). *Reykjavík gets into the proposition via the demands imposed by the meaning of the verb 'rain'.*

Might there not be occasions on which the location of dancing is a *nonaccidental* unarticulated constituent of the proposition expressed by a use of a sentence containing the verb 'dance', a scenario in which the location of the *dancing* is of such importance to the conversation that a good case could be made for saying that the truth-value of the proposition expressed is sensitive to the location of the dancing? Construction of a convincing example is not easy. Taylor is very cautious here, saying only that "such conversational relevance as the location of a dancing enjoys is not a direct consequence of lexically generated requirements on semantic completeness" (2001, 54). In the absence of a convincing example, I am strongly inclined to stick my neck out here and say that there are *no* scenarios of the sort I just described: if a location of a dancing is an unarticulated constituent of the proposition expressed by a use of a sentence containing the verb 'dance', this is always accidental, the location getting into the proposition expressed by virtue of something *other* than the dancing.[62] To explain why I say this, I want to look at a purported counterexample I raised earlier involving the verb 'pour'.

On the relevant usage, and in the crucial respect, 'pour' is no different from 'dance', but its use as a pseudo-weather verb reveals some important points. In the simplest cases, it looks as if no unarticulated location is a constituent of the proposition I express by uttering (24):

(24)   I poured the tea yesterday.

If Ósk and I take turns pouring afternoon tea, wherever we happen to be, and if we take afternoon tea just once each day, I may convey to her that it is her turn today by uttering (24). The *location* of my tea-pouring yesterday does *not* seem to be an unarticulated constituent of the proposition I express: that proposition is true if we were in our favorite café when I poured our tea, but equally if we were at Sindri's house, or in Russian submarine cruising the depths of the Indian Ocean watching Mary dance the tango. Of course Ósk may well try to recall where we were yesterday afternoon at around 4:00 PM in order to satisfy herself that it is really her turn to pour, but *that* is not the issue. So far, so good, then: the mere fact that the conversational participants may home in on a particular location when one of them has uttered (24) is not sufficient for making that location a constituent of the proposition expressed.

As noted earlier, there might be contexts in which the location is an unarticulated constituent. If Ósk and I take tea *twice* every day, once at a friend's house outside Reykjavík, and once in Reykjavík at our favorite café, and if it is only in the Reykjavík café that we ritually alternate the pouring, could I not use (24) to express the proposition that I poured the tea *in Reykjavík* yesterday? (Or, perhaps, the proposition that I poured the tea *in this particular café in Reykjavík* yesterday?) If so, then wouldn't Reykjavík would be an unarticulated constituent of the proposition I express? And given how easy it was to construct this scenario for an utterance of (24), in principle couldn't we construct an analogous scenario for an utterance of Taylor's (22), where the verb is 'dance' rather than 'pour'?

We need to exercise caution. It is far from clear that my use of the verb 'pour' is directly implicated in the presence of an unarticulated location in the modified scenario involving Ósk and the tea pouring. The culprit is surely my use of the *incomplete description* 'the tea'. When I utter (24) in the unmodified scenario, I was using 'the tea' in the sense of something like "the tea we drank together yesterday." In the modified scenario, I was using it in the sense of "the tea we drank together *in Reykjavík* yesterday" (or, if we are in the Reykjavík café at the time, "the tea we drank together *here* yesterday," for example). In summary, the presence of the unarticulated location appears to have nothing to do with the verb 'pour' itself, or with the metaphysical fact that tea pourings takes place at locations. And it is my contention that any attempt to cause trouble for examples involving the use of the verb 'dance' will actually involve smuggling in an unarticulated constituent in a similar way. In summary, I think Taylor is absolutely right about 'dance' and right to see it as contrasting with 'rain'.

There is a residual question involving 'pour'. Do we have the same verb in (the following?

(25)   It's pouring now [said in connection with the weather].

(26)   It's pouring well now [said in connection with a teapot whose spout has been repaired].

(27)   Ósk's pouring well [said in connection with Ósk's tea pouring].

I think we do. Unlike 'rain', 'pour' is not really a weather verb. It's basically an action verb, and the way it is used in (25) and (26) is surely derived from its use in sentences like (27)—which is not to say that one might first learn its use in, say, (25). The situation is roughly inverted with 'rain', its use in (27′) and (26′) derived from its use in sentences like (25′):

(25′)   It's raining now [said in connection with the weather].

(26′)   It's raining down his face [said in connection with the blood from a cut above someone's eye].

(27′)   Ósk's raining tears [said in connection with her crying].

'Rain' is a genuine weather verb, which is why its use demands a location (or quantification over locations).

The considerations just adduced suggest that Taylor and I may be disagreeing with Perry on one point, or at least that we are describing the presence of the unarticulated constituent in the proposition expressed by an utterance of (25′) in a way that is more linguistic than any description Perry might be willing to use here. Perry suggests that, since the use of no component of (25′) stands for Reykjavík when I use the sentence to express the proposition that it's raining now in Reykjavík, it must be my use of *the sentence as a whole* that is about Reykjavík. Fair enough, but I agree with Taylor that the *presence* of a location in that proposition is something demanded by a particular *component* of the sentence, namely, the verb 'rain'. It is mandated by the meaning of the verb 'rain'. It is as much a metaphysical fact about dancings that they take place at locations as it is a metaphysical fact about rainings that they do. So the simplest metaphysical considerations alone will not give us all we need to explain the existence of an unarticulated location in a rain statement. At the very least we need something like Taylor's idea of a *theme* or *undergoer*. Does this mean making a *syntactic* claim? That is something I shall take up later.

About and Concerns

Consider my utterances of (1) and (2) again:

(1)   Reykjavík has more than 100,000 inhabitants.

(2)   Every capital city has more than 100,000 inhabitants.

The proposition I express by uttering the singular sentence (1) is location-singular. The one I express by uttering the general (quantified) sentence (2) is location-general. But one might argue that there is a respect in which the proposition I express by uttering (2) is, nonetheless, location-*dependent*. Suppose I am using (2) to make a claim about capital cities *in Europe*, not capitals in the whole world, or capital cities, if there are such, on Mars or elsewhere in the universe.[63] We have a classic case here of what is often called "incompleteness," a phenomenon pervasive in the interpretation of quantified phrases.[64] If our conversation has been about European cities and my intention in uttering (2) is to be understood as claiming that every capital city in Europe has more than 100,000 inhabitants, then it is tempting to say that Europe is a constituent of the proposition I expressed. If our conversation has been about cities more generally and my intention in uttering (2) is to be understood as claiming that every capital city on the planet has more than 100,000 inhabitants (and I have no intention to be understood as making a claim about capital cities, if there are such, on other planets) it might be tempting to say that that the Earth is a constituent of the proposition I expressed.

At least the temptation might be there if the conversational participants have conceptions of other planets and so on.[65] We are at the heart, here, of what seems to me one of the most pressing and ill-understood issues in the philosophy of language and mind: the richness of propositional content. How do we tell just how much stuff gets into the contents of the thoughts we entertain and express? I do not pretend to have an answer to this question; indeed, it seems to me currently intractable. What is certain, however, is that it is something that has bothered Perry for a long time. For there is a rather different approach one might take to uses of (2), one that Perry (1986, 2001), and also Barwise and Perry (1983), have floated in connection with the narrowing of domains and horizons. To use Perry's terminology, the statement I make when I utter (2) might be said to *concern*, say, Europe, even if it is not *about* Europe.[66] Abstracting from temporal matters again, Perry's idea is that a statement is *about* a location if the proposition expressed contains that location as a constituent. By contrast, a statement *concerns* a location if the proposition expressed does not contain that location but is merely evaluated for truth or falsity *with respect to it* (rather than with respect to the Great Location, as it were). Some serious issues must be confronted if this proposal is go gain traction because it appears to involve what is sometimes called a *relativized* conception of truth: the statement that every capital city has more than 100,000 inhabitants is not itself true or false but true relative to some locations and false relative to others.

Perry's *about-concerns* distinction corresponds closely to the *explicit-implicit* distinction I talked about in *Descriptions*, and it will be useful to examine the distinctions together.[67] When confronted with the interpretation of utterances of sentences containing incomplete quantifier expressions such as 'every city', 'no capital city', or 'the table', philosophers tend to say one of two things. (i) "There's always an *implicit background restriction* on the domain over which a quantifier expression ranges" is one old reply. (ii) "The utterance is *elliptical* for an utterance of some richer or more *explicit* sentence the speaker could readily supply" is another. Call these the *implicit* and *explicit* replies, respectively. Incompleteness seems to concern slippage between language and the world, so dealing with it would seem to involve either tinkering with language, or else tinkering with the world. When we tinker with *language*, we do something about the quantifier's *matrix*, which we might represent abstractly as $\phi(x)$ when the nominal in question is ϕ (e.g., 'capital city'). When we tinker with the *world*, we do something about the *objects* that (potentially) satisfy the matrix. If we tinker with $\phi(x)$ itself, we are adopting an "explicit" approach to the problem; if we tinker with the objects potentially satisfying it, we are adopting an "implicit" approach.

The distinction between the world-tinkering, implicit approach and the language-tinkering, explicit approach corresponds to a difference in focus with respect to the parts of a DP. Suppose 'every capital city' has the structure we can rough out thus:

(3) $[_{DP}[_D$ every$][_{NP}[_A$ capital$][_N$ city$]]]$.

The determiner D 'every' is the head of the whole DP. The implicit response purports to explain how we get away with using incomplete DPs by focusing on how the head node, D, or its projection, DP, is to be interpreted. If the quantificational structure of 'every capital city is ψ' is represented in our formal language *RQ* as follows,

(4)   [*every x*: *capital-city*(x)] $\psi(x)$

then there are *two* quantifiers to look at, the unrestricted quantifier *every x*, corresponding to the D node, and the restricted quantifier [*every x*: *capital-city x*], corresponding to the DP node. The implicit, world-tinkering, approach explains incomplete usage by limiting the number of objects potentially satisfying *capital-city*(x); and the fact that there are two quantifiers to consider means there are (at least) *two* ways of effecting the required delimitation. Let r be some subset of the objects in the domain of quantification, for example the things on Earth ('r' for 'restricted'). In *RQ* we can represent the two ways of delimiting the domain as follows, subscripting 'r' onto the quantifier whose domain is to be delimited:

(4')   [*every x_r*: *capital-city x*]$\psi(x)$ ('*every x* (in r) such that x is a capital city is such that $\psi(x)$').

(4")   [*every x*: *capital-city x*]$_r\psi(x)$ ('*every x* such that x is a capital city (in r) is such that $\psi(x)$').

I prefer a simple 'r' rather that the variable-containing '$x \in r$' to avoid the suggestion that in (4') and (4") the descriptive content itself is modified, as it is in, say, (4'''):

(4''') [*every x: capital-city*(x) & $x \in r$] (*'every x* such that x is a capital city and $x \in r$ is such that $\psi(x)$').

For as I said in *Descriptions*, a central tenet of the implicit approach is that it "leaves the descriptive content untouched" (1990, 95). In (4'), the *unrestricted* quantifier *every x* ranges over the things in r; in (4") the *restricted* quantifier [*every x: capital-city* (x)] ranges over the things in r. If r is a proper subset of the total domain over which quantifiers range, then the use of (2) to say something that *concerns* Earth (without being *about* Earth) can, in principle, be explained.

In effect, the implicit-concerns approach yields a relativized notion of truth. For it would seem that the proposition expressed by someone using (4) is true or false only relative to some domain or other. And this seems to do serious violence to the traditional conception of proposition. Propositions are absolute bearers of truth values, the things we express using declarative sentences on given occasions, the contents of our statements and beliefs. Standardly, the truth value of a proposition does not vary with time or place. But on the implicit approach, thus described, the same proposition may have different truth values relative to different locations. The proposition someone expresses by uttering (2) right now is false relative to Europe, or to the Earth; relative to some other planet it may be true; relative to one group of countries on Earth (those making up the United Kingdom, for example), it might be true; relative to another (the OPEC countries, for example), it might be false (I have not checked). And so on. This certainly seems like a radical proposal, one involving a significant departure from the usual way of going about business. For on the implicit-concerns approach, propositions themselves—or at least some of them—are not true or false *absolutely*.[68]

No *syntactic* thesis is implied by the implicit-concerns approach. It is certainly compatible with the thesis that the English DP 'every capital city' contains an aphonic expression corresponding roughly to the subscript r in our formal language, just as it is compatible with the syntactic thesis that *what you hear is what you get*. That is, the postulation of an aphonic in 'every capital city' corresponding to r in (4') or (4") is no part of the implicit approach itself, it is, rather, a particular *syntactic* proposal for *implementing* it, one that might be motivated or rejected on *syntactic* grounds.

An interesting version of the implicit approach was provided by Barwise and Perry (1983). Quite generally, they suggest, statements are evaluated for truth or falsity not in connection with the whole world, but in connection with *parts* of it, which they call *situations*.[69] To simplify matters in a way that does not bear on present concerns in any threatening way, let us continue prescinding from time and think of situations as just regions of space, locations of whatever size. Drawing upon Barwise and Cooper's (1981) work on generalized quantifiers, Barwise and Perry define a persistent statement as one whose truth persists as the situation in connection with which evaluation takes place is enlarged. On this account, an utterance of (5) is persistent:

(5) Some capital city has more than 100,000 inhabitants.

Not so an utterance of (2):

(2) Every capital city has more than 100,000 inhabitants.

The idea Barwise and Perry want us to entertain is that the statement someone makes by uttering (2) could be *true* in connection with the United Kingdom, but *false* in connection with Europe, or the Earth, or the entire universe. Any *particular* utterance of (2) is made *in* some situation S and intended to be evaluated *at* some particular situation S', which need not be identical to S, and which may be smaller than the entire universe. And it is this fact, or so it is suggested, that explains how distinct utterances of (2) work.[70]

Before looking briefly at a problem for the implicit-concerns approach, let us turn to the explicit-about approach. The explicit approach leaves the world alone. It purports to explain the felicitous use of (2) by looking not at the nodes occupied by quantifiers in 'every capital city' but at the node occupied by the nominal 'city'. The basic idea is explicitly *modal*: the utterance of the nominal is elliptical for an utterance of at least one richer nominal the speaker *could have* used and *could* produce if asked to be more explicit. Utterances of (2) are understood as if they were utterances of things like the following:

(2′) Every capital city *in the United Kingdom* has more than 100,000 inhabitants.

(2″) Every capital city *in Europe* has more than 100,000 inhabitants.

(2‴) Every capital city *on Earth* has more than 100,000 inhabitants.

That is, the proposition expressed by a use of (2) is actually *about* a place and will contain it as an unarticulated constituent.[71]

Just as there is no *syntactic* thesis implied by the implicit/concerns response, so none is implied by the about/explicit response. There is no implication, for example, that expressions are transformationally deleted between levels of grammatical representation in a Chomskyan grammar—indeed, on standard assumptions there *could not be* such a syntactic thesis because such deletions would violate the principle of *recoverability*, which requires deleted elements to be recoverable from linguistic context.[72] Like the implicit approach, the explicit approach is meant only to describe how speakers intend their utterances to be *interpreted* on particular occasions and to describe the interpretations hearers do seem to get. It involves no *cognitive* claim about the mechanisms whereby hearers manage to *come up with* particular interpretations on particular occasions: that is something for a theory of the pragmatic, inferential processes involved in utterance interpretation to explain.

So what are we to say about a typical utterance of (2)? Will it be *about* a location or will it just *concern* one? Can one utterance of (2) be about a location while another merely concerns one? These are extraordinarily difficult questions. Probably there is not enough in Perry's discussions of locations, persistence, intentions, and the about/ concerns distinction to pin on him anything too definite here, and probably this is a good thing because every move here is fraught with complications. But the general picture I get from isolated remarks and from recollections of discussions with him when I was a student is roughly this: to the extent that some particular location forms part of the content of the communicative intention behind an utterance of (2), we should construe the location as a constituent of the proposition expressed. Of course, this only pushes the question back: when does a location form part of the content of the communicative intention behind an utterance of (2)? Perhaps all we can do is proceed with cases for now. If I am being questioned by Martians about the different countries on Earth, for example, I might use (2) to express the (false) proposition that every capital city on Earth has more than 100,000 inhabitants. Now suppose I tell them about continents and the like and try to explain what Europe is. When they explicitly ask me questions about Europe and its cities, I might use (2) to express the (false) proposition that every capital city *in Europe* has more that 100,000 inhabitants. In these scenarios it does not seem particularly far-fetched to say that Earth and Europe, respectively, are unarticulated constituents of the propositions I express. Similarly, when I return to Earth and face questions about my trip to Mars, I might report on the twenty-three Martian countries using (2) to express the proposition that every Martian capital has more than 100,000 inhabitants. Similarly someone might use (2) to make a bold conjecture about the whole universe, and in such a case I suppose the whole universe would be a constituent of the proposition expressed. (Would this be that different from having *no* unarticulated location as a constituent?)

But what of more down-to-Earth cases? Can't we imagine very ordinary situations in which speakers use (2) with no concept of Earth playing any part in the intention behind the utterance? Would the average speaker using (2) *construe himself* as implicitly referring to Earth? What about someone who has an ancient conception of heavenly bodies and knows nothing about the Earth being one of a number of planets? What should *we* as theorists say about the propositions *we* ourselves express in down-to-Earth cases? These are difficult questions, and I know of no easy answers.

I am skeptical about a *unitary* or *general* concerns/implicit approach, because of examples like the following:[73]

(6)   Every country sent a relief team to every island.

(7)   The Russian voted for the Russian.

Suppose we have been talking about Europe's response to a hurricane that has hit the five islands making up the Republic of Taora in the South Pacific. I might utter (6) to express the proposition that every country *in Europe* sent a relief team to every island *of Taora*. The explicit approach handles this well: the proposition expressed is *about* Europe and *about* Taora, and both are unarticulated constituents of that proposition. But the implicit approach has to overcome an obstacle. There is no situation or part of the world that my use of (6) *concerns*, no situation or part of the world with respect to which the proposition (or propositional function) I express using (6) is true. Europe won't do, because it contains hundreds of islands (I wasn't claiming, in part, that every country in Europe sent a relief team to Capri, Guernsey, and Texel). Nor will any particular portion of the South Pacific containing Taora, for I was talking about *European* countries. We need a situation that contains at least Europe and Taora, but once we have that we will have a situation that is too big (even if we permit it to be a discontinuous situation, a fusion of the Europe situation and the Taora situation, and nothing else). It's as if we need one situation while we focus on 'every country' and a completely different one when we focus on 'every island', changing situation in midutterance, as it were. But that idea makes no sense in light of the way I have described the implicit approach, for its defining feature is the idea of evaluating one entity with respect to another; more precisely it is the idea of evaluating a proposition (or propositional function) for truth or falsity not with respect to the entire world but with respect to just some part of it.

Why not say that we evaluate the proposition for truth or falsity with respect to a *pair* of situations, ⟨the Europe situation, the Taora situation⟩? People are quick to say this because there is no *technical* problem with evaluating one thing with respect to a pair of things. (We've all read our Tarski.) But what does that even *mean* in the present context? A consistent formalism does not answer any philosophical questions about interpretation.[74] What would be the interpretation of my utterance of (6′) for example?

(6′)   Every country sent every relief team to every island.

On the explicit approach, I express the proposition that every country *in Europe* sent every relief team *it sent to Taora* to every island *of Taora*. On the implicit approach, is the proposition (or propositional function) that every country sent every relief team to every island evaluated for truth or falsity with respect to a *triple* of situations, ⟨the Europe situation, the relief teams sent to Taora by European nations situation, the Taora situation⟩? No, this cannot be quite right: relief teams sent to Taora by European nations need to be relativized to individual nations that sent them, so the second of the situations in the triple must actually be parameterized to the individual nations in the first situation in the triple. Something like that, at any rate. No doubt with enough formal machinery one could concoct something that would have the right mathematical features, but an account of the interpretation process based on this is surely over-intellectualized, and the initial attraction of the implicit approach has now gone up in smoke. The original and very intuitive idea of evaluating for truth or falsity at some small portion of the world (as if checking whether one has the ingredients for a cake by restricting one's search for butter, milk, eggs, and flour to the contents of a single kitchen [rather than searching in the world at large]) has metamorphosed into the highly unintuitive idea of evaluating for truth and falsity at some rather odd concoction of various parts of the world, some parameterized to others (as if checking whether one has the ingredients for a cake by restricting one's search to the contents of one kitchen for milk, the contents of another elsewhere in town for eggs, and the contents of kitchens recently visited by people who ate any part of any chicken that laid any of the eggs taken from the second kitchen for butter and flour). How could such an idea possibly form part of theory of interpretation in any interesting sense? I am inclined to think that situation sculpting of this sort will yield no remotely useful way of dealing with (6) and (6').

Things are not much better if we see things *dynamically*. Every time a nominal is encountered, a new situation is invoked and that nominal is evaluated at that situation. But again, relativization of situations is going to be required and the overintellectualization of the interpretation process rears its head. The idea of a background situation shifting with every new nominal that is uttered strikes me as unlikely to help us understand anything about utterance interpretation.[75]

The situation with (7) is similar. Suppose we use it to explain how one of the boxing judges voted in a boxing match between a Swede and a Russian. There is no situation containing exactly one Russian and two distinct Russians. So again, two situations will be needed, one the situation containing judges for this boxing match, the other containing the boxers in it. Perhaps this example demonstrates the attraction of a combined implicit-explicit approach: the proposition I express is that the Russian judge voted for the Russian boxer, and this proposition *concerns* a particular boxing match. On the combined approach, every utterance is evaluated against an implicit background situation, meaning there is less explicit work to be done.

When you initiate a conversation, there is some onus on you to make sure enough of a background situation is either in place or quickly inferable to get things moving. You call me on the telephone and, after announcing your identity, you say, "Are you going to Ragga's party tonight?" not "Are you going to it tonight?" A background has now been created. In an effort to persuade me to come along, you say, "It will be really good. Steindór is going to sing." Now you use 'it' instead of 'Ragga's party'. And I know that you mean Steindór is going to sing *there*. The real issue between the implicit and explicit approaches concerns how much content gets into our thoughts and how much is, somehow or other, "left out." I suspect little remains for philosophers and linguists to do in this domain. The interesting question is one for cognitive psychology: how much content makes it into my thoughts when I speak and comprehend, and what do I evaluate the truth and falsity of my thoughts against? The idea of the background situation shifting with every new nominal that is uttered strikes me as pretty ridiculous, but perhaps cognitive psychology will prove me wrong. So, for what it is worth, I shall continue working with the explicit approach, perhaps combined with the implicit approach (drawing the line in each case where its strikes me as plausible) and wait until cognitive psychology tells me how much of the postulated explicit content should be explained away implicitly.

Let us turn to (8) and (9):

(8) It rained last week in Reykjavík.

(9) It rained last week everywhere I went.

The location-singular proposition I express using (8) is location-dependent, indeed *Reykjavík*-dependent. No problem there. Now suppose I drove from Reykjavík to Akureyri last week and took no other trip, and suppose it rained the whole way (and also rained when I was stationary in both Reykjavík and Akureyri). The proposition I express by uttering (9) is location-*general*: if I had driven only from Reykjavík to Höfn instead, or only from Cairo to Alexandria for that matter, and it had rained the whole way, *the proposition I just expressed by uttering (9) would still be true*. Although the location-singular proposition I expressed by uttering (8) is location-dependent, indeed Reykjavík-dependent, the location-general proposition I express by uttering (9) is not: there is no particular location x (for example, Reykjavík) such that the proposition's truth or falsity in actual and counterfactual situations depends upon how things are with x.

Now imagine a situation in which a prolonged drought hits western North America. (I am here adapting an example due to Récanati 2001—to use *against* him!) The situation is particularly dire on the island of Recanto (a republic located a few hundred miles off the coast of northern California). Rain has become so very rare and important in Recanto that rain detectors have been disposed all over its 200 square miles (the island is roughly oval-shaped, about twenty-four miles long and twelve miles wide). Each detector triggers an alarm bell at the meteorological office in San Juan (the capital) when it detects rain. There is a single bell, and the location of the rain detector that has been triggered is indicated by a light on a board. After months of drought, the bell eventually rings. Hearing it, the weatherman on duty, who is in an adjacent room at the time and cannot see the board, exclaims,

(10)   It's raining.

It would be wrong to say the proposition the weatherman expressed is true if, and only if, it is raining (at the time of his utterance) in some place or other, wrong to say he expressed a location-independent proposition. Why? Because he expressed a *Recanto*-dependent proposition, one that is true if, and only if, it is raining somewhere or other *on Recanto*. Rain in Reykjavík is simply not relevant.

   Following instructions, the weatherman calls the president of Recanto on a hot line as soon as he hears the bell. "Mr. President," he says excitedly, "I have some good news: it's raining." The president replies that this is indeed good news and asks the weatherman for more information:

(11)   Where is it raining?

Now the president's use of (11) does *not* indicate that he did not fully grasp the proposition the weatherman expressed. The weatherman expressed the Recanto-dependent proposition that it is raining *somewhere or other on Recanto*, and this proposition is the one the president grasped before asking his question. Similarly, when the weatherman replies, "If you will excuse me for just a moment, Mr President, I will go and find out," he is not indicating that he does not know which proposition he himself expressed earlier, for that was the proposition that it is raining *somewhere or other on Recanto*. What the president is seeking is a useful specification of a *smaller location*, a smaller part of *Recanto* within which the rain is falling, and reasonable answers might be "on the north coast" or "out in Punta Rosa." The proposition the weatherman first expressed when he uttered (10) contains an unarticulated constituent, *Recanto*; and the proposition he expresses when he utters (12),

(12)   It's raining out in Punta Rosa.

contains the "smaller" constituent, *Punta Rosa*.

Existentialism and Nihilism

The Recanto example is a variation of one used by Récanati (2001) to draw quite the *opposite* conclusion from the one I have just drawn. Récanati holds that under certain special circumstances someone can use (1):

(1) It's raining.

to express a location-independent proposition, a proposition that does *not* contain an unarticulated location. Is this because he thinks it can be used to express the location-*general* proposition that it's raining *somewhere or other*? Or because he thinks it can be used to express a proposition that is neither location-*singular* nor location-*general*? I think Récanati has in mind the former, but, either way, his example is unconvincing.

Let me put to one side for a moment what I take to be two hopeless positions. *Truth-conditional existentialism* is the position that a use of (1) always expresses the location-*general* proposition that it's raining *somewhere or other*. By contrast, *truth-conditional nihilism* is the position that a use of (1) always expresses a proposition that is neither location-*singular* nor location-*general*. (Existentialism seems plain false to me, and nihilism plain confused. I give my reasons later.) There may well be people who hold one or the other of existentialism and nihilism (or some conflation of both), but Récanati's position seems to be neither. Récanati does not argue that the proposition a speaker expresses by uttering (1) *never* contains an unarticulated location. Indeed, it seems to be his point that in the ordinary sorts of cases discussed in the literature the proposition expressed *does* contain such a location. But what he is doing is *engineering a highly out-of-the-ordinary case* that has the appearance (to him, at least) of not involving an unarticulated location. In summary, he seems to want to allow that *some* uses of (1) express location-singular propositions whilst others express location-general propositions. And to the latter extent, he has some affinity to the truth-conditional existentialist, who maintains that the proposition expressed is *always* location-general.

It is important not to tangle four quite separate distinctions here, (i) the distinction between *singular* and *general*, which has application in the realm of both sentences and propositions, (ii) the distinction between *singular* and *dependent* in the realm of propositions, (iii) the linguistic distinction between *arguments* and *adjuncts* (is 'here' an argument or adjunct in 'it's raining here'?), and (iv) the distinction between an argument *position* and an argument *role*, the former a linguistic notion, the latter a metaphysical one.

Here is Récanati's example:

Perry says that the contextual provision of a place is semantically mandatory for interpreting a weather statement like 'It's raining'.... But must we really accept Perry's claim, thus construed? Can we not imagine a context in which 'It is raining' would be evaluable even if no particular place were contextually singled out? I have no difficulty imagining such a context. I can imagine a situation in which rain has become extremely rare and important, and rain detectors have been disposed all over the territory (whatever the territory—possibly the whole Earth). In the imagined scenario, each detector triggers an alarm bell in the Monitoring Room when it detects rain. There is a single bell; the location of the triggering detector is indicated by a light on a board in the Monitoring Room. After weeks of total drought, the bell eventually rings in the Monitoring Room. Hearing it, the weatherman on duty in the adjacent room shouts: 'It's raining!' His utterance is true, iff it is raining (at the time of utterance) in *some place or other*. (2001, 317 [emphasis added])

Récanati's words "some place or other" suggest he agrees with the existentialist on the truth conditions of the weatherman's use of (1): the proposition the weatherman expresses is location-independent, it contains no unarticulated location because it is *location-general*.[76] But surely it is *false* that the weatherman's utterance is true if, and only if, it is raining, at the time of utterance, "some place or other." Raining on one of Jupiter's moons? On a planet orbiting some distant star? On a space station so gigantic and diverse that it has developed its own weather system with evaporation, cloud, and precipitation? The weatherman's utterance is true, rather, if, and only if, it is raining somewhere or other *on Earth*, or whatever territory is under consideration, and to that extent it is location-*dependent* even if it is not location-singular. A location *is* required, and without it there is no proposition to be evaluated for truth or falsity. In its crucial respects, Récanati's example seems no different from our Recanto one: Recanto is a location that is part of many larger locations (North America, the northern hemisphere, Earth, etc.), and so is the Earth (being part of the solar system, our galaxy, etc.).[77] Second, notice that Récanati's claim cannot actually be a claim about unarticulated *constituents*, for, by Récanati's own lights, the proposition the weatherman expresses by uttering (1) *does* contain unarticulated constituents, albeit unarticulated *properties* rather than an unarticulated location. The proposition the weatherman expresses is not, on his account, the one he would have expressed had he uttered (1'), but (according to Récanati's own words) the proposition he would have expressed had he uttered (1''):

(1')   It's raining on Earth.

(1'')   It's raining some place or other.

Now the relationship (1'') bears to (1') is none other than the relationship an existentially quantified sentence stands to a singular instance, the relationship (2'') bears to (2'):

(2′) Perry sneezed.

(2″) Somebody or other sneezed.

If I utter (2′), I express a singular proposition about Perry, a proposition that has Perry himself and the property of sneezing as constituents. Now, I take it no one would insist that the proposition I express by uttering (2″) contains only *one* constituent, the property of sneezing, the proposition containing no constituents whatsoever corresponding to 'somebody or other' (or any of its parts). The transition from the proposition expressed by my use of (2′) to the one expressed by my use of its existential generalization (2″) is a transition from a singular proposition to a general one, not a transition from a proposition that contains two constituents to one that contains only one. In a familiar notation, it is a transition from (3′) to (3″):

(3′) ⟨PERRY, SNEEZED⟩.

(3″) ⟨⟨SOME, PERSON⟩, SNEEZED⟩.

The propositional situation is no different with the transition from the proposition expressed by my use of (1′) to the one expressed by my use of its existential generalization (1″): it is a transition from a singular proposition to a general one, not a transition from a proposition that contains two constituents to one that contains only one:

(4′) ⟨EARTH, RAINING⟩.

(4″) ⟨⟨SOME, LOCATION⟩, RAINING⟩.

Récanati's claim is that, although one *can* (and usually *does*) use (1) to express a location-singular proposition, in the scenario envisaged the weatherman is using (1) to express the location-general proposition (4″), but the truth or falsity of his claim has *no bearing on the matter of whether or not there are unarticulated constituents* of the propositions expressed by uses of sentences containing the verb 'rain'. No one, certainly not Perry, is going to deny that one can express *location-general* propositions using sentences containing the verb 'rain' any more than he or she are going to deny that one can express *general* propositions using sentences containing the verb 'sneeze'. However you look at it, (4′) and (4″) *both* contain unarticulated constituents relative to uses of (1). That is, however you look at it, Taylor is vindicated: the presence of a location or range of locations in the proposition expressed by a use of (1) is something demanded by a particular *component* of the sentence, namely, the verb 'rain'—which expresses a relation with two argument *roles*, one for time, the other for location, whether singular or general. (It is still *sub judice*, however, whether there is a level of syntactic representation (LF, say) at which 'rain' has two argument *positions* one for some type of temporal expression, the other for some form of locative; and *sub judice* whether 'here' and 'in Reykjavík' occupy argument positions when appended to 'it's raining'.) The fact that the latter role may be filled by something other than a *particular* location (for example, in (4″) the proposition that it's raining *somewhere or other*) is neither more nor less interesting than the fact that one of the two argument roles of the relation expressed by 'sneeze' may be filled by something other than a *particular* person (for example in (3″), the proposition that *somebody or other* sneezed).

The remaining question, then, is whether the weatherman's use of (1) in Récanati's example really *does* express the fully general, wholly existential proposition (4″). Surely not, for then the weatherman's utterance would be true as long as rain is coming down somewhere or other in the universe and false only if no rain is coming down anywhere in the universe. So Récanati's position seems incorrect.[78]

If the weatherman's use of (1) does not express (4″), then truth-conditional existentialism is false. What about truth-conditional nihilism? I have encountered nihilist sentiments enough in talks and lectures by people who seem to be professing existentialism that something needs to be said about it. The nihilist idea is that a use of (1) expresses a proposition that is *neither location-singular nor location-general*, the proposition that it is raining *punkt*. This view is truly hopeless. A proposition, by our ground rules, is something that is true or false. The proposition that it is raining (now) in Reykjavík has a truth-value, false as it happens. And the proposition that it is raining (now) somewhere or other on Earth has a truth-value, true presumably. What about the proposition that it is raining (now) *punkt*? Is it true or false? The reason we don't answer "true" or "false" is that the only way we can construe the question as worthy of one of these answers is if we construe it not as a *punkt* question at all, but as a question about the proposition that it is raining *somewhere in particular*—Reykjavík, for example—or as a question about the proposition that it is raining *somewhere or other*, on Earth, for example. The question whether it is raining (now) *punkt* has no answer because it is not a genuine question.

It will not do to just trot out the following alleged "T-sentence" in defense of the *it's raining punkt* thesis, or any other thesis:[79]

(5)   'It's raining' is true iff it's raining.

For one thing, (5) does *not* qualify as a T-sentence: it does not specify the truth conditions of *any* utterance of (1), including, in particular, my utterance of (1) in Reykjavík at noon on November 5, 2002, the truth conditions of which are that its raining in Reykjavík at noon on November 5, 2002. Claims to the contrary are confused. Only *relative to a location* does it even make sense to consider 'it's raining' having either a truth *value* or a truth *condition*.[80] The problem iterates, of course. Since the right-hand side of

(5) does not have a truth condition, neither does (5) as a whole, and so it fails to specify the proposition I express when I utter (1) right now intending to communicate that it is raining in Reykjavík.[81] In a nutshell, (5) is about as useless a "T-sentence" as the following:

(6)   'Mike is foreign' is true iff Mike is foreign.

(7)   'Mike is ready' is true iff Mike is ready.

(8)   'Mike's horse is gray' is true iff Mike's horse is gray.

Wheeling out (5)–(8) with a view to repudiating unarticulated constituents of the proposition expressed by uses of the quoted sentences betrays confusions about what T-sentences and truth conditions are.

Suppose a purported truth-theorist were to say to us that (5) *is* a "general T-sentence" that can be instantiated in various ways: every utterance is made by a speaker s, at a time t, and location l, and an understanding of the "general T-sentence" (5) requires taking this basic fact into consideration. Statement (5) is to be understood as

(5′)   'It's raining'$_{\langle s,t,l \rangle}$ is true iff it's raining at t, in l.

But (5′) is not a T-sentence either: it is merely a universally quantified schema that individual T-sentences may instantiate. For example, (9) instantiates it:

(9)   'It's raining'$_{\langle \text{Stephen Neale, noon, Nov 5, 2002, Reykjavík} \rangle}$ is true iff it's raining at noon, November 5, 2002, in Reykjavík.

Whatever its faults, (9) is at least a T-sentence, at least within certain systems that take sentences-relative-to-assignments to be bearers of truth and falsity. But it's not a *true* T-sentence because I could utter (1) at noon on November 5, 2002, in Reykjavík to say something that is true if, and only if, it's raining in *Genoa* at that time. The location of the rain relevant to the truth or falsity of such an utterance of (1) would not be the location of the utterance, so an additional parameter would need to be added to the schema (5′) of which (9) is an instance, call it $l′$. The value of $l′$ on a given occasion is not a function of l, though it may often *be* l.

Using (9) to specify the proposition I express when uttering (1) right now intending to communicate that it's raining in Reykjavík just concedes the game to Perry, for within the aforementioned framework the actual specification of the proposition in question is surely given by the right-hand side of (6), which makes it very clear that the proposition in question is the Reykjavík-dependent proposition that it's raining *in Reykjavík*.[82]

At some point we shall need to ask whether I *referred* to Reykjavík when I uttered (1). Certainly I used no (overt) expression to do so. But perhaps that does not answer our question. Let us put unarticulated constituents to one side for a while and focus on referring in seemingly simpler cases.

Anchoring

Many philosophers write as if (or even argue that) understanding what a speaker S said on a given occasion by uttering a sentence X with its conventional meaning is a matter determined by the meaning of that sentence and a "context," in a sense of this frequently invoked word that is meant to make it more than simply a label for whatever it is that "bridges the gap" between the meaning of X and what S said by uttering X on that occasion. For example, it is frequently claimed that all one needs to bridge the gap is some sort of formal object, an "index" or "context" in the form of an ordered n-tuple that secures the references of a few annoying "indexical" pronouns ('I', 'you', and 'he', for example) and one or two other "indexical" words that have a somewhat pronominal nature ('here' and 'now', for example).[83]

Although formal contexts may have a useful *methodological* role from time to time, they are strictly irrelevant to a proper theory of utterance interpretation. For various semantic and syntactic purposes, it is often desirable—if not mandatory—to abstract or idealize away from facts to do with particular speech situations—"pragmatic" or "contextual" factors, as they are sometimes called—in order to get on with a particular piece of work. And, as long as caution is exercised, there is no harm in this. For example, *with certain restricted purposes in mind*—and without any sort of absurd commitment to the idea that such entities play a role in utterance interpretation—formal "indices" can be introduced to serve as "contexts" with which sentences can be paired in order to "anchor" or "co-anchor" the interpretations of certain "context-sensitive," or broadly "indexical" expressions. The usual idea is to construe such expressions as free variables that have values only relative to indices. Famously, this idea has been used to capture model-theoretically the validity of inferences whose premises and conclusions are stated using indexical sentences.[84] It is paramount in such work to keep things tightly under control in the following sense: the logician wants a mechanism that can (a) scan a set of sentences for occurrences of symbols on some pre-existing list of devices that do not carry their values with them and then (b) use an index to assign a value to each occurrence of such a symbol. If this goes well, logical deductions can proceed (assuming a semantics for items of a preselected "logical" vocabulary, of course). If there is still slippage after the index has made its assignments, on standard assumptions there is only one solution: posit further indexical symbols in the sentences involved, symbols which are invisible in surface syntax yet revealed by an analysis of their "logical forms," then try again.[85]

In the philosophy of language, indices have a methodological role, for they can be used to anchor or co-anchor indexical and anaphoric expressions and so allow work to proceed more easily on *other* expressions and on what people say (and imply for that matter) by uttering them on given occasions. There is, however, an idea that has emerged from work on indexical logics for which we can have little sympathy. This is the idea that sentence meanings and contexts can be paired to provide something of *empirical* significance: what a *sentence X says relative to a context C*.[86] We must not lose sight of certain facts. First, as far as utterance interpretation is concerned, such "contexts" are strictly irrelevant. Utterances do not come with such devices attached that anchor or co-anchor indexical, demonstrative, or anaphoric pronouns. The hearer has plenty of *pragmatic* work to do, much of it rightly called inferential, albeit inferential in a way that is steered by the meanings of individual words. A few passages from Evans (1982, 1985) summarize the situation well:

All that the conventions governing the referring expression 'he' insist upon, in any given context, is that the object referred to should be male. (1982, 312)

There is no linguistic rule which determines that a 'he' or a 'that man' refers to *x* rather than *y* in the vicinity, or that it refers to someone who has just left rather than someone who has been recently mentioned. (1985, 230–231)

'This' and 'that' are even less specific, contributing merely the vaguest suggestion of a contrast between nearer and further (in some generalised sense). . . . [*Footnote*: Often the *predicate* does more to narrow down the range of possible interpretations of the referring expression than does the referring expression itself. . . .] (1982, 312)

Let me take another example: the expression 'you': If a speaker addresses a remark to someone, saying, "You are a crook," it is surely clear that an identification is called for on the part of the audience: in order to understand the remark, it is not enough to know that there is one, and only one, person whom the speaker is addressing, and that the speaker is saying of that person that he is a crook. . . a quite specific *kind* of identification is called for; the person addressed has not understood the remark unless he realizes that the speaker is saying that *he* is a crook. . . . understanding the remark requires the hearer to know *of* an individual that he is being addressed. (1982, 314)

Nothing about the meaning of the word 'you' tells you that you are being addressed.[87]

Quite generally, there is something artificial about construing the meanings of, for example, 'I', 'we', 'you', 'he', 'she', 'it', 'they', 'this', 'that', 'these', 'those', 'here', 'now', 'there', 'then', 'today', 'yesterday', and 'tomorrow' as functions from contexts to references. The meanings of these devices—as Evans (1982, 1985), Russell (1940), Perry (1978, 2001), and Sperber and Wilson (1986) stress—are just perspectival *constraints* on references, more precisely perspectival constraints on the *referential intentions* with which the devices can be used. I am astonished at how much mainstream philosophy of language ignores this. We need to distinguish two ideas about formal contexts: one sensible, the other silly. The silly idea is that utterances come with prepackaged "contexts" that provide values for indexical expressions. The sensible idea is what I call *methodological anchoring* (*anchoring*, for short). For various pragmatic, semantic, and syntactic purposes, it is often helpful, perhaps even mandatory, for a theorist to abstract from certain "contextual effects" or "pragmatic factors" in order to get on with a piece of work, and so it is sometimes useful to use an "index" as a way of anchoring the interpretations of indexical expressions that are not, at that moment, the objects of primary concern, *even though the theorist knows the interpretation of these indexicals is not as straightforward as invoking an index might suggest*. If one is working on definite descriptions, for example, one might want to prescind, as much as possible, from the effects of, say, indexical pronouns occurring inside nominals; and if one is working on 'and', for example, one might want to prescind, as much as possible, from the effects of, say, indexical pronouns occurring inside conjuncts or inside the matrices of descriptions. To this end, we might use an index to anchor or coanchor these expressions, to keep their special features and the complexities they introduce out of the picture as it were.[88]

A certain amount of care is needed in the use of the word 'semantic' when indices are used to anchor (or coanchor) indexical expressions. To the extent that we are investigating the conventions governing a word whose role cannot be set out clearly without taking into account the conventions governing other expression(s) with which it combines to form larger expressions, we may find it convenient to talk about the (derived) conventions governing the larger phrases with respect to a particular index. For example, if the semantics of 'the' is being investigated, it is often useful, sometimes essential, to anchor indexicals so that *other* contextual effects may be monitored. And, although we may want to talk about the "linguistic meaning" of, the "semantics" of, or the "conventions governing" an indexical or any other expression, we may also wish to talk about its "semantic value" relative to a particular index, the object conveniently assigned to it by an index in order that work on pressing matters is not held up needlessly. There is no harm in such talk as long as everyone is clear about what is going on. "Semantic values," in this sense, are just *stipulated interpretations*, and the anchoring it involves is quite consistent with the idea that the interpretation of indexical expressions is basically a pragmatic matter only steered by semantic constraints.

Talk of sentences-relative-to-indices has some *methodological* value: artificially anchoring a limited range of expressions enables us, as theorists, to prescind from certain limited contextual issues and so get on with other business. To the extent that "what is expressed" ("what is said") by a sentence ϕ relative to an index C approximates the proposition the speaker expressed (what the speaker said) by uttering ϕ on a given occasion (certain basic features of which C is taken to model), such entities are harmless enough. But, when it comes to putting together the pieces of a theory of interpretation, we cannot rest content with the artificial anchoring of certain indexicals: we want an account of how they are actually dealt with in the interpretation process. Even when we have such an account, however, we will still not have a full specification of what the speaker said because of the myriad ways in which what is said is underdetermined even relative to fixing the interpretations of indexicals.

The Weather Game

My father called me around 6 PM (GMT) this evening from England. Being British, he did not neglect to inquire about the weather here in Reykjavík: "How's the weather there," he asked. Now I could easily have replied by uttering (1):

(1)   It snowed today.

But, in fact, I replied with (2):

(2)   It snowed here today.

In much of the literature, it is taken for granted that I would have expressed the same proposition by uttering (1) as the one I did, in fact, express by uttering (2). This is not self-evident, however, partly because the matter of a purported aphonic in the underlying syntax of both (1) and (2) needs resolving.[89] Let us for the moment assume that there is no aphonic, indexical, locative in (1) or (2).

My utterance of (2) seems like a familiar sort of case in which the linguistic meaning of a sentence underdetermines the proposition the speaker expressed by uttering it, a case in which the hearer must use information not encoded in the sentence itself in order to identify that proposition. What did my father do, in very general terms, when he identified what I was saying by uttering (2)? The short answer is that he identified the sentence I used and integrated the *semantic* information encoded in that sentence with various pieces of *non*semantic information he obtained from elsewhere (such as the information that I am in Reykjavík). At present, we have very little idea about the mechanics of *how* he did this—that is a question to be answered by a theory of the cognitive processes involved in utterance interpretation—but we do most certainly know this is *what* he did.

One thing my father had to do was associate a particular place, Reykjavík, with my use of 'here', since that is where I am (and was when he called). There is nothing in the meaning of the word 'here' to connect it to Reykjavík, for otherwise it would surely mean what 'in Reykjavík' means, which it does not. (Moreover, the fact that I could have performed an equally successful speech act in the circumstances by uttering (1), which contains no overt locative expression, demonstrates that it is not the presence of the word 'here' itself that makes it the case that the hearer must identify the location I am talking about in order to grasp the proposition I expressed. See below for discussion.) In this particular case, my father is able to home in on Reykjavík rather easily via a conspiracy of the following:[90]

i. his confidence that I am the speaker;

ii. his confidence that I am in Reykjavík;

iii. his confidence that I am attempting to answer his question, which was about the weather here in Reykjavík;

iv. his tacit knowledge that when a speaker uses 'here' he is constrained to be referring to his own location or surroundings—at the moment of use or reuse or whatever in the case of recordings for answering machines or voice mail—the boundaries of which may vary considerably from occasion to occasion.

It is a task for cognitive science to establish how (i)–(iv) come together in my father's head to yield an interpretation. The mere existence of expressions like 'here', 'there', 'now', 'then', 'I', 'you', 'he', and so on, means that the semantic information encoded in a sentence ϕ does not always provide all of the information necessary for the hearer to identify what someone is saying by uttering ϕ on a particular occasion. Additional information must be picked up by listening, watching, remembering, and even deducing, and, as such, identifying what someone is saying involves rather more than identifying the words uttered and their syntactic arrangement, retrieving the meanings of the words from one's lexicon, and projecting from these in accordance with the identified linguistic structure.

This does not mean, of course, that philosophers and linguists who have reflected on the use and structure of language have nothing useful to say to the cognitive scientist whose job it is to construct a theory of interpretation that explains how this form of informational integration takes place and how it delivers the results it does. They can at least specify what the *aim* should be in any particular case, specify the type of information that must be drawn upon, and characterize the information encoded in particular sentences. In the case at hand, the cognitive theory must explain *how* my father arrived at the conclusion that I was saying that it snowed in Reykjavík today (assuming this is, in fact, what I am saying).[91]

Now consider a different scenario. My father and I are playing an elaborate game we call *the weather game*. It is played like this. I start out in London and must return there within thirty days, making stops in Nairobi, Sydney, and Vancouver, and I must move at least 500 miles every (GMT) day. I am allowed to take any commercial airplane, train, or boat, and my father has a vast array of timetables at his disposal on the Internet, as well as world weather reports. No matter where I am, I must call him every day at 6 PM (GMT) from a secure, untraceable, satellite telephone I carry with me, and give him a weather report. My father has to guess where I am. If he gets it in five attempts, he wins the day's round; if he does not, I do. Silly, but there you go.

Day one, today. I flew from London to Reykjavík. At the allotted hour my father asks me for the relevant weather report, I utter (2). He starts to ruminate. Since it is only the first week in November, I must have gone north to see snow, he conjectures; and then he runs through a few possibilities drawing upon information he has about geography, transportation possibilities, my past travels, family trips, places I have good friends or professional commitments, and so on: Edinburgh, the Faroes, Reykjavík, Oslo? Question: has my father grasped the proposition I expressed? Or is his aim in the game quite rightly described as *guessing the proposition I expressed*. In the context of the weather game, we are strongly inclined to say that he *understands me* perfectly, for it is accepted that I will use the word 'here' (and perhaps also the word 'there' if I am sufficiently far ahead in the game and don't mind giving him an occasional clue by talking about the weather in a place I passed through earlier in the day or a place I plan to visit tomorrow) without expecting him to recognize immediately where I am (was or will be). That's part of the game. But our question is: Does my father grasp the proposition I express? What proposition *did* I express: the location-dependent (i.e., Reykjavík-dependent) proposition that it snowed today *in Reykjavík*? Or the location-independent proposition that it snowed today *in my current location*. The former seems to me to be the correct answer, 'here' being rigid and 'my current location' being flaccid. (And surely I can say something true by uttering the sentence 'my current location might not have been Reykjavík'.) On the basis of my utterance of (2), my father is able to more or less immediately grasp the location-independent proposition that it snowed today in my current location, and he must use that (and a lot of other things) to identify the location-dependent, (i.e., Reykjavík-dependent) proposition that I am expressing.[92]

Suppose that I had omitted the word 'here' when talking to my father, using (1) instead of (2), in an obvious modification of the actual case and an equally obvious modification of the case involving the weather game. In the modification of the actual case, the situation would not have been dramatically different (similarly if my father had not heard the word 'here' because of static on the line or a drop in volume or my mumbling or whatever). Of course, the presence of the word 'here' imposes a constraint on the interpretation of utterances of (2) that is not imposed on the interpretation of utterances of (1). This is evident from the fact that my father might go on to relay the information that it snowed in Reykjavík today to my mother by uttering (1), but not by uttering (2), since he is not in Reykjavík.[93] Now, according to Perry, I would have expressed the same proposition as the one I expressed when I uttered (2): the proposition that it snowed in Reykjavík today. Because there is no expression in (2) by the utterance of which I would be referring to Reykjavík, we must say with Perry that Reykjavík would be an unarticulated constituent of that proposition. (Remember, for now we are operating on the assumption that there are no aphonics in (1) and (2).)

Would my father have faced some new difficulty in interpreting my utterance that he did not face in connection with my utterance of (2)? Like (2), (1) can be used by a speaker to say that it snowed today somewhere other than Reykjavík, but it has an additional degree of freedom: unlike (2) it can be used by a speaker to say that it snowed today somewhere other than *where the speaker is*. That is why my father can use it in England to pass on information about the weather in Reykjavík. The absence of the word 'here' in (1) means that the knowledge mentioned in (iv) above is unhelpful in interpreting utterances of this sentence. And *in principle* this means my father's task is more difficult. In practice, I suppose it would not have been any harder at all. The confidence mentioned in (iii) would seem rather more significant in the case of an imagined utterance of (1) than it was in the case of my actual utterance of (2); indeed it was not strictly necessary in the actual case, given (i), (ii), and (iv).

Now back to the weather game. Is there any reason to think that, by uttering (1) when playing the weather game, I express a proposition any different from the one I express from the same location, at the same time, (a) by uttering (2) when playing weather game, or (b) by uttering (1) when not playing the weather game? Not really. In each case the proposition I express is surely the Reykjavík-dependent proposition that it snowed in Reykjavík today.

Now back to the original dialogue with my father. Given the wording of his question and the fact that he knows where I am—*he* called *me*, after all—using (1) instead of (2) to reply would have been perfectly natural in the circumstances. But suppose I had used (3):

(3)   It snowed in Reykjavík today.

This would have been slightly less natural; at the same time, it is difficult to deny that I would still have expressed the proposition that it snowed in Reykjavík today. So what would the slight unnaturalness in my use of (3) consist in? Perhaps not much more than the unnecessary use of a name. When we are talking about a person, we naturally slip into the use of pronouns when confusion on the part of the audience is unlikely.

Similarly with places, except that instead of, say, 'in Reykjavík', we slip into 'there' or 'here'. Why do we have a choice between 'there' and 'here'? *Perspective*. My father's question, recall, was "How's the weather there?" It would have been fine for me to reply with (1); it was fine for me to reply, as I did, with (2); it would have been acceptable, if a little unnatural, for me to reply with (3); but it would have been quite unacceptable for me to reply with (4):

(4)   It snowed there today.[94]

Now suppose my father's question had been "How's the weather in Reykjavík?" (rather than "How's the weather there?"). If I had replied with (4), surely I would have given the impression that I was not in Reykjavík (my father called me on an Icelandic *mobile* number, so I could have used (4) intending just this implication). There are really two ways of thinking about this. We might say that I would have *conventionally implicated* (in Grice's sense) that I am not in Reykjavík, where a conventional implicature does not bear on the truth or falsity of what is said, of the proposition expressed, despite being triggered by the linguistic conventions governing the use of the sentence uttered.[95] Alternatively, we could say that I would have said *two* things, expressed *two* propositions, by uttering (4), the true proposition that it snowed in Reykjavík today, and the false proposition that I am not in Reykjavík.[96] Either way, one thing is clear: to use the word 'there' is not merely to refer to a location, it is to *locate oneself* with respect to that location, at least coarsely.[97] And, of course, the same is true of 'here'. Suppose my father's question had been "How's the weather in Reykjavík?" and I had replied with (2). We are faced with the same theoretical choice. We could say that I conventionally implicated that I am in Reykjavík, or we could say that I said that I am in Reykjavík (in addition to saying it snowed here today). I see no reason to come down on one side or the other at the moment.

We have two more sentences to take into account:

(5)   It snowed here in Reykjavík today.

(6)   It snowed there in Reykjavík today.

I could certainly have responded to my father's question with (5), but it might have seemed a little long-winded. Now (5) brings up an interesting question that appears to go beyond the questions we asked in connection with (2): would I have referred to Reykjavík *twice*, once with 'here', again with 'in Reykjavík' (or at least with the 'Reykjavík' part), and perhaps even a third time with the compound (if such it is) 'here in Reykjavík'? I propose to postpone discussion of this matter.

It would have been *extremely* unnatural, indeed quite infelicitous, for me to have answered using (6). As with (4), there would appear to be two ways of thinking about the infelicity. (i) I would have said something true (that it snowed in Reykjavík today) and only conventionally implicated something false (that I am not in Reykjavík). (ii) I would have said something true (that it snowed in Reykjavík today) and also *said* something false (that I am not in Reykjavík).

So we are left with a few questions: would I have expressed the same proposition by uttering any of (1)–(6)? Would I have referred to Reykjavík twice (or even three times) in some cases? If so, is that because I would have expressed two propositions? However we answer these questions, we do not have to say that any of pair (1)–(6) have the same *meaning* in any interesting sense, or the same communicative utility.

I want to avoid talking about reports (attitude or otherwise) as much as possible in this chapter, but a brief word is in order at the this juncture. My father could use any of the following except (2′) or (5′) to report what I said:

(1′)   Stephen said that it snowed today.

(2′)   * Stephen said that it snowed here today.

(3′)   Stephen said that it snowed in Reykjavík today.

(4′)   Stephen said it snowed there today.

(5′)   * Stephen said that it snowed here in Reykjavík today.

(6′)   Stephen said it snowed there in Reykjavík today.

The philosopher trying to provide a specification of what I said will probably choose (3′). Why? Because typically he will try to flush out certain *perspectival* features, and typically that means taking it easy with indexicals in his report. Why does he care about perspective? Because the philosopher is trying to play God, or at least trying to talk as if he has a God's eye view of things, and words like 'here' and 'there' cause God all sorts of problems. When specifying the proposition expressed, philosophers tend to use a sentence that *someone* else, *somewhere* else, and, if possible, *somewhen* else might be able use to do the same thing, choosing his sacrifices carefully. One only has to look at the notation of structured propositions to see how we flee from indexicals to the seeming safety of proper names. 'CICERO' and 'CATILINE' frequently occur within angled brackets as proxies for individuals:

⟨CICERO, ⟨DENOUNCED, CATILINE⟩⟩.

But 'HE' and 'HIM' do not. 'ROME' and 'REYKJAVÍK' get used, but 'HERE' and 'THERE' do not.

Now (2′) above can be used today only by someone in Reykjavík to specify the proposition I expressed, and to that extent it is *less useful* than (3′). But what about (1′)? Isn't this just as useful as (3′)? I could have used (1) to say that it snowed in Reykjavík today, so surely the philosopher can use (1′) today to specify what I said, wherever that philosopher may be. The problem is that (1') is *too useful*. It can also be used to specify what I would have said if I had uttered "it snowed" to say that it snowed in Rome (or New York, or . . .) today, so (3') is the one that will tend to be used by the philosopher.

It is worth noting, however, that sometimes indexical or anaphoric devices occur very naturally in reports, even when made by philosophers. This is particularly true when words being used to make certain things salient or words being used as variable-binders occur in the linguistic material leading up to the specification:

(7)   When he spoke from *Reykjavík* earlier, Stephen said it snowed there today.

(8)   *Jón* said to *Ósk* that he had found her scarf.

(9)   Maria approached *each man* individually and said to him that he looked tired.

Sometimes this makes it easier to identify unarticulated constituents, as in (7'), or virtually forces a particular identification, as in (7''), or really does force it, as in (7'''), which nonetheless feels as if it is missing a 'there':

(7')   When he spoke from Reykjavík earlier, Stephen said it snowed today.

(7'')   When discussing the weather in Reykjavík, Stephen said it snowed today.

(7''')   Concerning Reykjavík, Stephen said it snowed today.

Syntactic, Subsyntactic, Parasyntactic

Perry appears to presuppose no particular syntactic theory or to advance any particular syntactic thesis. In connection with (1),

(1)   It's raining.

Perry says,

we do not need to first find an expression, hidden in the "deep structure" or somewhere else and then do the semantics of the statement augmented by the hidden expression. Things are intelligible just as they appear on the surface, and the explanation we might ordinarily give in nonphilosophical moments, that we simply understand what the statement is about, is essentially correct. (1986, 211)

Perry is not claiming that it is false that (1) contains a "hidden," "covert," "silent," or "unpronounced" expression or that it is false that (1) has an underlying LF, one of whose components is an expression the use of which on a particular occasion refers to a location. His point is simply that it does not appear to be *necessary* to posit a hidden expression or an underlying level of, say, LF in order to provide an intelligible description or explanation of how an utterance of (1) is understood on a particular occasion. (Note the modal.) The sort of description or explanation that one might get from someone with no prior knowledge of LF or covert syntax, or from a philosopher who wishes to remain agnostic on thorny syntactic matters, is perfectly intelligible.

In a more recent work, Perry (1998) again takes into account only rudimentary grammatical ideas. There is "no morpheme" (1998, 9) in (1), he says, the use of which designates a place. In such a case,

We lack the materials we need for the proposition expressed by a statement, even though we have identified the words and their meanings, and consulted contextual factors to which the indexical meanings direct us. (1998, 8)

The task of identifying the unarticulated constituents of the proposition expressed by an utterance remains after all of the relevant semantic rules have been understood and applied. (1998, 10)

And in a recent book, he again says that there is "no morpheme" (2001, 45) in (1) whose use designates a place, adding,

When we have the syntax of [(1)] and the meanings of each of the component words, we still don't have the content. (2001, 45)

An unarticulated constituent ... is ... a constituent of the proposition that is not the referent of some morpheme in the statement. (2001, 47)

The most detailed statement on this topic I have been able to find in Perry's publications is contained in a footnote to a 1998 paper:

Calling this phenomenon "unarticulated constituents" instead of, say, "implicit reference" is simply meant to focus on what I think as the starting point of investigation, the question of how there can be a constituent in the proposition, with no corresponding expression in the utterance. I sometimes use the more common and traditional term 'implicit reference' for what the speaker does, that leads to there being a constituent that is unarticulated. But I think the term 'implicit reference' is sometimes thought to be necessarily connected to what I regard as special case. In some cases of implicit reference there is a feature, a trace, a sort of phantom expression, that serves in place of an expression, so the referred to constituent really isn't unarticulated. Linguists often agree on the criteria for and presence of such features; it is a robust phenomenon. But I do think that saying there is such a feature should amount to more than saying that we use an $n - 1$ place predicate for an n-ary relation. I am interested in the theoretical possibility and coherence of truly unarticulated constituents; I also hope, however, that I have found some convincing examples that they really occur. (1998, 9 n4)

The thought here seems to be when a philosopher (or linguist) finds a superficially n-place predicate R, uses of which appear to express an $n + 1$ place relation, it does not follow as a matter of semantics or metaphysics or anything else that linguists simply have no choice but to treat R as a predicate with $n + 1$ argument positions somewhere in their theories of *syntax*. A solid interpretive reason for thinking the proposition $\langle \ldots a \ldots \rangle$ expressed by a use of a sentence X contains a constituent a corresponding to no component of X's superficial form is not ipso facto a solid reason for postulating an aphonic expression in X's syntax, or supposing anything syntactic whatsoever. (Would that syntacticians were so easily moved by philosophers' interpretive claims!) We need to distinguish between the linguistic notion of a *predicate* and the metaphysical notion of a *relation* and to distinguish correspondingly between the linguistic notion of an *argument position* and the metaphysical notion of an *argument role* (Perry 2001, 47–48).[98] The discovery that the proposition expressed by a use X^u of a sentence X whose surface form appears to contain a predicate P with n argument *positions* to be occupied by n terms nonetheless involves $n + 1$ entities filling the argument *roles* of an $n + 1$ place relation $\mathfrak{R}$ expressed by the use P^u of P (P^u a portion of X^u) is not ipso facto a *syntactic* discovery. Some sort of argument about the nature of syntax and its role in the psychology of interpretation would be needed to reach that syntactic conclusion, an argument to the effect that no argument role of $\mathfrak{R}$ may be filled by anything other than the entity designated by the use of the occupant of an argument position of P. In the absence of such an argument, we are in familiar linguistic territory: if we take LF seriously, we postulate an additional argument position of P in X's LF occupied by an expression with no phonic realization if, and only if, such a postulation helps us explain syntactic facts, comports with other postulations, and quite generally appears to improve our grasp of the syntax of natural language. Philosophical speculation about the elements involved in interpretation is all well and good, necessary even, but it must go hand in hand with empirical investigations, which involve not just coverage of data, but also examination of the consequences of particular syntactic posits for other aspects of syntax.

Perry is, as he says, "interested in the theoretical *possibility* and *coherence* of truly unarticulated constituents" [emphasis added], constituents for which syntacticians have yet to provide (and perhaps never will provide) compelling syntactic reasons for treating as the occasion-specific values of corresponding syntactic components, constituents that may fall beyond the boundaries of the "robust phenomenon" of aphonics in syntax. And Perry hopes, he says, to "have found some convincing examples."

Let us look briefly at the "robust phenomenon" Perry alludes to. Examples that many linguists see as involving a "trace" or "phantom" expression include a good number of those that traditional grammars describe in terms of the "understood subject" of a subordinated verb. A classic example is (3), where it is natural to say that we have an embedded infinitival clause, just as in (2):

(2) Everyone wants [$_S$ Pavarotti to sing].

(3) Everyone^1 wants [$_S$ X_1 to sing].

We are surely dealing with a single verb 'want' in (2) and (3), and it is clear from the former that its syntactic complement is a whole clause, albeit one that occurs in the infinitive. We are therefore virtually forced into postulating an aphonic subject of an embedded clause in (3), an expression often called PRO, which has a meaning but no sound, an expression that is semantic but aphonic (the converse, if you like, of the 'it' in (1) which is phonic but asemantic). That PRO is semantic seems to be borne out by the fact that it seems to behave here as if were a variable bound by 'everyone'.[99] For the sake of argument, let us suppose that the best way of capturing the idea that there is an aphonic expression in (3) is to see a sentence as a pair comprising a PF and an LF, where the former is (roughly) a representation that expresses its phonology, and the latter a representation that expresses *all* syntactic properties relevant to interpretation. The interpretation of PRO is required, by the syntax and the meaning of the verb 'want', to proceed by way of the interpretation of the subject of 'want' in (3).[100]

So far, so good. The postulation of an aphonic in (3) is certainly not just a funny way of saying that "we use an $n - 1$ place predicate for an n-ary relation." So the *general* question before us is the intelligibility of the following idea: the regular use of sentences X whose principal predicate is (even at LF) an n-place predicate to express propositions containing an $n + 1$ relation as a principal constituent. And the *particular* question before is whether Perry is right to think that a sentence containing 'rain' or 'snow' as its main verb is such a sentence. I am aware of no argument against the intelligibility of the *general* idea. Indeed, I have no idea how one might even *begin* to construct such an argument, for I know of nothing in syntactic theory that undermines it. We must examine particular cases and see if there are particular syntactic considerations that move us.[101]

Let us turn now to an illuminating discussion by Ken Taylor (2001). The core of the story about interpretation Taylor favors is called "Parametric Minimalism," a label borrowed from Récanati (1993). According to Taylor,

A sentence typically sets up a semantic scaffolding which constrains, without determining, its own contextual completion. The sentence does so by containing a variety of parameters the values of which must be contextually supplied in some more or less tightly constrained way. Sometimes the to-be-contextually-evaluated parameter is explicitly expressed in the syntax of the sentence. This is the case with explicit indexicals, demonstratives and also with verb tenses. Sometimes, however, the to-be-contextually-evaluated parameter is "suppressed" or hidden. Saying just where such parameters hide is a difficult matter—one perhaps better left to linguists than to philosophers. But I venture the hypothesis that some unexpressed parameters hide in what we might call the subsyntactic basement of suppressed verbal argument structure. (2001, 53)

I am uncertain whether Taylor is using 'unexpressed' and 'suppressed' interchangeably, but nothing I say is going to turn on this. Here is the interpretation of Taylor I like. Parameters may be *expressed* or *unexpressed*, and among the latter are those that are *suppressed*. We can leave it open whether all unexpressed parameters are suppressed parameters, restricting the immediate hypothesis to the existence of *some* unexpressed parameters that are merely *suppressed* (hidden in the subsyntactic basement) but in principle detectable by *linguistic* means, that is, as a result of empirical work in generative grammar. We can also leave open whether there might be unexpressed parameters of a use of a sentence that go beyond argument structure but are nonetheless constrained by the semantic scaffolding of the sentence used. That is, we can leave open whether the underarticulation of the proposition expressed by the sentence used to express it may outstrip the fixing of parameters *ex*pressed and *sup*pressed, for there may be unexpressed parameters that have nothing to do with argument structure per se. If this is what Taylor means, then I think I am in complete agreement.[102]

According to Taylor, as I am interpreting him, the verb 'rain' has a "lexically specified," but "syntactically unexpressed," argument place of which we have "tacit cognition." I take this as loose shorthand and interpret Taylor as meaning by it that the lexical properties of 'rain' determine that it expresses a *relation* that has a syntactically unexpressed argument *role*. Here are Taylor's own words on the matter:

The view which I favor supposes that the verb 'to rain' has a lexically specified argument place which is θ-marked THEME and that this argument place takes places as values. This is a way of saying that the subatomic structure of the verb 'to rain' explicitly marks rainings as a kind of change that places undergo. Now from the point of view of sentence-level syntax such lexically specified parameters are what I call subconstituents rather than constituents. Though subconstituents need not be expressed as sentence-level constituents, they make their presence felt by "demanding" to be assigned a contextually supplied value. Thus though [(1)] is missing no syntactically mandatory sentential constituent, nonetheless, it is semantically incomplete. The semantic incompleteness is manifest to us as a felt inability to evaluate the truth value of an utterance of [(1)] in the absence of a contextually provided location (or range of locations). This felt need for a contextually provided location has its source, I claim, in our tacit cognition of the syntactically unexpressed argument place of the verb 'to rain'. (Taylor 2001, 53)

This is very compressed, of course, but I like what I *think* are the main ideas (which can, perhaps, be spelled out in various ways). I would like to think Taylor means something like this, or would at least view this way of putting matters as in harmony with his own, once his prose is decompressed in a way that purges it of what is, strictly speaking, infelicitous talk of argument *places*: (i) A use of a verb *V* expresses a relation with n mandatory argument *roles* (in Perry's sense). (ii) The lexical structure of V specifies for each of its n roles, the sort of thing that may occupy that role. (iii) The lexical structure of V also specifies some number m of mandatory argument *positions in syntax*. (iv) There is no requirement that $m = n$. (v) Some of V's argument positions are specified to be individually connected to individual argument roles. (vi) Although argument roles and argument positions are in a sense made for one another, there is no requirement that for every argument role of the relation expressed by a use of V there is a corresponding argument position in syntactic structures containing V. (vii) Nor is there any requirement that for every argument position in syntax there is a corresponding argument role. (viii) A proposition is expressed by a use of some expression $E(V)$ containing V only if *every* argument role is occupied. (ix) $E(V)$ is a sentence only if *every* argument position is occupied. There is no commitment in any of this to aphonic syntactic elements ensuring that for every argument role there is an argument position. And that seems right to me. It is an empirical issue in any given case whether or not a particular occupant of an argument role (the occupant being a constituent of the proposition expressed by virtue of being such an occupant) is projected from the occupant of some particular argument position in syntax. In the case of my utterance of (1), the story is as follows. As a matter of fact $m = n$, but not because each of the argument position occupants is associated with exactly one of the argument role occupants and vice versa. $m = n$ because we have exactly one unarticulated constituent (Reykjavík) and exactly one nonprojecting articulant ('it')—that is, exactly one argument role occupant (Reykjavík) with no corresponding argument position occupant, and exactly one argument position occupant ('it') with no corresponding argument role occupant. At least that is the way it looks at first blush. We can leave it as an empirical question whether work in syntax will reveal an argument position in the syntax of (1) occupied by an expression corresponding to Reykjavík, qua occupant of an argument role. What we cannot do is simply *conclude* that there must be such a position in order to render intelligible the idea that Reykjavík occupies the argument role it does in the proposition I express by uttering (1).

According to Récanati (2001), what Taylor says about 'rain'-sentences is flawed. Concerning Taylor's proposal, Récanati says,

I think such an analysis is unavoidable once we accept Perry's claim that, to evaluate [(1)], we need a place. Or at least, it is unavoidable if we understand that claim as follows: for any token u of the complete sentence 'It is raining', it is necessary, in order to evaluate u, to be given a place. If the necessity concerns all tokens, it is a linguistic property of the sentence-type, hence, presumably, it arises from the internal lexical structure of the verb 'to rain'. (Récanati 2002, 317)

As we saw earlier, on the basis of a rather underdescribed and underanalyzed scenario involving a rain-monitoring room, Récanati rejects the thesis that a location is always required in order to interpret an utterance of a 'rain'-sentence, and this leads him to reject Taylor's description of the lexical structure of 'rain'.

If that is right, there is no need to posit a lexically specified argument-role for a location in the sub-atomic structure of the verb 'rain': 'Rain' is like 'dance' and other action verbs, contrary to what Taylor claims (2001, 54). That raining must take place somewhere or other is a metaphysical fact, not a linguistic fact. That fact does not prevent an utterance like [(1)] from expressing a fully determinate proposition even if no place is contextually provided. (Récanati 2002, 317)

There are three problems here. First, Récanati's rain-monitoring room argument for the rejection of a mandatory location is ineffectual, and when an argument of the same general form is spelled out in any sort of detail—for example, the one involving the rain-monitoring room on the island of Recanto—the only conclusion that comes into focus is the negation of the one Récanati is arguing for. So, in the absence of a convincing example of true loctionless rain statement, there is every reason to think the antecedent of Récanati's opening conditional is false. Second, the difference between 'rain' and 'dance' that Taylor stresses is robust, as we saw earlier. Third, the fact that it is just as much a metaphysical fact that raining must take place at a location as it is a metaphysical fact that dancing must, shows nothing whatsoever about locations as constituents of propositions expressed by 'rain'- and 'dance'-sentences. Taylor is right to insist that its location is to a raining as its dancer is to a dancing (not as its location is to a dancing).

Récanati goes on:

When a particular place is contextually provided as relevant to the evaluation of the utterance, that is for pragmatic reasons, not because it is linguistically required. In such cases, therefore, the place is a genuine unarticulated constituent. When we say "It's raining" and mean: It's raining in Paris, the location is an unarticulated constituent of the statement, just as, when we say "Look! He is eating" and mean: He is eating the dangerous mushroom, the mushroom is an unarticulated constituent. This is very different from cases of 'completion' where, as Taylor puts it, a subatomic variable "makes its presence felt by 'demanding' to be assigned a contextually supplied value." (Récanati 2002, 318)

Now it is important to realize that Taylor does not talk of a subatomic *variable*, he talks of a subatomic *parameter*. The difference is crucial and again comes from Perry. On the linguistic side of the coin, we have argument positions, singular terms, and variables, and, on the metaphysical side, argument roles, objects, and parameters. So Taylor is not making a claim about a *variable*—a syntactic object—making its presence felt; he is, rather, making a claim about a *parameter* making its presence felt through meaning. And, just as one cannot infer from the existence of an argument role of a verb to a corresponding argument position, so one cannot infer from the existence of a parameter in a proposition expressed by a use of a sentence to the existence of a corresponding variable in that sentence. (This is something I shall say more about later.)

Récanati's appropriation of 'unarticulated constituent' and his use of 'genuine unarticulated constituent' compound problems here.[103] Récanati appears to want to reserve Perry's expression 'unarticulated constituent' for constituents that are not mandated by argument roles, but, because of his conflation of parameters and variables, he appears to equate the idea of a propositional constituent mandated by an argument *role* of a relation expressed by a verb with the idea of a propositional constituent mandated by an argument *position* of a verb (at LF). And this equation is something Taylor is careful not to assume, which is why it would be rash to claim that Taylor's position on 'rain' is no more than a notational variant of the position that the LF of a 'rain'-sentence contains an argument position for a location variable.

Covert Operations

Perry's notion of an unarticulated constituent has been criticized by Stanley (2000). It is unclear to me, however, whether Stanley's arguments against unarticulated constituents amount to more than the platitude that whenever Perry (or anyone else) posits an unarticulated constituent, it will always possible to drum up a semiformal, semi-English formula that contains a variable whose value we could take to be the purported unarticulated constituent. Stanley's main claims are these:

all effects of extra-linguistic context on the truth-conditions of an assertion are traceable to elements in the actual syntactic structure of the sentence uttered...there are no convincing examples of what John Perry has called "unarticulated constituents." (2000, 391)

The standard examples motivating the existence of unarticulated constituents are not persuasive...for each alleged example of an unarticulated constituent there is an unpronounced pronominal element in the logical form of the sentence uttered whose value is the alleged unarticulated constituent. (2000, 410)

The occurrence of 'logical form' in the second passage is important. It crops up again in Stanley's definition of 'unarticulated constituent':

x is an unarticulated constituent of an utterance *u* iff (1) *x* is an element supplied by context to the truth-conditions of *u*, and (2) *x* is not the semantic value of any constituent of the logical form of the sentence uttered. (2000, 410)[104]

In the present context, Stanley's switch from talk of the *proposition expressed* by a use of a sentence to talk of the *truth conditions* of an utterance of a sentence is unproblematic, and we should have no complaint: *truth conditions* will have unarticulated constituents, as it were, relative to particular uses or utterances of sentences. There are, however, things to tidy up before we can examine Stanley's biconditional. First, his talk of "an unarticulated constituent of an utterance *u*" in the passage just quoted must be a slip—*propositions* and *truth conditions* have unarticulated constituents, not utterances—and it can be fixed by construing it, in the present context, as "an unarticulated constituent *of the truth conditions* of an utterance *u*." Second, something needs fixing in the following gloss: unarticulated constituents, says Stanley, are "elements supplied by context to the truth conditions of utterances, elements which are not the semantic values of any constituents in the actual structure of natural language sentences" (2000, 410). Now it is no part of Perry's claim that there is no expression in natural language one can use to refer to Reykjavík, of course, and Stanley surely recognizes this. So, by "the actual structure of natural language sentences," Stanley must mean what he could have expressed more clearly using "the actual structures of the natural language sentences used in making those utterances." Third, if we are to get anywhere at all, we shall have to overlook the following bizarre statement: "An unarticulated constituent analysis of an expression is closely related to the claim that the expression is an indexical in the narrow sense of the term" (2000, 411). There can be no coherent talk of an expression *E* with the following two properties: (i) some people claim *E* is indexical; (ii) some people provide an "unarticulated constituent analysis of" *E*. Something α is an unarticulated constituent of a proposition $\langle \ldots \alpha \ldots \rangle$ expressed by a use of some sentence *X* precisely if there is *no expression E* that is part of *X* that has α as its value on this use. So Stanley's talk of "an unarticulated constituent analysis of an expression" makes no sense.

The real problem I see with Stanley's biconditional concerns "logical forms." Perry does not talk of a sentence's "logical form" in his description of unarticulated constituents; yet a notion of logical form, indeed a *particular notion of logical form imported from a favored type of syntactic theory*, is at the heart of Stanley's definition of an unarticulated constituent and vital to his broadside against Perry and others who accept UT.[105] By the "logical form" of a sentence, Stanley has in mind a *phrase marker* in the sense of generative grammar.[106] As he puts it, a sentence's logical form is "a special sort of linguistic representation" (2000, 391), its "actual syntactic structure" (2000, 391), its "real structure" (2000, 392), which is "revealed by empirical inquiry" (2000, 392) and which "is, in fact, quite distinct from its surface grammatical form" (2000, 392). It is striking that Stanley *refrains* from explicitly identifying a sentence's logical form with its LF but does *not* refrain from saying he is using 'logical form' in accordance with what he claims is "standard" usage in syntactic theory:

> syntax associates with each occurrence of a natural language expression a lexically and perhaps also structurally disambiguated structure which differs from its apparent structure, and is the primary object of semantic interpretation. In accord with standard usage in syntax, I call such structures *logical forms*. (2000, 393)[107]

In short, the logical form of an English sentence is a genuine of representation of syntactic structure ripe for interpretation, something generated by a syntax or grammar for English.

Let me say, straight away, that I am in harmony with Stanley on one important point: I too advocate "logical forms" construed as syntactic structures distinct from surface structures that are the inputs to semantic interpretation, and this has always put me at odds with Perry.[108] So I have no qualms with the general syntactic framework Stanley wishes to use in his own theorizing. But Stanley wields the framework itself as a *weapon*. And this is unhelpful at best.

Many linguists explicitly *reject* syntactic frameworks that posit logical forms in Stanley's sense. At Perry's home institution alone, all sorts of theories have bloomed that explicitly reject "logical forms," reject aphonics in syntax, reject the idea of a level of syntactic representation as removed from surface appearances as logical forms (in Stanley's required sense) are meant to be, or reject the idea of more than one level of syntactic representation.[109]

Within the Chomskyan Principles and Parameters framework, some versions of theories that posit Logical Form, or LF, as a bona fide level of syntactic representation are effectively positing logical forms in the sense Stanley is talking about. To be sure, there are plenty of substantive internecine debates amongst such LF theorists—about whether LFs are really rich enough to be objects of semantic interpretation, about whether a sentence's LF is the *only* object of semantic interpretation, about whether all quantifiers (and possibly even proper names) undergo raising at LF, about whether all information about quantifier scope is really present at LF, about the precise statement of the binding theory, about which principles of the binding theory the different types of aphonics fall under, about island constraints on movement and interpretation, about purported advantages of a copy theory of movement, and so on.[110] But none of this touches the fact that there is something approximating a "standard" use of 'logical form', or at least 'Logical Form' *among these LF theorists*, even if important details are fiercely debated and different stances are taken on the nature and shape of an overall theory of meaning.

The first question to ask here is whether it is for substantive or merely expository reasons that Stanley refrains from calling the logical forms he is talking about LFs.[111] This is a matter about which we need to be absolutely clear. Stanley gives us no syntactic theory of his own, yet he makes *syntactic* claims about logical forms containing aphonic expressions for which he claims to have *syntactic* evidence; and he dismisses views, such as Perry's, that he claims are undermined by this syntactic evidence.[112] Obviously, one cannot start making such claims and dismissals if one has no theory whatsoever in mind about what these syntactic structures look like. So presumably Stanley has in mind *some* syntactic theory (or at least *some* syntactic analyses that can be stated in *some* syntactic theory or theories). One can certainly appeal to LF in setting out one's own proposals and do so without giving *all* of the details of one's favorite account of LF. But one cannot get away with claiming that *syntactic theory* writ large demonstrates the correctness of one's position and the falsity of all rival positions without getting into the thick of an empirical theory of syntax and explaining *why* one's theory is the only one that can be taken seriously.

Stanley may be refraining from saying he is talking about LFs for any of the following reasons, or for certain combinations of them:

(i) He *does* mean LFs but does not want to get drawn into exposition, assuming many of his readers are familiar enough with talk of LF to make the connection. (ii) He *does* mean LFs but wants to avoid getting into internecine debates about quantifier raising, Binding Theory, types of aphonics, and the like.[113] (iii) He *does* mean LFs but wants to leave the door open for other syntactic theories that may posit phrase markers with the properties he ascribes to logical forms. (iv) He does *not* mean LFs but "logical forms" in some other unnamed syntactic theory. (v) He does *not* mean LFs, because he has nothing particularly specific in mind by "logical form," just a general idea that involves positing "logical forms" containing aphonic variables and that might be approached through any of a number of possible syntactic theories.[114]

Whatever Stanley's theoretical and dialectical intentions, one thing is clear: without making *some* assumptions about the syntax of his "logical forms," he has no meaningful argument against Perry or anyone else when it comes to unarticulated constituents, for his arguments purport to demonstrate on *empirical grounds* the presence of an aphonic in a sentence's syntactic structure, specifically in its "logical form," that has as its value on a given occasion precisely the entity said by Perry (or whomever) to be an unarticulated constituent.

Anyone who has taken a logic course can produce semi-first-order, semi-English "logical forms" containing variables meant to be bound by quantifiers as a way of explicating the truth conditions of uses of English sentences, perhaps even in ways that respect certain syntactic features of the original English sentences deemed to be of semantic relevance. Philosophers do this sort of thing all of the time; it is one of the stock techniques for making ourselves clear, whatever the subject matter. But this is precisely what Stanley claims *not* to be doing. He says in no uncertain terms at the beginning of his paper that *his* "logical forms" are empirical posits of syntactic theory, phrase markers.[115]

When we examine Stanley's arguments, it becomes clear they are beholden to the correctness of not only a syntactic theory of a certain type, but also the correctness of certain *syntactic theses* meant to form part of a theory of that type. For better or worse, we can call this type of theory an *LF theory*. The thing that links the various proposals about LF in the literature and the myriad analyses of the LFs of particular sentences is the idea that a sentence's LF is grammatically real, a syntactic representation generated in a systematic way by the grammar and systematically related to X's superficial form (its PF, say) via certain well-defined syntactic operations. And it is just *this* that Stanley is presupposing, effectively welding his central point, his definition of an unarticulated constituent, and his arguments against them, to the success of some LF theory or other.

It is one thing to posit a particular LF for a particular sentence and show how its existence could play an important role in explaining a certain phenomenon or datum of an interpretive nature. It is quite another to claim that there is *no possibility* of explaining the phenomenon or datum without positing the LF in question; for this is tantamount to a claim *about* syntax (and other things), a claim to the effect that only LF theories are viable. And, of course, it is precisely *this* claim that many linguists reject, particularly at Stanford. Thus, Stanley's arguments must be aimed as much at syntacticians as at philosophers and cognitive scientists who postulate unarticulated constituents, and it would be as well for him to acknowledge this. But it was precisely because Perry was *not* making major syntactic assumptions that he introduced unarticulated constituents in the way he did. And it is wrong of Stanley to say the notion of an unarticulated constituent as *he, Stanley*, defines it is the one "used by Sperber and Wilson (1986), Récanati (1993), and Bach (1994)" (2000, 409, n.20).[116] Further, it is highly misleading to add that Crimmins (1992) is

substantially more cautious than the other advocates of unarticulated constituents. His target is not the view that all context-dependence is traceable to logical form, as I have presented this thesis, but the much more implausible view that contextual effects on truth-conditions are restricted to providing the values of expressions in the apparent structure of the sentence. Therefore, he should not be assimilated to my targets. (Stanley 2000, 409, n.20)

Stanley makes it clear that Perry *is* one of his targets:

A similar point does not hold of the article in which the vocabulary was introduced, Perry (1986), since, in his (1998), Perry is clear that the phenomenon of interest to him is what he calls a "truly unarticulated constituent," which is not the value of an unpronounced item in the actual structure of a sentence (cf. his footnote 4). (2000, 409–410, n.20)

Perry and Crimmins, however, are both neutral on the vexed matter of the correct shape of a syntactic theory (see below), and the wedge between them that Stanley is trying to drive amounts to nothing.[117]

Let us turn now to Stanley's discussion of Perry's discussion of uses of (1):

(1)   It's raining.

Stanley errs at the outset by attributing to Perry a particular syntactic thesis about the logical form of (1). In setting out Perry's argument for the presence of an unarticulated location in the proposition expressed by a use of (1), Stanley begins as follows:

Here is an argument for the existence of unarticulated constituents due originally to John Perry. Consider the sentence: [(1)] 'It's raining' [example indented]. According to this argument, it is plausible that [(1)] contains a covert temporal variable, so that it's true representation is more like 'It is raining (t)' [example indented]. (2000, 414–415)

This is extraordinary. *Nowhere* in Perry's discussions do we find him saying that (1) contains a "covert temporal variable"! Indeed, Perry's initial assumption seems to be that (1) does *not* contain a covert temporal variable, as we can see from what he actually *says* rather than relying on Stanley's reconstruction:

In order to assign a truth-value to my son's statement [his use of (1) above], as I just did, I needed a place. But no component of his statement stood for a place. The verb 'raining' supplied the relation $rains(t, p)$—a dyadic relation between times and places, as we have just noted. The tensed auxiliary 'is' supplied a time, the time at which the statement was made. 'It' does not supply anything, but is just syntactic filler [Footnote omitted]. So Palo Alto is a constituent of the content of my son's remark, which no component of his statement designated; it is an unarticulated constituent. (1986, 206)

As far as propositional constituents are concerned, then, there is a contrast for Perry, between, on the one hand, the relation and the time, both of which are *articulated explicitly* by overt parts of the sentence uttered (the verb and the tense, respectively), and, on the other hand, the location that is *unarticulated*. Stanley's claim that Perry talks about a "covert temporal variable" in his argument is false and liable to foster (a) the (false) impression that Perry is assuming an LF theory of syntax that posits *some* covert/aphonic expressions, in particular covert temporal variables, and (b) the (false) impression that Perry's argument for an unarticulated *location* of the proposition expressed by an utterance of (1) is meant to demonstrate the existence of a propositional constituent corresponding to no location variable in (1)'s LF. Perry is clear in the passage just quoted that it is the *overt* tense of the verb that contributes a time to the proposition expressed. To see Perry as claiming that it is not this overt tense but some "covert temporal variable" that contributes the time is to engage in wild distortion.[118]

As to syntax, all Perry actually claims, as we saw earlier, is that (i) the proposition expressed by a use of (1) contains a location corresponding to no obvious component of (1), and (ii) that it is not *necessary* to see (1) as containing an aphonic ("phantom") locative expression in order to appreciate this point. The purported existence of an aphonic *temporal* variable in the LF of (1) plays no role whatsoever in Perry's argument, and to claim it does is highly misleading.

Here is how Stanley sets out what he takes to be the second part of Perry's argument:

But what an utterance of [(1)] asserts is not just that it is raining at a certain contextually provided time. Rather, it asserts that it is raining at a certain contextually provided time at a certain contextually provided place. But surely it is implausible to posit a place variable in addition to a temporal variable. It is surely more plausible to supply the place to the truth-conditions of an utterance of [(1)] directly, without mediation of a variable. (2000, 415)

Here Stanley presents Perry as contrasting covert temporal and locative variables: "it is implausible to posit a place variable in addition to a temporal variable"; and he has Perry reasoning that it is "surely more plausible to supply the place... without the mediation of a variable." This is all wrong: Perry is not postulating (or endorsing anyone else's postulation of) one covert variable (a temporal one) while rejecting the postulation of another (a locative one). It simply will not do to portray Perry as making claims about LFs that might be refuted by appealing to more ideas about LFs.[119]

Stanley has a positive proposal, however, and he claims to have *syntactic* evidence for it and against unarticulated constituents. But, before getting to that evidence, we need to examine the general idea of indexical, locative aphonics.

Indexicals, Variables, Aphonics

Let us abstract from matters of tense and time in order to focus on location. The idea we shall need to examine is that the LF of (1) contains, as Stanley claims, an indexical, locative, aphonic, which I shall call *loc* (italicization indicating aphonicity), that something like (1′) is (1)'s LF:

(1)   It's snowing.

(1′)   It's snowing *loc*.

This is pretty uninformative as to syntactic structure, of course, and I make no claim about the structure of the LF Stanley assigns to (1) because he says nothing about it—

which is striking, given that his thesis is basically a *syntactic* one. Of course, since *loc* is meant to be an empirical posit of the "actual syntactic structure" of the sentence we standardly represent as (1), there must be some empirical fact of the matter as to *where* in the sentence *loc* actually occurs for which there is some empirical evidence. For the sake of having something to work with, I assume, without prejudice, that *loc* is meant to be understood as occupying an argument position of 'snowing', so I have placed it after the verb in (1′)—speaking linearly, and informally, it is where we would place 'here' or 'in Reykjavík'.

Before we investigate the syntactic and semantic properties of *loc*, we need to get clearer about the general semantic background Stanley is assuming in his attack on Perry's unarticulated constituents. Here is Stanley's picture.

(a) The proposition expressed by a sentence X relative to a context c is a proposition determined by, and only by, two things: (i) the denotations relative to c of the elements of X's LF and (ii) a set of context-invariant compositional operations on these denotations, determined by, and only by, the structure of X's LF.

(b) The effects of extralinguistic factors on the proposition expressed by X relative to c are restricted to the provision of denotations to some fixed set of expressions that are "context-sensitive" ("indexical," in a broad sense of the word), "primitive expression[s] whose denotation[s] [are] supplied entirely by context, perhaps guided by a linguistic rule" (2000, 400).

(c) Among these expressions are "indexicals," in a narrow sense of the word, expressions possessing "the characteristics shared by such words as 'I', 'here', and 'now', but not by 'this', 'that', 'she', and 'he', such as resistance to bindability by variable-binding operators" (2000, 400).

(d) There are three types of overt expressions whose denotations are context-sensitive (indexical, in the broad sense):

First, there are expressions which are obviously indexicals in the narrow sense of the term, words such as 'I', 'here', 'you', 'now', and their brethren. Secondly, there are expressions which are obviously demonstratives, such as 'this' and 'that'. Third, there are expressions that are obviously pronouns, such as 'he' and 'she'. Overt expressions that are in none of these classes are not context-dependent. (2000, 400)[120]

Now one can perfectly well accept (d)—assuming the notions of being "obviously" indexical, "obviously" demonstrative, and "obviously" pronominal can be given some content—without accepting Stanley's next claim:

(e) Any other type of context-sensitivity is attributable to the presence of aphonics in syntax:

If the truth-conditions of constructions containing [overt expressions that are in none of three classes mentioned in (d)] are affected by extra-linguistic context, this context dependence must be traced to the presence of an obvious indexical, demonstrative, or pronominal expression at logical form, or to a structural position in logical form that is occupied by a covert variable. (2000, 400)

Thus Stanley reaches the following position:

(f) There are no unarticulated constituents of propositions expressed: "for each alleged example of an unarticulated constituent there is an unpronounced pronominal element in the logical form of the sentence uttered whose value is the alleged unarticulated constituent" (2000, 410).

Let us use the subscript n to indicate when we are using indexical in what Stanley calls the "narrow" sense (whatever this finally amounts to). It is perfectly coherent to maintain that: (i) no phonic is itself an indexical unless it is an indexical$_n$, a demonstrative, or a pronoun; (ii) the LFs of at least some sentences contain aphonics; (iii) some of these aphonics are indexical; and (iv) not all potential differences in the propositions expressed by (or of the truth conditions of) distinct uses of a sentence X are attributable to the presence in X's LF of phonic or aphonic indexicals to which different values are assigned on these different uses of X. Perry's proposal that distinct propositions may be expressed by distinct uses of (1) because these propositions contain different unarticulated locations is compatible with (i)–(iv). This is not to say Perry *has* to accept them: as I have stressed already, Perry is making no claims he thinks *syntacticians* need to examine. Only Stanley is doing that.

I am inclined to accept (i)–(iv). Specifically, I find (ii) and (iv) compelling, given the empirical evidence, and I see (i) and (iii) as plausible empirical hypotheses, well worth treating as true until we find evidence to the contrary. My saying this, however, amounts to *very little* in the absence of clear *criteria* of what is involved in being indexical and in being indexical$_n$, or at least in the absence of empirically explicable (but not necessarily finalized) *lists* of which expressions are indexical and which are indexical$_n$. Without one or the other of these, accepting any of (i), (iii), or (iv) does not add up to much. More important for present concerns, nor do Stanley's claims (b), (d), and (e). Furthermore, claim (e) requires something else to give it serious content: an account of what it means to say that the occupant of a syntactic position in a sentence's LF is a *variable* (covert or otherwise), something that requires laying some syntactic cards on the table. And given that Stanley holds covert variables to be "bindable" by quantifiers, he will also need to tell us precisely what is involved—*syntactically and semantically* speaking—in a variable (covert or otherwise) being bound at LF, which will require laying down a few more syntactic cards, as well as some semantic ones.

Evidently, being an aphonic variable at LF has something to do with being a *pronominal* (rather than an indexical*ₙ* or a demonstrative), for Stanley claims, recall, that "for each alleged example of an unarticulated constituent there is an unpronounced *pronominal* [emphasis added] element in the logical form of the sentence uttered whose value is the alleged unarticulated constituent" (2000, 410). Stanley need not supply an entire syntactic theory, of course, but he does need to give us enough to justify talk of occurrences of *loc* and talk of variables and variable-binding at LF. The aphonic *loc* is a real *expression*, after all, so we need to be told *where* it occurs in a sentence that is alleged to contain it. And, given that syntacticians have painstakingly investigated, for a quarter century or more, the syntactic constraints on binding that hold in natural language, we need to be told what syntactic constraints on binding Stanley is assuming if *loc* can function, as he claims, as a bound variable.[121] We also need to be told about the *interpretation* of LFs containing bound expressions: a simple pointer to a favored account of the interpretation of binding in the first-order predicate calculus would certainly count, but all sorts of complexities are notoriously involved in effecting a simple mapping from the notion of binding assumed to be operative in the language of the calculus to one satisfactory for LFs of English sentences.[122] Postulating an expression that is aphonic may absolve one from saying anything about its *phonology*, but it does not absolve one from saying something with some content about its syntax and semantics!

Before Stanley's claims about *loc* can be given content enough to make them objects of serious examination, we need from him something substantial about *loc*'s syntactic category, its distributional properties, and its interpretation. And if the story about its interpretation involves the possibility of being *bound*, the syntactic questions take on a particular urgency as it is well known that syntactic structure places stringent conditions on binding possibilities. Remember we are not talking about semi-first-order, semi-English "logical forms" used to explicate truth conditions of uses of English sentences. Rather, we are talking about posits of syntactic theory. Stanley leaves us in no doubt whatsoever that he sees himself as making *empirical* claims about the *actual* syntactic structures of English sentences. And this imposes an empirical burden: whenever he posits an aphonic element, Stanley must construe himself as doing empirical work in *syntax* as much as anything else, as advancing a particular syntactic thesis for which he has syntactic evidence.[123] It simply will not do to terrorize philosophers with claims to the effect that their semantic or pragmatic proposals are incompatible with the empirical facts uncovered by syntacticians, while failing oneself to deliver the syntactic goods needed to justify such claims.

Remember, Perry is advancing no thesis in generative syntax. He is simply pointing out, labeling, and explaining the interpretive significance of the fact that there can be a constituent of the proposition expressed by a use of a sentence X to which no obvious or (at least uncontentious) component of X (or portion of a tokening X^u of X) itself corresponds. When the smoke has cleared, Stanley is *agreeing* with this and then making a vague syntactic suggestion that linguists may or may not consider worth turning into something of substance.[124]

The logical forms Stanley is talking about, and all of their components, are empirical posits of generative syntax for which there is meant to be syntactic evidence. This includes, of course, all *aphonics* and all components said to be variables capable of being bound by quantifiers. According to many LF theorists, there are plenty of aphonics in natural language that act like variables. This is, perhaps, most easily seen by examining the following:

(2)   Everyone wanted [$_S$ Maria to sing].

(3)   Everyone wanted [$_S$ everyone to sing].

(4)   Everyone wanted [$_S$ —to sing].

In (2) and (3) we find the infinitival clauses 'Maria to sing' and 'everyone to sing' subordinated to the main verb. The subject of those infinitival clauses are 'Maria' and 'everyone', respectively. But where is the subject of the infinitival clause in (4)? It will not do, notice, to say (as was sometimes said by some linguists) that we have here a case in which the second occurrence of equivalent noun phrases is deleted, an idea that would incorrectly predict (4) to be equivalent to (3). (4) is naturally read as meaning *everyone x wanted x to sing*. This can captured, and syntactic harmony can be nicely restored, if the infinitival clause in (4) is construed as having an aphonic expression in subject position functioning as a variable bound by 'everyone'. Many linguists call this aphonic PRO:

(4′)   Everyone[1] wanted [$_S$ x_1 to sing].[125]

We have here a simple example in which syntactic considerations suggest the presence of an aphonic, which semantic considerations welcome.[126]

The primary syntactic evidence for *loc*, according to Stanley, is the fact that it can be picked up and bound by quantifiers. And this just reinforces the point that Stanley needs to tell us precisely what is involved, *syntactically and semantically* speaking, in a variable (covert or otherwise) being bound at LF. In the present context, an informal appeal to a semi-first-order, semi-English representation containing a variable that is supposed to be doing the work of a purported aphonic in an English sentence X is only as good as the underlying assumptions about the relation between such a representation and the phrase marker that is $X's$ LF. The matter of what is involved in talk of variable-binding in LFs will be taken up later. Right now, let us try to get clear about what is involved in talk of indexicality.

Neither 'Here' nor 'There'

It is all well and good to come up with examples of indexical and indexical$_n$ expressions, but one would like some understanding of *what is involved* in being an indexical and in being an indexical$_n$ and what lies behind the existence of indexicals. First some seemingly small points that will be important later. Stanley gives us a *partial list* of indexical$_n$ expressions—'I', 'here', 'you', 'now', and their brethren (2000, 400)—and a *necessary* condition on being indexical$_n$—resistance to bindability by variable-binding operators (2000, 400).[127] We are not told which expressions are the "brethren" of 'I', 'here', 'you', 'now'. Perhaps Stanley means to include the strict case variants 'me', 'my', and 'your'. Perhaps also the absolute possessive forms 'mine' and 'yours'. How about the reflexive forms 'myself' and 'yourself'? (This would immediately raise issues about any adequate notion of binding—see below). And the number variants, 'we', 'us', 'our', 'ours', and 'ourselves'.[128] Are 'there' and 'then' brethren of 'here' and now'?[129]

Stanley explicitly excludes 'this', 'that', 'he' and 'she' from his list of indexicals$_n$. This suggests he would be inclined to exclude 'there' (or posit two homophonic words, one an indexical, the other a variable). And what of 'today', 'yesterday', and 'tomorrow'? They do not seem to be bindable, so perhaps Stanley would count them as brethren, or at least cousins, of the four words in his list.

What is involved in indexicality? The indexicals that dominate discussions in the philosophy of language are, in Russell's (1948) language, *egocentric* or *perspectival*: they are used to present things (by which I mean at least objects, persons, times, and places) perspectivally. There are all sorts of intricacies in this area that need to be taken into account in any adequate description of what I am trying to get at, but a few rough and ready remarks will suffice for present purposes. When a speaker refers to a location by uttering 'here' or 'there', in so doing he indicates some sort of *proximal* or *distal* perspective he has to it. (This is not to say anything additional to the location makes it into the proposition he expresses.) Similarly when he refers to an object using 'this' or 'that'. And similarly when the speaker uses 'now' and 'then' to refer to times, the distance now measured temporally rather than spatially. (The distal 'then' can be used to refer to a time past or a time future, and the tense of the accompanying verb is typically used to indicate the *direction*.) When a speaker uses 'today', 'tomorrow', or 'yesterday', he also *describes*, or perhaps *circumscribes* the distance.

Personal pronouns such as 'I', 'you', and 'he' are also used to indicate perspective. Reichenbach (1947) proposed to capture what he seems to have regarded as the locative flavor of these words by taking the utterance as a point of reference, yielding his "token-reflexive" theory of indexicals.[130] More neutrally, we might say that when a speaker uses 'I' to refer to someone, in so doing he indicates the *perfectly proximal* perspective he has to that person, the *self* perspective. When he uses 'you' or 'he' to refer to someone, in so doing he indicates a perspective to that person that is *not* perfectly proximal, even when referring to himself (as he may). With 'you' this perspective gives rise to a *second-order* perfectly proximal perspective, this being the characteristic of second-person pronouns. With 'he' it does not. (Thus, the hearer does not take the speaker to be referring to himself with 'you' or 'he' unless there is some special reason for him to be doing so.)[131] The gendering of third-person pronouns can be treated as a functional embellishment; similarly, the gendering or numbering of second-person pronouns in those languages that avail themselves of these things.[132]

I am strongly inclined to conclude that indexical words are *essentially* perspectival, that perspective is the *hallmark* of indexicality. This appears to be Perry's (1986) view, for he talks of just *two* ways in which an *articulated* constituent may get into the proposition expressed by an utterance of some sentence *X*. It is given either *directly* or *relationally* by the meaning of some component of *X*. More specifically, the meaning of a component of *X* is either of such a nature that that it supplies the *same propositional constituent* on any occasion of use, or else of such a nature that it indicates the *same relationship to the speaker* on any occasion of use, different propositional constituents bearing the relationship in question to the speaker on different occasions of use (1986, 209). This is Perry's way of drawing the distinction between *eternal* and *context-sensitive*, and it seems that if an expression is context-sensitive that is because it is used to express some fixed relation to the speaker that different things may bear on different occasions.[133]

The perspectival nature of the expressions just mentioned appears to *explain* their indexicality in a way nothing else does. So whenever someone proposes treating a particular expression as an indexical, we do well to inquire into the perspective it indicates. Whenever we find an expression that is used to refer to different things on different occasions of use, we should always ask ourselves what it is about this expression that makes it behave in this way, and we should not be satisfied with the answer that it just does. With the indexicals just mentioned, the answer is clear: they are designed for presenting things perspectivally, and also, if Kaplan (1989a, 1989b) and Perry (1979, 1986, 2001) are right, in a *direct* manner, that is, without contributing perspectival or otherwise descriptive elements to the proposition expressed. In summary, we should be skeptical about any claim to the effect that an expression (phonic or aphonic) is indexical if the expression is not perspectival in some way. This is one reason I am deeply skeptical about "contextualist" accounts of the meaning of 'know'. The idea that this verb is indexical in some way makes a mockery of the idea of indexical expressions.

Having zero phonology would do nothing to reduce any mockery. Yet the idea of an indexical that lacks both perspective *and* phonic form (and which also fails to describe or name) is the heart of Stanley's syntactic jihad against unarticulated constituents. The alleged aphonic *loc* in (1) is *not* perspectival. Certainly it is not an aphonic version of 'here'. Suppose I am talking to Ken Taylor on the telephone. He is in his office at Stanford, sitting with John Perry. John asks Ken to ask me how the weather is in Reykjavík today. I respond to Ken's question with (1), and then Ken uses the same sentence to report the news to John. Reykjavík is an unarticulated constituent of the proposition *I* expressed and of the proposition *Ken* expressed. Now, although Ken and I used the same sentence—namely (1)—there is no phonic indexical locative we could have *both* used in place of (or as well as) the purported aphonic. I would have had to use 'here', whereas Ken would have had to use 'there'. So neither 'here' nor 'there' is strictly synonymous with (has the same character as) *loc*, because the aphonic has the perspectival character of neither phonic. If Ken and I had wanted a common piece of English we could have used 'in Reykjavík' or 'where Stephen is'—hardly colloquial in the circumstances, but that is not the issue. But neither of these is synonymous with (identical in character to) *loc* either, because sentence (1) may be used to talk about somewhere *other* than Reykjavík or *other* than where I am (I may ask Ken how the weather is in Palo Alto, and he might respond with (1), using *loc* to refer to Palo Alto). It should be clear, then, that if there really is a locative aphonic in (1)'s LF, it differs from any extant *phonic* locative, indexical of English—and not just in being aphonic. There is no knock-down argument against the existence of *loc* here, just a serious worry: what would explain the existence of an indexical that lacks perspective (and phonology, to boot) and does not *name* or *describe* a location either?

Let that be our first question, then, for anyone who would posit *loc*: (i) How do we explain the existence of an expression that has no phonic properties and is used to refer to something in no particular way whatsoever? Further questions come straight to mind: (ii) Are there *perspectival*, aphonic indexicals in natural language? If not, why not? (iii) Are there aperspectival, *phonic* indexicals? If not, why not? (iv) Is it just an accident that no phonic of English has the same meaning (character) as *loc*? Are there natural languages that possess phonics with the same meaning as *loc*? If not, is there some deep reason for this? (v) Could we stipulate a new *phonic*, locative, indexical, 'loke', which could thrive in English as a synonym for *loc*? (vi) If so, would the occurrence of 'loke' in (1″) occupy the syntactic node that *loc* is supposed to occupy in (1′)?

(1″)   It's snowing loke.

(vii) Would (1″) function just like its 'loke'-free counterpart? If so, what would prompt the choice of one over the other? (viii) Would 'loke' allow of *doubling-up* the way 'here' and 'in Reykjavík do in (5)?

(5)   It's snowing here in Reykjavík today.

(6)   It's snowing loke here today.

(7)   It's snowing loke in Reykjavík today.

Or, for that matter, *trebling-up*?

(8)   It's snowing loke here in Reykjavík today.

Location, location, location!

A good interpretive reason for the double-up in (5) was given earlier: 'here' presents a location from a perspective, whereas 'Reykjavík' presents it by name, and 'the capital of Iceland' presents it by description.[134] So there is no communicative redundancy. One can straightforwardly convey information by uttering (5) that one would not straightforwardly convey by dropping 'here' or 'in Reykjavík'. But *nothing* would be lost by dropping the aperspectival, adescriptive, anominal 'loke' in any of (6)–(8). No *communicative need* would be served by for the phonic 'loke'. It is not used to describe, name, or signal a perspective; it is simply used to refer.[135] Recalling something I said earlier, 'loke' is useless by virtue of being too flexible, so to speak. All it has going for it is its phonology and the fact that is used to refer to a place. Draining it of its phonology does not improve matters, of course, and the product is just *loc*. This might well make one wonder whether any communicative need is served by the purported aphonic *loc*, with which 'loke' was supposed to be synonymous. That a location is a constituent of the proposition expressed by an utterance of (1) is something signaled by the use of the verb 'snow' with its standard meaning. *All* of the work seemingly done by 'loke' and *loc* has been done already by the weather verb; 'loke' and *loc* are useless.

The idea of expressions with phonic properties but no communicative utility is not hard to get one's mind around. Nor is the idea of expressions with communicative utility but no phonic properties. But the idea of expressions with neither communicative utility nor phonic properties? The idea is strained. We are involved in an empirical enterprise, so we cannot prejudge the issue, of course. Nonetheless, the default assumption should *not* be that there *are* such expressions. The reasoning here is Chomskyan: the logical problem of language acquisition becomes more tractable the more we can narrow the range of options (up to a limit of course), the more narrowly constrained linguistic theory becomes, whether we are talking about options involving syntactic categories, syntactic operations, parameters, levels of representation or whatever.[136] So, ceteris paribus, we should posit such things, as far as is possible, only when there are strong empirical reasons for doing so, when doing so appears empirically unavoidable or narrows other options. If we are going to posit expressions with phonic properties but no communicative utility, this should be because we have been led to them by strong empirical considerations, not simply because the idea of such expressions is not itself incoherent. Knowledge of the meaning of the verb 'snow' is enough to signal that a location is involved in a use of (1)—it expresses a relation between times and places after all. So if there really is an aphonic *loc* in (1), its existence will have to be justified on *syntactic* grounds, and that means getting clear about its syntactic category, its binding properties, the node it occupies and how this node stands to those occupied by 'here' and 'in Reykjavík' in (5).

Notice that I have been talking about expressions with neither *communicative utility* nor phonic properties, not expressions with neither *semantic properties* nor phonic properties. The latter appear to be ruled out on minimalist assumptions (according to which an expression is something that has a role at LF or PF, often enough both). To claim that *loc* has no communicative utility is not to claim it has no *semantic* properties. By hypothesis it does: it is used to refer to locations, and its use contributes a location to the proposition expressed. At least that is Stanley's idea. The point I am making is just this: given that 'rain' and 'snow' express dyadic relations between times and places, and given that *loc*, if it exists, indicates nothing of a *perspectival*, *nominal*, or *descriptive* character, why think it is in virtue of the assignment of a value to such an expression that the proposition expressed by a use of (1) contains a location as a constituent? Surely the null hypothesis should be that the use of the verb 'snow' demands a location, given what it means, just as Taylor (2001) suggests. Nothing is gained by the presence of *loc*, unlike by the presence of 'here' or 'there' or 'in Reykjavík' or 'in the capital of Iceland'.

The general point can be reinforced with the help of a quick thought experiment, the full morals of which will emerge later. Suppose we were to find a dialect of English that contained a singular term not found in our own dialects, 'pers'. We notice speakers of this dialect using sentences like the following:

(9)   Pers is here.

(9′)   Give it to pers.

(9″)   Have you seen pers's new shoes?

When we ask about 'pers', a speaker who uses it tells us it is a singular pronoun, an indexical that is used to refer to persons of either gender. Great, we think, a third-person pronoun, neutral as to gender. Then we hear him use two more singular terms with which we are unfamiliar, 'mers' and 'fers'. We ask him about them, and he says they are the masculine and feminine versions of 'pers'. We are baffled and say to him that we find this rather odd, given that they have 'he' and 'she' (and 'him' and 'her') in their dialect and that they seem to use them just as we do. Now it is *his* turn to be baffled; he tells us 'he' and 'mers' are not synonyms and that 'she' and 'fers' aren't either. Before we can follow up, one of his friends, *A*, arrives, and the following conversation takes place:

A: Hi, Bob, how is mers?

B: Fine thanks. And fers?

A: Fine, thanks. And your wife?

B: Fers has a bad cold.

A: Pers is sorry to hear that. Has mers had one too?

B: No, I've been fine. Mers didn't catch fers's cold.

We go over the conversation together and finally we see what is going on: 'pers' is not only neutral as to gender, but is also neutral as to *person*. So are the gendered 'mers' and 'fers'. They lack *perspective*.

   We are not going to find a dialect of English containing 'pers' of course—not because such a dialect is logically impossible, but because phonic indexicals lacking perspective are useless. Even the gendered 'mers' and 'fers' are pretty useless. To be sure, the referent of a use of 'mers' has to be (or at least be presumed to be) male, but for a language like English which has *personal* indexicals like 'I', 'you', and 'he', there is going to be no call for impersonal ones.

   Let us push this to the limit: a wholly aperspectival indexical that can be used to refer to anything whatsoever. Useless.

   Now let us bring predicates into the picture. Forget about perspective for a moment. If a language contains wholly indexical singular terms and wholly indexical one-place predicates, it contains wholly indexical sentences. Suppose we came across a dialect of English that had such expressions and so had a simple subject-predicate sentence that is wholly indexical, a sentence composed of a wholly indexical singular term 'i' and a wholly indexical predicate 'f' (pronounced like the letters 'i' and 'f' in the word 'if'):

(10) $[_S[_{DP}\ i][_{VP}\ f]]$.

We, who have just come across 'i' and 'f' for the first time, ask a speaker of this dialect to explain their meanings (characters) to us. He says that 'i' can be used to refer to any type of object whatsoever, male or female, animate or inanimate, concrete or abstract. We think we are close to having 'i' under control: it is synonymous with either 'this' or 'that', but its use appears to lack the rudeness that accompanies some uses of 'this' and 'that' when used in connection with people (unless we add a nominal, as in 'that man'). I say as much to our speaker, and he says that I am wrong, that the whole point of 'i' is that it is less constraining than 'this' or 'that', that it involves no proximal or distal locative perspective. It is wholly aperspectival. Then he tells us about the predicate 'f': it can be used to express any property whatsoever. Furthermore, it is also wholly aperspectival. So, on one occasion, a speaker might use (10) to say that London is pretty and on another to say that Paderewski is musical; on one occasion to say that he is feeling ill, on another to say that he is feeling much better; and so on. Would we say these people are unbelievably brilliant or unbelievably stupid? Surely (10) is so useful that it is useless; its versatility is its downfall, because it can be used to say anything that can be expressed in subject-predicate form. One may as well grunt. Indeed, I hereby decree my grunts synonymous with (10). Ludicrous, of course.

Now let's take away the only thing 'i' and 'f' have going for them: their phonology. That is, replace them with aphonics i and f. Surely we have reached an absurd terminus: an aphonic, aperspectival wholly indexical singular term and an aphonic, aperspectival wholly indexical predicate. It is hard to imagine two linguistic expressions put together to form a more useless expression than (11).

(11) $[_S [_{DP} i][_{VP} f]]$.[137]

Let us return to example (5), which brings up another question:

(5)   It's snowing here in Reykjavík today.

Are people who hold that every constituent of the proposition expressed by a use of a sentence X is the value of some item in X's LF attracted to the converse: that on a use of X, every item of X's LF has a value that is a constituent of the proposition expressed by a use of X? (Put aside obviously pleonastic occurrences of words such as 'it' in 'it's raining', and 'there' in 'there's a fly in my soup'.) On the face of it, a traditional compositional semantics will say that, relative to my use of (5) now, or relative to a context with me as speaker and Reykjavík as location, Reykjavík is the referent of *both* my use of 'Reykjavík' and my use of 'here'. Does that mean Reykjavík itself occurs *twice* in the proposition expressed? If 'here in Reykjavík' is itself a syntactic constituent of (5)—I have no firm opinion on this matter—then perhaps it too has Reykjavík as its value on this use. Would this be the product of composition, the value of 'here' (Reykjavík) combining with the value of 'in Reykjavík' (Reykjavík) to produce the value of 'here in Reykjavík' (Reykjavík)? What then of the alleged aphonic *loc*? Does it have its own special position in syntax that no phonic may occupy? If so, then on the hypothesis at hand would it require a value not only on my use of (1) but also on my use of (5)? Would Reykjavík get into the proposition once, twice, three times, four times, or five times? On Stanley's account, all of these appear to be live options until enough is said about (a) the LF of (5), and (b) the ways in which the compositional instructions associated with its structure determine the proposition expressed by a use of (5), to eliminate some of them.

What all of this brings out yet again is the need to say *something* about the "actual syntactic structure" of sentences containing weather verbs if one is going to claim that they contain the aphonic *loc*. Is *loc* an *argument* of a weather verb (does it occupy an argument position of the verb)? Is the position *loc* occupies one that may be occupied by a phonic? Can it be occupied by 'here in Reykjavík'? Or does *loc* itself appear in (5) *alongside* 'here in Reykjavík'? Or as *part* of it? One cannot simply ignore these questions. They are cries for enlightenment on how *loc* is meant to fit into syntactic and semantic theory, and a reminder that it is doubly egregious to claim that Perry and others who have posited unarticulated constituents argue as follows:

First, some linguistic construction is provided whose truth-conditional interpretation is mediated by context. Then, it is argued that it is inconsistent with current syntactic theory to postulate, in the logical form of the relevant construction, expressions or variables the semantic values of which context could provide. (Stanley 2000, 398)

First, this is decidedly *not* what Perry and company do. Second, Stanley doesn't actually tell us what syntactic theory declares or what syntactic structures he himself is assuming in giving his own analyses of the weather sentences Perry discusses. As far as Stanley's proposal that there is an aphonic *loc* in (1)—and, presumably, in (5)—is concerned, we are completely in the dark on all syntactic and semantic matters of substance, and as such we cannot construe it as a serious contribution to syntactic or semantic theory. All we have been given is a handful of semi-first-order, semi-English representations, some containing quantifiers and variables, representations which may illuminate the truth-conditions of uses of sentences (1) and (5) for those who are in some doubt about them. No sermon about "actual syntactic structure" that is "revealed by empirical inquiry" is needed to do *that*.

Until the syntax and semantics of *loc* are spelled out, claims to have provided syntactic evidence for its existence must be taken with a large grain of salt. If there is syntactic evidence for *loc*, probably it will not revolve entirely around the syntax of weather *verbs*. Consider:

(12)   There will be more snow/rain tomorrow.

(13)   Tomorrow will be a windy/rainy/foggy/cloudy/overcast day.

The philosopher who goes along with Perry and Taylor explains why the propositions expressed by utterances of (12) and (13) are location-involving as follows: raining is a binary relation obtaining between times and places, and the verb 'rain', the noun 'rain' and the adjective 'rainy' are devices for expressing this relation in verbal, nominal, and adjectival ways; hence, the propositions expressed by uses of sentences containing these expressions will contain a location.[138]

If every component of the proposition expressed by an utterance of X is the value of some syntactic object in X's LF, presumably we will find *loc*—or at least something that does the sort of work *loc* is meant to do—in the LFs of (12) and (13). Where it would occur is not obvious. Since I placed it after the verb 'snow' in (1), I shall place it after the weather noun or adjective here:

(12′)   There will be more snow/rain *loc* tomorrow.

(13′)   Tomorrow will be a windy/rainy/foggy/cloudy/overcast *loc* day.

And this would mean that *loc*—or whatever the purported aphonic is—is not always the occupant of the argument place of a *verb*. Similar considerations apply to the following:

(14)   It's cold/hot/humid/sticky.

(15)   It's dark/light already.

(16)   It's noon/midnight.

(17)   I rise at dawn/I enjoy a martini at sunset.

Would the following be close to the LFs of (14)–(17)?

(14′)   It's cold/hot/humid/sticky *loc*.

(15′)   It's dark/light already *loc*.

(16′)   It's noon/midnight *loc*.

(17′)   I rise at dawn *loc*/I enjoy a martini at sunset *loc*.

All of this might suggest to the *loc*-theorist that a generalization is being missed, that the aphonic in a weather sentence is the product of a rather general fact about sentence structure, perhaps about *verbal* structure: the most basic function of language is to express thoughts about things at times and places, and as such a basic sentential frame comes with an intrinsic, aphonic temporal indexical and an intrinsic, aphonic locative indexical, *loc*.[139]

But there are problems down this road. First, Taylor's (18) would now contain *loc*, uses of the sentence evaluable for truth or falsity only when some particular location is its value:

(18)   Laura danced the tango all night last night.

(18′)   Laura danced *loc* the tango all night last night.

And that, as we saw earlier, is plain wrong. The mere fact that every dancing takes place at a time and at a place does not mean a location is a constituent of the proposition expressed by a 'dance'-sentence.[140]

Second, there are all sorts of sentences that are used to talk about things that do not, as a matter of their metaphysical nature, involve specific locations:

(19)   Lead is heavier than copper.

I suppose both problems could be solved by brute force, existential closure for (18), and universal closure for (19), *loc* functioning as a variable:

(18″)   ($\exists loc$) Laura danced *loc* the tango.

(19″)   ($\forall loc$) Lead is *loc* heavier than copper.

We appear to have reached the following position. (i) Stanley (2000) claims that every constituent of the proposition expressed by (or the truth conditions of) a use of a sentence X is the value of some expression occurring in X's LF. (ii) He agrees with Perry (1986) that the proposition expressed by (or the truth conditions of) a use of (1) contains a location, and hence, by (i), that the LF of (1) contains an expression, the use of which on a given occasion refers to a location. (iii) This can be intended as no more than a thesis in generative syntax. (iv) But Stanley gives us no information about what he calls the "actual syntactic structure" of (1) beyond claiming that it contains *loc*; and yet he claims to have empirical evidence for what the actual syntactic structure of (1) *is*, for he claims to have syntactic evidence that it contains *loc*. (v) What all of this means is that when we come to evaluate the argument Stanley thinks he is using to undermine Perry's proposal, we are going to be examining an argument based on Stanley's syntactic evidence for the actual syntactic structure of (1), a syntactic structure he fails to provide. (vi) If *loc* really exists, it is a strange type of indexical: not only is it aphonic, it is aperspectival. It is used to refer to a location in no particular way whatsoever. Unlike the indexicals 'here' and 'there', it indicates no perspective; unlike 'Reykjavík', it is not used to refer in the way a name is; and unlike 'the capital of Iceland', it is not used to pick out a location by description. To boot, you can't hear it.

Does this mean it is pointless examining Stanley's *argument*? No. We know already that without an account of the LF of (1) the argument can have no conclusion with real empirical content. But there is a very important lesson to be learned from looking at its confused initial premise.

Binding and Relativization

The principal argument Stanley uses against Perry's unarticulated constituent analysis of the interpretation of utterances of (1) takes off from a warm-up argument involving the relativized interpretation of utterances of (2):

(1) It was raining.

(2) Everywhere I went, it was raining.

We can render reasonably transparent the relativized interpretation of (2) using the semiformal, semi-English (2′):

(2′) [*every x: location x: I went to x*] *it was raining in x*.

The two main assumptions in the warm-up argument are these:

(a) The *mere existence* of this reading of (2) demonstrates conclusively that the sentence involves "implicit binding," which means it contains an aphonic variable in syntax, call it *loc*, bound by 'everywhere I went last week' in (2)'s LF:

(2″) [Everywhere I went][1] it was raining loc_1.

Implicit binding means *explicit* binding, as it were, at LF.

(b) If there is a variable *loc* bound by 'everywhere I went' in (2)'s LF, *loc* must also appear in (1)'s LF. Whereas it is bound in (2)'s LF, it is free in (1)'s LF and so interpreted as an indexical. (The same aphonic device, *loc*, may occur as an indexical or as a bound variable.)

Assumption (a) is not a claim about how best to capture the truth-conditions of a use of (2), remember, but an *empirical* claim about the "actual syntactic structure" of (2), to be revealed by empirical work in syntax. And Stanley claims to have syntactic evidence for his syntactic claim.

There are three immediate problems here.

(i) Throughout, Stanley conflates two distinct notions, *variable-binding* and *relativization*. There is no intrinsic connection between these notions. Relativization is a purely *interpretive* phenomenon. Variable-binding is a phenomenon with both *interpretive* and *syntactic* dimensions. Most important, variable-binding is neither necessary nor sufficient for relativization. Variable-binding is no more than a method that has been used in the explication of certain forms of relativization. Hence assumption (a) is false.[141]

(ii) Since Stanley claims to be mounting an argument against Perry which appeals to variables and binding at LF, then the notion of binding he appeals to had better be one whose domain of operation is LF.[142] This means specifying the LF of (2) and the syntactic constraints on binding that well-formed LFs must satisfy. Stanley specifies neither, for he does not say what syntactic category *loc* belongs to, *where* in (2)'s LF it occurs, whether or not it falls under the Binding Theory (and, if so, under which principle it falls), whether it bears case, or whether the quantified expression 'everywhere I went' binds *loc* from a position to which it has been raised (by, e.g., Quantifier Raising; see below). We get no details about (2)'s LF beyond the vague claim that it contains *loc*.

(iii) The third problem, which I am less concerned with here, is raised by Récanati (2001). What reason is there, Récanati asks, to think assumption (b) is true? It seems to presuppose that the LF of (1) is a constituent of the LF of (2). But it could well be that it is the presence of the quantified expression 'everywhere I went', which occurs as a sentential operator in (2), that triggers the appearance of a variable in (2)'s LF. Because (1) does not contain such an operator, no such variable is generated. Hence, assumption (b) is false. For the sake of argument, let us just accept assumption (b) and so ignore problem (iii).

Stanley claims to have syntactic evidence for the claim that (2)'s LF contains an aphonic variable *loc* bound by 'everywhere I went'. But in fact the evidence offered is *purely interpretive*: the mere existence of the undisputed, relativized interpretation of (2)! Surely no one is going to argue with the well-known *interpretive* fact that (2) has a relativized interpretation. The question is whether anything of *syntactic* significance follows immediately from this. Stanley assumes without argument that it does.

If one's conception of the logical forms of English sentences is just of formulae in some semi-English, semiformal language that can be used to explicate truth conditions and perhaps even a few aspects of truth-conditional structure, a language that draws upon certain devices and structural features of formulae of the predicate calculus, one is naturally going to produce "logical forms" in which the relativization introduced by quantified expressions of English is captured using formulae containing bound variables. We should take care here to distinguish broader and narrower notions of *variation* associated with quantificational expressions. Variation is exemplified in (3):

(3)   Every man danced with some woman.

On the surface at least, (3) contains quantifier phrases in the argument places of the verb 'dance'. There is a reading of (3) upon which women may *vary* with men, a reading upon which men are selected before women, so to speak, a reading upon which, as we say in the trade, 'every man' has large scope. In the predicate calculus representation of this reading—there is more than one such representation, of course—we find bound variables in the argument positions of the predicate:

(4) $(\forall x_1)(man\ x_1 \supset (\exists x_2)(woman\ x_2\ \&\ x_1\ danced\ with\ x_2))$.

But it does not follow from the fact that we have developed an artificial language within which we can of capture the truth conditions of (one reading of) some English form X with an unambiguous and otherwise well-behaved formula that we have thereby uncovered the (or a) phrase marker for X, generated by the syntax of English posited by our best syntactic theory.

It is quite common in linguistics and philosophy to produce formulae in artificial languages that more closely reflect potential phrase markers of the English sentences they are meant to semantically illuminate than formulae of the predicate calculus. One way of doing this is to replace the unrestricted unary quantifiers by restricted quantifiers headed by quantificational determiners as in (3') (suitable semantic axioms being provided, of course):[143]

(3') $[every\ x_1\colon man\ x_1]\ [some\ x_2\colon woman\ x_2]\ (x_1\ danced\ with\ x_2)$.

Again, the argument positions of the predicates are occupied by variables, but it does not follow from the mere fact that we have developed a niftier way of capturing truth conditions of (one reading of) (3) with an unambiguous and otherwise well-behaved formula of a modified formal language containing restricted quantifiers (call the language *RQ*) that we have *thereby* uncovered the actual syntactic structure of (3). (Would that it were this easy to refute variable-free semantics!)

Many syntacticians who accept the LF hypothesis take (3)'s LF (on the reading we have been assuming) to be something that (3') usefully approximates, with something closer to (3'') giving the structure of the LF in question:

(3'') $[_S[_{DP}$ every man$]^1\ [_S[_{DP}$ some woman$]^2\ [_S\ e_1\ danced\ with\ e_2]]]$.

Here, the quantifier phrases are "raised," by which is meant (roughly) that they occupy syntactic positions from which they behave semantically like the restricted quantifiers in (3'), binding the occurrences of e, which behave as variables. If, as many LF theorists (myself included) maintain, a sentence is best seen as a pair consisting of a PF and an LF, then $\langle(3), (3'')\rangle$ is a sentence. One simply cannot tell whether Stanley goes along with this as he provides no syntactic details for the "logical forms" he wields against Perry.

The point of immediate interest is that the LF (3'') contains variables which do not appear at PF, the positions the variables occupy at LF being occupied by the quantifiers themselves at PF, almost as if the quantifiers have descended and smothered their respective variables.[144] But not all syntacticians see things this way, for there are those—particularly at Perry's institution—who see surface syntax as good enough for semantic interpretation, and there are plenty of accounts of the semantics of (3) that produce readings equivalent to (3′) without treating (3) itself as containing any variables in its syntax, so it is hardly a *given* of syntactic theory, an established empirical fact, that there are variables in the syntax of (1). I myself am rather attracted to the LF hypothesis, but I am not going to start telling syntacticians who *aren't* that the empirical facts refute them. And, rather more to the present point, I am not going to start terrorizing philosophers with exaggerated claims to the effect that their postulations of unarticulated constituents fly in the face of empirically established syntactic facts discovered over in the linguistics department.

It is, perhaps, *closer* to a given of syntactic theory that there is a variable in the syntax of (5) on the reading given by (5′):

(5)   Every man danced with some woman he knew.

(5′)   [*every* x_1: *man* x_1] [*some* x_2: *woman* x_2 & x_1 *knew* x_2] (x_1 *danced with* x_2).

For it seems to be held by almost everyone who cares about these matters that the occurrence of the pronoun 'he' in (5) must have some semantic role or other, and that when (5) is understood with truth conditions captured by (5′) that role is exhausted (or close to exhausted) by its acting as a variable bound by 'every man'.[145] Even many theorists who want their semantics to run off surface syntax and those with no particular interest in LF are tempted to see *this* particular form of variation as explained in part by the presence in the surface from of an ordinary English phonic, 'he', that acts as a bound variable. (This was the view of Quine 1960a and Geach 1962, of course, long before talk of the syntactic-level LF.)

The type of variation exemplified in (5) is what I have elsewhere called *relativization*.[146] In *RQ* representations of truth conditions, the characteristic feature of relativization is the presence in one quantifier of a variable bound by a higher quantifier. It is this that formally captures the relativization in *RQ*. And, in the particular example we are considering, the relevant variable in (5′) corresponds directly to the pronoun 'he' in (5).[147] The LF theorist might offer something akin to (5″) as the official LF of (5):

(5″)   [$_S$[$_{DP}$ every man]^1 [$_S$[$_{DP}$ some woman he$_1$ knew]^2 [$_S$ e_1 danced with e_2]]].

The point I wish to stress here is well-known but rarely stated explicitly: although relativization can represented in *RQ* using bound variables, there is no intrinsic connection between variable-binding and relativization. The binding of a variable in natural language syntax is neither necessary nor sufficient for a relativized interpretation.

That it is not *sufficient* is easily demonstrated. Wherever we find a sentence S containing a pronoun whose interpretation appears to be well explained on the assumption that it functions as a variable bound by a quantifier, we can replace the quantifier in question by a name (or some other singular term) to produce a sentence S' in which the interpretation of the pronoun is well explained on the assumption that it functions as a variable bound by the name in S' corresponding to the quantifier in S. Consider:

(6)   Every man loves himself.

(7)   Ringo loves himself.

A naive answer to the question of how the pronoun functions in the singular case (7) is that it is coreferential with 'Ringo', that it is a special type of referring expression whose reference is determined by 'Ringo'. But something is missed on such an analysis. Surely 'himself' functions *identically* in (6) and (7), a single closed predicate 'loves himself'—understood as $\lambda x(x\ loves\ x)$—occurring in both sentences.[148] That is, in effect (6) and (7) are both used to make claims involving the following condition *x loves x*. (6) is used to say the condition is true of every man, and (7) to say it is true of Ringo. So, if the occurrence of 'himself' in (6) is functioning, in some way to be elucidated, as a bound variable, shouldn't we at least countenance the idea that the occurrence in (7) is functioning in this way (rather than as a device of coreference)?[149] Arguably, this would explain the immediacy of the following inference:

(8)   Every man loves himself; Ringo is a man; so Ringo loves himself.

Examples involving propositional attitudes and VP-deletion appear to confirm the need for singular, nonrelativized binding, as we can see by examining bound possessives. Consider (9) and (10):

(9)   Every man loves his wife.

(10)   Ringo loves his wife.

On one use of 'his' it is a device of anaphora, bound by 'every man' in (9). And if the singular binding hypothesis is correct, there is a reading of (10) upon which 'his' is bound by 'Ringo'. (9) and (10) are used to make claims involving the condition *x loves x's wife*.[150] (9) is used to say it is true of every man; and (10) to say it is true of Ringo, the common predication being $\lambda x(x\ loves\ x's\ wife)$. Arguably, that explains the immediacy of the following inference:

(11)   Every man loves his wife; Ringo is a man; so Ringo loves his wife.

So if 'his' is really functioning as a bound variable on one reading of the quantified example (9), shouldn't we at least countenance the idea that it also functions in this way, rather than as a device of coreference, on one reading of the singular example (10)?[151] Evidence that this is correct comes from reflecting on possessives in attitude contexts.[152] Suppose we embed (9) and (10) under 'Mary thinks':

(12)   Mary thinks [every man]^1 loves his$_1$ wife.

(13)   Mary thinks Ringo^1 loves his$_1$ wife.

The bound variable treatment of the pronoun in (12) delivers a reading we can represent in RQ with (12'):

(12')   *Mary thinks ([every x: man x] (x loves x's wife)).*

This captures the fact that a use of (12) is true (on one of its readings) if, and only if, Mary thinks every man is an own-wife's lover. The analogous reading of a use of (13) is true iff Mary thinks Ringo is an own-wife's lover, but that reading is *not* captured by saying that 'Ringo' and 'his' are coreferential, for on such an account the use of (13) could be true if Mary believes that Ringo loves the wife of some man she sees but does not realize is Ringo.[153] So even if 'his' can be used as a device of *de jure* coreference, we still appear to need to take into account its use as a bound variable, which means we have variable-binding without relativization.

   The case of VP-deletion provides further confirmation. The literature on VP-deletion is vast and consensus is not easy to find, but traditionally deletion is subject to a stringent parallelism condition on form and interpretation.[154] As Heim and Kratzer put it, "A constituent may be deleted at PF only if it is a copy of another constituent at LF" (1998, 250), moreover a copy *interpreted in the same way*.[155] Consider (14):

(14)   Ringo loves his wife, and Paul does too.

There are two quite distinct readings of (14) because the second conjunct may be interpreted as either (15) or (16):

(15)   *Paul(λx(x loves x's wife)).*

(16)   *Paul(λx(x loves Ringo's wife)).*

The former is usually called the *sloppy* reading, and the latter the *strict* reading. If a constituent may be deleted only if it is a copy of another cointerpreted constituent at LF, the existence of the sloppy reading of (14) would appear to provide good evidence for a reading of the second conjunct of (14) upon which its VP is interpreted as (λx(x loves x's wife)), and this means treating 'his' as a bound variable, which means we have variable-binding without relativization.

That variable-binding in natural language syntax is not *necessary* for relativized inter-pretations is also well known and easy to demonstrate. Indeed, this fact forms the basis of a whole style of *variable-free* semantic theorizing. Quine (1960b) famously presented an insightful way of reformulating the first-order predicate calculus without variables, and the method may be generalized.[156] In the study of natural language, variable-free systems have been developed by Szabolcsi (1989), Jacobsen (1999), and others.[157] Unless Stanley can produce an incoherence argument against variable-free theories, their existence demonstrates that the existence of relativized readings of natural lan-guage sentences does not in and of itself entail variable-binding in natural language *syntax*.[158]

Even in the work of those who are perfectly accepting of variable-binding in natural language syntax, we find relativization without variable-binding. Classic examples are found in discussions of donkey anaphora, where we find pronouns that lie outside the scopes of the quantifiers upon which they are anaphoric and hence are incapable of being bound by those quantifiers. In order to appreciate the relevant examples, first consider (17) and (18), in which the anaphora involves a pair of sentences, that is, in which the expressions anaphorically linked appear in distinct sentences linked with a connective:

(17)   John bought *exactly one donkey*, and Paul vaccinated *it*.

(18)   If John buys *exactly one donkey*, then he pays cash for *it*.

As Evans (1977) points out, construing the pronouns in these examples as variables bound by the quantified DPs upon which they appear to be anaphoric, by giving the quantifiers large scope, yields the wrong results. Someone who utters (17), for example, would not be claiming that only one donkey satisfies (19):

(19)   *John bought x and Paul vaccinated x.*

This is so because that claim is consistent with John buying two donkeys, while the claim made by uttering the original conjunction in (17) is not.

The reason the pronouns are not bound by the quantifiers upon which are ana-phoric, says Evans, is that the pronouns are not within the quantifiers' scopes, those scopes being restricted to the embedded sentences containing the quantifiers.[159] On Evans's account, the pronouns in (17) and (18)—and, indeed, all others apparently anaphoric on quantified expressions that do not bind them—form a natural group in *having their references fixed rigidly by descriptions*, singular or plural as the case may be. In (17), for example, 'it' has its reference fixed by the 'the donkey John bought'; and in (18), 'it' has its reference fixed by 'the donkey John buys.' Evans calls such pronouns E-types.[160] Evans's theory assumes something that is surely correct: the hearer can

readily comprehend a particular use of the superficially simple 'it' as having its reference fixed by the rather more complex expression 'the donkey John bought', for
example.

Examples (17) and (18) do not themselves involve relativization, but one does not
have to look far in Evans's own discussion (or in the vast literature it has spawned) to
find examples that do. If a use of the pronoun 'it' may have its reference fixed by nonrelativized description 'the donkey John bought', surely we are going to find examples
in which a use of 'it' has relativized reference, that is, reference fixed by a relativized
description such as 'the donkey he bought'. Indeed, they are not hard to find, for being
in a distinct *sentence* from a quantifier is not the only way for a pronoun to fall outside
the quantifier's scope. It can lie outside by virtue of lying in a distinct VP, as in (20),
where two VPs are conjoined by 'and':

(20)   Every man owns exactly one donkey and feeds it at night.

Or by lying in the VP of a main clause when the quantifier lies in the VP of a relative
clause:

(21)   Every man who owns exactly one donkey feeds it at night.

Again, giving 'exactly one donkey' large scope and construing 'it' as a variable it binds
yields the wrong result in both (20) and (21) (and in countless others). Someone uttering (20) would not be saying that exactly one donkey satisfies *every man owns x and
feeds x at night*. And someone uttering (21) would not be saying that exactly one donkey satisfies *every man who owns x feeds x at night*. In both cases, the pronoun 'it' is not
bound by its purported antecedent, 'exactly one donkey', because it does not lie within
the purported antecedent's scope. On Evans's E-type account, in uses of (20) and (21)
'it' has its reference fixed by the description 'the donkey he owns', the interpretation of
'he' relativized to objects that 'man' is true of in the use of (20), and objects that 'man
who owns exactly one donkey' is true of in the use of (21). So although the occurrences
of 'it' in (20) and (21) are not themselves bound, interpreting them still involves recognizing relativization, because the interpretation of 'he' in the description that fixes the
referent of 'it' is relativized to other items.

For present concerns, the important point here is that although Evans presents a
theory that is meant to deliver the correct relativized readings of (20) and (21), he
makes no claim about the existence of a variable in the underlying syntactic structures
(or "logical forms") of (20) or (21) that corresponds to 'he' in the reference-fixing description 'the donkey he owns', a variable that is bound by the subject quantifier.[161]
Nor do those philosophers who claim that Evans's E-type pronouns are in fact D-type
pronouns, that is, pronouns that *go proxy for descriptions* (rather than having their refer-

ences fixed by them) and, as such, can be viewed as limiting forms of incomplete descriptions.[162] Consider the following progressions:

(21) Every man who owns exactly one donkey feeds it at night.

(21′) Every man who owns exactly one donkey feeds the donkey at night.

(21″) Every man who owns exactly one donkey feeds the donkey he owns at night.

Utterances of (21) and (21′) may well be understood as elliptical for, as shorthand for, as proxies for utterances of (21″). The interesting point here, which I discussed at length in *Descriptions*, is that the description for which the pronoun 'it' and the incomplete description 'the donkey' are taken to be proxies may itself contain a pronoun, moreover a pronoun understood as a bound variable. The truth conditions of utterances of (21), (21′) and (21″) might be captured using the following formula of our semiformal language:

(21‴) [every$_x$: villager x & [just one$_y$: donkey y] x owns y]
       [the$_y$: donkey y & x owns y] x feeds y at night.

This is not an LF, of course, but it may correspond quite closely to the LF of (21″). The description is Russellian but *relativized* in the sense that uniqueness is relative to choice of villager who owns exactly one donkey. This sort of relativization should occasion no surprise, and I embraced it in *Descriptions* in much the same way that Mates (1973) and Evans (1982) embraced it in similar examples. The processes at work in interpreting an incomplete description or a descriptive pronoun are pragmatic and richly inferential, and it is clear hearers have no trouble coming up with (21″) when quizzed about (21) or (21′).

One can call the D-type approach to (21) an "implicit binding" approach if one so desires, as long as the word 'implicit' is not being used to lull unsuspecting philosophers into thinking the concept of concern is a *syntactic* one, in the sense of involving the *explicit* binding of an aphonic variable in the LFs of (21) and (21). No such syntactic component of this sort is constitutive of the basic D-type proposal, and nothing in the particular D-type analyses offered by Davies (1981), Ludlow and Neale (1991), and Neale (1990, 1993) commits them to capturing the relativization in the D-type analyses of (20) and (21) by having the LFs of these sentences contain the description 'the donkey he owns' with 'he' bound by the subject quantifier. This is certainly one option that might be explored, of course, but it opens up a very serious gap between LF and PF.[163]

Interestingly, Stanley and Szabó (2000) appeal to the D-type theory presented in *Descriptions* to mount an argument against Westerståhl's (1985) view that aphonic quantifier domain variables cohabit syntactic nodes with determiners (in order to show that the view is "theoretically inferior" to their own view, according to which these variables cohabit nodes with common nouns). They recognize that on this D-type theory the pronoun of note is "a proxy" for a description, and they claim this account "elegantly captures" the required reading as long as the domain variable cohabits a node with the noun—and not if it cohabits a node with the determiner—but they do not point out that on that same account, and by the very principle they cite and invoke,[164] the occurrences of 'it' in (20) and (21) are D-type pronouns with relativized interpretations. Of course, if they *had* pointed this out, then, given their assumption that relativization can be captured only by variable-binding at LF, they would have had to say one of the following: (a) that the D-type theory they appeal to does *not* posit a bound aphonic at LF and is therefore an *inadequate* theory by virtue of being incapable of capturing relativized readings; or (b) that the theory *does* posit a bound aphonic at LF and so is actually a *precursor* of sorts to their own theory, the sentences it analyzes providing more evidence—"syntactic" evidence in their view—for their own position.

The relativized readings involved in relative clause donkey anaphora are well-known, and the sort of D-type theory Stanley and Szabó appeal to is meant to provide analyses of them; so their failure to discuss relativization in connection with D-type pronouns is striking. It is vital to know where Stanley and Szabó stand on relative clause donkey anaphora as the whole style of argument—the so-called Binding Argument—that both Stanley (2000) and Stanley and Szabó (2000) use against positions other than their own (including Perry's unarticulated constituent account of 'it's raining') actually assumes that the E-type and D-type analyses either do not exist or fail, despite explicitly invoking one of them in their argument against a rival theory of domain restriction.[165]

Perhaps there is an unstated psychological doctrine behind the assumption that relativization requires an actual bound variable at LF, despite the existence of accounts of relativization in the literature that do not postulate aphonic bound variables at LF: it is impossible to entertain quantified thoughts without bringing before the mind in some way actual natural language sentences containing variables bound by quantifiers. Evidence for such a doctrine would have to come from psychology, and I am aware of none. The following, even if true, would not guarantee the truth of the doctrine: it is impossible to entertain quantified thoughts without standing in some suitable relation sentences of Mentalese that contain the Mentalese counterparts of bound variables. Language of thought theorists would almost certainly hold this view—Fodor, and Sperber and Wilson, for example—but nothing follows directly about the syntax of the sentences of English, Icelandic, Xhosa and so on that are regularly used to communicate such thoughts.

Similarly, if I can utter a sentence X to say that p and thereby *conversationally impli-cate* that q, where the implicated proposition can be *described* using a natural language sentence Y containing an expression understood as a variable bound by quantifier, it does not follow that X contains an expression understood as a variable bound by quan-tifier. It is difficult to believe that relativized interpretations of utterances are going to present problems for the general cognitive mechanisms involved in interpretation given that these mechanisms must also be capable of revealing conversational implica-tures, ironic interpretations, metaphorical interpretations, jokes, and so on. A little rel-ativization is child's play.

That something similar to the aforementioned psychological doctrine may lie be-hind Stanley's variable-binding assumption, is suggested by remarks he makes in con-nection with (2):

(1)   It was raining.

(2)   Everywhere I went it was raining.

Since the supposed unarticulated constituent...is not the value of anything in [2], there should be no reading...in which the unarticulated constituent varies with the values introduced by ['everywhere I went']. Operators in a sentence only interact with variables in the sentence that lie within their scope. But if the constituent is unarticulated, it is not the value of any variable in the sentence. Thus its interpretation cannot be controlled by operators in the sentence. (2000, 410–411)

Stanley appears to be assuming here that it would be impossible for a hearer to inter-pret someone uttering (2) as saying something that might be expressed using the hid-eous philosophers' sentence, (2*):

(2*)   For every place I went, it was raining at that place

—unless the "actual syntactic structure" of (2) contained a variable for 'everywhere I went' to bind. And he assumes that it would be impossible for a hearer to interpret someone uttering (21) as saying that every man who owns exactly one donkey feeds the donkey he owns at night unless the "actual syntactic structure" of the VP 'feeds it at night' in (21) contains a variable that 'every man who owns a donkey' binds:

(21)   Every man who owns exactly one donkey feeds it at night.

The psychological thesis is dubious, and it is odd Stanley presupposes it. I suspect no plausible argument for it can be given, but the question is one for cognitive psychology to investigate.

At best, then, Stanley can be construed as (i) pointing to some well-known data, (ii) offering a vague syntactic proposal for the LFs of the sentences involved in the data, and (iii) claiming that even if utterances of (1) can be interpreted in the absence of an aphonic locative in the sentence's LF, interpreting utterances of (2) cannot. The claim in (iii) is pretty explicit:

It is easy to see how an object or a property could be provided by pragmatic mechanisms: it need only be made salient in the context either by the speaker's intentions, or contextual cues, depending on one's account of salience. However, denotations of bound variables are odd, theoretically complex entities. It is difficult, if not impossible, to see how, on any account of salience, such an entity could be salient in a context. Certainly neither it, nor instances of it, could be perceptually present in the context. It is equally difficult to see how speaker intentions could determine reference to such an entity. (Stanley 2000, 414)

The main claim here seems to be that the unarticulated constituent analysis of (1) is straightforward, whereas the unarticulated constituent analysis of (2) is too "complex" to be acceptable. But it's difficult to ascertain whether Stanley is talking metaphysics or epistemology/psychology here, for he seems to be running together various things we have been careful to keep apart. For one thing, objects and properties are not "provided by pragmatic mechanisms," although they are *identified* by hearers *using* pragmatic mechanisms (whatever these amount to); for another, salience is not the important issue; and for another, nobody's intentions ever made anything or any location salient, and the *speaker's* intentions are no exception.

Let us begin with (1). The location that Perry takes to be an unarticulated constituent of the proposition a speaker expresses by uttering (1) is *determined by* the speaker's intentions, the formation of these intentions themselves constrained by such things as knowledge of lexical meanings and syntax, expectations, beliefs, estimations of salience, maxims of conversation, and so on (as discussed earlier). The hearer's job is to *identify* the place the speaker intended, and such things as knowledge of lexical meanings and syntax, expectations, beliefs, estimations of salience, maxims of conversation, and so on are things he uses, or can use, in this task. So, from the point of view of metaphysics, things are simple: the unarticulated constituent is a single location. From the point of view of psychology, things are just as simple: the hearer has to identify a single location.

Now to (2). First, the metaphysics. Stanley says "denotations of bound variables are odd, theoretically complex entities." It is difficult to assess the import of this remark in the absence of Stanley's own semantics for bound occurrences of *loc*. Recall that on Stanley's picture, (a) the proposition expressed by a sentence X relative to a context c is a proposition determined by, and only by, two things: (i) the denotations relative to c of the elements of X's LF and (ii) a set of context-invariant compositional operations on these denotations, determined by, and only by, the structure of X's LF; and (b) the effects of extralinguistic factors on the proposition expressed by X relative to c are restricted to the provision of denotations to some fixed set of expressions that are indexical (in the broad sense). Since Stanley countenances bound variables, it seems he is committed to expressions that do indeed have these "odd, theoretically complex entities"—whatever they are—as their denotations. Quantifiers too will have complex denotations.[166] So will all manner of expressions. So Stanley's gripe appears not to be metaphysical.

Is it epistemological or psychological? If so, we will have to work hard to describe it clearly as it is surely Stanley's view that speakers and hearers *do* grasp or understand general/quantificational propositions containing these "odd, theoretically complex entities" as constituents—unless, of course, Stanley is engaged in a purely formal exercise unconnected to the empirical exercise of throwing light on our knowledge of language and on the mechanisms involved in utterance interpretation. According to Stanley, it is "difficult to see how speaker intentions could determine reference to such an entity." But if we can bear propositional attitudes to general propositions, then we can bear propositional attitudes to general propositions. If there is problem here, it concerns the tension between the idea that bearing a propositional attitude to a proposition involves bearing certain cognitive relations to each of its parts and the idea that bound variables have denotations that are constituents of propositions. *And this has nothing whatsoever to do with unarticulated constituents or relativization*, for it is just an instance of an old problem about the relation between language and thought that has vexed us since Frege, one that shows no signs of going away. In effect, Stanley is assuming that it is impossible for a monolingual English speaker to grasp the proposition someone expresses by uttering (21) unless (21)'s LF is something like (21″); or grasp the proposition someone expresses by uttering (2) unless (2)'s LF is something like (2′), perhaps (2″).

This all reinforces the point that the most pressing questions here are in psychology and the philosophy of mind rather than in the mechanics of quantification and binding, which seem relatively well understood for now. Perry's commonsense proposal about unarticulated constituents of the propositions we express using sentences of natural language appears to be untouched by anything Stanley says. Moreover, Perry's work on this topic, as well as his earlier joint work with Barwise on quantification and resource situations, forces us to confront what I take to be some of the most difficult and most important questions facing anyone working in the philosophy of mind and the philosophy of language. (i) *The Inside-Outside Question*: When we judge what someone has said on a given occasion by uttering some sentence *X* to be true (false), just how rich is the propositional content? How much of any seeming underarticulation is to be explained in the manner suggested by those who have talked about *explicit-elliptical-about* approaches to certain data, and how much in the manner suggested by *implicit-background-concerns* approaches. (The two approaches are not mutually exclusive, of course.) (ii) *The Underprojecting Question*: Can we make sense of the idea that our thoughts, sentences of Mentalese perhaps, also underdetermine their own propositional contents? Perry has suggested they can; Fodor has argued that they cannot. (I have steered well clear of that topic, for it seems to me that a rather long essay might be required just to get the question clearly in focus.) We owe Perry a great debt for his bold forays into this terrain and his thought-provoking hypotheses. Like it or not, unarticulated constituents are here to stay, and, with luck, our judicial system will come to appreciate this.

Acknowledgments

It is an honor to contribute a piece to this volume celebrating the work of my dissertation adviser John Perry. Most of the chapter was written at the University of Iceland in 2002–2003, while I held a fellowship from the John Simon Guggenheim Foundation. The first half was revised considerably in 2004 in light of a seminar John Hawthorne and I taught on contextualism at Rutgers University. Discussions in Reykjavík with Donald Davidson, Ólafur Páll Jónsson, Mikael Karlsson, Jón Ólafsson, Ken Safir, and Höskuldur Þráinsson were extremely helpful. So were discussions with Kent Bach, Emma Borg, and, especially, Robyn Carston and Ken Taylor in October 2002 at a conference in Genoa, where a slice of the material was presented. So too were discussions with Eliza Block, Deniz Dagci, Kevan Edwards, John Hawthorne, Damon Horowitz, Angel Pinillos, Adam Sennet, Ted Sider, Robert Stainton, in the autumn of 2004. John MacFarlane, Michael O'Rourke, Adam Sennet, and Jason Stanley provided me with some useful late comments that helped me fix a few problematic paragraphs. Several works published in 2002 or later—Breheny 2002, Carston 2002, MacFarlane 2003, 2005, Stanley 2002a and 2002b—are discussed only in footnotes added or expanded in 2004–2005. Reorganization and rewriting—but I think no change in my position—would have been necessary to address in the text points raised in or by these interesting works, so footnotes must suffice. I gratefully acknowledge the generous support of Rutgers University, the University of Iceland, and the John Simon Guggenheim Foundation.

Notes

1. *Smith v. United States*, 113 S. Ct. 2050 (1993). This particular case was brought to my attention by Doug Husak. It is discussed briefly by Scalia (1997) and by Sosa (2001), in his review of Justice

Scalia's book. I analyze the case in some detail in *Linguistic Pragmatism*, in the context of a discussion of Scalia's *textualism*. To cut a long story short, (a) I think Scalia is basically right on the issue, but (b) his textualism seems to me in need of repairs if it is to survive serious scrutiny and at the same time comport with the opinion Scalia himself expresses in *Smith*. (The repairs involve the distinction between expressed and unexpressed intent and Scalia's talk of "objective intent.")

2. Justice O'Connor wrote the majority opinion, in which Chief Justice Rehnquist and Justices White, Blackmun, Kennedy, and Thomas joined. Justice Blackmun filed a short concurring opinion. Justice Scalia wrote a dissenting opinion, joined by Justices Stevens and Souter.

3. Bach 1981, Donnellan 1968, Evans 1982, Husserl 1913/1970, Neale 1990, 2004, Quine 1940, Sellars 1954.

4. Sperber and Wilson 1986 and 1995, Wilson and Sperber 1981. See also Carston 1988 and 2002, Neale 1990 and 2004, and Récanati 1989, 1993, and 2001.

5. Perry 1986, 1993, 1998, and 2001. See also Crimmins 1993, Crimmins and Perry 1989, and Récanati 2001.

6. For discussion, see Schiffer 2003.

7. If we are to make sense of the phenomenon of utterance interpretation, we shall need to take more seriously than many philosophers do the *epistemic asymmetry* of speaker and hearer and the *dovetailed* nature of their respective tasks in the communicative setting. Identifying what the speaker is saying is not simply a matter of identifying *X* and recovering its linguistic meaning, if only because of the existence of pronouns. It is important to separate the epistemological and the metaphysical here. The important metaphysical question is this: what *determines* what a speaker said on a given occasion? And the Gricean answer I subscribe to is this: certain specific *intentions* the speaker had in producing his utterance. These intentions are referential and predicational, and they are severely constrained by the speaker's tacit grasp of syntax, of the meanings of the words he uses, and of the way rational, co-operative beings function, his beliefs about the audience, about the context, and about the topic of conversation, and probably a whole lot more. The important epistemological question is: What knowledge or information does a hearer use in *identifying* what the speaker said? And the Gricean answer I subscribe to is this: his tacit grasp of syntax, of the meanings of the words used, and of the way rational, co-operative beings function, his beliefs about the speaker, about the context, and about the topic of conversation, and just about anything else he can get his hands on.

It is pointless searching for a notion of "what is said" that transcends the two notions that actually play a role in a theory of interpretation: (i) what the speaker intended to say and (ii) what a reasonably well-informed, rational interpreter of the speaker's remark takes the speaker to be saying. When all goes well (i) and (ii) coincide, and it is the *potential for this coincidence* that gives rise to talk of "what is said." It is a mistake to think of "what is said" as some third thing upon which (i) and (ii) are supposed to converge, and it is only a form of linguistic bewitchment that makes "saying" appear more basic than "intending to say." Similarly for referring. There is nothing to be gained by looking for a notion of "reference" that transcends the two notions that actually play a role in a theory of interpretation: (i) what the speaker intended to refer to and (ii) what a reasonably well-informed, rational interpreter of the speaker's remark takes the speaker to be referring to. When all goes well (i) and (ii) coincide, and it is the *potential for this coincidence* that gives rise to talk of "reference." It is a mistake to think of "what is referred to" as some third thing upon which (i) and (ii) are supposed to converge; again it is only a form of linguistic bewitchment that makes referring appear more basic than intending to refer. For discussion, see Neale forthcoming.

8. The subject of the verb 'refer' in '*X* may be used to refer to *Y*' is not *X*. See note 37.

9. Binding relations are not always forced by syntax. For example, English permits a subject or a nonsubject expression to bind a reflexive pronoun. Thus, (i) may be read with 'himself' bound by 'every bishop' or by 'some cardinal';

(i)   [every bishop]^1 told [some cardinal]^2 a story about himself$_{1/2}$.

Not all languages permit this (e.g., German and Icelandic do not), reflexives often being subject-oriented. For a discussion of this and related matters that bear on the present discussion, see Neale 2005.

10. The word 'issues' was suggested to me by Perry many years ago in roughly this context.

11. If 'bank' is the superficial form of a single, ambiguous word, then identifying what *S* is saying when he utters, "I'm going to the bank" involves identifying which *meaning S* has in mind for 'bank'; if 'bank' is the superficial form of two distinct, unambiguous words then identifying what *S* is saying involves identifying which of the two *words S* is using. The latter view seems more useful in theorizing about language and is the one I shall assume.

12. The idea that certain constituents of propositions expressed by sentences relative to contexts of utterance are actually *determined* by those contexts just adds insult to injury here, involving as it does a horrible conflation of epistemology and metaphysics.

13. It has been common in philosophy to follow Frege and Russell in talking about names and other singular terms *referring*, *denoting*, *designating*, or *standing for* things and to see the relation in question as playing a pivotal role in a theory of meaning. I suspect this way of talking is the cause of a good deal of trouble. It is worth noting that not all straightforward uses of so-called referring expressions involve referring. As Wittgenstein notes in the *Philosophical Investigations*, if I say, "Peter, please pass me the pepper," it seems incorrect to say I was *referring to* (talking about, saying something about) Peter. I was *addressing* him, not referring to him. The question "Who was the speaker referring to with *X*?" needs to be replaced here with "Who was the speaker addressing as/using *X*?" There is much to say about this matter, but not here.

14. Crimmins and Perry (1989, 267) seem to be alluding to something like this distinction. The distinction I am trying to get at here is one articulated nicely by Stephen Schiffer in a seminar we taught together. Schiffer distinguishes *Referring-By* and *Referring-In*, the latter being conceptually prior to the former: I can refer to *X in* uttering a sentence (or perhaps just a phrase) α even though there is no part, β, of α, such that I referred to *X by* β. But I cannot refer to *X by* an expression β

unless β is a part of some expression α *in* the uttering of which I referred to X. It seems clear that when I talk of "S referring to X *with* β," I am just invoking Schiffer's notion of *Referring-By*, and when I talk of "S referring to X in uttering α," I am just invoking Schiffer's notion of *Referring-In*. Schiffer suggests something like the following as preliminary analyses to be explored and refined: S refers to X *in* uttering α if, and only if, in uttering α, S means that p, where 'that p' stands for some X-dependent proposition. S refers to X *by* (i.e., *with*) α if, and only if, $\exists R \exists x(S$ uttered '...α...' intending H to recognize, at least partly on the basis of H's knowing that R(α. x), that (i) S was referring to something in uttering '...α...' and (ii) that x was the thing to which S was so referring. Schiffer is surely right that as far as a theory of interpretation is concerned, the *conceptually* prior notion of *Referring-In* is the one that does the final work, but *Referring-By* will be *epistemically* prior in many cases, the hearer taking the speaker to have referred to X in uttering α because he takes the speaker to have referred to X with β, where β is a constituent of α.

15. The situation with (4) seems similar to certain cases that both Perry and I have discussed elsewhere, for example 'the mayor, Þórólfur Árnason' or 'Egil, son of Skallagrim' (Barwise and Perry 1983; Neale 1999). Because of the patronymic system, Icelandic names raise an interesting issue here. 'Jón Ólafsson' might be regarded as a proper name or as something English speakers might render as 'Jón, Ólaf's son'. Certainly there was a time when 'Jón Ólafsson' was more like 'Jón, Ólaf's son' than it is today.

16. See Carston 2002, Fodor 2001, Récanati 2001, Sperber and Wilson 1986, 1995, and Neale 2004. The issue of whether characters (rather than contents) can be composed is ultimately uninteresting.

17. It is an empirical theory of utterance interpretation in this sense that Sperber and Wilson and other relevance theorists are trying to construct.

18. As far as natural language itself is concerned, trying to build pure *content* begins to look about as futile as trying to build pure *character*.

19. See Lewis 1979, 1996, Cohen 1999, DeRose 1999, and MacFarlane 2003, 2005.

20. See Stanley 2000, 2002a, 2002b and Stanley and Szabó 2000.

21. See, e.g., Barwise and Perry 1983, Kaplan 1989a, 1989b, Montague 1974, Perry 1977, 1979, 1986, 1998, 2001, Reichenbach 1947, and Russell 1948.

22. See Lewis 1979, 1996, Cohen 1999, DeRose 1999, and Stanley 2000, 2002a, 2002b. Stanley also claims to have "syntactic" arguments for the existence of his silent, indexical expressions and against the existence of Perry's unarticulated constituents. But these arguments are not obviously distinguishable from the trivial point that, whenever Perry or anyone else posits an unarticulated constituent, it is possible to concoct a semiformal, semi-English formula that contains a variable whose value we could take to be the purported unarticulated constituent. This matter is discussed below.

23. See Grice 1970, 1981. See also Quine 1940, where he anticipates both Strawson's argument and Sellars's response. See also Husserl 1913/1970.

24. Part of this manuscript was published in 1981 and again (with cuts) in 1989 as "Presupposition and Conversational Implicature."

25. Kripke's position is quite different from the position Grice (and I, following him) took, for it revolves around a distinction between semantic reference and speaker's reference, a distinction that seems to me to have no useful role in a theory of language use. It seems to me, as it seemed to Grice and Strawson, that the notion of reference we need in a theory of language is speaker's reference and that any word-based notion is at best derivative. On the account of reference I favor it is perfectly acceptable to say that I referred to Reykjavík when uttering "it's raining" even if there is no part of the sentence I used to refer to Reykjavík.

26. In Neale 1990, I tried to remain neutral on the nature of propositions, stopping short of committing myself to the view that they contain objects (and properties) themselves as constituents, rather than being entities built up in some way from object-dependent senses in Evans's (1982) sense. This was one reason I eschewed Perry's terminology. (Another reason was that often I was privately construing the formulae of the language of restricted quantification I was using to systematically set out truth-conditions to be semi-English, semiformal renderings of sentences of the language of thought, and, unlike Perry, I was not willing to countenance the idea of sentences of the language of thought underdetermining their own contents. I had trouble with that idea when I was Perry's student, and I still have trouble with it.) These days I am less worried about cashing out object-dependence in terms of objectual constituency, indeed I see no serious alternative since I now believe Evans's ideas about object-dependent senses to be unworkable.

27. These sentences are quantificational, of course, and stand to (2) as 'I saw someone' stands to 'I saw him'. The matter of quantified weather sentences will be taken up in due course.

28. We can leave it open for now whether *all* unarticulated constituents are things implicitly *referred* to. It is quite consistent to hold (a) that *properties* may be unarticulated constituents and (b) that when we speak we do not exactly *refer* to properties. If I say, "Perry snores," I might reasonably be said to be *talking about* or *saying something about* Perry, and this seems to underpin talk of my *referring to* him. It seems odd, however, to say I am *talking about* or *saying something about* snoring, hence odd to say that I was *referring to* it. (Under the spell of their own theoretical uses of ordinary terms, some philosophers might be happy to say that when I utter "Perry snores" I am indeed talking or saying something about snoring: I was saying of it that Perry participates in it.)

29. Acoustic phonetics concerns the acoustic properties of the sounds we produce in speaking, auditory phonetics the effects these sounds have on the perceptual apparatus involved in receiving them.

30. The portion after the ellipsis in (1) is actually given as a distinct meaning, but this does not seem particularly important for my immediate purposes.

31. I say *perhaps* because delicate syntactic matters concerning syntactic deletion (syntactic ellipsis) need to be examined here. According to certain theories, including the theory to which I myself am most partial, it is arguable that there is an underlying level of syntactic representation (LF) at which the sentence I utter when using (5) to express the proposition that Akureyri gets less

rain that Reykjavík contains the words (or something doing the work of the words) 'than Reykja-vík', which are deleted at the surface (PF). See below.

32. I am indebted to Adam Sennet for exposing a weakness in an earlier formulation. In the formulation above, a great deal of work is being done by the verb 'correspond'. If clause (b) of the definiens were "among the portions of X^u that represent the constituents of $\langle \ldots a \ldots \rangle$, there is no portion that represents a" a problem would arise. As noted earlier, I may use sentences such as (i) and (ii) to express propositions containing *two* occurrences of Reykjavík (assuming the conception of propositions mentioned earlier):

(i)   Most citizens think the mayor is underpaid.

(ii)   The mayor doesn't realize that it's raining.

If we replace 'the mayor' in tokenings of (i) and (ii) by 'the mayor of Reykjavík', we will, in each case, have portions of tokenings that represent Reykjavík. But intuitively we still want to say that these propositions have constituents that are unarticulated relative to these tokenings of the sentences in question. Any patch would seem to require taking into account *position* or *occurrence*, pairing *portions* of X^u (where there are such) with *constituents* of $\langle \ldots a \ldots \rangle$. Hence, my use of the verb 'correspond' above. This might alarm some who endorse unarticulated constituents because it might seem to smuggle in an ellipsis (or explicit) approach to unarticulated constituents according to which a is an unarticulated constituent of $\langle \ldots a \ldots \rangle$ relative to X^u only if there is a natural expansion $E(X)$ of X with the following property: if $E(X)$ rather than X had been used to express $\langle \ldots a \ldots \rangle$ the tokening $E(X)^u$ would have a portion corresponding to and representing a. My own view of the matter is that an ellipsis (explicit) approach *is* required, but I do not want anything here to turn on this. Perry, Carston, and Sperber and Wilson say things that suggest they might be unhappy with this.

33. Let me say right away that this is not meant to exhaust the application of Perry's concept in the realm of thought, but, because I am not confident I have clear pictures of the issues Perry is using unprojected constituents to address (the *de se*, continued belief, self-location, self-knowledge, self-deception, and so on), I shall steer clear of them here and focus on what I think I *do* understand, which is quite enough work.

34. To say this is not to say that the resulting theories are always more *constrained*. (See Chomsky 1981.) There are all sorts of delicate issues one could take up here about the nature and of syntactic rules, the nature and number of levels of representation, the nature of phonological, syntactic, and semantic evidence for syntactic hypotheses and so on, but they can be ignored.

35. Perry's own words: Perry 1986, 1993, 1998, 2001 and Crimmins and Perry 1989. See also Crimmins 1992, which I take to be a reliable guide.

36. The importance of such a distinction was impressed upon me by Stephen Schiffer. For discussion, see below and note 14.

37. Thus, I assume (i)–(iv) are interpreted in parallel fashion:

(i)   I used Pashtu to welcome the chief.

(ii)   I used an arcane word to stress my/his point.

(iii) I used an indexical to refer to Reykjavík.

(iv)   I used 'here' to refer to Reykjavík.

I welcomed the chief, *I* stressed my point, and *I* referred to Reykjavík; Pashtu, an arcane word, an indexical, and the word 'here' were my tools. In the parlance of generative linguistics, 'use' is here a subject-control verb; that is, each of (i)–(iv) contains an infinitival clause whose subject is an aphonic bound by the subject of the main clause:

(i') I^1 used Pashtu [$_S$ PRO_1 to welcome the chief].

That subject control is what is involved is reinforced by (v) and (vi) because Principle A of Chomsky's (1981, 1986) Binding Theory requires a reflexive to be bound by an expression that is a constituent of (roughly) the smallest clause containing it:

(v)   I used 'I' to refer to myself.

(v') I^1 used 'I' [$_S$ PRO_1 to refer to $myself_1$].

(vi)   Every officer used 'I' to refer to himself.

(vi') [Every officer]^1 used 'I' [$_S$ PRO_1 to refer to $himself_1$].

(Very roughly, reflexives cannot be "too far away" from their antecedents, and nonreflexives cannot be "too close" to them, putting the two in virtual complementary distribution as far as interpretive dependence is concerned. For a discussion of the Binding Theory aimed at philosophers, see Neale 2005.)

38. Indeed, it seems in harmony with what Crimmins and Perry (1989, 267) say about reference. See below for discussion.

39. I have no intention of sorting the logical grammar of 'statement', 'utterance', 'use', 'remark', 'assertion', 'question', 'inscription', 'expression', 'interjection', 'speech act' and so on here. I am, however, willing to say that someone who utters "Perry's use of 'it's raining' was true but far too loud," "Perry's statement was well timed and quite pertinent," "the content of Perry's utterance was proportional to its volume," or "Perry's remark was justified and broke a window," is making a category mistake, and that "Perry's question was hostile" is ambiguous— did he quietly ask whether your current theory of personal identity was as idiotic as your previous one, or did he make menacing gestures while screaming into your ear, "Would you like some chocolate?" When 'utterance' is used for the object/product in, say, 'my utterance of X', at least some of the time it is replaceable by 'what I said by uttering X' or by 'what I said by my utterance of X', in which 'utterance' is used in the sense of act/process. And it is for this reason, I think, that many of us are drawn to talk of true or false utterances. There are many other adjectives that we put alongside 'statement', 'remark', 'utterance', 'use' and so on: 'reassuring', 'frightening', 'intelligent', 'hurtful', 'courageous', 'bold', 'rude', 'sentimental', 'loud', 'ironic', 'metaphorical', for example. We must exercise caution here: in many cases we are predicating something of what the speaker said, of the fact that something was said, of the speaker's act of saying what he said, or of the particular words used in the act. (If Bill, who has been knocked down by a bus and seems close to death, manages to utter the words 'I am dying', his

utterance, his statement, his remark, or his use of these word may be reassuring in one sense but not in another.)

40. It seems a good idea to me to use different words for the parts of propositions and the parts of sentences the way Perry does. I did this in *Facing Facts*, but I chose the reverse usage, 'constituents' for the parts of sentences (following the usage of linguists) and 'components' for parts of facts, propositions. I adopt Perry's usage here.

41. The only place I detect any trouble is where Perry says that "the constituents of my statement that I am sitting are me, the present moment, and the relation of sitting" (1986, 207). Replacing 'statement' by 'sentence', 'use of the sentence' or 'utterance' here leads to nonsense; but that this is not what Perry intends seems clear from the fact that he uses the locution 'the statement that'. On the seemingly safe assumption that Perry does not mean to be positing a new class of entities, 'statements', halfway (as it were) between uses of sentences and propositions, I am inclined to think he has simply tried to compress too much into this remark. If he were being less elliptical he would have written "the constituents of the proposition that I am sitting, i.e., the proposition expressed by my use of 'I am sitting', are me, the present moment, and the relation of sitting."

A final remark on 'statement': when Perry talks simply of "a component of a statement," he appears to be talking about a component of a sentence used (to make the statement); but when he talks of a component of a statement *designating something*, he appears to be talking about a component of a sentence *as* used on a particular occasion.

42. See also Crimmins 1992 (16).

43. The repeated parenthetical 'right now' was calculated to be sufficiently irritating that you will (a) feel only relief if I assume it henceforth, and (b) feel disinclined to complain that I am over-looking *times* when I suppress reference to them in later discussion. Suppose I use (i)

(i)   It rained here today

at 6 PM GMT—Reykjavík is on GMT year-round—to answer a question about the weather in Reykjavík, i.e., using 'here' to refer to Reykjavík and 'today' to refer to today (November 5, 2002). The word 'today' is not the only temporal element I used. I used the *past* tense, and in so doing I indicated that I was talking about something that happened *prior* to the time of utterance. Nothing about the meaning of 'today' guaranteed this (witness the sentence 'it will rain here today'). The past tense and 'today' narrow things down in a way that *neither* does alone. With a draconian and somewhat artificial degree of precision, let us say that by using 'today' at 6 PM, I indicated only that I was talking about something happening no earlier than eighteen hours prior to my speaking and no later than six hours afterward. By using the past tense marker I indicated something happening *prior* to the time of my speaking. So it was only by my use of the *combination* that I indicated that the happening I was talking about—raining in Reykjavík—occurred during the eighteen hours prior to my speaking.

Virtually all of the important points I make here could be made using an example such as (ii) in which a time is nailed down:

(ii)   It rained on November 5, 2002.

But there is now quite a literature involving examples like (1), most of it making the same tempo-rary temporal and tense-related idealizations I am making here, so I work with examples like (1) to preserve continuity with that literature, making it easy for me to quote Perry (1986, 1998, 2001), Bach (2001), Récanati (2001), Stanley (2000), and Taylor (2001) without boring remarks indicating changes.

44. For discussion, see Kaplan 1978, 1989a, and 1989b. I take it that the pleonastic 'it' in 'its rain-ing' and 'there' in 'there's a fly in my soup' are not interesting.

45. Neale 1990 (105 n.16; 114 n.46; 116 n.54).

46. Neale 1990 (115, n.54). The actual example I used was of an utterance of

(i)   The president looks ill.

There is no "guarantee" I said, that just because I am in the United States when I utter this sen-tence my utterance is to be understood as elliptical for an utterance of 'the U.S. president looks ill'. It could easily be elliptical for an utterance of, say, 'the French president looks ill', for example, during a discussion about the health of French politicians. I added that Husserl (1913/1970) was surely wrong when he said that a German using 'the emperor' (back in 1913) would be talking about the emperor *of Germany*. We don't want to say that the speaker's *nationality* determines an unarticulated constituent here!

With respect to sentence (ii) from footnote 32, we could easily construct a scenario in which Perry expresses a proposition containing two distinct unarticulated constituents, Reykjavík and Keflavik, for example, and just as easily construct one containing Reykjavík twice.

47. Don't fret about the indefinite article: it is no part of the concept of *being a mayor* that only one thing can be mayor of something at any one time. Sparta had two kings, and semantically this is no more bizarre than California having two senators. One could always write it into the law of some country that there is to be only one king at any one time, just as one can write it into law that there is to be only one senator of a certain state, only one mayor of a certain town, only one general in a particular army, or one headmaster of a certain school, but such acts do not alter the *meanings* of 'king', 'senator', 'mayor', 'general', or 'headmaster'.

48. It is sometimes said that one difference between 'eats' and 'devours' is that the latter has no intransitive use. This is surely wrong. We should not be misled by the fact that intransitive uses of the general eating verb 'eat' are very useful and so frequently encountered ('I've eaten already') to into thinking intransitive uses of the more specific eating verb 'devour' are ungrammatical. It does not take much imagination to come up with a scenario in which 'I have already devoured' is nat-ural. (Cf. 'I have already consumed' and 'I have already imbibed'.)

49. I have here assumed that in predicates of the form 'is the F', 'the F' functions as a Russellian description. Nothing turns on this, but the idea has been questioned by Geach (1962), Fara (2001), and others.

50. (6″) and (7″) raise the question whether it would in any event be correct to think that the *nouns* themselves co-occur with aphonic arguments, for there is not even the semblance of an incompleteness problem to be solved with uses of these sentences. But this is an artifact of the

examples, involving as they do, indefinite descriptions, hence determiners that are persistent in the sense of Barwise and Cooper 1981 and Barwise and Perry 1983. For discussion, see Neale 2004.

51. As John Hawthorne has pointed out to me, there is the matter of *the king of the gypsies*. I find nothing metaphorical in talk of a nomadic people having a king or a mayor; but some informants do, so I won't push this.

52. See Stanley 2000, 2002a, 2002b and Stanley and Szabó 2000.

53. A *phonic* is an element of syntax that has phonetic properties; an *aphonic* is one that does not. Since 'aphonic' is both an adjective and a noun, it is well suited to our discussion, enabling us to avoid such nominal mouthfuls as 'phonologically empty element' and 'phonetically null element', as well as the adjectival mouthfuls 'phonologically empty' and 'phonetically null'. (All aphonics are homophonic, I suppose, but it does not follow that all aphonics affect the totality of phonic features of a sentence in the same way.) Since 'indexical' is also an adjective and a noun, 'indexical aphonic' and 'aphonic indexical' are strictly interchangeable. However, for purposes of *emphasis*, one may be better than the other in certain contexts. Mutatis mutandis 'aphonic variable' and 'variable aphonic'.

54. This position is advocated by Stanley (2000) and criticized by Récanati (2001) and Carston (2002). For discussion, see below. I say in 'much the same way' rather than 'in exactly the same way' above because the alleged aphonic does not have the same use conditions as the phonic 'here': unlike the phonic, the alleged aphonic can be used straightforwardly to refer to locations other than the one the speaker is in. (I say "straightforwardly" because it is possible to have what I shall call *map* uses of 'here': I am writing this footnote in New York, but I could point to the spot representing Reykjavík on a map and say "I wrote most of this paper here," meaning Reykjavík rather than New York.)

55. As Chomsky (1995) stresses.

56. It does not follow that names are not rigid in Kripke's (1980) sense, as Chomsky appears to think.

57. By 'possible states of the world' I mean what many philosophers mean by 'possible world', a phrase that can lead people with certain propensities into saying (and then endorsing and defending) seemingly exciting and bizarre things that more down-to-Earth vocabulary might never have suggested to them.

58. Mutatis mutandis the propositions I express by uttering (i) and (ii):

(i)   The capital of Iceland has over 100,000 inhabitants.

(ii) The king of Iceland is bald.

Of course, strictly speaking, the propositions are location-dependent by virtue of being *Iceland*-dependent, but it is not the referential expressions *inside* the subject phrase that we are winking at, so the propositions are not singular. It would be a lame objection to Russell's theory of descriptions to point out that since the proposition someone expresses by uttering "the king of France is bald" depends for its existence upon the existence of France, we do not uniformly express general propositions when we use sentences with descriptions as subjects.

59. For discussion, see Neale 1990 (ch. 2).

60. There is, of course, a perfectly good sentence one would use to express the proposition that it's raining somewhere or other:

(i)   It's raining somewhere or other.

But even here, 'somewhere or other' will typically be taken to be elliptical (for, say, 'somewhere or other in Iceland') or to be interpreted relative to a restricted domain.

61. I take it that Taylor says "the contextual provision of a place or *range* [emphasis added] of places" to take into account quantified as well as singular weather statements. This seems right to me, and I will follow Taylor to indicate this where appropriate.

62. Michael O'Rourke has suggested the following possible counterexample. *A*: How's the night-life in Provo? *B*: Well, we're dancing! (Compare: *A*: How's the weather in Provo? *B*: Well, it's raining.)

63. Of course, it is not difficult to imagine a scenario in which I intend to be expressing the "more general" proposition that every capital city in the universe has more than 100,000 inhabitants.

64. The label comes from talk of incomplete definite descriptions ('the capital city', etc.).

65. See Perry's (1986) discussion of *Z*-landers.

66. Perry 1986 (214–215).

67. I heard a version of Perry's 1986 paper at Stanford before I had completed my first draft of ch. 3 of Neale 1990. Where Perry, at the time, was trying to shed some light on self-knowledge and egocentric space, I was labelling two traditional approaches to incompleteness I had encountered in the literature. As I worked with Perry on drafts of ch. 3 in 1986–1987, I contemplated bringing in his about-concerns distinction but shied away, thinking it would complicate matters and necessitate digressions on locations, situations, and self-knowledge.

68. It is sometimes claimed that we are all relativists of a sort about truth, that no one takes propositions to be true or false absolutely because the same proposition can be true at one possible world and false at another. (See, e.g., MacFarlane 2003.) This claim seems to me deeply misguided, the product of allowing oneself to be steered more by machinery than by the philosophical problems engendering it. To express an interest in the *truth* of a proposition is to express an interest in how things *are*, not an interest in how things *have to be*. (To be interested in how things *have to be* is to express an interest in *necessary truth*.) A proposition is true or false depending upon how things are. If it makes you happy to construe this as true or false *relative* to the way things are, so be it; but don't try to sell this as a form of relativism! (Similarly for talk of truth in a model.) Within a semantic framework that appeals to the machinery of possible worlds, the surrogate for a proposition's being true ("relative to the way things are") is its being *true at the actual world*,

where the actual world is conceived as one of an indefinite number of ways things could have turned out. But the perfectly sensible idea that we can, within such frameworks, represent a *proposition's* being true in this way appears to have become inextricably bound up in some minds with the discovery that there is a role in certain logics for talk of a *sentence's* being true or false (expressing a truth or falsehood, expressing a true or false proposition) with respect to collections of parameters ("circumstances of evaluation") that include worlds and times (and perhaps locations), to engender the unsound idea that there are interesting choices to be made about *the nature of propositions*: we might view them as true or false relative to worlds, or relative to worlds and times, or relative to worlds, times, and locations, or relative to worlds, times, locations, and aesthetic standards, and so on. Call these beasts "propositions" if you like, but don't confuse them with propositions! Why not call them exactly what they are: *propositional functions*?

69. The semantic theory built around these entities is called *situation semantics*, and the theory of the nature and structure of situations themselves is called *situation theory*.

70. Formally, Barwise and Perry (1983) take *partial* possible worlds to be the entities relative to which propositions are evaluated for truth and falsity, and this adds an interesting twist to any charge of truth relativism of the sort mentioned in note 68. Barwise and Perry's framework evolved considerably in the 1980s, and it is tricky trying to transpose the underlying suggestion for use in frameworks that involve propositions. But with some liberty, we might say the following. As far as (2) is concerned, the idea is *not* that someone uttering (2) expresses different propositions according as the speaker is talking about the UK, Europe, Earth, or the entire universe—the proposition that every capital city in the UK has more than 100,000 inhabitants, the proposition that every capital city in Europe has more than 100,000 inhabitants, and so on. Rather, the idea is that the *same* proposition is expressed. But doesn't this open the theory up to the charge that it does violence to the notion of a proposition by making the truth or falsity of a proposition a relative notion? Formally a proposition is still true or false depending upon how things are, so the answer "No" might seem plausible on the grounds that no *new parameter* is being invoked. But it might be countered that talk of *part* of the way things are is indeed the invocation of a new parameter.

71. So, on the explicit response, someone producing an utterance of an incomplete DP (e.g., 'every citizen' or 'the president') is understood as expressing what he *would have* expressed more explicitly had he uttered a richer ("complete") DP (e.g., 'every U.S. citizen', 'the U.S. president'), a DP he *could have* used in place of the incomplete one. The explicit strategy is sometimes called the *ellipsis* strategy in the literature, presumably in deference to the suggestions made by Quine (1940) and Sellars (1954), who talk, respectively, of *elliptical uses* and *elliptical utterances* of descriptions. For detailed discussion, see Neale 2004.

72. For unfathomable reasons, Stanley and Szabó (2000) read just such a syntactic thesis into the summary of the explicit response in *Descriptions*, and by implication into the explicit responses of Quine (1940), Sellars (1954), Bach (1981), Davies (1981), and Evans (1982), among others. For discussion, see Neale 2004.

73. See Soames 1986 and Westerståhl 1985.

74. The situation here is reminiscent of the situation in modal logic when people thought having a full axiomatization and later a model theory answered the philosophical questions about the interpretation on 'necessarily *Fx*'. See the postscript to ch. 4 of *Descriptions*, expanded ed.

75. But see O'Rourke 2003.

76. The same words appear at the beginning of the paragraph immediately following the one just quoted:

the fact that one can imagine an utterance of 'It's raining' that is true iff it's raining (at the time of utterance) in some place or other arguably establishes the pragmatic nature of the felt necessity to single out a particular place, in the contexts in which such a necessity is indeed felt. If that is right, there is no need to posit a lexically specified argument-role for a location in the sub-atomic structure of the verb 'rain': 'Rain' is like 'dance' and other action verbs, contrary to what Taylor claims (2001, 54). That raining must take place somewhere or other is a metaphysical fact, not a linguistic fact. That fact does not prevent an utterance like [(1)] from expressing a fully determinate proposition even if no place is contextually provided. (2001, 317)

Taylor is right, I believe, and Récanati wrong about 'rain' and the properties it shares with 'dance'.

77. Surely Récanati would agree that it would be poor methodological practice to centre a theory of interpretation on the unusual, out-of-the-ordinary case he constructs, and then treat the usual, run-of-the-mill cases as involving a complexity or oddity of some sort. It would make more sense to see the unusual, out-of-the-ordinary case as involving a complexity or oddity. So really the strongest moral Récanati would be entitled to draw from his intuition that the proposition the weatherman in his example expresses does not contain an unarticulated location, is that under certain unusual circumstances it is just about possible to abstract from a location. And *that* moral does not conflict with point made by Taylor, that in the interpretation of a use of a sentence containing the verb 'rain', the lexical structure of the verb itself is "the source of the felt need for the contextual provision of a place or range of places where a raining happens" (2001, 54). But, once this is conceded, it might as well be conceded that the alternative description of the proposition expressed in Récanati's unusual, out-of-the-ordinary case, the one according to which the weatherman's utterance is true if, and only if, it is raining somewhere or other *on Earth* is considerably more attractive. It conforms more closely to our intuitions and preserves a unitary account of utterances involving the verb 'rain': there is *always* an unarticulated location (or range of locations). Could Récanati tip the methodological scales in the other direction by modifying his example, making it more science fictitious? Suppose rain has become extremely rare and important in *the entire universe* (whatever exactly that amounts to), trillions of detectors, etc. Would he now have a potential counterexample to the unarticulated location hypothesis? It is far from obvious we would, for it would not be unreasonable to maintain that the entire universe (rather than, say, Earth or Recanto) is an unarticulated constituent of the proposition expressed.

78. In response to the present paper, Récanati recently sent me a paper in which he expresses a worry about the existential quantification in the sort of informal glosses I have been using in monitor-room examples (e.g., 'it's raining somewhere or other on Earth'). The worry, as I understand it, is this (I have changed 'Paris' to 'Recanto' and shifted to my own monitor-room example in order to make the right comparison): usually when we use 'it's raining in Recanto' to say that

it's raining in Recanto, we are not just saying that it's raining *somewhere or other* in Recanto, but that it's raining "*over* Recanto (i.e., at most sublocations in the Recanto area)." Thus, a difference between monitor-room examples and the more usual examples, one that Récanati seems to think undermines the position I am taking in the text. Why? Because, "Clearly in the [monitor-room] example, the sentence 'it's raining' does not mean that it's raining over Recanto.... The weatherman's utterance only means that it's raining *somewhere* in Recanto." There is an error in Récanati's thinking: assuming that facts about uses of 'it's raining in X' carry over to uses of 'it's raining'. The assumption Récanati needs is, in fact, false. It may well be true that when we use 'it's raining in X', we are normally saying something that is true if, and only if, it's raining at most sublocations in the X area (actually this seems to too strong, but let that pass), but *nothing* follows about our uses of 'it's raining', and for an obvious reason, if what Perry has been saying is true: the proposition one expresses by uttering 'it's raining' (unlike the proposition one expresses by uttering 'it's raining in X') must contain an unarticulated constituent. What is characteristic of monitor-room examples is the *complexity* of this constituent, which could be articulated using 'somewhere or other in X'.

79. I am not entirely sure, but this may be something that Cappelen and Lepore endorse. I have difficulty getting their position clear, in some places it seems like a version of existentialism, in other places a version of nihilism, and in still others a version of neither.

80. "False!" the advocate of "T-theorem" (5) cries: "A sentence can have a truth condition even if it lacks a truth-value." But I did not assume that no sentence can have a truth condition unless it has a truth-value; I assumed only that if a particular sentence can have a truth-value only relative to a location then it can have a truth condition only relative to a location, an assumption whose denial leads to obvious contradiction.

81. It is no response to this to say that it is obvious that 'it's raining iff it's raining' is true. It is *not*, since neither its left- nor its right-hand side has a truth-value or a truth condition except relative to an index. (To claim, as I think Cappelen and Lepore would, that this remark runs together truth conditions and *verification* conditions is to confuse the metaphysical question of whether 'it's raining iff it's raining' is evaluable for truth or falsity with the epistemological question of whether anyone can determine the truth value of 'it's raining'. Verification is simply not the issue.) And once an index is brought in, the game is up again.

82. Of course, I do not think sentences-relative-to-indices are actually the right sorts of things to be evaluated for truth or falsity within a theory of utterance interpretation.

83. The word 'indexical' is itself part if the problem, suggesting as it does that interpreting such devices involves merely looking something up in an "index." People can be more influenced by labels than they sometimes realize.

84. A lot here turns on one's conception of logic, and my wording evinces a particular stance, though not one I want to insist on: logical relations hold among *what is expressed* by token sentences of a formal system not among sentences themselves. (Various issues about the notion of formal validity and inference rule must be faced by people who hold this view of logic.) The point I am making in the text is not dependent upon this stance. Cf. discussions of the difference

between the logical form of a proposition and the logical form of a particular sentence used to express that proposition.

85. It is, perhaps, tacit recognition of this fact that has led some philosophers to conclude that there is no hope of producing a theory of *utterance interpretation* without positing all sorts of aphonic, indexical elements in the underlying syntax of natural language sentences. We may use anything we like to throw light on the syntax of natural language, but we must never lose sight of the fact that discerning the syntactic structures of our sentences is an empirical exercise. Certainly the idea of aphonics in syntax is not objectionable in itself. On the assumption that syntax relates sound and meaning, we must certainly allow for the possibility of elements that have sound but no meaning ('it' in 'it's raining'?) or meaning but no sound (the understood subject of 'leave' in 'Tom wants to leave'?). And there can be little doubt today that great advances in our understanding of syntax have been made by those such as Chomsky, who have not shied away from the idea of aphonic items in syntax and argued for their existence and explanatory value. But we cannot simply *assume* that whenever we encounter some feature of what is said that does not appear to correspond to any element or feature of the sentence uttered it follows that there is some element in underlying syntax waiting to be exposed.

86. I am putting aside here some very real concerns about talk of *sentences* saying things relative to contexts. I am skeptical about the value or relevance of the use of the verb 'say' assumed in this way of talking to the project of constructing a theory of utterance interpretation, unless it is understood as a stylistic variant of talk of *speakers* saying things by uttering sentences on given occasions. Judgments about what a *speaker* said, and about whether what he said was true or false in specified situations, constitute the primary data for a theory of interpretation, the data it is the business of such a theory to explain. What a speaker *says* and what he *implies* (e.g., conversationally implicates) on a given occasion are the things that together constitute what the speaker *means*, and a theory of interpretation is meant to explain the role of linguistic meaning and inference in the hearer's identification of what the speaker meant. No one has intuitions about *what is said by a sentence X relative to a context C* or about the truth or falsity of X relative to C unless this is just a formal way of talking about what the speaker said by uttering X on a particular occasion—the occasion that C is being used to partially model or approximate. If such talk is straightforwardly transposable into talk about what the speaker said, then we can accept its empirical significance. If it is not so transposable, then its empirical significance must be justified in some other way, from *within* the theory of interpretation by reference to some empirical role it is required to play in an explanation of what a speaker says and implies by uttering X on a given occasion, in much the same way that notions such as LF, scope, and binding are motivated from within. If some such motivation is forthcoming, we should be only too happy to listen. I suspect it will not be forthcoming because the notion of what a *sentence says* relative to a context is going to be too thin and overly detached from speakers' communicative intentions to carry any empirical weight. Nonetheless, I adopt a wait-and-see approach. We are involved in an empirical enterprise, after all.

87. As soon as we introduce anaphoric pronouns—those that are linked in some interpretive fashion to other expressions (their "antecedents")—matters become more complicated. The reflexive

'himself' *must be* interpreted via an antecedent; the nonreflexives 'he', 'him', and 'his' *can be* so interpreted (under certain conditions).

88. Carston (2002) implicitly anchors in her examinations of 'pragmatic enrichments' in connection with utterances of conjunctions (indeed, it is what she implicitly does throughout). Similarly, Evans implicitly anchors in *The Varieties of Reference* (and elsewhere), Sperber and Wilson do it throughout *Relevance* (and elsewhere), and I do it explicitly in ch. 3 of *Descriptions* in connection with the effects of indexicals appearing in definite descriptions. Chomsky also does something analogous to anchoring in every work in which he discusses pronouns. (I say "analogous" because of Chomsky's concerns about reference).

89. If as, for example, Stanley (2000) has suggested, (1) contains such a device, does this mean that (2) also contains it? Or does it mean the position the device occupies in (1) is occupied by 'here' in (2)? Is 'here' an argument or an adjunct in (2)?

90. To say that he homes in on Reykjavík is not to make the cognitive claim that he has to mentally convert 'here' into 'in Reykjavík' in his head in order to interpret my utterance. Nor is it to make the syntactic claim that although 'here' appears in (2)'s PF, its LF contains the expression 'in Reykjavík' (a syntactic operation turning 'in Reykjavík' into 'here'). Both claims strike me as bizarre, and the latter would seem to conflict with standard assumptions in syntax: (2) could no longer be viewed as the PF of a unique sentence, for otherwise it could not be used to say that it snowed today somewhere other than Reykjavík! (2) would have to be treated as the PF of thousands of distinct sentences, something that would not in this case obviously comport with the usual ideas about the relation between PF and LF.

91. Appeals to formal contexts do not answer the *how* question. Such appeals are fine for formalizing inference or methodological anchoring and co-anchoring, but contexts make precisely no contribution to answering the *how* question beyond helping the theorist state clearly what the *how* question *amounts to* in certain easy cases. An utterance of a sentence is generally made by a person, at a time and place, with a particular audience in mind. But all this means is that information about the environment in which an utterance is made can be exploited reasonably systematically by the hearer in identifying what the speaker said. It does not tell us *how* such information is integrated with semantic information to yield interpretations; it just tells us what the result of the integration has to be for the hearer to get it right. A formal context provides nothing more than help for the theorist in *describing* the proposition expressed. The answer to the *how* question has to flow from a general theory of the ways various cognitive abilities produce interpretations of utterances.

92. This being philosophy, someone is sure to disagree with this characterization. It might be argued, for example, that my father immediately grasped the proposition I expressed because a special use of 'here' has evolved in the weather game according to which it is understood as if it were an occurrence of the descriptive phrase 'in my current location'. One consequence of this position would be that, in the context of the weather game, I could say something true right now (in Reykjavík) by uttering, "It is not necessary that if it snowed here today, then it snowed here today" (different scopes for 'here' on the hypothesis in question, or one traditional use of

'here' and one special, descriptive, game use). My father's task on this account would be to identify a location-dependent proposition that went beyond the proposition expressed. I see no merit to this view, only unpalatable modal and epistemological consequences, some of which could be dealt with, I suppose, by "actualizing" ('my actual, current location'). Anyway, I am not interested in pursuing this option.

93. I am putting to one side the case of deferred ostension when, for example, my father points to southwest Iceland on his globe while uttering (2).

94. Which is not to say that one could not cook up a scenario in which replying with (4) would have been less unacceptable, indeed quite pointed.

95. See Grice 1989. Within the modification of Grice's framework I favor, this would be a case of implying something *by uttering X* without implying it by *saying* whatever it was that was said (by uttering *X*). See Neale 2005, forthcoming.

96. Multiple proposition theories have been popular of late, and Perry (1993) has done his fair share to motivate them. (See also Barwise and Perry 1983, Frege 1892/1952, Grice 1989, Karttunen and Peters 1979, O'Rourke 1998, Neale 1999, and Stalnaker 1978.) Within the sort of pragmatist framework I favor, there does not seem to be much of a problem involved in saying that I would have expressed two propositions by uttering (4) in response to my father's question as the framework is not beholden to the strictures governing traditional compositional theories of meaning. According to a traditional theory of the direct reference variety, relative to a context *C* the semantic content of 'there' in (4) is just a location that, like the semantic content relative to *C* of every other expression in (4), constitutes its contribution to the semantic content relative to *C* of (4) itself (i.e., its propositional content relative to *C*, the proposition it expresses relative to *C*). This effectively forces the traditional theorist to opt for a conventional implicature account or a presuppositional account of the speaker's location relative to the location that is the semantic content of 'there' relative to *C*. Unless, of course, the traditional theorist maintains that there would have been a *double* reference to Reykjavík if I had uttered (4). Is that conceivable? See below.

97. There is one context in which the locating of the speaker with respect to the place he is referring to with 'there' breaks down. Consider a philosophical discussion here in Reykjavík about the proposition I expressed when I uttered (1) or (2) or (3). Mike might say, "Stephen referred to Reykjavík and said of it that it was raining there." The occurrence of 'there' in the sentence Mike uttered is surely interpreted as anaphoric on 'it', itself anaphoric on 'Reykjavík'. It seems clear that locatives do have bound occurrences, just like pronouns:

(i)   [Every politician]^1 charms some of the people who work with him$_1$.

(ii)   [Every city]^1 charms some of the people who live there$_1$.

(On the most plausible theories of anaphora, 'him' and 'there' in (i) and (ii) remain bound when the respective quantifiers are replaced by names such as 'John' and 'Reykjavík' [see Neale 2005].) In (ii), 'there' can be replaced by 'in it' (if the nominal were 'island', 'mountain' or 'planet' rather than 'city', the appropriate substitution would be 'on it'). There would appear to be no reflexive form of 'there', presumably as there are no suitable structures in which 'there' can be understood as locally bound by a subject locative:

(iii) [Every city]^1/Reykjavík^1 is destroying itself$_1$.

(v) [Every city]^1/Reykjavík^1 *is going there$_{*1}$.

98. See also Barwise and Perry 1983.

99. See Chomsky 1986, 1995, and 2000. The postulation of expressions that are aphonic despite having syntactic roles and semantic properties is surely no more or less problematic than the postulation of expressions that are asemantic despite having syntactic roles and phonological properties (e.g., 'it' in 'it's raining'). The idea of an expression that is phonetically *and* semantically empty is more difficult to gets one's mind around, and on the interpretation of Chomsky's present framework I endorse—syntax is whatever it is that relates PF and LF—the possibility of such an expression is straightforwardly excluded. The discovery or postulation of *any* linguistic expression constitutes a contribution to syntax and its existence is justified only if it is doing something at LF or PF. Consequently, the discovery or postulation of an *aphonic* expression must be justified by its role at LF. To this extent, it will contribute in one way to the project of producing a theory of utterance interpretation. The point, however, should not be exaggerated. Discovering or postulating occurrences of a bound aphonic PRO has very clear consequences for a theory of interpretation: an expression has been discovered or posited that is understood as a bound variable, effectively answering all questions about its interpretation on a particular occasion, given a general account of binding. Contrast this with the discovery or postulation of an *indexical* aphonic, one even more flexible in its interpretation than the indexical phonics 'this' or 'that' or 'he' (when used to make independent reference). The interpretation of an utterance of a sentence containing an occurrence of an aphonic indexical is always going to be a full-fledged *pragmatic* (i.e., inferential matter) the semantics of the aphonic itself placing only nondeterministic constraints on interpretation. This matter will be taken up shortly.

100. Compare (3) with the following:

(i) Everyone^1 promised John [$_S$ PRO$_1$ to sing on Sunday].

(ii) John asked everyone^1 [$_S$ PRO$_1$ to sing].

In (i), PRO would appear to be bound by the subject of 'promise'; in (ii) it would appear to be bound by the object of 'ask'.

101. Famously, Davidson (1967) suggested that the "logical form" of an English sentence containing an *n*-place action verb contains an $n + 1$ place predicate, the additional argument position occupied by a variable ranging over events. The logical form of (i), for example, might be (ii):

(i) Brutus stabbed Caesar

(ii) $(\exists x)(stabbed(Brutus, Caesar, x))$

where (ii) is read as something like 'there is an event x such that x is a (past) stabbing of Caesar by Brutus'. Question: Did Davidson originally intend this proposal as a claim in generative grammar about a level of syntactic structure, about *deep structure* as it was called at the time? Answer: That was not how he originally conceived of it. But when philosophers and grammarians traded ideas and began to explore the idea that a superficially *n*-place verb might be an $n + 1$ place verb at deep structure or (later) at LF and to view his proposal as abstractly capturing facts about "real" syntactic structure, he was prepared to see syntactico-semantic arguments for variables ranging over events at LF as lending support to his proposal.

102. I deliberately refrain from listing Taylor with the people I called *linguistic pragmatists* in Neale 2004, 2005 because I am not entirely sure his position does not admit of an interpretation quite different from the one I am providing here. If the interpretation I offer here is accurate, then his position seems to me entirely correct—which is not to say that I agree with Taylor on how to classify every parameter in every potential example. The more I look at Taylor's paper, the more I think that what I have in mind by 'blueprint' in the paper just mentioned is what he has in mind by 'semantic scaffolding'. That our positions might be closer than I once thought was in fact suggested to me by Taylor in conversation.

103. Perry (2001) himself has commented on the appropriation.

104. Stanley (2002a) renews his attack on Perry and unarticulated constituents without using 'logical form' in his initial definition. But see below.

105. In more recent work, Stanley (2002a) is initially more cautious in his definition of unarticulated constituent, which does not contain the expression 'logical form':

an entity (object, property, or function) e is an unarticulated constituent relative to an utterance u if and only if (a) e is a constituent of the proposition . . . expressed by u, and (b) e is not the value of any constituent in the expression uttered in u, and (c) e is not introduced by context-independent composition rules corresponding to the structural relations between the elements in the expression uttered. (2002a, 150 n.2)

But once Stanley gets down to business, "logical form" in the sense he takes from syntactic theory is soon invoked. Perry is not explicitly listed amongst the *targets* of the more recent paper, however; Stanley says that "most prominently" his targets are

Kent Bach, Robyn Carston, François Récanati, Dan Sperber, and Deirdre Wilson . . . [who] hold that . . . the proposition expressed . . . contains . . . elements that are not the value [*sic*] of any constituent of the sentence uttered, nor introduced by composing those values. Instead these elements are provided directly by context. Loosely following John Perry, I shall call such elements unarticulated constituents. (2002a, 150)

The fact that Stanley says he is only "loosely" following Perry in this more recent work does not seem to bear on the matters I am discussing here. The looseness Stanley alludes to stems from the fact that some of the people he lists state particular underdetermination claims in terms of Mentalese, and from the fact that certain forms of underdetermination are not readily restated in terms of unarticulated constituents. It is important to recognize that the looseness Stanley alludes to does not stem from his introduction of the notion of "logical form."

106. Stanley (2002b, 367) and Stanley and Szabó (2000, 247) explicitly say that a logical form is a phrase marker.

107. See also Stanley and Szabó 2000:

We will call the output of the syntactic processes that is visible to semantic interpretation a logical form. A logical form is a lexically and structurally disambiguated ordered sequence of word types, where word types are individuated by semantic and syntactic properties. Logical forms are phrase markers. (247)

Note the use of "phrase marker." This passage (with an insignificant stylistic change) recurs in a more recent paper by Stanley (2002b, 367).

108. Neale 1990, 1993, 2005. My position on the precise *nature* of these logical forms, knows as LFs, has not remained constant, however. In the 1993 paper, I explored the idea that LFs are rich enough to be evaluated for truth and falsity, but elsewhere my position is that they do not carry enough information to be evaluable for truth or falsity, they are merely the grammar's contribution to representations that have truth values.

109. See, for example, Bresnan 1982, 2001, Gazdar, Pullum, Klein, and Sag 1985, Kaplan and Bresnan 1982, and Sag and Wasow 1999. I do not mean to be *endorsing* any of these particular syntactic theories or suggesting that *Perry* endorses any of them. I am just pointing out that there are plenty of working syntacticians who reject logical forms in Stanley's sense.

110. PRO, for example, does not appear in case-marked positions (verbs in the infinitive do not assign nominative case to their subjects), but other aphonics appear only in case-marked positions; and different aphonics fall under different principle of the Binding Theory. On LF, see, for example, Aoun 1985; Baltin 1987; Chomsky 1981, 1986, 1995; Higginbotham 1980, 1983; Higginbotham and May 1981; Hornstein 1984; Huang 1982, 1995; Larson and Segal 1995; Ludlow 1989; May 1985; and Neale 1994. Huang's 1995 article (called "Logical Form") provides a nice overview of the main issues.

111. Stanley and Szabó (2000) do not say the logical forms they are talking about are LFs either. Nor does Stanley do so in his more recent papers on the topic (2002a, 2000b).

112. In more recent work, Stanley says of the aphonic "pronominals" he is positing that their "existence can be demonstrated by purely syntactic tests" (2002, 150). In fact, the tests Stanley marshaled all involve *interpretation*.

113. In the semiformal, semi-English sentences Stanley uses to represent his "logical forms," quantifiers have not been raised. Because he says so little about the syntax of "logical forms" and gives virtually no structural information about the things he writes down as particular "logical forms," it is hard to know whether the failure to have raised quantifiers is for expository simplicity or part of some undeclared empirical thesis.

114. Stanley recently communicated to me that he does mean logical forms to be understood as LFs.

115. Recall his talk on pp. 391–392 about the empirical discovery of "real structure." See also Stanley and Szabó 2000 (247). Stanley and Szabó say they realize that

some semanticists and philosophers use their semantic theories to interpret structures that differ greatly from the syntactic structures produced by plausible syntactic theories for natural language. (2000a, 246)

And they lament the difficulty they see philosophers have in giving up the idea that

one can freely construct alternative semantic structures for various natural language sentences without being constrained by empirical evidence from linguistics. Such a view ... is tantamount to the endorsement of the hypothesis that syntax is a superficial feature of language, detached from the way we understand the utterances of others. We find this hypothesis implausible in the extreme. (2000a, 245)

See also Stanley 2002b (367).

116. It is incorrect to claim that those who accept UT employ the following general strategy in arguing for underarticulation:

First, some linguistic construction is provided whose truth-conditional interpretation is mediated by context. Then, it is argued that it is inconsistent with current syntactic theory to postulate, in the logical form of the relevant construction, expressions or variables the semantic values of which context could provide. (Stanley 2000, 398)

The truth of the matter is just this: some linguistic construction X is *noticed* whose truth-conditional interpretation *appears* to outstrip what is given by composing the semantic values of X's parts (some of which are fixed only in context) in accordance with X's syntactic structure. And, in the absence of pre-existing reasons given by syntacticians for thinking there is some structural fact about X that has been *missed*, it would appear that the role of extralinguistic considerations in fixing truth-conditional content goes beyond supplying values to a handful of indexical expressions. UT is not something that has been gleefully embraced in some intellectual game but something that a number of serious philosophers and linguists reluctantly accepted in the face of problematic examples and conceptual pressures, something they then sought to understand.

117. There is, of course, a famous paper by Crimmins *and* Perry (1989) on unarticulated constituents (in the contents of attitude ascriptions) and cross-referencing confirms the existence of a position common to both of them individually.

118. Récanati (2001) interprets Perry correctly:

To evaluate a statement of rain as true or false, Perry says, we need both a time and a place, but the statement 'It's raining' explicitly gives us only the two-place relation (supplied by the verb) and the temporal argument (supplied by the present tense). The location argument must be contextually supplied for the utterance to express a complete proposition. (2001, 307–308)

119. There is further distortion of Perry's proposal in Stanley's claim that,

According to the unarticulated constituent analysis, the structure of [(1)] is as in [(2)]. Therefore, its truth-conditions would be given by a clause such as:

R: 'It is raining(t)' is true in a context c if and only if the denotation of 'rains' takes $\langle t, l \rangle$ to the True, where l is the contextually salient location in c.

Clause R is a standard unarticulated constituent clause. It captures the intuition that the place variable [*sic*] is supplied directly by context, rather than first to a variable in the logical form of [(1)]. (2000, 415)

If the first occurrence of 'variable' in the last sentence of this passage is an infelicitous hangover from a botched cut-and-paste, then the remark at least makes sense. (It seems plausible to me that Stanley, an editor, or a typesetter just slipped here.) But clause R is certainly *not* a "standard unarticulated constituent clause," and not Perry's in particular: it is a clause that can be maintained only by someone who holds that (1) has an LF that contains a *covert temporal variable.*

In a more recent paper, Stanley (2002a) argues against unarticulated constituents again and says the following, which may be intended to justify his 2000 description of Perry's position:

I have heard it said that, for Perry, an unarticulated constituent is one that is not the value of a *pronounced* element. But Perry (1986) argues for the thesis that there are unarticulated constituents of thoughts. If the values of phonologically null representational elements were unarticulated, then *every* semantic value of a mental representation would be an unarticulated constituent. (2002a, 150 n.1)

But this is quite unfair. The issue of whether or not there are unarticulated constituents of *thought* contents—*unprojected* constituents, as I called them earlier—is simply not to the point. When someone says, "for Perry, an unarticulated constituent is one that is not the value of a *pronounced* element," it should be clear to a charitable reader genuinely seeking to understand the remark (when made by a competent philosopher familiar with the issues) that the speaker is talking about unarticulated constituents *of the propositions we express by uttering sentences of natural language.* To deny this is rather like denying that someone who says, "every bottle is clean," when talking about the bottles he has been asked to clean, is saying something true on the grounds that there are some dirty bottles elsewhere in the world. (The matter of quantifier domain restriction is one that Stanley (2000, 2002a, 2002b) and also Stanley and Szabó (2000) address, their position being that a nominal (e.g., 'bottle') "cohabits" its syntactic nodes with an aphonic domain variable.)

120. In more recent work, Stanley adds a fourth category, "context-dependent quantifiers such as 'many' and (perhaps) 'that'" (2002a, 150).

121. See Chomsky 1981, 1986; Higginbotham 1983; Evans 1977, 1980; Heim 1988; Heim and Kratzer 1998; May 1985; Reinhart and Reuland 1993; and Reuland 2001.

122. See Heim and Kratzer 1998 and Neale 2005 for accessible but detailed discussion.

123. In more recent work, Stanley explicitly acknowledges this: "syntactic structure cannot simply be postulated on semantic grounds. Rather, evidence of a syntactic sort must be available" (2002b, 368).

124. Nothing in Stanley's (2002a, 2002b) more recent papers suggest there is any need for me to temper this claim.

125. The purported binding does not require the subject of the main verb to be quantificational:

(4″)   John[1] wanted [$_S$ x_1 to sing].

(4′) and (4′) attribute the same property to every man and John. The truth of (4′) requires that every man satisfy 'x wanted x to sing', and the truth of (4″) requires that John satisfy it.

126. I have suppressed various complexities for the sake of exposition.

127. The claim that 'I' and 'you' are not bindable is not actually self-evident, given that the notion of binding we are interested in is one needed to sustain talk of the LFs of sentences being the objects of semantic interpretation. It is arguable that the second occurrence of 'I' in 'I know I am awake' is bound by the first in the requisite sense.

128. It is somewhat misleading to think of the difference between 'I' and 'we' as one of pure number. As Lyons (1969, 277) notes, the word 'we' usually has the force of (roughly) 'I and one or more other persons'. The other persons may or may not be the addressee(s); some languages, however, use two phonologically unrelated pronouns for our 'we', according as the relevant persons distinct from the speaker are the addressees or not.

129. It is arguable that 'there' can be bound. Recall the following perfectly well-formed and interpretable sentences:

(i)   Reykjavík[1] enchants many people who live there[1].

(ii) [Every city][1] enchants some people who live there[1].

130. For discussion, see Kaplan 1989a and Perry 2001.

131. Differences signaled by choice of honorific (e.g., French *tu* and *vous*) may be thought to signal different "perspectives" of a sort, involving social distance.

132. There is the vexed matter, of course, of whether the gender of a pronoun (even a bound one) contributes systematically to the truth conditions of what is said.

133. As Mark Sainsbury puts it:

In using an indexical, one exploits a perspective on the world. One locates an object by reference, ultimately, to one's own position in space or time. In interpreting a use of an indexical, one needs to locate its user's perspective within one's own.... One needs to identify the perspective, not suppress it. (2002, 146)

See also Colin McGinn:

All the [essential] indexicals are linked with I, and the I mode of presentation is subjective in character because it comprises the special perspective a person has on himself. Very roughly, we can say that to think of something indexically is to think of it in relation to *me*, as I am presented to myself in self-consciousness. (1983, 17)

134. If Russell is right, Reykjavík is not articulated by the description, unlike Iceland and the property of being capital.

135. Of course, one can use *other* words with 'loke' to indicate perspective: 'here', 'there', 'come', 'go', 'bring', 'take', and so on. The verbs just mentioned bring up some interesting locative issues. First, there are dialectal differences. For most speakers of British English, 'bring' and 'take' are perspectival in a way they are not for most speakers of American English. Consider (i) and (ii):

(i)   Bring the receipts to the bank.

(ii) Bring the luggage out to the car.

If I am the speaker, (i) and (ii) are both bad for me unless I am already at the bank or out by the car (or at least think I will be by the time, or very close to the time, the addressee arrives with the requested items). *Bringing to* is toward, *taking to* is away from, just as *coming* is toward and *going* is away from. Not so for many speakers of American English, for whom (i) and (ii) are fine even if they never intend to set foot near a bank or car again. (Matters are complicated by the fact that perspective transfer is possible in an almost logophoric way.)

136. See Chomsky 1980, 1981, 1995, 2000.

137. The existence of an aphonic, aperspectival wholly indexical expression functionally quite similar (but not identical to) to (11) is the heart of Stanley's account of quantifier incompleteness or quantifier domain restriction. For the syntactic details, he directs the reader to Stanley and Szabó 2000. (See also Stanley 2002b for a schematic account.) The interpretive incompleteness associated with the utterance of a DP is to be explained on the assumption that it contains a com-

plex aphonic domain variable "assigned" a value "by context" and composition. We can call this a syntactic proposal with semantic import or a semantic proposal implemented syntactically; it doesn't matter. What is key, however, is that it has a very clear *syntactic* dimension. Although the variable is syntactically real, it is not attached to, dominated by, or associated with either of the quantificational nodes, D ('the') or DP ('the table'), in 'the table' as one might have thought; rather, it 'cohabits' a node with the common noun N ('table'). The variable is complex element they represent as $f(i)$ a compound of two variables, one individual, i, the other functional, f:

(i) $[_{DP}$ the $[_{NP}$ $[_{N}$ $\langle$man, $f(i)\rangle]]]$.

(I take the liberty of italicizing Stanley and Szabo's variables in accordance with my own policy of italicizing aphonics. And I take the liberty of setting out their proposal assuming the DP hypothesis; nothing turns on this.) Here is the idea:

The value of 'i' is provided by context, and the value of 'f' is a function provided by context that maps objects onto quantifier domains. The restriction on the quantified expression 'every man' . . . relative to context would then be provided by the result of applying the function that context supplies to 'f' to the object that context supplies to 'i' (2000, 251–252)

They go on:

Since we are taking quantifier domains to be sets, relative to a context, what results from applying the value of 'f' to the value of 'i' is a set. Relative to a context, 'f' is assigned a function from objects to sets. Relative to a context, 'i' is assigned an object. The denotation of '$\langle$man, $f(i)\rangle$' relative to a context c is then the result of intersecting the set of men with the set that results from applying the value given to 'f' by the context c to the value given to 'i' by c. That is (suppressing reference to a model to simplify exposition), where '$[\alpha]_c$' denotes the denotation of α with respect to the context c, and '$c(\alpha)$' denotes what the context c assigns to the expression α: $[\langle$man, $f(i)\rangle] = [$man$] \cap \{x: x \in c(f)(c(i))\}$. (2000, 253)

It is for expository simplicity only, however, that Stanley and Szabo treat quantifier domains as sets. They make it clear that in order to deal with a certain form of counterexample, on their final theory quantifier domains are "intensional entities such as *properties*, represented as functions from worlds and times to sets" (2000, 252).

   The problem with this proposal is that from the point of view of a theory of utterance interpretation it is, in fact, *merely syntactic*. The values "context" "assigns" to the individual variable 'i' and the functional variable 'f' in any particular case are unconstrained. Neither 'i' nor 'f' is perspectival or descriptive. Thus, '$f(i)$' is wholly aperspectival, wholly adescriptive, and wholly aphonic. Because it concerns the interpretation of nominals, the theory posits n occurrences of the wholly aphonic, wholly aperspectival, wholly indexical expression $f(i)$ as part of the logical form of every sentence containing n common nouns. On this account, interpreting an utterance of a sentence containing n nouns involves identifying the values "context" has "assigned" to each of the n occurrences of '$f(i)$' via identifying the values "context" has "assigned" to n occurrences of the wholly aperspectival, adescriptive, aphonic expression 'i' and n occurrences of the wholly aperspectival, adescriptive, aphonic expression 'f'. So the proposal is nothing more than an pointlessly formal and absurdly syntactic way of saying that interpreting an utterance of, say,

(ii)   Every philosopher explained several theories to every linguist

involves identifying which philosophers, which theories, and which linguists are being talked about. But that is precisely what the explicit-about approach involving unarticulated constituents has been saying all along, but without the syntactic palava. It will not do to claim, with Stanley (2002a, 158, n.12) that the explicit-about approach "simply amounts to a re-description of the phenomenon to be explained, rather than an account of it," *if* the implication is that this is less of an account than positing an aphonic, aperspectival, adescriptive domain variable that takes on whatever value is required to make things work out correctly. Neither the explicit nor the implicit approach, nor Stanley and Szabó's contextual variable, approach constitutes a *theory* in any sense relevant to a theory of interpretation. Whichever way we go here, all of the work is done by pragmatic inference. A theory that posits the existence of aphonic aperspectival, adescriptive domain variables in syntax is essentially a *syntactic* proposal concerning the LF of a sentence that may be uttered on different occasions to say different things, and it should not be confused with a theory that explains *how hearers* manage to interpret nominals. Interpretation of any postulated context-sensitive expression on a given occasion of utterance is itself a *pragmatic, richly inferential* matter, the product of integrating linguistic and nonlinguistic information, something that is done by a pragmatic theory. (However you look at it, it's magic, and it betrays a misunderstanding of the issues to complain that on the explicit approach the hearer performs an act of magic no counterpart of which the hearer performs on an approach that requires the hearer to supply properties or sets or whatever as values for aphonic aperspectival, adescriptive domain variables.) As far as interpretation of incomplete matrices is concerned, the only substantive difference between the unarticulated constituent theorist and someone who postulates aphonic aperspectival, adescriptive elements cohabiting nodes with common nouns is that the latter insists that the search for and integration of contextual information in the interpretation process is triggered syntactically. I know of no good argument that an item in syntax is *necessary* for such a search and or for such integration to take place—such an argument would have to come from psychology. Merely pointing to the well-known phenomenon of "implicit binding" certainly does not *demonstrate* the existence of aphonic variables. (See below.)

138. What about 'Rainy days and Mondays always get me down'? A quantified case, to be sure.

139. Alternatively, one might pursue the idea of an aphonic *event* variable in logical form. This was, in fact, the way Davidson originally suggested dealing with weather sentences in the mid-1990s, prompted by a talk Perry gave at Berkeley on unarticulated constituents. The logical form of a weather sentence, Davidson suggested, is like the logical form of an action sentence, it contains an event variable to which temporal predicates ('today', 'at midnight', etc.), locative predicates ('in the bathroom', 'in Reykjavík'), and perhaps even manner predicates ('with great intensity') may be attached. Of course, this involves positing in addition to an aphonic event variable in the logical form of, say, (1), an aphonic locative *predicate*, itself 'indexical' in so far as its interpretation could vary from utterance to utterance (e.g., it could be understood as 'in Reykjavík', 'in the Berkeley hills', and so on), and for this reason Davidson thought the price to high. To the best of my knowledge, Davidson never came up with an account of Perry's examples he found satisfactory.

140. It would smack of desperation to say that for certain verbs it is entirely optional whether *loc* has to have a referent on a particular occasion use. That would require coming up with compelling cases in which a particular location is required in order to evaluate the proposition expressed for

truth or falsity. We failed in that quest earlier, and I hazard this was not for lack of imagination in constructing examples. Cf. Ósk and the tea-pouring.

141. I cannot have been alone in being startled upon first reading Stanley's main claim. The notion of implicit binding is so well known, so familiar to anyone who has worked on donkey anaphora, at least since Evans's (1977) pioneering work on the phenomenon. Evans explains the interpretation of various examples in terms of (predicted) implicit binding but nowhere says this forces us to acknowledge aphonic variables in the actual syntactic structures of sentences. To get from implicit binding to aphonic variables in syntax requires an *argument*, presumably a very complex one. Let me be very clear about one thing. I am all in favor of Stanley constructing a theory in which the interpretation of, say, (2) proceeds by way of interpreting an aphonic variable in its actual syntactic structure; what I am opposed to is the dismissive idea that the mere presentation of such a theory is ipso facto a proof of its correctness and a demonstration of the failure of any theory not positing such a syntactic structure.

142. "The output of the syntactic processes that is visible to semantic interpretation" (Stanley and Szabó 2000, 247).

143. Barwise and Cooper 1981; Higginbotham and May 1981; May 1977; Neale 1990. Alternatively one could use the binary quantifiers of Davies 1981, Evans 1977, 1982, and Wiggins 1980.

144. Notice that the problem of how to unify the semantics of transitive verbs, prepositions, and any other expressions that, in surface syntax at least, may take singular terms and quantifiers as arguments disappears on this account, as the variables left by quantifier movement are singular terms.

145. Why the parenthetical qualification? Because it is arguable that the gender and number of a bound pronoun is not semantically inert. For simplicity, in (5') I have suppressed the fact that relative clauses, even when truncated as in (5), are typically seen as introducing more binding, relative pronouns acting as abstraction operators. See Quine 1960b; Evans 1977; and Heim and Kratzer 1998.

146. Neale 1990, 2004.

147. It should be clear that relativization is narrower than variation per se. Example (3) exemplifies variation without relativization in my sense. With some quantifiers, variation may be induced only via relativization. Consider (i):

(i)   Everyone mocks the mayor.

The semantics of 'the', on Russell's account, involves uniqueness, so read as (i') there is no variation:

(i')   [*every* x_1: *person* x_1] [*the* x_2: *mayor* x_2] (x_1 *mocks* x_2).

But, of course, the incomplete description in (i) can be understood as relativized:

(i'')   [*every* x_1: *person* x_1] [*the* x_2: x_1's *mayor* x_2] (x_1 *mocks* x_2).

Further familiar examples are discussed below. For discussion of this topic, see Beghelli, Ben-Shalom, and Szabolcsi 1997.

148. Geach 1962, 1972; Heim 1988; Heim and Kratzer 1998; Neale 2005; Partee 1975; Salmon 1986, 1992; Soames 1990, 1994; and Wiggins 1976. λ is the *lambda* (or *abstraction*) operator. On the usage adopted here, $\lambda x(x \; snores)$ and $\lambda x(x \; loves \; x)$ are one-place predicates. Thus, *John*$(\lambda x(x \; loves \; x))$ is a sentence.

149. Why do I say "in some way to be elucidated"? Hasn't enough been said? Not yet. In order to explicate binding by a singular term we need to mirror the *abstraction* introduced by quantification that explicates binding by quantifiers. (See Soames 1989 for discussion.) We could do this by treating names as quantifiers, perhaps in the manner of Montague (1974) or Barwise and Cooper (1981). If one is determined to resist the idea that names are quantifiers, the relevant abstraction can be captured in other ways. One increasingly popular idea is that (i) the intransitive verb 'snores' is understood as having the structure of the formal device $\lambda x(x \; snores)$; and the transitive verb 'loves', is understood as having the structure of the formal device $\lambda y(\lambda x(x \; loves \; y))$; (ii) in consequence, the predicate 'loves himself' really has a structure something like that of the formal predicate $\lambda x(x \; loves \; x)$, assuming an interpretive principle for the reflexive pronoun that distinguishes it from its nonreflexive counterparts in forcing $y = x$, so to speak; and (iii) to say that a pronoun β is bound by some expression α is to say that α merges with (is concatenated with) verb phrase whose λ-operator binds β. See Heim and Kratzer 1998 and Neale 2005.

150. See Soames 1990, 1994.

151. And, if that is right, in order to preserve as much strict compositionality as possible, shouldn't we see all predicates as ultimately devices of abstraction, 'snores' expressing $\lambda x(x \; snores)$, 'loves' expressing $\lambda y(\lambda x(x \; loves \; y))$, and so on?

152. Castañeda 1966, 1967, 1968; Partee 1975; Salmon 1986, 1992; and Soames 1989, 1990, 1994.

153. See Soames 1989, 1994.

154. For discussion of VP-deletion, see Keenan 1971, Sag 1976, and Williams 1977. For more recent, user-friendly discussions of linguistic ellipsis, see Heim and Kratzer 1998 and May 2002.

155. Stanley and Szabó (2000) appear to accept this, saying of VP deletion that it is "a syntactic phenomenon, due to some sort of syntactic rule of reconstruction or copying, or PF deletion under a syntactic parallelism condition" (226, n.9).

156. See Dosen 1988 and Peregrin 1995, 2000.

157. See the papers in Boettner and Thümmel 2000.

158. In a footnote, Stanley (2000, 400, n.13) suggests that the substance of his main claim is unaffected by the existence of variable-free systems. In variable-free systems, he says, (i) variables are eliminated in favor of operators, and (ii) whenever his own theory postulates aphonic variables in the syntax of some sentence X, a variable-free theory will have to posit aphonic operators or functionals somewhere in X. Several issues could be taken up here, but I will mention just two. First, Stanley's remarks on this topic make it look as though the substance of his main claim is that there must be aphonics in syntax, not the original claim (that every purported unarticulated

constituent is the value assigned to some aphonic item in syntax). Second, the principle motivation for variable-free systems is a desire to run a genuinely compositional semantics on surface structure and overcoming well-known compositional difficulties for systems containing bound variables, phonic or aphonic. To the best of my knowledge, no one has presented any sort of argument for the thesis that variable-free systems cannot be produced without positing aphonic operators in syntactic structure. The truth of the thesis is not obvious to me, nor, I think, is its truth presupposed in the variable-free tradition. It is an interesting open question whether a genuinely compositional semantics can be run on surface forms, and of course much turns on what is understood by "compositional." This is an area fraught with technical difficulties.

159. A pronoun can be bound only by an expression that c-commands it.

160. On Evans's account, the larger group to which E-type pronouns belongs also includes descriptive names such as 'Julius', introduced by a description such as 'the man who invented the zip'. See Evans 1982, 1985 for discussion.

161. I say Evans's E-type theory is "meant to deliver" the correct relativized readings of (20) and (21) because certain contortions are required to make the theory fly. To speak very loosely, the relativized description that fixes the relativized reference of the pronoun must be invoked at the right point in the interpretation in order to get the required relativization. There are various problems here. See Soames 1989 and Neale 1990. These problems do not affect the D-type theory discussed below.

162. D-type theories are presented by Cooper (1979), Davies (1981), Ludlow and Neale (1991), Neale (1990, 1993), and Parsons (1978). One of the main reasons for going D-type is that scope ambiguities of the sort found with overt descriptions can now be explained:

(i)   The mayor is a Republican. He used to be a Democrat.

(ii) A man robbed Mary. The FBI think the local police think he is from out of town.

163. Just as there is no commitment in the D-type idea itself to LFs containing spelled out descriptions where PFs contain just pronouns, so there is no commitment in the idea to the view that the description for which a particular D-type pronoun goes proxy can be extracted by some automatic procedure from the immediate linguistic context. In Neale 1990, 1993, 1994, I toyed with the idea of specifying the understood descriptive content of D-type pronouns using a simple algorithm and pointed to problems suggesting retrieval was a looser pragmatic matter, perhaps guided or shaped by formal factors and strong interpretive heuristics. A default procedure or heuristic seems to yield extremely good results in very many cases.

What should LF theorists who advocate D-type accounts of unbound anaphora say about the LFs of (21), (21$'$) and (21$''$)? This is something I took up in Neale 1993. Given the role LFs are supposed to play in syntactic theory, I suggest roughly the following:

(i)   [every^1 villager$_1$ who^3 [[[just one]^2 donkey$_2$]^2 [$_S$ e_3 owns e_2]]$_1$]^1 [it]^2 [$_S$ e_1 feeds e_2 at night].

(i$'$) [every^1 villager$_1$ who^3 [[[just one]^2 donkey$_2$]^2 [$_S$ e_3 owns e_2]]$_1$]^1 [the^2 donkey$_2$]^2 [$_S$ e_1 feeds e_2 at night].

(i″) [every[1] villager₁ who[3] [[[just one][2] donkey₂][2] [$_S$ e_3 owns e_2]]₁][1] [the[2] donkey₂ e_1 owns e_2][2]
     [$_S$ e_1 feeds e_2 at night].

In (i) 'it' has been raised, which goes hand in hand with its interpretation as a quantifier, indeed as a description, a full descriptive content for which the speaker expects the hearer to come up with pragmatically, just as with the incomplete description in (i′).

164. Neale 1990 (182 and 266), cited and used on their page 257.

165. The arguments used by Stanley (2002a, 2002b) assume the same. The plot thickens here. First, Stanley and Szabó (2000) fail to see their alleged refutation of the "explicit" approach to incomplete descriptions would, if successful, ipso facto be a refutation of the theory of D-type anaphora they appeal to in their argument against Westerståhl, as D-type pronouns are essentially limiting cases of incomplete descriptions. Stanley and Szabó, however, do not actually present any argument against the explicit approach: they attack an implausible syntactic implementation of that approach I doubt anyone has ever held, according to which a sentence whose PF contains an incomplete description like 'the table' contains a complete description such as 'the table at which we are now sitting' at LF. (For discussion, see Neale 2004.) But this misfire does not actually get them off the hook. Either they construe the D-type theory they claim to be using in their argument as involving the appearance of definite descriptions at LF where there are only D-type pronouns at PF, or they do not. Either way, there is trouble. If they do, then their argument against the approach they *mistake* for the explicit approach will be ipso facto an argument against what they *take* to be the D-type theory they appeal to. If they don't, then they are accepting that there can be relativization without variable-binding.

166. In a paper that Stanley points us to for more detail, Stanley and Szabó (2000) say they adopt a generalized quantifier account of determiners (of the sort proposed by Barwise and Cooper 1981 and others) according to which they express relations between sets. Stanley (2000, 419, n.31) takes the restrictions on quantifier domains to be intensional entities.

References

Aoun, J. 1985. *A Grammar of Anaphora*. Cambridge, Mass.: MIT Press.

Bach, K. 1981. "Referential/Attributive." *Synthese* 49: 219–244.

———. 1994. *Thought and Reference*. Reprint edition. Oxford: Oxford University Press.

Baltin, M. 1987. "Do Antecedent-Contained Deletions Exist?" *Linguistic Inquiry* 18: 579–595.

Barwise, J., and R. Cooper. 1981. "Generalized Quantifiers and Natural Language." *Linguistics and Philosophy* 4: 159–219.

Barwise, J., and J. Perry. 1983. *Situations and Attitudes*. Cambridge, Mass.: MIT Press.

Beghelli, F., D. Ben-Shalom, and A. Szabolcsi. 1997. "Variation, Distributivity and the Illusion of Branching." In A. Szabolcsi (ed.), *Ways of Scope Taking*. Dordrecht: Kluwer.

Böttner. M., and W. Thümmel. 2000. *Variable-Free Semantics*. Osnabrück: Secolo-Verlag.

Breheny, R. 2002. "The Current State of (Radical) Pragmatics in the Cognitive Sciences." *Mind and Language* 17: 169–187.

Bresnan. J. 1982. *The Mental Representation of Grammatical Relations*. Cambridge, Mass.: MIT Press.

———. 2001. *Lexical-Functional Syntax*. Oxford: Blackwell.

Carston, R. 1988. "Implicature, Explicature, and Truth-theoretic Semantics." In R. Kempson (ed.), *Mental Representations: The Interface between Language and Reality*. Cambridge: Cambridge University Press.

———. 2002. *Thoughts and Utterances*. Oxford: Blackwell.

Castañeda, H. N. 1966. "'He': A Study in the Logic of Self-Consciousness." *Ratio* 8: 130–157.

———. 1967. "Indicators and Quasi-Indicators." *American Philosophical Quarterly* 4: 85–100.

———. 1968. "On the Philosophical Foundations of the Theory of Communication: Reference." In P. French, T. Uehling, Jr., and H. Wettstein (eds.), *Contemporary Perspectives in the Philosophy of Language*. Minneapolis: University of Minnesota Press.

Chomsky, N. 1976. "Conditions on Rules of Grammar." *Linguistic Analysis* 2: 303–351.

———. 1980. *Rules and Representations*. Oxford: Blackwell.

———. 1981. *Lectures on Government and Binding*. Dordrecht: Foris.

———. 1986. *Knowledge of Language: Its Nature, Origin, and Use*. New York: Praeger.

———. 1995. *The Minimalist Program*. Cambridge, Mass.: MIT Press.

———. 2000. *New Horizons in the Study of Language and Mind*. Cambridge: Cambridge University Press.

———. 2002. *On Nature and Language*. Cambridge: Cambridge University Press.

Cohen, S. 1999. "Contextualism, Skepticism, and the Structure of Reasons." *Philosophical Perspectives* 13: 57–89.

Cooper, R. 1979. "The Interpretation of Pronouns." In F. Heny and H. Schnelle (eds.), *Syntax and Semantics*. Vol. 10: *Selections from the Third Gröningen Round Table*. New York: Academic Press.

Crimmins, M. 1992. *Talk about Belief*. Cambridge, Mass.: MIT Press.

Crimmins, M., and J. Perry. 1989. "The Prince and the Phone Booth: Reporting Puzzling Beliefs." *Journal of Philosophy* 86: 685–711.

Davidson, D. 1967. "The Logical Form of Action Sentences." In N. Rescher (ed.), *The Logic of Decision and Action*. Pittsburgh: University of Pittsburgh Press. Reprinted in Davidson 1980.

———. 1980. *Essays on Actions and Events*. Oxford: Clarendon Press.

Davies, M. 1981. *Meaning, Quantification, Necessity*. London: Routledge and Kegan Paul.

De Rose, K. 1999. "Contextualism in Epistemology: An Explanation and Defence." *Noûs* supplement 13: 57–89.

Donnellan, K. 1966. "Reference and Definite Descriptions." *Philosophical Review* 75: 281–304.

———. 1968. "Putting Humpty Dumpty Back Together Again." *Philosophical Review* 77: 203–215.

Dosen, K. 1988. "Second-Order Logic without Variables." In W. Buszkowski, W. Marcizsewski, and J. van Benthem (eds.), *Categorial Grammar*. Amsterdam: Benjamins.

Elbourne, P. 2001. "E-Type Anaphora as NP-Deletion." *Natural Language Semantics* 9: 241–288.

Evans, G. 1977. "Pronouns, Quantifiers, and Relative Clauses (I)." *Canadian Journal of Philosophy* 7: 467–536. Reprinted in Evans 1985.

———. 1980. "Pronouns." *Linguistic Inquiry* 11: 337–362.

———. 1982. *The Varieties of Reference*. Oxford: Clarendon Press.

———. 1985. *Collected Papers*. Oxford: Clarendon Press.

Fara, D. G. 2001. "Descriptions as Predicates." *Philosophical Studies* 102: 1–42.

Fodor, J. 2001. "Language, Thought, and Compositionality." *Mind and Language* 16: 1–15.

Frege, G. 1892/1952. "Über Sinn und Bedeutung." *Zeitschrift für Philosophie und Philosophische Kritik* 100: 25–50. Translated as "On Sense and Meaning." In P. Geach and M. Black (eds.), *Translations from the Philosophical Writings of Gottlob Frege*. Oxford: Blackwell.

Gazdar, G., E. Klein, G. Pullum, and I. Sag. 1985. *Generalized Phrase Structure Grammar*. Oxford: Blackwell, and Cambridge, Mass.: Harvard University Press.

Geach. P. T. 1962. *Reference and Generality*. Ithaca, N.Y.: Cornell University Press.

———. 1972. *Logic Matters*. Oxford: Blackwell.

Grice, H. P. 1961. "The Causal Theory of Perception." *Proceedings of the Aristotelian Society* (supplement) 35: 121–152. Reprinted in Grice 1989.

———. 1969. "Utterer's Meaning and Intentions." *Philosophical Review* 78: 147–177.

———. 1970. "Lectures on Logic and Reality." University of Illinois at Urbana.

———. 1981. "Presupposition and Conversational Implicature." In P. Cole (ed.), *Radical Pragmatics*. New York: Academic Press.

———. 1989. *Studies in the Ways of Words*. Cambridge, Mass: Harvard University Press.

Heim, I. 1988. *The Semantics of Definite and Indefinite Noun Phrases*. New York: Garland.

———. 1990. "E-Type Pronouns and Donkey Anaphora." *Linguistics and Philosophy* 13: 137–178.

Heim, I., and Kratzer, A. 1998. *Semantics in Generative Grammar*. Oxford: Blackwell.

Higginbotham, J. 1980. "Pronouns and Bound Variables." *Linguistic Inquiry* 11: 679–708.

———. 1983. "Logical Form, Binding, and Nominals." *Linguistic Inquiry* 14: 395–420.

Higginbotham, J., and May, R. 1981. "Questions, Quantifiers, and Crossing." *Linguistic Review* 1: 41–80.

Hornstein, N. 1984. *Logic as Grammar*. Cambridge, Mass.: MIT Press.

Huang, C.-T. J. 1982. "Move *WH* in a Language without *Wh*-movement." *Linguistic Review* 1: 369–416.

———. 1995. "Logical Form." In G. Webelhuth (ed.), *Government and Binding Theory and the Minimalist Program*. Oxford: Blackwell.

Husserl, E. 1913/1970. *Logische Untersuchungen, Zweiter Band*. 2nd ed. Halle: Niemeyer. Translated by J. N. Findlay. London: Routledge and Kegan Paul.

Jacobson, P. 1999. "Towards a Variable-Free Semantics." *Linguistics and Philosophy* 22: 117–184.

Kaplan, D. 1978. "Dthat." In P. Cole (ed.), *Syntax and Semantics*. Vol. 9: *Pragmatics*. New York: Academic Press.

———. 1989a. "Afterthoughts." In J. Almog, J. Perry, and H. Wettstein (eds.), *Themes from Kaplan*. New York: Oxford University Press.

———. 1989b. "Demonstratives." In J. Almog, J. Perry, and H. Wettstein (eds.), *Themes from Kaplan*. New York: Oxford University Press.

Kaplan, D., and J. Bresnan. 1982. "Lexical-Functional Grammar: A Formal System for Grammatical Representation." In J. Bresnan (ed.), *The Mental Representation of Grammatical Relations*. Cambridge, Mass.: MIT Press.

Karttunen, L., and S. Peters. 1979. "Conventional Implicature." In C. K. Oh and D. Dinneen (eds.), *Syntax and Semantics*. Vol. 11: *Presuppositions*. New York: Academic Press.

Keenan, E. 1971. "Names, Quantifiers, and the Sloppy Identity Problem." *Papers in Linguistics* 4: 211–232.

Kripke, S. 1977. "Speaker Reference and Semantic Reference." In P. A. French, T. E. Uehling, Jr., and H. K. Wettstein (eds.), *Contemporary Perspectives in the Philosophy of Language*. Minneapolis: University of Minnesota Press.

———. 1979. "A Puzzle about Belief." In A. Margalit (ed.), *Meaning and Use*. Dordrecht: Reidel.

———. 1980. *Naming and Necessity*. Cambridge, Mass.: Harvard University Press.

Larson, R., and G. Segal. 1995. *Knowledge of Meaning*. Cambridge: MIT Press.

Lewis, D. 1979. Scorekeeping in a Language Game. *Journal of Philosophical Logic* 8: 339–359.

———. 1986. "Elusive Knowledge." *Australasian Journal of Philosophy* 74: 549–567.

Ludlow, P. 1989. "Implicit Comparison Classes." *Linguistics and Philosophy* 12: 519–533.

Ludlow, P., and S. Neale. 1991. "Indefinite Descriptions: In Defence of Russell." *Linguistics and Philosophy* 14: 171–202.

Lyons, J. 1969. *Introduction to Theoretical Linguistics*. Cambridge: Cambridge University Press.

MacFarlane, J. 2003. "Future Contingents and Relative Truth." *Philosophical Quarterly* 53: 321–336.

———. 2005. "Making Sense of Relative Truth." *Proceedings of the Aristotelian Society* 105: 321–339.

Mates, B. 1973. "Descriptions and Reference." *Foundations of Language* 10: 409–418.

May, R. 1977. "The Grammar of Quantification." Doctoral dissertation, Massachusetts Institute of Technology.

———. 1985. *Logical Form: Its Structure and Derivation*. Cambridge, Mass.: MIT Press.

———. 2002. "Ellipsis." In *Macmillan Encyclopaedia of Cognitive Science*. London: Macmillan.

McGinn, C. 1983. *The Subjective View*. Oxford: Blackwell.

Montague, R. 1974. *Formal Philosophy: Selected Papers of Richard Montague*. R. Thomason (ed.), New Haven, Conn.: Yale University Press.

Montague, R. 1974. "The Proper Treatment of Quantification in Ordinary English." In R. Thomason (ed.), *Formal Philosophy: Selected Papers of Richard Montague*. New Haven: Yale University Press.

Neale, S. 1990. *Descriptions*. Cambridge, Mass.: MIT Press.

———. 1993. "Grammatical Form, Logical Form, and Incomplete Symbols." In A. D. Irvine and G. A. Wedeking (eds.), *Russell and Analytic Philosophy*. Toronto: University of Toronto Press.

———. 1994. "Logical Form and LF." In C. Otero (ed.), *Noam Chomsky: Critical Assessments*. London: Routledge and Kegan Paul.

———. 1999. "Colouring and Composition." In R. Stainton (ed.), *Philosophy and Linguistics*. Boulder, Colo.: Westview Press.

———. 2004. "This, That and the Other." In A. Bezuidenhout and M. Reimer (eds.), *Descriptions and Beyond*. Oxford: Oxford University Press.

———. 2005. "Pragmatism and Binding." In Z. Szabo (ed.), *Semantics versus Pragmatics*. Oxford: Oxford University Press.

Neale, S. Forthcoming. *Linguistic Pragmatism*. Oxford: Oxford University Press.

O'Rourke, M. 1998. "Semantics and the Dual-Aspect Use of Definite Descriptions." *Pacific Philosophical Quarterly* 79: 264–288.

———. 2003. "The Scope Argument." *Journal of Philosophy* 100: 136–157.

Parsons, T. 1978. "Pronouns as Paraphrases." Unpublished manuscript.

Partee, B. 1975. "Deletion and Variable Binding." In E. Keenan (ed.), *Formal Semantics of Natural Languages*. Cambridge: Cambridge University Press.

———. 1989. "Binding Implicit Variables in Quantified Contexts." In C. Wiltshire, B. Music, and R. Graczyk (eds.), *Proceedings of the Chicago Linguistics Society 25*. Chicago: Chicago Linguistic Society.

Peregrin, J. 1995. *Doing Worlds and Words*. Dordrecht: Kluwer.

———. 2000. "Variables in Natural Language: Where Do They Come From?" In M. Böttner and W. Thümmel (eds.), *Variable-Free Semantics*. Osnabrück: Secolo-Verlag.

Perry, J. 1977. "Frege on Demonstratives." *Philosophical Review* 86: 474–497. Reprinted in Perry 2000.

———. 1979. "The Problem of the Essential Indexical." *Noûs* 13: 3–21. Reprinted in Perry 2000.

———. 1986. "Thought without Representation." *Proceedings of the Aristotelian Society* (supplement) 60: 137–151.

———. 1993. *The Problem of the Essential Indexical and Other Essays*. Oxford: Oxford University Press.

———. 1998. "Contexts and Unarticulated Constituents." In *Proceedings of the 1995 CSLA-Amsterdam Logic, Language, and Computation Conference*. Stanford, Calif.: CSLI Publications.

———. 2000. *The Problem of the Essential Indexical and Other Essays*. Expanded ed. Stanford, Calif.: CSLI Publications.

———. 2001. *Reference and Reflexivity*. Stanford, Calif.: CSLI Publications.

Quine, W. V. 1940. *Mathematical Logic*. Cambridge, Mass.: Harvard University Press.

———. 1960a. "Variables Explained Away." *Proceedings of the American Philosophical Society* 104: 343–347.

———. 1960b. *Word and Object*. Cambridge, Mass.: MIT Press.

Récanati, F. 1989. "Referential/Attributive: A Contextualist Proposal." *Philosophical Studies* 56: 217–249.

———. 1993. *Direct Reference: From Language to Thought*. Oxford: Blackwell.

———. 2001. "What Is Said." *Synthese* 128: 75–91.

———. 2002. "Unarticulated Constituents." *Linguistics and Philosophy* 25: 299–345.

Reichenbach, H. 1947. *Elements of Symbolic Logic*. London: Macmillan.

Reinhart, T., and E. Reuland. 1993. "Reflexivity." *Linguistic Inquiry* 24: 657–720.

Reuland, E. 2001. "Primitives of Binding." *Linguistic Inquiry* 32: 439–492.

Russell, B. 1948. *An Inquiry into Meaning and Truth*. Harmondsworth: Penguin.

Sag, I. 1976. Deletion and Logical Form. Ph.D. diss., Massachusetts Institute of Technology.

Sag, I., and T. Wasow. 1999. *Syntactic Theory: A Formal Introduction*. Chicago: University of Chicago Press.

Sainsbury, M. 2002. *Departing from Frege: Essays in the Philosophy of Language*. London: Routledge.

Salmon, N. 1986. "Reflexivity." *Notre Dame Journal of Formal Logic* 27: 401–429.

———. 1992. "Reflections of Reflexivity." *Linguistics and Philosophy* 15: 53–63.

Scalia. A. 1997. *A Matter of Interpretation: Federal Courts and the Law*. Princeton, N.J.: Princeton University Press.

Schiffer, S. 2003. *The Things We Mean*. Oxford: Oxford University Press.

Searle, J. 1969. *Speech Acts*. Cambridge: Cambridge University Press.

———. 1979. *Expression and Meaning*. Cambridge: Cambridge University Press.

———. 1980. "The Background of Meaning." In J. R. Searle, F. Kiefer, and M. Bierwisch (eds.), *Speech Act Theory and Pragmatics*. Dordrecht: Reidel.

Sellars, W. 1954. "Presupposing." *Philosophical Review* 63: 197–215.

Soames, S. 1986. "Incomplete Definite Descriptions." *Notre Dame Journal of Formal Logic* 27: 349–375.

———. 1989. "Review of Gareth Evans, *Collected Papers*." *Journal of Philosophy* 89: 141–156.

———. 1990. "Pronouns and Propositional Attitudes." *Proceedings of the Aristotelian Society* 90: 191–212.

———. 1994. "Attitudes and Anaphora." *Philosophical Perspectives* 9: 251–272.

Sosa, D. 2001. "The Unintentional Fallacy." *California Law Review* 919: 932–936.

Sperber, D., and D. Wilson. 1981. "Irony and the Use-Mention Distinction." In P. Cole (ed.), *Radical Pragmatics*. New York: Academic Press.

———. 1986. *Relevance: Communication and Cognition*. Oxford: Blackwell.

———. 1995. *Relevance: Communication and Cognition*. 2nd ed. Oxford: Blackwell.

Stalnaker, R. 1978. "Assertion." In P. Cole (ed.), *Syntax and Semantics*. Vol. 9: *Pragmatics*. New York: Academic Press.

Stanley, J. 2000. "Context and Logical Form." *Linguistics and Philosophy* 23: 391–434.

———. 2002a. "Making It Articulated." *Mind and Language* 17: 149–168.

———. 2002b. "Nominal Restriction." In G. Peters and G. Preyer (eds.), *Logical Form and Language*. Oxford: Oxford University Press.

Stanley, J., and Z. Szabó. 2000. "On Quantifier Domain Restriction." *Mind and Language* 15: 219–261.

Strawson, P. F. 1950. "On Referring." *Mind* 59: 320–344.

Szabolcsi, A. 1989. "Bound Variables in Syntax (Are There Any?)." In R. Bartsch, J. van Benthem, and T. van Emde Boas (eds.), *Semantics and Contextual Expression*. Dordrecht: Foris.

———. 1994. "The Noun Phrase." In F. Kiefer and K. Kiss (eds.), *Syntax and Semantics 27: The Syntactic Structure of Hungarian*. New York: Academic Press.

———. 2003. "Binding on the Fly: Cross-Sentential Anaphora in Variable-Free Semantics." In G.-J. Kruijff and T. Oehrle (eds.), *Resource-Sensitivity, Binding and Anaphora*. Dordrecht: Kluwer.

Taylor, K. 2001. "Sex, Breakfast, and Descriptus Interruptus." *Synthese* 128: 45–61.

Westerståhl, D. 1985. "Determiners and Context Sets." In J. van Benthem and A. ter Meulen (eds.), *Quantifiers in Natural Language*. Foris: Dordrecht.

Wettstein, H. 1981. "Demonstrative Reference and Definite Descriptions." *Philosophical Studies* 40: 241–257.

Wiggins, D. 1976. "Identity, Necessity, and Physicalism." In S. Körner (ed.), *Philosophy of Logic*. Berkeley, Calif.: University of California Press.

———. 1980. "'Most' and 'All': Some Comments on a Familiar Programme, and on the Logical Form of Quantified Sentences." In M. Platts (ed.), *Reference, Truth, and Reality*. London: Routledge and Kegan Paul.

Williams, E. 1977. "Discourse and Logical Form." *Linguistic Inquiry* 8: 101–139.

11 Reflections on *Reference and Reflexivity*

Kent Bach

In *Reference and Reflexivity*, John Perry tries to reconcile referentialism with a Fregean concern for cognitive significance. His trick is to supplement referential content with what he calls "reflexive" content. Actually, there are several levels of reflexive content, all to be distinguished from the "official," referential content of an utterance. Perry is convinced by two arguments for referentialism, the "counterfactual truth-conditions" and the "same-saying" arguments, but he also acknowledges the force of two Fregean arguments against it, arguments that pose the "coreference" and the "no-reference" problems. He sees these as genuine problems for referentialism and does not share Howard Wettstein's (1986) view that semantics has "rested on a mistake," the mistake of thinking that semantics is obliged to come to grips with "cognitive significance" and, in particular, to explain the fact that coreferring terms can differ in cognitive significance and that terms lacking in reference can still have cognitive significance. Perry points out that "there is nothing in [the arguments for referentialism] to show that the official content, rather than the reflexive content, is the key to understanding the cognitive motivation and impact of utterances" (Perry 2001, 193).[1] In other words, "a theory of direct reference provides no argument for ignoring reflexive content, and, properly understood, has no motivation for searching for such an argument." Thus Perry uses the notion of reflexive content to complement referentialism with a theory of cognitive significance.

Frege drew a fundamental distinction between the reference of a term and the means by which its reference is determined. In his view, however, it is not the references themselves but the means by which they are determined that enter into propositions ("Thoughts") expressed by sentences in which the terms occur. So we might call Frege an 'indirect reference' theorist. Echoing the introduction to Kaplan's "Afterthoughts" (1989a), Perry stresses that 'direct', as it occurs in 'direct reference', does not imply that "the mechanism of reference is unmediated by the relation of fitting identifying conditions" (188). Identifying conditions can play a significant role in direct reference semantics even though they are not propositional constituents, that is, make no (direct) propositional contribution. Even though indexicals (including demonstratives) and proper names contribute their referents, an utterance containing such a term can have, in addition to its referential content, reflexive content involving the condition for identifying the referent.[2] So, for example, if you utter, "I am hungry," your utterance has as its referential content the singular proposition[3] that you are hungry as well as the reflexive content that the speaker of that utterance is hungry. This explains how it is that, if I hear your utterance without knowing who produced it (I might hear it coming from a distant street corner), I am still in a position to know that it is true if the person producing it is hungry.[4] And, if someone calls me on his cell phone and says, "I'm going to give this man your sandwich. He is hungry," if he is referring to you, the content of the second part of his utterance is the same as that of your utterance of 'I am hungry'. But I might not know that. Still, I know that his utterance is true if the man he is referring to is hungry, and I could coherently suppose it to be true even if, though he is referring to you, I don't think your utterance of 'I am hungry' is true.

This is a simple illustration of Perry's approach. It would be unfair to complain that he doesn't present a systematic defense of his syncretic view, which he dubs the "reflexive-referential" theory. His aim is to sketch its main features and explain how it works. I will not be focusing on it directly, but instead on some of Perry's underlying assumptions and arguments. First, there are his two arguments for referentialism, neither of which seems to show what he thinks they show. Then there is his account of identity statements, which provides an excellent example of how his reflexive-referential theory is supposed to work but also seems to illustrate some difficulties for it. Next, I will look at certain claims Perry makes about the contents of allegedly referential singular terms: proper names, and indexicals and demonstratives. This discussion will invoke the familiar distinction between reference by an expression and reference by a speaker in using an expression. It is easy to confuse the first, which is semantic, with the second, which is pragmatic. Indeed, in the next section I will take up the semantic-pragmatic distinction itself and Perry's conception and application of it. In that connection, I will look at why he attributes contents to utterances rather than to sentences and at the roles played by context in his account. Finally, I will raise some questions about his view of propositional attitude reports and its relation to his account of semantic content and of cognitive significance.

One disclaimer: I will not be discussing many of Perry's interesting and suggestive ideas about what he calls information games, cognitive paths, and notional networks. Indeed, it may very well be that these objections, however valid, have more terminological than substantive implications for these ideas and require merely that they be recast.

The Arguments for Referentialism

Perhaps because his aim is to combine referentialism with a theory of cognitive significance, Perry does not critically evaluate the two arguments he endorses in favor of referentialism, the arguments from counterfactual truth-conditions and from same-saying. Consideration of them will point to the importance of distinguishing speaker reference from semantic reference and to the risks in relying on intuitions about what is said.

In expounding the argument from counterfactual truth-conditions, Perry stresses that "we need to keep clearly in mind the difference between the conditions under which an utterance is true, and the conditions under which what is said by the utterance (or, perhaps better, what the speaker says, in virtue of making the utterance) is true" (85). As he points out, "we can separate these, by considering counterfactual circumstances in which the utterance is false, but what is said by the utterance is true." This is illustrated by an example from Kaplan (1989b, 512–513), who points to Paul and utters, "He now lives in Princeton, New Jersey." If Kaplan had uttered the same words but pointed to someone else, someone who lived in Santa Monica, California, and who he mistook for Paul, what Kaplan would have said would have been false. But he would have said something else. What he actually said would still have been true, even though he wouldn't have said it. The counterfactual circumstances with respect to which what Kaplan actually said would have been false are those in which Paul, the man Kaplan actually pointed to, did not live in Princeton. Similar examples can be given involving proper names and their alleged associated descriptions (5).

This argument does not show that indexicals and demonstratives are directly referential but, at most, that they are rigid.[5] Being rigid may be necessary for being directly referential, but it is not sufficient. For all this argument shows, names and indexicals, instead of contributing their references to propositions expressed by sentences in which they occur, could just as well have rigid descriptive contents, just like rigid definite descriptions, such as 'the square of 3' or 'the actual inventor of the zipper'. So the counterfactual argument does not show that indexicals or names are directly referential. As far as reference is concerned, the most that it shows is that the *speaker's reference* in *using* an indexical or a name is rigid. That is, if a speaker who makes a statement uses a name or indexical to refer to a certain individual, were he to have used it to refer to someone else, perhaps because he mistook that person for the one he actually referred to, he would have made a different statement; his actual statement could have a different truth value only if the individual he actually referred to were different.

As for the same-saying argument, it is basically an appeal to intuition. Perry relies on the fact that "we need to say things whose truth or falsity turns on the same objects having the same properties, or standing in the same relations" (5). For example, regardless of what descriptions (or identifying conditions) different people associate with the name 'Clinton' when uttering, say, "Clinton likes pickles with his hamburgers," they "have said the same thing if what [they] each say is true if Clinton likes pickles with his hamburgers, and false if he doesn't." Unfortunately, this argument assumes that if two speakers ascribe the same property to the same individual, they are saying the same thing altogether. Intuitively, that may often seem to be a distinction without a difference, but sometimes substituting one term for another, coreferring term does make an intuitive difference. Ask typical nonphilosophers to compare utterances of sentences like these:

(1a)   Eminem is insecure

(1b)   Marshall Mathers is insecure

and they are likely to indicate that what a speaker says in uttering (1b) is different from what someone says in uttering (1a). Even people who know that Eminem is Marshall Mathers, but know that others don't, are disinclined to suppose that speakers of (1a) and of (1b) are saying the same thing. Intuitively, there is a difference between saying that Marshall Mathers is insecure and saying that Eminem is insecure, even though the same property is ascribed to the same individual and the two utterances are true under the same actual and counterfactual circumstances. Intuitively, different things are said, at least according to people not prejudiced by philosophical theories. The claim that (1a) and (1b) have the same "official" content depends on who's officiating.

Identity Statements and Reflexive Content

Whereas the referential content of an utterance is the proposition it expresses, its "official" content, as best I can tell a reflexive content of an utterance is any proposition derived from the referential content by replacing one or more constituent with its identifying condition. So, for example, a reflexive content of an utterance of 'I love you' is the proposition that the speaker of that utterance loves the addressee of that utterance. Similarly, a reflexive content of an utterance of 'I love Sally' is the proposition that the speaker of that utterance loves the person the convention exploited by that use of 'Sally' permits the speaker to designate (108). These are propositions one could know to be true without knowing the referential contents of the relevant terms, but Perry is making a much stronger claim about reflexive contents. He suggests that in certain cases they comprise the contents of utterances when the referential content does not capture all, or even much, of what the speaker is trying to convey.

Identity statements provide an excellent example. They figure centrally in Frege's puzzle, illustrated by the sentences in (2).

(2a)   Marshall Mathers is Eminem.

(2b)   Eminem is Eminem.

These have the same referential content but differ in their information value, hence their cognitive significance. It is important to note that this difference does not depend on the triviality of (2b), that it is of the form '$a = a$'. Suppose that Eminem adopted a new stage name, 'Sniff Kitty'. Then (3a) and (3b) would also differ in cognitive significance from (2a).

(3a)   Marshall Mathers is Sniff Kitty.

(3b)   Eminem is Sniff Kitty.

Indeed, the sentences in (1), as well as 'Sniff Kitty is insecure', would also all differ in cognitive significance. In any case, Perry thinks that identity statements are a special case, because of their triviality: "In the case of identity statements, the triviality (true or false) of the referential content triggers a default mechanism; the default, referential, candidate is trivial, so we look for something meatier at the intentional or reflexive level" (163). So if you utter (2a), whose referential content is a necessarily true but trivial singular identity proposition about a certain white rapper, you are implicitly making a further claim. This claim is an informative, contingent claim to the effect that your use of the two names exploits conventions that together permit one to designate the same individual. That is Perry's version of it, anyway. Another, simpler candidate for the relevant reflexive content, one that requires less familiarity with Perry's account of names, is the proposition that the referent of 'Marshall Mathers' is (identical to) the referent of 'Eminem'. This too is an informative, contingent proposition that is distinct from the official, referential content of an utterance of (2a).

Why does Perry think there is something special about identity statements? "In the most central cases," he writes, "referential content will get at the information the speaker wishes to convey. What is said is what is said about the subject-matter; it is how the world has to be for the statement to be true, given the facts about meaning and reference" (119).[6] But there are exceptions. "The very nature of language gives rise to sentences the meaning of which guarantees they will not fit the general picture.

Identity statements using names and indexicals are a case in point. They will virtually never be used with the intent of conveying their referential content, which will always be necessarily true or necessarily false" (119–120). Identity statements are one example, but there are obvious others, such as those in (4):

(4a)   Marshall Mathers is as wealthy as Eminem.

(4b)   Shaquille O'Neal is no taller than The Big Aristotle.

In Perry's view, "the referential content is the *default* candidate for what is said, but in certain circumstances other levels of content can be, as I will put it, raised to *subject matter*. In cases where referential content will always be trivially and necessarily true or false, the default is overridden. Identity statements trigger the mechanism that replaces the default. We raise some salient empirical content to subject matter" (121).

It is not clear why Perry thinks that this phenomenon is in the "very nature of language." It sounds more like a Gricean quantity implicature—ostensibly asserting a triviality can best be explained on the supposition that one means something that is more informative. Nevertheless, although "language has a core function, which is not to convey information about utterances, or about words, or about languages, or about meanings, or about context, but about the things the words stand for, their subject matter, the reflexive contents are possible because of the architecture of language" (119). It seems to me that they pertain to the nature of language use. I take it that in attributing the possibility of reflexive contents to the architecture of language, Perry is alluding to meaning rules and the identifying conditions they determine for reference; however, insofar as speakers can use a sentence to convey contents other than its semantic content—for example, by exploiting the very fact that they are uttering that sentence—their communicative intentions and their listeners' ability to identify these intentions play a role too. But this takes us beyond semantics to pragmatics.

Even so, Perry is tempted to loosen his conception of "official content" when he writes, "It seems that our concept of what is said is simply too useful to be confined to referential content in all cases. Semantics makes available a system of contents, reflexive and incremental. We choose among them, pragmatically" (163). This way of looking at things is puzzling. How can how "pragmatic" choice affect semantic content? Why should the official content depend on what is useful, or on what speakers are likely to mean? Rather than suppose that what is said is not always confined to referential content, it seems more sensible to suppose that what a speaker says is not always what he means. If Perry is right that utterances of identity sentences are generally made with some further aim than to assert their necessarily true or necessarily false contents, the more natural explanation, in the fashion of Grice, is that the speaker is saying one thing and meaning something else. There is nothing inherently problematic about the fact that with certain sentences this is typically the case.[7]

This way of looking at the matter has an interesting consequence for Perry's picture, for, when a speaker says one thing and means something else, the flow of information is from the first to the second.[8] When Perry introduces the notion of reflexive content, he makes it sound as though it comes in prior to referential content, not as what is being conveyed but as something that can be gleaned from an utterance even if one is not in a position to identify the referents. In his explanation of the informativeness of identity statements, on the other hand, reflexive content comes in after referential content. To appreciate the difference, compare the following two situations. First, suppose you read a postcard that says, "I wish you were here," but the signature and the name of the addressee are badly smudged. Then the referential content is unavailable to you. Still, you can glean from its reflexive content that the speaker wished, at the time of writing, that the intended reader were where the speaker was. However, this is not what the writer was trying to convey. If nothing had been smudged (and if, say, the postcard was addressed to you), you could have grasped the referential content by way of exercising your linguistic competence on the reflexive content, that is, that he (the writer) wished you were there. Now consider a quite different case. Suppose you see a friend walking in the rain and offer her a ride in your car. After she gets in, you say, "I could have been Gene," suggesting to her that she could have mistaken you for your evil twin Gene. Here the reflexive content of your utterance, of 'I' in particular, does enter into what you are trying to convey, to the effect that the person speaking to her then could have been Gene. This is quite different from the situation with the partially illegible postcard.

Compare the two roles of reflexive content. In the one case, reflexive content plays a kind of transitional, computational role between meaning and referential content. Ordinarily, one is able to ascertain the referential contents of utterances containing indexicals, and one does not stop to contemplate their reflexive contents. Moreover, the reflexive content is not what the speaker intends to be conveying (and he does not specifically intend the hearer/reader to take it into account in figuring out what he intends to be conveying). The postcard example is the exception that proves the rule, since in that situation the reflexive content is as far as the reader gets. In the evil-twin example, reflexive content plays a very different role, because it is what the speaker intends to be conveying. In this case, the hearer recognizes the speaker's intention to be conveying something distinct from the referential content, and recognizing that requires recognizing the referential content first. This is more like a case of conversational implicature.[9]

Let me conclude this section with a point that echoes my doubt about the same-saying argument discussed in the previous section. Perry treats identity statements (and other trivially true or trivially false statements) as a special case because their referential content is typically not the conveyed content. But there are other special cases in which what intuitively is the official content is not the referential content but not the reflexive content either. Here is a (false) identity statement and a counterfactual identity statement in which the speaker is likely to be conveying something other than either referential or reflexive content:

(5a)   Marlowe was Shakespeare.

(5b)   Marlowe might have been Shakespeare.

These are statements that claim that Marlowe was, or might have been, the author of the works of Shakespeare, not that he was the person the convention exploited by that use of 'Shakespeare' permits the speaker to designate (or anything of the sort). Then there are statements like these:

(6a)   In 1964 Cassius Clay became Muhammad Ali.

(6b)   In 1964 Muhammad Ali became Cassius Clay.

Intuitively, (6a) seems true and (6b) seems false. I am not claiming here that intuitions about (5) and (6) are correct. The point, rather, if these intuitions are incorrect, as referentialism predicts, then intuitions cannot be taken at face value as reliable evidence about what is said or about semantic content. One can't rely on them when they support one's view and dismiss them when they do not.

Are Singular Terms Inherently Referential?

Perry's strategy for solving the problem of cognitive significance for proper names, indexicals, and demonstratives is to attribute to uses of them (and to utterances of sentences containing them) reflexive as well as referential contents. Whereas referential contents are their "official" contents, their reflexive contents account for their cognitive significance. Here I will not try to assess the internal merits of Perry's reflexive-referentialism but rather will focus on two of his underlying assumptions. In the next section, I will take up his assumption that utterances of sentences, not sentences themselves, have semantic contents, but in this section I will question his assumption that names, indexicals, and demonstratives are inherently referential. The most obvious problem with this assumption is that these terms have nonreferring uses, uses that nonetheless seem perfectly literal. It is not obvious how a referentialist is to explain this. Also, when indexical or demonstrative reference depends on the speaker's intention, it is not clear how to explain that as a semantic rather than pragmatic phenomenon. We should not be misled by the ambiguity of the phrase 'indexical reference', which can mean either reference by an indexical or reference (by a speaker) in using an indexical; 'demonstrative reference' is similarly ambiguous and also suggests that the reference involves a demonstration. After a brief discussion of names, we will look more fully at questions pertaining to indexicals and demonstratives.[10]

Proper Names

Perry's discussion of proper names is limited to standalone occurrences of them, when they are generally used to refer. He does not consider their predicative use or, in particular, their occurrence within quantifier phrases. He uses a few examples of such phrases, for example, 'that David Lewis' (56), 'the David in question' (103), and 'two David Kaplans' (108, 111), but in his account of names he does not mention them. They pose an obvious problem for referentialism, because they seem to involve perfectly literal uses of proper names and should not be dismissed arbitrarily as peripheral.[11] So Perry needs to show either that proper names are systematically ambiguous or that these other uses are not literal. Perhaps he would argue that they are a kind of a reflexive use.[12]

Perry posits "permissive conventions" to explain how proper names refer. Now it is obvious that when an individual is named, an association is established between the name and the individual, but what follows from that? Perry thinks it shows that names (directly) refer. His argument is simply this: "the conventions of language assign names directly to objects, and the propositions containing the names are about those objects" (4). This argument is based on two claims he makes later, that linguistic conventions for proper names "associate them with objects, rather than conditions on objects" (102) and that assigning a name to an individual establishes a permissive convention enabling us to designate the individual named (103).[13]

Obviously names are associated directly with objects—somebody names them. But it hardly follows that propositions containing names are about those objects, that these are singular propositions. That is an entirely separate question. Also, it is far from clear that naming an object establishes a permissive convention for designating. Naming is a conventional act establishing that a certain object has a certain name—this much is a matter of convention—but there does not seem to be an additional convention for referring or any need for one. Compare the naming conventions with the convention for having a Social Security number. Aside from the fact that you get your Social Security number from the government rather than your parents, having a certain Social Security number is the same sort of conventional fact as having a certain name. Even so, we generally do not refer to people by their Social Security numbers. Still, it is easy to imagine circumstances in which we would—say, if names were kept secret and we were introduced to people by their Social Security numbers, or if Social Security numbers were much easier to remember than proper names (imagine that proper names were all at least a hundred syllables long and we didn't use nicknames). In those circumstances, we would expect people to refer to one another by their Social Security numbers. And no special convention would be needed to permit that—people would just do it and recognize when others do it. Similarly, there could be conventions giving names to individuals even if the names were not used to refer to their bearers (maybe they would be used only on things like address labels, luggage tags, and tombstones). If they came to be used to refer, no additional convention would be needed to explain that.

Indexicals and Demonstratives

Perry distinguishes "automatic" indexicals (Kaplan called them "pure" indexicals), such as 'I' and 'today', from "discretionary" indexicals, notably third-person pronouns and demonstratives (60). His account of their meanings and of how these determine reference relative to context presupposes that these terms are all inherently referential (this does not entail that they always succeed in referring). However, although that may be true of automatic indexicals, discretionary indexicals all have nonreferring uses.[14] Here are a few typical examples of such uses:

(7)   Most golfers wear tacky clothes, but *they* don't realize it.

(8)   Always savor your first sip. *That*'s usually the best one.

(9)   (Fire chief: The fire may have been caused by an arsonist.)
       Police chief: If so, *he* will be arrested and prosecuted.

These uses of 'they', 'that', and 'he' are not referential, but they all seem to be perfectly normal, literal uses.[15] But, if they are used literally, whether or not they are used referringly, then these terms are not inherently referential. To show that they are requires showing either that they are systematically ambiguous, with both referential and nonreferential meanings, or that their nonreferring uses are not really literal. This is a very simple and obvious argument, but, as far as I know, it has never been directly rebutted. Rather, referentialists either ignore nonreferring uses or, if they mention them, just stipulate that their account does not apply to such uses, as if this excuses them from giving a uniform account of the meanings of these terms or else showing either that these terms are ambiguous or that their nonreferring uses are not literal. Perry doesn't mention these uses.

Moreover, Perry agrees with Kaplan and many others that the "reference" of a discretionary indexical depends on the speaker's referential intention. If so, how can the reference in question really be semantic rather than merely just a case of speaker reference?[16] In explaining why some indexicals are discretionary, Perry writes, "The designation of an utterance of 'that man'...is not automatic. The speaker's intention is relevant" (62). Several men may be standing together, and "which of them I refer to depends on my intention" (notice that Perry switches from "the designation of an utterance of 'that man'" to "which of them *I* refer to"). But this is already getting into the domain of pragmatics, as is implicit when he explains, "If I intend to secure uptake on the part of my listeners, and them to think of the person to whom I am at least trying to refer, I must do something to make the man salient" (62), unless the object of reference is already salient.[17] If the speaker's referential intention plays a key role and its fulfillment (the hearer's recognition of it) requires something's being salient or being made salient, the relevant intention is part of the speaker's communicative intention, and we are beyond semantics. I will expand on this point in the next section.

The resulting picture is a far cry from Kaplan's official doctrine that demonstratives have characters that can be represented as functions from contexts to contents. That doctrine works smoothly only for pure or automatic indexicals, where values of a short list of contextual parameters determine content. Speaker intention is not another contextual parameter. The meaning of a discretionary indexical or a demonstrative imposes a constraint on the speaker's referential intention, but even within a context there may be several individuals any of which the speaker might intend to use a certain indexical or demonstrative to refer to. Perry takes this "directing" intention, as Kaplan called it (1989a, 582), to be "the intention to refer to an object X simply in virtue of the meanings of one's words and the context, both pre-existing and supplied by the speaker" (60). However, if in the context there are different candidates for being the reference, then obviously context can't determine the reference.[18]

Now consider the distinction Perry draws between two types of context, "narrow" and "wide."[19] It corresponds to the distinction between automatic and discretionary indexicals. Narrow context consists specifically "of facts about which things occupy the essential roles involved in the utterance, which I will take to be the agent, time and position" (59), whereas wide context is anything else relevant to determining what the speaker is trying to convey. Determining of this sort is what the audience does to ascertain what the speaker is uttering, saying, or trying to convey. This is *epistemic* determination. In contrast, the role of context in the narrow sense, to provide values of parameters for determining the reference of context-sensitive expressions, is *constitutive* determination.

The stark difference between constitutive and epistemic determination suggests narrow versus wide context is a distinction in kind. However, something Perry says in the course of introducing the distinction suggests that it is one of degree: "Any indexical will identify an object by a role that it plays in the lives of the speaker and his listeners. And all of these roles will in some way connect with the utterance the speaker makes, for this is the starting point of the cognitive paths on which the speaker relies. But given that, the roles vary tremendously in how intimately they are related to the utterance" (59). However, whereas the reference of an automatic indexical is determined by linguistic meaning as a function of context, the reference of a discretionary indexical (or rather, as I will argue, what the speaker refers to in using it) is a matter of the speaker's intention, not a function of context. Contextual information, information that is mutually salient, is what the speaker exploits in forming his intention to use a certain expression to refer to a certain individual and what his listeners rely on in order to identify that individual, but it does not play a constitutive role. In the course of forming an intention to refer to something and choosing a term to refer to it with, to make his intention evident a speaker exploits what is antecedently salient in the speech situation or makes something salient by demonstrating it or with the words he uses (the gender of a pronoun, the nominal in a demonstrative phrase, or even the predicate in the sentence), but this is to enable his listeners to determine (ascertain) what he is referring to. It involves what Perry calls the "pragmatic use of context," whereby we "interpret the intention with which the utterance was made" (60). But it is important to realize that (wide) context does not determine what the speaker's intention is but merely helps the hearer figure it out. Of course, for this intention to be reasonable, the speaker needs to utter something in that context such that his audience, taking him to have such an intention and relying on contextual information that they can reasonably take him to intend them to take into account, can figure out what that intention is.

Now consider how salience figures in Perry's account of the content of a demonstrative phrase: the "basic content of [an utterance of 'that ϕ'] is the identifying condition, being the salient ϕ to which the speaker of [that utterance of 'that ϕ'] directs attention" (77). It is clear that Perry takes the property of being salient to be part of the meaning of demonstrative phrases. Yet the role of salience is clearly pragmatic. A speaker who wishes to use a simple demonstrative or demonstrative phrase to refer to something needs to make sure that the intended referent is salient not because the meaning of 'that' requires this but because otherwise his audience would not be able to figure out what he is referring to. If he uses the demonstrative to (try to) refer to something that isn't salient, he is not misusing the word 'that', in the sense of using it to mean something it doesn't mean (as he would if, say, he thought 'surreptitious' meant what 'syrupy' means). Rather, he would be committing the pragmatic mistake of trying to refer to something that his listener would have no reason to take him to be referring to. It would be like correctly using arcane words knowing full well that one's audience was unfamiliar with them. Obviously it is not part of the meaning of arcane words that they be uttered only to people who understand them.

The moral here is that there is no fact of the matter, independent of the speaker's referential intention, as to what a discretionary indexical refers to.[20] There is no question as to what the reference is beyond what the speaker intends to refer to and what his audience takes him to refer to (different members of his audience might take him differently). It is only because there is generally no discrepancy between the two that there seems to be a fact of the matter, hence that we can describe (the use of) the discretionary indexical as itself referring rather than merely as being used to refer. Again, we should not be misled by the ambiguity of the phrase 'indexical reference', which can mean either reference by an indexical or reference (by a speaker) in using an indexical.

Attributing semantic properties to utterances of sentences and to specific uses of their constituents, in particular, any discretionary indexicals (including demonstratives) that occur in them, commits a version of what Barwise and Perry called the "fallacy of misplaced information," that is, "the idea that all the information in an utterance must come from its interpretation" (1983, 34). In this case, the fallacy is the idea that utterances have semantic contents in their own right, as opposed to the semantic contents of uttered sentences and the contents of speaker's intentions in uttering them. This is a fallacy because the fact that a certain expression is being used on a given occasion, and with a certain intention, is a pragmatic fact. It, and any further facts attendant on it, do not provide a source of linguistic information but, rather, a basis for inferring the speaker's communicative intention. Intentions don't endow expressions with semantic properties. Expressions have semantic contents, perhaps relative to contexts, independently of the speaker's intention in using them. Otherwise, the speaker would have to know *his* intention in order to know *their* semantic contents.

Here's another way to put the same point. Sentences and their constituent expressions have semantic properties. That is, they encode information that competent speakers know. This information can be contextually variable, but it is still information associated with expressions considered as linguistic types (tokens of linguistic types carry no additional *linguistic* information).[21] Utterances of sentences do not encode information but provide the persons to whom they are directed with evidence for speakers' communicative intentions. This is a very different way of carrying information, and the information so carried plays a very different role. Whereas someone who understands a sentence grasps its semantic content (relative to the context) by virtue of associating certain information with it (and, where necessary, applying values of contextual parameters into lexically mandated slots), to understand an utterance is to identify the communicative intention with which it is made, and that is a matter of inference, not of reading off information.

A corollary of the previous point is that the meanings of discretionary indexicals are not utterance-reflexive. Of course, the intention with which such a term is used is, trivially, an intention the speaker has in making the utterance, but that does not literally make the (constitutive) determination of the reference utterance-reflexive: the indexical itself refers only in the Pickwickian sense that the speaker uses it to refer.

Why Utterance Semantics?

Perry attributes various sorts of contents to utterances. But do utterances really have various contents, and in a way that is semantically relevant? Also, to some extent it seems that what Perry distinguishes as different contents are really different ways of characterizing the same content, from different perspectives or to different degrees of specificity.[22] Finally, it is not clear why he attributes all these contents to utterances and why, in particular, he is unwilling to attribute semantic contents to sentences rather than only to utterances of them. As I see it, his picture of how the different contents come into play encourages a misleading view about the nature of utterances and their relations to what speakers do in producing them and what hearers do in understanding them. Indeed, it tends to blur an independently motivated semantic-pragmatic distinction, one that Perry himself appears to recognize. Although he stresses the difference between what a speaker says and what a speaker conveys in saying it—or what might otherwise be inferred from the fact of the utterance—it seems to me that in certain ways he underplays this difference.

Utterances and Speech Acts

Treating one utterance as having various contents obscures the fact that there are different acts with different contents. Suppose, for example, that an utterance is not literal, as with a likely utterance of 'Bees are electric dewdrops'. Then what the speaker says and what the speaker asserts are two different things. Which is supposed to be the content of his utterance? If it is what the speaker asserts, some such thing as that bees on flowers deliver shocking sensations when touched, then the utterance content would count as semantically relevant even though the utterance is not literal. That can't be right. But, if it is what the speaker says, that bees are electric dewdrops, then the speaker's communicative intention can't play a role in determining what that is, because the intention comes in only at the illocutionary level. Perry does not mention the distinction, familiar from speech act theory and originating with Austin (1962), between locutionary and illocutionary acts, but he does have occasion to invoke speakers' communicative intentions (as well as salience, another pragmatic notion) as determinants of utterance contents, as in his account of discretionary indexicals. At any rate, the distinction between locutionary and illocutionary acts applies to most utterances, and acts of each type have contents. To be sure, one and the same utterance is the performance of both a locutionary and an illocutionary act (more than one if there is an indirect illocutionary act being performed along with a direct one) and is a perlocutionary act too, but still it is misleading to speak simply of utterance contents as if there were no such distinction to be drawn. Only the content of the locutionary act is relevant to semantics, and this is what is said, strictly speaking. However, intuitions about what is said tend to be insensitive to the locutionary/illocutionary distinction, and to the distinction between what is said and what is merely implicit in what is said.[23]

Do Semantic Contents Belong to Utterances?

Syntactic and phonological features belong to linguistic expressions, not to utterances of them. So, for example, speakers with different accents can utter an expression in different ways, thereby producing different-sounding tokens of the expression, but the expression still has the same phonological features. Why should semantic features be any different? In particular, why attribute semantic contents to utterances of expressions rather than to the expressions themselves, as is commonly done, even by referentialists?[24] Here is Perry's explanation: "Contents belong to particular utterances, and should not be confused with meanings, which belong to types of expressions. Meanings are the rules that assign contents to the uses of expressions—that is, to particular utterances" (17). Why does Perry suppose that utterances, rather than sentences, have contents? Because meanings "may exploit contextual factors, and assign different contents to different utterances of the same expression. So content is an attribute of individual utterances" (70).

This rather sketchy argument ignores Kaplan's well-known distinction between utterances and sentences-in-contexts (1989b, 522) and his arguments that favor attributing semantic contents to sentences-in-contexts rather than to utterances. He argues that if semantics is to help explain entailment and formal validity in respect to sentences containing indexicals or demonstratives, it cannot very well take utterances as its subject matter. Citing such obvious facts as that "utterances take time, and [one speaker's] utterances of distinct sentences cannot be simultaneous" (1989b, 546), Kaplan argues that utterance semantics would get the wrong results. He proposes a somewhat idealized conception of context to make allowances for sentences that can be true but cannot be truly uttered ('I am not uttering a sentence'), sentences (or sequences of sentences making up an argument) that take so long to utter that their truth values can change during the course of the utterance, and sentences that are too long to utter at all. Sentences have contents, relative to contexts, but contexts here are not to be taken as contexts in which sentences are actually uttered. Contexts must be construed more abstractly. As Kaplan points out, utterances of sentences such as 'I know a little English' or 'I am alive' are always true, even though their contents are not. Similarly, utterances of sentences such as 'I don't know any English' and 'I am deceased' are always false—they cannot be true relative to a context in which they are uttered—but these sentences can still express truths relative to contexts. For some reason, Perry does not mention, much less rebut Kaplan's arguments (or others') that favor attributing semantic contents to sentences-in-contexts rather than to utterances.[25]

These arguments and special examples aside, there are general reasons for being wary of utterance semantics. Perry makes clear that by 'utterance' he means an intentional act by a speaker (or by extension, a writer or even gesturer), not a token of a linguistic type.[26] But, if one would rather attribute content to the intentional act of uttering a sentence than to the sentence being uttered, one might as well attribute the content to the speaker's intention.[27] So, in regard to Perry's claim that utterances have multiple contents,[28] it would seem that these putative utterance contents are really the contents of different intentions on the part of the speaker (except for those that are really sentence contents). But if that's the correct way of putting things, then to say that utterances have multiple contents is just to say that they can be made with multiple intentions, each with its own content (presumably intentions don't have multiple contents). So, insofar as putative contents of utterances are really contents of intentions, the different contents are really contents of distinct items.

Also, utterances are often nonliteral and/or indirect and perhaps almost always not strictly literal.[29] Presumably it is not the business of semantics to account for the contents of utterances that are not strictly literal, because in such cases the speaker is trying to convey something that is not predictable from the meaning of the uttered sentence (or, if it is ambiguous, from its operative meaning), relative to the context. Otherwise, anything that a speaker means would count as semantic content, however far removed it is from what the sentence means. But semantic content is independent of whether an utterance is strictly literal or not. Indeed, it is independent of any linguistic errors (misspeaking, linguistic misunderstanding) on the part of the speaker. So it might as well be regarded, in the usual way, as a property of sentences, albeit relative to contexts.

Semantics and Pragmatics

Perry accepts a semantic-pragmatic distinction, but it is not clear how, or under what conditions, his different levels of utterance content count as semantic or pragmatic.[30] In fact, it is not clear what for him counts as semantic and what as pragmatic. In the only place where he is explicit about it, Perry writes, "there is an intuitive distinction between what someone literally said and what is conveyed when we take into account why she said it. Traditionally, the first is included in semantics, the second in pragmatics" (48–49). He then briefly mentions the speaker's reasoning in choosing what to say and the hearer's reasoning in figuring out why she said it. He describes the hearer's reasoning as "a species of inference to the best explanation." If we accept Grice's conception of communication (Perry never mentions Grice), presumably what makes it special is that it is reasoning the speaker intends him to engage in, partly on the basis that he is intended to.

I share this conception of the semantic-pragmatic distinction.[31] In my view, the semantic-pragmatic distinction fundamentally concerns two different types of information associated with an utterance of a sentence. Semantic information is linguistically provided (encoded in the sentence), though it can be sensitive to narrow context; pragmatic information is generated by, or at least made relevant by, the act of uttering the sentence. This way of characterizing pragmatic information generalizes Grice's point that what a speaker implicates in saying what he says is carried not by what he says but by his saying it and sometimes by his saying it in a certain way (1989, 39). The act of producing the utterance exploits the information encoded but by its very performance creates new or at least invokes extralinguistic information. This extralinguistic information (wide context) includes the fact that the speaker uttered *that* sentence and did so under certain mutually evident circumstances and with a certain communicative intention for the hearer to identify under those circumstances.

From this perspective, viewing utterance content as semantic tends to fudge the semantic-pragmatic distinction. That is because the pragmatic fact that a speaker uttered something and did so with a certain intention affects the content of an utterance. Perry's contention that the "official" content of an utterance is referential might seem take this into account, but, as argued in the previous section, the fact that with

demonstratives and most indexicals reference depends on the speaker's communicative intention indicates that reference in using them is not a merely semantic matter.
That is, speakers use them to refer—they do not refer by themselves.

Also, it seems that Perry's liberal construal of what counts as semantic is driven
partly by a controversial underlying assumption. He implicitly assumes that for any
utterance of a sentence, the semantic content must be a complete proposition. This
explains why, I think, when something needed to yield a complete proposition is missing from the sentence, Perry posits an unarticulated constituent to fill the gap.[32] There
is no reason, however, to assume that sentences, just because they are syntactically
well-formed, must be semantically complete.[33] In contrast, assertive utterances of
complete sentences do express propositions. So Perry's view that unarticulated constituents play a semantic role even when they're not lexically or syntactically mandated requires holding that semantic contents are assigned not to sentences but to
utterances.

Demonstratives and Utterance Semantics

These observations about semantics, pragmatics, and reference suggest a way of out a
certain dilemma posed by sentences containing multiple occurrences of a demonstrative. As Kaplan recognized, such occurrences pose challenges for both utterance semantics and for the sentences-in-context approach. Manuel Garcia-Carpintero (1998)
has taken up these challenges, though his aim, as a proponent of utterance semantics,
is merely to show that it fares no worse than sentences-in-context semantics. He considers the following examples. Suppose that, while pointing first to one tree branch
and then to another, a speaker utters (10) or (11).

(10)   *That* is an elm and *that* is a beech.

(11)   *That* is older than *that.*

She may be referring to two different trees or, perhaps, unwittingly to one and
the same tree twice. This poses a problem, for it seems that the two occurrences of the
same word 'that' in the same sentence are used in the same context. Recognizing the
problem, Kaplan treats the two occurrences as having distinct characters; however,
Garcia-Carpintero argues, this implausibly treats them as, in effect, occurrences of
two different words (as when Kaplan uses subscripts in his formal semantics). Garcia-
Carpintero also considers two other strategies, what Braun (1996) calls the "context-
shifting" strategy, which treats the occurrences as being in different contexts, and
Braun's own "three-meaning" strategy, which treats 'that' as having a fixed meaning but variable character, depending in part on associated demonstration, and finds

them, depending on their precise formulations, either empirically inadequate or at least as problematic as utterance semantics (and in some cases merely notational variants thereof). So he concludes that utterance semantics is no worse off than the sentences-in-context approach. But how well off is either one? Leibniz and Candide may have thought that this is the best of all possible worlds, but it doesn't follow that this world is a good one. Similarly, Garcia-Carpintero has not shown that either utterance semantics or the sentences-in-context approach is a good one, at least if the latter attributes (context-relative) references to demonstratives themselves. The way out, as I have suggested, is not to ascribe references to demonstratives or to their uses, but to say, simply, that speakers use them to refer. This means, of course, that (utterances of) sentences containing them do not have referential propositions as their semantic contents.

What Is Said, Saying What Is Believed, and Cognitive Significance

In this section, I will briefly take up Perry's view on belief reports, with its assumption that, if a speaker is being sincere, what is said is what is believed. I will question this assumption as well as Perry's view that belief reports contain separate information about what is believed and how it is believed. Also, I will wonder whether Perry's view on belief reports is consonant with his views about cognitive significance.

Perry appears to equate "what is said" or "the proposition expressed" by an utterance, at least if it's a statement, with the content of the belief being conveyed by the speaker, at least if the utterance is literal. Like many others he simply "assume[s] that what a sincere speaker says is what he believes" (19). There is, however, good reason to doubt that the content of every statement is even a possible belief content. Suppose the content of a statement is a singular proposition. Then, as Schiffer (1977) has argued, it cannot be the complete content of a belief. Singular propositions are perfectly good propositions all right—they just aren't the sorts of things that we believe. That is, they do not comprise complete contents of possible beliefs. If they were things we can believe, then (assuming that proper names are directly referential) to believe that Eminem is a rapper and to disbelieve that Marshall Mathers is a rapper would be to believe and disbelieve the same thing (and without committing any logical mistakes). So would, to take a perhaps more familiar and more puzzling example, believing that Paderewski had musical talent and disbelieving that Paderewski had musical talent. It seems, then, that utterances of (12a) and (12b) can both be true, as can the pair in (13).

(12a)   Dubya believes that Eminem is rapper.

(12b)   Dubya disbelieves that Marshall Mathers is a rapper.

(12c)   Dubya believes that Marshall Mathers is a rapper.

(13a)   Peter believes that Paderewski had musical talent.

(13b)   Peter disbelieves that Paderewski had musical talent.

One strategem for explaining this is to suppose that believing is a three-term relation between agents, things believed, and ways of believing them, and that in a belief report of the form 'A believes that S', in which only the first two terms of this relation are explicitly represented, the way of believing that p is an unarticulated constituent of the belief report. Perry still endorses this approach (96–99), a version of which was advanced by Crimmins and Perry (1989) and then developed in detail by Crimmins (1992).

In this way Crimmins and Perry reconcile referentialism with intuitions about the truth conditions of belief reports. They suppose that the 'that'-clauses of standard belief reports merely specify what is said to be believed and that how it is believed (the notions and ideas involved) is merely implicit in the belief report. The "how" is included as an unarticulated constituent, and is semantically relevant, affecting the truth or falsity of the belief report. Thus they disagree with Salmon (1986), who contends that this information does not enter into the semantic content of the belief report but is merely "pragmatically imparted," as well as with Soames (most recently in his 2002, chs. 6 and 8). Although this view conflicts with common intuitions about the truth conditions of belief reports, Salmon and Soames maintain that these intuitions, the antisubstitution intuition in particular, are responsive to pragmatic factors, not just to the strictly semantic contents of belief reports. So, for example, if (12a) is true, then so (12c), but it would be misleading to utter (12c) rather than (12a).

One apparent problem with Crimmins and Perry's view is that there is no syntactic basis for the claim that belief reports implicitly refer to ways of taking propositions (or to notions and ideas of constituents of propositions). Presumably Perry would insist that there can be elements of semantic content that do not correspond to anything in the syntax, but this, as we saw in the previous section, requires an unduly liberal conception of semantics. Then there are Schiffer's (1992) well-known objections to the Crimmins and Perry view, which Schiffer (1977) himself had originated as the "hidden-indexical" theory.[34] The main virtue of this view is that it comports compara-tively well with common intuitions. In contrast, as Perry remarks, the Salmon and Soames "bite-the-bullet" approach "requires accepting that many prima facie false belief-reports are true'' (97). It seems to me, however, that having no syntactic basis for ascribing an extra argument place to belief reports, merely in order to preserve intuitions about truth values, just reflects a different taste in bullets.

In any case, both views assume that the 'that'-clause of a true belief report fully specifies the content of one of the agent's beliefs. But this "specification" assumption, as I call it (Bach 1997), is questionable and conflicts with intuition too. So, for example, it seems that to believe that Marshall Mathers is a rapper is not to believe the same thing as that Eminem is a rapper. This is the simplest and most straightforward explanation of the apparent fact that a great many people who believe that Eminem is a rapper do not believe that Marshall Matters is a rapper. Both of the referentialist views mentioned above deny that this is a fact and locate the difference not in what is believed but in how it is believed.

Once we accept the intuition that believing that Marshall Mathers is a rapper and believing that Eminem is a rapper is to believe two different things, it is a short step toward conceding that when someone utters, "Marshall Mathers is a rapper," he is saying something different from what he would say if he uttered "Eminem is a rapper." This conflicts with referentialism, and with Perry's same-saying argument. But we saw in the section "The Arguments for Referentialism" that the intuitive support for that argument isn't all that strong—intuitively, ascribing the same property to the same individual is not necessarily to say the same thing.

An alternative for referentialism is to deny that what is said must be what is believed. After all, if what is said is a singular proposition, it cannot be what is believed. It is only on the assumption that the 'that'-clause of a true belief report fully specifies something that the agent believes that it even seems plausible to suppose that belief reports report not only what someone believes but how he believes it.[35]

To all this Perry might reply that believing that Eminem is rapper and believing that Marshall Mathers is a rapper have not only referential but also reflexive contents. He might suggest that although their referential contents are the same, their reflexive contents are different. He could say that our intuitions about truth values are sensitive to both. But then Perry would need to explain how beliefs can have two kinds of contents (and not merely one content characterized in different ways), how it is that notions and ideas, as representations with contents, themselves comprise (reflexive) contents of beliefs, and how the reflexive as well as the referential contents of attributed beliefs get into the (referential) contents of belief reports.

I will close this section with a question. In Perry's view, belief reports implicitly provide information about how what is believed is believed. This information is about the notions and ideas under which the agent is being said to believe it. So suppose that someone reports correctly that Mother Goose believes that Jack loves Jill. Then they are tacitly referring to certain of Mother Goose's notions of Jack and Jill (and to her idea of the relation of loving). Now suppose that Mother Goose asserts, "Jack loves Jill." In Perry's view the cognitive significance of this statement consists not in its referential content but in its reflexive content. But this concerns information about permissive conventions for using 'Jack' to refer to Jack and 'Jill' to refer to Jill. This may be the cognitive significance of Mother Goose's statement to her listeners, but clearly it is not its cognitive significance for Mother Goose. So my question is how, in Perry's view, does the cognitive significance of a statement to the hearer tie in with the notions and ideas that the speaker has of the constituents of the proposition expressed by the statement?

The same question arises regarding discretionary indexicals and demonstratives. As Perry explains, in connection with an example involving two uses of demonstratives in which the same object is unwittingly referred to, "the reflexive contents of the beliefs are not the same as the reflexive contents of the statements that express them—given the reflexive nature of the contents they could not be" (95). He suggests that in this case two different "perceptual buffers" are associated with, respectively, the speaker's uses of 'this' and of 'that'. Here he says that the buffers "govern" the uses of the demonstratives, which he describes as a "causal connection." It is not clear, however, how this causal connection is effected independently of the speaker's intentions.

Perry's strategy for explaining cognitive significance runs into a special problem with the second-person pronoun 'you'. As Richard Heck has pointed out, "there is no such thing as a second-person belief. . . . Of course, I can identify someone descriptively, as the person to whom I am now speaking, and may have beliefs whose contents involve that descriptive identification. But that is not what I mean to deny. . . . The phenomenon of the second-person is a linguistic one. . . . The word 'you' has no correlate at the level of thought" (2002, 12). That is, although there is a linguistic rule that determines its reference, relative to a context, as the addressee, there is no corresponding second-person way of thinking of someone. (Perhaps Martin Buber would disagree.)

All these examples illustrate my question: if the reflexive content of the use of a referring term provides its cognitive significance for the hearer, what is the connection between this reflexive content, which is a linguistic matter, and the ways in which the speaker using the term thinks of the referent?[36] For most terms, there is no unique way of thinking of the referent that is systematically correlated with the meaning of the term or the reflexive content of its use.

Summing Up

I have argued for a number of points regarding Perry's reflexive-referentialism and his way of stating it. Here are the main ones:

(1) Perry's arguments for referentialism and the intuitions they're based on are rather shaky. The argument from counterfactual truth-conditions conflates being rigid with being directly referential and depends on intuitions that are insensitive to the distinction between linguistic reference and speaker reference. The argument from same-saying relies on selective intuitions. Contrary intuitions compete with the intuitions that support the referentialist conception of "official" content.

(2) In particular, there is solid intuitive resistance to referentialism about identity statements and about belief reports involving proper names and/or indexicals. Intuitions about what is said and about what is believed individuate things said and things believed more finely than referentialism allows.

(3) Referentialism holds that the semantic ("official") contents of proper names, and of indexicals and demonstratives, are their references. All of these expressions, however, have nonreferring uses, which Perry does not consider, much less reconcile with his referentialism. As for indexicals, only the references of pure indexicals are determined as a function of context, in the *narrow* sense. So the problem arises of how, when a discretionary indexical (or demonstrative) is used to refer, its semantic content could be affected by the speaker's referential intention. As part of his communicative intention, this intention plays a pragmatic role (in forming his referential intention and choosing a term to use to implement it, the speaker exploits context in the *wide* sense, information that the audience relies on it to identify the intended referent). But if reference is determined by the speaker's intention and this intention plays a pragmatic role, then the term does not refer—it is only used to refer.

(4) Perry's formulation of reflexive-referentialism is cast in the framework of utterance semantics, as opposed to a semantics of sentences-in-context. Unfortunately, he does not explain why he favors the first over the second, and he does not address the well-known difficulties for utterance semantics posed by Kaplan and others. Also, relying on a notion of utterance content tends to obscure the fact that a given utterance involves the performance of several speech acts, each with its own content. People's intuitions about "what is said" tend to be insensitive to these theoretical niceties and tend not to distinguish what is said, which is the content of the locutionary act, from the contents of illocutionary acts, which are matters of speakers' communicative intentions and can be performed directly or indirectly, literally or nonliterally. Besides, it

seems that any contents that are attributable to utterances are really contents of sentences (relative to contexts) or of speaker's intentions, in which case the notion of utterance content has no autonomous role to play.

Reference and Reflexivity develops and consolidates many of John Perry's ideas regarding the nature, types, representation, and flow of information about particulars. Many of these ideas are very suggestive, but I have not examined them here. Instead of looking at Perry's big picture, I have focused on some of the claims and assumptions in the philosophy of language that underlie this picture as he presents it. I am not suggesting that he couldn't frame it differently and even more effectively.

Notes

1. All page references to Perry are to Perry 2001.

2. It should be noted that Perry, like most direct reference theorists, focuses entirely on singular terms and ignores the problem of cognitive significance for general terms and kind terms. It is not clear how his account would generalize to such terms.

3. Singular propositions, which have individuals as constituents, are commonly contrasted with general propositions, which are quantificational. It is worth noting, as Perry does (28), however, that this distinction is not exclusive, because a proposition may be particular with respect to one argument slot and general with respect to another, as with the proposition that most National League pitchers fear Barry Bonds.

4. We can go further and abstract from the time of the utterance. If I see a scrap of paper with the words 'I am hungry' on it and have no idea not only who wrote them or when, I am still in a position to know that it is true if the person who wrote those words was hungry at that time.

5. Although Kaplan's phrase 'direct reference' is widely used, the presence of the word 'direct' strikes me as redundant, at least from a Russellian point of view. For if an expression refers at all, it refers directly. If it doesn't refer directly, it doesn't refer at all but merely denotes, as with definite descriptions, which Russell analyzes as quantificational. Of course, Kaplan (1989a, 1989b) is concerned to contrast his view with Frege's, on which *both* names and descriptions refer indirectly and their senses, not their references, enter into Thoughts expressed by sentences in which they occur. So the distinction between direct and indirect reference does clarify the difference between Kaplan's and Frege's view, but on neither of their views, nor on Russell's, do some terms refer directly and others indirectly. In other words, the distinction between direct and indirect reference is useful for contrasting different types of theories but not, within any given theory, for contrasting different types of referring expressions.

6. This reminds one of Frege's observation that "If words are used in their ordinary way, what one intends to speak of is their reference."

7. Our intuitions certainly can't be trusted in this regard (see Bach 2002b and Thau 2002, ch. 4). Intuitions about literal content are especially unreliable when there is a recurrent pattern of non-

literality associated with particular locutions or forms of sentence, as with what I call *standardized nonliterality* (Bach 1987/1994, 77–85) and the more commonly recognized phenomenon of *standardized indirection* (Bach and Harnish 1979, 192–219), including what Grice called *generalized conversational implicature* (1989, 37–39), as amply illustrated by Levinson (2000).

8. This doesn't mean that real-time processing occurs in that order (see Bach 1994, sec. 8, and 2001a, sec. 3). See also O'Rourke 2003.

9. Actually, there are two kinds of case here. In one, what is conveyed is merely the reflexive rather than the referential content. The individual constituents of the singular proposition (what is said) do not enter into what is conveyed. In the other case, what is conveyed is, in effect, an annotated version of what is said. It too is a singular proposition, but one containing additional information. It is an example of what I call a "conversational impliciture" (Bach 1994), because it is a beefed-up version of what is said.

10. I will not discuss definite descriptions, except to note the following. Perry characterizes them as contributing "identifying conditions" rather than the individuals thus identified to propositions expressed by sentences in which they occur (26). He also characterizes identifying conditions as "modes of presentation" of individuals (102). This suggests a Fregean picture, on which descriptions have both a sense and a reference, though of course Perry rejects such a picture for proper names (Frege assimilates the two, counting definite descriptions as Eigennamen). More important, he implicitly rejects Russell's theory of descriptions, according to which they are quantifier phrases. This is a bit puzzling, because Perry holds that sentences containing definite descriptions express general propositions (26).

11. Burge anticipated such an attitude when he described the "appeal to 'special' uses whenever proper names do not play the role of individual constants [as] flimsy and theoretically deficient" (1973, 437). He too was arguing for a unified account of names, one that can handle their various uses.

12. I have defended the view that proper names have reflexive meanings, that they express the property of bearing themselves (Bach 2002a). By employing the same pragmatic strategy that Kripke (1977) uses to explain away the apparent semantic significance of the referential-attributive distinction regarding definite descriptions, I argue that names are not essentially referring terms. Kripke applies this strategy to argue that the fact that definite descriptions are commonly used referentially does not show that semantically they refer; I argue likewise for proper names. It is interesting that this is the same sort of strategy that two of the most prominent Millians, Salmon (1986) and Soames (2002), use to explain away the antisubstitution intuition about names in attitude contexts, for they, too, exploit the fact that people's intuitions are often insensitive to the distinction between the semantic content of a sentence and what it is used to convey. It is ironic that the very distinction these referentialists exploit to save the Millian view can be used to undermine its intuitive basis.

Why does it often seem to people that names themselves refer? When you use a name to refer, generally the property of bearing the name does not enter into what you are trying to convey. For example, if you say, "Aristotle was the greatest philosopher of antiquity," presumably you are not suggesting that having the name 'Aristotle' had anything to do with being a great philosopher. Rather, you intend the property of bearing that name merely to enable your audience to identify who you are talking about. In this respect, proper names are like most definite descriptions, which are incomplete and generally used referentially. When we use them to refer to specific individuals, the properties they express are incidental to what we are trying to convey.

13. The reflexive contents Perry ascribes to utterances of names include such conventions (108). Later, in chs. 7 and 8, where he develops the idea of notion networks and takes up the no-reference problem, he amends his view to allow for cases in which there is no actual object to which a name in use has been assigned (because the object is fictional or downright nonexistent). The reflexive contents he attributes to utterances of sentences containing such names are propositions about notion-networks. These do not, however, seem to be the sorts of propositions that ordinary users of names are cognizant of. Quite the contrary, it seems that the only people capable of entertaining such propositions are Perry and his readers. In effect, he is building his theory of proper names into their reflexive contents.

14. I will not be discussing demonstrative phrases (so-called complex demonstratives), but King (2001) has made a very strong case that they are quantifier phrases, not singular terms, and suggests the same for simple demonstratives.

15. Neale has made a very strong case that unbound pronouns used anaphorically function like definite descriptions, not referring terms (1990, chs. 5 and 6).

16. One of Kaplan's "Afterthoughts" was that the speaker's "directing" intention rather than demonstration is decisive in determining demonstrative reference (1989a, 582–584). I defended this view (in Bach 1992) against Marga Reimer's (1991) contention that Kaplan, in "Demonstratives" (1989b), was right the first time.

17. Perry mentions four ways of being salient: being an object of the speaker's perception or action, being an object of audience's perception, being part of an anaphoric thread, or being related in an obvious way to a salient object.

18. Perry recognizes that not just any intention to refer to a certain individual is of the relevant sort. The relevant one is what he calls the "lowest level intention" (61)—that is, the one that relies for its recognition merely on contextual facts and not on the speaker's collateral beliefs, which he cannot reasonably expect the hearer to take into account. In the course of discussing such examples as Kaplan's Carnap-Agnew case, I have suggested a similar conception of distinctively referential intentions (Bach 1992).

19. I have noted the same distinction myself (Bach 1999, 72, and 2001b, 29), but I argue that only narrow context is semantically relevant.

20. In fact, Perry does not say that indexicals and demonstratives refer but that uses or utterances of them refer. As a matter of usage, it strikes me as a bit odd to speak, for example, of the use of 'that' as referring, and much more natural to say that a speaker uses 'that' to refer. But I am making a substantive point. This way of talking is not only a bit odd but unnecessary. Speakers use expressions to refer; their uses of expressions don't literally do anything. And to the extent that expressions refer (contrary to Strawson's 1950 insistence that referring is not something an expres-

sions does but only something that someone can use an expression to do), as with pure indexicals, we can say that they refer relative to contexts. But discretionary indexicals and demonstratives do not do that. And to say that uses of them refer is just a awkward and misleading way of saying that speakers use them to refer.

21. Any additional information carried by tokens is not encoded but is signaled by their specific features. For example, how a certain word is pronounced might signal the presence of an implicature. In such cases, it is the fact that the speaker pronounced it in that way that provides the basis for the hearer's inference to the implicature.

22. Perry's comment that "propositions are abstract objects we use to classify cognitive states" (20) makes me wonder whether he would regard this as a genuine issue. Although he often describes propositions as "what is believed" (or as "what is said"), this comment suggests that he thinks that beliefs and other propositional attitudes are not really relations to propositions, except in the Pickwickian sense in which temperatures are relations to numbers (relative to a temperature scale). If so, there is no real difference between believing two distinct propositions and having one belief state that can be classified more or less finely by those two propositions.

23. I develop and defend these points about what is said in Bach 2001b, 2002b.

24. Here I am alluding to the well-known views of Salmon (1986), Kaplan (1989a, 1989b), Richard (1993), Braun (1996), and Soames (2002).

25. Perry does respond to Kaplan in Crimmins and Perry 1989, but not to Richard (1993, 143–145), who argues against Crimmins and Perry's utterance semantics. However, Crimmins (1995) offers a reply to Richard, and Garcia-Carpintero (1998)—in response to Kaplan, Richard, and Braun (1996, 151f.)—argues that utterance semantics fares no worse than sentences-in-context semantics, at least with respect to the sorts of problems raised by those philosophers. The arguments below, however, suggest other, less technical reasons favoring sentences-in-context semantics.

26. He observes that tokens are epistemically basic but insists that utterances are semantically basic (37). I agree with him about tokens. In my opinion, token semantics is, well, token semantics.

27. At one point Perry writes, "Utterances are semantically basic; it is from the intentional acts of speakers and writers that the content derives" (37). But surely the contents of intentional acts derive from agents' intentions and not the other way around.

28. Perry means this literally. He doesn't mean merely that they have multiple truth conditions. He does, however, observe "the concept of 'truth-conditions of an utterance' is a relative concept" (80). That is, there is no such thing as "*the* truth conditions of an utterance." This could mean merely that the one content of an utterance can be characterized, in the form of truth conditions, to a greater or lesser degree of specificity. They could be given in terms of referential contents, any of Perry's reflexive contents, or in even weaker ways (for example, 'Trees have leaves' is true iff whatever is designated by 'trees' have whatever is designated by 'leaves'; or true iff the proposition it expresses is true). No one would object to the claim that there is no such thing as *the* truth conditions of an utterance, but Perry is making a stronger claim, that utterances literally have multiple contents associated with them.

29. As I have suggested in "Speaking Loosely" (Bach 2001a), we rarely make fully explicit what we mean. Even when we use our words literally, we generally don't use our sentences literally.

30. Perry accepts something like Kaplan's distinction between presemantic (or metasemantic), semantic, and pragmatic (or postsemantic) matters. He is clear on what is presemantic, namely, whatever is relevant to determining (in the sense of ascertaining) the linguistic meaning of the uttered sentence. This is an issue when, for example, there is homonymy or ambiguity. Obviously, if someone utters a sentence like 'I saw her duck under the bridge', it is not part of the semantic content of the sentence that the speaker is using it one way rather than other. And, as Perry explains, it is a presemantic matter which words are being used and, if there is structural ambiguity, which syntactic structure is operative (40).

31. See Bach 1999. I would make one qualification. Consider that what someone intends to convey may be nothing more that what he literally said. Even then, that he intended to convey anything at all is a pragmatic matter, to be ascertained in essentially the same way as any other communicative intention. This is why, contrary to a widespread misconception, Gricean maxims or conversational presumptions, as I prefer to regard them, are operative *whenever* we use language to communicate, not just in implicature and other indirect speech acts and in nonliteral utterances.

32. As I understand Perry, unarticulated constituents, insofar as they are not lexically or syntactically mandated, are constituents not of contents of sentences but of propositions the speaker is trying to convey. Jason Stanley (2002) argues against unarticulated constituents so construed but believes that hidden argument slots are lexically or syntactically mandated in many cases in which Perry probably would not think they are so mandated.

33. I have developed this point elsewhere (Bach 1994). See also Borg 2005.

34. Schiffer's objections are based on what he calls the "candidate," the "psychological reality," and the "logical-form" problems. The first two problems concern what sorts of things the relevant modes of presentation (ways of taking propositions and ways of thinking of their constituents) could plausibly be, such that speakers could plausibly be supposed to make tacit reference to them. The logical form problem, which is related to the syntactic problem, is that there ought to be occurrences of 'believes' where its three-place form is explicit, but there do not seem to be.

35. As for the nature of believing itself, recently Michael Thau (2002, ch. 3) has offered reasons to doubt that there is a viable distinction to be drawn between the "what" and the "how" of believing.

36. Perhaps Récanati's distinction between linguistic and psychological modes of presentation is relevant here (1993, ch. 4).

References

Austin, J. L. 1962. *How to Do Things with Words*. Oxford: Oxford University Press.

Bach, K. 1987/1994. *Thought and Reference*, revised with postscript. Oxford: Oxford University Press.

———. 1992. "Intentions and Demonstrations." *Analysis* 52: 140–146.

———. 1994. "Conversational Impliciture." *Mind & Language* 9: 124–162.

———. 1997. "Do Belief Reports Report Beliefs?" *Pacific Philosophical Quarterly* 78: 215–241.

———. 1999. "The Semantics-Pragmatics Distinction: What It Is and Why It Matters." In K. Turner (ed.), *The Semantics-Pragmatics Interface from Different Points of View*. Oxford: Elsevier.

———. 2001a. "Speaking Loosely: Sentence Nonliterality." In H. Wettstein (ed.), *Midwest Studies in Philosophy*. Vol. 25. Oxford: Blackwell.

———. 2001b. "You Don't Say?" *Synthese* 128: 15–44.

———. 2002a. "Giorgione Was So-called Because of His Name." In J. Tomberlin (ed.), *Philosophical Perspectives* 16: 73–103.

———. 2002b. "Seemingly Semantic Intuitions." In J. K. Campbell, M. O'Rourke, and D. Shier (eds.), *Meaning and Truth*. New York: Seven Bridges Press.

Bach, K., and R. Harnish. 1979. *Linguistic Communication and Speech Acts*. Cambridge, Mass.: MIT Press.

Barwise, J., and J. Perry. 1983. *Situations and Attitudes*. Cambridge, Mass.: MIT Press.

Borg, E. 2005. "How to Say What You Mean: Unarticulated Constituents and Communication." In R. Elugardo and R. Stainton (eds.), *Ellipsis and Non-sentential Speech*. Dordrecht: Springer.

Braun, D. 1996. "Demonstratives and Their Linguistic Meanings." *Noûs* 30: 145–173.

Burge, T. 1973. "Reference and Proper Names." *Journal of Philosophy* 70: 425–439.

Crimmins, M. 1992. *Talk about Beliefs*. Cambridge, Mass.: MIT Press.

———. 1995. "Contextuality, Reflexivity, Iteration, Logic." In J. Tomberlin (ed.), *Philosophical Perspectives* 9: 381–399.

Crimmins, M., and J. Perry. 1989. "The Prince and the Phone Booth: Reporting Puzzling Beliefs." *Journal of Philosophy* 86: 685–711.

Garcia-Carpintero, M. 1998. "Indexicals as Token Reflexives." *Mind* 107: 529–563.

Grice, P. 1989. *Studies in the Way of Words*. Cambridge, Mass.: Harvard University Press.

Heck, R. 2002. "Do Demonstratives Have Senses?" *Philosophical Imprint* 2: 1–33.

Kaplan, D. 1989a. "Afterthoughts." In J. Almog, J. Perry, and H. Wettstein (eds.), *Themes from Kaplan*. Oxford: Oxford University Press.

———. 1989b. "Demonstratives." In J. Almog, J. Perry, and H. Wettstein (eds.), *Themes from Kaplan*. Oxford: Oxford University Press.

King, J. 2001. *Complex Demonstratives: A Quantificational Account*. Cambridge, Mass.: MIT Press.

Kripke, S. 1977. "Speaker's Reference and Semantic Reference." *Midwest Studies in Philosophy* 2: 255–276.

Levinson, S. 2000. *Presumptive Meanings: The Theory of Generalized Conversational Implicatures.* Cambridge, Mass.: MIT Press.

Neale, S. 1990. *Descriptions.* Cambridge, Mass.: MIT Press.

O'Rourke, M. 2003. "The Scope Argument." *Journal of Philosophy* 100: 136–157.

Perry, J. 2001. *Reference and Reflexivity.* Stanford, Calif.: CSLI Publications.

Récanati, F. 1993. *Direct Reference: From Language to Thought.* Oxford: Blackwell.

Reimer, M. 1991. "Do Demonstrations Have Semantic Significance?" *Analysis* 51: 177–183.

Richard, M. 1993. "Attitudes in Context." *Linguistics and Philosophy* 16: 123–148.

Salmon, N. 1986. *Frege's Puzzle.* Cambridge, Mass.: MIT Press.

Schiffer, S. 1977. "Naming and Knowing." *Midwest Studies in Philosophy* 2: 28–41.

———. 1992. "Belief Ascription." *Journal of Philosophy* 89: 490–521.

Soames, S. 2002. *Beyond Rigidity.* Oxford: Oxford University Press.

Stanley, J. 2002. "Making It Articulated." *Mind and Language* 17: 149–168.

Strawson, P. F. 1950. "On Referring." *Mind* 59: 320–344.

Thau, M. 2002. *Consciousness and Cognition.* Oxford: Oxford University Press.

Wettstein, H. 1986. "Has Semantics Rested on a Mistake?" *Journal of Philosophy* 83: 185–209.

Part III

12 Thinking the Unthinkable: An Excursion Into Z-Land

Eros Corazza

In "Thought without Representation" (1986), Perry argues that one can think about an item without having to represent it. One can entertain thoughts without representation insofar as the *aboutness* of someone's thought need not be articulated. As paradigmatic examples, Perry invites us to consider sentences like:

(1a)   It rains.

(1b)   It's 3:00 PM.

(1c)   Events ξ and φ are simultaneous.

Imagine that these sentences are uttered by a five-year-old child—it is unlikely that a five-year-old child utter (1c) though; our child is more likely to utter something like: "This and that happens at the same time." It is a safe claim that (i) our child speaks about a relevant location without designating it, (ii) our child picks out a time relative to a time zone without thinking of the latter, and (iii) our child can characterize two events as simultaneous without being aware of Einstein's theory and, thus, without knowing that simultaneity is relative to a frame of reference. By the same token, one can argue that our child's thoughts—that is, the thoughts he or she entertains while uttering these sentences—are, in a way we should specify, related to the items tacitly referred to or presupposed. In this chapter, I investigate the different ways a thought can be related to and be about a given item without representing it.

Varieties of Implicitness

To begin, let us contrast sentences (1a)–(1e) and sentences (2a)–(2e):

(1a)   It is raining.

(1b)   Jane is not strong enough.

(1c)   Jon is late.

(1d)   Joe is too tall.

(1e)   It is 5 PM.

(2a)   * Jane devours.

(2b)   * Jeff gave.

(2c)   * Mary manages.

(2d)   * Joe founded.

(2e)   * Sue opens.[1]

Sentences (1a)–(1e), unlike sentences (2a)–(2e), are syntactically complete and, as such, they are well formed. In order to become well-formed sentences, (2a)–(2e) must be completed; (2a) should become 'Jane devours *a hamburger/all her cookies/...*' (2b) 'Jeff gave *up his job/a hand to Mary/away his car/Mary a kiss/...*' and so forth.

Sentences (1a)–(1e), though syntactically complete, are *conceptually incomplete*. To understand an utterance of (1a), one needs to know *where* it is raining, while to understand an utterance of (1b) one needs to know *for what* Jane is not strong enough. Insofar as these sentences are usually used to talk about things not mentioned—things merely presupposed or taken for granted—one may suppose that these sentences are also semantically underdetermined. The story, as I understand it, goes as follows. When one understands an utterance of a sentence like (1a)–(1e), one grasps a proposition. What one grasps, however, *transcends* what the words uttered mean. Hence, for an utterance of a conceptually underdetermined sentence to express the proposition one grasps, it must be *completed* or *enriched*.

I shall distinguish between conceptually underdetermined sentences and semantically underdetermined ones and claim that a semantically underdetermined sentence entails a conceptually underdetermined or incomplete sentence, but not vice versa. Thus, a conceptually underdetermined sentence can be semantically determined or complete. As a paradigmatic example of a semantically underdetermined sentence, we can quote, 'It is raining,' 'It is 5 PM', and so forth. For the utterance of a sentence such as 'It is raining' to be true or false, a location must be furnished. As a paradigmatic example of a conceptually underdetermined (though a semantically determined) sentence, we can quote 'Jane is late', 'Joe is too young'. Utterances of these sentences are understood insofar as one knows *for what* one is late and too young. It goes without saying that a semantically determined sentence need not be conceptually underdetermined. Utterances like "It's 3:00 PM CET," "Today/Now is raining in Paris/here," not to mention utterances of eternal sentences such as '2 + 2 = 4' or 'On Monday June 25, 2001, CE, it was sunny in Paris', are conceptually determined. To understand an utterance of any one of these sentences (be it context sensitive or not), one does not have to add further information. All the relevant information is conveyed by an element present in the utterance of the relevant sentence.

Before going further it may be worth mentioning that some people may object to the distinction between a *conceptually* incomplete (or underdetermined) sentence and a *semantically* incomplete (or underdetermined) one. People who defend a radical form of contextualism tend to argue that all (or at least most of) the sentences we end up using are *semantically* incomplete. Thus Carston, among others (see, for instance, Searle 1978 and Travis 1985), claims:

I think that public-language systems are intrinsically underdetermining of complete (semantic evaluable) thoughts because they evolved on the back, as it were, of an already well-developed cognitive capacity for forming hypotheses about the thoughts and intentions of others on the basis of their behavior. (Carston 2002, 30)

Though I am sympathetic with radical contextualism, I maintain that we should distinguish between conceptual indeterminacy and semantics indeterminacy for the following reason. Although there are infinitely many way a given utterance can be conceptually completed, semantic completion must be triggered by a syntactic element present either at the surface or logical form level of the sentence. In short, semantic completion, unlike conceptual enrichment, is syntactically triggered. On the other hand, conceptual completion, unlike semantic completion is free. The situation, as I view it, can be summarized as follows.

A propositional constituent may be the value of:

1. a phonetically realized element of an utterance, that is, a spoken or written element;

2. a phonetically unrealized element of an utterance, that is, an unspoken or unwritten element, present nonetheless at the level of logical form as an implicit argument;

3. a phonetically unrealized element of an utterance, that is, an unspoken or unwritten element, not present at the level of logical form as an implicit argument.

The notion of logical form I have in mind comes from the Chomskyan school: it is the level of syntactic representation, representing the properties relevant for semantic interpretation. Logical form so understood (or LF, as it is commonly characterized) aims to capture the syntactic structures relevant to a semantic interpretation.[2] One of the main tasks this conception faces is to determine how much of the semantic structure of a natural language is manifest in its syntax. Hence, if we apply this notion of logical form to a semantically underdetermined utterance, the main question concerns whether the phonetically unrealized elements are syntactically represented or not. I shall defend the view that all the semantically relevant elements are represented at

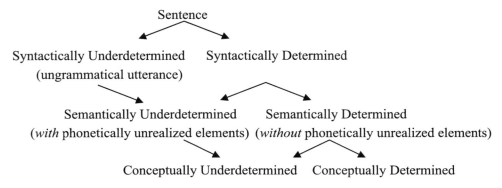

Figure 12.1

the LF level. In other words, I shall argue that, for the purposes of semantics, all the relevant propositional elements are the value of either a phonetically realized element or an implicit argument. The propositional elements not triggered by a phonetically realized element or an implicit argument can be dealt with as either pragmatically imparted or as background presuppositions upon which a given speech act occurs. In this chapter I shall mainly concentrate on propositional constituents that are semantically triggered, that is, triggered by, either phonetically realized or unrealized, elements present at the LF level.[3] The chart in figure 12.1 summarizes the distinctions I propose. The truth conditions of an utterance of a semantically underdetermined sentence such as 'It is raining' can be cashed out using the biconditional:

'It is raining' is true (in English) iff it is raining at time T and location L,

where the relevant location is usually given by the location of the utterance (but need not be so given) and the time by the present tense verb 'is'. For an utterance of a meteorological sentence such as 'It is raining' or 'It is storming' to express a full and evaluable proposition, *a* location must be supplied. The truth conditions of the utterance of a semantically determined, but conceptually underdetermined, sentence such as 'Jane is late' can be represented by the biconditional:

'Jane is late' is true (in English) iff Jane is late at time T.

To process the truth condition of an utterance of this sentence we do *not* need to add for what Jane is late.[4] The eventual conceptual enrichment does not affect the truth value of the proposition expressed. The proposition communicated in this case may be richer than the one expressed. In that case, the proposition communicated differs from the one expressed.

This difference between sentences such as 'It is raining', on the one hand, and others such as 'Jane is late', on the other, seems to suggest that the predicate 'rain' (in English) is a two-place predicate which must be completed by *a location* and *a time* and can *only be so completed*, while the predicate 'late' (in English) need not be semantically completed in a specific way.[5] I take it to be a meaning fact of English that 'rain' *always* picks up a location, whereas 'late' does not specify the particular thing or class of things for which one (or something) is late. In other words, from a semantic viewpoint there is not a particular, specific, way verbs and adjectives such as 'late', 'eat', 'short', 'strong', and so forth must be completed. With meteorological verbs such as 'to rain', 'to storm', and the like, on the other hand, the completion is not free but syntactically triggered. As we shall soon see, these verbs θ-mark a location as their subject—that is, their thematic role can only be a location. We can, for instance, say:

(3a)   Jane is *late* and will thus miss the train.

(3b)   The trains in England are often *late*.

(3c)   Jon is always *late* in submitting his scripts.

(3d)   Joe was *late* for the meeting.

(3e)   Each time Sue arrives home *late* at night she calls her parents.

(3f)   This year, the rain season in Zambia is *late*.

One of the basic ideas I shall develop in this chapter is that semantically underdetermined sentences have an implicit argument operating on some contextual parameters such as time, location, agent and possible world. As we shall see in the section "Meteorological Verbs," in the case of the verb 'to rain' the contextual parameter is θ-marked as a location by the verb. On the other hand, conceptually underdetermined but semantically determined sentences do not have implicit arguments operating on contextual parameters. Succinctly, whereas semantic completion is triggered by an implicit argument, the conceptual completion may not be so triggered. The conceptual completion of a semantically determined sentence "is free," and, as such, it is best viewed as *additional* information. The latter ends up in the proposition communicated but it is not, properly speaking, expressed and, most of all, it does not end up in the proposition expressed.

In this chapter I concentrate on semantically underdetermined sentences and I shall address the following two questions:

(Q1)   How does a semantically underdetermined sentence get completed in order to express a fully determined proposition?

(Q2)   Does one need a mental representation of all the constituents that end up in a
       fully determined proposition?

As I just said, I shall claim that the utterance of a semantically underdetermined
sentence expresses a fully determined proposition insofar as (i) it exploits parameters
available from the context and (ii) the context-exploitation is triggered by hidden or
implicit arguments present at the level of the logical form. These implicit arguments,
however, need not be represented by the speaker and/or hearer. Thus, one can think
about something without having to represent it. One's thought can be about a given
time zone, for instance, without representing it.

Varieties of Context Exploitation

Since Castañeda's (1966, 1967), Kaplan's (1989), and Perry's (1977) studies, it is common knowledge that utterances of sentences like:

(4a)   *I* am busy

(4b)   *Today* Jane will be *here*

(4c)   *This book* is rather expensive

(4d)   *She* is always very well dressed

are context-sensitive. If you utter (4a), you say that *you* are busy, whereas if I utter it I
say that *I* am busy. In uttering (4c), one picks out as an object of discourse the relevant
book one demonstrates/points at/…In short, if we change the context of utterance,
such as the agent, time or location, we usually end up with different referents and
we express different propositions. We can call sentences like these *indexical sentences*.
Utterances of sentences like:

(5a)   A *local* pub is promoting German beer

(5b)   Vieira is one of many *foreign* players playing in the Premiership

(5c)   Jane believes that Jon is an *enemy*

(5d)   Maria is one of many *immigrants* in the United States

are also context sensitive. The relevant location of the pub in (5a) is provided by the
context of the utterance, whereas Vieira in (5b) is foreigner vis-à-vis English citizens,
and so on. The intuitive way to understand these utterances is that the predicate itself
is context sensitive and, thus, that the context sensitivity of the utterance is triggered by the fact that the predicate is relational. The natural way to understand these
predicates is to view them as two-places predicates: a location is local vis-à-vis some-

one, *local* (p, x), a person is an immigrant vis-à-vis some country, *immigrant* (c, x). The dictionary registers that 'local' means "existing in or belonging to the area where you live, or to the area you are talking about," that 'immigrant' means "a person who settles as a permanent resident in a different country," that "a foreigner is someone who belongs to a country which is not your own," and so forth.[6] Utterances of sentences like

(1a)   It rains

(1b)   It's 3:00 PM

(1c)   Events ξ and φ are simultaneous

are also context sensitive, but, unlike (4) and (5), there is no element in the utterance that operates on context to designate a particular item. In (4) the context sensitivity is triggered by the presence of indexical expressions ('I', 'here', 'today', 'this book') and in (5) by the presence of the relational predicates ('local', 'foreigner', 'enemy'). In (1), though, we do not seem to have elements triggering the context sensitivity. Where, then, does it come from? How do the relevant location, time zone, and frame of reference get referred to, and, thus, end up in the proposition expressed? To borrow Perry's (1986) terminology, we can say that the relevant location, the relevant time zone and the relevant frame of reference tacitly referred to in (1) are *unarticulated constituents* of the propositions expressed:

The unarticulated constituent is not designated by any part of the statement, but is identified by the statement as a whole. The statement is *about* the unarticulated constituent, as well as the articulated ones. (Perry 1986, 174)

In this case, I say that the place is an *unarticulated constituent* of the proposition expressed by the utterance. It is a constituent, because, since rain occurs at a time in a place, there is no truth-evaluable proposition unless a place is supplied. It is unarticulated, because there is no morpheme that designates that place. (Perry 2001, 33)

In an utterance of 'It is raining here', the relevant location is picked out by the indexical 'here', while, in an utterance of 'It is raining', it is picked out, following Perry's suggestion, by the utterance as a whole. What does it exactly mean to claim that an utterance *as a whole* can single out a given location? To this specific question I now turn.

Meteorological Verbs

I suggested that meteorological predicates such as 'rain', 'snow', 'storm', and so forth have an implicit argument for a location and that they should thus be treated on a par with relational adjectives such as 'local', 'foreigner', 'enemy', and so forth. To stress the fact that the latter do have an implicit argument at work, I invite you to consider the following utterances:[7]

(6a)   A local bar is selling cheap beer.

(6b)   A reporter for the *Times* got seriously drunk. A local bar was selling cheap beer.

(6c)   Every sport fan watched the Super Bowl in a local bar.

There are different ways in which we can understand how the relevant location is provided. In (6a) it is provided by the location where the utterance occurs; in (6b) it is provided by the previous linguistic discourse, that is, the location of the reporter for the *Times*; in (6c) it is dependent of the domain of the quantifier. A natural way to understand the different ways in which 'local' works in these utterances, following Condoravdi and Gawron (1986), is to treat them as working like a relational predicate with an implicit argument. The implicit argument triggers the contextual interpretation. In (6a), it works as a free variable and as such receives an indexical or deictic interpretation; in (6b), it works as an anaphoric pronoun and as such gets a discourse anaphoric reading, while in (6c) it works as a bound variable and thus receives a bound variable reading.

We can easily see a parallel between these utterances and utterances containing meteorological verbs:

(7a)   It rains.

(7b)   Every time Jane goes on vacation, it rains (where she happens to be).

Whereas in (7a) the relevant location is provided by the location where the utterance occurs, in (7b) it depends upon (and varies with) the domain of the quantifier. As in the analysis proposed for 'local', the natural way to understand utterances such as (7a) and (7b) is to posit a hidden argument place for a location, so that the implicit argument place for the verb 'to rain' in (7a) works as a free variable, whereas in (7b) it works as a variable bound by the quantifier.[8]

This interpretation, though, faces difficulties. *Every* action or event occurs at a *time* and *location*, so one could go on and argue that every verb should present an argument place for a time and another for a location. Consequently, every verb is at least a two-place predicate. For the time being, let us forget the time—the latter being conveyed by the verb tense—and focus on the locational argument-place. To put it in a nutshell, the difficulty runs as follows: if every verb presents an argument place for a location, then the position I am defending is trivial, for then verbs such as 'to sleep', 'to eat', 'to run', 'to kiss', and so forth *must* have an argument for a location as well. But then, contrary to our intuition, nothing would differentiate meteorological verbs like 'to rain', 'to storm', 'to snow', and the like from other verbs. To put it slightly differently, if we infer that we have to postulate an argument place for a location in 'to rain' from the fact that it always rains *in some location*, then we should also posit an argument place for a location for 'to sleep', for one always sleeps *in some location*. What is the story, if any, enabling us to differentiate meteorological verbs form all the other verbs? What is the peculiarity that would make 'to rain' a two-place argument, while making 'to sleep' one-place?

There are two ways in which one can tackle this difficulty. First, one can focus on the competencies required to master the language games involving meteorological terms. Second, one can focus on the metaphysics of locations.

I begin by focusing on the competencies involved when meteorological verbs are at play. It is a peculiarity of these verbs that they convey information about the weather condition *at some given location*. The location where it rains/storms/snows/thunders/...affects our life and actions. If it rains/storms/snows/...where we are located, we act differently to how we would if it had rained/stormed/snowed/...miles away from where we are (this is the main reason why weather reports are always linked to a limited location/region). It seems, then, that one is competent with meteorological terms insofar as one acts and reacts to weather reports in an appropriate way, that is, insofar as one links the weather condition to a given location. On the other hand, the location where one ate dinner last night is not (usually) cognitively relevant. If one asks a visiting friend, "Did you already have dinner?" with the intent to invite her out, the location the addressee ate her dinner is irrelevant. If someone asks about the weather conditions, however, the location *is* relevant and becomes the focus of attention. In a nutshell, while the subject of an utterance such as "It is raining" is a location, the subject of an utterance such as "Jon slept with Jane last night" is not a location but Jon.

It seems that (i) with meteorological verbs, the location plays a cognitive role which it does not play with verbs such as 'to eat', 'to sleep', and so forth and (ii) a competent speaker immediately links a meteorological verb to a given location and understands the message insofar as she can make this link, whereas she does not (and often need not) do so with other verbs.

This does not prove, however, that it is intrinsic to the lexicon of meteorological verbs that a location needs to be furnished, that is, that there is an argument place for a location. As a matter of fact, the dictionary does not report that there must be an understood location accompanying 'to rain' and the other meteorological verbs. The competence argument does, though, contribute some evidence in favor of the presence of an argument place for a location in meteorological verbs.

From a metaphysical, or ontological, viewpoint, one can stress the difference between meteorological verbs such as 'to rain', 'to storm', and so forth and verbs such as 'to run', 'to eat', and so forth in focusing on the property or relation they stand for. It should not be controversial to claim that meteorological properties are properties of locations; this amount to saying that a location is the "subject" that undergoes meteorological change. If this is the case, then meteorological verbs *do* require an argument for locations inasmuch as the latter are the subjects of these verbs. On the other hand, even if eating and running—like raining and storming—always take place in a location as well, they cannot be viewed as modifiers of the location. With verbs such as 'to rain' and 'to storm', the location can be viewed as the agent/subject undergoing a given modification, whereas with intransitive verbs such as 'to eat' and 'to run' or transitive verbs such as 'to kiss' and 'to give' the location of the activity cannot be viewed as the agent/subject undergoing modification. In the latter case, the agents/subjects are not locations. The subject/agent of 'is running' may be Jon, Jane, the train, and so forth. It cannot be a location.[9] In other words, the noun phrase that completes or saturates open sentences such as 'x runs', 'x kissed y', and so forth cannot pick out locations, whereas the noun phrases that complete utterances of sentences such as 'x rains...' *must* stand for locations. In many cases, as we saw, sentences such as these can be saturated by 'it'. The latter may be viewed merely as a syntactic filler, taking the place of the subject. We need 'it' because English, unlike Italian and Spanish, for instance, is not a pro-drop language, that is, it does not allow the subject of a finite clause to remain unexpressed. Because 'it' contributes nothing to the meaning of the sentence in which it appears, its presence is required only for structural reasons. The asymmetry between meteorological verbs and action verbs—for example, 'to eat', 'to beat', 'to sleep', 'to fall', and so forth manifests itself in the fact that the former, unlike the latter, do not take a grammatical subject. Locations enter the picture in very different ways. When a meteorological verb is uttered, locations enter the scene as the subject, whereas when other verbs are uttered, the location merely enters the picture as the background upon which the subject(s) of the verb either acts or experiences a given event.

The same story can be told using the notion of *Theta-Role* (θ-*Role*). It is often said that the lexical information associated with a lexical item must specify the syntactic category by which the thematic roles are realized. A first distinction can be made between the subject arguments and object arguments. While the subject argument does not affect the θ-Role of the object, the choice of the latter does, as it is illustrated by:[10]

(8a) Jeff broke a leg last week

(8b) Jeff broke a vase last week,

where the choice of the complement determines the θ-Role of the subject. In (8b), Jeff can be considered to be the AGENT, whereas he cannot in (8a) (where he is the subject who undergoes the event)—to be sure, if Jeff were to work as a wrestler or an enforcer for the loan shark, he could be the agent doing the action, that is, breaking someone else's leg. In these cases, it is said that the verb θ-*marks* the subject indirectly, whereas in the latter case, it is θ-marked compositionally, that is, it is determined by the semantics of the verb and other VP constituents. In some other cases, however, the verb θ-marks the constituent directly: 'to shut', for instance, directly θ-marks a subject and a patient. This seems also to be the case with meteorological verbs: 'to rain', 'to snow', 'to storm', and the like directly θ-mark the subject. The latter can only take locations as values, namely, its thematic role must be a location.[11] On the other hand, the θ-Role of verbs such as 'to kiss', 'to run', 'to sleep', and so forth is not θ-marked as a location.

There is, then, an asymmetry between meteorological verbs and other verbs with respect to the way locations enter the picture. The best way to capture this asymmetry is to posit an argument place for a location in the case of meteorological predicates.

Implicit Arguments and Representation

I now turn to the second question I asked at the beginning. I shall defend Perry's idea that one can think about an item without having to represent it. In particular, one can think about an unarticulated constituent without representing it. This thesis seems to contrast with the idea that, at the LF level, or subsyntactic level, there is an implicit argument that works like a free variable standing for the unarticulated constituent.

As I have already noted, by "logical form" I mean the syntactic structure of a given class of sentences. In *Tractarian* terminology, we can say that this structure reflects the structure of the propositions expressed by utterances of these sentences. Hence, I take propositions to be structured entities whose structure, is reflected by the logical form of the sentences expressing them. A sentence of the subject/predicate form Fa reflects the form of the proposition expressed, whose constituents are the object a and the property F. The LF of a relational sentence like 'Jane kisses Jon', $R(a, b)$, reflects the structure of the proposition expressed. This idea is cashed out in the tree in figure 12.2. The LF of a quantified sentence such as 'Every man smokes', $(x)(\mathrm{Man}(x) \rightarrow \mathrm{Smokes}(x))$ can be represented by the tree shown in figure 12.3. An ambiguous sentence such as:

(9a)   Jane saw Jon with the binoculars

can be represented as either the tree shown in figure 12.4, or the tree shown in figure 12.5. What about Perry's idea that one need not have a representation of all the

Propositional Structure:

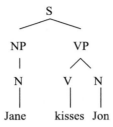

Propositional Constituents: <Kiss, Jane, Jon>

Figure 12.2

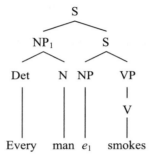

Figure 12.3

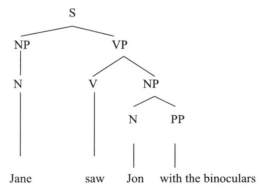

Figure 12.4

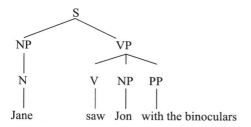

Figure 12.5

constituents ending up in the proposition expressed? How do we represent the logical form of a sentence such as 'It is raining'? The notion of LF I have been assuming is usually committed to the view that LF is a mental representation. Hence, if an argument place is represented at the level of LF, it is *mentally* represented. The position I am defending, then, seems to contradict Perry's claim that one need not represent the location when one utters, 'It is raining'.

As far as I can see, there are at least two ways one can accept the position I propose and yet defends Perry's claim. First of all, one could argue that the position that postulates the presence of argument places at the level of LF is not committed to the assumption, without further argument, that one must represent all the syntactic structure that mirrors the structure of the proposition in order to express the latter. A child can easily express the proposition *that it is raining* without representing either the location where it is raining or the structure of the sentence. Our child merely *exploits* the linguistic resources at her disposal and, in so doing, comes to utter the sentence 'It is raining'. It is because *in English*—the language our child uses and exploits—the sentence has such and such a structure and that 'to rain' is a two-place predicate that our child refers to the relevant location and expresses the relevant proposition. Our child can do so without representing either the structure of the proposition or all of its constituents. This can be understood as the phenomenon of *deferentiality*. As Putnam and Kripke told us, one can refer to Gellman and Feynman (or to an elm or a beech) without knowing who Gellman and Feynman are, or even without knowing that they were physicists. One can competently use 'elm' and 'beech' without being able to tell an elm from a beech. With the same token, one can argue that one can refer to a given location without mentioning it or even representing it. In short, one can express a proposition having a given structure and a given location as constituent in virtue of exploiting the linguistic resources at one's disposal. Along this line, the notion of LF is independent of the mental representation one may have. LF is understood to be the logical form of English *qua* natural, objective language. Along this line one could argue that LF is akin to lot of other mental properties that are, at least in part, dependent on external circumstances. This (externalist) position would, no doubt, be in conflict with the notion of LF *qua* psychological reality, as it is usually conceived within the Chomskyan tradition.[12]

Second, the position I am defending is also consonant with the view that logical form *qua* syntactic properties relevant to semantic interpretation *is* a psychological reality and yet can salvage Perry's claim that one's thought may be about something without one having to represent it. Understood this way, LF can be viewed as the mental representation explaining the (grammatical) understanding and capacities of an agent speaking a given language. Even if we understand logical form this way, we do not commit ourselves to the thesis that one cannot refer to (and think about) a given item without representing it. The presence of implicit arguments representing the unarticulated constituents do not commit us to the view that an agent ought to think of the unarticulated constituents of the proposition expressed in order to refer to (and for the thought to be about) them. Logical form, understood along this line, is unconscious:

> the unconsciousness of mental grammar is still more radical than Freud's notion of the unconscious: mental grammar isn't available to consciousness under *any* conditions, therapeutic or otherwise....if at least some other processes in the mind are not open to consciousness, it shouldn't be too distasteful to say that parts of language ability are unconscious too. (Jackendoff 1994, 19)

Unconscious representation is not, properly speaking, representation. At least, unconscious representations are not the kind of representations associated with language and propositional attitudes, that is, they are not the representations one is aware of when one entertains them. One cannot claim that she was unconsciously thinking about something. I can meet someone and tell her, "Last night I thought/wondered/talked/...about you," but I cannot tell her, "Last night I *unconsciously* thought/wondered/talked/...about you." The paradox entailed by a sentence such as 'I am (now) unconsciously thinking about X' should further underline the fact that the unconsciousness of mental grammar and logical form entails that one does not need to represent the items picked out by implicit arguments. It is worth noticing that a third-person attribution such as 'Jane is unconsciously thinking/dreaming/wondering/...about X' also sounds paradoxical, or at least it would make sense only among some very inspired psychologists and/or cognitive scientists. The awkwardness of attributions like these should further contribute to the point I am making; that is, one can use an *n*-place predicate without having to think of all the predicate's places, that is, without having a (conscious) representation of each parameter of the corresponding relation. When unarticulated constituents are involved, what gets represented at the level of logical form are *implicit* arguments. An implicit argument is not what comes to one's mind; when one thinks about a relevant location using a sentence such as 'It is raining', one need not call to one's mind the implicit argument for the location. If one were to call to one's mind the implicit argument, one would make them explicit and hence the relevant location would no longer be an *unarticulated* constituent. It is even possible (and is in fact often the case) that a child, for instance, is unable to recover and articulate all the constituents of a given proposition (i.e., she may not be disposed to articulate the unarticulated constituents). In other words, it is conceivable that a child is unable to go from 'It is raining' to 'It is raining here' and thus to articulate the unarticulated constituent. On the other hand, someone who goes from the former to the latter would move from an unarticulated to an articulated thought constituent and thus from a thought without (full) representation (i.e., without a representation of a location) to a thought in which the relevant location is represented. It is in this sense that I claim that the unarticulated constituent becomes represented.[13]

Perry claims that we can even imagine a whole community that is unable to articulate some of the constituents that end up in their propositions. He invites us to imagine an isolated community, living in a location called Z-land. Members of this community never travel or communicate with members of other communities; they do not even have a name for Z-land. After all, they do not need to name their own location, insofar as they do not have to distinguish it from other locations. The important thing is that members of this community are unable to say, "It is raining here." If Z-landers desire to report the weather condition when they face rain, all they can say is "It is raining." Perry's moral is:

It would be natural to treat Z-landers' uses of the sentence *It is raining* as having Z-land as an unarticulated constituent. But what secures Z-land, rather than, say, San Francisco, as the unarticulated constituent of their discourse about rain? It is simply that the perception that gives rise to the beliefs that *It is raining* expresses are perceptions of the weather in Z-land. Z-land is a constituent of the practice, or language game, in which the sentence *It is raining* plays a role. There is no need to postulate a concept or idea of Z-land as a component of their thought, to secure the connection to Z-land. The connection is secured by the role of the whole belief in their lives. . . .

The Z-lander's beliefs have a simple job to do. All of the information (or misinformation) they get about the weather, through observation or reports of others, is about Z-land. All of the actions they perform, in light of their weather beliefs, take place in Z-land. The connection between the place about which they receive weather information, and the place whose weather determines the appropriateness of their action, is guaranteed by their life-style, and need not be coordinated by their beliefs. (Perry 1986, 177–178)

The first reaction that comes to my mind when considering this scenario is to argue that in Z-landish, unlike in English, 'rain' is a one-place predicate. When (in English) we utter, "It is raining," we express the proposition that it is raining at a given location at the time of utterance, while the Z-landers' utterance of the homophonic sentence 'It is raining' expresses the proposition that it is raining at the time of utterance. Hence, the truth conditions of these homophonic sentences, are cashed out as:

- 'It is raining' is true (In English) iff it is raining *at location L and u_t*
- 'It is raining' is true (In Z-landish) iff it is raining *at u_t*,

where 'u_t' stands for the time of the utterance. The English and Z-lander semanticists would thus look at things differently. Whereas we consider 'rain' to be a predicate expressing a two-place relation between times and locations, the Z-lander semanticists would consider it to be a predicate expressing a property of time.

Perry recognizes that there is a distortion in treating the Z-landers' use of 'It is raining' on a par with our own use. At the same time, however, Perry insists on the fact that the possibilities the Z-landers fails to recognize are real. Perry seems thus to commit himself to a realist position with respect to properties and relations. That is, rain is a two-place relation regardless of whether we use a two-term predicate while the Z-landers use a one-term predicate.[14] As a consequence, Perry proposes a kind of mixed analysis:

Suppose we accept the Z-lander semanticist's opinion as to the object of the Z-landers' attitude— what they assert with a use of *It is raining* and what they believe when they hear such a statement from a reliable source—but stick to our view of what those objects are. Then we would say that the Z-landers assert and believe propositional functions, rather than propositions. What would be wrong with this? (Perry 1986, 178)

Following this suggestion, an utterance of the Z-landish sentence 'It is raining' is true if the propositional function it expresses is true relative to Z-land:

For the Z-landers' discourse about weather, a statement is true if the propositional function it expresses is true relative to Z-land. Z-land comes in not as an unarticulated constituent each Z-landish weather statement is about, but as a global factor that all Z-land discourse about the weather concerns. (Perry 1986, 179)

To be sure, this characterization allows us to record the difference between the linguistic practice in Z-land and our own. Why, though, Perry does not accept the position I have suggested—that 'rain' in Z-landish is a one-place predicate and an utterance of 'It is raining' in Z-landish expresses the proposition that it is raining at the time of utterance? Succinctly, why does Perry not accept the idea that 'It is raining' in English and 'It is raining' in Z-landish do not have the same truth-conditions? After all, the Z-landers' meteorological language games differ from our own. In the Z-landers language game, for instance, questions of the form 'Where is it raining?', 'Where will it snow tomorrow?' and so forth do not exist.

As I understand it, Perry's considerations rest on the assumption that, when describing the way members of a given community use their language, we can take an external stance and yet understand how they rationally use and master their own language. The question that springs to one's mind is whether this is a plausible stance or whether one should instead take an internal stance and describe the community's linguistic activity from inside their own practice. Thus, the question runs as follows: In analyzing the Z-landers' use of 'It is raining', can we take our semanticist's viewpoint or are we constrained to take the Z-lander semanticist's one?

Since the kind of knowledge that is at issue when we use sentences like 'It is raining' is a sort of implicit knowledge, akin to a practical ability, a kind of knowing-*how*, the best way to capture it seems to be from the Z-landers' viewpoint.[15] Actually, if one's goal is to capture the Z-landers use of 'It is raining' and the way they linguistically interact with each other and their surroundings, one is constrained to deal with the way *they* understand each other and the way *they master their* language.[16] To do so, however, it seems that we must take the Z-landers' viewpoint:

[O]ne human being can be a complete enigma to another. We learn this when we come into a strange country with entirely strange traditions; and, what is more, even given a mastery of the country's language. We do not *understand* the people. . . . We cannot find our feet with them. . . . If a lion could talk, we could not understand him. (Wittgenstein 1952, 223)

It may be worth noticing that, if we follow Wittgenstein on this issue, we ultimately ought to accept that our form of life is the nonlinguistic context essential to understanding our linguistic activity, for "to imagine a language is to imagine a form of life" (1952, sect. 7), "what has to be accepted, the given, is—so one could say—forms of life" (1952, 226).

What I have just said does not rule out the fact that our semanticist can describe the Z-landers' linguistic activity and come out with a plausible story (i.e., a story that provides a set of rules that *fit* the Z-landers' linguistic behavior). These rules, though, do not account for the way in which Z-landers *actually* follow rules, for the relation between a rule and the behavior (linguistic or not) it guides is not of the same kind as the relation between a scientific hypothesis and its evidence. The former, unlike the latter, is (to borrow Wittgenstein's terminology) an *internal* relation, that is, a relation whose *relata* cannot be disentangled. Our semanticist's rules, which "enable" her to explain the Z-landers' linguistic behavior, are merely explanatory hypothesis purporting to describe their linguistic activity.

Because Perry does not take the Z-landers' viewpoint, he does not consider the predicate 'rain' in Z-landish as a one-place predicate. The only alternative Perry can envisage is the one in which Z-land is a context-*in*sensitive unarticulated constituent of the Z-landers' weather condition. This way, whenever a Z-lander utters, "It is raining," she would inevitably express a proposition having Z-land as a constituent. The truth-condition of the Z-landish 'It is raining' would thus correspond with

- 'It is raining' is true (in Z-landish) iff it is raining *in Z-land at u_t*.

To dismiss this possibility, Perry invites us to imagine a scenario in which Z-landers become nomads and start migrating:

> If their use of 'It is raining' is keyed to their surroundings, we would have to say its meaning had changed, or that their reports were now false, whenever the weather in their new environments deviate from that in Z-land. Neither of these steps seems plausible. What we have contemplated is a change in their surroundings, not a change in the meaning of their sentences. (Perry 1986, 179–180)

Perry's argument rests on the assumption that Z-landish does not change. Why, though, should we accept this assumption? In particular, why cannot we suppose that Z-landish evolves and 'to rain' becomes a two-place predicate when the nomads adapt to their new situations and migrations? Languages do evolve. In a nutshell, why cannot we suppose that Z-landish becomes just like English? After all, after their migrations the nomads will come to entertain beliefs that they can express with utterances of sentences such as 'It is raining *here*', 'It is raining *here* while it may not be raining *where* our relatives are', 'It was not raining so much *where* we were before', and so forth. Z-landers *do* have words like 'here', 'there', and so forth—that is, words enabling them to locate objects in space—so it will not be difficult for the nomads to apply these words to their weather conditions as soon as they start moving and realize that the weather condition may change with a change of location. To sum up, unlike Perry, I believe that the Z-landish sentence 'It is raining', unlike the English one, *is* semantically determined. If, as I suggested, we take the Z-lander semanticist's viewpoint, we can easily account for this phenomenon.

If I am right, then we can easily recognize the presence of implicit arguments at the level of logical form and, yet, admit that one need not articulate the unarticulated constituents and thus need not have a (conscious) mental representation of all the items that end up in the proposition one expresses using a semantically underdetermined sentence.

The general moral is that Perry should not be scared by the presence of implicit arguments (i.e., arguments at work when meteorological verbs are used) for implicit arguments do not undermine Perry's thesis that one can have thoughts without representation. The same, or a similar, story can be told about time zones. If we turn the clock back a few centuries, people did not have conceptions of a time zone and so the latter were not unarticulated constituents of their utterances involving times. Their language games involving time probably rested on an absolutist conception of time, that is, on the view that time statements are not relative to a time zone. Even if this is not historically accurate, we can easily imagine a linguistic community that, like the Z-landers, never travels and does not need to have time statements relative to time zones.

Other cases of unarticulacy, such as 'simultaneous', are best understood as a kind of background or presupposed information, which does not need to be implicitly referred to. If so, we do not need to postulate the existence of implicit arguments referring to frames of reference. If one considers (following Wittgenstein) that a linguistic community operates with a plurality of variegated language games, the fact that not all implicit information can be captured within a single and simple framework should not come as a surprise. In some language games, the implicit information is confined to the background assumptions or presuppositions upon which the linguistic act occurs. In other language games, the implicit information is captured in postulating implicit arguments at work during the speech act. In neither case, though, are we forced to assume that the speaker and/or hearer must represent all the constituents that either end up in the proposition expressed or which operate as background assumptions and presuppositions enabling the speech act. The context upon which the speech act occurs bridges the gap and fills in the relevant information in saturating the implicit arguments. It is this contextual phenomenon that makes one's thought *about* something (such as a location or a time zone) and *not* the alleged representation the speaker entertains.

Acknowledgments

This paper originated from an idea I tried to articulate in a talk I gave at the workshop on Perry care of the Institute of Cognitive Sciences in Lyon (June 1999). Thanks to the audience for the valuable criticisms. The first version of this paper was written while visiting the *Institut Jean-Nicod*, supported by a fellowship from the Research French Ministry in June–July 2001 (no. 303553L). To both institutions I express my gratitude. Discussions with Dick Carter, Jérôme Dokic, Jonathan Gorvett, Pierre Jacob, Pascal Ludwig, Elisabeth Pacherie, Adriano Palma, John Perry, Joëlle Proust, François Recanati, Dan Sperber, and Isidora Stojanovic have been very helpful. Parts of this paper were presented at the Institute Jean-Nicod. Thanks to the audience for comments. For written comments, I would also like to thank Emma Borg, Jérôme Dokic, John Perry, François Recanati, and Mark Whitsey. As usual, I am alone responsible for the subsisting mistakes.

Notes

1. I have been told by cricket fans that "Sue opens" is an acceptable statement (e.g.: "What position does Sue play? Sue opens"). I do not have strong intuitions either way on this matter; at first sight, it looks to me that this is either a case of ellipsis and, as such, it goes short for something like "Sue opens the game" or it is an idiomatic use of language, tied to cricket- and baseball-related games. In some other context, one could also say "Mary manages" alone in response to the question: "How does Mary do it?" just as one could also say "Jeff gave" in response to the question "Did some of you give Jane some money?" In these cases, too, the answers are elliptical and, as such, short for "Mary manages *to do it*," "Jeff gave *some money*."

2. For an accurate and well-developed account of LF, see May 1985.

3. Roughly, the picture I have in mind is that, in the case of the utterance of a semantically determined (but conceptually underdetermined) sentence, two or more propositions are expressed: the semantically encoded proposition and the pragmatically imparted ones. The latter are the result of a pragmatic enrichment of the semantically encoded proposition operated by the speaker and/or audience.

4. Cf. Jacob 1999, for a similar distinction. These truth-conditions can be spelled out in terms of utterances. Furthermore, truth should also be relativized to situations. We would thus have:

If u is an utterance of 'Jane is late' and s is the situation in which u occurs, then [u is true *iff* Jane is late relative to s].

Thus, Jane could be late to catch the train and yet not be late to join the army. For the sake of simplicity, I ignore these subtleties here. I discuss the way truth conditions must be relativized to situations and the picture that emerges, which I label *Situational Contextualism*, in Corazza 2004 (introduction).

5. Recanati (2002) proposes an example in which a speaker utters "it is raining" on hearing a bell signaling that it is raining *somewhere*. It seems to me that such a sentence would not make much sense within our community. Within our everyday practices, it does not make sense to utter "It rains" when we do not know where it is raining. To be fair, though, Récanati asks us to imagine a scenario in which it rarely rains, and, as a consequence, many rain detectors have been placed around the globe. Each detector triggers an alarm bell in the Monitoring Room when it detects rain. Furthermore, Récanati asks us to imagine the presence of a single bell—the location of the triggering detector is indicated by a light on a board in the Monitoring Room. After a few weeks without rain, the bell rings and, upon hearing it, the weatherman on duty in the adjacent room shouts, "It rains!" Following Récanati, the weatherman's utterance is true iff it is raining (at the time of utterance) *in some place or other*. In such a situation, it seems that an utterance such as "It

rains" has a raison d'être, even if no specific location is considered. My reply is rather simple and straightforward: in such a situation, the verb 'to rain' would not have the same meaning as our own verb. In Wittgensteinian fashion, we could say that, in the scenario imagined by Récanati, the weatherman does not play the same language game as the one we play when the verb 'to rain' is involved. We would not be speaking the same language. More on this in the last section, where I discuss Perry's Z-lander scenario.

6. See *The New Shorter Oxford English Dictionary.*

7. I am borrowing this example from Condoravdi and Gawron (1996).

8. As far as I know, the first who suggested that when binding is possible we have to postulate an argument place for the alleged unarticulated constituent is Barbara Partee (1989). For more on the binding argument and the way it suggests the presence of tacit arguments at the level of LF, see Stanley 2000. For a criticism of the binding argument see Récanati 2002. Récanati's main argument is that it forces unwelcome consequences. In particular, it forces us to postulate the presence of argument places where, intuitively, there is none. Récanati invites us to consider an intransitive verb such as 'to eat', which denotes the property of eating. In that case, he argues, the contextually provided constituent results from free enrichment and not from the semantics of the verb, for in its intransitive reading 'eat' is not a two-places predicate, but in a sentence such as 'Jon ate' binding can occur:

(i)   Jon is anorexic, but whenever his father cooks mushrooms, he eats.

The intuitive way to understand it is that Jon eats *them*, i.e., *the mushrooms his father has cooked.* Examples like this seem to prove that intuitive binding, per se, does not entail the presence in the logical form of an argument place and, therefore, that the binding argument is not compelling. As we will soon see, though, my claim that we have to posit an argument place for a location when meteorological verbs are involved does not rest, unlike Stanley, on the binding argument. I can thus welcome Récanati's argument.

9. It may be worth mentioning that in some uses 'to run' can take a location as a subject: 'Chicago is running behind LA in population', 'That field there is running a close second to the one we saw yesterday and I may have to buy both!' These cases can be classified as idiomatic (or metaphorical). As such they are peculiar of English. Actually, they cannot be directly translated into other languages. In Italian, for instance, a word to world translation of 'Chicago is running behind LA in population' generates 'Chicago sta rincorrendo LA in popolazione', which, though grammatical, is senseless. This should suggest that when a verb like 'to run' takes a location as a subject it is used idiomatically or metaphorically.

10. For a more accurate discussion, see Haegeman 1994 (71), from whom I am borrowing the example.

11. Taylor presents a similar view: "I venture the hypothesis that some unexpressed parameters hide in what we might call the subsyntactic basement of suppressed verbal argument structure. Take the verb 'to rain' as an example. The view that I favor supposes that the verb 'to rain' has a lexically specified argument place which is θ-marked **THEME** and that this argument place takes

places [locations] as values. This is a way of saying that the subatomic structure of the verb 'to rain' explicitly marks raining as a kind of change that places [locations] undergo" (Taylor 2001, 53).

12. One could argue that the deference involved in the 'Gellman'–'Feynman' or 'elm'–'beech' cases differs from the deference involved in unarticulated constituents and that, in the case of 'It rains *here*', there can be deference just as in the case of 'It rains'. To begin with, I do not believe that one can defer, as far as reference is concerned, when one uses indexical expressions. One cannot say, for instance, "You are kind" and defer to someone else (an expert?) to fix the reference of the pronoun 'you'. The same applies in the case of 'here', 'now', 'today', and the like. One may not know which day it is or what location one is in, but in simply uttering 'now', 'today', or 'here', one immediately picks out and identifies the relevant location/time. Indexical thoughts are *perspectival*, whereas thoughts involving proper names and other terms are not (see Corazza 2002). Thus, I do not object to the fact that the kind of deference involved in the Kripke-Putnam example differs from that involved in the case of unarticulated constituents. Like all indexical thoughts, thoughts containing unarticulated constituents are perspectival. The deference involved does not concern the reference-fixing mechanisms. One's thought may be about a given location simply because the thought occurs in that very location, yet one need not represent the latter, i.e., one need not represent the implicit argument at work. Dokic (2002) spells out a theory of situated thoughts that could be adopted to account for the view that a thought can be about something simply by being situated in a given location. Thus, when one utters, "It is raining here," one represents and refers to the relevant location, simply by the act of uttering "here." We cannot deny that, in this case, one has a '*here*'-thought, just as one has an 'I'-thought when one uses the first person pronoun. When one utters "It is raining," on the other hand, one's thought is still about the relevant location, for it too occurs in that very location. Yet one does not represent the latter insofar as one utters no words standing for it; there is no morpheme one entertains standing for the relevant place. Thus, one may not have a '*here*'-thought. The unarticulated constituent at work in these cases need not be represented. It is in this sense that we can say that a child, for instance, can use meteorological verbs in a deferential way (i.e., without realizing that they are two-place predicates). That is to say, one can exploit a two-place predicate without knowing it, or even while believing it to be monadic.

13. Perry has suggested a third option to me. LF can be viewed as a combination, reached by accommodation of our linguistic institutions (both individual and community-wide) with the facts about how things work in the world. Although the two positions I have described can be viewed as externalist (LF depends on language-*qua*-social-entity) versus internalist (LF depends on language-*qua*-psychological-entity), this third option is a hybrid. As such, it is probably the more plausible, insofar as it recognizes that both internal and external constraints contribute in determining the LF of a relevant class of sentences. Without entering into the details and merits of the three options, it is worth noticing that they are *all* consonant with the view that implicit arguments need not be represented by the speaker and/or audience.

14. If one were to adopt a nominalist stance and assume conceptualism about properties, one would reject Perry's argument insofar as we could not have a nonlinguistic access to properties. If

so, in Z-landish and in English 'rain' would not have the same meaning. For a defense of conceptualism about properties, see Dokic 2001.

15. In assimilating the knowledge at issue with the use of 'It is raining' to a knowing-how ability I simply mean that, like most of our linguistic knowledge and behavior, this knowledge is akin to a practical capacity: thus the knowledge involved in the use and understanding of 'It is raining' bears some similarities with the knowledge involved in riding a bicycle or in swimming. Furthermore, this knowledge cannot be dissociated from the practical capacities one engages when using and or hearing this sentence. One can be said to master the use of 'It is raining' when one, in his own community, behaves in an appropriate way when using and or hearing it, e.g., when one takes an umbrella before going out, does not plan for an outdoor party, etc.

16. "This account can only be given in terms of the practical ability which the speaker displays in using sentences of the language; and, in general, the knowledge of which that practical ability is taken as a manifestation may be, and should be, regarded as only implicit knowledge" (Dummett 1993, 101).

References

Borg, E. 2005. "Saying What You Mean: Unarticulated Constituents and Communication." In R. Elugardo and R. Stainton (eds.), *Ellipsis and Non-sentential Speech*. Dordrecht: Springer.

Carston, R. 2002. *Thoughts and Utterances: The Pragmatics of Explicit Communication*. Oxford: Blackwell.

Castañeda, H.-N. 1966. "'He': A Study in the Logic of Self-Consciousness." *Ratio* 8: 130–157.

———. 1967. "Indicators and Quasi-Indicators." *American Philosophical Quarterly* 4: 85–100.

Condoravdi, C., and M. Gawron 1986. "The Context Dependency of Implicit Arguments." In K. Makoto, C. Piñón, and H. de Swart (eds.), *Quantifiers, Deduction, and Context*. Stanford, Calif.: CSLI Publications.

Corazza, E. 2002. "Temporal Indexicals and Temporal Terms." *Synthese* 130: 441–460.

———. 2004. *Reflecting the Mind: Indexicality and Quasi-Indexicality*. Oxford: Oxford University Press.

Dokic, J. 2001."Conceptualism about Properties: A Defense." Unpublished manuscript.

———. 2002. "Steps Toward a Theory of Situated Representations." Unpublished manuscript.

Dummett, M. 1993. *The Seas of Language*. Oxford: Oxford University Press.

Haegeman, L. 1994. *Government and Binding Theory*. Oxford: Blackwell.

Jackendoff, R. 1994. *Patterns in the Mind*. New York: Harper Collins.

Jacob, P. 1999. "Unarticulated Constituents and Explicit Content." Unpublished manuscript.

Kaplan, D. 1989. "Demonstratives." In Almog, J., J. Perry, and H. Wettstein (eds.), *Themes from Kaplan*. Oxford: Oxford University Press.

May, R. 1985. *Logical Form: Its Structure and Derivation*. Cambridge, Mass.: MIT Press.

Partee, B. 1989. "Binding Implicit Variables in Quantified Contexts." *Proceedings of the Chicago Linguistic Society* 25: 342–365.

Perry, J. 1977. "Frege on Demonstratives." *Philosophical Review* 86: 474–497.

———. 1986. "Thought without Representation." *Proceeding of the Aristotelian Society* 60: 137–152.

———. 1997. "Indexicals and Demonstratives." In R. Hale and C. Wright (eds.), *Companion to the Philosophy of Language*. Oxford: Blackwell.

———. 1998. "Indexicals, Context and Unarticulated Constituents." In Aliseda, A., R. van Glabbeek, and D. Westerståhl (eds.), *Computing Natural Language*. Stanford, Calif.: CSLI Publications.

———. 2001. *Reference and Reflexivity*. Stanford, Calif.: CSLI Publications.

Récanati, F. 2002. "Unarticulated Constituents." *Linguistics and Philosophy* 25: 299–345.

Searle, J. 1978. "Literal Meaning." *Erkenntnis* 13: 207–224.

Stanley, J. 2000. "Context and Logical Form." *Linguistic and Philosophy* 23: 391–434.

Taylor, K. 2001. "Sex, Breakfast, and Descriptus Interruptus." *Synthese* 128: 45–61.

The New Shorter Oxford English Dictionary. Oxford: Clarendon Press. 1993.

Travis, C. 1985. "On What Is Strictly Speaking True." *Canadian Journal of Philosophy* 15: 187–229.

Wittgenstein, L. 1952. *Philosophical Investigations*. Oxford: Blackwell.

13 Thinking about Qualia

Brian Loar

John Perry's *Knowledge, Possibility, and Consciousness* (2001) is a wonderful essay in sophisticated theory and lucid explanation. Perry defends physicalism about phenomenal qualities against a contingent of well-known antiphysicalist arguments with incisive and original constructions, and with admirably gentle and constructive polemics. The upshot is a compelling essay in how to think about the exasperating topic of qualia. Alas many of us, including me, have our own difficult ways of conceptualizing these topics, and I fear that in this short chapter the argument is denser than I would like it to be. It is easy to admire Perry's lucidity but not so easy to emulate it. The chapter proceeds as follows. I will first consider, not for the first time, the instructive antiphysicalist arguments of Saul Kripke and Frank Jackson, in the hope that counterarguments will produce some useful structures. The rest of the chapter is an attempt at saying what *phenomenal concepts* are, and how we think about qualia, with some indication why that topic is, as it seems to me, at the core of the debate about qualia.

Kripke's Argument

Saul Kripke's argument against physicalism begins with the observation that if the phenomenal property of pain were identical with a physical property (e.g., C-fiber stimulation), then that statement would be a posteriori; and, of course, it would be *necessary*. What might explain this combination? Some unproblematic identities are apparently similar (e.g., "heat = molecular motion"), which is necessary and a posteriori. In Kripke's framework, if a statement is a posteriori, its mode of presentation (as I will call a certain proposition) must be *contingent*. In the present case, the mode of presentation is say [the cause of heat-sensations = molecular motion]. That is contingent. The contingency of that mode of presentation makes the statement a posteriori, even though the statement as a whole is necessary.

By contrast, the phenomenal concept of pain conceives pain under a noncontingent mode of presentation (e.g., feeling painful). And the mode of presentation of "C-fiber stimulation" is, plausibly, C-fiber stimulation itself. (There are accounts of the semantics of theories on which at least some theoretical terms come out thus.) So the psychophysical identity would have to be a posteriori and yet have a noncontingent mode of presentation. According to Kripke, this does not make sense.

How then might a defender of physicalism reply? There are two ways. First, find a contingency in the statement that explains its a posteriori status. Second, deny that being a posteriori implies having a contingent mode of presentation.

As I understand it, a certain argument of Perry's takes the first way.

The reflexive content that captures the additional demand that the new belief places on the world is simply that the reference of his stimulated C-fibers concept and the inner state he is in and is attending to are one and the same. There is nothing contradictory or incoherent about the content of his current state at this reflexive level, since we are abstracting from the sensation his inner attention buffer is of. (182)

So the a posteriori status of an identity statement of the form "C-fiber stimulation is identical with *that* internal state of mine" can be explained by the following contingency. The statement has a reflexive content that *abstracts from* the demonstrative phrase's referring to the sensation of pain. That the reflexive content is true is contingent, for what it refers to is contingent. (I think this is the point, but I may not have got it right.)

But I worry about the following objection. The antiphysicalist may say that even though Perry does provide a factor that is a posteriori and contingent, there is another a posteriori mode of presentation (of the psychophysical identity) that does not correspond to something contingent. Think the thought in question—"C-fiber stimulation is identical with *that* internal state of mine"—*without* abstracting from the sensation of pain. That is a posteriori and is, if true, necessarily true. A supporter of Kripke may say that this configuration is incoherent, and, because it is implied by the psychophysical identity, that that identity statement is also incoherent.

The second answer to Kripke denies that being a posteriori requires having a contingent mode of presentation. This is the reply I will defend. The basic point is that being a posteriori is not a modal-semantic property but a psychological-cognitive property, or, to put it another way, a matter of conceptual role. The conceptual role of the phenomenal concept *feeling like that*, and the conceptual role of the verbal-theoretical concept of C-fiber stimulation, are conceptually independent. That is all one needs to explain the a posteriori status of the identity. The phenomenal concept of feeling pain and the theoretical concept of C-fiber stimulation are such empirically independent sorts of concept that the metaphysics of their references are, on the face of it, beside the point. Even if two such concepts connote the same mode of presentation, that is, a certain property, there is no reason to suppose that those concepts should thereby be connected a priori. A related point is this. A physicalist about phenomenal properties will be a physicalist about phenomenal concepts. According to the physicalist, the phenomenal *concept* of pain will be deeply connected with the neural underpinnings of pain itself, whereas the theoretical concept of C-fiber stimulation will be connected with language-cognitive centers and not with pain centers. The antiphysicalist assumption that a posteriori connections between phenomenal and theoretical concepts must imply contingent property relations—modes of presentation in that sense—should then appear unmotivated to the physicalist. (These reflections will I think be congenial to Perry, and that is a reason to suppose I may not have got his reply to Kripke right.)

It will be useful now to have a look at Jackson's *Mary* argument and then to consider its relation to Kripke's argument and to the more general picture.

Jackson's Argument

Mary the brilliant scientist has been confined to a black and white room. She has learned all there is to know about the brains of normal people like us, who know what seeing red is like. She emerges, she experiences seeing red things, and she thereby learns what we have been experiencing all along, that is, what it is like to experience the quale that Perry calls Q_{wow}—what it is like to see red. According to Jackson, if Q_{wow} were a physical property, Mary would already have known that other people had it. But, upon her emergence, Mary has learned a new fact about what other people have been experiencing. Because that would not be so were physicalism true, Jackson concludes that a form of property dualism is true. Phenomenal properties are real, and they are not physical or functional properties.

Perry's reply is that the argument commits "the subject matter fallacy." It is true that Mary learns something new about us, but this implies property dualism only if she has learned a *new subject matter*. That would mean her learning that the rest of us have had a property that she did not know about, under any description, before she left the black and white room. Perry agrees that it is correct to say that Mary "learns something new" and that this is a matter of Mary's having a new true thought. But the physicalist should say that that knowledge is new because it involves a new *concept*. That is a matter of what Perry calls new *reflexive content* (what I will call below a new phenomenal concept). This does not imply that she has learned something about a new property, because Mary's new knowledge is compatible with the new concept's referring to a property she already knows about under a different concept, a certain physical property. One may ask why this isn't a new subject matter at a different level. Perry's reply, I believe, is that the new knowledge is not about new concepts; it rather *uses* new concepts.

Even so, it may be said, what appears new to Mary is the phenomenal quality itself. She points to an instance of Q_{wow} and comments: so that is what seeing red is like. But Perry's point is that how Mary conceives things—in particular her attending to an instance of Q_{wow}—is a function of what concept she *deploys* rather, and not what concept she thinks about. We may point out that when she first experiences Q_{wow} she says "so *that* is what it is like; that is how they have been experiencing it." She is able to make this judgment it seems only because she has a certain phenomenal concept. She is attending to the experience by way of a novel concept.

But there is still something puzzling here, two things in fact. The first is that qualia have the properties they appear to have quite independently of how we conceive of them. Indeed, Perry speaks of knowing the subjective characters of sensations (what they are like) and their being independent of our attending to them. And this may seem inconsistent with saying that what is new is at the level of reflexive contents. The second puzzle is this. It is not easy to say what phenomenal concepts are without mentioning phenomenal properties themselves. Indeed, it may seem that understanding phenomenal properties is required for understanding phenomenal concepts.

At this point, I should say that I am uncertain about how Perry formulates his point about reflexive content. Reflexive content is a matter of demonstrative thinking; and the question it raises is whether a purely demonstrative mode of presentation can *reflect* the unique quality of a phenomenal concept. The line of reply to the dualist we are considering seems to put the weight of phenomenality on demonstrative *concepts*. But if those concept-tokens have the simple demonstrative form "that property," how can they reflect the vast varieties of phenomenal properties? Phenomenal concepts must differ as variously as phenomenal properties differ, and the omniconcept "that" can achieve this only if its uses are somehow grounded in phenomenal properties. Perry points out that thinking about qualia involves attending to *images* and *Humean ideas*. And they are representations of qualia. But it would be odd to suppose that qualia get their characteristic flavor in part from Humean ideas, odd to regard the vivid as engendered by the faint.

And yet Perry must be right in holding that what Mary acquires on her emergence from the room is a new *conception* of a property that she already thought about under a theoretical description. Later I will propose that a phenomenal concept is a recognitional concept, grounded in a disposition to recognize positive and negative instances of a certain phenomenal property. And such a recognitional concept stands in an intimate relation to whatever phenomenal properties it serves to recognize. In exercising a phenomenal recognitional concept, instances of the corresponding phenomenal property will trigger the concept, as if announcing its belonging. This is how a vivid quale may appear to be a component of a phenomenal concept. I say "may appear" to note that the quale is not, in my view (see below), in fact such a component. When Mary emerges and experiences the phenomenal property Q_{wow}, she seems perhaps to exercise a phenomenal concept that includes that property. A more cautious formulation is that the new experience engenders a new concept. Armed with that new concept, Mary has the thought that Q_{wow} is what the rest of us have been experiencing. That thought is new because that recognitional concept is new and because that Q_{wow} is a new experience for her. Perry's idea of recognitional/identificatory concepts may lead to the same analysis.

I am, however, not confident that I know how such concepts are intended to work. When Mary emerges, she conceives things in a new way. Jackson takes that to imply that she knows a new fact. We have interpreted this to mean that she has a novel way of thinking about an old fact. Is there yet a way of making it reasonable for Jackson to insist that it is a new fact and not a new conceptualization of an old fact? Well there is, if phenomenal concepts are dependent on phenomenal properties; something like this emerges in what follows. New concepts then, one might suppose, imply new facts. But this doesn't work: one must be careful about the use of 'new'. What is uncontroversially new about Q_{wow} is that it is newly instantiated by Mary. That hardly implies that it is new in the sense of her not having conceived of it earlier under some concept or other.

The Jackson argument leaves itself open to the objection that what is new is the deployment of a new concept. At this point, it is not clear what backup argument might insist that nevertheless phenomenal concepts cannot have physical properties as their references. The Kripke argument produces a conceptual-metaphysical connection: a posteriority must derive from a contingent mode of presentation. It may seem that this thesis could fit handily into the Jackson argument: phenomenal concepts refer to physical propositions only if they have physical modes of presentation, for such concepts are one-dimensional. But then we must face the elusiveness of physicalism: phenomenal concepts will always evade proof of the physical nature of their references. This is true, but it is not an argument. The antecedent physicalist, in Perry's phrase, has long ago conceded that. There is no refuting a determined dualist. But the antecedent physicalist position is at least as strong, more so in fact, if you take the whole picture into account.

Phenomenal Concepts as Recognitional Concepts

A familiar way of expressing physicalism about the mental makes physicalism a matter of supervenience, whether the mental supervenes on the physical. It is, however, generally agreed among qualiphiles, physicalist, and dualist alike that all of physical fact and theory, couched in physical language, does not conceptually entail anything about qualia. So, if physicalism is coherent, supervenience in the foregoing sense must not imply conceptual supervenience. A familiar move invokes instead "metaphysical supervenience." Nevertheless, some philosophers, including me, do not understand the idea of nonconceptual metaphysical supervenience, except as a matter of property identity.[1] Physicalism then becomes an identity thesis (i.e., that all properties are physical properties).

When we think about qualia or phenomenal properties directly, we do so using phenomenal concepts. The question how phenomenal concepts are constructed and how they work has become central in recent discussions. There are apparent differences about how phenomenal concepts determine reference to phenomenal properties and how those concepts are able to conceive of qualia "directly." Phenomenal concepts are somewhat unusual, and they are idiosyncratic enough to make antiphysicalists suppose that perhaps there is a weakness here in the physicalist position.

We often use descriptions to point to phenomenal properties—"dull toothache." But phenomenal concepts are not descriptive, and we conceive of qualia rather as we experience them. There is no independent mode of presentation that mediates our phenomenal concepts and qualia; it is as if, in using those concepts, we are directly acquainted with qualia. Invoking "acquaintance" is intuitively apt here, but not as a theoretical term that we might philosophically explicate. It is a phenomenological concept, and physicalists are entitled to it on that understanding. They may say that, just as pain is identical with a physical state, so being acquainted with a phenomenal property is identical with being in a suitably structured physical state. But even if we regard the notion of acquaintance as a mere manner of speaking and not a proper object of physicalist identification, it still gives us a handle on the phenomenology of phenomenal concepts: we can understand those concepts as focusing our acquaintance with phenomenal properties.

It seems that a phenomenal concept of a quale Q is unique in the following sense, that there cannot be two cognitively independent phenomenal concepts of Q. It is tempting to register this by saying that the quale is a *component* in some sense of one's phenomenal concept of Q, that nothing else is needed to individuate that concept and that the remaining features of the concept are shared with all other phenomenal concepts.

A dualist may suppose that merging the last two ideas gives us an account of phenomenal concepts: we refer to qualia via acquaintance with them, phenomenal concepts somehow incorporate phenomenal properties, and there is nothing more to those concepts than that. Although this can be said—and it does capture something intuitive about phenomenal concepts—it is not illuminating. Physicalists can hardly be satisfied with it, even if we add "and this is all physical." We also want an untrivial account of what makes a concept the concept of a certain phenomenal property. The question may be put thus: by virtue of what does a person have a phenomenal concept of a particular quale?

In earlier papers (1997, 2003b) I proposed that phenomenal concepts are a kind of *recognitional concept*. Such concepts are constituted by dispositions to assert and to deny instances. The thesis that there are such concepts cannot be tested by seeing whether the idea works for socially established concepts such as 'horse'. These are not recognitional concepts, which is not to say that there cannot be recognitional concepts of horses. Recognitional concepts are individuated in several dimensions, and one of them is perspectival. These concepts are from a point of view, and they are not always enduring. There is no fixed perspective for recognitional concepts in general. But I won't discuss the theory of reference in this chapter. What I say about phenomenal concepts depends on the coherence of the idea of recognitional concepts and corresponding suppositions about reference.

All we have to go on directly are quale instances or tokens. Even if our phenomenal *concepts* were innate or in some sense psychologically natural, the question remains what constitutes them. A reason for holding phenomenal concepts to be recognitional concepts is that a theory of phenomenal concepts should explain how phenomenal concepts manage to refer to phenomenal properties of varying degrees of generality. Some phenomenal concepts are maximally specific—for example, the concept of unique green or its phenomenal counterpart unique green*—whereas others come in less specific degrees of generality: there is the broad phenomenal concept of pain, the less general concept of toothache, and the still more specific concept of dull toothache. It again might be said that these relations of determinable-determinate are psychologically *natural*. The question remains, what draws the lines? What constitutes these concepts? A commonsense answer is simply that they are certain recognitional concepts, constituted by acceptance and rejection (or, better, by "determinate" acceptance and rejection.) Perhaps "constituted" isn't quite right; at an unconscious level there may well be factors that explain how we group phenomenal properties together in familiar intuitive ways. What we are looking for then might simply be how such concepts manifest themselves consciously. The answer, it seems to me, is as recognitional concepts.

From the perspective of the physicalist qualiphile, the structure of a phenomenal concept should be the same for both antiphysicalist and physicalist. Of course, the antiphysicalist needn't agree; he could insist that there is an ineffable relation between a phenomenal concept and a phenomenal property and that no philosophical explication is required. But even though the dualist may take that line, the idea of recognitional concepts and the corresponding notion of reference can I think be coherently accepted by him. A dualist could accept my account of the nature of phenomenal concepts. But the physicalist should, if possible, give a constructive account of phenomenal reference. For according to the physicalist, a phenomenal property is identical with a physical property and a person's having a phenomenal concept of a quale is the same as her standing in a certain reference relation to whatever physical property that quale is identical with. The recognitional ability will, of course, apply itself according to our phenomenal take on those physical properties. We will not be noting nonphenomenal physical resemblances.

If physicalism is true, however, our sorting dispositions will have physical properties as their focus, though not in physical terms. That must be a component of any story we tell about what would count as evidence that physicalism is true. Reference relations are crucial in any kind of empirical psycho-physical investigation. And, of course a sorting relation will be, if it turns up the right sort of physical properties, referential.

Again, however, we must note that the general idea of phenomenal reference as recognitionally based is compatible with antiphysicalism. The two issues—the nature of phenomenal concepts, on the one hand, and physicalism, on the other—appear to be independent.

In noting the specificity and breadth of phenomenal concepts we should keep in mind the vast array of actual and possible qualia and phenomenal concepts. It seems sensible to suppose that we are born perhaps not with an innate repertory of all those phenomenal concepts but at least with a structured ability to form them. It is not interesting to be told that our phenomenal concepts simply have systematically differing scopes, as a brute fact. It is a conceptual achievement that our concepts are thus, and it would be somewhat odd if we lacked even a shallow story.

It seems to me commonsensical that a phenomenal concept must be grounded in a disposition to apply the concept in certain cases and to deny it in others, to judge when it is applicable and when not—yes for this, no for that. Phenomenal concepts are—on the surface, at least—concepts that differ entirely in virtue of one's constitutive dispositions to apply or deny them in certain phenomenal circumstances. Recognitional concepts are a kind of concept of which there are countless examples. Paradigms are visual concepts whose references are kinds of flora or fauna for which we lack names. Unlike phenomenal concepts, these concepts do not pick out their references directly. Consider the difference between visual and tactile concepts of surface types, which are mediated by visual and tactile perceptual experiences. We can speak of those experiences as modes of presentation of the corresponding visual and tactile recognitional concepts; or we might mean by "modes of presentations" the concepts themselves, as psychological or cognitive entities. Those concepts are able to play cognitive roles by virtue of a mechanism we do not know about. Somehow those perceptual experiences are focused by conceptual processes, and they become, by virtue of conceptual molding, perceptual recognitional concepts, and thereby fit into the frames of thoughts.

We can say that the phenomenological character of such perceptual recognitional concepts is determined by those different visual and tactile experiences and not by their references. I proposed elsewhere (2003b) that we are able to take two perspectives on our experiences, what we can call *transparent* and *opaque*. From the transparent perspective, the phenomenology of our visual experiences and concepts is object directed. But the previous remark concerns the phenomenology of visual experiences and concepts from the opaque perspective; from it one discerns experiences as they are internally individuated, that is, as qualia.

The difference between those perceptual recognitional concepts and phenomenal concepts is that the phenomenological character of phenomenal concepts are determined by the character of the phenomenal property thereby referred to, and that is identical with its mode of presentation—on the understanding of a mode of presentation on which it is a component of a concept and not a concept itself. But on the understanding on which it can be identified with a concept (in a psychological sense of 'concept'), the mode of presentation itself plays a conceptual, cognitive role. This observation applies not only to modes of presentation of phenomenal concepts but also to those of the perceptual concepts mentioned above.

Earlier we posed the question how a theory of phenomenal reference might account for the varying generality and specificity of phenomenal properties. It is clear that recognitional concepts vary in the requisite way. How are we able to acquire such a vast variety of recognitional dispositions? That we do not know. Philosophy can only speak of quality spaces and innate dispositions to classify certain resemblances. In any case, the vast wealth of such resemblances among kinds of external objects is matched with an equally vast wealth of qualia types. In both cases sortal dispositions underpin concepts.[2]

Are phenomenal concepts—those recognitional concepts—demonstratives? Phenomenal concepts do naturally involve a use of demonstratives in thought. We may mean by 'type-demonstrative' two different semantic entities. The first is the *unassigned* demonstrative. This has a general use, and that general use has no single reference attached to it. There is also what we can call the *assigned* type-demonstrative: it has the same use and reference on each occasion of its use and may have the form "one of *them*." Memory ties the different occurrences together. The reference of such a type demonstrative is determined by a classifying disposition, and so we can say that it, that assigned demonstrative, is a recognitional concept. When I say "that kind of animal," the use of the demonstrative is mediated by, let's say, an optical relation and other relations (e.g., of location) to instances of the referred to type. So the assigned demonstrative is determined by contextually determined relations and a recognitional disposition. And it is natural to think of recognitional concepts as having a qualifying condition: not just "that," but also "that kind of animal." These factors, and the nature of the observed entities, determine the reference of that assigned demonstrative, a certain kind of animal. All of this carries over to phenomenal concepts, which are a kind of applied demonstrative.

What I am calling a *phenomenal concept* has two dimensions: there is the phenomenal property on which it focuses—the concept's reference—and there is its conceptual role, which depends on its having psychological properties whereby it causally interacts with other concepts. In the case of phenomenal concepts, these are intimately related.

In Perry's analysis, the concepts with which we think about phenomenal properties are demonstratives. Here is his understanding of how demonstratives in general work. Statements that contain demonstratives have two sorts of content, "subject matter" and "reflexive content." The former is truth-conditions of the sort determined by references. Reflexive content can also be called reflexive truth-conditions (129). Consider 'that man is F', where the demonstrative is backed by a visual demonstrative that focuses on a certain man. The reflexive truth condition is expressed as follows: the thought "that man is F" is true iff *the man to whom the thinker of that thought is visually attending* is F. The phrase 'that man . . .' expresses the reflexive reference conditions of the demonstrative 'that man'. Perry's account of reflexive truth-conditions assigns to reflexive reference conditions two roles. One is their role in determining, given the context, the reference of 'that man'. The other is what Perry calls "cognitive significance" (131) and what I will call *conceptual role*.

Phenomenal concepts are counted by Perry as demonstratives. "When we are attending to a subjective character in the subjective way ... we use our flexible demonstrative, 'this', as in 'This feeling is the one I've been having'. Let's label this use of 'this' as an inner demonstrative: 'this$_i$'" (146). (That demonstrative, as we have seen, plays a central role in Perry's response to the Mary argument.) Clearly, reference here is to a phenomenal property: "this feeling." And the question arises how a demonstrative of this sort manages to refer to a phenomenal property. When Mary leaves the black and white room, she experiences what it is like to see red, that is, like *this$_i$*, where 'this$_i$' refers to a phenomenal property. Perry says that Mary's "new knowledge is a case of recognitional or identificational knowledge" (147). That seems to point to the kind of recognitional concepts to which I have been suggesting phenomenal concepts belong. In another passage he says, "Many of our concepts of sensible properties, such as being red, have a demonstrative/recognitional core. In normal daylight conditions most of us can simply look at a nearby object and say with a great deal of confidence whether or not it is red" (141). The "core" is perhaps intended to be a *personal* concept of red that is *constituted* by one's identifying dispositions. If that is so, then these demonstrative concepts are pretty much what I mean above by recognitional concepts. But we should note that Perry also mentions other factors as components of our acquaintance with the phenomenal properties. "It should be no surprise that we can have *complex concepts of universals, involving images, Humean ideas*" (142). This apparently suggests that there are phenomenal concepts that refer to properties by virtue of factors other than recognitional abilities. Something like this complication is found in related forms in other writers, and we will turn to it shortly.

This may be the place to note an argument of David Chalmers that phenomenal concepts cannot be demonstratives (Chalmers 1996). Suppose that P is a phenomenal concept and D is any demonstrative concept. According to Chalmers it will always be possible for one rationally to deny the identity "$P = D$." It follows that P cannot be one of the Ds. The intuitive idea seems to be that a demonstrative does not reveal the essence of what it picks out, whereas a phenomenal concept does. But this argument does not apply to the recognitional concepts that we have proposed to be identical with phenomenal concepts. Chalmers's point would be true only if a recognitional phenomenal concept can be, as it were, phenomenally blank, that is, that one can grasp the concept without thereby grasping the phenomenal property it stands for. But I do not think that is possible. Perhaps there is an ambiguity in what counts as "demonstrative," and one use of that may be simply to refer to concepts that are, for whatever reason, natural to express using 'that' and the like. The basic topic of my account however is not demonstratives in some precise sense but recognitional concepts. More on the idea of blank demonstratives below.

Type Modes of Presentation

Apart from being recognitional concepts, have phenomenal concepts any other essential features? There have been proposals for other factors. To begin with, it is natural to ask whether phenomenal concepts have modes of presentation, and if so what they are. If we were to follow a suggestion of Kripke's, we might say that the phenomenal concept "pain" has as its mode of presentation the feeling of pain itself. This could simply convey the idea that a phenomenal concept does not have a contingent mode of presentation; but it also has a positive point, as we will see.

Should we say that phenomenal concepts have "noncontingent" modes of presentation? If so, then the mode of presentation of the phenomenal concept of pain (i.e., pain) is identical with the concept's reference (i.e., pain). By contrast, the mode of presentation of a visual recognitional concept is contingently related to its referent. But the idea of a noncontingent mode of presentation is not trivial, for it and contingent modes of presentation play similar cognitive roles. The visual recognitional concept of a ping-pong ball employs a visual state in a familiar way. Not only does that perceptual factor track the concept's *reference* (a certain spherical type), but it also determines the conceptual role of that visual concept. A corresponding factor apparently determines, in crucial part, a phenomenal concept's role in thought.[3] The property pain has a similar role in determining the pain-concept's role in thought. This similarity of conceptual role appears to justify speaking of the property pain as both mode of presentation and reference of the phenomenal concept of pain.

So a phenomenal concept has as its mode of presentation the very phenomenal property it picks out. But this cozy circle does not explain how a given phenomenal concept *refers* to a given phenomenal property, for it does not answer the fundamental question, which is how the owner of that concept is able to refer to the phenomenal property of pain.

Do type modes of presentation really explain the epistemic roles of phenomenal concepts? It seems that token modes of presentation—present pains and pain memories—are what really do the work. But that is all right. The type determines what is causally relevant, or at least what on the surface seems causally relevant. That relation between token and type is normally present in causal interaction, and it allows an ordinary causal relevance, and hence conceptual role, to phenomenal types—but, of course, we should say, to phenomenal types as they fit in the frame of a concept.

Present-day proponents of a certain sort of "two-dimensional semantics" seem to suppose, like Kripke, that what is a posteriori and a priori is a matter of (as I would put it) what proposition is *expressed* by a thought. But it seems to me more to the point to say that what is a posteriori or a priori is a matter of concepts and their relations and that concepts are not fully determined by propositional factors, even at the level of what is expressed. Concepts have cognitive-psychological features in addition to whatever propositional factor they express—that is, whatever gives the concept a conceptual role. So it seems to me that what makes a judgment a posteriori is not something semantic-*cum*-modal—not a matter of a proposition and its contingency—but something we may call *psychological* or *cognitive*. Again, it is the sort of thing that we can speak of as having a functional or conceptual role.

From the foregoing remarks it should be clear that invoking phenomenal type modes of presentation as an underpinning of phenomenal concepts is a matter of making economic use of what we already have, and this is not incompatible with the spirit of the idea that phenomenal concepts are simply certain recognitional concepts. We will see below why it may appear that further factors, such as token modes of presentation, ought to be regarded as also required or are also available for grounding a different sort of concept.

Consider the thesis that phenomenal properties are determined solely by certain recognitional dispositions, what we may call the simple dispositional theory of phenomenal concepts. It may seem that the simple condition is compatible with being satisfied by a self-directed blind-sight concept, for, of course, the mere disposition to judge "there it is again," as it were in the dark or without feeling, evidently does not suffice for grounding a phenomenal concept. One might accidentally catch a kind in one's net, but it will not be a quale. Exercising a recognitional disposition is obviously compatible with being attuned to a property of which one is not phenomenally conscious. Some seem to have thought that the simple theory implies that that is all there is to what I am calling a phenomenal concept, and then the question becomes what we must *add* to the recognitional concept to give us a genuine phenomenal concept.

In an earlier paper (1997), I proposed the following: "one can focus attention on the phenomenal quality [of] cramp feeling by way of a token cramp feeling...particular cramp feelings and images can focus one's conception of the phenomenal quality of cramp feeling." "As for self-directed blindsight concepts...they differ from phenomenal concepts [in] that they [blindsight concepts] lack...phenomenal 'token modes of presentation'." The idea then is that what determines a phenomenal concept is complex, combining a certain recognitional disposition and a token mode of presentation. The two together were supposed to suffice for a genuine phenomenal concept.

Although I now think that token modes of presentation are not components of phenomenal concepts, the notion that they are is espoused by several philosophers, and so I will address the issue.

Token qualia have been supposed to play two roles in fashioning phenomenal concepts. The first we have just seen, that token qualia are components of phenomenal concepts with other essential components. But in another role, token qualia seem to be offered as the primary ingredient of phenomenal concepts. This has been proposed by several philosophers (e.g., Perry, Block, and Papineau).

Perry writes, "there is a way of attending to a subjective character that is possible only when one is having an experience of which it is the subjective character." Again, "Suppose now that you are demonstratively identifying the property of being red, pointing at a red object, and saying, 'This color is red'. If you are correct you have referred to [the color red]" (141). I read the two passages (perhaps mistakenly) as saying that we can refer to a property by way of referring to a token of that property.

In a recent paper, Ned Block (2002) proposes that a phenomenal concept must contain an instance of a phenomenal experience (what I am calling a phenomenal token) and that a phenomenal concept of a phenomenal property P must somehow embed a token of P. The notable thesis is that one can have a phenomenal concept of P by virtue of having an experience that is P. On his view, this phenomenal token is not meant to be added to a recognitional concept, for recognitional dispositions are not determinants of phenomenal concepts. The experience is a component of the phenomenal concept, it seems, raw and unconceptualized, and that is what explains the cognitive role of the phenomenal concept. Perry says something more elaborate that, on one interpretation, seems close in spirit to the point. He says, "it should be no surprise that we can have complex concepts of universals, involving images, Humean ideas, typical instances, causes, effects, the expressions that stand for the universal, and so forth. We can have different concepts of the same universal." As noted above, the relevant part is "concepts of universals, involving images, Humean ideas." This might seem to imply that there is a concept of a phenomenal property that is determined by a visual experience, and another one by a visual memory. But how should we interpret this, token-type wise? On a natural interpretation, images include say visual token color experiences, and Humean ideas include visual memories of specific color experiences. This assumes that one cannot have a memory of red in general, which seems wrong. One can have such a memory, but I am inclined to think that a recognitional disposition goes along with it. How else does one get the full generality? Each would determine a concept of a universal only if, it seems, tokens of universals determine universals, or (a new idea) that memories of a shade of red might determine the universal red. We will see how, on a certain interpretation, this seems to be plausible in a moment. But I will suggest that it does not give us concepts of experience-universals other than recognitional concepts of them.

Those uses of quale tokens suggest that awareness of an instance of a phenomenal property (red*, say) is enough to give one the phenomenal concept of that phenomenal property. There are at least two ways to understand this. The first is downright puzzling. The second is intelligible, but it does not give us an alternative to the idea that a phenomenal concept is a recognitional concept.

1. The idea seems to be that by focusing attention on an instance of a quale one can thereby acquire a phenomenal concept, by virtue of that focusing's determining a phenomenal property—that is, the reference of that phenomenal concept. But that raises an old problem. Does a token of a light shade of red* determine the quale red*, the quale light red*, the quale "warm-colored*"? It doesn't determine any single such phenomenal property as it were metaphysically. So there is a puzzle as to what these philosophers have in mind. My suggestion (1997) that "one can focus attention on the phenomenal quality [of] cramp feeling by way of a token cramp feeling" raises similar problems, at least when generalized.

2. There is an interesting psychological phenomenon that deserves mention. It may even explain the intuitions that motivate the ideas above. A new phenomenal concept *can* be psychologically determined by a single token.

Consider what happens when you see a new kind of tropical fish at the aquarium, or when an experienced bird watcher sees a new kind of bird. One has the feeling that one will be able to recognize *another one of those creatures* when one see it, and this turns out to be right, which is to say, on future occasions one easily judges "there's another one" and also "that's not one." It seems that there must be an interesting psychological basis for this, though of course it is not our point to pursue how it works. The present idea is that it might explain the foregoing intuitions without any problematic metaphysical determination of type by token. But at the same time the phenomenon is dependent on recognitional concepts. I would put the structure of that conceptual capacity thus: attending to an instance of a certain kind somehow generates a dispositional concept that determines a phenomenal concept. Again how this is possible, what the underlying psychology is, one does not know. In any case, the phenomenon in question does not support the idea that you can focus attention on an instance of a phenomenal property and thereby fix a phenomenal property without thereby generating a recognitional concept. If that were possible, we would need nothing dispositional to determine perceptual type reference. But a token of a property does not metaphysically determine that property uniquely.

The task then is to explain how purely recognitional concepts can be phenomenal concepts while at the same time to answer the blank demonstrative worry. I will mention another role for token-qualia, and for phenomenal memories, in what I hope is a realistic account of what it is like to think about a phenomenal property.

The worry has been that a mere recognitional concept, directed at one's inner states, cannot (on its own) be a phenomenal concept, because it could not be distinguished from blank demonstrative concepts. ("There it is again. I don't know what I'm tracking, but they say I'm on to something.") This worry, it seems to me, is unmotivated, when one considers the setting in which phenomenal concepts are normally deployed.

Before turning to the relevance of qualia tokens, we should keep in mind the role of qualia in what we have called *type modes of presentation*. As Papineau (2003) puts it, "the 'involvement' of phenomenal states in phenomenal concepts is a matter of the concepts simultaneously both using and mentioning the states." More specifically, as I have just suggested, the conceptual role of a phenomenal concept is determined by the phenomenal property it stands for, by virtue of the latter's role in the phenomenal concept. Does this answer the worry about blank demonstrative concepts? Not really, for the question is just whether phenomenal concepts can be identical with certain recognitional concepts. The foregoing remarks about phenomenal modes of presentation does not answer this question. It will apply to genuine phenomenal concepts; but the question is what constitutes them.

Answering this question requires keeping in mind the *setting* in which phenomenal concepts are fashioned and deployed. Suppose your nose is itching. This has a distinctive feel and—as with the tropical fish—you are confident, unless you have a poor memory, that you will recognize that experience (type) when it recurs. You have implicitly fashioned a phenomenal concept, and that means, according to my account, that you have a disposition to say "yes" (here it is again) or "no" (a different feeling) or "borderline" (rather peculiar). Is that recognitional confidence like a blank demonstrative experience? This is an odd question. Here you are saying yes to a lively experience, and you are asked whether what you are experiencing is like not having any sensation at all. But if the answer to this is obvious, so is the answer to the question whether your recognitional concept is indistinguishable from a blank demonstrative concept. A recognitional concept is grounded in dispositions to respond to certain experiences. It would, intuitively, be a different concept if it involved a disposition to say yes to the taste of pineapple or to something phenomenally blank.

Notice that what distinguishes the itchy recognitional concept from the fruity one is not any particular token experience. Rather, an experiential type is built into each of these recognitional concepts. But of course this is not news; it is already present in our understanding of those concepts.

Notes

1. For some remarks about this see Loar 2003a.

2. Diana Raffman has argued (1995) that phenomenal concepts cannot be recognitional concepts. The basis of the argument is that we are able to discriminate but not to reidentify most fine-grained shades of colors; our memories are not up to it. But, at the same time, we are able to conceive those fine-grained shades. A quick and crudely brief response is that it is false that we have *phenomenal concepts* of those shades. For a fuller reply see Loar 1999 (120–123).

3. In a recent paper, Ned Block (2002) calls this a "cognitive mode of presentation."

References

Block, N. 2002. "The Harder Problem of Consciousness." *Journal of Philosophy* 99: 1–35.

Chalmers, D. 1996. *The Conscious Mind.* Oxford: Oxford University Press.

Loar, B. 1997. "Phenomenal States." In N. Block, O. Flanagan, and G. Güzeldere (eds.), *The Nature of Consciousness.* Cambridge, Mass.: MIT Press.

———. 1999. "Should the Explanatory Gap Perplex Us?" In T. Rockmore (ed.), *Proceedings of the Twentieth World Congress of Philosophy*, vol. 2. Bowling Green, Ohio: Bowling Green State University Press.

———. 2003a. "Phenomenal Intentionality as the Basis of Mental Content." In M. Hahn and B. Ramberg (eds.), *Reflections and Replies: Essays on the Philosophy of Tyler Burge.* Cambridge, Mass.: MIT Press.

———. 2003b. "Qualia, Properties, Modality." In E. Sosa and E. Villanueva (eds.), *Philosophical Issues 13: Philosophy of Mind.* Oxford: Blackwell.

———. 2003c. "Transparent Experience and the Availability of Qualia." In Q. Smith and A. Jokic (eds.), *Consciousness.* Oxford: Oxford University Press.

Papineau, D. 2003. "Reply to Kirk and Melnyk." *SWIF Philosophy of Mind.* Http://lgxserver.uniba.it/lei/mind/forums/004_0004.htm.

Perry, J. 2001. *Knowledge, Possibility, and Consciousness.* Cambridge, Mass.: MIT Press.

Raffman, D. 1995. "On the Persistence of Phenomenology." In T. Metzinger (ed.), *Conscious Experience.* Thorverton, U.K.: Schöningh/Imprint Academic.

14   A Refutation of Qualia-Physicalism

Michael McKinsey

Recent defenders of reductive physicalism such as Brian Loar (1990, 1997) and John Perry (2001) have adopted an intriguing new strategy:[1] (1) accept as so much common sense (nearly) everything that property-dualists want to say about sensory qualia, including the central claims that sensory qualia determine "what it's like" to have a given sense experience, and that persons are directly aware of these qualia in the having of such experiences; (2) contend that, although these common sense facts about qualia may show that our ways of thinking and speaking about qualia are *conceptually* different from our ways of thinking and speaking about physical properties of the brain, these facts do *not* show that sensory qualia *themselves* (as opposed to our ways of thinking and speaking about them) are distinct from physical properties of the brain; (3) use this contention to turn aside the few existing arguments against reductive physicalism by such property dualists as Kripke (1972), Nagel (1974), Jackson (1982), and Chalmers (1996); and finally (4) insist that sensory qualia are in fact just identical with physical properties of the brain so that, consequently, the facts about the sensory qualities of conscious experience are nothing over and above physical facts about the brain. I will call the view that incorporates this strategy *qualia-physicalism*, or *Q-physicalism* for short.

In this chapter, I will argue that Q-physicalism is false. I agree that in the case of *some* words, notably indexical pronouns, proper names, and natural kind terms, there is an important semantic distinction between (a) the word's conceptual or linguistic meaning and (b) the particular contribution, which I call "propositional meaning," that the word makes to the propositions expressed by use of sentences containing the word. This distinction makes it possible, in principle, for there to be predicates that have distinct conceptual meanings and that nevertheless ascribe or predicate the same properties. However, or so I shall argue, the conceptual facts about predicates that ascribe sensory qualia, on the one hand, and predicates that ascribe physical properties to the brain, on the other, are sufficient to guarantee that the logical properties of what we say (i.e., the propositions we express) when we ascribe sensory qualia to our experiences are quite different from the logical properties of what we say (i.e., the propositions we express) when we ascribe physical properties to the brain. It follows that propositions about the sensory qualities of conscious experience, and hence the facts that make these propositions true, are *not* the same as any physical propositions and facts about the brain. Hence, Q-physicalism is false.

The question of whether Q-physicalism is true or false is crucial to our understanding of the mind-body problem. This is because the phenomenal qualities of sense experience are so difficult to incorporate in a physicalist worldview, and it seems to me that Q-physicalism is the only form of *reductive* physicalism that is capable of taking qualia seriously. The Q-physicalists, in contrast for example to defenders of functionalist views of mental properties, can agree with nonreductivists like myself that sense experiences are distinguished by their qualitative features, features that determine "what it's like" to have the experience in question.

The Q-physicalist's distinctive claim is of course that these qualitative features of sensations are identical with physical properties of the brain, and it is this claim that I'm most interested in refuting.[2] If I am right, then sensory qualia are not identical with any physical properties of the brain. Sensory qualia, I take it, are also not functional properties that logically supervene upon physical properties, since no functional property is sufficient to determine "what it's like" to have any given sense experience.[3] Thus, if Q-physicalism is false, then it surely seems that sensory qualia are not reducible in any way to physical properties, and so no form of reductive physicalism is true: the phenomenal properties of sense experience, and the propositions and facts involving the ascription of such properties, are properties, propositions, and facts "over and above," and are not reducible to, any physical properties, propositions, or facts. So if I am right, only non-reductive forms of physicalism have a chance of being true.

My arguments against Q-physicalism will rely crucially on claims about logical possibility, and in this respect they will resemble some of David Chalmers's (1996) recent important arguments against reductive physicalism. Certainly, my discussion will be very much akin to Chalmers's, both in its spirit and in its conclusion. As we shall see, however, the concept of logical possibility on which I will rely is significantly different from the concept that Chalmers uses, making my arguments quite different from his and allowing me to avoid certain objectionable assumptions about possible worlds that Chalmers's arguments require. I will discuss Chalmers's concept of logical possibility in detail below, after I have given my arguments against Q-physicalism.

Descartes's Argument for Substance Dualism

In order to motivate and explain the concept of logical possibility on which I will be relying, it will be useful to consider an argument that I think may capture Descartes's chief reason for believing that he is not a physical object.[4] To state the argument succinctly, let 'd' be a name of Descartes, and define the property P as follows:

x has P =$_{df}$ it is possible that: x exists, and there are no physical objects.

Then the argument is simply:

(D1) d has P.

(D2)   No physical object has P

Therefore,

(D3) d is not a physical object.

This argument certainly has a valid form. Moreover, each of its premises, taken separately, is plausible. Premise (D1) is plausible because, as Descartes argued at length in *Meditation II*, it is consistent with all he knows for certain about himself as a thinking thing that he is a disembodied mind in a purely spiritual universe, so it certainly does not *logically follow* from the assumption that Descartes exists, that there are any physical objects. In this sense, then, it is possible that Descartes exists in a world devoid of physical objects, and premise (D1) is true.

Premise (D2) is also plausible, but for a quite different sort of reason. Any physical object, it seems, would have to have a physical *nature*, or essence; such an essence would be a physical property without which the object in question could not exist. Thus no physical object could exist in a possible world in which it lacks its physical essence. Hence no physical object could exist in a possible world devoid of physical objects, for the simple reason that no physical object could exist in a possible world in which it itself is not a physical object. So, in this sense, premise (D2) is true.

By now, however, the reader should have begun to suspect that Descartes's argument equivocates on two senses of the word 'possible'. Premise (D1) is true when 'possible' is understood in a very weak sense to mean "logically possible." In this weak sense, a proposition is logically possible just in case it is logically *consistent*, that is, fails to logically imply a contradiction. Let us say that a proposition p *logically implies* a proposition q just in case there is a correct deduction of q from p, a deduction whose only premises other than p are either logical truths or other necessary, conceptual truths that are knowable a priori, and every step of which immediately follows from previous steps by a valid rule of inference.[5] Then we can say that it is *logically possible* that p if and only if the proposition that p fails to logically imply any explicit contradiction (of the form (q & $\sim q$)). Note also that it follows from these definitions that if a proposition p fails to logically imply a proposition q, then it is logically possible that (p & $\sim q$).[6] (Note that these senses of logical implication and logical possibility are *broadly*, rather than strictly, logical, because I assume that these senses can apply or fail to apply by virtue of necessary a priori conceptual truths that may not be strict logical truths.)

As we have seen, premise (D1) is true, given that the property P is understood in terms of mere logical possibility. But premise (D2) is *false* when 'possible' is understood in this weak sense. For just as the existence of Descartes fails to logically imply that there are any physical objects, so the mere existence of *any* object x fails to logically imply that there are physical objects, *whatever* that object x's actual nature happens to be. Consider, for instance, the large, battered, old oak desk at which I am now writing, and call it "Fred." Fred is, of course, the very paradigm of a physical object. But the simple singular proposition about Fred to the effect that Fred exists does *not* logically imply that there are any physical objects: no logical or conceptual truths that are knowable a priori will allow us to prove that there are physical objects, given merely the assumption that Fred exists.

Of course, we know that Fred has a physical nature, because Fred is a large oak desk. Even so, it no more *follows* from Fred's existence that there are physical objects, than it follows from Descartes's existence that there are such things. In fact, in my view, Descartes and Fred are in exactly the same boat, for, just like Fred, Descartes also has a physical nature. It's just that in the case of neither object does it follow from the object's mere existence that the object has a physical nature.

The sense of 'possible' in which premise (D2) is true is much stronger than mere logical possibility. I will call this stronger sense "metaphysical possibility." A proposition p is *metaphysically possible* just in case there is a (metaphysically) possible world w such that p is true in w. Because every physical object has a physical essence, no physical object can exist in a possible world in which there are no physical objects. So premise (D2) is true in this sense: for no physical object is it metaphysically possible that that very object exists, even though there are no physical objects.

But taken in this sense of 'possible' premise (D1) is at best highly controversial, and Descartes has given us no reason whatever to believe that it is true, for Descartes has provided support for only the weak claim that his existence does not logically imply that there are physical objects. In addition, as Father Arnauld pointed out, the fact that Descartes could not *prove* that he has a physical nature from premises about himself that he knew with certainty, hardly shows that Descartes *does not in fact* have a physical nature.[7]

Arnauld was justifiably very puzzled as to why Descartes should have thought otherwise. The solution to the puzzle would seem to be that, in discovering that his existence as a thinking thing failed to logically imply that there are physical objects, Descartes assumed that he had also discovered a sense in which it is *possible* for him to exist as a disembodied mind in a purely spiritual universe. What Descartes failed to notice, however, is that this was a *new* sense of possibility, a sense quite different from the then traditional, metaphysical sense that Arnauld had in mind. In this traditional sense (no doubt inherited from Aristotle), what is possible is not determined by logic alone, but also by facts about the *natures* of things, where some of these facts can only be known a posteriori.

Descartes's discovery of a new kind of possibility (and a corresponding new kind of necessity) was certainly an historically important event, because it seems to have eventuated in the Humean idea that the necessary truths are just the *analytic* truths, an idea that has been so dominant in the recent past. But unfortunately, Descartes immediately *confused* his important new sense of possibility with the old sense: for again, as Arnauld pointed out, nothing about Descartes's nature follows from the mere logical possibility that Descartes exists in a world devoid of physical objects.

I intend the distinction between metaphysical and logical possibility, as I have explained these notions, to apply only to *propositions*, rather than to *worlds*.[8] Earlier I used the notion of a possible world to explain a proposition's being metaphysically possible as meaning that the proposition is true in some (metaphysically) possible world. Thus, any metaphysically possible proposition must also be logically possible, because, of course, no logically impossible (inconsistent) proposition is true in any possible world. But the converse does not hold: a proposition, such as the proposition that Descartes is not a physical object, can be both logically possible and metaphysically *im*possible.

This might suggest that a logically possible proposition is one that is true in some *logically* possible world and that, therefore, the metaphysically possible worlds are simply a proper subclass of the logically possible worlds. Like many others, however, I find this suggestion to be counterintuitive.[9] For instance, given that water is necessarily composed of H_2O molecules, there is no metaphysically possible world in which water is not H_2O. But according to my definition, it is certainly logically possible that water is not H_2O. Should we then say that, in some *logically* possible world, water is not H_2O? Apparently not. Because water cannot exist without being composed of H_2O molecules, it seems wrong to suppose that in *any* member of *any* subclass of the possible worlds, water exists and yet is not composed of H_2O. Thus the concept of logical possibility that I am using requires me to *reject* any inference from a premise of the form 'it is logically possible that p' to a conclusion of the form 'for some possible world w, it is true that p in w'. (In this respect, my concept of logical possibility contrasts sharply with that of Chalmers, which I will discuss at length below in the sections "Chalmers's Concept of Logical Possibility" and "Chalmers's Zombies.") For me then, the class of possible worlds = the class of metaphysically possible worlds, and thus I *accept* inferences from premises of the form 'for some possible world w, it is true that p in w' to conclusions of the form 'it is metaphysically possible that p', and vice versa.[10]

A Cartesian Argument against Q-Physicalism

We have seen that Descartes's argument from logical possibility fails to support *substance-dualism*, the view that persons are not physical objects. Nevertheless, considerations regarding logical possibility of the sort that Descartes used to argue against substance-dualism do suffice, I believe, to show that *type-dualism* is true, where type-dualism is the view that many mental properties, propositions, and facts are distinct from any physical properties, propositions, and facts. In particular, considerations of the sort that Descartes adduced are sufficient to show that sensory qualities of experiences are not physical properties of any sort and hence that Q-physicalism is false.

Let us say that a property is a *physical property* just in case possession of that property by a concrete entity such as an object, event, or state logically implies that the object, event, or state in question is itself a physical entity, that is, an entity that has a location in physical space.[11] As I am using the term, *propositions* are the abstract semantic contents, or meanings, expressed by the declarative sentences of natural languages. Propositions are what such sentences can be used to *say* or *assert*, and they are also the contents of cognitive attitudes, such as *thoughts* and *beliefs*. Propositions are also, I assume, the ultimate bearers of truth-value: the truth or falsity of a proposition p determines the truth or falsehood of any sentence that expresses p and of any thought or belief that has p as its content. By a *physical proposition*, I will mean a proposition that logically implies the existence of physical entities. Thus, any proposition that ascribes a physical property to an object, event, or state will be a physical proposition. By a *physical fact*, I will mean a fact that corresponds to, or is the objective correlate of, a true physical proposition.[12] As I use the term, facts are precisely as intensional and fine-grained as the true propositions to which they correspond. Thus, for me, the fact that p = the fact that q only if the proposition that p = the proposition that q.

As I say, Descartes's discussion in the *Meditations* concerning what he could consistently doubt given incorrigible knowledge of himself and many of his mental states, acts, and experiences, suffices to show that Q-physicalism is false. For Descartes's discussion shows that ever so many true propositions concerning one's mental states, acts, and experiences fail to logically imply the existence of one's own body and indeed fail to logically imply the existence of even so much as a single physical object. Suppose, for instance, that a given person x feels a sharp pain. It certainly does not seem to *logically follow* from the assumption that x feels a sharp pain that x is a physical object. Hence it certainly *seems* that possession of the mental property of feeling a sharp pain by x does not logically imply that x is a physical object, and, if so, then this mental property is simply *not* a physical property, and, in particular, it is not a physical property of the brain. Hence, Q-physicalism is false.

The Q-Physicalist's Reply

Defenders of Q-physicalism will no doubt fail to be impressed by this simple, not to say simple-minded, argument. They would perhaps immediately respond by accusing the argument of "begging the question" against their view. After all, on their view, the phenomenal properties that we truly ascribe to ourselves and to our mental experiences just *are* physical properties of the brain. So the true propositions asserted by such ascriptions, propositions about ourselves and our mental experiences—our feelings of pain, for example—just *are* physical propositions about our brains. So contrary to what Descartes thought, these propositions logically imply the existence of physical objects after all.

But how could Descartes (like the rest of us) have missed so many of the *logical* implications of the mental propositions that he knew incorrigibly and, apparently, understood so well? The Q-physicalist is ready with an answer. Consider the forms of sentence that we normally use to describe the qualitative features of sensations, for example a form such as

(P) X feels a sharp pain.

According to the Q-physicalist, a sentence of this form would ascribe a property that is in fact a physical property of the brain. Apparently, the idea is that the brain in question would be the brain of the person whose sense experience is being described (see, for instance, Perry 2001, 36–37). So a sentence of the form (P) might ascribe the same property as some sentence written in neurophysiological language, such as

(B)   The C-fibers of X's brain are firing to degree n.

Now the Q-physicalist is quick to point out, indeed insist upon, the fact that sentence forms like (P) and (B) are radically different from each other in semantically important ways. Thus, it is obvious, as everyone can agree, that (P) and (B) have quite different linguistic *meanings*. A language such as English could contain sentence forms with the meaning of (P) and yet completely lack expressions with the meaning of (B), and vice versa. Thus, speakers of such a language could have perfect understanding of the meaning of a sentence form like (P) and yet fail completely to understand any sentence form with the meaning of (B), and vice versa.

In short, the Q-physicalist points out, the forms (P) and (B) are *conceptually* different: the concepts one must have to understand (P), such as the concepts of *feeling* and *pain* are admittedly quite different from the concepts required to understand (B), such as the concepts of *brain* and *C-fiber*. Nevertheless, this conceptual difference is consistent with the possibility that these forms express, and are used to predicate, one and the same *property*. And this is just what the Q-physicalists seem to be claiming: sentence forms like (P) and (B), despite their conceptual differences, can nevertheless be used to ascribe one and the same physical property. (See, for instance, Loar 1990, 81–85; see also Perry 2001, ch. 3, 68–69. Perry could put this point by emphasizing that while such forms as (P) and (B) differ radically in what he calls their *reflexive* contents, they can nevertheless coincide in their *subject-matter* content, which in this case would be the common physical property represented by the forms.)

Now it certainly seems that any two sentences that ascribe the same properties to the same objects must express the same propositions as well as state the same facts. That this is so follows from a very plausible and commonly endorsed Fregean principle of compositionality for propositions, namely,

(FRE)   The proposition expressed by a given sentence is a *function* of, or is determined by, the properties ascribed by the predicates contained in the sentence.

It follows from (FRE) that if two sentences differ only in that the sentences contain distinct predicates, then if the predicates ascribe the same property, the sentences must express the same proposition. On the Q-physicalist hypothesis we're considering, the predicates contained in (P) and (B) ascribe the same property, and so instances of (P) and (B) concerning the same person must express the same proposition. It then follows that the propositions expressed by such instances of (P) and (B) must share all their logical properties in common.

In particular, the proposition that the C-fibers of one's brain are firing to degree n *logically implies* the existence of brains and C-fibers. But if instances of (P) ascribe the same property as instances of (B), then by our Fregean principle (FRE) such instances that concern the same object must express the same propositions, and hence the propositions expressed must have all the same logical properties. Therefore, the proposition that one feels a sharp pain, being identical with the proposition that the C-fibers of one's brain are firing to degree n, must also logically imply the existence of brains and C-fibers, and so if Q-physicalism is true, then it is *not* logically possible after all that one can feel a sharp pain, even though there are no such things as brains and C-fibers.

Of course, as Descartes's discussion in the *Meditations* shows, it certainly does not *seem* to logically follow that there are such things as brains and C-fibers, given merely the premise that one is feeling a sharp pain. This appearance is due to the fact that one cannot construct an a priori deduction, one based on understanding of concepts and meanings alone, from the mere assumption that one is feeling a sharp pain to the conclusion that there are brains and C-fibers. The Q-physicalist contends, however, this failure of a priori deducibility is fully explained by the *conceptual* differences between such linguistic forms as (P) and (B). What Descartes's discussion shows is merely that it is *conceivable* that one might feel a sharp pain even though there are no such things as brains and C-fibers. But again, this is not really even *logically* possible, given that the forms (P) and (B) do in fact ascribe the same property.

Notice that, if the Q-physicalist is right, then one's inability to construct an a priori deduction from the assumption that one feels a sharp pain to the conclusion that there are brains and C-fibers does *not* by itself show that the proposition assumed fails to *logically imply* this conclusion, in my sense of 'logically imply'. For given the Q-physicalist's thesis that the proposition that one is feeling a sharp pain is *identical* with the proposition that the C-fibers of one's brain are firing to degree n, it follows that there is *a* correct deduction from this proposition as premise to the conclusion that there are brains and C-fibers. It is just that in order for one to *know* (a priori) that this deduction is correct, one must *conceive* the premise *as* the proposition that the C-fibers of one's brain are firing to degree n. If instead one *conceives* the premise *as* the proposition that one is feeling a sharp pain, then one will be unable to tell (a priori) that this premise logically implies that there are brains and C-fibers.

I think that most philosophers, myself included, would agree that conceivability is an unreliable guide to what is *metaphysically* possible. (See, for instance, Yablo 1993.) But we've just seen that Q-physicalists must apparently say in addition that conceivability is also an unreliable guide to what is *logically* possible. Now that conceivability does not guarantee logical possibility is far from being obviously correct, and, as far as I know, no Q-physicalist has explicitly defended it. Yet as we've just seen, the Q-physicalist's distinction between the *concept* and the *property* expressed by a mental predicate does provide the basis of such a defense. Moreover, as we shall see, there is a grain of truth in this defense. For Chalmers's (1996) hypothesis that conceivability at least guarantees logical possibility is in fact wrong: as we shall see, there are cases in which it is conceivable that p even though it is *not* logically possible that p.

Two Forms of Q-physicalism

Although the defense I just stated on behalf of such Q-physicalists as Loar and Perry does closely resemble, and is certainly consistent with, what the Q-physicalists have actually said in print, I can't be certain that all or even any of the Q-physicalists would agree with the defense exactly as I've stated it. The crucial claim of the form of Q-physicalism just defended is that mental predicates such as that found in the form (P) are actually used to *predicate* or *ascribe* sensory qualities that turn out to be identical with physical properties of the brain, properties that would also be ascribed by such a complex neurophysiological predicate as that found in the form (B). This claim is required for the application of our Fregean principle (FRE), which then has the further consequence that the mental propositions and facts expressed and stated by instances of such forms as (P) turn out to be identical with physical propositions and facts, since they turn out to be identical with neurophysiological propositions and facts expressed and stated by instances of such forms as (B).

To have a name for this form of Q-physicalism, I will call it *predication of qualia–*physicalism, or PQ-physicalism for short. Although I think it is natural to take the Q-physicalists to be defending and endorsing PQ-physicalism, there is another view that they (or some of them) may have in mind instead. As far as I can tell, the Q-physicalists never speak of phenomenal mental predicates as *predicating* or *ascribing* physical properties. Rather, they pretty uniformly say that phenomenal concepts and predicates *refer* to (what turn out to be) complex physical properties of the brain. (See, for instance Loar 1990, 84, and Perry 2001, 64.) So perhaps these Q-physicalists would not agree that any phenomenal mental predicates actually *predicate* neurophysiological properties and would prefer to say instead that such predicates merely *refer to*, or perhaps merely *involve* reference to, physical properties of the brain. I will call this view *reference to qualia–*physicalism, or RQ-physicalism for short.

Although I think that both PQ-physicalism and RQ-physicalism are false, we shall see below that they are different views with different implications, and so they are false for different reasons. In particular, PQ-physicalism entails, while RQ-physicalism does not, that the mental propositions expressed by instances of such forms as (P) are identical with physical propositions about the brain expressed by instances of such forms as (B). Thus, PQ-physicalism entails, while RQ-physicalism apparently does not, that instances of such forms as (P) logically imply the existence of such things as brains and C-fibers. The version of Q-physicalism defended earlier was really PQ-physicalism. I will at this point continue my discussion of PQ-physicalism, argue that it is false, and then later turn to discussion of RQ-physicalism.

Two Types of Meaning

Both forms of Q-physicalism that we have identified must rely on what is by now a well-known distinction between two types of meaning that I call *linguistic* meaning and *propositional* meaning. Our current understanding of this distinction is due primarily to the seminal work on indexical and demonstrative pronouns by David Kaplan (1978, 1979, 1989) and John Perry (1977, 1979).[13] I have elsewhere described and defended this distinction in some detail for the cases of indexical pronouns, proper names, and natural kind terms. (See McKinsey 1984, 1987, 1994, and 1999.) On my account, the linguistic meaning of a word is the meaning that the word has in a given language, by virtue of a semantic rule of the language that governs the word's use. For instance, the linguistic meaning of the indexical pronoun 'I' in English would seem to be provided by a rule of reference such as

(I)   For any token α of 'I' and any object x, α is to refer to x if and only if $x =$ the speaker of α.

By contrast, the *propositional* meaning of a word is the specific semantic contribution that the word makes toward determining which proposition is expressed by a sentence containing the word. The distinction between linguistic and propositional meaning is easiest to see in the case of indexicals like 'I', since such pronouns can be used with a *single* linguistic meaning (provided by a rule like (I)), while that very meaning requires the pronoun's propositional contribution to *vary* from one occasion of use to another (as Frege 1956 first pointed out). For instance, a sentence such as 'I am watering the lawn', though it has a single linguistic meaning, will express different propositions on different occasions of use, depending on the identity of the speaker and the time of utterance. Hence, distinct utterances of 'I' must be taken to make distinct propositional contributions in distinct utterances of an indexical sentence such as 'I am watering the lawn'.

Because the proposition expressed (on an occasion) by a sentence containing an indexical pronoun seems to be determined by that indexical's *referent* (on that occasion), the most plausible view is that an indexical's propositional meaning (on an occasion) just *is* its referent (on that occasion). So, in the case of indexicals, the distinction between linguistic and propositional meaning boils down to the distinction between (linguistic) meaning and *reference*. And because the linguistic meaning of an indexical pronoun is given by a rule like (I) that determines the indexical's referent (on an occasion), we have in this case the consequence that *linguistic meaning determines propositional meaning*.[14] A term whose linguistic meaning determines that the term's propositional meaning (on an occasion) just *is* the term's referent (on that occasion) is what I call a *genuine term*.[15] The proposition expressed by a sentence containing a genuine term is a *function* of the term's referent. Such propositions are standardly called *singular* propositions, and genuine terms are standardly said to *directly refer* to their referents.

So far, we've seen that a sentence containing an indexical, a sentence such as 'I am watering the lawn', can have a single linguistic meaning even though it can be used to express many different propositions. But, for our present purpose of evaluating PQ-physicalism, the more important semantic fact is that different indexical sentences, with different linguistic meanings, can be used to express the *same* proposition. For instance, suppose that a friend looking for my house calls me on his cell phone, saying, "I'm in your neighborhood but I can't find your house. . . . Wait, there's a guy at the end of the block. . . . *he's watering the lawn*." I then reply (on my cell phone), "That's odd, *I'm watering the lawn*, too." In fact, of course, I'm the man my friend sees at the end of the block, and so he and I have said the same thing, expressed the same proposition, with our different sentences ('he's watering the lawn' and 'I'm watering the lawn'). Moreover, although each of us has perfect understanding of the (linguistic) meaning of all the sentences being uttered, it may well be that, at least at first, neither of us realizes that we've asserted the same proposition. The reason why this can happen is that sometimes, the proposition one expresses is determined by the *referent* of a word one has used, even though the referent of that word is not determined *completely* by the word's linguistic meaning alone. For instance, suppose that the linguistic meaning of the demonstrative 'he' is given by the semantic rule

(He)   For any token α of 'he' and any object x, α is to refer to x if and only if x = the male that the speaker of α demonstrates by uttering α.

Then in the case described, the fact that I'm the referent of my friend's utterance of 'he' is determined partly by the meaning of his utterance of the pronoun 'he' and partly by the (nonsemantic) fact that I happen to be the man my friend sees down the block, so that as it turns out, I am in fact the male my friend has demonstrated with his utterance of 'he'. Being at first unaware of these nonsemantic facts, I don't at first realize that my friend has said that I'm watering the lawn.

This case involving indexical pronouns bears important similarities to what the PQ-physicalist wishes to say about the semantic relations between such sentence forms as (P) and (B) above. (Similarities of this sort are emphasized and described in various useful ways throughout the text of Perry 2001.) Perhaps a person (Descartes, say) could have complete understanding of the linguistic meaning of an uttered instance of '*X* feels a sharp pain' and yet still be unaware of certain important nonsemantic facts that in part determine what proposition is expressed by that utterance. And perhaps these nonsemantic facts, together with the linguistic meaning of (P), have the result that the person's utterance of an instance of (P) expresses the same proposition as an instance of (B). In such a case, perhaps, the person has—though with no awareness of having done so—actually asserted a proposition that *logically implies* the existence of such things as brains and C-fibers. This could happen, if the *linguistic* meaning of the predicate 'feels a sharp pain' were such as to allow it to turn out that the predicate's *propositional* meaning just is the property ascribed by instances of (B), namely, the property of having a brain whose C-fibers are firing to degree n. (Or, in Perry's terminology, this could happen if the *reflexive* content expressed by the predicate were such as to allow it to turn out that the predicate's *subject-matter* content just is the physical property ascribed by instances of (B). See Perry 2001, 68–69.)

The Case of Proper Names

Perhaps, then, the distance between linguistic and propositional meaning allows for the possibility that the propositions we express with the words we use have *logical* properties of which we are ignorant, properties of which we can have no a priori knowledge, since the conceptual meanings of the words we use can by themselves provide no basis for knowledge of the properties in question.

This possibility is even more strongly suggested by the case of *proper names*. The modal evidence that Kripke (1972) provided to show that every proper name is a rigid designator (a term that refers to the same object relative to every possible world) is also strong evidence that names, like indexicals, are genuine terms. If so, then two sentences that are just alike except for containing distinct names must express the same proposition if the two names have the same referent. But two such sentences that express the same proposition might well have different conceptual meanings, if the names themselves have different linguistic meanings.

The classic example of this is of course provided by identity sentences such as 'Hesperus = Hesperus' and 'Hesperus = Phosphorus' ('H = H' and 'H = P', for short). Given that the names 'Hesperus' and 'Phosphorus' are genuine terms that have the same referent, these two sentences, despite appearances, must express the same proposition. From the apparent difference in "cognitive value" of such pairs of identity sentences, Frege (1966) reasonably inferred that the members of such pairs must express different propositions. But as we've just seen, one who holds as I do that names are genuine terms must give some other explanation of why 'H = H' and 'H = P' differ in cognitive value.

One possibility is that 'Hesperus' and 'Phosphorus', though both are genuine terms whose referent (the planet Venus) is their only propositional contribution, also have distinct *descriptive meanings* that determine, or fix, the names' reference in Kripke's 1972 sense.[16] Perhaps, suppose, the linguistic meanings of 'Hesperus' and 'Phosphorus' are given by the following different descriptive reference rules:

(HES)   For any token α of 'Hesperus' and any object x, α is to refer to x if and only if $x =$ the heavenly body that appears brightest on the western horizon in the evening.

(PHOS)   For any token α of 'Phosphorus' and any object x, α is to refer to x if and only if $x =$ the heavenly body that appears brightest on the eastern horizon in the morning.

Given this hypothesis about the meanings of 'Hesperus' and 'Phosphorus', the sentences 'H = H' and 'H = P' will differ in linguistic meaning and in "cognitive value," even though the sentences express the same proposition. But notice that on this same hypothesis, one cannot know a priori that the sentences *do* express the same proposition. Certainly, one can know, just on the basis of knowledge of meanings alone, that, *if* the sentence 'H = P' is true, then it expresses the same proposition as 'H = H'. But one cannot know that 'H = P' expresses a truth, without first knowing that the two reference-fixing descriptions in the rules (HES) and (PHOS) are uniquely satisfied by the same object, and such knowledge of course requires a posteriori empirical investigation.

As a consequence of our semantic hypothesis, it follows that various *logical* properties of the proposition that H = H (that is the proposition that H = P) can be hidden from view and not *a priori* accessible, even to one who has perfect understanding of the linguistic meanings of the relevant sentences. For instance, the proposition that H = H *logically implies* the proposition that H = P (since every proposition logically implies itself), even though this logical fact cannot be known a priori. Also the proposition that H = P is a *logical truth*, since it is the same as the proposition that H = H (and the proposition that P = P), though, again, this cannot be known through consideration of conceptual meanings alone. And finally, the proposition that H ≠ P is *not logically possible*, since it is identical with the logically impossible proposition that H ≠ H (and that P ≠ P), though again, one cannot know a priori that it is not logically possible that H ≠ P.[17]

This last case is especially important for the PQ-physicalist's defense of his view. For reasons that I will explain below, it certainly is *conceivable* that H ≠ P. Surely everyone, whether Q-physicalist or type-dualist, can agree with this. But as we've just seen, since the names 'Hesperus' and 'Phosphorus' are coreferential genuine terms, it turns out (a posteriori) that in fact it is *not* logically possible that H ≠ P. Thus, contrary to Chalmers's view, conceivability is no guarantee even of mere logical possibility. (See the section "Chalmers's Concept of Logical Possibility" below for further discussion of this point.)

Why PQ-Physicalism Is False

So the semantic facts about proper names and indexicals, based on the distinction between linguistic and propositional meaning, have the consequence that some of the most important logical properties of propositions can be hidden from a priori investigation, even for a person who has perfect understanding of the linguistic meanings of the sentences that express those propositions. That the propositions we express in ordinary language could have such hidden logical properties is of course one of the PQ-physicalist's crucial assumptions, since, as we've seen, the PQ-physicalist claims that an instance of say '*X* feels a sharp pain' would in fact express a proposition that, unbeknownst to ordinary speakers, logically implies the existence of such things as brains and C-fibers.

But does the existence of support for this crucial assumption make it reasonable to believe even that PQ-physicalism *might* be true? Not really. The fact that some logical properties of some propositions can only be known a posteriori shows at most that there is perhaps room in logical space for the *sort* of semantic view that the PQ-physicalist wants to endorse. But what any PQ-physicalist owes the rest of us is an *actual account* of the semantics of phenomenal predicates, an account that is based on real semantic evidence and that actually explains how the PQ-physicalist's incredible hypothesis—that phenomenal predicates actually ascribe complex, perhaps completely unknown, neurophysiological properties—could possibly be true.

Instead, PQ-physicalists can offer us only a mere *analogy* that they allege to hold between phenomenal predicates, on the one hand, and indexical pronouns, proper names, and (as we shall discuss below) natural kind terms, on the other. No defender of Q-physicalism has ever provided any evidence to support this analogy, however, and in fact the analogy breaks down in rather spectacular ways.

Imagine a tribe of prehistoric hominids who communicate in a rudimentary language about, among other things, each others' cognitive states and sensations. Their language contains a predicate that means exactly "feels a sharp pain," but, being quite ignorant of anatomy, these hominids have no concept of the brain and certainly no concept of C-fibers. Nevertheless, according to PQ-physicalism, when our hominids use their predicate to say that a given person feels a sharp pain, the proposition asserted is identical with the proposition that the C-fibers of the person's brain are firing to degree n. And so, even though our hominids *have no concepts* of either brains or C-fibers, they are capable of using their language to assert the proposition that the person has a brain whose C-fibers are firing to degree n. Surely, however, this consequence is just preposterous! Our hominids can obviously assert nothing about brains and C-fibers, *because they have no concepts of these things.*[18]

Notice that there is nothing about the semantics of indexicals and proper names that at all supports the idea that the conceptual meanings of our words could be so radically distant from the logical implications of what we say as in the case of the hominids just described. One who says that H = H may indeed be unaware that she is saying something that logically implies that H = P, but there is nothing whose existence is logically implied by the proposition in question of which an understanding speaker is incapable of conceiving. It is true in this case that an understanding speaker of "H = H," who thereby asserts the proposition that H = P might be unable to conceive *that* H = P, because she might not have the concept expressed by 'Phosphorus'.[19] Still, the speaker can conceive *of* Phosphorus, because she can conceive *of* Hesperus, and of course, Hesperus = Phosphorus. I am not suggesting that one who asserts a proposition with understanding must be able to conceive of that proposition in *every* possible way in which it *can* be conceived. Rather, I'm saying that, if a person can assert with understanding a proposition that formally involves or immediately implies the existence of a certain kind of thing (such as brains or C-fibers), then the person must have at least *some* way of conceiving of that kind of thing.

To avoid a certain sort of misunderstanding, I should emphasize that I am *not* assuming in my argument that our primitive hominids have no concept of the property of having a brain whose C-fibers are firing to degree n. Because the hominids by assumption do have a concept of the property of feeling a sharp pain, and because the PQ-physicalist asserts that this property is identical with some neurophysiological property (such as that of having a brain whose C-fibers are firing to degree n), I would beg the question to just *assume* that our hominids have no concept of the latter property. But I am not making this assumption.

Rather, I am assuming only what should be common ground, namely, that our hominids have no concept that applies to all and only *brains* and no concept that applies to all and only *C-fibers*. (I take it to be obvious that one could have the concept of a sharp pain, without having any concept whatever that picks out either brains or C-fibers.)

Thus, it is clear, and should be common ground, that our hominids cannot assert with understanding that anyone has a *brain*, or that anyone's body contains *C-fibers*, because they have no concepts of either brains or C-fibers. Yet PQ-physicalism implies that our hominids *can* assert with understanding propositions to the effect that the C-fibers of given persons' brains are firing to degree *n*. But again, this is just absurd. If one has no concepts of the relatively simple properties of being a brain or being a C-fiber, then one certainly cannot assert (with understanding) any proposition that predicates a complex property which in turn is constructed (say, truth-functionally) out of those simpler properties.[20]

What is absurd about the PQ-physicalist's semantic hypothesis is that, according to this hypothesis, we have given meanings to some of the words of our language (namely, certain mental predicates) that allow us to use these words to in effect say things having logical implications that we cannot really understand or even conceive of. This is absurd because it violates the basic purpose for which we have language in the first place. We give meanings to our words so that we can communicate and say things that we understand, whose truth-conditions we can know in advance. Imagine the case of a person Mutt, who whimsically introduces a new predicate 'whatever' into his language, declaring that it is to be used to predicate whatever is his friend Jeff's favorite property. Not, you understand, that 'whatever' is to *mean* "has Jeff's favorite property"; rather, it is to *predicate* the relevant property, whatever it is. So suppose that the relevant property is that of being a bachelor. Then, whenever Mutt utters a sentence of the form '*X* is whatever', he's actually saying that a given object is a bachelor and is thus asserting of that object that it is an unmarried male of marriageable age. Of course, neither Mutt nor anyone else (with the possible exception of Jeff) has the slightest idea that this is what Mutt is saying. But it is surely just absurd to suppose that we could use words with meanings such as this, because, in doing so, we'd be using words with meanings that *prevent* ourselves and others from understanding what we're saying in using the words—and then we'd be undermining the very purpose for which we give meanings to words in the first place.

The PQ-physicalist's semantic hypothesis allows there to be an implausibly huge gap between one's understanding of an expression's linguistic meaning and one's understanding of what can be said, what sorts of propositions can be asserted, by use of that expression. It is clear that there must be some *constraints* on the kind of semantic relations that can hold between linguistic and propositional meaning, constraints that the PQ-physicalist is wantonly flouting. We have seen that PQ-physicalism implies the absurd consequence that one who asserts the proposition that a given person feels a sharp pain would also be asserting a proposition that *immediately*, *formally*, implies the existence of kinds of things such as brains and C-fibers, of which the speaker might be completely unable to conceive. To block this sort of consequence, I would propose the following reasonable constraint:

(CONS)   A semantic hypothesis must not imply that a speaker *S* could use a sentence with a given linguistic meaning, having perfect understanding of that meaning, to assert or express a proposition *p*, even though *p* formally implies the existence of objects of a given kind *K* such that *S* has no way to conceive of *K*s (where *p* is logically possible and it is not logically necessary that *K*s exist).[21]

Here, by 'formally implies' I mean *strictly* logical implication, as opposed to the broadly logical notion that I explained earlier and that I have been calling "logical implication."[22]

But What about H_2O?

Recent defenders of Q-physicalism seem to commonly assume that ordinary natural kind terms such as 'water' predicate (or "refer to") the same properties as complex theoretical terms such as 'H_2O', which describe the physical natures of members of the relevant kinds. (See, for instance, Lycan 1990, 120 and Loar 1997, 599.) Of course, it goes without saying that the terms 'water' and 'H_2O' have quite different conceptual or linguistic meanings. So if these terms did indeed predicate (or "refer to") the same property, then PQ-physicalists would have an important additional analogy on which to base their claim that ordinary phenomenal predicates can ascribe complex physical properties to the brain.

It is easy however, to see that, for the same reason that the PQ-physicalist's semantic hypothesis about phenomenal predicates is false, it is also false that 'water' and 'H_2O' predicate (or "refer to") the same property. When one of our primitive hominids says, for instance, that a given gourd *g* contains water, she is not asserting the proposition that *g* contains H_2O. As before, she cannot assert this proposition with understanding because she has concepts of neither H_2O, hydrogen, nor oxygen. Hence the proposition that *g* contains water is not the same as the proposition that *g* contains H_2O: whereas the latter proposition formally implies the existence of H_2O molecules, hydrogen atoms, and oxygen atoms, the former proposition formally implies none of these things. Hence the property of being water is not the same as the property of being H_2O.

Q-physicalists who assume that 'water' and 'H_2O' predicate the same property may be laboring under the impression that this result was "shown" by Kripke's (1972) and Putnam's (1975) seminal discussions of the semantics of natural kind terms. This is just wrong. All the semantic evidence adduced by Kripke and Putnam can be accounted for by a semantic theory that fails to have this alleged consequence. For instance, I have proposed elsewhere (McKinsey 1987) that the linguistic meaning of 'water' is provided by a "property-fixing" rule of the following sort:

(W)   For any token φ of 'is water', and any property F, φ is to predicate F if and only if there is a unique natural kind K such that (in the actual world) the watery stuff found in our environment belongs to K, and F = the property of belonging to K.

Here, 'watery stuff' is a euphemism for a conjunction of surface qualities that ordinary speakers associate with 'water'. Use of the indexical expression 'our environment' allows me to distinguish the meaning that 'water' has in the English spoken by *us*, the inhabitants of Earth, from the meaning of 'water' in the English spoken by our counterparts on the Twin Earth of Putnam's (1975) famous example.[23]

According to (W), the *propositional* meaning of 'water' is the property of belonging to K, where K is the natural kind to which samples of water actually belong. But notice that the property of belonging to K is *not* the same as the property of being composed of H_2O molecules, for the simple reason that having the former property does not logically imply having the latter. There is to be sure an important relation between these two properties, but it is not that of *identity*. Rather, it is that of (metaphysically) necessary equivalence. What scientists discovered is that being water, that is, belonging to K, is necessarily determined by being composed of H_2O molecules. Because membership in a given natural kind is an essential property of anything that has it, it has turned out to be a (metaphysically) necessary truth that water is composed of H_2O molecules.

Another reason why some Q-physicalists may have assumed that 'water' and 'H_2O' predicate (or "refer to") the same property is that they have assumed that the necessarily true sentence 'Water is H_2O' is an *identity*-sentence. Of course, if this were a true identity-sentence, then it would have to express the necessary identity of the type *water* with the type *H_2O*, and so the truth of the sentence would imply that 'water' and 'H_2O' refer to the same types (properties). But, again, this is simply wrong. The sentence 'Water is H_2O' does not (falsely) assert that the types *water* and *H_2O* are identical, for this sentence does not involve reference to, is not *about*, abstract types at all. Rather, the sentence is about *water*, the liquid *stuff* that we drink and bathe in, and it says simply that all stuff that is water (i.e., that belongs to K) is composed of H_2O molecules. (See McKinsey 1987, 31, and Burge 1972.)[24]

So we may conclude that, like the semantics of indexicals and proper names, the semantics of natural kind terms also provides no support for the PQ-physicalists' semantic hypothesis about phenomenal predicates.

Why RQ-Physicalism Is False

I have argued that PQ-physicalism is false on the grounds that when we use mental predicates to ascribe sensory qualities, the propositions we express and assert do not formally imply the kinds of physical consequences that according to PQ-physicalism these propositions must imply. Now PQ-physicalism has this kind of false consequence only because it holds that the mental predicates in question *ascribe* or *predicate* sensory qualities that are identical with complex physical properties of the brain. But as I mentioned earlier, it is not altogether clear that Q-physicalists such as Loar and Perry would agree with PQ-physicalism, because they tend to use the vocabulary of *reference*, rather than predication, to state their view.[25]

So we should consider RQ-physicalism, a view which does not claim that phenomenal predicates ascribe or predicate properties that turn out to be physical properties of the brain. Rather, RQ-physicalism claims that such mental predicates somehow involve *direct reference* to sensory qualities of experience, where these qualities turn out to be identical with complex physical properties of the brain. RQ-physicalism is a much more abstract and inexplicit sort of view than PQ-physicalism, which is quite explicit and straightforward about what it is claiming. PQ-physicalism just takes phenomenal predicates and concepts at face value, assumes that these predicates and concepts predicate or ascribe sensory qualities, and then adds that the qualities predicated happen to be complex physical properties of the brain.

By contrast, RQ-physicalism says that our uses of phenomenal predicates and concepts somehow involve direct reference to sensory qualities that turn out to be complex physical properties of the brain, but it does not explain how this direct reference (as opposed to predication) goes, and it is quite inexplicit as to how any mental predicates could have such a logical form that there is only direct reference to, rather than predication of, the relevant sensory/physical properties. But, abstract and inexplicit as it is, RQ-physicalism has interesting logical features that make it worth discussing. In particular, RQ-physicalism has the distinct advantage of failing to imply any of the false consequences that I used to argue against PQ-physicalism.

For definiteness, let's consider the possibility that a mental attribution of the form

(P)   X feels a sharp pain

might express a proposition of the form "X has N," where N is a singular term, such as a proper name or demonstrative pronoun, which refers directly to a certain sensory quality (namely, the one allegedly mentioned in the predicate contained in (P)). In fact, let's just give this quality a name, say, 'Charley'. Then the idea is that instances of (P) express propositions of the form

(C)   X has Charley.

Of course, the RQ-physicalist adds that the name 'Charley' refers to a sensory quality that in fact turns out to be a complex physical property, perhaps the very same neurophysiological property as the one that is *predicated* by instances of our old friend

(B)   The C-fibers of X's brain are firing to degree *n*.

But there is a big difference between propositions of the form (C) and propositions of the form (B), for, unlike propositions of the form (B), propositions of the form (C) do not formally imply the existence of such things as brains and C-fibers. This is not implied, even if the name 'Charley' contained in (C) refers to what is in fact a complex physical property. For instances of (C) say only that a given object X bears the relation of *having* (of instantiating or exemplifying) to *that property*. Because, unlike instances of (B), instances of (C) do not ascribe or predicate the physical property in question, instances of (C) do not say or formally imply anything about what that property is, or about what its physical nature is. So instances of (C) do not formally imply the existence of brains, or C-fibers, or any other sort of physical object.

Thus a form of RQ-physicalism that says that mental attributions such as (P) express propositions of the form (C) that are *about* sensory/physical properties appears to be a view that is perfectly consistent with all Cartesian intuitions to the effect that mental attributions in general fail to logically imply any physical propositions. Thus my earlier objections to PQ-physicalism fail to apply to RQ-physicalism. Still, I think it is fairly easy to see that RQ-physicalism is false, for the simple reason that it gives a false account of the semantics of most phenomenal predicates, such as the predicate contained in (P), 'feels a sharp pain'. This predicate, just like other predicates, neither refers to nor contains any other terms that refer to properties of any sort. Rather, predicates like this, just like other predicates, are used to predicate and ascribe properties, not to refer to them.

One important difference between predicates and referring expressions like proper names and demonstratives is that, unlike referring expressions, predicates can be *modified* by adjectives and adverbs so that, as a result, predicates can have complex structures and bear important logical relations to each other. RQ-physicalism cannot do justice to this simple fact. Consider for instance the RQ-physicalist's suggestion that instances of (P) ('*X* feels a sharp pain') have the same logical form as instances of (C) ('*X* has Charley'). If this suggestion were true, then it would be impossible to explain why instances of (P) all logically imply instances of

(Q)   *X* feels a pain.

For if we apply the RQ-physicalist's hypothesis about (P) to the case of (Q), then instances of (Q) would have the logical form of

(D)   *X* has Dudley,

where 'Dudley' names some property distinct from the property named by 'Charley'. But of course no instance of (C) can logically imply an instance of (D), given that the imbedded names have distinct properties as referents. Even if we assume that 'Charley' names the property of feeling a sharp pain and 'Dudley' names the property of feeling a pain, the implication cannot go through, because (C) and (D) function to effectively *hide* the logical structures of any properties that they might name.[26]

Recall that for the RQ-physicalist, the main advantage of the suggestion that phenomenal predicates might refer to properties in the manner of names or demonstratives is that this suggestion blocks the formal implication of any implausible physical consequences that uses of phenomenal predicates clearly do not have. But the great *dis*advantage of this same suggestion is that it blocks not only bad, unwanted, logical implications, but *also* the logical implications that uses of phenomenal mental predicates really do have.

So Q-physicalists face a serious dilemma. They can endorse PQ-physicalism, accepting the fact that phenomenal concepts and predicates can be used to predicate and ascribe complex mental properties, thus doing justice to the fact that phenomenal mental predicates can bear important logical relations to each other. On this alternative, the Q-physicalist must identify the property ascribed by a predicate such as 'feels a sharp pain' with a complex physical property of the brain. But then it follows that ordinary ascriptions of sensory qualities to persons and experiences must express complex physical propositions about the brain so that, when we make such ascriptions, we are asserting propositions that formally imply the existence of kinds of things of which we may be incapable of conceiving. This consequence, I take it, defies credulity.

On the other hand, the Q-physicalist can avoid this absurd consequence by instead endorsing RQ-physicalism, insisting that phenomenal mental predicates do not predicate complex physical properties, but rather merely *refer* to such properties. But then, as we've just seen, the Q-physicalist's view conflicts with the fact that phenomenal mental predicates can and do in fact ascribe complex mental properties that bear important logical relations to each other.

Whichever of these two sorts of view the Q-physicalist chooses to endorse, the view endorsed is false. Hence, Q-physicalism is false.

I have never seen these two forms of Q-physicalism distinguished from each other, so it may well be that the defenders of Q-physicalism have simply *conflated* the two views, thus tacitly assuming that they could have the advantages of both views and the disadvantages of neither. A conflation of this kind is of course fostered by the Q-physicalists' unfortunate tendency to say that phenomenal concepts and predicates *refer to* (rather than predicate) sensory qualities. So the mistake at the root of Q-physicalism may simply be a confusion of *reference* and *predication*.

Chalmers's Concept of Logical Possibility

In the above discussion, chiefly in my argument against PQ-physicalism, I have relied crucially on the notion of logical possibility that I explained earlier. In this respect, my treatment of these issues resembles that of Chalmers (1996), who also relies on a concept of logical possibility in his arguments against reductive physicalism. But my concept of logical possibility is significantly different from Chalmers's. One major difference is that for me, logical possibility is a property of *propositions*, whereas for Chalmers, it is a property of what he calls "statements." Although he does not say so explicitly, Chalmers seems to take statements to be a species of *sentence*, because, as he uses the term, "statements" are said to have meanings and to have words as parts.

Chalmers's concept of a sentence's being logically possible is based on a distinction that he makes between two types of meaning. In his terminology, every word (or "concept") and every sentence (or "statement") has both a *primary* intension and a *secondary* intension. This distinction is the same as, or at least very similar to, the distinction that I described earlier between linguistic meaning (primary intension) and propositional meaning (secondary intension). In effect, from my point of view, a sentence (or "statement") is said by Chalmers to be logically possible if and only if it satisfies one of two conditions: either (i) the proposition that the sentence actually expresses (the sentence's secondary intension) is true in some possible world or (ii) the sentence's linguistic meaning (its primary intension) is such that, in some possible world w, if the sentence were used in w with that meaning, it would express a proposition that is true in w. For instance, the sentence 'Water is not H_2O' actually expresses a necessary false-hood, and so it does not satisfy the first of the above two conditions (its "secondary intension" is not true in any possible world). Nevertheless, Chalmers counts 'Water is not H_2O' as logically possible, because it could be used with its actual linguistic meaning (its "primary intension") to express a truth. For instance, in a possible world in which the watery stuff in our environment is not composed of H_2O molecules but rather of, say, XYZ molecules, 'Water is not H_2O' would express a truth, and so Chalmers counts the sentence as logically possible.

I would also count the sentence 'Water is not H_2O' as logically possible, but for a quite different reason. Extending my notion from propositions to sentences, I would say that the sentence is logically possible because the proposition that the sentence *actually* expresses (its "secondary intension") is logically possible. This proposition in turn is logically possible because it is logically consistent, that is, does not logically imply a contradiction.

Both Chalmers's concept of logical possibility and mine count 'Water is not H_2O' as logically possible, though for different reasons. In other cases, however, the two con-cepts diverge in their application. As we saw above, it is logically possible in my sense that Descartes is not a physical object, but Chalmers provides no sense in which the sentence 'Descartes is not a physical object' is logically possible. For on the one hand, the proposition actually expressed is true in no possible world (because Descartes is in fact a physical object, as Chalmers and I agree). On the other hand, there also seems to be no world in which the sentence *could* express a truth, given its actual linguistic meaning. The reason why 'Water is not H_2O' can express a truth is that the sort of con-tingent description that fixes the reference of 'water' (e.g., 'the watery stuff in our envi-ronment') can, in some nonactual but possible world, refer to stuff that is not H_2O. But as I've argued at length elsewhere, most ordinary names like 'Descartes' (and unlike 'Hesperus' and 'Phosphorus') have no descriptive meanings in the public language (see McKinsey 1984, 1994, 1999). So there is in this case no distinction between the proposition actually expressed by 'Descartes is not a physical object' and other propo-sitions that the sentence could express, given its actual meaning.[27] For we have to ei-ther take this sentence to have *no* linguistic meaning (no primary intension), because it contains a name that has no meaning in the language, or we have to take the sentence's linguistic meaning to be a function of the actual *referent* of 'Descartes', in which case the sentence's primary and secondary intensions are identical. In either case, the sentence expresses a truth in *no* possible world given its actual meaning, and so the sentence is not logically possible in Chalmers's sense.

Now I take it that a sentence like 'Descartes is a physical object' expresses a paradigm of a posteriori metaphysical necessity. Hence its negation should be taken to express a paradigm of something that is metaphysically but *not* logically impossible. Because my concept of logical possibility implies, but Chalmers's does not, that it is logically possible that Descartes is not a physical object, it seems to me that my concept has a distinct advantage over his.

We have just seen that something can be logically possible in my sense without being logically possible in Chalmers's sense. It also happens that something can be logically possible in Chalmers's sense without being logically possible in mine. As we saw earlier, because the proposition that H ≠ P is the same as the proposition that H ≠ H, it follows on my account that it is *not* logically possible that H ≠ P. But on Chalmers's account, this is logically possible, for, given that the linguistic meanings (primary intensions) of the (unusual descriptive) names 'Hesperus' and 'Phosphorus' are provided by reference-fixing semantic rules like (HES) and (PHOS) above, the sentence 'H ≠ P' will express a truth in any possible world in which the relevant contingent reference-fixing descriptions are satisfied by distinct planets. Chalmers agrees with me that the names in question may well have their references fixed by description in this way. So it follows from his account that it is logically possible that H ≠ P.

The "two-dimensional" semantics appealed to by Chalmers in his account of logical possibility is similar to, if not the same as, the semantic view of singular and natural kind terms that I described earlier and that I've been defending for many years. (See McKinsey 1978a, 1978b, 1984, 1987, 1994, 1999.)[28] So it's interesting that Chalmers should use this two-dimensional semantics to motivate a concept of logical possibility that is so different from the concept that I've proposed above and elsewhere (McKinsey 1991a, 1991b). Again, on my account, a sentence expresses a logical possibility just in case the proposition that the sentence *actually* expresses is logically consistent. Whether the sentence in question, like 'H ≠ P', *could* express a truth given its actual meaning is for me strictly irrelevant to whether or not the sentence in fact expresses a logical possibility. To be sure, that such a sentence *could* express a truth may explain why that sentence *appears* to express a logical possibility, but in my view, it's a mistake to infer, as Chalmers seems to do, that the sentence actually does express a logical possibility in any interesting sense.

On the other hand, if a sentence *p* could express a truth given its actual meaning, then, in my view, it does indeed follow that it is *conceivable* that *p*. On the theory of cognitive ascriptions that I've defended elsewhere (McKinsey 1986, 1994, 1999), the *linguistic* meaning of a given sentence *p* can semantically determine what cognitive property is expressed by cognitive predicates that contain *p* (such as 'thinks that *p*' and 'believes that *p*'), and this can be determined *independently* of the proposition that the sentence *p* actually expresses. In particular, on my theory, this happens when the relevant sentences contain (unusual) proper names that have descriptive meanings, meanings of the kind provided for the names 'Hesperus' and 'Phosphorus' by such reference-fixing rules as (HES) and (PHOS).

Thus, in the actual world, if one conceives (thinks) that H ≠ P, then the content of one's thought is in fact an inconsistent proposition. But, in another possible world *w*, one could have *exactly the same thought*, also thinking in *w* that H ≠ P, and be thinking something true, because the content of one's thought in *w* is a different, consistent proposition that is true in *w*. The proposition in question would of course be the proposition expressed in *w* by 'H ≠ P', given the sentence's actual (descriptive) meaning. Thus, on my theory of cognitive ascriptions, it is conceivable that H ≠ P, because it is possible to truly conceive (think) that H ≠ P. (See McKinsey 1999, esp. 351–352, n.13.)

In general, it is conceivable that *p* just in case it is possible to consistently conceive (think) that *p*, where there are two different ways in which one can consistently conceive (think) that *p*: either (i) the proposition that *p* (the proposition actually expressed by '*p*') is in fact logically possible in my sense, or (ii) there is a possible world *w* in which one could have the very same thought that *p*, where one's thought that *p* is true in *w*. Note the structural similarity of this account of conceivability to Chalmers's account of logical possibility. Also note that on this account, in contrast to that of Chalmers, its being conceivable that *p* is necessary but *not* sufficient for its being logically possible that *p*.

Chalmers's Zombies

The argument against reductive physicalism on which Chalmers seems chiefly to rely is based on the logical possibility of *zombies*. A zombie is by definition a creature that is physically, molecule-for-molecule, identical with some actual human being but that completely lacks *consciousness* and so never has any mental experiences characterized by sensory qualia (there is nothing that it is like to be a zombie). Now, by my lights, it is indeed logically possible that there are zombies, at least in my sense of "logically possible," for it seems to me that even the totality of physical facts that I for instance would share in common with my zombie twin would be insufficient to logically imply any mental facts about my conscious states. It follows of course that none of these mental facts about me are identical with any physical facts, because, if any mental fact about me *were* identical with a physical fact, then it *would* be logically implied by the totality of physical facts about me (for the simple reason that this mental fact would be one of the totality of physical facts and would logically imply itself).

But while I agree that this simple argument is sound, I'm afraid that it's not very persuasive. A defender of reductive physicalism like the PQ-physicalist would no doubt find the argument question-begging, because the PQ-physicalist's view is that mental facts about a person's conscious states just *are* physical facts about the brain. This is one reason why I prefer my earlier arguments against Q-physicalism to the zombie argument. Recall that my earlier argument against PQ-physicalism does not merely *claim* that facts about conscious states fail to logically imply any physical facts about the brain. Rather, my argument provides a reason for this claim, by pointing out that if facts about conscious states logically imply physical facts because the former facts are *identical* with complex physical facts about the brain, then pedestrian facts about conscious states that people state every day would (absurdly) formally imply the existence of kinds of things of which we may not even be able to conceive.

Notice that my argument and the zombie argument in effect proceed in opposite directions. The zombie argument contends that the physical facts can (logically) occur in the absence of facts about consciousness. My argument contends conversely that facts about consciousness can (logically) occur in the absence of the physical facts. At one point (1996, 147–148), Chalmers contends that this difference makes the zombie argument preferable to arguments like mine. It is true, as he points out, that the zombie argument is more *general* in its application. Although arguments like mine, if sound, refute only *identity* theories such as PQ-physicalism, the zombie argument, if sound, refutes both identity theories and weaker forms of reductive physicalism on which the mental facts merely logically *supervene* upon the physical facts, such a theory as

(LS)   The totality of physical facts that hold in the actual world *logically implies* all of the mental facts that also hold in the actual world.

(See Chalmers 1996, 41–42.)

But the fact that the zombie argument, if sound, refutes both identity theories such as PQ-physicalism and supervenience theories such as (LS) does not, it seems to me, give the zombie argument any distinct advantage over arguments like mine. For one thing, as I say, the zombie argument is not very persuasive. For another, the only form of reductive physicalism yet proposed that is not an identity theory and that is strong enough to entail (LS) is *functionalism*, and, as I remarked earlier, there are ample independent grounds for rejecting functionalism.

I should emphasize that so far, I've stated the zombie argument using only *my* sense of logical possibility. The argument is weak when understood this way, but it is *much weaker* if understood in terms of Chalmers's concept of logical possibility. In order for it to be logically possible in Chalmers's sense that there are zombies, it must be true *in some possible world* that there are zombies, given either the primary or secondary intensions of 'there are zombies'. I admit to having some difficulty distinguishing the primary and secondary intensions of this sentence, and so I strongly suspect that the intensions are identical in this instance. But in any case, it seems to me that it is very implausible, or at least highly controversial, to suppose that there is a possible world in which it is in any sense true that there are zombies.

Consider my zombie twin and me at the moment when each of us stubs his toe on a chair leg. Our toes are damaged in exactly the same way, and, as a result, exactly the same nerve impulses are transmitted to our brains, which end up being in exactly the same state. Only, of course, although we are in molecule-for-molecule identical brain states, I feel excruciating pain in my toe while my zombie twin feels nothing! This *seems* to be at least *logically* possible in my sense: we certainly cannot *deduce*, using logic alone, that my zombie twin must feel pain and hence that the scenario is contradictory. But is it *really possible* that he feels no pain? In describing this scenario, have we *really* described part of a possible world? I very much doubt it.

Chalmers, I should emphasize, never gives any good reason at all to believe that there are possible zombie worlds. He only contends (correctly) that it is *conceivable* that there are zombies, pointing out frequently (and correctly) that there is no *incoherence* or *inconsistency* in the supposition that there are zombies (1996, 94–99). But this of course only supports the conclusion that zombies are logically possible in *my* sense. It does not at all support the conclusion that in some possible world it is true that there are zombies. One might as well argue, repeating Descartes's error, that because it is not contradictory to suppose that Descartes is not a physical object, there is *therefore* some possible world in which Descartes exists as a purely spiritual being![29]

The problem is that Chalmers's sense of logical possibility forces him to confuse logical and metaphysical possibility, whether he wants to or not. In his sense, the contention that zombies are logically possible entails that there are possible zombie worlds, and since the possible worlds = the metaphysically possible worlds, it follows that zombies are metaphysically possible. But this is just too much to swallow.[30] For the claim that zombies are metaphysically possible contradicts not only all the forms of physicalism that we've so far considered, it also contradicts a view that some property dualists including myself believe may well be the truth about the relation between the mental and the physical. This is the view that, although mental properties, propositions, and facts are neither identical with nor otherwise logically reducible to physical properties, propositions, and facts, the mental may nevertheless *metaphysically supervene* upon the physical. A simple way to express this view would be:

(MS)   The totality of physical facts which hold in the actual world *metaphysically entails* all of the mental facts which also hold in the actual world.

If we count (MS) as a form of physicalism, then it is certainly the weakest form we've yet considered. That is, (MS) is entailed by all of the other forms, although it entails none of them. I am myself strongly inclined to believe that (MS) is true. Certainly, (MS) deserves further serious consideration of the sort recently provided by Nagel (2000).

Chalmers's zombie-argument is unconvincing because it proves too much. The assumptions required by the argument are so strong and controversial that they contradict not only clearly *false* forms of reductive physicalism such as Q-physicalism, but also nonreductive forms of physicalism such as (MS) that are likely to be true. By contrast, when the zombie argument is understood in terms of my sense of logical possibility, its premises are perfectly consistent with nonreductive views such as (MS).

Conclusion

Q-physicalists invoke the distinction between concepts and properties, a special case of the distinction between linguistic and propositional meaning, as a way of countering plausible Cartesian intuitions to the effect that propositions that ascribe sensory qualities to our experiences do not logically imply the existence of such complex physical things as brains, neurons, and C-fibers. PQ-physicalists in particular maintain that propositions ascribing sensory qualities must logically imply complex physical propositions about the brain, where these implications are hidden from any a priori investigation that is based on understanding of conceptual meanings alone.

I have agreed that there is a grain of truth underlying the PQ-physicalist's position: research in referential semantics concerning indexical pronouns, proper names, and natural kind terms does show that some of the logical properties of the propositions we assert by use of such terms can be hidden from a priori investigation. However, I've argued that the PQ-physicalist goes too far. For if PQ-physicalism were true, then many commonplace ascriptions of sensory qualities to experiences would formally imply the existence of kinds of things of which the speakers cannot, and perhaps never could, conceive. As a remedy for the PQ-physicalists' semantic excesses, I proposed (CONS), a reasonable constraint on how linguistic meaning can be related to propositional meaning.

A second version of Q-physicalism, RQ-physicalism, claims that we never use mental concepts and predicates to *ascribe* or *predicate* sensory qualia; rather, we only use such concepts and predicates to *refer* to sensory qualia, where these qualia turn out in fact to be complex physical properties of the brain. RQ-physicalism does avoid the semantic excesses and absurd consequences of PQ-physicalism, but it does so only at the expense of implying the false consequence that phenomenal mental predicates are never used to ascribe complex mental properties that can bear important logical relations to each other.

Because both forms of Q-physicalism are false, Q-physicalism is false. So the phenomenal qualities of sense experience are not identical with any physical properties of the brain. Nor, I take it, do such qualities logically supervene upon the physical properties of the brain, or indeed upon any other physical properties. Hence, it seems to me that no form of *reductive* physicalism is true. Phenomenal properties, as well as the propositions and facts that involve such properties, exist 'over and above' the physical properties, propositions and facts. But again, it does nevertheless seem likely that such nonphysical phenomenal properties, propositions, and facts are somehow *metaphysically* necessitated or entailed by physical properties, propositions, and facts about the brain. But I confess that I do not have the slightest idea of how or why this could be so.

Acknowledgments

For useful discussions of these matters, I am grateful to my students in Philosophy of Mind (winter term, 2002), especially David Stylianou, John Turri, and Matthew Zuckero, and to Erin Anchustegui, David Baggett, David Chalmers, Mark Huston, Lawrence Lombard, Lawrence Powers, Bruce Russell, Sean Stidd, and Åsa Wikforss.

Notes

1. Others endorsing or at least suggesting this sort of strategy include Lycan (1990), Levine (1993), Conee (1994), and Hill (1997).

2. While holding a type-identity theory for sensory qualia, the Q-physicalist need not hold that *all* mental properties are identical with physical properties. For instance, some Q-physicalists might want to endorse a mixed form of reductive physicalism, holding that, whereas sensory qualia are identical with physical properties of the brain, *cognitive* mental properties are multiply

realizable functional properties that logically supervene upon, but are not identical with, physical properties.

3. See, for instance, the classic refutations of functionalism by Block (1978) and Goldman (1993).

4. The argument I have in mind occurs in *Meditation VI*. See Descartes 1977, vol. 1: 190. I discussed this argument in McKinsey 1991a and 1991b. See also Burge 1988. My version of Descartes's argument was inspired by an argument that Alvin Plantinga once proposed, defended, and attributed to Descartes (see Plantinga 1970, 485–486, and 1974, 66–69). A similar version of Descartes's argument, also inspired by Plantinga, was proposed and usefully discussed by Michael Hooker (1978). (Thanks to Bill Stine for referring me to Hooker's paper.)

5. This is the same as the definition that I gave of 'conceptually implies' in McKinsey 1991a (152) and 1991b (14).

6. For suppose that it is not logically possible that $(p \& \sim q)$. Then $(p \& \sim q)$ logically implies a contradiction, and so it is a logical truth that if p then q; but then p logically implies q (since, in conjunction with the logical truth that, if p then q, p immediately implies q by *modus ponens*). So, if p does *not* logically imply q, then it *is* logically possible that $(p \& \sim q)$. I make implicit use of this principle at various points in the text.

7. For Arnauld's objection, see Descartes 1977, *Objections IV*, vol. 2: 81.

8. Thus, my distinction is similar to Chalmers's, who applies his distinction only to what he calls "statements" and not to worlds (1996, 68). But apparently, Chalmers's "statements" are just *sentences*, or perhaps sentences as used assertively, so that his distinction unlike mine applies to neither propositions nor worlds. I'll discuss the differences between Chalmers's distinction and mine more fully in sections 10 and 11 below.

9. See for instance Chalmers 1996 and Hill and McLaughlin 1999.

10. This leads me to strongly suspect that the notion of logical possibility as I'm understanding it, the notion that Descartes discovered, even though it is a perfectly fine and useful notion, may not correspond to any actual meaning of the word 'possible'. Perhaps, then, it would be less confusing or misleading if we used other terminology instead, such as 'logically consistent'. However, because the expression 'logically possible' in the sense I'm using it has become so well entrenched, I'll continue to use it this way, while recommending caution. In particular (unfortunately), it should not be assumed that "it is logically possible that p" entails "it is possible that p."

11. To avoid trivial satisfaction by contradictory properties, we should add that the property is one that it is logically possible for an object to possess.

12. Strictly, these definitions are more naturally taken to define what we might call *basic* physical propositions and facts, with the nonbasic physical propositions and facts being either truth-functions or generalizations of the basic ones. Ignoring this distinction should not affect the discussion to follow.

13. See also Pollock 1982. The basic distinction at the level of whole sentences had earlier been made in the seminal papers by Strawson (1950) and Cartwright (1961). The most thorough and

plausible recent treatment of indexicality that I know of is Perry 1997. My distinction between linguistic and propositional meaning is very similar to, though slightly more general in its application than, Kaplan's famous (1989) distinction between *character* and *content*. My distinction is also (as far as I can tell) the same as Perry's distinction between *reflexive* and *subject-matter* content. See Perry 2001 (ch. 3).

14. This consequence stands in sharp contrast to Frege's (1966) view that *sense* determines reference, since Frege identified sense with propositional meaning, and denied that a term's sense could ever be identical with its referent (see McKinsey 1984, 1987).

15. The concept of a genuine term is of course the same as Russell's (1959) concept of a "logically proper name." But, whereas Russell held that (some) indexicals are genuine terms, he denied, as Frege did, that ordinary proper names are genuine terms. While Kaplan (1989) in effect showed that Russell was right about indexicals, Kripke (1972) showed that Russell was wrong about names.

16. I have discussed the theoretical importance of this possibility in various places. See McKinsey 1986, 1994, and 1999.

17. Points similar to these, based on the distinction between the *proposition* that H = P versus the *sentence* 'H = P', occur in Tichý 1983.

18. For an application of a similar point to a defense of Jackson's (1982, 1986) argument about Mary, see Anchustegui 1997 (83–84). After writing the first version of this paper, I discovered that Tichý (1983, 235) had raised a similar objection to Kripke's (1972) view that the sentence 'Heat is molecular motion' expresses a necessary a posteriori truth. Tichý claims that Kripke's view implies that the sentence 'Phosphorus is hot' says that Venus's molecules move fast. I am not myself sure that Kripke's view does imply this, but I agree with Tichý that if it does, then the view is false. I am grateful to John Turri for referring me to Tichý's paper.

19. That this is a possibility is a consequence of the theories of names and cognitive ascriptions that I've defended in McKinsey 1994 and 1999. See the section "Chalmers's Concept of Logical Possibility" below.

20. My thanks to Mark Huston, John Turri, and Åsa Wikforss for discussions that led to the preceding two paragraphs.

21. The parenthetical qualification is necessary to rule out contradictory propositions that logically imply any proposition whatever, as well as to rule out Ks whose existence is logically necessary and hence logically implied by any proposition whatever.

22. Thus a proposition p formally implies a proposition q just in case there is a correct deduction of q from p, a deduction whose only premises other than p are strict logical truths, and every step of which immediately follows from previous steps by a logically valid rule of inference.

23. Though (W) is really the same as my proposal of 1987 (23), I have borrowed the useful phrase 'watery stuff in our environment' from Chalmers (1996, 56–61).

24. After writing this chapter, I learned that Scott Soames (2002) has recently argued at length and with great plausibility for a view of natural kind terms that is similar in several important respects to the view I am suggesting here and that I had explained and defended in McKinsey 1987. In particular, Soames argues very persuasively (in ch. 9) that natural kind terms are *predicates* rather than *names*. (His arguments complement the argument I had given for the same conclusion.) This in turn leads Soames to endorse, as I do, the view that a sentence like 'Water is H_2O' expresses a universal generalization, rather than a numerical identity (see ch. 11). Finally, Soames also argues, as I do, that 'water' and 'H_2O' do not predicate the same property, but on the different grounds that if they did then (absurdly) 'Water is H_2O' would express the same proposition as 'Water is water' (276–279).

25. Another reason to think that Loar and Perry might endorse RQ-physicalism is the emphasis that both place on the idea that our cognitive access to sensory qualities is *demonstrative* in nature. See Loar 1997 (597), and Perry 2001 (64). I think that this emphasis on demonstrative reference to sensory qualities is misleading. According to Perry, when one says, "For a feeling to be a pain is for it to be like *this*," one would be demonstratively referring with 'this' to a *property*, in this case the property of being a pain (which Perry thinks is also a "physical aspect of a brain state"). But this is wrong, for a feeling to be a pain is not for that feeling to be like *the property* of being a pain. (What is it for a feeling to be like a property, anyway?) Rather, for something to be a pain is for it to be like other particular feelings, or *tokens*, of pain. So when one says, "For a feeling to be a pain is for it to be like *this*," one is using '*this*' to refer demonstratively to a particular token or experience of pain and *not* to a property.

26. Note that it won't help to suppose that (P) means "X has Dudley and Dudley is sharp." If (P) did mean this, then (P) would imply (D) all right. But this hypothesis about (P) makes no sense, since it makes no sense to say that the property of feeling a pain (i.e., Dudley) is sharp. At best, only *particular* pains (tokens) can be sharp.

27. Even if we take seriously the proposal I've defended elsewhere, that the reference of a particular use of a name like 'Descartes' can be determined by a contingent description that is privately associated with the name by its speaker, we still don't get the right results regarding logical possibility in Chalmers' sense. (See McKinsey 1978a, 1978b, and 1984. Chalmers 1996 [84] indicates that he would take my proposal seriously.) For instance, suppose that the reference of a speaker's use of 'Descartes' is fixed by a description like 'the famous philosopher I've heard of named "Descartes"'. Because this description can be satisfied only by someone of whom the speaker has *heard*, it can only be satisfied in a world in which physical objects exist. So in no possible world in which the reference of 'Descartes' is fixed by such a description will the sentence 'Descartes exists and there are no physical objects' express a truth. Thus, this sentence would not be logically possible in Chalmers's sense, but it would actually express a proposition that is logically possible in my sense.

Chalmers has suggested to me (in correspondence) that the logical possibility of 'Descartes is not a physical object' can be explained on his view by the fact that the *de se* sentence 'I am not a physical object' can be true in a possible world W that is centered on some purely spiritual being X (see also Chalmers 2002a, 612). But this suggestion seems quite irrelevant to the issue. First, the objection I am raising does not concern the logical possibility of the *de se* sentence 'I am not a physical object', but rather concerns the logical possibility of the different sentence, 'Descartes is not a physical object'. Second, because Descartes is a physical object in every possible world in which he exists, the purely spiritual being X is of course *not* Descartes. But then I fail to see how the possible existence of some purely spiritual being *other than* Descartes could be at all relevant to making it true that it is logically possible that *Descartes* is not a physical object.

28. The two-dimensional idea in semantics ultimately derives from Kripke's (1972) concept of reference-fixing by description, as well as Kaplan's (1989) distinction between character and content. Application of the idea to modality occurs in Segerberg 1973, Stalnaker 1978, and Davies and Humberstone 1980.

29. Chalmers has pointed out to me (in correspondence) that he has in fact given an argument for the conclusion that there are possible zombie worlds. This argument assumes as premises (1) the obvious fact that zombies are conceivable and (2) the principle that conceivability entails logical possibility (in Chalmers's sense of "logical possibility"; see Chalmers 1999 and 2002b). However, I can find no argument either in *The Conscious Mind* or in Chalmers's more recent papers to support his controversial and apparently false thesis that conceivability entails logical possibility (in his sense).

30. Others who express dissatisfaction with Chalmers's zombie argument, for similar reasons, include Yablo (1999) and Perry (2001, ch. 4).

References

Anchustegui, A.-M. 1997. Qualitative Content and the Mind-Body Problem. Ph.D. dissertation, Wayne State University.

Block, N. 1978. "Troubles with Functionalism." In C. W. Savage (ed.), *Minnesota Studies in the Philosophy of Science*. Vol. 9. Minneapolis: University of Minnesota Press.

Burge, T. 1972. "Truth and Mass Terms." *Journal of Philosophy* 69: 263–282.

———. 1988. "Individualism and Self-Knowledge." *Journal of Philosophy* 85: 649–663.

Cartwright, R. 1961. "Propositions." In R. J. Butler (ed.), *Analytic Philosophy*. Vol. 1. Oxford: Basil Blackwell.

Chalmers, D. 1996. *The Conscious Mind*. Oxford: Oxford University Press.

———. 1999. "Materialism and the Metaphysics of Modality." *Philosophy and Phenomenological Research* 59: 473–496.

———. 2002a. "The Components of Content." In D. Chalmers (ed.), *Philosophy of Mind: Classical and Contemporary Readings*. Oxford: Oxford University Press.

———. 2002b. "Does Conceivability Entail Possibility?" In T. Gendler and J. Hawthorne (eds.), *Conceivability and Possibility*. Oxford: Oxford University Press.

Conee, E. 1994. "Phenomenal Knowledge." *Australasian Journal of Philosophy* 72: 136–150.

Davies, M., and L. Humberstone. 1980. "Two Notions of Necessity." *Philosophical Studies* 38: 1–30.

Descartes, R. 1977. *The Philosophical Works of Descartes*. Vols. 1 and 2. Trans. E. Haldane and G. Ross. Cambridge: Cambridge University Press.

Frege, G. 1956. "The Thought: A Logical Inquiry." Trans. A. M. Quinton and A. Quinton. *Mind* 65: 289–311.

———. 1966. "On Sense and Reference." In P. Geach and M. Black (eds.), *Translations from the Writings of Gottlob Frege*. Oxford: Oxford University Press.

Goldman, A. 1993. "The Psychology of Folk Psychology." *Behavioral and Brain Sciences* 16: 15–28.

Hill, C. 1997. "Imaginability, Conceivability, Possibility, and the Mind-Body Problem." *Philosophical Studies* 87: 61–85.

Hill, C., and B. McLaughlin. 1999. "There Are Fewer Things in Reality Than Are Dreamt of in Chalmers's Philosophy." *Philosophy and Phenomenological Research* 59: 445–454.

Hooker, M. 1978. "Descartes' Denial of Mind-Body Identity." In M. Hooker (ed.), *Descartes: Critical and Interpretive Essays*. Baltimore: Johns Hopkins Press.

Jackson, F. 1982. "Epiphenomenal Qualia." *Philosophical Quarterly* 32: 127–136.

———. 1986. "What Mary Didn't Know." *Journal of Philosophy* 83: 291–295.

Kaplan, D. 1978. "Dthat." In P. Cole (ed.), *Syntax and Semantics*. Vol. 9. New York: Academic Press.

———. 1979. "On the Logic of Demonstratives." In P. French, T. Uehling, and H. Wettstein (eds.), *Contemporary Perspectives in the Philosophy of Language*. Minneapolis: University of Minnesota Press.

———. 1989. "Demonstratives." In J. Almog, J. Perry, and H. Wettstein (eds.), *Themes from Kaplan*. Oxford: Oxford University Press.

Kripke, S. 1972. "Naming and Necessity." In D. Davidson and G. Harman (eds.), *Semantics of Natural Language*. Dordrecht: D. Reidel.

Levine, J. 1993. "On Leaving Out What It's Like." In M. Davies and G. Humphreys (eds.), *Consciousness: Psychological and Philosophical Essays*. Oxford: Blackwell.

Loar, B. 1990. "Phenomenal States." *Philosophical Perspectives* 4: 81–108.

———. 1997. "Phenomenal States." In N. Block, O. Flanagan, and G. Güzeldere (eds.), *The Nature of Consciousness*. Cambridge, Mass: MIT Press.

Lycan, W. 1990. "What is the 'Subjectivity' of the Mental?" *Philosophical Perspectives* 4: 109–130.

McKinsey, M. 1978a. "Kripke's Objections to Description Theories of Names." *Canadian Journal of Philosophy* 8: 485–497.

———. 1978b. "Names and Intentionality." *Philosophical Review* 87: 171–200.

———. 1984. "Causality and the Paradox of Names." *Midwest Studies in Philosophy* 9: 491–515.

———. 1986. "Mental Anaphora." *Synthese* 66: 159–175.

———. 1987. "Apriorism in the Philosophy of Language." *Philosophical Studies* 52: 1–32.

———. 1991a. "Anti-Individualism and Privileged Access." *Analysis* 51: 9–16.

———. 1991b. "The Internal Basis of Meaning." *Pacific Philosophical Quarterly* 72: 143–169.

———. 1994. "Individuating Beliefs." *Philosophical Perspectives* 8: 303–330.

———. 1999. "The Semantics of Belief Ascriptions." *Noûs* 33: 519–557.

Nagel, T. 1974. "What Is It Like to Be a Bat?" *Philosophical Review* 82: 435–450.

———. 2000. "The Psychophysical Nexus." In P. Boghossian and C. Peacocke (eds.), *New Essays on the A Priori*. Oxford: Clarendon Press.

Perry, J. 1977. "Frege on Demonstratives." *Philosophical Review* 86: 474–497.

———. 1979. "The Problem of the Essential Indexical." *Noûs* 13: 3–21.

———. 1997. "Indexicals and Demonstratives." In R. Hale and C. Wright (eds.), *Companion to the Philosophy of Language*. Oxford: Blackwell.

———. 2001. *Knowledge, Possibility, and Consciousness*. Cambridge, Mass.: MIT Press.

Plantinga, A. 1970. "World and Essence." *Philosophical Review* 79: 461–492.

———. 1974. *The Nature of Necessity*. Oxford: Oxford University Press.

Pollock, J. 1982. *Language and Thought*. Princeton, N.J.: Princeton University Press.

Putnam, H. 1975. "The Meaning of 'Meaning'." In K. Gunderson (ed.), *Minnesota Studies in the Philosophy of Science*. Vol. 7. Minneapolis: University of Minnesota Press.

Russell, B. 1959. *The Problems of Philosophy*. New York: Oxford University Press.

Segerberg, K. 1973. "Two-dimensional Modal Logic." *Journal of Philosophical Logic* 2: 77–96.

Soames, S. 2002. *Beyond Rigidity*. Oxford: Oxford University Press.

Stalnaker, R. 1978. "Assertion." In P. Cole (ed.), *Syntax and Semantics*. Vol. 9. New York: Academic Press.

Strawson, P. F. 1950. "On Referring." *Mind* 59: 320–344.

Tichý, P. 1983. "Kripke on Necessity A Posteriori." *Philosophical Studies* 43: 225–241.

Yablo, S. 1993. "Is Conceivability a Guide to Possibility?" *Philosophy and Phenomenological Research* 53: 1–42.

———. 1999. "Concepts and Consciousness." *Philosophy and Phenomenological Research* 59: 455–463.

Part IV

15 Situating Semantics: A Response

John Perry

Introduction

I am very grateful to Michael O'Rourke and Corey Washington for envisaging and putting together this volume and for their kind and careful introduction. I also want to thank the contributors for their essays—indeed, in some cases, almost monographs.

At first I was surprised to find O'Rourke and Washington crediting me with a systematic philosophy. I don't think they thought of me this way during their years as graduate students at Stanford. O'Rourke, who discussed intention and reference in his dissertation in ways that continue to influence me[1] and has illuminated a number of issues about the semantics-pragmatics interface, was familiar with my work in the philosophy of language. Washington's dissertation involved an intense look at quotation[2] and a devastating if somewhat abstract critique of a species of theories of content. When I suggested "reading some of my stuff," Washington thought I was encouraging him to borrow books from the shelves of my office, which he proceeded to do. This isn't criticism—far from it. I like graduate students to do their own thing, and while they are doing it to learn about what other philosophers are thinking and to tell me about them, and especially to tell me what's plausible and what's not so plausible. If they spend a lot of time worrying about what I'm doing, I become anxious. Better to have distant strangers staring at your naked thoughts than folks who are going to make comments to your face and refute you in real time.

At any rate, I think the charge of systematicity is a conclusion O'Rourke and Washington came to only when they took on the job of reading virtually everything I have written, having decided to write an introduction to this book. As far as I know, the three of us are unique in having read almost everything I have written, and I greatly appreciate their efforts. Actually Washington is working on a second Ph.D., mostly about ants and other small creatures, so I'm not sure he read everything, but I appreciate his taking time off from ants to absorb as much as he did. O'Rourke, on the other hand, is merely a committed husband, father, teacher, philosopher, and university servant, and so presumably has lots of spare time on his hands.

After the initial shock, I've come rather to like O'Rourke and Washington's conclusion, too, and have been trying to live up to it. For, if I indeed have a systematic philosophy, or the beginnings of one, it is in spite of being a most unsystematic philosopher. As I see it, one problem led to another, with little respect for fields, or the knowledge I had to work with, propelling me, each time I thought I had more or less mastered some important literature, into some new and large area of ignorance. The process continues. Still, the thought of having a systematic philosophy has been helpful in reading the essays. It seems to me that at times some of these insightful essayists fail to fully grasp (what I like to think of as) the power and charm of some of my views. I think this is partly because they do not see how naturally these views fit into the bigger picture about information, meaning, and the mind that I have, or don't see that picture as compelling as I do. So, as I go through the essays, I feel free to digress from time to time to explain the relevance of, and, I hope, convey the charm of this picture.

For the purpose of my comments, the essays divide into three groups. First, Patricia Blanchette and Genoreva Martí offer essays on topics dear to my heart, and don't criticize anything I have said—God bless 'em. Blanchette argues that the sorts of puzzles about identity that arise in mathematics, and the sorts of thoughts some mathematicians have had about them, provide no reason for abandoning universal identity; as is common with her fine essays,[3] part of this one is devoted to getting us to a yet deeper understanding of Frege's central ideas, especially about identity. Martí emphasizes the distinction between the indiscernibility of the identical, a metaphysical principle that ought to be as secure as any, especially if, following Blanchette, we see no reason to waver from the simple an straightforward concept of identity, and the principle of substitution, which has to do with reference, sentences, and truth and simply doesn't seem to be true for natural languages like English. She finds reasons for thinking it even less true than one might have thought. This essay is one in a series by Martí on very basic issues about reference, naming and describing; readers of Perry 2001b will remember my debt to earlier essays in the series.[4] In various drafts I have tried some variations on themes that Blanchette and Martí raise, but given issues of time and space and wit, I have decided to instead focus on essays in the second category.

These are essays that discuss my work, with varying degrees of enthusiasm, or lack thereof. Most of these concern issues in the philosophy of language: Kent Bach, Peter Ludlow, Cara Spencer, Eros Corazza, François Recanati, Kenneth Taylor, Herman Cappelen and Ernie Lepore, and Stephen Neale. Virtually all of them spend at least some time on the issue of the interface between semantics and pragmatics, "what is said," and similar issues. Indeed, had I not at various times said "I am the person spilling the sugar" and "It is raining," this would be a slim volume. These topics coincide with what I have been working on, so I spend a lot of time discussing these papers. Loar and McKinsey have some reservations about my handling of qualia and the identity theory that Loar and I favor, and I spend some time discussing these.

Neale's wonderful essay was the last to arrive. Mostly he does a better job defending my views than I do, while at the same time setting them in a richer framework of considerations about linguistic theory than I have any hope of doing. So, apart from defending my use of 'utterance', I've excused myself from saying much. Considering Neale's essay and the others, this book should provide all the insights and thoughts about rain and locations that the world is likely to need for some time. Or so one might suppose.

Robert Audi's essay comprises the third category: he doesn't criticize anything I have said so far but rightly senses in me a devotion to Hume-inspired naturalization project about reason, theoretical and practical, and about this he has very grave and insightful reservations. In various drafts I have played with attempts to use Audi's fine essay as a springboard for sketching a deep, penetrating, and promising approach to these matters, but nothing suitably deep, penetrating, and promising has yet emerged. I have hopes, and thank this old friend, who has given so much to so many areas of philosophy over the years, for his fine essay.

The Reflexive/Referential Theory (Bach)

In his essay, Bach criticizes most of the central doctrines of Perry 2001b, so discussing his characteristically vigorous, insightful, and clear essay will provide an opportunity to review some of these. Bach complains that I don't evaluate the arguments for referentialism. In fact I spend a good bit of the last chapter doing so, arguing for at least part of Bach's own conclusion that these arguments do not show as much as many referentialists think they do; my brand of "critical referentialism" maintains that statements with names and indexicals typically express "singular propositions" and that this is a key insight of the referentialist tradition. But, I argue, the sort of cognitively relevant machinery that is needed to deal with Frege's insights is available at the level of reflexive truth conditions. More worrisome is his claim that, in taking utterances to have semantic properties, I ignore important results of David Kaplan's, so I will start there.

Utterances

Bach says of my use of 'meaning' for properties of expression types and 'content' for properties of utterances:

> Perry...ignores Kaplan's well-known distinction between utterances and sentences-in-contexts (1989b, 522) and his arguments that favor attributing semantic contents to sentences-in-contexts rather than to utterances....Citing such obvious facts as that "utterances take time, and [one speaker's] utterances of distinct sentences cannot be simultaneous" (1989b, 546), Kaplan argues that utterance semantics would get the wrong results. He proposes a somewhat idealized conception of context to make allowances for sentences that can be true but cannot be truly uttered ('I am not uttering a sentence'), sentences (or sequences of sentences making up an argument) that take so long to utter that their truth values can change during the course of the utterance, and sentences that are too long to utter at all. Sentences have contents, relative to contexts, but contexts here are not to be taken as contexts in which sentences are actually uttered. Contexts must be construed more abstractly. As Kaplan points out, utterances of sentences like 'I know a little English' or 'I am alive' are always true, even though their contents are not. Similarly, utterances of sentences such as 'I don't know any English' and 'I am deceased' are always false—they cannot be true relative to a context in which they are uttered—but these sentences can still express truths relative to contexts. For some reason Perry does not mention, much less rebut Kaplan's arguments. (409–410)

I ignored Kaplan's reasons for using sentences in context as the content-bearers in his logic of demonstratives, because I don't explore the logic of indexicals and demonstratives. Contrary to what Bach says, Kaplan offers no arguments to the effect that utterances don't have semantic contents, and I would be surprised if he holds this view. He offers reasons for abstracting from utterances when one wants to do logic, not when one wants to do the philosophy of language in general. Thus I see no basis for the word 'rather' Bach uses in describing Kaplan's conclusion as the view that semantic contents should be attributed to sentences-in-contexts "rather than to utterances."

The argument that Bach offers as Kaplan's is surely strange. The premise is that utterances of sentences like 'I know a little English' or 'I am alive' are always true, even though their contents are not. So the premise attributes contents to utterances, contents that determine semantic values, truth, and falsity. The conclusion, however, is that semantic contents cannot be attributed to utterances; that they must be attributed to sentences in context *rather than* to utterances. But the most that follows is that to do logic we need the concept of sentences in context having contents, in addition to utterances.

Kaplan's theory is most naturally interpreted as providing us *not only* with what we need for logic, but also something we need to do the semantics of utterances, and this use of his theory seems to be the basis of the premise of Bach's argument. We apply Kaplan's theory to utterances by supposing that his contexts model facts about utterances: the agent *of* an utterance, the time *of* an utterance, the *location* of an utterance and the world *of* an utterance—that is, what else is going on.

This use of the theory is surely licensed by Kaplan's informal exposition in Kaplan 1989b. Sentences in context *model* utterances, and like all good models Kaplan's discards the properties deemed irrelevant to the task at hand—in this case, logic. Kaplan's key constraint on *proper* contexts is that the agent be at the location at the time in the world. Without this constraint, there wouldn't be much of a logic. 'I am here now' would not be a theorem in the logic of demonstratives. The natural motivation for the constraint is the structure of utterances: the constraint is a property of utterances preserved in the model.

Given this understanding of Kaplan's theory, we get an explanation of the fact every utterance of 'I am alive' is true—that is, has a true content. An utterance of this sentence involves an agent using the sentence 'I am alive' at a location, at a time, in a world. Its content will be that the agent is alive at the time. Assuming that being alive is a necessary condition of using English sentences, this content will be true.

In the philosophy of mind and language generally, and surely in pragmatics, we need to be concerned with causal relations between contentful states and events, and so we need to attribute contents to concrete states and events. My beliefs, desires, and intentions are causes of my utterance, and when things go well the referential content of my utterance will match the content of my belief. If I intend for my utterance to be understood by you, and to convey more or less than it says by way of implicature, then I intend my utterance to have effects on you with further contents. You should acquire, or at least consider, a belief with the same referential content as my utterance, and the implicature you derive should have the referential content that matches the implicature I intended for you to have. To come up with a theory that does this, we need to attribute contents to utterances, their causes, and their effects.

There is nothing in my theory that precludes us from attributing contents to pairs of contexts and sentences for the purposes of logic, and nothing in Kaplan's theory that I can find, and I doubt very much anything in his intentions, that precludes us from attributing contents to utterances.

Identity

My treatment of identity problems is a source of pride, so it is dismaying to find Bach using these problems in his arguments against my theory. Bach's example is

(1a) Eminem is insecure.

(1b) Marshall Mathers is insecure.

He notes that ordinary folk would take different things to be said. He then says, "The claim that (1a) and (1b) have the same 'official' content depends on who's officiating." This is cute, but I don't get it. "Official content" is a term I use for referential content, so I don't understand who else gets to officiate. Surely if you asked ordinary folk whether (1a) and (1b) have the same official content, you'd get a blank stare. And I think if you asked them whether the same thing was said, after explaining that Eminem and Marshall Mathers are the same guy, the response that different things were said would be far from universal, especially if an insightful and persuasive teacher like Kaplan were there to guide the intuitions.

My view is that we usually take "what is said" to be referential content, and that this fact underlies the intuitions that referentialists such as Kripke, Donnellan and Kaplan mine. That's why I call it "official"; it has authority behind it. But "what is said" is more complex than that, and sometimes diverges from referential content. I didn't offer a full account of "what is said," but I did exploit the divergence in my account of identity statements. Because Bach quotes most of what I say, I won't repeat it; it seems as plausible to me when he quotes it as when I wrote it. I do discuss "what is said" more below.

Bach thinks Gricean reasoning is important here, and I agree. However, there are some ambiguities in the phrase 'Gricean reasoning.' This phrase first brings to mind the reasoning that gets us, within Grice's theory of implicatures, from what is said to what is implicated by application of his principles and maxims. A second, more inclusive reading extends it to other accounts of how the inferences to the intentions of the speaker take place, as are found in Relevance Theory,[5] or among theorists who think that all that we need is inference to the best explanation. Finally, in the past twenty years or so, the need for reasoning about intentions prior to arriving at what is said, that is, prior to the "input" for reasoning about implicatures, has been emphasized, by Bach, Récanati, relevance theorists and others.[6] And, to return to David Kaplan for a moment, in "Afterthoughts" he adopts a "directing intentions" theory of demonstratives so that the speaker's intention is determinative in getting to the content—that is what is said or "the proposition expressed." Even at this basic stage of interpretation, assigning referents to demonstratives, broadly Gricean reasoning about intentions takes place.

The triviality of the identity statement triggers a search for what the speaker meant to convey—the first sort of Gricean reasoning. When we try to treat the information conveyed as a case of Gricean implicature, however, we find a weakness or at least a theoretical lacuna at the heart of Grice's theory. According to Grice the listener looks for an explanation of the fact that the speaker has said "that S." If what is said is the referential content, then the inferential project will be the same for "that S" and "that S'" if S and S' have the same referential content. Since utterances of (1a) and (1b) could have quite different implicatures, identity statements pose a problem for Grice's theory.[7]

The reflexive/referential theory gives us just what we need to deal with the problems identity poses for Grice's theory. The reflexive contents of (1a) and (1b) are different and provide different inputs for Gricean reasoning. Suppose A says "Eminem is insecure" and B replies,

(2a)   I agree. Eminem is insecure.

(2b)   I agree. Marshall Mathers is insecure.

Replies (2a) and (2b) could give rise to quite different implicatures because they have different reflexive contents, even though official contents are the same. The relevance of the utterance of the second sentence of (2b) is explained by the fact that the speaker wishes to convey the information that 'Marshall Mathers' is a name for Eminem.

My theory, it seems to me, should be a boon to us Griceans, but not if my theory is interpreted in the way Bach does.

When Perry introduces the notion of reflexive content, he makes it sound as though it comes in prior to referential content, not as what is being conveyed but as something that can be gleaned from an utterance even if one is not in a position to identify the referents. In his explanation of the informativeness of identity statements, on the other hand, reflexive content comes in after referential content. (401)

The last part is a misunderstanding. The way I make it sound is the way it is. If we say "Eminem is Marshall Mathers," the official content, the referential content, is the same as if we said "Eminem is Eminem." There is no way to get from that content to different reflexive contents. And no need to. They are right there, available to anyone who perceives the utterance and understands how English works. What comes after the recognition of the triviality of the official content is the realization that some other content may be what the speaker wants his listener to focus on. But this alternative content is not inferred from the official content; rather, what is inferred from the triviality of the official content is that some other available content is the key to figuring out what the speaker is trying to convey.

Bach uses reflexive content in the discussion of several examples. He seems to find it objectionable that reflexive contents can be all of the following: a feature of utterances we usually don't explicitly focus on as we figure out what the speaker is trying to convey; something we stop to notice and focus on when we don't have all the facts to figure this out (the postcard); a candidate for what the speaker may be trying to convey (the evil twin). Why the utility of the theory is supposed to count as an objection to it eludes me.

Reference

I believe many of Bach's complaints reflect his commitment to his own very nuanced and subtle view, which in turn supports a terminology that he has developed and uses with great consistency.[8] Probably when I am older and wiser I'll see things his way, for experience shows there is always a lot to be learned from Bach. But given my present level of wisdom, Bach's theory is sometimes seems so subtle that I can't grasp it, and so often can't see the point of his complaints. For example he says, with gnomic finality:

Speakers use expressions to refer; their uses of expressions don't literally do anything. And to the extent that expressions refer (contrary to Strawson's [1950] insistence that referring is not something an expressions does but only something that someone can use an expression to do), as with pure indexicals, we can say that they refer relative to contexts. But discretionary indexicals and demonstratives do not do that. And to say that uses of them refer is just a awkward and misleading way of saying that speakers use them to refer. (420–421)

Strawson's remark I understand, or thought I did. I believe it is reflected in my theory in a number of ways: reference is a concept connected with content, which is a property of utterances, which are acts by people, not expression types. I do not say that indexicals such as 'I' refer, but that utterances of them do. This, however, is a major sin in the Bachian orthodoxy; people refer to things, utterances do not. Neale also doesn't like the idea of attributing saying and referring and such to utterances. One might say more generally, I suppose, that people accomplish things by acting, their acts don't accomplish anything. The National Rifle Association tells us that guns don't kill, people do; Bach can say, Charlton Heston-like, "acts don't refer to people, people do." But I can reply, "That's true, but people refer by performing intentional acts, that is, utterances, and utterances have properties that make it much easier to refer." If we want to cut down on murder, regulating guns is a good idea; if we want to cut down on reference, eliminating utterances would go a long way.

The main reason I have for taking utterances as central, however, and deviating from our ordinary ways of speaking a bit, is the point mentioned above, about fitting the philosophy of language into a general theory about the flow of informational content and other kinds of content.

Explaining his reservations about my concept of discretionary indexicals, Bach says:

The moral here is that there is no fact of the matter, independent of the speaker's referential intention, as to what a discretionary indexical refers to. There is no question as to what the reference is beyond what the speaker intends to refer to and what his audience takes him to refer to (different members of his audience might take him differently). It is only because there is generally no discrepancy between the two that there seems to be a fact of the matter, hence that we can describe (the use of) the discretionary indexical as itself referring rather than merely as being used to refer. Again, we should not be misled by the ambiguity of the phrase 'indexical reference', which can mean either reference by an indexical or reference (by a speaker) in using an indexical. (407)

I don't think I use the phrase 'indexical reference' ambiguously; indexical reference means reference by a speaker in using an indexical.

I think, *pace* Bach, there not only appears to be, but often is a fact of the matter, as to what a discretionary indexical refers to. I do not think it depends on uptake by the audience, but on what I call, following or interpreting Kaplan (1989a), the "directing intention."[9]

There is certainly a contrast to be made between what a speaker intends to refer to and what he succeeds in referring to, if anything. (I talk about this more below.) I may intend to refer to Gene, pointing at his evil twin. I don't refer to Gene, but to his evil twin. Only my directing intention determines to whom I refer. I intend to refer to Gene *by* referring to the person I am looking at, attending to, and demonstrating. The low-level directing intention shouldn't be glommed together with other things I intend to do *by* carrying it out; the phrase 'speaker's intention', which can be applied to either the directing intention or other things one intends to do *by* carrying out the directing intention, can mislead us here.

From Essential Indexicals to the Reflexive/Referential Theory (Ludlow, Spencer, and Recanati)

The essays by Ludlow, Spencer, and Recanati provide an occasion for discussing the connections among the reflexive/referential view and the views I put forward in Perry 1977 and 1979. Spencer does a nice job of recalling the historical context and motivations of Perry 1979 and the motivations for extending the "two-tier" view developed there to handle indexicals to other phenomena. In my own thinking, this extension happened in a couple of stages. For a while I played with the idea of treating names as indexicals.[10] Then, in Barwise and Perry 1983, Barwise and I distinguished between the "discourse situation," which was relevant to pure indexicals, the "connecting situation," which gave the requisite second tier for demonstratives and names, and "resource situations" of various sorts, used for the interpretation of names, nouns, and definite descriptions. Finally, in the reflexive/referential theory, the phenomenon of reflexivity, that is, of conditions of truth and reference that are conditions on the utterance itself, is quite general, and indexicality is seen as just one special case of it.

Root Canals and the Reflexive/Referential Theory

I'll start with an example Ludlow borrowed from Arthur Prior:

(3)   I am thankful that my root canal is over with.

First consider:

(4)   My root canal is over with.

Let's imagine Ludlow saying this on July 8, 2004, and Prior saying it on July 8, 1954. Call these utterances of (4) u_L and u_P. If we take the first person and the past tense to work in fairly standard ways, simplify things by assuming each of these fellows was thinking about their only root canal and give ourselves a few liberties in wording, we get two propositions expressed by the two utterances respectively:

P_L: That there be a unique root canal on a tooth of **Ludlow**'s, and it was over before **July 8, 2004.**

P_P: That there be a unique root canal on a tooth of **Prior**'s and it was over before **July 8, 1954.**

I use 'be' as a tenseless way of speaking, and use roman boldface to indicate the constituents of a proposition. So the two utterances express singular propositions about the speaker of the utterance and the time of the utterance. If one believes that such singular propositions are expressed by such sentences, then one cannot very well deny that someone else could express the same propositions with different sentences. As a matter of fact, I just did this, with the two sentences in the that-clauses above. And I could just say, typing on July 8, 2004:

(5)   Ludlow's root canal is over.

(6)   Prior's root canal was over.

Although my use of (5) expresses the same proposition as Ludlow's use of (4), it seems that the two utterances are importantly different. Ludlow's utterance certainly conveys to the listener the information that the speaker is the one whose root canal is over, and it shows that the speaker is aware that it is his root canal that is over. Even if Ludlow said (5), it would not convey this information, and not show that Ludlow himself was aware of it. Perhaps he is still groggy and suffering from mild and temporary amnesia after a powerful anesthetic, and doesn't know that his own root canal is over but sees on the whiteboard in the oral surgeon's office that Ludlow's is.

There seem to be two quite different groups of "doxastically similar" people that we can use Ludlow's utterance of (4) to identify. There is the group of people, including Ludlow and Prior, but not me, who are aware that their root canal is over. And there is the group of people, including me and Ludlow, but not Prior, who know that Ludlow's root canal is over. There are those, that is, who are in the same kind of (partial) belief state as Ludlow, the state one is in when one believes that one's own root canal is over. And there are those who believe the same proposition that Ludlow does, that Ludlow's root canal is over.

The properties that define these two different groups project on to other properties in different ways. All, or at least most, members of the first group will feel relief. I'm sure Prior was relieved in 1954, just as Ludlow was in 2004. However, not everyone who believes that Ludlow's root canal is over will feel relief. Probably no one in this group of cobelievers in P_L other than Ludlow himself feels relief as intense as he does; many may have some milder positive emotion: "I'm happy for Peter that he has that behind him." Many have no significant emotional involvement in Peter's dental work, and it's possible, though unlikely, that some victims of his quick wit and dialectical prowess are saddened to see Ludlow's pain and angst come to an end, and would just as soon that the root canal had gone on for a week or two longer.

We take what a person says as a good guide to what they believe, and we expect what they believe to play an important part in explaining what they do. So Ludlow's belief that his root canal is over explains his relief, his willingness to pay the dentist's bill, his willingness to resume chewing nuts with his right molars, and so forth. But what about his belief does the explanatory work? It doesn't seem that it is the proposition believed, for we saw that I could believe that very same proposition, that Ludlow's root canal was over, and that wouldn't explain my feeling relieved, paying the dentist, or changing my chewing habits. And even if Ludlow believed it, in the way we imagined him doing when he emerges groggy and amnesiac, that wouldn't explain his doing these things.

Moreover, it seems that Prior's belief, in a different proposition, would explain his doing the same sorts of things: feeling relief, paying his dentist, changing his chewing habits. As Spencer rightly observed, none of these actions will be motivated, for Ludlow or Prior, simply by their beliefs that their root canals are over. If Ludlow believes the truce he has made with assassins that are after him comes to an end when the root canal is over, he will feel anxiety, not relief. If a main motivation in his having the operation was to bilk the oral surgeon who stole his girlfriend in college, he won't pay. And if he doesn't know that root canals leave the tooth without sensation, he won't change his chewing habits. Still, when we think of the state that Ludlow and Prior were in, and supplement it with the normal auxiliary beliefs, the actions I mentioned make sense.

What I take the example to show is that we can assert the same proposition in different ways and that these different ways of asserting correspond to different ways of believing the same proposition. The way I now get at the differences is in terms of reflexive and referential truth conditions of utterances and beliefs.

Consider Ludlow's and Prior's utterances of (4), $\mathbf{u}_L$ and $\mathbf{u}_P$. There is a certain property that each of these must have, in order to be true:

$C^*(u)$: u is such that there is a person x, an event e, and a time t such that:

(i) x is the speaker of u;

(ii) e is a root canal of x's

(iii) t is the last time at which e occurs;

(iv) t is earlier than the time of u.

Instantiating $C^*(u)$ onto $\mathbf{u}_L$ and $\mathbf{u}_P$ we obtain two quite different propositions, that $C^*(\mathbf{u}_L)$ and that $C^*(\mathbf{u}_P)$. These are what I call the *reflexive contents* of the two utterances, given only the meaning of (4).[11]

Finally, there are the *referential contents* of $\mathbf{u}_L$ and $\mathbf{u}_P$, the conditions that they must meet to be true given, in addition to the meaning of (4), the facts about the identities of the speakers and the time the utterances occurred. These are

P_L: That there be a unique root canal on a tooth of **Ludlow**'s, and it was over before **July 8, 2004.**

P_P: That there be a unique root canal on a tooth of **Prior**'s and it was over before **July 8, 1954.**

The referential content of $\mathbf{u}_L$ gets at what people have in common who believe what Ludlow says when he utters (4). The reflexive truth-condition gets at what Ludlow's utterance and Prior's have in common. The point of recognizing the reflexive contents I'll get to in a bit.

It is pretty clear, of course, that Ludlow could be relieved that his root canal was over but not tell anyone about it. It is not only the content of his utterance we need to worry about, but also the contents of his thoughts and beliefs. What correspond to indexicals in our beliefs are not words with a special conventional meaning, but notions and ideas that are tied to what I call "epistemic and pragmatic roles." Our self-notions, for example, are store information we get in "normally self-informative ways" and motivate actions that are "normally self-effecting."[12] When we find out information about ourselves in other ways, and realize it is we ourselves we are getting information about, that information is also associated with our self-notions. Similarly, things we are aware of through memory will be associated with our idea of being in the past; things we are perceiving will be associated with our idea of being present.

I will consider thoughts rather than beliefs, since Ludlow's concerns focus on issues of time and tense. Thoughts are fleeting, whereas beliefs typically endure, so such issues are clearer with respect to thoughts. Consider the Ludlow's and Prior's *thoughts*, τ_L and τ_P, that their utterances express. The common structure of the thoughts we can represent with,

∃e such that e happened to **SELF**, e is a root canal, and **PAST**(e).

where **SELF** is a self-notion, and **PAST** is an idea of the past. We assume that Ludlow had this sort of thought on July 8, 2004, and expressed it with (4), and similarly for Prior in 1954. The reflexive truth-condition of any thought τ of this sort is:

$C^{**}(\tau)$: τ is such that there is a person x an event e and a time t such that

(i) x is the owner of τ;

(ii) e is a root canal of x's;

(iii) t is the last time at which e occurs;

(iv) t is earlier than the time of τ.

$C^{**}(\tau)$ gets at what Ludlow's and Prior's thoughts have in common, the condition they must satisfy to be true, given only the cognitive role of such thoughts. Thoughts like this project onto the various emotions, actions and other thoughts we noted, and the reflexive truth-conditions show the rationality or normality of this.

The referential contents of τ_L and τ_P, are the conditions that have to be met for the thoughts to be true, given, in addition to their cognitive roles, that facts that τ_L belongs to Ludlow and occurred on July 8, 2004, whereas τ_P belongs to Prior and occurred back in 1954. They are, in fact, our old friends, P_L and P_P, the referential contents of their utterances.

So τ_L and τ_P have the same referential contents as u_L and u_P, but this does not get at all that is required for the utterances to express the thoughts. We need reflexive contents for this. Although the reflexive truth conditions of the thoughts and utterances are *not* the same, there is an intimate connection between them:

Given that the speaker of u = the owner of τ and the time of u = the time of τ, u will meet condition C^* if and only if τ meets condition C^{**}.

It is, of course, a pretty solid fact that when an utterance expresses a thought, these identities hold. The relation between the owner of a belief and the speaker of an utterance is an example of what David Israel and I call an architectural relation.[13]

Now suppose that Ludlow has a root canal scheduled for Wednesday, but it is cancelled for some reason or other. On Friday he says, "If I'd had a root canal Wednesday, by now I would have been relieved that it was over." Consider the possible world in which Ludlow did have his root canal on Wednesday. In that possible world, Ludlow, the speaker, on Friday, the day of the utterance, is relieved that the root canal he had Wednesday is over. No utterance has to occur in the possible world. The counterfactual situation is the same one at issue if I had said to Ludlow, the following Monday, "If you had had a root canal last Wednesday, by Friday you would have been relieved that it was over." In the counterfactual situation, Ludlow will have to have a thought with a structure like the one given above, the sort that would lead him to utter (4) if he felt like expressing it. But nothing out of the ordinary needs to be carried along with the referential content to understand the possibility Ludlow has in mind. So, while Ludlow thinks this counterfactual situation is a problem, I don't quite see why.

This then is how the reflexive/referential theory treats (4). Now let's consider

(3)   I am thankful that my root canal is over with.

I will assume that there is a subset of beliefs, which we may call "thankfuls." One is thankful that S, if one believes that S, and that belief causes, in the way that thoughts about the end of unpleasant episodes do, feelings of gratitude and relief. This isn't a very sophisticated theory of thankfuls, but perhaps it will do for discussing the issues at hand. Now, applying and adapting the second version of the theory Crimmins and I put forward in Crimmins and Perry 1989[14] we have:

The referential content of Ludlow's utterance of (3) at **t** is that Ludlow has a thankful thought τ at **t**, involving a self-notion **SELF** and an idea of the past **PAST**, and τ has the reflexive content that $C^{**}(\tau)$, (and hence the referential content that **Ludlow**'s root canal end prior to **July 8, 2004**).

The Relation of the Reflexive/Referential Theory to Others

The reflexive/referential theory shares with my earlier essays on these subjects the leading idea that we believe propositions in certain *ways*; we can believe the same proposition in different ways: the way normal Ludlow believes versus the way groggy Ludlow believes that Ludlow's root canal is over; the way normal Ludlow believes it and the way the rest of us believe it. We can believe different propositions in the same way: Ludlow and Prior, each believing that his root canal is over. It is the way we believe propositions that fit into the descriptions of mental states that project on to the more basic actions we are motivated to perform and thus provide the basis for explaining action. Without some such distinction, we cannot properly distinguish between states and properties when discussing the attitudes. States, the way I use the term, are properties that are intrinsic or internal to the agent; he could have these properties, and so be in the same states, even if his relations to the rest of the world, causal, environmental, and so forth, were quite different. The 'can' here is logical or metaphysical; it might be unlikely, or even causally impossible, that Ludlow should be in the state he is, and have thought τ_L, if he hasn't visited a dentist and had a root canal, but it is logically possible that he be in that state, without those things happening. Attitude properties, on the other hand, are typically not states, since they depend on relations to things outside the believer. An agent will believe the things he does, want the things he does, see the things he does, and so on, in virtue not only of the states he is in but also the wider situation in which he finds himself. For example, my attitude property of *believing that* **Ludlow**'s *root canal is over*, requires that my belief state be about Ludlow, and this isn't just a matter of what goes on inside of me, but also a matter of Ludlow having interacted with me in the past in a way that was crucial to the formation of my idea of him.

How do we get at the attitude states? The picture is that the attitude states *plus* facts about how the agent fits into the world yields the attitude properties, the properties involved in our ordinary indirect classifications of minds in terms of incremental content. Conversely, in the reflexive/referential theory, we add to the ordinary classifications in terms of propositions believed or asserted, by quantifying over the objects and properties external to the utterance or state itself. The content properties we end up with can be as "narrow" as we need it to be for a given explanatory issue.

I explored a number of alternatives along the way to the reflexive/referential theory. In Perry 1979 I called the abstract objects we need in addition to propositions "roles." Then as now I thought roles characterize cognitive structures and states by what they require of objects in the world given the role they play in the agent's life—the role of being the object perceived, or the person talked to, or being the agent herself. Propositions, conceived of as set of possible worlds, or functions from worlds to truth values, or singular propositions, characterize my beliefs in terms of the conditions they put on their subject matter, independently of the roles they play in the life of the agent.

Roles were originally inspired pondering Kaplan's *characters*, which are functions from quadruples of agents, times, positions, and worlds—what he calls "contexts"—to propositions, and serve to model the meanings of sentences. The character of "my root canal is over" yields, in context c, the proposition *that* **the agent of c**'s root canal is over at **the time of c**.

A later candidate for getting at the "narrow" facts about utterances and cognitive states is the concept of meaning developed in situation semantics. In the version in Barwise and Perry 1983, the linguistic meaning of 'my root canal is over' is a relation [[my root canal is over]] (d,c,P) among discourse situations, connecting situations, and described situations. Discourse situations have to do with who utters the sentence and when, connecting situations with the circumstances that determine the reference of names and demonstratives, and described situations give us the proposition expressed. (Actually, we didn't have propositions in Barwise and Perry 1983—we talked about "the interpretation" instead of the "proposition expressed" or "what is said," but I'll ignore those complications, mostly now of only historical interest.) So we have [[my root canal is over]] (d,c,P) iff there is an agent x, and a time t, such that x says "my root canal is over" at t in d, and P is the proposition that x's root canal is over by t. On the other hand,

[[Ludlow's root canal is over]] (d,c,P)

holds if the speaker's use of 'Ludlow' in d at t is connected in c to someone who has been through a root canal that is over by t. In chapter 10 of Barwise and Perry 1983, we developed a theory of mental meanings, or *schemata*, for representing the narrower contents of beliefs, based on these ideas.

A key difference between the approach of papers such as Perry 1977 and those of Barwise and Perry 1983 and Perry 2001b, is the appreciation of Spencer's point that the two-tiered approach does not pertain only to indexicals and that there is a need for more machinery than is supplied by Kaplan's contexts.

Thus a variety of abstract objects can be used to help us characterize the belief state: the character of 'my root canal is over', the property of being a person whose root canal is over, the relation between discourse situations and propositions expressed that English associates with 'my root canal is over', and so forth. Picking one's favorite suitable abstract object to do the classifying job is one thing. But what should we call the relation that the agent has to this object? It's clear that we shouldn't call it "belief." Or so it seemed, and seems, so to me. (I pick up on these issues below, when I discuss Recanati and relativized propositions.)

In Perry 1977, I suggested that Frege, should he want to modify his view conservatively, should divide two jobs he assigned to his concept of *sinn*: serving as the mind characterizers, that get directly grasped, and graspings of which are mental states in the causal realm, and serving as the propositions, the *gedanke*, that get to be objectively true and false. The mind-characterizers would be functions from contexts to the *gedanke*.[15]

This is the view that I arrived at, considering "essential indexical" examples. I sometimes call it the "two-tier view"; Spencer is quite right that, once we have seen the need of it for indexicals, it is fairly easy to see that it is needed for other kinds of beliefs. The two-tiered, or multitiered, picture simply reflects the anatomy of incremental content; indexicals push this structure in our faces, but do not exhaust it. Now I want to explain the connection between this view, and my current theory, developed in Perry 2001b, about reflexive and referential contents. I like to think of all of this in terms of *reflexive truth-conditions* of an utterance or a belief.

Thus, with a little squinting and ignoring subtleties, we can say that these formulations get at the same phenomena:

i. (Kaplan-inspired)

a. An utterance u of 'My root canal is over' has the character that yields the content *that a's root canal is over by t*, where a is the speaker of the utterance and t is the time of the utterance.

b. So Ludlow's utterance of 'My root canal is over' at **t** has the content that **Ludlow**'s root canal be over by **t**.

ii. (Reflexive/referential theory: Reichenbach- and Kaplan-inspired)

a. An utterance u of 'My root canal is over,' is true iff there is an x and a t such that x is the speaker of u and t is the time of u and x's root canal is over by t.

b. So, given that Ludlow is the speaker of **u** and **t** is the time of **u**, **u** is true iff **Ludlow**'s root canal is over by **t**.

The reflexive/referential account is basically an application of the anatomy of content.[16] The utterance **u** is an event, a signal in the broad sense, that has informational content relative to various constraints to which an English speaker is attuned. Truth-conditions classify the utterance in terms of success conditions. The reflexive content gets at the success conditions relative to the constraints provided by the conventions of English, the referential content gets at them relative to these constraints plus connecting facts. The connecting role is *being the speaker of*, which Ludlow plays, so we get the incremental informational content, the referential truth-conditions.

Reflexive Contents

In the reflexive/referential treatment, unlike the earlier ones, we have *three* things to worry about, the reflexive truth-conditions of utterances of 'my root canal is over', given the meaning, which is a descendant of characters, roles, and meanings; the reflexive content of Ludlow's utterance of it—that's the new thing; and the referential content, what he said. This new thing, the reflexive content, seems to me to be a useful tool in understanding communication and planning and reasoning about what is said and what is implicated (in Grice's sense) by utterances. It is *not* a candidate for *what is said* or *what is believed*. In particular, I do *not* hold that what explains the difference between Ludlow and me, when we both believe that Ludlow's root canal is over, is that he believes the *reflexive* content of his remark. If he thinks about it, he will no doubt believe it. That is, he will believe, of his own utterance of 'my root canal is over', that it is uttered by someone whose root canal was over by the time of the utterance. But I will also believe this proposition, if I think about it. So belief in reflexive content does not get at what is special about Ludlow's assertion or belief and the mental state that motivates it.

In his essay, Ludlow appears to think that I intended the reflexive content to be *the proposition believed* when one uses the first person or other demonstratives and indexicals. However, this was not my intention. The singular proposition P_L is still my candidate for that, and the character or meaning of 'I'm glad my root canal is over' is still my candidate for what Prior and Ludlow's utterances have in common that gets at their common beliefs state. The main use of the reflexive content is something quite different.

The main purpose of the reflexive content of utterances is to help us understand the whole process of communication, from belief, to utterance, to uptake on the listener's part, to belief. One important part of this is how understand the connections between the contents of beliefs and the contents of the assertions that express them, which we considered above. Here I'll indicate how these contents are essential to understanding utterances.

Consider this conversation:

JP: Peter, would you like a caramel?

PL: I'm glad my root canal is over!

PL says that he is glad his root canal is over and implicates that he would like a caramel. 'Implicates' is of course Grice's word for something that Peter means to convey but does not say. Rather, I am to see that he intends for me to believe that he would like a caramel, because this is part of the best explanation of how what he said fits into the conversation in a helpful, relevant, way.

Here is my account of how this works. I know English and I hear Peter's utterance **u**, and because I know English I know its reflexive truth conditions:

u is true iff the speaker of **u** is glad that his root canal is over.

This much is a matter of applying the semantics of English to the utterance **u**. And, I maintain, it is at this point that semantics has done its job. The rest of the work is done by observation and reasoning about intentions.

I observe that the speaker of **u** is the person across the table from me, whose mouth is moving as I hear the words, so I reason,

Given that the speaker of **u** is the fellow across the table, **u** is true iff the fellow across the table is glad that his root canal is over.

I realize that the fellow across the table from me is the person I just offered a caramel to, and so I reason,

Given that the fellow across the table is the fellow I just offered a caramel to, **u** is true iff the fellow I just offered a caramel to is glad his root canal is over.

So far, my reasoning has been based on my knowledge of English and observation. Now I begin to think about *why* he might have said what he did. I think he heard my offer and assume that he intends his reply to be conversationally appropriate. If so, it should tell me whether or not he wants a caramel. His reply entails that he no longer has a problem with his teeth that he once had. Everyone knows that caramels should be avoided by people who have problems with their teeth. Because he knows I know all of this, he will expect me to think he intends to accept a caramel. So the simplest explanation is that by saying that he is glad his root canal is over he intends for me to understand that he wants one by recognizing that intention. So I give him one. This picture of the central role that utterances and their reflexive contents play in communication has implications for the semantics/pragmatics distinction, an issue that concerns many of the essayists, as we shall see.

Recanati's Approach

Before leaving the basic issues connected with Perry 1979, I want to comment on something Recanati says, which doesn't seem quite right. He says:

there are a number of options available. First, we can make the belief relation triadic: we can say that propositions are believed under "guises" or "modes of presentation". Replacement of an indexical by a non-indexical expression in the asserted sentence affects the guise, even if the proposition expressed is the same. The problem is solved because a rational subject may both believe and disbelieve the same proposition, provided he believes it under one guise (P) and disbelieves it under another guise (Q). This is the solution advocated by Perry himself, and by most philosophers in the so-called Russellian camp. Alternatively, we can keep the belief relation dyadic, but, departing from Russellianism and the "coarse-grained" individuation of propositions in terms of objects and properties, follow Frege in building propositions ("thoughts") out of "senses" or modes of presentation, thus making them directly answerable to cognitive considerations. For that solution to work, special, nondescriptive senses of the sort invoked by the "neo-Fregeans" must be associated with indexical expressions. A middle course is also available (Recanati 1993, 1995). We can keep the belief relation dyadic by incorporating the modes of presentation into the singular proposition, alongside the objects and properties of which they are modes of presentation. The resulting "quasi-singular proposition" will be truth-conditionally equivalent to, but cognitively distinct from, the original singular proposition. (122–123)

The charm of the second and third options eludes me, for each fails to make the distinctions between role-based characterization and subject matter-based characterizations that seems to me to be essential to solving the problem. That is, if we follow Recanati and pack both relational modes of presentation and subject matter into a quasi-singular proposition, our attitude properties will not get what agents who believe the same thing have in common, or what those who believe in the same way have in common.

Recanati continues:

There is yet another option. . . . We can shift to 'relativized propositions', as Prior suggested in his treatment of tensed sentences. According to Prior, tensed sentences express propositions which are true or false only relative to a time. (123)

In Perry 1979, I said it would not work to take relativized propositions, which we can think of as functions from contexts to truth-values rather than from worlds to truth-values, as the objects of belief. But David Lewis seems to have done just this, as Recanati observes. What I said was right, however, and Lewis's view can easily lead us astray.

Lewis (1979) chose properties as the abstract objects to characterize belief states. Properties, conceived generally, are a lot like relativized propositions; we need an agent and time and we get a truth-value. Lewis used the word 'self-ascribes' for the relations a believer has to these properties. A believer he takes to a person-stage rather than a person. So Ludlow—or, more precisely, one of his stages—self-ascribes the property of *being one whose root canal is over*. Lewis's theory begins, as he noted, as simply a stylistic variant of my Kaplan-inspired account. We say that Ludlow self-ascribes this property, rather than saying that he accepts 'my root canal is over', or is in the belief state characterized by the role or character of this sentence. Ludlow self-ascribes this property and thereby believes that his root canal is over as of July 8, 2004. Prior self-ascribed the same property and thereby believed that his root canal was over as of July 8, 1954.

Lewis built on this initial move, and added a number of other wrinkles that streamlined things within his overall metaphysics, and made his account much different than mine. The agents are person-stages, not persons. And, because he thinks that other possible worlds are concrete and that no one exists in more than one of them, he can treat all beliefs as involving self-attributions. When normal Ludlow believes that his root canal is over, he self-attributes the property of *being one whose root canal is over*. When groggy Ludlow, looking at the whiteboard, believes that Ludlow's root canal is over, or when I believe that Ludlow's root canal is over, we self-attribute *being in a world in which Ludlow's root canal is over*. However, this doesn't work if we are in more than one world, and Ludlow exists in some worlds where his root canal is over, and others where it continues. You can't just take Lewis's theory of "de se belief" by itself and add it to some other, perhaps more commonsensical, conception of the universe.

But the key point is that self-attribution of a property is *not* belief, but a component of belief. I think many philosophers have thought they could adopt Lewis's view, if they agreed that beliefs expressed with indexicals involve self-attribution of properties. But unless they swallow the whole metaphysics, they have really just adopted a version of my view, and should be careful not to confuse self-attribution with belief.

Semantics, Pragmatics, and What Is Said[17]

A number of the articles are concerned about the implications of various things I have said for the nature of pragmatics and of semantics and their "interface." I think Bach is exactly right in saying that I haven't ever had a very clear position on this, but I will try to develop one here that fits naturally with the main ideas in Perry 2001b and elsewhere, and the picture of content sketched above, even though it may be somewhat different from what I have said or implied in the past. This thinking reflects recent work with Kepa Korta and incorporates many of his ideas.[18]

On my view, utterances are the subject matter of both pragmatics and semantics. Utterances are intentional acts of speaking, writing, or signing, usually for the purpose of communication and usually in service of further goals, such as developing a plan, persuading someone to do something, teaching, learning, passing the time, or whatever. The utterance is an act by the speaker, which the listener interprets, using many tools that are used for interpreting all sorts of actions, and some that are specific to language. Pragmatics and semantics need to tell us how various properties of utterances relate to one another. The philosopher of language should study these issues from the usual philosophical perspectives, logical, epistemological, metaphysical, ontological, ethical, and so forth. The issue of the interface between semantics and pragmatics has to do with the properties of utterances with which each discipline deals. As I see it, semantics pertains to what is special about language, the use of words and grammatical forms with conventional meanings.

For a long time, the concept of "what is said" seemed like a natural dividing line; semantics gets us to what is said, in virtue of the words used, how they are combined, and their meanings; pragmatics takes over and figures out what acts were done, or what implicatures were conveyed, in or by saying what was said. But this has gotten problematic. As promised in the section on Bach, we need to think a bit more about what is said.

Perhaps the best way to start is by way of Recanati's recent book *Literal Meaning*.[19] Recanati's scheme for understanding current debates about semantics and pragmatics has been deservedly influential. He sees the range of positions as having two poles, literalism and contextualism: The literalist holds that

> we may legitimately ascribe truth-conditional content to natural language *sentences*, quite independently of what the speaker who utters this sentence means.... [Contextualism] holds that *speech acts* are the primary bearers of content. Only in the context of a speech act does a sentence express a determinate content. (3)

Recanati goes on to distinguish a number of intermediate positions. The minimalist admits to get to truth-conditional content we need to supplement conventional meanings with contextually determined values for indexicals, and perhaps some other kinds of "saturation." Cappelen and Lepore (2005) advocate a form of minimalism (although they do not think that their concept of semantic content should be identified with "what is said," which they take to be a pragmatic concept). The view that Taylor advocates in the essay in this book also seems to be a form of minimalism; for Taylor, what is "strictly and literally said" pays attention to intentions only when called for syntactically, where this calling starts from the lexicon in the "subsyntactic basement." Recanati and relevance theorists are far over to the contextualist side. Both camps call on Grice. Literalists use Grice's ideas to create a sort of shock absorber between our intuitions about what someone says and what their theories deliver as semantic content; the intuitions confuse semantic content with conversational implicatures. The contextualists see (broadly) Gricean reasoning about speaker's intentions involved throughout the process of interpretation.

In discussing the reflexive/referential theory, Recanati (2004) sketches an approach that seems to me quite plausible, and capable of doing justice to both literalist and contextualist insights and theoretical ambitions. He is discussing an utterance of the sentence 'I am French'.

> the reflexive proposition is determined *before* the process of saturation takes place. The reflexive proposition can't be determined unless the sentence is tokened, but no substantial knowledge of the context of utterance is required to determine it. Thus an utterance u of the sentence 'I am French' expresses the reflexive proposition that *the utterer of u is French*. That it does not presup-

pose saturation is precisely what makes the reflexive proposition useful, since in most cases satu-ration proceeds by appeal to speaker's meaning. . . . The reflexive proposition is admittedly distinct from that which the speaker asserts . . . but why is this an objection? [The reflexive proposition] comes as close as one can get to capturing, in propositional format, the information provided by the utterance in virtue solely of the linguistic meaning of the sentence 'I am French'. (65–66)

This is pretty much the approach I will develop. First a caveat: I do not hold that an utterance *u* of 'I am French' *expresses* the proposition that *the utterer of u is French*. I de-scribe that proposition as giving the reflexive truth-conditions of *u*, or being the reflex-ive content of the *u* (with meaning fixed). These truth conditions are available to any competent speaker and, I think, need to be appealed to in understanding both the gen-eration of and the comprehension of the utterance. But I do not claim or think it is what is said or is the proposition expressed.

What Kepa Korta and I propose is that the reflexive content, with meaning fixed, be taken as the *semantic content* in the sense in which a literalist wants such a thing for theoretical purposes, that is, constructing a compositional, truth conditional theory of meaning. On the issue of "pragmatic intrusion" into semantic content, then, I am more radical, more minimal, than those, like Cappelen and Lepore (2005), who factor in contextually determined values for indexicals, and a number of other things (resolu-tion of reference for demonstratives and names, resolution of ambiguity and vague-ness) that, as far as I can see, would have to be based on speaker's intentions. On the other hand, on the issue of what is said, I am over on the contextualist side. The first step in developing these ideas is to discuss some issues about what is said and replace it, or explicate it, with a concept that Korta and I call locutionary content.

Saying and Locutionary Content

Korta and I suggest replacing or explicating it the ordinary concept of what is said, for theoretical work, with the concept *locutionary content*. This is based loosely on Austin's concept of a locutionary act.

Our ordinary concept of what is said has (at least) three pressures on it, which push in different ways. An example of Kaplan's will help to identify these pressures. A pro-fessor is lecturing in a room that for a long time has had a picture of Rudolf Carnap hanging behind the podium. The lecturer doesn't know that it has been recently replaced with a picture of Spiro Agnew. He points behind himself, without looking, and says, "That's a picture of the greatest philosopher of the twentieth century." Assuming, for the sake of argument, that Carnap was the greatest philosopher of the twentieth century, we can ask: has he said something false, about a picture of Agnew, or something true, about a picture of Carnap?[20]

The first pressure is *forensic*. We use our ordinary concept of "what is said" to distribute responsibility for the effects of one's utterances. A competent English speaker who heard our professor might go out and buy a picture of Agnew and tell his friends it is a picture of the greatest philosopher of the twentieth century. When one of them laughs at him, and says he is a fool, he might return to our professor and complain that he had been misled. The professor said something false. We certainly sympathize with the audience member, at least I do. The professor replies that he didn't *intend* to say *that*. But didn't he say it nevertheless? Phrases such as 'he inadvertently said', and 'He didn't mean what he said', and the like suggest to this possibility.

Another pressure is psychological. Saying things is a way of expressing our beliefs and desires. At least when we are sincere, the content of what we say seems intimately connected to the content of the main belief that motivates it. It is probably this pressure that leads Neale to say that he can't see that our concept of saying comes to anything other than what we intend to say (359). Our professor might respond to the complaining picture-buyer, "I'm sorry you took me to say something so silly. It was definitely my fault, for not looking. But I was actually talking about another picture that used to hang there, of Carnap, so what I really said was true." I also sympathize with the professor, although in this case I think he is wrong. The connection between what one intends to say and what one says is not so simple.

The third pressure is theoretical, and comes from a role that "what is said" has often played, in demarcating the interface between semantics and pragmatics. On this view, what is said is something like the "output" of the "semantic component." This then is "input" to the "pragmatic component" which uses Gricean reasoning to figure out what the speaker may have meant to *convey* by saying what he did. On this view, intentions shouldn't enter into what is said; it should simply be a matter of the content determined by the semantical rules of the language.

On the original view of the semantics/pragmatics distinction, brought into analytical philosophy by Morris and Carnap, semantics deals with *types* of expressions, not utterances; pragmatics deals with what is peculiar to utterances (including, in Carnap's formulation, most of what we now call "cognitive science" and much else). This use of the word led early investigators of indexicals, like Bar-Hillel, to call what they were studying "pragmatics." Using Kaplan's terminology, on this conception semantics would end with the analysis of the character of the type of expression used in an utterance, whereas the content, which turns on the context of the utterance, would be a matter of pragmatics. What is said would then belong to pragmatics, not semantics.

Kaplan conceived himself to be doing semantics, however, and this is the picture of the interface that has been popular for some time. Semantics gets us to the content of an utterance, to what is said, all of which is determined in an intention-free way, given the identity of the words used, the way they are combined, the rules of language and objective facts about the speech situation. It seems even more like semantics if we interpret what he gives us as a theory not of utterances but of sentences-in-context, a theory of the interaction between two abstract objects.

Demonstratives put pressure on this picture. Kaplan (1989b) does not deal with "true demonstratives," such as 'this' and 'that', in his formal semantics. In the informal discussion, however, he develops a theory in which the *demonstration* determines the demonstratum in an objective way; intentions are relevant only as evidence. Proper names also put pressure on this picture. It seems that *which* David a speaker refers to when he says, "David is brilliant," is a matter of how he intends to use the name 'David'. Kaplan offers us a theory of proper names, however, according to which each person named David has a different name. Once we have identified the word used, intentions are not relevant. So, it seemed that the intention-free conception of semantics, and semantics as delivering what is said, could be maintained, even when the facts of particular utterances that determined the semantic values of indexicals and demonstratives and names were taken into account. Using Recanati's terminology, we could say that it seemed that saturation could be intention-free.

This has proven rather illusory, however. Kaplan (1989a) gives up his demonstrations theory in favor of a "directing intentions" theory, acknowledging that intentions have a role in determining reference and are not merely evidence for interpreting demonstrations. Even with most indexicals, perhaps all except 'I', intentions seem relevant, as a number of writers have pointed out. When we use 'now' and 'here' semantics may dictate that the moment and location of the utterance be included in the stretches of time and space that are designated, but the extent of those stretches seems to be a matter of the intentions of the speaker. The stretch of time relevant to an evaluation of 'Now we walk upright', is likely to be different than that relevant to 'Now I must run to the meeting'. Even 'today' and 'tomorrow' seem to involve intentions. Suppose I am in Palo Alto talking to Syun in Tokyo, when it is 5 AM Tuesday my time and 9 PM Tuesday his time. "I'll get it to you today," I promise. Does 'today' mean the twenty-four-hour period of time that comprises Tuesday in California (in which case I have nineteen hours to complete my task) or the twenty-four-hour period that comprises Tuesday in Tokyo (in which case I have only three)? It seems a matter of my intentions.

The conflicts among the three pressures involve the role of intentions. Sorting this out is the virtue of the positive view that Korta and I are developing. The basic idea is that a locutionary act is an act of using language to express a proposition, the locutionary content, which is determined by (i) the conventions governing the words and combinations of words that the speaker uses; (ii) the speaker's intentions to use some of those conventions to refer to objects or predicate properties as permitted by the conventions; (iii) further facts about the things thus referred to or predicated. Because the role of intentions is limited, we do not end up with a "Humpty Dumpty" theory, in which anyone can say anything they want with any expression they choose, simply by having the intention to do so. We separate off the forensic aspects of saying; the locutionary content does not depend on how one's listeners take what one says. We give conventional meanings an honorable but limited role; we give up on the ideas of an intention-free route from the words and constructions used to what is said.

Let's return to Kaplan's example. Our professor knows English and realizes that the conventions governing 'that' permit him to refer to a great variety of things that play various roles in his life at that point. One thing you can do with 'that X' is to refer to the object of type X that you are pointing to. So he intends to refer the picture he is pointing to, the picture of Agnew. This is the intention relevant to part (ii) in the paragraph above. Now he also intends to refer to a picture of Carnap. This is not a type-(ii) intention, but something he plans to carry out by fulfilling his type-(ii) intention. He intends to refer to the picture of Carnap *by* referring to the picture he points to. (It is type-(ii) intentions, ones that directly exploit language, that I think Kaplan means by "directing intentions." But whether that is the right interpretation of Kaplan's intentions, it is what I will mean.) Referring to the picture he points to is a subgoal; it is part of the professor's plan to refer to the picture of Carnap, which is part of a plan to express a proposition about the picture of Carnap, which is no doubt part of a further plan, to secure uptake on the part of the audience, have them understand his views about Carnap, and perhaps implicate that Heidegger, Sartre, Quine, Rorty and Kripke are not so important as various other speakers have suggested.

So our professor's intentions play an important role in what he says, but only some of them, the type-(ii) intentions. Then the facts of type (iii) take over. The picture he points to is not the picture of Carnap he intended to point to, but a picture of Agnew, so that is what he in fact refers to, contrary to his intentions. The locutionary content of his utterance is that the picture of Agnew is a picture of the greatest philosopher of the twentieth century.

In this case, the locutionary content agrees with the ordinary, forensically imbued, concept of what is said. But it isn't because of forensic considerations that we obtained this result. The locutionary content did not depend on what people would take him to say, but simply on conventions, type-(ii) intentions, and type-(iii) facts.

Consider a somewhat different example. I go into the department lounge to get a cup of coffee and check my mail. Some graduate students are in an animated conversation:

A: Aristotle was a very rich man, but ruthless.

B: Nonsense. He was rich, but he was very kind.

They are in fact talking about Aristotle Onassis, but I take them to be talking about the philosopher. So I say, "Aristotle was not rich, but he was kind." The word 'Aristotle' has been assigned by conventions to a number of people over the course of time, including Aristotle the great philosopher and Aristotle Onassis. I intend to exploit the former convention to refer to the great philosopher. The locutionary content of my utterance is that the ancient philosopher was not rich but was kind, even if everyone naturally takes me to be talking about Aristotle Onassis, and I could be perhaps held responsible for saying something about Aristotle Onassis, if the fact that someone understood me that way led to horrible consequences. In this case I don't think our ordinary concept of "what is said" gives a determinate answer, but the locutionary content is clear.

Let's consider a series of Kripke-inspired examples. Elwood sees Jones mowing Smith's lawn and takes the person he sees to be Smith. Smith is in fact in seeding another part of the lawn, out of sight. (In discussing these examples, and from now on, I'll just use 'says' for locutionary content, unless I indicate otherwise.)

A. Elwood intends to say that Smith is mowing a lawn, by saying "He is mowing a lawn." Elwood's plan is to refer using 'he' to the person he sees mowing a lawn, a type-(ii) intention, and thereby refer to Smith. The plan miscarries, because of his false belief that the person he sees is Smith. Elwood says (truly) that Jones is mowing a lawn, which is not what he wanted to say.

B. Elwood intends to say that Smith a mowing a lawn, by saying, "He is mowing a lawn." In this case, Elwood has been thinking about Smith, and intends to use 'he' to refer to the person he is thinking about, a type-(ii) intention, and thereby refer to Smith. The false belief that he sees Smith mowing a lawn is evidence for what he says, but not part of his plan for saying it. Elwood says what he intended to say, that Smith is mowing a lawn, which is false.

C. Elwood intends to say that the man he sees is mowing a lawn, by saying "Smith is mowing a lawn." He has a type-(ii) intention to use 'Smith' to refer to Smith and plans by doing that to refer to the man he sees. He doesn't say what he intended to say, which was true, but that Smith is mowing a lawn, which is false.

D. Elwood has a limited grasp of English. He thinks he knows how to say that some-one is mowing a lawn; he thinks a way to do this is to say, "is seeding a lawn." As before, he wrongly believes the man he sees is Smith. He intends to say that the man he sees is mowing a lawn. He says, "Smith is seeding a lawn." He doesn't say what he intended to say. He says that Smith is seeding a lawn, which is true.

Semantic Content and Reflexive Truth Conditions

Given this conception of what is said, it is not the natural dividing point between semantics and pragmatics. Semantics has to do with the conventional meanings of words and modes of combination. Its most central part is truth-conditional semantics. Truth-conditional semantics gives us the truth-conditions of utterances in terms of the constraints imposed by these meanings. So conceived, semantics can give us *utterance-bound descriptions* of what is said, but cannot usually provide *utterance-free* descriptions of what is said. That is, in my terminology, semantics gives us the reflexive truth-conditions of utterances.

Consider an example of Grice's from "Logic and Conversation." He says, concerning the sentence 'He was in the grip of a vice',

Given a knowledge of the English language, but no knowledge of the circumstances of the utterance, one would know something about what the speaker had said, on the assumption that he was speaking standard English, and speaking literally. One would know that he had said, about some particular male person or animal x, that at the time of utterance (whatever that was), either (1) x was unable to rid himself of a certain kind of bad character trait or (2) some part of x's person was caught in a certain kind of tool or instrument (approximate account, of course).[21]

Thus, what one knows about the utterance of "He is in the grip of a vice," merely on the basis of knowledge of its conventional meanings, falls short of what one needs to know in order to fully identify what is said. One has only an *utterance-bound* way of getting at it. Conventions don't tell you whom was referred to with 'he', or at what time it was said. And they don't tell you *which* conventions the speaker was exploiting, the ones that allow one to use the phrase 'in the grip of a vice' to talk about tools, or the ones that allow one to use the same expression to talk about character traits. To whom the speaker refers, and with which meaning he uses the word, are matters of intentions of the speaker. Limiting ourselves to semantics, we can identify what the speaker said, the locutionary content, only reflexively, as conditions on the utterance: what was said was true if there was a time and a person such that the time is the time of the utterance, the person is the one the speaker uses 'he' to refer to, and that person at that time is in whichever of the two conditions 'in the grip of a vice' can be used for, that the speaker intended to predicate (approximate account, of course).

This is a rather limited, and perhaps quite radical, conception of semantics. Herman Cappelen and Ernie Lepore, in their (2005) book, tell us that their view, which they call "semantic minimalism," takes the following thesis as the core of truth-conditional semantics:

In order to fix or determine the proposition semantically expressed by an utterance of a sentence S, follow steps (a)–(e):

a. Specify the meaning (or semantic value) of every expression in S (doing so in accordance with your favorite semantic theory . . .).

b. Specify all the relevant compositional meanings rules for English (doing so also in accordance with your favorite semantic theory . . .).

c. Disambiguate every ambiguous/polysemous expression in S.

d. Precisify every vague expression in S.

e. Fix the semantic value of every context sensitive expression in S.[22]

But, on my view, semantics is more minimal than this. Clauses (c), (d) and (e) go too far. It is the business of semantics to specify the meanings, but not to disambiguate them; that is a matter of the speaker's intentions. It is the business of semantics to give us the ways vague expressions can be precisified, and trace out the effects of such precisification on truth-conditions, but not to provide a prespecification for them; that is up to the speaker's intentions. And the semantic value of context sensitive expressions is also not for semantics to decide; it will be a matter of objective facts about the utterance and more facts about intentions.

Here is another example to illustrate these ideas. Let **u** be an utterance of 'I am tired' in English, the meanings of the words and the mode of composition involved are given, but not the speaker, time, and so forth. In the terms of Perry 2001b, the Content$_M$ of **u** is:

(7)   That *the speaker of **u*** is tired *at the time of **u***.

Statement (7) is, of course, a *reflexive* content of **u**, since it puts conditions on **u** itself Content$_M$ is a species of reflexive content: the truth conditions of the utterance given only the facts about meaning.

Two utterances, **u** and **u′**, of 'I am tired' by different people will not have the same *content*, reflexive or locutionary, and they may differ in *truth-value*. This difference is reflected in the difference between (7) and (8):

(8)   That *the speaker of **u′*** is tired at *the time of **u′***.

Suppose you find a note **n** that reads "I am tired." You don't know who wrote it, or when, but you assume it is written in English. On the Cappelen and Lepore account you *do not* grasp the semantic contribution of the sentence, for you do not have the information necessary, on their theory, to grasp "the proposition semantically expressed." But, of course, you do, and you can report it:

Note **n** is true iff the person who wrote it was tired at the time he wrote it.

Suppose Tom wrote the note at noon Wednesday. If you knew that fact, which semantics alone cannot give you, you could say,

Note **n** is true iff Tom was tired Wednesday.

The proposition that Tom was tired Wednesday is the locutionary content of the note (the Content$_C$ or the referential content in Perry 2001b). It is what is required of the world for the note to be true given *not only* that it was written in English, *but also* that Tom wrote it on Wednesday. With the sentence 'Tom was tired Wednesday' you can actually *express* the proposition Tom expressed with the note. Without that information you cannot *express* that proposition, but you can give an *utterance-bound* or *reflexive* characterization of it.

Suppose the note is instead "I'll fix the car soon." What does the speaker mean by "soon"? It is a vague expression. Cappelen and Lepore would claim that we don't grasp the semantic content unless we can fix what counts as "soon". But surely we do grasp the *utterance-bound* truth conditions:

The note is true iff the author of the note fixed the car he is referring to within the length of time that counted as upper bound of what counted as "soon" according to his intentions.

Suppose you get an e-mail from Gretchen that says, "David has made an amazing discovery." There are a lot of Davids. You don't know which one Gretchen is referring to with her use of 'David': David Kaplan, David Hills, David Israel? You respond, "David who?" Your response can be understood precisely because you *do* grasp utterance-bound truth conditions of the e-mail:

This e-mail is true iff the David the author it was referring to with 'David' has made a great discovery.

Saying and Implicating

Now let's turn to Grice's distinction between *what is said* and *what is conversationally implicated*. The paradigm is often supposed to be like this. I hear and understand the meaning of the words; I resolve the ambiguities and nambiguities,[23] I resolve the references and thus arrive at what was said. At that point, I can begin doing real Gricean pragmatics, reasoning about why what was said, was said. But this is confused. One does not need to be able to *express* what someone said, in order to begin reasoning about why they might have said it. An utterance-bound description will do.

Suppose Kent Bach and I have just participated in a symposium. We each gave a paper. Grice beamed during Kent's talk and looked irritated and uncomfortable during mine. Grice approaches us after the session and says to Kent, "I liked your paper." I hear this as "I liked your mumble" and am not sure whether he is speaking to Kent or to me; Kent is busy talking to someone else, so perhaps Grice is talking to me, but he seems to be aiming his remark more at Kent; perhaps he doesn't notice that Kent's attention is diverted.

I can already describe what Grice said as "what Grice said." That's pretty uninformative. More helpfully, I can describe it as "that he liked something—whatever the word that I heard as "mumble mumble" stands for—that belonged to or had something to do with the person he was talking to." That's an utterance-bound truth-conditional description. I get at the truth-conditions reflexively, in terms of facts about the utterance and its speaker. Based on the meaning of 'liked' and the likelihood that what I heard as 'mumble' was 'paper', I get a little further: that his remark was true iff it was directed at someone whose paper he liked. Combining that with what I noticed during the talk, I strongly suspect he is talking to Kent and intending to convey just what he says. But before being sure, I give him a chance to add something like "the jokes were by far the best part," which might affect the likely implications and make it conceivable that he was talking to me. Finally, once I figured out what he said, and that he didn't mean to imply any less than what he said, and so that he was talking to Kent and not to me, I could describe Grice's utterance this way to Kent: "Grice said that he liked your paper." That's an expressive description. I not only get at the truth conditions of what Grice said; I do so in a way that expresses the very proposition that Grice expressed, from my point of view and given my conversational situation.

To review and sum up. I adopt a minimalist conception of semantics, as the study of meaning, paradigmatically by way of how the meanings of words and ways of combining them constrain the truth-conditions of utterances. This means that, when semantics has done its job, we will typically only have an *utterance-bound* conception of what is said—the sort that the reflexive/referential theory deals with—even when we limit what is said to locutionary content, sparing ourselves the worry of how others react to the utterance. Such an utterance-bound conception of what is said is all we need to get started on Gricean reasoning about what is further implicated (or reasoning about what speech act was performed); resolving what is said and what is implicated is more a matter of back-and-forth reasoning based on constraints on two unknowns than a matter of achieving the solution to the problem of what is said and then feeding it into the question of what is implicated.

Unarticulated Constituents (Recanati, Corazza, Cappelen and Lepore, Taylor)

A Trendy Idea?

I introduced the term "unarticulated constituents" in a paper called "Thought without Representation." My main philosophical target at the time was to understand how we should think about "selfless" thought we have, as when we think "He's to the right" or "That's a long ways away." It seemed to me that there are thoughts, roughly express-ible with these sorts of sentences, in which the person who is doing the thinking is not explicitly represented. They differ, that is, from the thoughts we could get from them, through the step of "self-introduction," namely, "He is to *my* right" and "That is a long way from *me*." It seemed to me that the selfless thoughts were closely tied to per-ception and action and might be the only sorts of thoughts which animals and small children and adults in certain situations need to have. So, I wanted to be able to say, in a way I thought I could understand, that the person having the thought is an unarticu-lated constituent of the first kind of thought and that the steps of self-introduction and self-elimination preserves the content but changes the form of the thought.

In fact, the literature has mainly focused on two other uses of the idea of unarticu-lated constituents. To introduce the idea of unarticulated constituents in interpretation of thought I showed that they made sense in the interpretation of language. I used the example of 'It's raining'. I said that when I say, "It's raining," my utterance will be true or false because it is raining or not raining in some particular place, the one I am talk-ing about. That place is an unarticulated constituent of proposition expressed by my utterance, or so I said. A lot has been written about rain since then, and I'm very proud of being able to draw the attentions and imaginations of philosophers to this impor-tant meteorological phenomenon.

The second use involved belief-reports. Mark Crimmins and I (1989) claimed that be-lief reports involve unarticulated constituents. If I say "Pierre believes London is quite ugly," to use Kripke's wonderful example, I describe what Pierre believes relative to one or the other of his ideas, or *notions*, of London. If I am describing what he believes in virtue of the ideas connected with the notion of London he acquired as an adult, when he visited there and was shocked by how ugly the neighborhoods he visited were, the notion that is tied to his use of the word 'London', then I am right and my utterance is true. If I am describing what he believes via the notion he acquired as a child, when he was told stories, in French, about how beautiful London was, a notion that is tied to the French name for London, 'Londres', but not to 'London', then what I have said is false. Our theory was a little more complicated than that, but that will do for now. Crimmins (1992) develops and defends a sophisticated version of this theory.

Both of these uses of the idea of unarticulated constituent have drawn some criticism. This is not surprising with the case of belief reports, which of course is a major source of controversy in philosophy at least since Frege and Russell. I'll discuss these in the next section. But the passion that my views about "It is raining" have elicited are somewhat surprising. These passions are evident in something Cappelen and Lepore once said, calling my view UCP, for "unarticulated constituent position." They found the view annoyingly popular, saying:

UCP, to say the least, is trendy. Philosophers invoke it in epistemology and ethics to account for diverging intuitions about knowledge and moral claims; in semantics to solve puzzles about rigidity and belief attribution, diverging intuitions about modal and subjunctive claims, and in metaphysics to avoid apparent paradoxes surrounding our use of vague expression; in the philosophy of mind to defend a view about the self as represented in thought—not to mention linguists and linguistically oriented philosophers who have elicited UCP to account for a rather wide range of linguistic intuitions that had gone hitherto neglected in the literature. In short, UCP is all the rage in philosophical and linguistic circles.[24]

It would be a thrill to think that all of these innovations actually stem from my little paper. I think, however, that the idea of an unarticulated constituent occurred to a number of people, as a necessity for dealing with a wide range of phenomena; for once I invented some terminology that people liked. At any rate, the quote from Cappelen and Lepore certainly makes the idea of unarticulated constituents sound like a good one. Not all trends are bad.

Before explaining how I see unarticulated constituents, it will be helpful to consider two related issues. The first, which comes up in the essays by Eros Corazza and François Recanati, has to do with the phenomenological and external viewpoints on thoughts and utterances.

The Phenomenological versus the External Viewpoint

Consider a young child, call her "Jamaica," who has learned to tell time. That is, she can look at a clock or a watch and report, based on the position of the hands, "It is nine o'clock" or "It is quarter to one." She knows that at least some "o'clocks" occur twice in a day; she has been up both at 7:00 AM and 7:00 PM and knows the difference. She knows that when it is light at 12:00 it is noon, and when it is dark and 12:00 it is midnight. She may have only the vaguest idea that there are such things as 1:00, 2:00, and 3:00 AM, since she isn't allowed to stay up until those times. And she has no idea about time zones, and the general relativity of o'clock properties to location.

There are two inquiries we should undertake to understand Jamaica's cognitive and linguistic situation, and how it will change, as she gets older. First, there is the phenomenological. What is it like for Jamaica to pick up information about o'clock properties, use this information, and report it? Then there is the external viewpoint. Given my somewhat richer understanding of o'clock properties, how do I account for the utility and limits of Jamaica's way of thinking and speaking?

Suppose Jamaica and I are at the lake fishing. We both know that we should be back at the cabin for lunch at one. We both look at our watches and see the big hand at nine and the little one a bit before one. We both think "it's quarter to one, time to start back." We both say, to the other kids, "It's quarter to one, time to start back." Neither of us think, "It's quarter to one Pacific Time." Jamaica can't think it, because she doesn't have the necessary knowledge and concepts. I could think it, but I don't because this more complicated form of thought is triggered only when the difference in time zones is relevant to the use I am making of the information.

When such considerations are relevant, I am capable of employing what we might call "time-zone introduction and elimination rules." If my thought, "It is quarter to twelve" is true, then the more complicated thought, "It is quarter to twelve in Z" is also true, where 'Z' designates the time zone about which I picked up information. In the case in question, where I looked at the watch on my own wrist, this will be the time zone I am in—assuming I haven't forgotten to reset the watch after a trip.

For the purpose at hand, getting to lunch and telling others to, all of them in the same time zone as me, this ability is of no use. Suppose, however, that Jamaica and I are listening, without watches, to a radio station from some distant place that's on Mountain Time. They announce, "It's quarter to two." I think "It's quarter to two Mountain Time, so it's quarter to one Pacific Time, so it's quarter to one. Time to go to lunch." Jamaica, on the other hand, breaks into tears because she thinks we have missed lunch. My additional knowledge and concepts are useful, in this more complicated information game.

Now I, as a philosopher, want to explain how this all works, and in particular to explain why Jamaica's way of thinking works when it does, and comes up short when it does. For this I need to take the external viewpoint. I look on Jamaica as player of an information game in which one gets information about the place one is at and uses it to guide action relative to that same place. She has the skills to make the discriminations and distinction necessary to play that game. I identify the information she gets from her watch within my richer system, with the proposition "It's quarter to one Pacific Time." I note that lunch will be served at one o'clock Pacific Time. The extra parameter, reflected in my system of concepts, but not in hers, is part of the explanation of why her way of thinking and acting works when it does. It also explains why it breaks down when it does, as when she broke into tears, thinking she had missed lunch. She doesn't have the knowledge and concepts necessary to use information about the o'clock properties somewhere else, suitably distant, to guide her action in accord with the o'clock properties of the place where she and her lunch find themselves.

Corazza thinks that taking this external viewpoint is misguided. He refers to Wittgenstein. I have to admit, I just don't get it. I would have thought that Wittgenstein's point ought to be that we will never know what it is *like* to be a lion; the best we can do is to take an external viewpoint, and try to understand the "language games" and "forms of life" of the lion in our own terms. When Wittgenstein describes language games, he does so from an external viewpoint; he doesn't limit himself to the vocabulary of 'Slab', 'Block', and so forth when explaining how the Builder's game works, for example. We understand the Builders when we realize that when the boss says "Slab" he wants a slab brought to where he is working; this is how *we* describe the success conditions of his order, since *we* can imagine and describe a lot of other possibilities; it's not how the boss thinks; he presumably manages to think this whole thought by thinking little more than "Slab," since his thought doesn't have to deal with all the other possibilities that noun would leave open in our language—making a slab, carrying a slab away, and so forth. We can *also* imagine being limited in language and thought the way we would be if we only had a language of nouns like the builders.

We don't know what its *like* to be a bat, in a pretty clear sense; we also don't know what its like to be a lion, though perhaps we can come closer. The life of a good bloodhound, with its incredibly sensitive sense of smell and limited color vision, seems completely alien to me; I can barely sniff the difference between merlot and prune juice. Still, we can understand a lot about bats, lions, and dogs and the way their worlds differ from ours by studying and describing, within *our* conceptual scheme, how *they* handle information; what things in the environment (accessible to us only by instruments, or perhaps by using the bloodhounds themselves) they can discriminate with their senses; how they group phenomena together that we may not (that which affords eating for a lion is somewhat different than that which affords eating for me); and so forth. To get a handle on LionSpeak we'll have to understand a lot about the needs and capacities of lions. Imagining what its like to be a lion will be helpful, just as imagining what its like to be Jamaica is helpful in understanding her tears. But the external viewpoint seems to me quite essential and in no way to get in the way of also taking the phenomenological viewpoint, insofar as that is possible.

It is in this mismatch of the classificatory scheme required by some agents for some information game, and the richer scheme necessary for the theorist, philosopher or grandfather, to explain why the game works, given the information available and the range of actions involved, where the need for unarticulated constituents arises.

The Persistence of Facticity

A second preliminary issue comes up in Recanati's essay. After writing Barwise and Perry 1983, in response to various problems we knew we had while writing the book, and others that critics carefully explained to us, Barwise and I and others working with us on situation theory moved away from trying to model situations as set theoretical constructions out of objects, properties and locations, in favor of treating situations as primitives and trying to come up with a theory of them that could be used as a basis for theories of information, action, and semantics. I think of situations as chunks of reality, paradigmatically connected regions of space-time, which can be classified by a method of individuation and classification—this would be direct as opposed to indirect classification. The methods of individuation and classification—that is, a domain of objects and properties—provides us with basic possibilities, or states of affairs, or *infons*, in the happy phrase of Devlin (1991), designed to make them sound less philosophical and metaphysical and more suitable for cognitive science. Infons can in turn be thought of as a pair of an issue and an answer, where an issue is an n-ary relation paired with a sequence of n objects, and an answer is "true" or "false," or 1 and 0. Where a relation is located, it is convenient to put the argument place for the time, place, or spatiotemporal location before the relation, more or less as we did in Barwise and Perry 1983. An infon can be symbolized as, for example, $\langle$Palo Alto, July 11, 2005, rains, 0$\rangle$. This infon or state of affairs is *made factual* by the situation that is going on around me as I write on that date in Palo Alto. I'll write:

$s \models \langle$Palo Alto, July 11, 2005, rains, 0$\rangle$

The *opposite* infon is $\langle$Palo Alto, July 11, 2005, rains, 1$\rangle$. So we have

$s \not\models \langle$Palo Alto, July 11, 2005, rains, 1$\rangle$

The situation in Palo Alto now makes it *nonfactual* that it is raining. Let σ' be the opposite of σ; that is, the state of affairs that gives the opposite answer to the same issue. One axiom we will want is that

$s \models \sigma$ iff $s \not\models \sigma'$.

On the other hand, s does not determine whether

$\langle$San Francisco, July 11, 2005, rains, 1$\rangle$

is factual:

$\neg s \models \langle$San Francisco, July 11, 2005, rains, 1$\rangle$.

$\neg s \not\models \langle$San Francisco, July 11, 2005, rains, 1$\rangle$.

$\neg s \models \langle$San Francisco, July 11, 2005, rains, 0$\rangle$.

$\neg s \not\models \langle$San Francisco, July 11, 2005, rains, 0$\rangle$.

But it seems that every issue should be resolved by some situation or other:

$\forall \sigma \; \exists s \; s \models \sigma$ or $s \models \sigma'$.

Although the situation in Palo Alto doesn't determine whether it is now raining in San Francisco, a larger situation, the one in the whole Bay Area, does determine this. Perhaps there is a largest situation, the world, which resolves every issue; what exactly ought to drive us to that intuitive conclusion, I'm not sure. But at any rate, it seems that the whole system of situations ought to be coherent, that is:

If $\exists s \; s \models \sigma$, then $\neg \exists s' \; s' \models \sigma'$.

Finally, it seems that facticity ought to persist through larger and larger situations, namely:

$\forall s, s'$ if $s \models \sigma$ and s is a part of s', then $s' \models \sigma$.

But it sometimes seems as if an utterance of a certain sentence can be true, relative to one situation, but false relative to another more inclusive situation. For example, we might think that "All copies of Barwise's *Handbook of Logic* are missing" is true, if we are talking about the situation in Tanner Philosophy Library, but not if we are talking about the situation in all of Stanford, since there is a copy in the Mathematics Library. In such cases I think we need find different infons that are at issue, as opposed to giving up the principle of the persistence of facticity. We might take the library and the university to be unarticulated constituents of the propositions expressed, or even the smaller and larger situations themselves. The latter route might be implemented by working with Austinian propositions, which consist of a situation and an infon; Barwise and Etchemendy (1987) explored Austinian propositions and Recanati is exploring other uses for them, which I applaud.

However, I don't think we want to use Austinian proposition for the salt and pepper case that concerns Recanati. The idea is that H and W are on opposite sides of the table. H says, "The salt is to the right of the pepper," and W says "The salt is to the left of the pepper." I would say that H and W are unarticulated constituents of the propositions they each express, and there is not contradiction, but agreement, in what they say. But how about just appealing to two different situations, H's and W's, and saying that the facts are as follows?

$S_H \models \langle$ right-of, salt, pepper, 1 $\rangle$
    $\models \langle$ left-of, salt, pepper, 0 $\rangle$.

$S_W \models \langle$ right-of, salt, pepper, 0 $\rangle$
    $\models \langle$ left-of, salt, pepper, 1 $\rangle$.

The problem with this is that, given persistence, any situation of which s_H and s_W are both parts will make factual both $\langle$ left-of, salt, pepper, 1 $\rangle$ and $\langle$ right-of, salt, pepper, 1 $\rangle$, which is incoherent. In suggesting this route, Barwise was playing with giving up persistence.

From my point of view, this is not a very good idea, because it leads to metaphysical havoc, which on the whole I dislike. (I'm not saying Barwise liked metaphysical havoc, but he was more of a conceptual and logical adventurer than I am, less frightened of the metaphysical abyss, because he had more intellectual tools to keep from falling over the edge.) The motivation for it is that from H's *point of view*, nothing has been left out or unarticulated—this is how the present point connects with the previous point. That is, the motivation is phenomenological. But phenomenology is only part of the data. As long as H sticks in his own perspective, he can make all the distinctions he needs to in order to decide which movements to make to get or pass the salt or pepper in terms of "right" and "left." That's fine, but not hard to explain. The perspective relevant to the results of moving his hands, and the perspective from which he sees are (almost) the same, and so the parameter of which perspective he is using for these two things can be left unarticulated in his thought, just as Jamaica didn't have to worry about time zones, and just as most of us don't have to worry about inertial frameworks, and so hardly ever mention or think about them.

As I analyze it, right-of is a relation that obtains between a person at a time and an object. H can use 'right of' as if it predicated a one-place relation, because, for certain purposes, such as directing our own movements, we don't need to keep track of the person relative to which objects are to the right and to the left. But to play a more complicated information game, such as helping W locate the salt and the pepper from her point of view, or communicating with W, or understanding how their remarks are consistent, it will be necessary make the parameter explicit, as we might naturally do by saying "it's to my right, but to your left."

So, I applaud Recanati's exploration of the use of Austinian propositions, but I recommend that he use them in ways that do not require giving up persistence. If this is done, then I don't think they can do the work that is done by unarticulated constituents.

Cappelen, Lepore, and the Myth of Unarticulated Constituents

Cappelen and Lepore maintain that when I utter "It is raining" I will in all likelihood "saliently assert" a proposition that has a location as a constituent, a location that is not referred to by any word, morpheme, or even any less audible and visible syntactic creature. So it sounds a lot like they agree with my doctrine of unarticulated constituents. But they think it is a myth (not, notice, a part truth, a near miss, a misplaced insight, or any else so honorable, but a *myth!*). Their reason for this is that they think there is a "location-neutral" proposition that does not have a location as a constituent, nor involve any sort of quantification over locations, that is "semantically expressed" by the words 'It is raining (at t)'. Call this proposition $\Re$.

In spite of the attempts at clarification, I must admit I'm not completely clear about $\Re$. I'm pretty sure that $\Re$ is true if it's raining somewhere on Earth at t. But is it true or false if it's not raining anywhere on Earth, but it is raining on Venus, or one of the moons of Jupiter, or a planet in a distant galaxy? To be location neutral, it seems it ought to be true if there is rain anywhere at all; if, as they say, "rain is going on at t." Their tutorial for get us to identify $\Re$ features the noun 'rain'; but the *phenomenon* of rain isn't limited to Earth, as far as we know; otherwise, we wouldn't be looking for water vapor on the planets and moons around our solar system. But so understood $\Re$ doesn't fit the description of their Rain-Ache universe, does it? Do these poor folk really get headaches when it rains, full stop? Or just when it rains on Earth? If the former, they will probably have to wear their yellow hats all the time; how will they know when to take them off? But in fact these folk place rain-detectors around "the entire globe." Where did the restriction to the globe—presumably our Earth?—come from? Could it be that Cappelen and Lepore have mistaken a proposition with the Earth as an unarticulated constituent for a location-neutral proposition? Should we speak of "the myth of the location-neutral proposition?"

Cappelen and Lepore are sure of one thing; $\Re$ is *not* just the proposition that it is raining somewhere. They don't want their proposition to be the one Recanati is worried about in his example of the rain-starved Earth, eager for signs of rain anywhere. So we know that $\Re$ is not that proposition.

They have a second reason for thinking that $\Re$ is not the proposition it is raining somewhere. They think my argument for unarticulated constituents depends on the premise that there is no proposition available constructed merely from the semantic resources made available by the components of the statements; that is, 'it', 'rains', and tense. Indeed, I did say "In order to assign a truth-value to my son's statement, as I just did, I needed a place." It is certainly possible to interpret this as an extremely stupid remark. I could have just used the apparatus of logic, and come up with a number of propositions that quantify over places: most obviously, that it is raining everywhere, and that it is raining somewhere. Then I could have assigned truth-values to my son's remark: false for the first interpretation, true for the second. Indeed, I could have assigned them fairly confidently without even getting up and looking out the window.

A more charitable interpretation is that I thought it was obvious that, as I put it, "What my son said was true, because it was raining in Palo Alto," and by the phrase "as I just did," I referred to this interpretation, the one that seemed (and seems) obviously correct to me; I had just used a place, Palo Alto, to assign a truth-value to that remark, and no articulated component of the sentence provided that fair city. Within the Cappelen and Lepore theory, it seems a sufficient explanation of where I went wrong to suppose that I mistook what was asserted for what they call the *semantic content*. And, if their theory is correct, I certainly made this mistake.

However, it is fairly clear to me that I still don't have a grasp of what $\Re$ is. I know it is not Recanati's candidate, and apparently not the proposition that it is raining on earth, even though that is the one the people with Rain-aches worry about. Why not just tell us under what conditions $\Re$ is true and Recanati's proposition is not?

Still, as far as their explanation goes, does it matter? The role $\Re$ plays in their theory really doesn't seem to require much of it; its truth-value, and truth conditions, whatever they are, are irrelevant to what my son meant to convey to me; they stand outside the whole informational transaction, which began with his looking out the window, and ended with my giving up on playing tennis, and going back to bed. What is needed is a semantic content that depends only on the components of the sentence and is so wildly irrelevant that I can begin trying to figure out what else, other than the semantic content, my son might have been trying to convey. One could, Carnap-like, have an assigned object, perhaps $\varnothing$, to use to get at the semantic content of all propositions where there might seem to be unarticulated constituents. The proposition that the null set is getting wet seems as irrelevant to the communicative transaction as $\Re$, whatever it might be, and that irrelevance seems to be the main requirement.

This irrelevance is my main problem with their theory. Granting the existence of $\Re$, why would we describe this proposition as the "semantic content" of an utterance of 'it's raining at t'? To be sure, the proposition is constructed of constituents (rain, and the time *t*) that are articulated in the utterance. But so what? As I showed in the original paper, *there is nothing in the nature of a compositional semantics for utterances that requires semantics to confine the constituents of contents to items articulated by the sentence.* This point is intended not merely as one about the weather, but is used in a variety of settings, from issues involving the self to criticisms of Davidson's arguments against reference.[25] To suppose that if such a proposition as ℜ can be found, *it* must be assigned the honorific "semantic content" is just to assume that this is not so, without, as far as I can see, any reason having been given at all.

Of course, if proposition ℜ played some honorable role in our use of language, that would be some reason to recognize it with the honorific "semantic content." I see no reason to suppose that this proposition enters the mind of any speaker or hearer of 'It's raining'. According to Cappelen and Lepore, when I say "it's raining today" I am semantically expressing ℜ, a proposition I don't believe, "in order to communicate a proposition [I] do believe." But what reason is there to assign ℜ any role in my plan? My utterance introduces some propositional constituents, today and the relation of raining at a location. And the listener figures out what location, if any, I am talking about. My plan for his reasoning, and his reasoning, won't come within a hundred feet of ℜ. Are the constraints on semantic content that lead them to postulating ℜ as the semantic content empirical in any way, or merely ideological?

Well, one might say, the listener needs a proposition to get started with any sort of Gricean pragmatic reasoning, and your plan needs to provide him with one. What is there besides ℜ? But this is a question to which the reflexive/referential theory provides a nice answer. If a person is talking about location *l*, his utterance at *t* of 'it is raining now' will be true iff it rains at *t* in *l*. My contemporary listener will know that I what I have said is true iff:

There is a location *l* such that (a) Perry is talking about *l* and (b) it is raining at *l* now.

If we are in Palo Alto, and have been discussing whether we can play tennis, the assumption that I am being relevant and helpful will lead him to the conclusion that I am talking about Palo Alto. If we are in Palo Alto and it is obviously sunny and bright, the quality maxim will lead him to wonder where else I might be talking about. In neither case do I or my hearer need to worry about ℜ.

Corazza, Rain, and Logical Form

Among utterances of grammatical sentences, Corazza distinguishes between those that are semantically incomplete and those that are conceptually incomplete. "It is raining" is an example of the semantically incomplete. To express a proposition we need a location. An utterance of the sentence will be true if it is raining in the location the speaker is talking about. The location is an unarticulated constituent of the proposition expressed. In all of this we agree.

In such a case of semantic incompleteness, Corazza says, the location will be unarticulated—that is, unwritten and unpronounced. But it will be called for by the grammar, however, at the level of logical form. The verb 'rains' specifies that locations will be the subjects of the property it introduces, and so a location must be specified, articulately, or inarticulately, by the context. This is sometimes called "hidden indexicality," and sometimes, as in the debates between François Recanati and Jason Stanley, the term 'unarticulated constituent' is reserved for constituents that are not only not articulated in my sense (more or less based on the meaning of 'articulate'), but also not called for at some level like logical form.

Hence Corazza does not disagree with me, but takes a position on something about which I am silent, somewhat agnostic, and sometimes skeptical, namely, whether unarticulated constituents have to be values for parameters introduced by language, in *logical form*. My definition of unarticulated constituent did not rule out some level such as logical form. It simply requires that at the level of visible or audible speech nothing called for them. In my original article, I tried to show that we don't *need* to find something invisible and inaudible in the grammar to explain how the constituent ends up in the proposition expressed, but I didn't rule out that such structures might be required for other respectable empirical reasons. Neale's discussion of this is animated and accurate. There are in fact many syntactic theories around, and not all of them provide a level of logical form; HPSG (Head-driven Phrase Structure Grammar), for example, a theory that is widely used by computational linguists, and built on sound philosophical principles for the most part, does not require a level of logical form, although it allows it.[26]

But suppose we agree with Corazza that 'rain' calls for a location because of facts about logical form. Still, where are *those* facts located? Corazza gives three alternatives: internalism, externalism, and a hybrid view. The two latter views do not require that a competent language user have a representation of the logical form of sentences she uses.

Consider Jamaica again. She says it is one o'clock. I say that what makes her statement true is that it is one o'clock Pacific Time, and that what makes her remark about Pacific Time is that that is the time zone the clocks she relies are set to, the time zone she is in, and the time zone the o'clock properties of which will determine when the things happen, like lunch, that she is using those clocks to arrive on time at. I don't see any reason for her to have a concept of time zones, or even a representation of them at some level inaccessible to consciousness connected with her mastery of English syntax.

Corazza's second category is conceptually incomplete utterances. All semantically underdetermined sentences are conceptually underdetermined, too, but not vice versa. In the case of a sentence that is conceptually underdetermined but semantically complete, the unarticulated constituents in a proposition attributed to the utterance are not syntactically triggered. An example is 'Jane is late'. Late for what? The answer to that question will not be triggered by the verb phrase 'is late' but will be an issue of pragmatics.

Suppose that we are all ready to hop in the car and go the Giants game, but Jane isn't here yet. The agreed on time to assemble comes and goes. "Jane is late," I say. I clearly mean, at some level, in some way, that Jane is late for our trip to the Giants game. I *need* not mean that. It might just have occurred to me that she hasn't handed in her term paper, and I might be providing that fact, in a conversationally inept way, as a possible explanation for why she is late for the game. Which I meant is up to me. But where does that intention go? If it is part of what is said, on the view we are developing, then it seems there should be a "hook" for it in the reflexive truth-conditions, which will be roughly:

The person the speaker is calling "Jane" is late by the time of utterance for some event that the speaker has in mind.

The hook would not come from logical form, if Corazza is right about the logical form of 'Jane is late'. So someone over on the literalist side of things, as I take Corazza to be, won't want that hook in semantic content and won't want the thing she is late for, the Giants game, to be part of what I say. Recanati, on the other hand, thinks it will be part of what is said, by a process of free enrichment.

If we take Corazza's position, we will have to suppose that my use of 'is late' predicates some not very obvious but perhaps not wholly implausible property of Jane: a very weak form of being late, perhaps just being late to something or other. Then part of what I convey, by Gricean implicature, will be that she is late to the salient event, the Giants game: Grice as shock absorber. My approach *can* accommodate Recanati's approach, and that is what I am inclined to think is the right way to go with this particular example. I won't pretend to understand all of the issues, and all the examples, for which "free enrichment" has been called on, however, so I think I'll just leave it at that for now. I will briefly return to this example below, while stretching Taylor's concept of the lexicon in ways he probably won't be too enthusiastic about.

Taylor, Rain, and the Lexicon

Taylor seems to assume that the way I use 'unarticulated constituents' precludes anything in grammar calling for them. His theory is that they are called for by thematic information in the lexicon, so he thinks he doesn't believe in any of them in my sense. But the way I use the term he does believe in some of them, especially the locations in propositions expressed by 'It's raining'. We agree that they are not articulated, in the way I and the dictionary use this term, that is, "put into words," "pronounced." I think they get into the proposition by being what the speaker is talking about; as I understand Taylor he would take that to be necessary but not sufficient. There also must be a hook in the lexicon that calls for a location as theme. So, like Corazza, he takes a view on something about which I was silent, in his case the lexicon rather than logical form. I rather like the lexicon.

Taylor chides me for oversimple thinking, when I said that it is merely the metaphysics of rain that calls for a location. I plead guilty—or nolo contendere, at any rate. I'll try to do better. The special status of locations derives, I think, from a combination of the nature of rain on earth and the way humans interact with it. Those facts are associated with the word 'rain', one way or another, by those who know how to use and interpret the word.

'Lexicon' is a synonym for dictionary. Nowadays we often have in mind not merely a dictionary that is designed to supply a human language user with the information she needs, in addition to what she already knows, to use a word correctly, but a dictionary designed to provide the information one thinks an artificial system will need to intelligently parse natural language sentences and deal with natural language discourse. One approach is to construct a lexicon so as to incorporate all sorts of general knowledge that we think is available to humans but needs to be made explicit for machines. This more inclusive concept of a lexicon or dictionary is relevant to philosophy, as it is part of the enterprise of making the implicit explicit.[27] A dictionary of this sort ought to tell us a lot about 'rain', including that for the most part humans will say "it rains" without further modification, when the rain in question in involves falling water, and the duration, intensity and other factors are within certain wide ranges. One assumes that unless frogs or oil or sulfuric acid are mentioned, it is rain consisting of falling water that is at issue, for example. The location, however, is not a matter of such defaults, nor can we get at what is said by quantifying it out; 'it's raining' doesn't mean it's raining somewhere, and it doesn't mean it's raining everywhere. All of this more or less follows Taylor—how much more and how much less is an issue for the next section—and seems right to me, and much better than saying, as I did, that it is a matter of metaphysics. So I can adopt Taylor's view, although I don't much like terminology like "subsyntactic basement" as this suggests an "internalist conception" in Corazza's sense, of the lexicon.

Modificational Neutrality

The next topic I want to discuss is Taylor on modificational neutrality.

Taylor's main example is 'is red'. He notes that there are lots of ways of being red; the way in which a book is red (it has red covers), the way in which dirt is red (through and through), the way in which a box of Sun-Maid Raisin box is red (it is the dominant color of the outside of the box). He then says:

The foregoing considerations will suggest to the various advocates of unarticulated constituents, free-enrichment, implicatures[28] and the like that a statement of the form:

[9] x is red

is semantically incomplete and must somehow be completed in context. But I want to suggest that instances of [9] are not so much semantically incomplete but rather what I'll call modificationally neutral. An utterance of [9] makes the weakest possible positive statement about the redness of x. It is not, for that reason alone, semantically incomplete, however. It just that there is no modifier $m'ly$ such that an utterance of (an instance of scheme) [9] will be strictly literally equivalent to an utterance of an instance of scheme [10]:

[10] x is $m'ly$ red.

Strictly, literally when a speaker asserts merely that x is red, she has asserted neither that x is wholly red, nor that x is partly red, nor that x is just a little bit red, nor that x is mostly red. In fact, she has asserted no modification of redness of x at all. She has simply asserted that x is red. However, because a modificationally neutral assertion of redness is the weakest possible assertion of redness possible, such an assertion would, in typical conversational contexts, be insufficiently informative. But the mutual recognition by speaker and hearer of the uninformativeness of the speaker's modificationally neutral assertion may well generate, by roughly Gricean means of a familiar sort, some more informative, because less modificationally neutral, pragmatic conveyances of one sort or another.

The fact that modificationally neutral assertions are minimally informative, together with the fact that speakers who make such assertions typically convey something more informative and less modificationally neutral, has, I believe, led many to see semantic incompleteness where there is only modificational neutrality. But the inference from neutrality to incompleteness is fallacious. Indeed, in the spirit of Perry himself, it is worth giving a name to the relevant fallacy. I will say that one commits a fallacy of misplaced modification when one infers from the modificational neutrality of a sentence to the semantic incompleteness of that sentence. One who commits a fallacy of misplaced modification is liable to believe that sentences with a perfectly determinate, though modificationally neutral semantic contents stand in need of contextual supplementation, even when there are no explicit or suppressed argument places for context to fix a value for. I suspect that all forms of so-called radical contextualism are founded on fallacies of misplaced modification. (229–230)

So let's consider something of form (9), say

(11)   That apple is red

According to Taylor, if I utter (11), I have not said that the apple is, say, of a red variety as opposed to green, nor have I said that it is red in the way that ripe apples of red varieties are. Instead, I have said something neutral between those two ways of being red, and a number of others besides—perhaps including being one of those dreaded Marxist apples, although Taylor doesn't mention that possibility.

I think Taylor's analysis of the phenomenon he has identified is coherent and even elegant, but not very convincing, and I wish to suggest an alternative, drawing on his concept of a lexicon that I found so attractive in the last section. As matter of fact, let's start by going back to rain.

As Taylor notes, just as there are lots of places it can be raining, there are lots of ways that it can be raining. It could be raining water, or violets, or cats and dogs, or oil, or sulfuric acid. The lexicon tells us that the location is thematized and so must be specified, whether articulated or not. An alternative treatment which some have considered is to apply something like the modificational neutrality thesis to locations. An utterance of 'It's raining', on this line, would strictly and literally say that it is raining somewhere or other, the weakest possible thing one can squeeze out of the words, or perhaps not, depending on what one thinks of Cappelen and Lepore's proposition $\mathfrak{R}$. The strategy is this: we look for the weakest possible thing and then use Gricean reasoning, that great shock absorber for jarring theories, to get to something sensible conveyed: because it is so silly to say that it is raining somewhere, which is almost a necessary truth, I try to come up with something more helpful or relevant that you were trying to convey. Taylor doesn't adopt this approach, quite rightly in my opinion.

But then, we need *something* besides the word 'rains' and the phenomenon of rain to highlight the location. Metaphysics alone, he rightly points out, won't do. Taylor suggests the lexicon, and I applaud, taking the lexicon to be a compilation of information about rain and the interest we have in it, relevant to understand what English speakers are trying to say when they use the word 'rain'.

But now what about the issue of whether its raining water, or oil, or tears, or cats an dogs, or violets? We *can* make clear which we are getting at by adverbial modification: "It's not raining rain, you know, it's raining violets." Will I then be committing the fallacy of misplaced modification if I suppose that with an unmodified assertion of 'It's raining' I can say that it's raining water? Does Taylor's theory imply that when I just say it's raining, I have just said it's raining in some neutral sense? And that I leave it to the listener to figure out what sort of rain I have in mind? A possible theory; but is it plausible?

I would prefer to use the lexicon in tandem with the approach to locutionary acts and contents developed above. When I look in the nearest dictionary, the *Shorter Oxford*, it seems to tell me that 'rain' has a default reading, which implies ordinary watery rain, and another related reading, where it can mean that some sort of thing, which is "specified," is falling in great quantities. As I read the dictionary, there are a number of things one *can* use 'is raining' to predicate of a location, and people will expect me to say so if it is not just ordinary water whose falling I'm telling them about. I'm inclined to think that whenever I have said "It's raining," I have in fact said, and not merely implied, that it's raining water.

Suppose I told my wife Frenchie, on the basis of hearing pitter-pats outside, "It's raining," and she went to look and said, "You're wrong. It's not raining. But there are violets falling all over the place." I reply, "Well, I didn't say it was raining rain, you know." I *might* be telling the truth; I might have noticed that it was the pitter patter of violets that I heard and intended to say something weak that allowed that possibility and was therefore true, while wanting her to discover the unusual nature of the rain on her own. But, it seems to me, given that I didn't notice the violets, I must have intended to mean raining rain by 'rain'. My reply was a joke or an evasion. "Well," Taylor might say, "that's just the sort of appeal to intuition that Grice taught us how to deal with." Perhaps, but I'm not convinced.

How about the intensity? I can say "It's raining" and then go on to add that it's raining quite hard, or barely sprinkling, and so on. Along this dimension, Taylor's strategy seems more plausible. What I am saying is quite weak; what I implicate in a given conversational situation may be more definite. Still, I am not completely convinced that I can't say "It's raining" and intend to say something stronger and more definite, say, that it is raining much harder than a mere sprinkle. Does the meaning of 'raining' require us to mean something weak, or permit us to say a great many things. I'm inclined to vote for freedom, but I'm not quite sure.

The issue here isn't lack of articulation. There is a phrase, 'raining', that stands for the conditions I am predicating, whether we decide that it must be the weak condition or can be some more specific and determinate way of raining that I have in mind. My main point, at any rate, doesn't turn on resolution of that problem. It is that we may find many things in the lexicon. We may find thematic rules: raining requires a location. We may find default rules: if nothing else is specified, 'is raining' predicates the fall of water. We may find permissive rules: 'raining' can be used to say of a location that it has many of a number of properties: sprinkling, mild rain, intense rain, monsoon-like rain, and so forth. We may find not-so-permissive rules: 'raining' can only be used to say of a location that rain is falling in weakest possible sense, anything from sprinkles to monsoons counts as rain. I don't see any general philosophical principles for being sure, in advance, what we will find. We need to look in the dictionary. So I can agree with Taylor that it's a fallacy to *automatically assume* we should go for a specific intention that takes us beyond a weak reading whenever we have the possibility of adverbial modification. But the conclusion, to which the fallacy would lead, may nevertheless be the correct one in many cases. Once we have the lexicon, and we realize that the reflexive/referential theory can give us an intention-free level of semantic content, and once we realize that intentions are needed to get to any plausible theory of locutionary content—needed for demonstratives, needed for names, needed for unarticulated constituents, needed for ambiguity, needed for vagueness—we no longer have any reason based on general principles and the needs of compositional semantics to eschew intentions as input to what is said. And so, to briefly return to Corazza and Jane who is late to the Giants game, I don't see any general principles that prevent us from following Recanati's approach, or any that require us to do so.

So I am inclined to suppose that in the lexicon, where we find out facts about the phenomenon "rain" and how humans interact with it, we find that there are defaults for the kind, perhaps for the intensity, and for other factors, but not for the location. If someone says "It's raining in Albuquerque," they have said that it is raining rain in Albuquerque, not violets or oil or meteorites.

Similarly, it seems to me that a good lexicon will do what Taylor does in his article, that is, distinguish among the kinds of properties that one can use 'is red' to predicate, and indicate the situations in which they are appropriate. A speaker will use the expression 'is red' to predicate one of these conditions, possibly, but one expects not very often, the very weak condition Taylor says we are always predicating. What the speaker predicates with 'is red' is up to the speaker, at least as far as the locutionary content goes.

Going back to rain, one might argue that I can cancel the implication that I have some specific form of rain in mind. "I don't mean to imply that it's raining rain, or violets, or cats and dogs, or manna from heaven, or anything in particular; I just mean it's raining." At one time, Grice thought that what one could cancel was not part of what was said. But it is at best a tricky test. Suppose Elwood is blushing at a political meeting, and I say, "Elwood is red—I don't mean to imply that he is a leftist." The cancellation clarifies in which sense I was using 'red'. I might say, "Elwood is red—and I don't mean to imply anyone pays attention to the books he writes." The cancellation clarifies which word I was using—'red' not 'read'.

The cancellation test is intuitively powerful, because we think of words having meanings that imply a set of necessary and sufficient conditions for their application;

if you can cancel a condition and still apply the word, it isn't necessary and not part of the meaning. But no plausible lexicon for a natural language will be built on this model. There are many other resources for getting at word meanings; default rules and others sorts of mechanisms that allow for nonmonotonic reasoning, for example. The cancellation test is at best problematic.[29]

To return to Taylor's apple, suppose I utter

(11)   That apple is red

in a situation in which the ripeness of apples has been under discussion. Doubtless I will be taken to have conveyed, one way or another, that the skin of the apple is red, so it can be assumed to be ripe. Is this something I said? Or something I merely implicated?

Those who would regard it as something I say, like me, will be inclined to look at it as follows. The word 'red' can be used to stand for a number of related properties (and some not so related, like being a Marxist). That is, we have permissive conventions that allow it to be used to express any of these properties. Which one a speaker expressed, and hence what he said, depends on his intention in using it. That intention would be discovered by broadly Gricean means, or relevance, or whatever generally we use to divine speaker's intentions. But, as I noted above, "Gricean reasoning" in this sense is not limited to discovering implicatures. The speaker, if attentive, will realize that the property of being red in the sense of being a sign of ripeness is what people will think he intended his use of 'red' to stand for, and, if attentive, will be more explicit about what he means if he has some other property in mind. But there is no reason to say "has a red skin" instead of just "red." Indeed, saying that would probably trigger an unwanted Gricean implicatures.

It is clear, or seems clear to me, that most of the conventions that govern words are permissive; we can use the words to stand for a number of things, often related, and it is our intention that determines which thing we use the word to stand for. Consider the first word in (11), 'that'. In Kaplan 1989a and Kaplan 1989b, David Kaplan goes through four theories of demonstratives, settling on the directing intentions view, as I noted above. There may have been a number of apples I could have referred to with 'that apple', which one I referred to is a matter of my intentions. As I interpret 'directing', this indicates that not just any old intention is determinative, but only the low level, type-(ii) ones. For example, I may mistake apple X for apple Y, where apple Y is of interest for some reason or another. I intend to refer to apple X with 'that apple' as a way of referring to apple Y. The first intention is my directing intention, and I do in fact refer to X. I fail to refer to apple Y; even though I had an intention to do so, it is not a directing intention.[30]

So it seems to me we should suppose that what I said was that the apple I intended to refer to with 'that apple' is, in the sense I intend to use 'is', red, in the sense in which I intend to use 'red'—namely and roughly, "has red skin." Even in so simple a statement as "that apple is red," there is a lot of intention discovery to do before we get to what is said, quite apart from what might be implicated. In other words, it seems to me that at least some cases of what Taylor calls "modificational neutrality" are not a matter of neutrality, but a matter of not using extra words to nail down what you are saying, when your intentions are pretty obvious.

Suppose Taylor asks me to fetch the red book from the table. There are four books on the table. One has uniformly red covers. One is by Marx. One has covers with the same pattern that is found on many raisin boxes. Those three are all in pristine condition; clearly no one has ever read them. There is a fourth book too, with brown covers, quite worn, marked up, with a bookmark in it. Clearly a much-read book. He wants me to get the one bound in red covers, and I figure this out and do so.

I would take him to have been using the word 'red' and not 'read', even though they sound the same; this is a fact about his intentions. I would take him to be using 'red' to stand for some color property, rather than for a political position; this is also a fact about his intentions. Both of these inferences about his intentions are part of determining what he said, "strictly and literally." I also take him to have the property of being bound in red covers in mind, because he is talking about books, so that the raisin-box like book doesn't qualify. On my view, this inference about his likely intentions also figures in to what he said. I can't see why intentions can come into determining what is strictly and literally said, by determining which words he used, and eliminating ambiguities, but from then on be consigned to limbo until we get to the point of worrying about what is implicated. On Taylor's view, they are so consigned. What he strictly and literally asks me to do would be satisfied by bringing him either the raisin box–colored book or the red book. I then use Gricean reasoning, in the sense of reasoning about why a person said what they said, to figure out that he wants to book bound in red. Well, it could be that things work this way. But once we realize we don't need to think this in order to have intention-free compositional semantics, is this really the most plausible theory?

Reporting Attitudes

When we get to the issue of reporting attitudes, there is much that is clarifying about Taylor's essay, but also much that is confusing. Although later on in his article Taylor demonstrates that he understands the Crimmins-Perry theory of belief statements, much of the rhetoric of the initial part of his paper suggests otherwise. Specifically:

First, in the Crimmins-Perry account, as in Barwise and Perry 1983, embedding a sentence in an attitude report does *not* affect the meanings or references of its parts or of the whole. That is, as we point out, and Taylor later acknowledges, the theory is semantically innocent in the Davidson-inspired sense of this phrase in Barwise and Perry 1983.

Second, *pace* Taylor, it is not our view that embedding a sentence introduces unarticulated constituents. There are all kinds of linguistic contexts in which sentences are embedded to yield new terms or sentences, as noted above. The need for unarticulated constituents arises not from the use of embedded sentences—a characteristic of many kinds of "indirect classification"—but from the subject and verb of the belief report. It is the fact that we are reporting a belief that gives rise to unarticulated constituents in what the reporter says.

The basic idea behind the Crimmins-Perry account of belief reports was that when we report beliefs, we are implicitly talking about a notion (or sequence of notions) and saying that the beliefs in question were beliefs held via those notions. Suppose we are discussing the situation of Kripke's Pierre, walking disgustedly down a dirty alley in London, and you say, "Pierre doesn't believe London is pretty." This strikes me as true. I can't speak for others, but my willingness, when working on Barwise and Perry 1983, to think that it was *really* false, because of the belief that Pierre acquired when he was reading about London in his French books, and retains, seems to have been motivated by the fact that Barwise and I had a theory about belief reports that made things come out that way. It never seemed like an insight that counted in favor of the theory, but a prima facie problem that the theory could *possibly* handle, by referring to Grice and a little hand-waving. The fact the Crimmins-Perry theory has it come out as *really* true, on the other hand, strikes me as a strong mark in favor of the theory, not a prima facie problem with it. Our theory, in its rawest form, said that we are talking about the notion of London Pierre acquired when he moved there and that is engaged whenever he walks out in London and perceives his environs. We saw in our article that one needed to retreat to more flexible view, where the *kind* of notion in question is implicit, not the notion itself. In almost all of the cases one encounters in real life and in philosophy, there are basically three kinds of notions involved: *perceptual* notions, like Pierre's as he walks the street and Miles Hendon's when he looks at Prince Edward Tudor dressed as a pauper,[31] *common* notions, the ones we have of people and objects that are tied to their names, their publicly recognized photographs, and the like, and what we might call *lost* notions, like the one I might have acquired of a new adult neighbor, when as a child, she played on my daughter's soccer team years ago. I didn't know the kid's name, and I don't realize that she is the same person who, grown up, has moved in next door.

Taylor does not explicitly say that Crimmins and I believe in the view he spends a good deal of time rather persuasively attacking, the view that the terms in a *de dicto* belief report are supposed to present the point of view of the person whose belief is being reported, and we do not. Our account holds that the notion, or type of notion, being discussed by the reporter—the unarticulated constituent of the belief report—is often a matter of pragmatics, that is, Gricean reasoning in the broad sense of the term. Thus consider:

Pierre believed that London was ugly.

Pierre believed that Londres was ugly.

The *Situations and Attitudes* strategy, and Taylor's, claims that the first strikes us as true, given Kripke's story, and is true, while the second strikes us as false but is actually true. The feeling of falseness pertains to the implicated proposition, recovered through Gricean reasoning, based on the noticeable use of the French word 'Londres'. On Taylor's theory, this implicated proposition would be a fulsomely *de re* proposition. On the Crimmins-Perry theory, broadly Gricean reasoning is involved at an earlier stage, in figuring out which type of notion the reporter is talking about, and the report not only seems true, it is true. Neither theory needs to rely on the sort of *de dicto* approach that Taylor attacks.

Taylor talks about "pragmatic alchemy." But the alchemy would seem to be the same, whether the unarticulated information is gathered by broadly Gricean reasoning on the way to what is said or as part of strictly Gricean reasoning after taking the reporter to have said something false. Spencer (2006) argues quite persuasively, by the way, that it is extremely difficult to provide an account of the Gricean implicatures of the sort we require in Barwise and Perry 1983 or that Taylor's theory requires.

As someone who thinks incessantly about recognition, in personal identity cases, and also with respect to people such as Mary (below, pp. 560ff.), my attention has been drawn to how many ways we have in English for talking about such phenomena. To extend the bite-the-bullet strategy to reports using some of these other expressions seems even less plausible than in the case of 'believes.'

Suppose we were to say, of Pierre walking down the street, telling us how he hates ugly London and hopes some day to visit beautiful Londres, things like this:

He doesn't recognize that this city is Londres.

He doesn't realize that London is Londres.

He doesn't take this city to be Londres.

If we bite the bullet, these reports say that same things as,

He doesn't recognize that this city is this city.

He doesn't realize that London is London.

He doesn't take London to be London.

Words and phrases such as 'recognize', 'realize', and 'take to be' seem to be fashioned, unlike 'believes', for focusing on mode of presentation rather than object presented. In terms of the three-story picture of cognition I have described in various places it seems to me that 'believes' is most happily used for describing third-story doxastic states and 'recognizes' for those involving the first story—that is, for cases involving recognition.

It's not that Taylor thinks that we can explain the informational transactions involving beliefs reports and related phenomena without appeal to ways of believing, or notions, or ideas or some such thing: see his account of denials of belief.

The lexicon is a very nice place to locate the differences between 'believes' and 'recognizes' and 'takes to be'. It should contain information about how people are attuned to the different ways they and other people can cognize the things they talk about and should provide the hooks necessary at the level of reflexive content to feed intentions about those things, however implicit, into what is said. That is, in sum, I don't see why Taylor, having let the nose of the unarticulated constituent camel under his tent with 'it rains' and having provided us, in the lexicon, with just the tool we need to convert talk about "what someone is talking about" from pragmatic alchemy to principled philosophy of language and in need of the same pragmatic alchemy (which just amounts to allowing what people are talking about to be relevant to what they say, as far as I can see) for his own account of denials of belief as we need for our account of assertions of belief, should be so hostile to the Crimmins-Perry approach.

Dealing with Qualia (McKinsey and Loar)

McKinsey and Loar discuss physicalist theories of qualia, and in particular the one I offered in Perry 2001a. McKinsey thinks that Loar and I both hold a form of physicalism which, while perhaps the most plausible form available, is nevertheless mistaken.

I took myself to be supplementing Loar's insights rather than disputing them. We agree, as he has argued persuasively, that the two ways we might think about the same brain state, one as part of our ordinary experience-based ways of thinking and talking about what goes on in us, and the other as a theory-embedded description of a brain event in some canonical scientific language, are so different that there is no basis for supposing that the relevant identity statements should be a priori. In Perry 2001a, I tried to trace arguments for such a strong connection to the mistake of not appreciating what a weak relation identity is from an epistemological point of view. If A = B, then there is just one thing that is both A and B: a strong metaphysical condition. But there doesn't need to be any connection between 'A' and 'B' that would allow one to figure this out, on the basis of their meanings. In this sense, identity is much weaker than logical supervenience.

In Perry 2001a, I also took myself to agree with much that Ned Block has said on the topic of qualia. But Block, like Loar, remains skeptical about aspects of my treatment having to do with "phenomenal concepts," and this issue is also relevant to McKinsey's criticisms. I'll begin by briefly recapping my view on some central issues, by looking at the knowledge argument, doing so in a way that focuses on the issue of phenomenal concepts.[32]

The Knowledge Argument and Phenomenal Concepts

In its simplest form, Frank Jackson's knowledge argument has three steps. Mary has *new* knowledge when she steps out of the black-and-white room and sees a red fire hydrant. But while in the black-and-white room, she knew *all* the physical facts relevant to color vision. Conclusion: her new knowledge is of a nonphysical fact. It is Mary's new knowledge that is the crucial step. Some physicalists deny that she has new knowledge. I do not deny this. Instead, I offer an account of Mary's new knowledge that is consistent with her knowing, in the black-and-white room, which qualia were which physical brain states.

Mary emerges from the black-and-white room, sees a fire hydrant, and has her first experience, call it E, of the type $Quale_{RED}$. She thinks, "This$_i$ experience is the type I have when I see, in these conditions, the color of that fire hydrant." She has a certain relation to the experience: she *has* it. A less inquisitive person might have left it at that, but she also *attends to* the experience. E is the referent of her thought "this$_i$ experience" because of the relations it has to her: it is the one she is having and attending to. She is having an experience of the color of the grass beside the fire hydrant too, but "this$_i$ experience" doesn't refer to that experience, because it is not the one to which she attends.

Mary forms a concept of the *type* of color experience E exemplifies. She notes that E is similar to the color experience she has of the fire engine parked nearby and not similar to the color experience she is having of the grass next to the fire hydrant. She can introduce a term, 'quale$_?$' and ask,

Is quale$_?$ = quale$_{RED}$?

Mary's concept quale$_?$ seems like a good candidate for what some philosophers call a "phenomenal concept," for it is tied to her current experiences of the fire engine and the fire hydrant; it is the type of color experience of which those two color experiences are instances. For example, Block says the following about phenomenal concepts:

A phenomenal concept of the experience of red is what Mary lacked in the black and white room and what she gained when she went outside of it. . . . A phenomenal concept is individuated with respect to fundamental uses that involve the actual occurrence of phenomenal properties. In these fundamental uses, an actually occurring experience is used to think about that very experience. No one could have a phenomenal concept if they could not in some way relate the concept to such fundamental uses in which the subject actually has an instance of the phenomenal quality.[33]

Since quale$_?$ is quale$_{RED}$, Mary is thinking about the same type of experience when she uses the two terms in thought or language. The referential relations are quite different; she is related to the same quale in two quite different ways. On the one hand, it is the quale that two of her current experiences exemplify. On the other, it is the quale that her textbooks referred to and identified as the type of experience normal people have in favorable light when they see red objects. Her conceptions of the two are different. She believes that quale$_{RED}$ is the one people with normal vision have when they see red things in favorable light, and she also believes—because my version of Mary is a physicalist—that quale$_{RED}$ is a type of brain state, B_{52} to be precise; that to experience quale$_{RED}$ is to be in brain state B_{52}. She believes quale$_?$ is the type of two of her present color experiences and is the quale caused in her in her present conditions by the colors of the surfaces of the fire hydrant and the fire engine. She also believes that *if* her vision is normal, and the present lighting is favorable, and this fire hydrant is, like most of them are, painted red, *then* quale$_?$ is quale$_{RED}$. Once she is confident that her vision is normal and conditions are favorable and no one has repainted the local fire hydrants and fire engines to fool her, she will believe that quale$_?$ = quale$_{RED}$.

 Once she draws this inference, she knows something new about quale$_{RED}$ that she didn't know in the black-and-white room, namely, that it is the type of color experience exemplified by her current experiences of the colors of the fire hydrant and the fire engine. Moreover, she knows that quale$_{RED}$ falls under her new phenomenal concept, quale$_?$. There is nothing threatening to physicalism in this. This is a relational fact about particular experiences that hadn't occurred when she was in the black-and-white room; it is not knowledge of some new fundamental property of $Quale_{RED}$ that was of necessity missed by her physicalist texts.

Perhaps Mary is so brilliant that she was able to predict that upon leaving the black-and-white room she would see a fire hydrant and a fire engine, both with their normal colors, in favorable light. She can introduce terms for the predicted experiences, say, E_H and E_E. So she had a way of referring to and thinking about the experiences she is now having and their common quale, $quale_{RED}$, before having them. But the referential relations, in virtue of which she was able to refer to these things and talk about them, are quite different than the referential relations that enable her to think and talk about them as "this$_i$ color experience" (attending to the hydrant), "this$_i$ color experience" (attending to the engine) and "$Quale_?$." She can ask herself whether this$_i$ color experience is E_H, this$_i$ color experience is E_E, and whether $Quale_?$ is the one she predicted, $Quale_{RED}$. She can figure out that they are. So she still has new knowledge that she didn't have before.

Does anything in all of this give Mary a reason to abandon her physicalist view, that $Quale_{RED}$ is B_{52}? I cannot see that it does. If her physicalist views are correct, and she is wearing a new-fangled autocerebroscope that produced visual images of the goings-on in her brain as she had her experiences, she would have to grant that she was seeing the very experiences she was having. She might think, "Goodness, *seeing* an experience of $Quale_{RED}$ through an autocerebroscope (which I've never done before) is certainly nothing like *having* an experience of type $Quale_{RED}$ (which I've never had before). But then, why should it be?"

When aging Isaac wishes to bless the elder of his twins, Esau, the younger, Jacob, pretends to be Esau and receives the blessing. "May God give you of the dew of heaven, and of the fatness of the earth, and plenty of grain and wine," Isaac says to Jacob, thereby managing to address to God the request that He give Jacob dew, fatness, grain, and wine, and so blessing Jacob—pretty effectively as it turns out—although Isaac thought he was blessing Esau. This illustrates two aspects involved in talking or thinking about an object. There is the referential relation; in this case, because he uses the word 'you', the fact that Isaac is addressing Jacob determines that it is Jacob that he refers to and has petitioned God about. Second, there is the conception of the referent that guides the thinking or speaking. In this case, the conception of Esau, the elder son, the hunter who has given Isaac lots of meat over the years guides what Isaac asks God to do for the referent and not the the conception of his younger son Jacob, who supplies only vegetables.

It is natural to use the term 'mode of presentation' in thinking about Isaac and Mary. Isaac had two modes of presentation of Jacob, as "this fellow" (or "you") and as "Jacob." That's why he could be ignorant of the fact that "You are Jacob." Mary had a number of different modes of presentation of $quale_{RED}$ as *the type of this$_i$ experience*, as *quale$_?$*, as *quale$_{RED}$*, assuming physicalism is true, as B_{52}, and, via the autocerebroscope, as *that$_{AC}$ type of experience*. That's why it counts as knowledge, when she learns that they are modes of presentation of the same quale.

In the general case, and the one usually relevant to directing intentions, our assertion or thought is about an object because that object stands in a certain relation to us, not because it fits our conceptions of the person or thing we take ourselves to refer to. That's why we can have misrecognition. Jacob's thought "You are my eldest son, Esau" is false because the person he is talking to is *not* Esau. His request, "May God bless you," is a request for God to bless Jacob, because Jacob is the person to whom he is talking. The point is not limited to demonstratives. When I say "Aristotle," I refer to a certain ancient Greek because of a complex relation I have to him, mediated by a network of linked thoughts and assertions, texts, encyclopedias, and lectures, even if my conception of him is a confused mixture of what I've been told about Socrates, Plato, and Aristotle.

Also, in the general case, we don't incorporate the referential relation into *what* is thought or said, the "propositional content." When I see Ned Block, and learn that he is tall, surely what I learn first and foremost is that the person I am seeing and attending to is tall. But I would ordinarily say "I learned that man was tall," where 'that man' is a device of direct reference. That is, I would identify what I came to believe with a proposition about Ned Block. As the reflexive/referential theory suggests, except when mistakes are made or recognition is slow, the way we perceive and the way we refer are not so important to us as what we perceived to be the case with the things we saw or what we claimed to be the case about the objects we refer to.

We learn the term 'mode of presentation', in its philosophical usage, from Gottlob Frege, in his *Über Sinn und Bedeutung*. Frege's example is of a point of intersection of three lines, A, B, and C, which bisect the three sides of a triangle. The descriptions 'the point of intersection of A and B' and 'the point of intersection of B and C' illustrate two modes of presentation of the same thing. With definite descriptions like these, there doesn't seem to be a referential relation involved, and the mode of presentation is reasonably supposed to be part of the proposition that is asserted or thought. For this reason, these modes of presentation are misleading as to the general case.

After the first paragraph of *Über Sinn und Bedeutung*, Frege could have developed a concept of modes of representation that incorporated the distinction between referential relations and conceptions, but the rest of the essay goes in a different direction. Frege's modes of presentation are, or somehow give rise to, propositional constituents that are nonrelational; that is, *sinne* that determine the same *bedeutung* for everyone, and are so suited to be constituents of objective *gedanken*. But referential relations simply don't work this way.

If we think that referential relations do not suffice to establish reference, but that reference really resides in a relation between a nonrelational, objective *sinn* and the referent, then we will have to find such a *sinn* whenever we have reference, and a different such *sinn* for each new mode of presentation. Applying this to Mary, she would need some nonrelational mode of presentation of her new experience *E*; it would not suffice simply to have it and attend to it. And she would need some new nonrelational concept of quale$_{RED}$; it wouldn't suffice to think of it as what the experiences she attends to have in common. I believe the Fregean idea that modes of presentation must be objective *sinne* lurks behind the knowledge argument.

McKinsey

The heart of McKinsey's paper is an argument that goes like this:

1. Consider Descartes in *Meditation II*. It is possible, for all he knows, that he has a pain but there are no brains or brain states and so he does not have the property of being in a certain brain state.

2. So it is possible, for all Descartes knows, that having a pain is not being in brain state.

3. Because it is possible, for all Descartes knows, that having a pain is not a brain state, it is logically possible that having a pain is not being in a brain state.

4. If it is logically possible that having a pain is not being in a brain state, then there is no brain state ϕ such that having a pain is identical with being in ϕ.

5. So Perry (and Loar) are wrong.

I do not think there is a reasonable sense of 'logical possibility' that can meet the demands this argument puts on it. I think McKinsey's use of this term is based on conflating the following conceptions of logical implication, which on my view need to be kept separate.

Let S and S' be representations of any kind, including sentences, utterances, or thoughts. S logically implies S' if:

Conception A. Representations (sentences, utterances or thoughts) S and S′ mean propositions P and P′, and if P is true, P′ must be true, or

Conception B. Representations S and S′ are so related by their meaning properties, that if S is true, S′ is true.

Consider the sentences

(12)   Cicero was bald.

(13)   Tully was bald.

I take utterances of these to express the same proposition, the singular proposition that a certain Roman, the one philosophers call "Tully" and "Cicero," was bald. So, in sense A, the latter follows from the former. I would not call this a matter of logic, but of meaning and metaphysics. Logic has to do with representations, the sorts of things we can manipulate on paper or that can occur in our minds in chains of reasoning. Propositions are a way of getting at the truth-conditions, success-conditions and other properties of representations, but they are not themselves something we write, erase, derive, and the like.

If, in dealing with the meaning of sentences, we have only the proposition expressed to work with, it looks like (12) implies (13) in sense B also. But, on my view, we are not limited to those properties to deal with the meanings of sentences, we have indefinitely many more reflexive properties. What these will be depends on one's semantic theory. Let's take a simple theory of (proper) names, that they have a sort of ambiguity characteristics of names, that I call "nambiguity." When a name is assigned to an object, a convention is established allowing some population to refer to that object with that name. Many names are subject to far more such conventions than even the most ambiguous of ordinary nouns and verbs have meanings, so nambiguity is worth distinguishing from ordinary ambiguity. We expect a good dictionary to give us all the meanings of nouns and verbs, but not all of the conventions that pertain to names, for example.

Given this theory, we have the additional semantic properties, for (12) and (13), of having truth conditions given the meanings of the predicate 'was bald' but abstracting from the meanings of either 'Cicero' or 'Tully' or both.

Associated with (12) is the truth condition that the convention exploited in (12) for 'Cicero' is such that the referent of this name was bald, while associated with (13) is the truth-condition that the convention exploited in (13) for 'Tully' is such that the referent of this name was bald. Relative to these semantic properties, (13) does not follow from (12).

So we have, as my version of Conception B:

Conception B′. Representations S and S′ are so related by their reflexive truth-conditions, with nambiguities unresolved, that if S is true, S′ is true.

Note that this property is one step in the direction of the ordinary concept of logical truth, which involves abstracting from the meanings of all of the constants in a sentence other than the logical constants.

Now consider

(14)   Gold is valuable.

(15)   Au is valuable.

Au is the term for gold that is used in the periodic chart of the elements. Someone could understand quite a bit about periodic charts and know, for example, that element 79 is Au and perhaps also know that its melting point is 1064.18°C, without realizing that element 79 is gold. It would be possible, for all such a person knew, that he owns a gold ring, but that he does not own a ring made of Au. From this it would follow that there was a logical possibility, by McKinsey's test, that gold is not Au. If we are going to find this logical possibility at level A, we will have to distinguish the propositions expressed by (14) and (15). On my account, we should instead note that nouns for substances, like 'gold' and 'Au', are assigned to them by conventions, and scientific descriptions like 'element 79' by a combination of conventions and structural facts. We can distinguish the reflexive truth conditions of (14) and (15) at the level at which those conventions are not fixed:

(14) is true iff there is a substance the term 'gold' stands for in English, and it is valuable.

(15) is true iff there is a substance the term 'Au' stands for in the language of chemistry, and it is valuable.

Starting with (14) and (15), we can account for what our subject learns, when he learns that gold is Au; that is, what possibility is eliminated when he gains this bit of knowledge. He learns that there is a single substance that both 'Au' and 'gold' stand for, and so that the substance his ring is made of, that he knows to be valuable, is also the one with atomic number 79 that melts at 1064.18°C.

Now of course this is the strategy that I would want to pursue with Descartes. He knows quite a bit about having a pain. He knows that it is a property he has, that it is unpleasant, that can be directly aware of it, and the like. He doesn't know that it is a brain state. For all he knows, it is not. I can't see any new problems that McKinsey poses for this view, beyond those discussed in Perry 2001a, except the claim that the semantics cannot recognize what he calls "predication."

But there is nothing in my approach that I can discern that requires to me to suppose that 'gold' in 'this ring is gold' or 'Descartes wore a gold ring' or 'Descartes's ring was solid gold' *refers* to the substance gold. I think there are properties such as being gold, being solid gold, being cheap gold, and the like that rings have and that we can predicate of rings. This would in no way preclude making the distinction between reflexive content, which corresponds to what the world has to be like for a predication to be true, where we do not fix the facts about which expressions predicate which properties, and the content we have with the facts about which expressions predicate which properties. If Descartes were transported to the twenty-first century and taught the basics of chemistry, he might understand in a general way what is predicated by 'this substance is pure Au' without realizing that what is predicated is the same thing that would be predicated with 'this substance is pure gold'.

I can't see then, that McKinsey has given arguments against "Q-physicalism," much less arguments that justify the abusive words like "stupid" that he heaps on us Q-physicalists. It may, of course, be that his own semantical view is so plausible that we should adopt it, even if it prevents us from saying that the substance gold and the substance Au are one and the same, and even if it leaves us in what would seem to be a rather not very illuminating metaphysical posture:

the phenomenal qualities of sense experience are not identical with any physical properties of the brain. Nor, I take it, do such qualities logically supervene upon the physical properties of the brain, or indeed upon any other physical properties. Hence it seems to me that no form of *reductive* physicalism is true. Phenomenal properties, as well as the propositions and facts that involve such properties, exist "over and above" the physical properties, propositions and facts. But again, it does nevertheless seem likely that such non-physical phenomenal properties, propositions, and facts are somehow *metaphysically* necessitated or entailed by physical properties, propositions, and facts about the brain. But I confess that I do not have the slightest idea of how or why this could be so. (498)

McKinsey's semantics may well be quite plausible, but, I must admit, I have not yet seen why I should accept it, rather than one like my own, which permits us to at least have at least a slight idea of why there should such a tight connection between the phenomenal and the physical.

Loar

Loar discusses responses to Kripke's argument on the part of physicalists. Loar distinguishes two responses to this argument: that there is a contingency in the statement that explains its a posteriori status; second, deny that being a posteriori implies having a contingent mode of presentation. He takes me, rightly, to defend a version of the first reply, while he favors the second. And he worries about the following objection to my view:

The antiphysicalist may say that even though Perry does provide a factor that is a posteriori and contingent, there is another a posteriori mode of presentation (of the psychophysical identity) that does not correspond to something contingent. Think the thought in question—"C-fiber stimulation is identical with *that* internal state of mind"—*without* abstracting from the sensation of pain. That is a posteriori and is, if true, necessarily true. (452)

Let me begin by saying how I take Kripke's argument. Kripke basically argues that a strategy he uses to explain the felt contingency of the statement "Heat is molecular motion" is unavailable to explain the felt contingency of the statement "Pain is vibrating C-fibers," and, in the absence of such an explanation, the prudent course is to take the felt contingency as strong evidence for a real contingency. Both 'heat' and 'molecular motion' are rigid designators, hence the statement is true in all possible worlds. However, we have a concept of heat as the cause of a certain range of sensations; although this concept does not *determine* the reference in each possible world, it fixes the reference in the actual world; we identify heat and explain the use of the word 'heat' by appealing to such experiences.

'Pain', like 'heat', is a rigid designator, and, if true, the statement, "Pain is C-fiber vibration" would be necessarily true. But we have no concept of pain as the *cause* of certain characteristic sensations, for pain *is* a sensation. There is no layer of reference-fixing, criterial, but nonreference determining sensations for pain, as there is for heat.

Before considering my response, let's look at Kripke's explanation of the felt contingency of "Heat is molecular motion." I think the phrase that there is "contingency in the statement" does not get at his view in a very precise way. The contingency is that the cause of such and such sensations is molecular motion. This is not the proposition expressed by "Heat is molecular motion," nor is it entailed by that proposition. It is quite a different proposition, whose connection with the proposition expressed is that it incorporates a concept that, in the actual world, uniquely characterizes heat and is in fact for most people a criterion for the presence of heat. It is an important mode of presentation of heat but does not provide the meaning of 'heat'.

The a posteriori nature of the statement "Heat is molecular motion" derives from the fact that our criterion for heat is not a necessary property of heat, but a property that plays a central role in our interactions with it in this world.

My response is that there are also back-up concepts or modes of presentation of pain, that are not only contingently related to pain, but are criterial, and explain the felt contingency of the connection between pain and C-fiber vibration and will be involved centrally in the discovery that pain is C-fiber vibration.

Following Ewing's advice to physicalists,[34] we could grab hold of a red-hot piece of iron and attend to the painful sensation it causes in us. The pain we feel, at that moment, will be the result of grabbing the iron, it will be that to which we are attending, and it will be that which we wish to cease and a great deal else. All of these descriptions of the pain are only contingently so, because had we not picked up the piece of iron, we would not have felt this kind of pain and so would not have been able to think of it, and identify it, in all of these ways.

It is sometimes said that pain is its own mode of presentation. This is at best a poor way of making the point that we do not think of pains as the cause of further sensations. But a mode of presentation is a way of thinking about something. In order to think about pain, I need not be in pain. When I remember being in pain, anticipate being in pain, think about the pain others are feeling, and the like, I employ a mode of presentation of pain that quite clearly is different than pain itself. A simple way to put it is that I employ my *idea* of pain. Most of us acquire this idea, the one that is a component of our later thoughts and memories of pain, by having pain of some sort, and it may well be that it is necessary to have pain to have this sort of idea of pain (which, for roughly these reasons, I call a "Humean" idea).

Let's return to the experience we imagine ourselves having as we follow Ewing's suggestion. We have a certain thought, "This sensation is pain." 'This sensation' we take to refer to the kind of sensation I am having, which is pain, and is so in every possible world. I note that there are, however, contingent truth-conditions for the statement at the reflexive level, roughly "the sensation attended to by the owner of this thought as part of having the thought is pain." Because the owner of that very thought could have been having a different sensation, this is contingent. (Perhaps it's not *obvious* that the owner of that very thought could fail to be in pain, for that fact might enter into the individuation of the thought. Since no one made this objection to my theory, however, I'll pass over it.)

Now I think that Loar feels that the mode of presentation of pain involved in this reflexive content—namely, *that sensation I'm having*—is not a very impressive candidate for an explanation of the felt contingency of "Pain is vibrating C-fibers" or even the felt contingency of "This sensation is vibrating C-fibers." I'd have to agree with that. It is, however, a necessary link to a more impressive candidate. The sensation I am now feeling, is the sensation caused by grasping the red-hot iron bar, the sensation I find extremely unpleasant, the sensation that is bringing tears to my eyes, the sensation others might have in similar circumstances and so forth. Note that the type of sensation, designated by 'this sensation', is only connected to these other modes of presentations of it, through the reflexive mode of presentation: *the sensation I am now having and attending to.*

We have then a rather rich mode of presentation of the sensation of pain that involves but is not limited to the reflexive content of the thought "This sensation is pain." This mode of presentation of pain can then be detached from the current experience of pain, but retained as a recognitional concept. This concept will be only contingently related to pain, and only contingently related to vibrating C-fibers. Suppose that an Australian philosopher has manipulated my brain and nerve endings so that, when I grab hold of a red-hot piece of iron, the sensation that I am caused to have is not the sensation of pain, but some extraordinarily bad taste, say some combination of lima beans and mud from the bottom of a mature pond. I form many beliefs about this experience, some true, some false. I believe truly that it is caused in me now by grabbing the red-hot iron; I believe rightly that it is very unpleasant; I believe rightly that it is a sensation I very much want to cease; I believe wrongly that it is pain and that it is the sensation others feel when they grab a red-hot iron.

Suppose that when all of this happens I have already felt pain many times. I am forced to grab the red-hot iron, in spite of my fear of what I will feel. Then I would be quite surprised to have the sensation of lima beans mixed with mud; perhaps somewhat relieved. I would not mistake it for pain, for I would remember what pain feels like. Whatever the mechanism for having a memory of what it is like to feel pain— whatever the implementation in our neurophysiology of Humean ideas—there is no reason to suppose that my abiding concept of pain, which allows me to recognize it when I have it again, involved pain itself, as opposed to some special sort of representation of pain. But, of course, remembering what it is like to have pain is not a matter, even partly, of remembering what further sensations being in pain causes in us.

Thus, I agree with Loar, and take the second strategy of the two he sketches, as well as the first. Our two concepts of pain, that of vibrating C-fibers and that of the sensation we have experienced many times, that we use in remembering, anticipating and recognizing the sensation, are quite different, parts of different language games, information games, and forms of life; there is no reason for the physicalist to suppose that there need be an a priori connection between them; if an elaborate metaphysical and semantical scheme such as Chalmers's seems to provide such a result, so much the worse for the scheme. Still, I am not happy to simply remain there. It seems we can have the ordinary concept of pain and fully grasp the neurophysiological concept of vibrating C-fibers and still doubt whether pain is vibrating C-fibers. That is, even if there is no metaphysical possibility, there is an epistemological possibility. And it is this epistemological possibility that is eliminated when we learn that, as a matter of fact, pain is vibrating C-fibers. It is this epistemological possibility that I feel we need to identify, to fully understand the physicalist story.

Loar's view may be connected to a worry that Block and Chalmers have; Block quotes Chalmers semiapprovingly as follows:

Chalmers (2003) argues that phenomenal concepts cannot be demonstrative concepts. The main argument could be put as follows: for any demonstrative concept, say 'this$_i$', this$_i$ has phenomenal property P would be news. But if the demonstrative concept was genuinely a phenomenal concept, there would be some claims of that form that are not news.[35]

This leaves me perplexed. As we saw, demonstrative phrases can be used to express different concepts in different situations. As Mary turns her attention from the fire hydrant to the lawn next to it, she might use the phrase 'this$_i$ color experience' for different concepts; the two concepts might be part of the same thought: "this$_i$ color experience is much more soothing than [turning her head back to look at the fire hydrant] this$_j$ color experience." But how exactly is it news to Mary, as she looks at the fire hydrant, that "this$_i$ color experience has phenomenal property P," if phenomenal property P is exactly the property she has never experienced until now, and is now experiencing, and attending to, and referring to with 'this$_i$ color experience'?

Conclusion

At times, in reading the more critical of the essays in this volume, I have been reminded of a story Abraham Lincoln told. Asked by a friend from Springfield how he liked being president, he said,

You have heard the story, haven't you, about the man who was tarred and feathered and carried out of town on a rail? A man in the crowd asked him how he liked it. His reply was that if it was not for the honor of the thing, he would much rather walk.

After all, I thought in these self-pitying moments, it's hard enough to write essays with a beginning and an end and mostly grammatical sentences in between; why on top of that do people have to read them and expect me to be coherent and persuasive? But such moments were comparatively rare, and, as I reach the end of this response I am overwhelmed by gratitude to those philosophers who have worked hard to understand and evaluate what I have had to say. I appreciate the opportunity to clarify my thoughts, even while I know that, thus clarified, they may strike others as even less plausible than before.[36]

Notes

1. See O'Rourke 1998, 2000, 2003.

2. See Washington 1992.

3. See Blanchette 1994, 1996, 1999.

4. See, especially, Martí 1995, 2003.

5. See Carston 2002.

6. See also O'Rourke 2003, where he makes the important point that inputs to the process of Gricean reasoning need not be complete propositions.

7. See Korta and Perry 2006.

8. See Bach 2004.

9. See Perry (forthcoming).

10. My reasons for abandoning the idea of treating names like indexicals are given in Perry 1980. David Kaplan's skepticism at the time about the idea was an important cause in abandoning it, and considering the reasons for doing so.

11. In the past I've used 'reflexive truth conditions' and 'reflexive content' more or less synonymously, but from now on I'll try to use the former for the *condition* and the latter for the proposition that an utterance instantiates its reflexive truth conditions. In this usage u_L and u_P have the same reflexive truth-conditions, but different reflexive contents.

12. For notions and ideas, see my (1989) paper with Mark Crimmins. See also Perry 2001a. For self-notions, see part III of Perry 2002.

13. See Israel and Perry 1991.

14. See Crimmins and Perry 1989 (225) as reprinted in Perry 2000.

15. I translate '*Sinn*' as '*sinn*', '*Gedanke*' as '*gedanke*', and so forth.

16. See Israel and Perry 1990 and 1991.

17. This section replaces an earlier version, in which these ideas were developed in the course of responding to a fascinating article by Herman Cappelen and Ernie Lepore. Their article was the first received by the editors; it took so long for the rest of the essays to be received, and then for me to formulate my responses, that it no longer did a very good job representing their latest thinking. I apologize for my slowness. It is a fine article, which I found very useful in clarifying my own thoughts about semantics and pragmatics and understanding the reservations some very bright philosophers have about it, and the issues involved in the debate. Kepa Korta and I discuss their ideas in Korta and Perry (forthcoming) which is part of a symposium on Cappelen and Lepore (2005).

18. See our 2006 and forthcoming.

19. Recanati 2004 especially pp. 65ff.

20. I discuss this example at (even) greater length in Perry forthcoming.

21. Grice 1989 (25).

22. See Cappelen and Lepore 2005 (144–145).

23. 'Nambiguity' is my term in Perry 2001a for the particular kind of ambiguity involved in proper names that to which many conventions of roughly the form "*N* may be used to refer to *x*" have been assigned.

24. This quote is from the withdrawn paper referred to in n. 18. I suspect this view isn't one they have changed their minds about. I love the quote too much to give it up, even if they have.

25. See Perry 1994.

26. See Sag and Wasow 1999.

27. Another approach for dealing with machines is to make available large corpuses of discourse and various powerful statistical methods for extracting information relevant to discourse interpretation from them, without any pretense that this is how humans work. Combinations are also possible.

28. Implic*i*tures are not implic*a*tures. 'Impliciture' is Kent Bach's term, for how his theory deals with intention-derived content that goes beyond semantic content but is not properly seen as implicature in the Gricean sense.

29. See Carston 2002.

30. See Perry forthcoming.

31. In Twain 2001.

32. Some of what follows is borrowed from Perry 2006 which is a discussion of Block 2006.

33. In Block 2006.

34. Ewing's remark is quoted and discussed in the first chapter of Perry 2001a.

35. In Block 2006.

36. I am thankful to the Stanford Humanities Center and the Center for Advanced Studies at the Norwegian Academy of Science and Letters for support in writing this essay.

References

Bach, K. 2004. "Minding the Gap." In C. Bianchi (ed.), *The Semantics/Pragmatics Distinction*. Stanford, Calif.: CSLI Publications.

Barwise, J., and J. Etchemendy. 1987. *The Liar*. New York: Oxford University Press.

Barwise, J., and J. Perry. 1983. *Situations and Attitudes*. Cambridge, Mass.: MIT Press.

Blanchette, P. 1994. "Frege's Reduction." *History and Philosophy of Logic* 15: 85–103.

———. 1996. "Frege and Hilbert on Consistency." *Journal of Philosophy* 93: 317–336.

———. 1999. "Relative Identity and Cardinality." *Canadian Journal of Philosophy* 29: 205–224.

Block, N. 2006. "Max Black's Objection to Mind-Body Identity." In D. Zimmerman (ed.), *Oxford Studies in Metaphysics*. Vol. II. Oxford: Oxford University Press.

Cappelen, H., and E. Lepore. 2005. *Insensitive Semantics*. Oxford: Blackwell.

Carston, R. 2002. *Thoughts and Utterances: The Pragmatics of Explicit Communication*. Oxford: Blackwell.

Chalmers, D. 2003. "The Content and Epistemology of Phenomenal Belief." In Q. Smith and A. Jakic (eds.), *Consciousness: New Philosophical Perspectives*. Oxford: Oxford University Press.

Crimmins, M. 1992. *Talk about Beliefs*. Cambridge, Mass.: MIT Press.

Crimmins, M., and J. Perry. 1989. "The Prince and the Phone Both: Reporting Puzzling Beliefs." *Journal of Philosophy* 86: 685–711.

Devlin, K. 1991. *Logic and Information*. Cambridge: Cambridge University Press.

Grice, H. P. 1989. *Studies in the Way of Words*. Cambridge, Mass.: Harvard University Press.

Israel, D., and J. Perry. 1990. "What Is Information?" In P. Hanson (ed.), *Information, Language and Cognition*. Vancouver: University of British Columbia Press.

———. 1991. "Information and Architecture." In J. Barwise, J. M. Gawron, G. Plotkin, and S. Tutiya (eds.), *Situation Theory and Its Applications*. Vol. 2. Stanford University: Center for the Study of Language and Information.

Kaplan, D. 1989a. "Afterthoughts." In J. Almog, J. Perry, and H. Wettstein (eds.), *Themes from Kaplan*. New York: Oxford University Press.

———. 1989b. "Demonstratives." In J. Almog, J. Perry, and H. Wettstein (eds.), *Themes from Kaplan*. New York: Oxford University Press.

Korta, K., and J. Perry. 2006. "Three Demonstrations and a Funeral." *Mind and Language* 21: 166–186.

———. Forthcoming. "Varieties of Minimalist Semantics." *Philosophy and Phenomenological Research*.

Lewis, D. 1979. "Attitudes de dicto and de se." *Philosophical Review* 88: 513–543.

Martí, G. 1995. "The Essence of Genuine Reference." *Journal of Philosophical Logic* 24: 275–289.

———. 2003. "The Question of Rigidity in New Theories of Reference." *Noûs* 37: 275–289.

O'Rourke, M. 1998. "Semantics and the Dual-Aspect Use of Definite Descriptions." *Pacific Philosophical Quarterly* 79: 264–288.

———. 2000. "In Defense of Common Content." *Philosophical Papers* 29: 159–188.

———. 2003. "The Scope Argument." *Journal of Philosophy* 100: 136–157.

Perry, J. 1977. "Frege on Demonstratives." *Philosophical Review* 86: 474–497. Reprinted in Perry 1993.

———. 1979. "The Problem of the Essential Indexical." *Noûs* 13: 3–21. Reprinted in Perry 1993.

———. 1980. "A Problem about Continued Belief." *Pacific Philosophical Quarterly* 61: 317–322. Reprinted in Perry 1993.

———. 1986. "Thought without Representation." *Supplementary Proceedings of the Aristotelian Society* 60: 263–283. Reprinted in Perry 2000.

———. 1993. *The Problem of the Essential Indexical and Other Essays*. New York: Oxford University Press.

———. 1994. "Davidson's Sentences and Wittgenstein's Builders." Presidential Address, *Proceedings and Addresses of the American Philosophical Association* 68: 23–37. Reprinted in Perry 2000.

———. 2000. *The Problem of the Essential Indexical and Other Essays*, exp. ed. Stanford, Calif.: CSLI Publications.

———. 2001a. *Knowledge, Possibility, and Consciousness*. Cambridge, Mass.: MIT Press.

———. 2001b. *Reference and Reflexivity*. Stanford, Calif.: CSLI Publications.

———. 2002. *Identity, Personal Identity, and the Self*. Indianapolis: Hackett.

———. Forthcoming. "Directing Intentions." In a festschrift for David Kaplan, edited by J. Almog and P. Leonardi. Oxford: Oxford University Press.

———. 2006. "Mary and Max and Jack and Ned." In D. Zimmerman (ed.), *Oxford Studies in Metaphysics*. Vol. II. Oxford: Oxford University Press.

Recanati, F. 1993. *Direct Reference: From Language to Thought*. Oxford: Blackwell.

———. 1995. "Quasi-Singular Propositions: The Semantics of Belief Reports." *Proceedings of the Aristotelian Society* (supplementary vol. 69): 175–194.

———. 2004. *Literal Meaning*. Cambridge: Cambridge University Press.

Sag, I., and T. Wasow. 1999. *Syntactic Theory: A Formal Introduction*. Stanford, Calif.: CSLI Publications.

Spencer, C. 2006. "Do Conversational Implicatures Explain Substitutivity Failures?" *Pacific Philosophical Quarterly* 87: 126–139.

Strawson, P. 1950. "On Referring." *Mind* 59: 320–344.

Twain, M. 2001. *The Prince and the Pauper*. Edison, N.J.: Castle Books.

Washington, C. 1992. "The Identity Theory of Quotation." *Journal of Philosophy* 89: 582–605.

Bibliography of John Perry's Publications

Books

1. 1978. *A Dialogue on Personal Identity and Immortality*. Indianapolis: Hackett. Translated in Spanish by A. Campiran as *Dialogo sobre la Identidad Personal y la Inmortalidad*. Cuadernos de Critica, Universidad Nacional Autónoma de Mexico, 1984. Also translated into Chinese and Korean.

2. 1983. *Situations and Attitudes*. With J. Barwise. Cambridge, Mass.: MIT Press. German translation by C. Gerstner as *Situationen und Einstellungen*. Berlin: Walter de Gruyter, 1987. Translated into Japanese. Tokyo: Tuttle-Mori, 1992. Translated into Spanish by J. I. Olmos as *Situaciones y Actitudes*. Madrid: Visor, 1992. Reprinted with a new introduction by CSLI Publications, 1999.

3. 1993. *The Problem of the Essential Indexical and Other Essays*. New York: Oxford University Press. (Expanded edition, Stanford, Calif.: CSLI Publications, 2000.)

4. 1999. *Problems d'Indexicalité*. Selected essays translated by J. Dokic and F. Preisig. Stanford and Paris: Editions CSLI: 1999.

5. 1999. *Dialogue on Good, Evil and the Existence of God*. Cambridge/Indianapolis: Hackett.

6. 2001. *Knowledge, Possibility and Consciousness*. Cambridge, Mass.: MIT Press.

7. 2001. *Reference and Reflexivity*. Stanford, Calif.: CSLI Publications. Spanish translation by K. Korta and R. Agerri as *Referencialismo Critico: Le Teoria Reflexivo-referencial Del Significado*. Stanford, Calif.: CSLI Publications.

8. 2002. *Identity, Personal Identity and the Self*. Indianapolis: Hackett.

9. 2002. *Contesti*. Lectures given in Genoa, translated by M. Vignola. Forward by C. Penco. Genova: De Ferrari & Devega.

Books Edited

10. 1975. *Personal Identity*. Berkeley: University of California Press.

11. 1985. *Introduction to Philosophy*. Edited with M. Bratman. New York: Oxford University Press. Rev. ed. 1993; 3rd ed. 1999; 4th ed. (edited with M. Bratman and J. Fischer) 2006.

12. 1989. *Themes from Kaplan*. Edited with J. Almog and H. Wettstein. New York: Oxford University Press.

13. 1990. *Situation Theory and Its Applications. Volume 1*. Edited with R. Cooper and K. Mukai. Stanford, Calif.: CSLI Publications.

14. 1994. *Berkeley's Three Dialogues*. Edited with D. Hilbert. Claremont, Calif.: Arete Press.

Articles and Chapters

15. 1963. "Paradoxical Logic." *Philosophy East and West* 13: 155–157.

16. 1967. "Equality and Education: Remarks on Kleinberger." *Studies in Philosophy and Education* 5: 433–445.

17. 1970a. "The Same F." *Philosophical Review* 79: 181–200. Reprinted in (8).

18. 1970b. "Review of Cornman and Lehrer, *Philosophical Problems and Arguments*." *Philosophical Review* 97: 578–580.

19. 1970c. "Review of David Wiggins, *Identity and Spatial Temporal Continuity*." *Journal of Symbolic Logic* 35: 447–448.

20. 1972. "Can The Self Divide?" *Journal of Philosophy* 69: 463–488. Reprinted in (8).

21. 1974a. "Review of *Three Paradoxical Aspects of Identity*, by Heinrich Behmann." *Journal of Symbolic Logic* 39: 359–360.

22. 1974b. "Review of *Universals*, by Nicholas Wolterstorff." *Journal of Philosophy* 71: 252–257.

23. 1975a. "The Problem of Personal Identity." In (10).

24. 1975b. "Personal Identity, Memory, and the Problem of Circularity." In (10). Reprinted in (8).

25. 1975c. "Reviews of Gustav Bergmann, *Sameness, Meaning, and Identity*, and Gustav Bergmann and Herbert Hochberg, *Concepts*." *Journal of Symbolic Logic* 40: 106–107.

26. 1976. "Review of Bernard Williams, *Problems of the Self.*" *Journal of Philosophy* 73: 416–428.

27. 1976. "The Importance of Being Identical." In A. Rorty (ed.), *The Identity of Persons.* Berkeley: University of California Press. Reprinted in (8).

28. 1977. "Frege on Demonstratives." *Philosophical Review* 86: 474–497. Reprinted in (3). Translated into Spanish as "Frege sobre los demonstratives," by L. Lecuona. In M. Valdés (ed.), *Pensamiento y Lenguaje. Problemas en la atribuci'on de actitudes proposicionales.* Instituto de Investigaciones Filosóficas, Universidad Nacional Autonóma de Mexico, 1996. Translated into German as "Frege Über Indexikalische Ausdrücke" by Joseph A. Tougas in *Conceptus Zeitschrift für Philosophie* 1995, 28: 147–183.

29. 1978a. "A Dialogue on Personal Identity and Immortality." In J. Feinberg (ed.), *Reason and Responsibility.* 4th ed. Encino, Calif.: Dickenson Publishing. Reprinted with revisions as (1).

30. 1978b. "Relative Identity and Relative Number." *Canadian Journal of Philosophy* 7: 1–14. Reprinted in (8).

31. 1978c. "Defenses for the Mind-Brain Identity Theory: Commentary on Puccetti and Dykes." *Behavioral and Brain Sciences* 1: 362.

32. 1979a. "The Problem of the Essential Indexical." *Noûs* 13: 3–21. Reprinted in *Philosophers Annual*, III, 1980. Reprinted in (3).

33. 1979b. "The Philosophical Problem of Personal Identity." *Stanford Observer*, March 1979: 3–4.

34. 1980a. "Belief and Acceptance." *Midwest Studies in Philosophy* 5: 533–542. Reprinted in (3).

35. 1980b. "A Problem about Continued Belief." *Pacific Philosophical Quarterly* 61: 317–322. Reprinted in (3).

36. 1980c. "The Situation Underground." With J. Barwise. In J. Barwise and I. Sag (eds.), *Stanford Working Papers in Semantics.* Vol. 1. Stanford, Calif.: Stanford Cognitive Science Group.

37. 1981a. "Semantic Innocence and Uncompromising Situations." With J. Barwise. *Midwest Studies in Philosophy* 6: 387–403.

38. 1981b. "Will Tommy Vladek Survive?" In F. D. Miller and N. D. Smith (eds.), *Thought Probes: An Introduction to Philosophy through Science Fiction.* Englewood Cliffs, N.J.: Prentice-Hall.

39. 1981c. "Situations and Attitudes." With J. Barwise. *Journal of Philosophy* 77: 668–691.

40. 1983a. "Castañeda on He and I." In J. E. Tomberlin (ed.), *Agent, Language, and World: Essays Presented to Hector-Neri Castañeda with His Replies*. Indianapolis: Hackett. Reprinted in (3).

41. 1983b. "Personal Identity and the Concept of a Person." In G. Floistad (ed.), *Chronicles of Institut International De Philosophie*. Volume 4: *Philosophy of Mind (Philosophy: A New Survey)*. The Hague: Martinus Nijhoff. Reprinted in (8).

42. 1983c. "Contradictory Situations." In F. Landman and F. Veltman (eds.), *Varieties of Formal Semantics: Proceedings of the 4th Amsterdam Colloquium, September, 1982*. Dordrecht: Foris.

43. 1985a. "Shifting Situations and Shaken Attitudes." With J. Barwise. *Linguistics and Philosophy* 8: 105–161 (also Report No. CSLI-84-13. Stanford University: Center for the Study of Language and Information, 1984).

44. 1985b. "Language, Mind, and Information." In B. H. Partee, S. Peters, and R. Thomason (eds.), *Report of Workshop on Information and Representation*. (Also Report No. CSLI-85-44. Stanford University: Center for the Study of Language and Information, 1985.)

45. 1985c. "Self-Knowledge and Self-Representation." *Proceedings of IJCAI-1985*. Mountain View, Calif.: Morgan Kaufmann.

46. 1985d. "Semantics." In A. Kuper and J. Kuper (eds.), *The Social Science Encyclopedia*. London: Routledge and Kegan Paul.

47. 1986a. "Perception, Action, and the Structure of Believing." In R. E. Grandy and R. Warner (eds.), *Philosophical Grounds of Rationality*. Oxford: Oxford University Press. Reprinted in (3).

48. 1986b. "Circumstantial Attitudes and Benevolent Cognition." In J. Butterfield (ed.), *Language, Mind and Logic*. Cambridge: Cambridge University Press (also Report No. CSLI-86-53, Stanford University: Center for the Study of Language and Information, 1986). Reprinted in (3).

49. 1986c. "From Worlds to Situations." *Journal of Philosophical Logic* 15: 83–107. Reprinted in (3).

50. 1986d. "Thought without Representation." *Supplementary Proceedings of the Aristotelian Society* 60: 263–283. Reprinted in (3).

51. 1988a. "Cognitive Significance and New Theories of Reference." *Noûs* 2: 1–18. Reprinted in (3).

52. 1988b. "Review of *A Border Dispute*, by John MacNamara." *Cognition* 30: 183–188.

53. 1989a. "Possible Worlds and Subject Matter: Discussion of Barbara H. Partee's 'Possible Worlds in Model-Theoretic Semantics: A Linguistic Perspective.'" In S. Allen (ed.), *Possible Worlds in Humanities, Arts and Sciences: Proceedings of Nobel Symposium, August, 1986, 65*. Berlin and New York: Walter de Gruyter. Reprinted in (3).

54. 1989b. "The Prince and the Phonebooth: Reporting Puzzling Beliefs." With Mark Crimmins. *Journal of Philosophy* 86: 685–711 (also Report No. CSLI-88-128. Stanford University: Center for the Study of Language and Information, 1988). Reprinted in *The Philosophers Annual*, XII, 1989. Reprinted in (3).

55. 1990a. "What Is Information?" With D. Israel. In P. Hanson (ed.), *Information, Language and Cognition*. Vancouver: University of British Columbia Press.

56. 1990b. "Individuals in Informational and Intentional Content." In E. Villanueva (ed.), *Information, Semantics and Epistemology*. Oxford: Basil Blackwell. Reprinted in (3).

57. 1990c. "Self-Notions." *Logos* 11: 17–31.

58. 1991a. "Fodor and Psychological Explanations." With D. Israel. In B. Loewer and G. Rey (eds.), *Meaning in Mind*. Oxford: Basil Blackwell. Reprinted in (3).

59. 1991b. "Actions and Movements." With David Israel and Syun Tutiya. *Proceedings of ICAI-'91*. Mountain View, Calif.: Morgan Kaufmann.

60. 1991c. "Il Filosofo e il computer." In L. Gallino (ed.), *Informatica e Scienze Umane: Lo Stato ADell'Arte*. Milan: Franco Angeli.

61. 1991d. "Information and Architecture." With David Israel. In J. Barwise, J. M. Gawron, G. Plotkin, and S. Tutiya (eds.), *Situation Theory and Its Applications*. Vol. 2. Stanford University: Center for the Study of Language and Information.

62. 1993a. "Williams on the Self and Its Future." In J. Perry and M. Bratman (eds.), *Introduction to Philosophy*, 2nd ed. New York: Oxford University Press. Reprinted in (8).

63. 1993b. "Executions, Motivations and Accomplishments." With David Israel and Syun Tutiya. *Philosophical Review* 102: 515–540.

64. 1993c. "Richly Grounded Symbols in ASL." With E. Macken and C. Haas. *Sign Language Studies* 81: 375–394.

65. 1994a. "Fodor and Lepore on Holism." *Philosophical Studies* 73: 123–138.

66. 1994b. "Davidson's Sentences and Wittgenstein's Builders." Presidential Address, *Proceedings and Addresses of the American Philosophical Association* 68: 23–37. Reprinted in (3), enlarged edition.

67. 1994c. "Introduction." In D. Hilbert and J. Perry (eds.), *Berkeley's Three Dialogues*. Claremont, Calif.: Arete Press.

68. 1994d. "Intentionality and Its Puzzles." In S. Guttenplan (ed.), *A Companion to the Philosophy of Mind*. Oxford: Blackwell.

69. 1995. "American Sign Language and Heterogeneous Communication Systems." With E. Macken and C. Haas. *Sign Language Studies* 89: 363–412.

70. 1996a. "Evading the Slingshot." In A. Clark, J. Ezquerro, and J. Larrazabal (eds.), *Philosophy and Cognitive Science: Categories, Consciousness, and Reasoning*. Dordrecht: Kluwer Academic Publishers. Reprinted in (3), enlarged edition.

71. 1996b. "Interfacing Situations." With E. Macken. In J. Seligman and D. Westerstahl (eds.), *Logic, Language, and Computation*. Vol. 1. Stanford, Calif.: CSLI Publications.

72. 1996c. "Where Monsters Dwell." With David Israel. In J. Seligman and D. Westerstahl (eds.), *Logic, Language, and Computation*. Vol. 1. Stanford, Calif.: CSLI Publications.

73. 1996d. "Self." *The Encyclopedia of Philosophy, Supplement*. New York: Simon & Schuster Macmillan.

74. 1996e. "Indexicals." *The Encyclopedia of Philosophy, Supplement*. New York: Simon & Schuster Macmillan.

75. 1996f. "Philosophy of Mind." *Microsoft Encarta Encyclopedia*. Redmond, Wash.: Microsoft Corporation.

76. 1996g. "Reflexivity, Indexicality and Names." *Korean Journal of Cognitive Science* 7: 95–112. Reprinted in (3), enlarged edition.

77. 1997a. "Indexicals and Demonstratives." In R. Hale and C. Wright (eds.), *Companion to the Philosophy of Language*. Oxford: Blackwell.

78. 1997b. "Russell's *The Problems of Philosophy*: An Introduction to Bertrand Russell, *The Problems of Philosophy*." New York: Oxford University Press.

79. 1997c. "Reflexivity, Indexicality and Names." In W. Kunne, M. Anduschus, and A. Newen (eds.), *Direct Reference, Indexicality, and Proposition Attitudes*. Stanford, Calif.: CSLI Publications and Cambridge University Press. Reprinted in (3), enlarged edition.

80. 1997d. "Rip Van Winkle and Other Characters." *European Review of Analytical Philosophy* 2: 13–39. Reprinted in (3), enlarged edition.

81. 1997e. "Disability, Inability and Cyberspace." With E. Macken, N. Scott, and J. McKinley. In B. Friedman (ed.), *Designing Computers for People: Human Values and the Design of Computer Technology*. Stanford, Calif.: CSLI Publications and Cambridge University Press.

82. 1997f. "Possible Worlds Semantics." *Routledge Encyclopedia of Philosophy*. London: Routledge.

83. 1997g. "Situation Semantics." *Routledge Encyclopedia of Philosophy*. London: Routledge.

84. 1998a. "Broadening the Mind: Review of Jerry Fodor, *The Elm and The Expert*." *Philosophy and Phenomenological Research* 58: 223–231. Reprinted in (3), enlarged edition.

85. 1998b. "Contexts and Unarticulated Constituents." *Proceedings of the 1995 CSLI-Amsterdam Logic, Language, and Computation Conference*. Stanford, Calif.: CSLI Publications.

86. 1998c. "Myself and I." In M. Stamm (ed.), *Philosophie in Synthetisher Absicht*. Stuttgart: Klett-Cotta. Translated into German as "Mein Selbst und 'Ich'" by V. Friesen and A. Newen. In A. Newen and K. Vogeley (eds.), *Selbst und Gehirn*. Paderborm: Mentis, 2000. Reprinted in (3), enlarged edition.

87. 1999. "Prolegomena to a Theory of Disability, Inability and Handicap." With D. Israel and E. Macken. In L. Moss, J. Ginzburg, and M. de Rijke (eds.), *Logic, Language and Computation*. Vol. 2. Stanford: CSLI Publications.

88. 2001a. "Time, Consciousness and the Knowledge Argument." In L. N. Oaklander (ed.), *The Importance of Time*. Dordrecht: Kluwer.

89. 2001b. "Frege on Identity, Cognitive Value and Subject Matter." In A. Newen, U. Nortmann, and R. Stuhlmann-Laeisz (eds.), *Building on Frege: New Essays about Sense, Content, and Concept*. Stanford, Calif.: CSLI Publications.

90. 2002a. "The Two Faces of Identity." In *Identity, Personal Identity, and the Self*. Indianapolis: Hackett.

91. 2002b. "Information, Action, and Persons." In *Identity, Personal Identity, and the Self*. Indianapolis: Hackett.

92. 2002c. "The Self, Self-Knowledge, and Self-Notions." In *Identity, Personal Identity, and the Self*. Indianapolis: Hackett.

93. 2002d. "The Sense of Identity." In *Identity, Personal Identity, and the Self*. Indianapolis: Hackett.

94. 2002e. "Review of Gilles Fauconner and Mark Turner, *The Way We Think: Conceptual Blending and the Minds Hidden Complexities*." *American Scientist* 90: 576–578.

95. 2003a. "Predelli's Threatening Note: Contexts, Utterances, and Tokens in the Philosophy of Language." *Journal of Pragmatics* 35: 373–387.

96. 2003b. "The Subject Matter Fallacy." *Journal of Applied Logic* 1: 93–105.

97. 2004a. "Precis of *Knowledge, Possibility and Consciousness*." *Philosophy and Phenomenological Research* 68: 172–181.

98. 2004b. "Reply to Critics." *Philosophy and Phenomenological Research* 68: 207–228.

99. 2004c. "Compatibilist Options." In J. K. Campbell, M. O'Rourke, and D. Shier (eds.), *Freedom and Determinism*. Cambridge, Mass.: MIT Press.

100. 2005. "Personal Identity, Memory and the Self." In W. Østreng (ed.), *Synergies: Interdisciplinary Communications*. Oslo: Center for Advanced Study.

101. 2006a. "Using Indexicals." In M. Devitt and R. Hanley (eds.), *The Blackwell Guide to the Philosophy of Language*. Oxford: Blackwell.

102. 2006b. "Mary and Max and Jack and Ned." In D. Zimmerman (ed.), *Oxford Studies in Metaphysics, vol. II*. Oxford: Oxford University Press.

103. 2006c. "Three Demonstrations and a Funeral." With K. Korta. *Mind and Language* 21: 166–186.

104. 2006d. "How Real Are Future Events?" In F. Stadler and M. Stöltzner (eds.), *Time and History: Proceedings of the 28th International Wittgenstein Symposium*. Frankfurt: Ontos Verlag.

105. 2006e. "Pragmatics." With K. Korta. *The Stanford Encyclopedia of Philosophy* (http://plato.stanford.edu/).

106. 2006f. "Stalnaker and Indexical Belief." In J. Thomson and A. Byrne (eds.), *Content and Modality: Themes from the Philosophy of Robert Stalnaker*. Oxford: Oxford University Press.

107. 2007. "Situating Semantics: A Response." In M. O'Rourke and C. Washington (eds.), *Situating Semantics: Essays on the Philosophy of John Perry*. Cambridge, Mass.: MIT Press.

108. Forthcoming. "Body, Mind, and Soul." In I. Kaplow (ed.), *Body and Soul*. Cambridge, Mass.: MIT Press.

109. Forthcoming. "Diminished and Fractured Selves." *Proceedings of the 2004 Phoebe Berman Institute for Bioethics Symposium on Personal Identity and Bioethics*. Baltimore: Johns Hopkins University Press.

110. Forthcoming. "Subjectivity." In B. McLaughlin, et al. (eds.), *The Oxford Handbook in the Philosophy of Mind*. Oxford: Oxford University Press.

111. Forthcoming. "Varieties of Minimalist Semantics." With K. Korta. *Philosophy and Phenomenological Research*.

112. Forthcoming. "Radical Minimalism, Moderate Contextualism." With K. Korta. *Protosociology: An International Journal and Interdisciplinary Project*.

113. Forthcoming. "The Pragmatic Circle." With K. Korta. *Synthese*.

Index